Rx. xx (D)

EARLY VICTORIAN METHODISM

THE CORRESPONDENCE OF
JABEZ BUNTING
1830–1858

UNIVERSITY OF DURHAM
PUBLICATIONS

EARLY VICTORIAN METHODISM

THE CORRESPONDENCE OF
JABEZ BUNTING
1830–1858

W. R. WARD

OXFORD UNIVERSITY PRESS

OXFORD   LONDON   NEW YORK

1976

Oxford University Press, Ely House, London W.1

OXFORD LONDON GLASGOW NEW YORK
TORONTO MELBOURNE WELLINGTON CAPE TOWN
IBADAN NAIROBI DAR ES SALAAM LUSAKA ADDIS ABABA
KUALA LUMPUR SINGAPORE JAKARTA HONG KONG TOKYO
DELHI BOMBAY CALCUTTA MADRAS KARACHI

ISBN 0 19 713140 9

© *University of Durham 1976*

PRINTED IN GREAT BRITAIN BY
ROBERT MACLEHOSE AND CO. LIMITED
PRINTERS TO THE UNIVERSITY OF GLASGOW

PREFACE

In recent years German scholars have been able to confer the accolade of a *Gesamtausgabe* upon an enviable number of nineteenth-century churchmen of the first and second rank; there is no immediate likelihood of the resources becoming available here to rescue Newman from his embarrassing isolation in publishers' favour. I am therefore all the more grateful to the Publications Board of the University of Durham for completing, in circumstances exceedingly discouraging for academic publishing, the modest memorial to Jabez Bunting and his brethren in the old Wesleyan itinerancy begun by the Royal Historical Society in *The early correspondence of Jabez Bunting 1820–1829*. For although Bunting was never a man to everyone's taste, and certainly not to every Methodist's taste, he was undoubtedly one of the first-rank churchmen of the nineteenth century. Though an intelligent man, Bunting contributed nothing to biblical or theological scholarship, and the connexion he served was loath to publish his by no means negligible sermons. His son did not complete his *Life,* and perhaps his best and most intimate memorial is constituted by the personal correspondence with the preachers and with the powers of the church and state through which he sustained the management of the connexion he reconstructed and then helped to break. The core of that correspondence during the years of his greatness is presented below. I must again thank Dr. J. C. Bowmer and the committee in charge of the Methodist connexional archives for giving me the run of their holdings and thus making possible the discovery and cataloguing of the Bunting collection. My best thanks are due to Mrs. Joan McQuillan for producing the typescript. The patience of my wife during the whole enterprise has exceeded even that of my good-natured colleagues; unlike them she has never taken me at a fancy-dress party for Jabez Bunting in disguise.

Durham, February 1975   W.R.W.

CONTENTS

INTRODUCTION

(1) THE BUNTING CORRESPONDENCE

(a) *Principles of Selection*

The letters which follow complete the publication of the core of the Bunting correspondence which was begun over a century ago by Jabez's second son Percy,[1] and resumed by the present editor in *The early correspondence of Jabez Bunting 1820–1829* edited for the Royal Historical Society.[2] When work for that edition began, it was believed that the surviving portion of the Bunting correspondence, which had been assembled by Percy Bunting for the purpose of writing his father's *Life*, ran to some 700 letters, about half of which merited publication. A combing of the holdings of the Methodist Church Archives and Research Centre at 25–35 City Road, London, EC1Y 1AA, however, revealed the existence of more than 4,000 letters to and from Jabez Bunting, and to these have been added photocopies of six other collections of Bunting's papers which had been dispersed in the United States of America. These letters have been catalogued and arranged, alphabetically by correspondents, in the boxes containing the general correspondence of the archives, and every letter may be traced by the card catalogue of correspondents at the Centre. A typewritten transcript of most of the letters with calendar entries for the remainder has been deposited in the Library of the University of Durham.

The fifteen years which followed Bunting's second election as President of the Wesleyan Methodist Conference (1828–29) represented the period of his greatest dominance in Methodist affairs. The correspondence is voluminous, and as Percy's *Life* got no further than the year 1829, being completed by four slight chapters by another hand, the letters have remained almost completely unpublished. The 345 letters published below are selected from some 2,000, most of them in-letters. It has not been possible to illustrate the collection as fully as in the period of the *Early Correspondence*, though by following the same principles of selection, a place has been found for most of the letters of permanent interest. Those which have been excluded fall into the

---

[1] T. P. Bunting, *The Life of Jabez Bunting D.D.* (London, 1858–87) [cited below as *Life of Bunting*].

[2] Camden 4th series vol. xi (London, 1972) [cited below as *Early Correspondence*].

following categories: (1) those of secondary importance, of no intrinsic value, or of purely local or personal interest: (2) those concerned with missions overseas (letters relating to negotiations with government on missionary matters, or concerning the impact of missionary organization on Methodism at home have been retained): (3) those concerning Scottish Methodism the mismanagement of which worried the connexional leadership increasingly in this period: (4) a very small number of letters which duplicate others included in the collection.

(b) *The character of the correspondence: its historical value*

Though in one respect unaltered, the character of the Bunting correspondence changes in numerous ways in this period. There is the old disproportion between in-letters and out-letters. The bulk of the preachers were discouraged alike by social habit and by the itinerant life from hoarding letters, and much of what remains of Bunting's side of the correspondence he himself preserved in copy or draft form. Moreover, finding that preachers were too apt to make use of his name in local battles, Bunting himself on occasion asked for the destruction of his letters.[1] It was on matters to which future reference might be required that he was most likely to keep drafts of his replies. In all this the correspondence of Bunting's hey-day does not differ from that of his youth and rise to pre-eminence.

In at least three respects, however, the correspondence changes markedly. Personal correspondence of the kind which is so informative in the days of Bunting's youth disappears almost altogether. This is partly a testimony to the degree to which Bunting sank his private personality in his official character, and parallels the decline in the most personal aspect of his official functions, his preaching.[2] But there was certainly personal correspondence within the Bunting family; and the dearth of this in the collection now was probably due to the deliberate action of Percy Bunting.[3] It is also likely that Jabez destroyed or that Percy removed whatever might be construed to the great man's discredit in the most explosive episode of his career, the great conflict with Dr. Warren (1834-35), which arose from the establishment of a seminary for training preachers. Bunting was even nearer to the centre of this fracas than he had been to that of the Leeds organ case in 1827-28,[4] and it is unlikely to be an accident that the Warrenite issue

---

[1] M.C.A. MSS. Jabez Bunting to Mr. Dredge, November 18, 1837.

[2] On this see *Early Correspondence*, pp. 12-16.   [3] cf. *Ibid.* p. 2.

[4] On this see W. R. Ward, *Religion and society in England, 1790–1850* (London, 1972) pp. 144-7.

figures much less fully in his correspondence. Apart from this, the collection seems to have suffered no more than random losses since it was first constituted, a circumstance which emphasizes the change in the character of the correspondence.

Methodist correspondence had always embraced matters of many various kinds, but the abiding impression left by reading large quantities of it, is that in Wesley's later years the matter of overriding concern was religion; in the generation following his death it was politics; and in the generation of Bunting's supremacy it was administration, notwithstanding that the steady establishment of connexional routine had relieved the preachers of the necessity for that desperate transmission of information which had characterized their correspondence in Bunting's younger days. This shift of emphasis implies no diminution of general interest. Behind administration was Church discipline, and, for Bunting, this 'equally with the dispensation of the word and sacraments [was] an institution of Christ'[1]; in this respect at least administration was a religious matter, and in a very real sense a function of the living Church. Moreover the 'thirties and early 'forties were the period of Bunting's greatest achievement. Settled permanently in London as secretary for foreign missions in 1833, Bunting was no longer even in outward appearance an ordinary member of the Wesleyan itinerancy, and around him clustered a series of new connexional developments which were to arouse violent controversy. The Missionary Society became a major business, one of the great nineteenth century charities. The decision to found the Theological Institution and give seminary training to prospective preachers was taken in 1834: it led on the one hand to Bunting's appointment as President of the Institution, and on the other hand to the great secession led by Dr. Warren. In 1835 came a great attempt to overhaul and codify connexional law and discipline, the most important piece of general legislation since the 'nineties, and Bunting's personal masterpiece. In 1839 the Centenary Fund was launched to commemorate the foundation of the United Societies by Wesley, the most conspicuous fruit of which consisted in buildings for the branches of the Theological Institution and for a London headquarters for the Missionary Society, a great endowment for the central administration of the connexion which showed only too clearly the way in which the balance in the Methodist polity was shifting. Moreover, as the letters below illustrate, Bunting and a few of his immediate colleagues in London were continuously engaged in diplomacy as well as administration: negotiations with the government about slavery, colonial administration and missions,

[1] *Sermons by Jabez Bunting* ed. W. L. Thornton (London, 1861–62) ii. 375, 379.

education and chapel trusts; negotiations with Anglican evangelicals about the Protestant crusade and with the evangelical Protestant rump about the Evangelical Alliance; negotiations with Scots evangelicals on matters which led to and followed from the Disruption. Moreover the Methodist connexional management like that of every other Church had particularly severe difficulties to face in the 1830's and contended vigorously with great general issues, political and social conflict, a diminishing popular appeal, the problem of realizing a Christian ethic among industrial populations in England or former slave populations in Jamaica. Ecclesiastical administration has not often raised as many issues of general interest as it did during Bunting's hey-day.

Many of the documents which follow bear directly upon these great themes, and especially upon the rhythm of inner tension and secession which accompanied the development of Bunting's central administration and discipline, tension which had its counterpart in secular bodies such as trade unions and friendly societies. There is much also about the doctrine of the ministry, which in these years reached its 'highest' Methodist form; about ministerial training, liturgy, and the discipline to be applied to ministers. In a wider sphere there are discussions of the nature of church membership, and the difficulties encountered by the Wesleyan conception of society membership through the class-meeting; the relations of the preachers to the flock are curiously illuminated by the issue of licensing the chapels for the solemnization of marriages, and their attitude to the local preachers is illustrated at length. There is much about relations between the churches, not only on public matters such as church rates and education, but on their co-operation and conflict at the grass-roots in all kinds of mundane concerns. There is much on those things which many of the preachers regarded as a rival religious appeal, teetotalism and revivalism in the organized American manner. Ireland is a continual anxiety. Above all, the daily difficulties of circuit life are seen through the eyes and in the terms of ordinary itinerant preachers and laymen. A large slice of English life from Yorkshire to Cornwall which has never been adequately treated by historians is vividly brought to life.

(c) *Editorial Practice*

The same editorial conventions have been followed as in the *Early Correspondence*. In the text of the letters punctuation and the use of capitals have been modernized and abbreviations have been expanded. In this period (unlike the 'twenties) no problem of modernizing spelling arises; apart from the occasional *lapsus styli*, ordinary Methodist preachers were fully as conversant as Bunting himself with the conventions of modern orthography. Pressure upon space has compelled the omission of many more passages (including, very often, long passages) from letters printed below than in the *Early Correspondence*; but passages have been omitted on the same principles which have governed the omission of letters from the collection. The subscriptions to the letters, none of which are of any significance, have also been omitted; the omissions are indicated by points (. . . . . .). Editorial additions to the text appear in square brackets ([ ]) or, in the case of emendations where the manuscript has suffered damage, in pointed brackets (⟨ ⟩). Brief biographical details are provided for all the preachers and almost all the laymen mentioned in the letters, and there are notes on the principal *explicanda*; in order very greatly to reduce the number of cross references, this information is given in footnotes on the first occasion of mention, and may be traced through the index. In the period of this volume, as today, the Methodist connexional year began on 1 September; a note that a preacher served in a particular station, 1838–39, for example, implies one year's service from 1 September 1838 to 31 August 1839. The Methodist Conference, however, met later than it now does, assembling for up to three weeks, late in July and early in August. A note that a preacher was President in 1838 or 1838–39 implies, therefore, a period beginning late in July 1838, and continuing for a year.

(2) METHODISM DURING THE HEY-DAY OF JABEZ BUNTING

The Leeds Protestant Methodist connexion, formed as a result of the great conflict over the Leeds Brunswick organ which dominates the latter part of the *Early Correspondence*,[1] was not the first Methodist reform connexion to be established,[2] but it marked a new stage in the development of the reform question, and a new hardening of Methodist differences of opinion about the constitutional power and pastoral status of the preachers. In the course of this conflict the 'high' Wesleyan doctrine of the Pastoral Office was formulated for the first time, by men such as John Beecham and Richard Watson,[3] who appealed skilfully

---

[1] See pp. 156 *seq.*

[2] This distinction falls to the Methodist New Connexion, formed in 1797.

[3] See e.g. J. Beecham, *An essay on the constitution of Wesleyan Methodism* (first published 1829; 3rd ed. London, 1851) and Richard Watson, *Theological Institutes* (London, 1829) iii. 361–9. For modern discussions: John Kent, *The age of disunity* (London, 1966) pp. 44–85: J. C. Bowmer, 'Church and ministry in Wesleyan Methodism from the death of Wesley to the death of Jabez Bunting' (Ph.D. thesis, University of Leeds, 1967): W. R. Ward, 'The legacy of John Wesley: the Pastoral Office in Britain and America' in *Statesmen, Scholars and Merchants* ed. A. Whiteman, J. S. Bromley, and P.G.M. Dickson (Oxford, 1973) pp. 323–50.

not only to scripture and Methodist history, but to *a priori* assumptions about the sovereignty intrinsic to bodies politic. The sovereign legislature of Methodism was Conference in which Wesley had chosen to exercise his plentitude of power with the preachers, and to which he had bequeathed his authority to appoint them to their annual stations. The Superintendent in each circuit exercised Wesley's general superintendence over the flock, and District Committees acting on behalf of Conference maintained (somewhat uneasily) his daily oversight over the connexion. This concentration of authority, it was maintained, was rooted in the New Testament. Christ had filled the whole Pastoral Office and transmitted his authority to his ministers. The pastor, wholly given up to the work, must feed and also rule the flock; his authority was *sui generis* and could not be shared with those who were not pastors, even if like Local Preachers or class leaders, they performed valuable spiritual functions. Concessions which had apparently been made to the lay interest in the Society in the Plan of Pacification (1795) or the Regulations of 1797 could not reduce or divide the pastoral power: they were simply procedural provisions designed to prevent abuse. To resist this position and the active central administration of Bunting's era, Methodist reformers could no longer rest content with the New Connexion *nostrum* of a Conference half composed of lay representatives, and wished to limit the omnicompetence of Conference by formal safeguards to circuit rights such as the New Connexion would not countenance. The Leeds Protestant Methodists, indeed, not only placed the oversight of local societies (including the power of expulsion from membership) in the Circuit Quarterly Meeting, but gave it the power to elect ministers (under the title of elders) for a year at a time. This arrangement was fatal to itinerancy as well as to separation, and it exemplified a process of power rising from below rather than descending from above which could not but be abhorrent to the apologists of 'high' Wesleyanism.

Methodist opinion was now presented with two radically different models of constitutional and spiritual organization around which other differences of opinion tended to polarize in the following generation. Bunting and the 'high' Methodist party proceeded in their domestic policies to consolidate the status and develop the work of the ministry: seminary training was followed by ordination by imposition of hands (1836)[1] and some itinerants adopted the preaching gown; the administrative authority of the preachers was extended in various directions (even while prominent laymen were given new scope in the raising and

---

[1] Missionaries leaving for overseas service had been ordained before departure ever since Wesley's death.

expenditure of connexional funds), and, when the connexion encountered fresh difficulties in holding and extending its congregations in the 'forties, anxious consideration was given to schemes of pastoral visitation, and of extending membership to adherents of the Society not meeting in class, thus bringing more of the congregation under direct ministerial authority. The external policies of Bunting's connexional management were complementary to all this; presenting Wesleyan Methodism as a church in its own right, they extended the range of spiritual services rendered to the flock (see no. 254 about the solemnization of marriages), built up a system of church schools under their own control, and re-acted violently when unchurched by the high-flown episcopalianism of the Tractarians. On the other side 'low' Methodists perceived the root of the connexion's troubles in the very institutionalization to which Bunting pinned his faith; they clung to the independence of the Sunday schools, many of which originated in the undenominational effort of the past, and still enjoyed much independence of ministerial control. They took up teetotalism, another undenominational move-ment of moral reform with roots in artisan enterprise; they retained the vision of Methodism as a great out-pouring of grace, even when it needed revitalizing by the American fireworks of revivalists like Caughey; and they signified their allegiance to the rising of the provinces against the central institutions of the England of their day, by being much more wholeheartedly devoted to liberal politics than was the Wesleyan community as a whole. In much the same way Bunting and his friends lent their support to the principle of church establish-ment in England and Scotland in the 'thirties, making it impossible for an outright disestablisher like Joseph Rayner Stephens to hold his ground in the ministry; hostility to establishment was common among 'low Methodists', and it was a serious set-back for Bunting's general schemes that in the 'forties he found himself supporting the Disruption in the Church of Scotland, and wishing in Conference that 'two thousand clergymen would leave the English Church in the same way'.[1]

The major theme of the correspondence which follows is the develop-ment and hardening of these attitudes, a process particularly hazardous in decayed city-centre congregations, in which the migration of substantial laymen to the suburbs left the entire burden of controlling radical opinion upon the shoulders of the ministry; a process which led to small secessions in defence of 'Derby faith' (1831) and Joseph Rayner Stephens (1834), to the formation of the large Warrenite Wesleyan Methodist Association (1835), and to the disastrous Wesleyan Reform secessions which began with the expulsion of Everett, Dunn and

[1] B. Gregory, *Sidelights on the Conflicts of Methodism 1827–52* (London, 1899) p. 348.

Griffith in 1849, and which speedily cost the connexion one-third of its membership. By this time the defence of the Pastoral Office had devolved upon John Beecham and men much younger than the aged Bunting. It was Methodist connexional ethics that a man might not be re-elected President (or indeed be reappointed to a circuit) for eight years after he had last served. Bunting had been elected every eight years from his first Presidency in 1820, serving for the fourth time in 1844. It was clear that he could not face the Reform holocaust in 1852, and so in 1851 he was hastily retired from the full-time work of the ministry, though an arrangement was made by which he could continue to put in as much work as his strength permitted in the Mission House. How had he fared personally with the years?

(3) JABEZ BUNTING

The hardening of Methodist sentiment towards and around Bunting had long been foreshadowed in the mind of the great man himself. 'I belonged to a school of revivalists in Manchester', he confessed to the Conference of 1846, 'not a good one, but good in its design'.[1] But this had been at the turn of the century; once he had given himself to the creation of an ecclesiastical system there was, notwithstanding his fertility in administrative resource, no room for basic development. And despite the constant appeal to Wesley made by Bunting and the exponents of the high Wesleyan doctrine of the ministry, even Wesley was overshadowed in the minds of the panegyrists at Bunting's graveside by the new ecclesiastical system.

> I plainly see that as the Wesleys were employed by providence to form the *Methodistic element*, so Jabez Bunting was used by the like providence to form the *Methodist Church*. All our ecclesiastical system has *his* impress gradually operating in it, and reducing it to harmonious unity. And it was all done deliberately, and upon a scale of large views.[2]

If, when the present correspondence opens in 1830, Bunting's mind was already fixed, so also was his personal situation. His unique influence in Methodist affairs combined with his active role in the Leeds organ case exposed him uniquely to the abuse of his enemies, personal and ecclesiastical, to '*public trials*, I had almost said *actual persecutions*'.[3] 'Cool-blooded persecution' of Bunting was indeed a way for the opposition in the connexion to keep their ranks in line, and in the

---

[1] *Ibid.* p. 403. For this period in Bunting's life see *Early Correspondence* pp. 10–11.

[2] M.C.A. MSS. *Funeral of the late Jabez Bunting* June 22, 1858. A printed order of service containing a MS. copy of part of one of the funeral addresses, probably by John Scott.

[3] M.C.A. MSS. Barnard Slater to Jabez Bunting, April 9, 1833.

correspondence which follows they appear in the eyes of the connexional management as 'our small friends', or more precisely as 'little
men, and selfish men, and jealous men and crafty men, and sneaks, and
slanderers, and all that tribe'.

If, by 1830, assailing or championing Bunting personally had become
one of the established rituals of Methodist corporate existence, the
dependence upon him of leading members of the connexion, both lay
and ministerial, had reached extraordinary proportions. William
Vevers would not even commence a description and defence of Methodist institutions without Bunting's leave:

> it would be an act of great indiscretion in me to publish on such a
> subject without a previous and *rigid* examination; and to whom can I
> apply but to one whose knowledge of our doctrines and discipline
> I regard as unequalled; and whose attachment to Methodism is
> unconquerable.[1]

If John McLean wanted advice how to deal with Scots who thought
that the eccentricities of Erskine of Linlathen and Campbell of Roro
could be found in Fletcher of Madeley and the old Wesleyan authorities,
it was to Bunting he turned to be put right.[2] A pompous circuit superintendent, in the toils with his District Meeting, wrote 'with most
sincere and scriptural respect. Solemnly and devoutly, if a Bishop
should write to a superior *Bishop* with becoming entreaty, even so do I
to you'.[3] Methodism's 'superior Bishop' was also in lay demand for
political purposes; his old friend Gilyard Scarth, besought him to
accept appointment to Leeds East in the name of the 'noble stand you
have taken against that overwhelming flood of democracy and misrule
which was so recently breaking in upon us almost everywhere'.[4] If
Bunting's own station was crucial, it was assumed right through the
connexion that his influence was decisive in the Stationing Committee
of Conference: leading laymen and circuit superintendents plied him
with statements of their requirements, and, as the years went by,
preachers who failed to receive the stations to which they felt entitled,
ascribed their disappointments to Bunting's unjust suspicions and
heaped bitter reproaches upon him. To one wild Irishman his case was
'unparalleled in any society known in Great Britain since its civilization,
except the Star Chamber or High Commission Courts, *steeped in the blood*

---

[1] M.C.A. MSS. Wm. Vevers to Jabez Bunting, April 13, 1830, cf. John Beecham to same,
November 15, 1834, *infra* no. 65.
[2] M.C.A. MSS. John McLean to Jabez Bunting, March 5, 1831.
[3] M.C.A. MSS. Thomas Ludlam to Jabez Bunting, December 19, 1836.
[4] M.C.A. MSS. W. Gilyard Scarth to Jabez Bunting, September 24, 1832.

of thousands ! ! !'[1] There is no evidence that Bunting used his power to manipulate a party in Conference, but it is not difficult to see how the suspicion arose that he did so.[2]

The personal acrimony which Bunting had already encountered was sufficient motive, had there been no other, for a display of modesty when, in 1833, he was pressed to accept one of the most prestigious appointments in the connexion of that day, one of the secretaryships for foreign missions.[3] In some of the current apologetic, foreign missions had come to figure almost as the *raison d'être* of the church, and twice already Bunting had been called to their rescue, once on his first appointment in London in 1803 with responsibility for sorting out the accounts, and again between 1813 and 1817 when he put the Missionary Society on a formal and efficient basis, with fund-raising by local auxiliary and public meeting. To complete the work he had already begun, and, as he always longed,[4] to reside permanently in London, were powerful inducements, but there is no reason to doubt a degree of genuine humility in his hesitation upon the brink. For Bunting had not yet come to the end of his personal elasticity; he was still welcome personally was well as officially in families about the connexion,[5] and the few surviving letters from his son, young Jabez, or more familiarly 'Bez', show that his father's devotion to the Pastoral Office did not upset a hearty family life in which 'jugged hare, cold beef, apple-tart and cheese' alternated with prayer, high spirits and hard work.[6]

The great clash with Dr. Warren which brought Bunting's influence

---

[1] M.C.A. MSS. George Hansbrow to Jabez Bunting, January 8, 1837. For two other cases of differing kinds, M.C.A. MSS. John Langston to Jabez Bunting, November 13, 1843: Thomas Cutting to Jabez Bunting, July 29, 1844.

[2] It is noteworthy that the same suspicions of the machinations of their elders were entertained by Bunting's friends in the days of their youth. 'There are certain senior brethren who endeavour to influence the juniors and secure their votes on all occasions, and one said he knew that in the neighbourhood of his seat last Conference, two senior brethren had about 40 young men to vote &c.'. M.C.A. MSS. Joseph Entwisle to Jabez Bunting, June 2, 1809. It is clear from nos. 280 and 323 *infra* that in Bunting's later years his friends came to demand a degree of manipulation.

[3] See *infra* no. 24.

[4] From the first Bunting thrived not only on the social prestige of the London congregations, but on the public business which came the way of preachers in metropolitan stations (M.C.A. MSS. Jabez Bunting to Richard Reece, October 13, 1803; Jabez Bunting to George Lomas, October 14, 1803; Jabez Bunting to Sarah Maclardie, November 5, 1803; Jabez Bunting to James Wood, September 17, 1810) and suspected that when he was out of London, missionary business was not 'done quite as well as it should be'. *Life of Bunting* ii. 83.

[5] This is, I think, the implication of the anxiety of the Ashworths of Halifax to have Bunting preach John Ashworth's funeral sermon and write his memoir in 1833. M.C.A. MSS. A. E. Farrar to Jabez Bunting, June 7, 1833.

[6] See *infra* no. 59, also M.C.A. MSS. Jabez Bunting junior to his mother, June 7, 1833, written across W. Dalby to Jabez Bunting, June 3, 1833.

in Methodism to its peak and left his system harder and hence more brittle than it had been before, saw the beginning of personal trials which cost him dear. When the warfare was at its height Bunting's wife, Sarah (née Maclardie), died. Blessed with a personal vivacity which he deliberately abjured, Sarah had done much to keep life sweet in Bunting's immediate circle, and her loss aggravated the burden Jabez must bear. 'Every heart knows its own bitterness' he complained to John Beecham, 'and many preachers in the neighbourhood, who are in little local difficulties, and want advice, insist on seeing me'.[1] Before long, as the letters which follow show, Bunting made a happy second marriage with a preacher's widow, but it was not the same. A stranger had replaced the life and soul of the Bunting family party; a kindly tone does not conceal the stiffness of Bunting's letters to his daughter Emma.[2] His son, William Maclardie, the preacher, who reproduced his father's worst mannerisms in the pulpit, but lacked the concentration of personal energy and conviction which formed the dynamite in his father's best preaching, ran out of steam in mid-life and became a supernumerary in 1849, two years before his father. That lively scamp, young Bez, who became a solicitor in Leeds, fell into some unspeakable (and unspoken) disgrace:

> We are truly sorry [wrote Alfred Barrett] on many accounts and especially on yours, that every effort to recover him to respectability and peace (to say nothing of what is higher) seems utterly unavailing. It is sometimes a relief in times of great anxiety, when we can know the worst of a thing; and that poor relief I am afraid is that which can only now be afforded you . . . it really does seem as if nothing but an act of sovereign and unusual grace would open poor Jabez's eyes to his real condition and make him a lowly penitent . . . As far as his position and circumstances are known in Leeds (they are not known extensively) there is but one feeling of sorrow for yourself, and regret that your declining life should be embittered from such a source . . .[3]

Bunting's other son, and biographer, Thomas Percival, a Manchester solicitor, was everything his father could desire; he fought with him into the last ditch in connexional battles; he entered so wholeheartedly into the dirty business of putting financial pressure on Samuel Warren as to make old Jabez tremble for his professional prospects;[4] and he

---

[1] See *infra* no. 100.

[2] E.g. M.C.A. MSS. Jabez Bunting to Emma Bunting, August 29, 1837.

[3] M.C.A. MSS. Alfred Barrett to Jabez Bunting, March 13, 1843. There is the same funereal tone in another letter: 'Permit an humble individual to cast in his meed of sympathy at this your hour of trial . . . to you that have been so long on the Mount trials are very heavy, but you *live* in the affections of a loving people'. M.C.A. MSS. Joseph Blake to Jabez Bunting, May 3, 1843.

[4] See *infra* no. 63.

created a home in Nelson Street which his father delighted to visit. What happened within the Bunting family was characteristic of what was happening to Jabez's personal relations generally in the years following the Warrenite clash. 'At the Leeds Conference of 1837 Dr. Bunting's absence for a single session brought business to a standstill, in so much that it must needs adjourn itself till his return',[1] yet he made it increasingly clear that he was the spokesman for 'the *élite* of our Connexion'.[2] Within the élite there were fewer and fewer with whom he was on terms of real intimacy, and in the end, as his health gradually deteriorated, the great Jabez, who owed his power in Methodism to the conviction of the bulk of the preachers that he would fight their battles, corporate and individual, for them, came himself to depend on a small knot of much younger men who revered him and his ideals, his son Percy, and men like F. J. Jobson[3] and Alfred Barrett who assured him of his 'affectionate and reverential respect'.[4] And, sadly but inevitably, not only did he find it harder to maintain civil relations with men of independent mind in Conference,[5] but as his ecclesiastical handiwork was torn apart by the Reform secessions of his old age, younger men who had been most anxious to make their way as his personal protégés turned sharply upon him.

> If you knew what students and young men do in this country [John McLean lectured him from Scotland] you would perhaps be a little less afraid of polemics than in your excessive good nature and Evangelical Allianceism I fear you are in danger of becoming. If you *are* consenting to be put out to nurse in your old days, either by old women or young men or *young women* you really must forgive those whom you have implicated in the teachings of your prime to take protection from the guns which may be fired at them from defences which is impossible *they* should ever consider to be other than sacred.[6]

By this time he was fairly caught between young men spoiling for a fight, and old men deploring the opening which Bunting's own legislation had given to the exercise of discipline.

> I beg and beseech you Sir [cried old Robert Melson] to consider the awful state of things into which we are brought! by *whom*! and by *what means*! Look at the laws of '35, like a man of understanding, and as

---

[1] Gregory, *Sidelights* p. 251.   [2] *Ibid.* p. 297.

[3] 'Be assured that I feel deeply the loss of your occasional society and conversation, by which I have been so often solaced and cheered, and for which an interchange of letters is now the only available substitute'. M.C.A. MSS. Jabez Bunting to F. J. Jobson, November 8, 1855 (cf. same to same, March 31, 1856).

[4] M.C.A. MSS. Alfred Barrett to Jabez Bunting, March 31, 1857.

[5] Gregory, *Sidelights* pp. 240–1. cf. M.C.A. MSS. Joshua Marsden to Jabez Bunting, June 17, 1834.

[6] M.C.A. MSS. John McLean to Jabez Bunting, December 17, 1857.

becometh the *Premier* for such a wise, holy, kind, merciful, loving and powerful body of people as the Wesleyans, who could never have supposed they were under the government of men and ministers of God who could have enacted and enforced laws so *opposed* to the Laws of *God* as revealed in the Scriptures of truth, had they not been informed of the fact.[1]

The strains which made it hard for Bunting to sustain personal relationships were intensified in 1840 by the financial crisis into which the business recession plunged his family with so many others. Limited to odd pence in his pocket for months on end, Bunting sought relief by discounting a bill drawn by Percy, against the Missionary Society funds; the bill bounced.

> While my heart aches at the thought of giving *you* additional pain or embarrassment [he wrote], I am now compelled by dire necessity to tell you that I am reduced to great distress for want of the other money due to me, and really *must* have it in a week or two, or I cannot longer avoid a disgraceful exposure of myself, involving one that must, I fear, be seriously injurious to you under present circumstances. Many of the tradesmen's bills are unpaid – Aunt Hale's lodging debts etc. are in arrear at Windsor – the Centenary [Fund] instalments are called for – I have more than anticipated for several quarters past all my coming receipts – Joe's claims appear to have no chance of liquidation, and, altogether I am involved in straits, which viewed in connexion with the too prominent position I am reluctantly compelled to retain before the public, often deprive me of rest, and always of comfort. What can I do? Or rather, what can *you* do? I should like to have a frank and clear account in writing, as to your prospects; for your speedy solvency or insolvency *involves my own*.[2]

Again, sadly but inexorably, the additional burden was followed by ill-health. 'I began seriously to fear that I am almost *done for*',[3] he complained in October 1840, and, although he proved to have many years of useful work still in store, he was never really well again. Early in 1842 he was required to stop work altogether, and bullied by his Mission House colleagues to delegate his duties.[4] Conference, where he had held the stage so long, upset him, and in 1843 he could not attend the Welsh Assembly.[5] 'I am fit for nothing just now' he confessed at the beginning of 1844, and a temporary improvement in his health in

---

[1] M.C.A. MSS. Robert Melson to Jabez Bunting, April 26, 1850.

[2] M.C.A. MSS. Jabez Bunting to T. Percival Bunting, June 4, 1840.

[3] See *infra* no. 192.

[4] M.C.A. MSS. R. Alder to Jabez Bunting, January 17, 1842: Elijah Morgan to Jabez Bunting, January 20, 1842; Jabez Bunting to J. E. Coulson, February 4, 1842.

[5] M.C.A. MSS. H. Hughes to Jabez Bunting, May 10, 1843: Jabez Bunting to Samuel Hill Smith, June 6, 1843.

the spring was undone by his emotional pother over the Dissenters' Chapels Bill.[1] But with the ministry dividing into parties, his friends could not let him off a fourth term as President at the Conference which opened in July 1844. The result was predictable. Though a by no means extinct volcano, Bunting erupted less fearsomely than of yore.

> Successive resolutions were carried against his warmly and strongly argued, and emphatically enunciated judgement, till at last, when it became plain that another motion to which he had earnestly objected would almost certainly be carried, he abruptly left the Chair, and declared he would sign the Journal, thus dissolving the Conference before the stations were confirmed and much of the most important business yet unfinished. Happily, he was persuaded to resume his seat, and made graceful, gentlemanly apology to the brother to whose answer to his question from the Chair he had refused to listen – but not to the Conference. On the contrary he held himself to be the aggrieved party.[2]

It was behaviour of this kind which convinced younger observers like Benjamin Gregory that the reason for the disaster which overwhelmed Methodism at the end of the decade was the unwarrantable personal power which Bunting had assumed. In fact Bunting was paying in personal terms the penalty already exacted from numbers of his friends for the insupportable demands of the Pastoral Office as he had pressed the entire ministry to understand and fulfil it; in the autumn he was ill again, afflicted with 'indications which threaten, if I am not careful, an approaching crisis'.[3]

Occupied 'by night and day'[4] in the great contest with Samuel Warren, and bereft of his wife, Bunting had never recovered his spring, and preaching, personal relations, and the conduct of business during an exceptionally difficult time, had all suffered. He could not be thrown again into the front line and in 1851 was made a supernumerary before the occasion of a fifth presidential term should arise. But the General Missionary Committee had ample material for a testimonial to active service.

> They are satisfied that the confidence reposed in this Society by the public of this country, and the Churches of Christendom at large, and the liberal pecuniary support which it has received, have been owing in no small degree to the unrestrained disinterestedness and zeal with which Dr. Bunting has, from the commencement devoted himself to its

[1] United Methodist Church Archives, Lake Junaluska, N.C. MS. Corr. of Jabez Bunting to James Wood, January 10, June 13, 1844.

[2] Gregory, *Sidelights* pp. 375–6.   [3] See *infra* no. 245.

[4] Southern Methodist University, Dallas, Texas. MS. letter of Jabez Bunting to J. S. Stamp, London, March 5, 1835.

management and direction. They are persuaded that Dr. Bunting's name and influence have been of the highest value to this Society in its intercourse with government at various critical periods in the history of its Missions. They bear in mind the triumph of Christianity exhibited in the maintenance of the Missions in the West Indies during the trying period of negro slavery; the abolition of that iniquitous system, and the subsequent enlargement of the Society's operations in the West Indies; the extension of the Missions in India, in western and southern Africa, in the regions of Australia and Polynesia, and in other parts of the world; in the promotion of which measures and operations Dr. Bunting has taken an active and prominent part as a member of this Committee.[1]

To Bunting's efforts to broaden the frontiers of Christ's kingdom, as well as to the consolidation and disruption of an ecclesiastical system at home, the letters which follow bear eloquent testimony.

[1] *Life of Bunting* ii. 360–1.

1 From John Scott[1]   *Liverpool, January 1, 1830*

Mr. Sands has acquainted you with the decision to which our Quarterly Meeting came on Tuesday, a decision which has given me great pleasure.[2] I now entertain the hope that you may succeed me in the superintendency of this circuit, and that those whom for some time I have had in charge will soon have the benefit of your invaluable ministry and pastoral direction – I am glad on their account. Then the vote was so nearly unanimous, the dissentients, in everything, even in ability for mischief, were so inconsiderable, and opposition was so completely silent, for not one word of opposition on any ground, was uttered, that I cannot but regard it as the further triumph of our holy and righteous cause over the wretched opposition which in the commencement of the year was arrayed against it. Permit me my dear Sir also to say that I rejoice in our decision on your account. Altho[ugh] endeavours had been made, after the Liverpool radical fashion as I have since learned, to secure votes against your coming, only because of hostility to your administration of Methodism (for the creatures own they have no other objection whatever against you, nay they even admire you in all other respects!) and with the intention I doubt not of making very public the defeat were our friends defeated, and so of keeping up and extending the unprincipled and wicked attempt to prejudice our whole connexion against you, because you are the most formidable enemy to the Methodist liberals. They are disappointed – they cannot proclaim our defeat – our triumph will be made known. I am aware that you can well afford to do without other praise than what has already been so generally awarded you, and may safely rely on the stability of that general regard which is so warmly cherished for you throug[h]out our connexion by all persons of wisdom and piety, so that in your own mind this may be of small account; yet I cannot feel

---

[1] John Scott (1792–1868), superintendent, Liverpool North Circuit, 1827–30. President, 1843 and 1852. President of Westminster Normal Institution, 1851–67.

[2] The Liverpool Quarterly Meeting had resolved to petition Conference to appoint Bunting their superintendent for the following year, and secured his consent. The background to this letter was the division of the Liverpool Circuit and the breakup of the circuit Leaders' Meeting required by a Conference deputation in 1825 (see *Early Correspondence* pp. 121–4). These methods of control weakened but did not annihilate the Liverpool radicals, and contributed to their great revolt in support of Dr. Warren in 1835.

indifferent to the fact that your character, talents, and usefulness have commanded a vote so nearly unanimous in a circuit where lately we had a large party marshalled in the very front of radicalism, and have imposed upon the very leaders of the faction a reluctant silence . . .

From the congregations that attend our ministry, the good feeling of the great part of our Society, and the low estate of the radical faction, we hope that the present quarter will, by God's blessing, keep up and swell the tide of our prosperity, and that you may find our circuit in a healthy and happy state should Divine Providence allot it as your station . . .

2   From John Rigg[1]   *Macclesfield, January 19, 1830*

. . . Of the agitated state of the first London West Circ[ui]t[2] you have heard. The flame was kindled by a Local Preacher,[3] and kept alive by his agency. For some time it burned beneath the surface; but when I arrived in London, the crust that kept it down was so thin, and the openings which it had made so numerous, that an eruption was certain. There was a time perhaps when it might have been extinguished with comparative ease; but that time unhappily had passed away. Of the infamous and inflammatory pamphlet which has issued from the London West Circuit, you have heard.[4] This disgraceful document is signed by thirty three or thirty four person[s], amongst whom are included the majority of our Local Preachers, who have raised themselves to a bad eminence, in this bad work. About thirty of those who had signed the Pamphlet were present at the Qu[arterl]y Meeting, and all, of course voted on the wrong side. From men so deeply pledged to oppose all that is constitutional in Methodism, nothing else could be expected; and yet this number was *barely* sufficient to give a wrong turn to the balance.

I assure you Sir I know not one person in the Circuit, whose judgment and principles are entitled to respect, who does not sincerely, and *strongly* desire you as a Pastor and Superintend[en]t. And could you,

[1] John Rigg, preacher, London (Great Queen St.) circuit, 1829–32. Became preacher, 1808. D. 1857.

[2] I.e. Great Queen St. circuit which had been affected by the serious disorders in the Southwark circuit which followed the refusal of Conference to give a constitutional clarification of the Special District Meeting proceedings in the Leeds Organ case. Cf. *Early Correspondence* pp. 213–25.

[3] Probably Robert Eckett (see *Early Correspondence* pp. 216–25).

[4] *Remarks on the resolutions of the Methodist Conference . . . relative to the discussions at Leeds . . .* (London, 1829). This was a remonstrance against the interpretation put on the Plan of Pacification (1795) by the previous Conference.

after what has taken place, consent to come to us, I have not the smallest fear, but you would be both useful and happy. On my own account I should rejoice in your appointment to Queen St[reet]; but I should rejoice, even more, on account of the Circ[ui]t. What are we to do? Is the Circuit to be ruined because a few men who are incurably prejudiced against the constitution of Methodism, have been able, and but barely able, to outvote its friends? Is not this the way to make the triumph of the faction complete, and to encourage them in their divisive proceedings? I am sure you have sufficient dignity of mind, and sufficient love to Methodism, and to religion, to enable you to despise, shall I say, or to pity many of those whose private feelings governed their public conduct. I assure you I should consider it an honor to be opposed by such persons, and with this honor it is probable even I may be crowned . . .

3   From John Beecham[1]   *Liverpool, Mount Pleasant, April 1*
                                                 [post-marked 1830]

Judging that you will be anxious to hear how we have got over the question, concerning the *Circular*[2] in *our* Quarterly Meeting also, I snatch a moment to give you a brief account of our proceedings. We had some doubt whether we should succeed so well as in the North Circuit, because our friends generally, have considered that circuit as more especially ⟨im⟩plicated in it; and this doubt was increased by the ⟨realis⟩ation that we should not take our few radicals by surp⟨rise⟩ as, to a certain extent, they did in the North. We had a strong muster; and the meeting got into charming tune, as we ascertained the extent of our prosperity during the quarter, it being found that we had 95 [members] nett increase, 94 on trial, and about 35 pounds surplus. When the *Circular* business was introduced, first one and then another spoke in terms of reprobation of it. Mr. Henshaw's[3] opinion being asked respecting it by one, he placed the iniquity of the *Circular* in a most forcible and impressive light, and excepting that afterwards he admitted that he

---

[1] John Beecham (1787–1856), preacher, Liverpool (South) circuit, 1828–31. Difficulties in the Liverpool (South) Quarterly Meeting had led Beecham to write the first of the great tracts on the Pastoral Office, *An essay on the constitution of Wesleyan Methodism* (Liverpool, 1829). He was President in 1850, and secretary for foreign missions, 1831–56.

[2] The *Circular to Wesleyan Methodists* was a paper published by the Liverpool radicals, 1830–1833, when it merged with the *Christian Advocate*.

[3] William Henshaw (1775–1841), superintendent, Liverpool (South) circuit, 1829–32. In his previous appointment as superintendent of the Sheffield circuit, 1827–29, Henshaw had distinguished himself by tactful handling of the disturbances caused by the Leeds radicals in the Sheffield and Barnsley area (see *Early Correspondence* pp. 182–5, 186–9).

thought the Conference had been misinformed on one point respecting the Leeds business he acquitted himself nobly. Old John[1] spoke; but an experiment I had made the preceding evening, in communicating to him a gentle hint respecting a certain part of his conduct or some other motive so far influenced him that he dared not to vindicate the *Circular*. He talked about the Leeds business, and argued that although he did not at all undertake to vindicate the publication, he thought it would be better not to adopt the motion of condemnation already made, but to leave the *Circular* to its fate; and he accordingly proposed as an amendment, that it be considered this day 3 months; and this was seconded by his right hand man on those occasions, who spoke in the same strain as himself. I was most solicitous respecting our friend Dean,[2] as to the view he would take of the propriety of our condemning it. He is by far the most talented of all who have ⟨b⟩een radically inclined on our side, and I knew if he entered heartily into our views on this subject, he would be of great service. At first, from the great love of peace which he now uniformly evinces he inclined to the opinion that we had better perhaps not notice it. He however was soon convinced that it was our duty to do so; and at the meeting, he followed old John, and in an excellent speech, he not only execrated the publication in stronger terms than any preceding speaker, but referring to the industrious dissemination of it among our people, he proved from our rules that any of our members or leaders being guilty of recommending it subjected themselves to expulsion from society by virtually breaking that rule which forbids evil speaking against ministers; and avowed it as his determination, that whoever might be found guilty of such conduct if amenable to his Leaders' Meeting, he would act the part of Attorney General against them. Bowers[3] and I thought it would tell better for the business to be managed by our friends; unless, however, we found it necessary to come up to their help. This however was far from being the case. Old John and his seconder withdrew their amendment, and the motion of our concurrence in the condemnatory resolution of the North Circuit, and the renewal of the vote of last Spring respecting the confidence of the meeting in the Conference was past nem. con. Old John had lifted up his hand for his own amendment, and another or two did not hold up their hands for the motion. The resolution is to be printed with that of the North in the public papers here, and on the cover of the Magazine . . .

[1] Probably John Russell, basket-maker, one of the Liverpool radicals (see *Early Correspondence* p. 119) who seceded to the Wesleyan Methodist Association.

[2] John Dean, a Methodist radical active at the time of the division of the Liverpool circuit, 1825. See *Early Correspondence* p. 119.

[3] John Bowers (1796–1866), preacher, Liverpool (South) circuit, 1829–31. Son of a Mayor of Chester. Governor of Theological Institution, Didsbury, 1843–63. President, 1858.

4 From George Marsden[1]   *Leeds, July 24, 1830*

It gives us pleasure to hear by various persons that you are in some measure recovering, though it be but slowly. The ways of Divine Providence are sometimes mysterious, as a depth which we cannot fathom; and why the Lord should have perm⟨itt⟩ed you to be laid aside at this par⟨ticu⟩lar season, eternity alone will reveal. There undoubtedly we shall see that divine wisdom directed all things well. How often in human life must we calmly leave what would be too painful for the mind, had we not a firm reliance on infinite wisdom and love.

You will have received an account of the most important stations. You deem it necessary to go to Liverpool and it may be right, but on many accounts it would have been desirable for you to have been in London. However you may occasionally come to any of the important meetings which will be held from time to time, in which the welfare of our connexion is very deeply involved.

It seems as if the preachers are a little divided respecting the appointment of the President. Dr. Clarke[2] is already arrived, and it is thought that he hopes to be elected. It is a little extraordinary that he should have arrived so early this year, when in general he comes to the Conference very late, and remains but a short time. Certainly it does bear the appearance of his having arrived here at an early period for the purpose conjectured. We hear that Mr. Stephens[3] is very ill and sometimes a little delirious, but the account may be exaggerate⟨d⟩. The representatives from Ireland ar⟨e⟩ Messrs. Tobias, Stewart, and T. Wau⟨gh.⟩ Yesterday the Stationing Committee m⟨et⟩ about 11 o'clock, and the Committee of eleven then entered on their work. This morning the School Committee are meeting, and the business is going on in a regular way. About 60 or 70 preachers are now in town. . . .

[1] George Marsden (1773–1858), superintendent, Bolton circuit, 1827–30. President, 1821 and 1831. The holograph of this letter is at Southern Methodist University, Dallas, Texas.

[2] Adam Clarke (1762–1832), b. Kilcronaghan, Co. Londonderry, ed. Kingswood school. One of the greatest of all Methodist scholars, he was widely read in classical and oriental languages, and employed by the Record Commission in editing Rymer's *Foedera*. He produced a valuable 8-volume scripture commentary, but his orthodoxy was always suspect to Bunting and his friends, on account of his denial of the eternal sonship of Christ, and his affection for John Taylor's *Key* (1745) to the apostolic writings, in which an anti-Calvinist view of original sin and atonement was developed. President, 1801, 1814, and 1822.

[3] John Stephens (1772–1841), superintendent, Birmingham circuit, 1829–32. President, 1827. Celebrated for his conservative and authoritarian attitudes.

5   From Edmund Grindrod[1]   *Leeds, August 2, 1830*

Up to the present the business of the Conference has proceeded generally with safety to all our great moral and religious principles. In one instance, the righteous jealousy of those who think aright, was awakened by a most injudicious, and almost impudent speech of Mr. Bromley,[2] den⟨y⟩ing the doctrine of Mr. Wesley's note on t⟨he⟩ Acts, on the Foreknowledge of God.[3] ⟨He was⟩ taken up with promptness and firm⟨ness⟩ and his conduct was remarked upon with that severity which it deserved, and the conversation to which it led was calculated to do good. The examination of the young men to be admitted [into] Full-Connexion is now nearly finished; they have acquitted themselves with very great credit . . .

Dr. Clarke has taken his departure from Leeds, but not until after many attempts to win either the affections or the future suffrages of his brethren . . .

We contended with our difficulties ⟨in the⟩ Stationing Committee until ⟨we w⟩ere all wearied out, and this may be one reason which accounts for the good speed which we have made in the Conference. It is not too much to say that we feel the lack of your master mind in every difficulty. Thank God my health is good. I rejoice, as do all the preachers, to hear a good account of you. We remember you in all our prayers.[4] . . .

6   From R. Wood[5]   *Salford, January 21, 1831*

When in Leeds, the week before last, I saw Brother D. Isaac,[6] and hand you the substance of one part of our conversation. After having asked after Methodist news in general, I enquired,

[1] Edmund Grindrod (1786–1842), superintendent, Hull circuit, 1829–32. President, 1837. The holograph of this letter is in the library of Duke University, Durham, N.C.

[2] James Bromley, superintendent, Huddersfield circuit, 1827–30. Connected himself with every opposition movement in Methodism, being a confidant of Warren in 1835. In 1837 he was charged before a District Meeting, Bunting being informed that 'there can be no doubt of his unfaithfulness. But whether we shall be able to fasten any charge upon him is to be seen' (M.C.A. MSS. John McLean to Jabez Bunting, May 8, 1837). Became preacher 1811 and ceased to be recognized at the Conference of 1850 when the reform secessions began.

[3] Presumably the comment on Acts ii. 23 in John Wesley's *Explanatory Notes upon the New Testament* (1754).

[4] The occasion for both the letter and the prayers was a broken leg occasioned by a fall, by which Bunting was confined to bed for many weeks and kept away from Conference. A young man, Philip C. Turner, was appointed to help him with his new duties as superintendent of the Liverpool (North) circuit.

[5] Robert Wood (c. 1788–1851), superintendent, Manchester (Irwell St.) circuit, 1830–32.

[6] Daniel Isaac (c. 1780–1834), superintendent, Leeds (West) circuit, 1829–32. Championing

'Do you hear who is likely to be our President next year?'

A. 'I have heard two or three conjectures respecting it, the most probable of which is Mr. Treffry'.[1]

Q. 'Did you hear any one conjecture that Brother Isaac would be raised to that honourable office?'

A. 'I dont know that I have. But that is quite out of the question; for I dont intend to be there at all'.

Q. 'You have not, perhaps, resolved that you *will not* be there'.

A. 'I have made no resolutions at all about it. But I have such an antipathy to travelling, and the distance is so great, and, as I am not removing, I have so little business there, that I do not intend to go'.

Q. 'I am glad to hear that you have made *no resolutions* on the subject. Of course if you should learn that it is the wish of your Brethren generally, that you should fill the chair, your anti-travelling objections may be waived, and you will not tell them, as you did last year, that you would not accept the office, if elected'.

A. 'O yes, I would. My mind is made up on that subject. I know very little of Conference business, and am every way so unfit for the place that, however obliged I might feel to my brethren for thinking of conferring that honour upon me, I could not accept it'.

Mr. Isaac, therefore, it seems, must be passed over. Mr. Treffry's probable station next year is so uncertain as to place an obstacle in his way, if there were no other. I understand, if his son recover, he wishes to go down to Penzance – too remote a corner of the kingdom for the President's residence. Where must we look next?[2] . . .

7   From William Leach[3]   *Bristol, February 14, 1831*

. . . I must if the Conference can accommodate me, have a circuit without so much travelling as I have had lately. The Bristol South Circuit is rather fagging. I rode 20 miles or near that yesterday, preached 3 times and gave the sacrament. It is a very natural division,

---

a very low view of the ministry in his *Ecclesiastical Claims* (1815), and hostile to instrumental music in church services at the time of the Leeds Organ conflict (1827–28), Isaac had long been regarded as a prospective leader of Methodist radicalism. He had, however, never gone into irretrievable opposition, as here he was refusing alliance with the dominant party in the connexion. Cf. *Early Correspondence* pp. 92, 169.

[1] Richard Treffry (1771–1842), superintendent, Leeds (East) circuit, 1829–32. Treffry became President three Conferences later, in 1833. Governor of Theological Institution, 1838–41.

[2] The next President was George Marsden, q.v.

[3] William Leach, superintendent, Bristol (Langton St.) circuit, 1829–31. D. 1846, aet. 67.

but a very inequitable one, both as to property and labour. I took the part to which the Superintendents for many years past had paid very ⟨litt⟩le attention. The chapels in a sad state, unsettled and of course unsafe.[1] Very little discipline had been known for years in many of the places. Good Mr. Entwisle[2] only went once in the weekday to one of the principal country places during his last year. I have had much to do; and the more as Brother Stead[3] is really a very delicate man, and cannot always attend to his places . . .

I have had an invitation to Burslem. What do you think of it? Is it not a very hard circuit? 1700 members and only two preachers . . .

8   To E. Grindrod   *Liverpool, March 2, 1831*

[Comments on Grindrod's MS.][4] . . . There are two points which have occurred to me as requiring perhaps some modification.

1. In what you say of the Ordination of God that a class of men, separated from all secularities, should be maintained in the Church, you are quite correct and scriptural; and you well vindicate the wisdom of the appointment. But may not some of the good and useful *Local* Preachers complain that you *tacitly* condemn the system under which *they* officiate who do 'entangle themselves in the affairs of this life'. Some brief sentence or short note may be desirable which, without compromising your great and sound principle (a principle now more than ever to be avowed and maintained) shall guard against any irritation of their feelings or prejudices, and shew that their case is the exception not the rule; an exception justified by the necessity which calls for it.

2. You properly state that the Church should not support ministers *in affluence*. But you proceed to assign reasons for the statement, the expediency of which I doubt. There is some weight in your apprehension that affluence would indispose us for laborious effort, would insulate us from the poor, etc. But if this danger be so great and insurmountable as you intimate, ought we not (to be consistent) to *refuse* admission into the ministry to any and every affluent candidate? I fear the Radicals may

---

[1] I.e. not secured to Conference by the Model Deed.

[2] Joseph Entwisle (1767–1841), superintendent, Bristol circuit, 1826–29. President, 1812 and 1825. On him generally, see [Joseph Entwisle, Jun.] *Memoir of Rev. Joseph Entwisle* (Bristol, 1848 and later eds.).

[3] Thomas Stead, preacher, Bristol (Langton St.) circuit, 1829–32. D. 1872, aet. 83. Brought into the ministry by Jabez Bunting.

[4] Shortly afterwards Grindrod published *The duties, qualifications and encouragements of class-leaders* . . . (London, 1831), but the MS. here referred to sounds more like that which eventually took shape as *A compendium of the laws and regulations of Wesleyan Methodism* (London, 1841).

quote your opinion as applicable not only *against affluence*, but *in favour* of short and scanty allowances to preachers. Does not your statement better rest on the ground that *the Church* cannot reasonably be expected to do more for its ministers than place them on the same pecuniary level with the *middle* class of its own members, those who are above poverty and yet still more remote from splendid affluence; and on the other ground, mentioned by you, that what can be spared, after a moderate support of ministers locally needed should be devoted to the extension of christian privileges in districts less favoured. To this might be added that ministers, of all persons, are most bound to be content with reasonable supplies from their people, and to let their moderation be known to all men. You see I take a distinction between those who have private property, and who, I think, ought not to be on that account abandoned to the invidious and low-minded reflexions of our small friends, and those who, being wholly dependent on their ministerial labours, have a just though limited claim to support.

Excuse the freedom of a friend. I *feel* indeed that *you* will require no apology.

. . . My own plans . . . are very uncertain as yet. I have not made such steady progress towards full recovery as I hoped for. I am indeed better and can walk a mile or more, and have for the last 3 Sabbaths *stood* to preach. But my foot and ankles swell much after every little effort and I have often considerable pain. If to avoid this or to relieve it, I rest much, then want of exercise disturbs my general health rather seriously. Thus I am in a 'strait betwixt two'. I hope as the spring and summer advance to do better. I suppose I must spend a good deal of time at Harrogate or Cheltenham, or both, in order to try the effect of an alterative course, steadily pursued. But how to leave my Circuit for so long a time, I know not; because, though I have Mr. Turner's[1] invaluable assistance, yet Mr. Newton's[2] frequent absences on the week-days leave me almost wholly bound to the duties of Superintendency which cannot here be intermitted with safety. We have, chiefly at Leeds Street, a bad radical faction, ever on the alert to seize any occasion of annoying us. I have already had two rencontres with them. One was caused by their attempt to have a public Exhibition of Sunday School children and a Tea-Meeting of Teachers *on Good Friday*, to the disparagement and neglect of

[1] Philip C. Turner, preacher, Liverpool (North) circuit, 1830–31 (cf. n. 4 p. 6 *supra*). Became preacher, 1821. Governor of Theological Institution, Didsbury, 1842–43, Richmond 1843–6. Ceased to be recognized 1846, after proceedings upon a charge of immorality.

[2] Robert Newton (1780–1854), preacher, Liverpool (North) circuit, 1829–32. President, 1824, 1832, 1840 and 1848. Newton who was reckoned to have raised more money for religious objects generally than any preacher of his day, was much engaged in public fund-raising for the Missionary Society.

c

our Sacramental Service and evening preaching on that day. Another arose from the effort of D. Rowland[1] and Co. to *force* me to nominate as Leeds Street Steward a man whom they had first *publicly* urged on us, by *conspiring* to *reject* at all hazards *any and every other man* but the one they had recommended. We have conquered in both cases; but the latter especially cost me much trouble and anxiety. Thank God, the great mass of the people are heartily with us, and at Brunswick we have prosperity and great comfort. Every seat is now let; and the congregation is uniformly good . . . [Stationing gossip.]

Now for the *Presidency*. It is a subject which seems to have interested already the anxieties of many brethren. Not a few have written to me on the subject suggesting the necessity of timely understanding and agreement, if possible, among those who look at the peace and character of the Connexion as much involved in the result. To Dr. C.[2] whom, as an old man, possessing many qualities well calculated to fascinate and to attract affection, one would like to please if possible, and whose *friends* will probably again clamour for his 4th election, not a few of the Preachers entertain *conscientious* objections. He is not *fairly* in the ranks as an itinerant; he has very objectionable peculiarities of opinion, which might embarrass him in his official duties, and make his election for a *fourth* time a virtual encouragement of what we deem heterodoxy; he has certainly *favoured* the late attempt to promote faction and rebellion against the Conference, not perhaps intentionally; but still his triumph would be in some degree that of the party who do not best love Methodism as it is; and he has for many years stood so much aloof from us, and known so little either of Circuit or Conference affairs, that he really seems *incompetent* to those duties of the Presidency which belong to the *intervals* of our actual Session. *In* Conference he could not go very far wrong; but *afterwards* he could not possibly do justice to his situation, especially living where he does, in a perfect corner, where he could seldom consult the brethren in difficult cases, and where no letter could reach him till many hours after its arrival in London, so that all *prompt* attention to pressing cases would be quite precluded. Such are the reasons urged against Dr. C. Now can we get over them? Will it be consistent with *public* duty, in spite of such reasons, to indulge our private inclinations and to gratify his wishes? This is the 1st question to

[1] David Rowland, sucessively ship-broker, tea-dealer, secretary to the Liverpool Pilots' Association and book-keeper; an active radical at the time of the division of the Liverpool circuit in 1825 (see *Early Correspondence* p. 119); became leader of the local Methodist reformers and seceded to the Wesleyan Methodist Association in 1835, but subsequently left it.

[2] Adam Clarke (cf. n. 2 p. 5 *supra*) had been in scholarly retirement at Millbrook near Liverpool for some years.

be solved: because if we *can* conscientiously elect the Doctor, then all is clear before us.

But if, with some of our wisest and soundest Brethren, we say that we *cannot* unite for Dr. C., what shall be done? If Mr. *Isaac* could have been induced to *submit* to an election, we could, I doubt not, bring him in very well. But he totally and peremptorily, though very respectfully declines; alleging incompetency, want of knowledge, dislike of travelling, etc.; and proposes *Treffry*. To this amiable and excellent man there are two objections:

1. The possibility that, in order to be near his son, he may be obliged to go to Penzance next year, a point too remote for a President's residence.

But 2., after all that passed at Southwark, making every kind allowance for Mr. Treffry's difficult situation there, his hostile or trimming colleagues etc., I doubt much whether it would strengthen the cause of Methodism to put *him* so soon into our highest office.[1] The Southwark Rads. have always *professed* to think him their friend, and boasted of his patience with them to the disparagement of men who shewed more firmness. Mr. Burdsall,[2] I think with you, is just now out of the question, both on account of his odd marriage, and of his inconvenient locality. Mr. Jos. Taylor,[3] I should most heartily support; but *he* objects to it as strongly as Mr. Isaac does; I doubt whether his health would not materially suffer from it; in Mr. Edmondson's[4] weak state, all the burden of Conference preparations etc. must rest on him this year; and then I learn with surprize and sorrow that he would not have the quite *unanimous* support of even *our own friends. All* of those, whom I designate by that term, would, I believe, be glad to unite for *you*; but the *Trimmers* would, I fear, be against you, on the ground that we should do nothing *just now* to irritate the grumblers, or give them occasion for fresh discussions. In spite of all the Radicals, and of their master, I shall *most zealously* advocate your election, if we see any probability of *uniting a large and respectable number* in your favour. For even if we be in a *minority*, as I own I apprehend we shall, we shall in that way better bear our *testimony* to good principles than by going with Dr. C.'s stream, merely to

---

[1] On Treffry's troubles in Southwark, 1827–29, see *Early Correspondence* pp. 213–25.

[2] John Burdsall, superintendent, Plymouth circuit, 1830–33. Became supernumerary, 1837. D. 1861, aet. 85.

[3] Joseph Taylor (1779–1845) preacher, Bristol (King St.) circuit, 1830–32; superintendent, 1832–3. A former missionary in the West Indies, and secretary for foreign Missions, 1818–24, Taylor became President in 1834.

[4] Jonathan Edmundson sen., superintendent, Bristol (King St.) circuit, 1829–32. D. 1842, aet. 75. The Conference of 1831 was to be held in Bristol, which must therefore find hospitality for the members and organize the business.

hide the fact of our defeat. This is what my mind has always wished and inclined to. If that cannot be, then why not look to Mr. Marsden?[1] It would much gratify him; we can depend on his substantial soundness; he has always *some* steady supporters, added to whom we might make a minority at least not despicable; and though he is not a *new* man, yet, in a case when his rival would be standing for the *fourth* time, that could be no just objection.

Grindrod, then, or Marsden, seems to me to be our watch-word. What others will think finally, on whose decision more depends than on my opinion, I cannot tell. Now let me have your cogitations, those of your correspondents, as *freely* and *confidentially*, as I have given mine, and those of my friends, to you. . . .

9 From Henry Davies[2]   *Camborne, March 26, 1831*

. . . In the course of the past quarter it has pleased the great Head of the Church to favour this circuit with a most extensive effusion of divine influence. Ev[e]ry place in the circuit, small and large, has participated in it; and as the present general result, my colleague and myself have given upwards of 1300 notes on trial, besides between two and three hundred notes of admission to Society Meetings etc., to young persons under 16 years old, who[m] I have deemed it expedient to place in select juvenile classes, under the care of suitable persons, without at once placing them in the same state as adults. The great work commenced the 16th of January and continued about eight weeks. In some places, it is going on still. Our society being previously upwards of 1400 we have thus given tickets and notes to more than 2750 persons. The present revival is distinguish[e]d from all others which have occurred in this part of the county, by its duration. That which took place seventeen years ago, did not at Camborne, continue more than three or four days.[3] We cannot expect the whole of these persons to stand fast; nevertheless, as it appears to me, we ought to think of applying to the next Conference for an additional preacher. This, Sir, I have stated to the brethren here. And as I am most desirous of being favoured with your opinion and counsel on the subject, permit me to lay before you the reasons on which I found the opinion.

[1] George Marsden became President, 1831.

[2] Henry Davies (1789–1870), superintendent, Camborne circuit, 1830–32. Davies, despite the sentiment of his last paragraph, remained at Camborne a second year.

[3] At Redruth nearby, the revival of 1814 continued without a break for nine days and nights, and was accompanied by abnormal physical manifestations. M.C.A. Tyerman MSS. iii. fo. 355; *Monthly Repository* 1814, pp. 377–8.

In the first place, I do not see how two preachers can give the quarterly tickets in a methodistical way; I have been necessitated, in several instances, to adopt a more summary mode, to give each individual his ticket or note, and then give a general address. This is unsatisfactory to one's own mind, as well as contrary to our standing regulation. On this I will not enlarge. In the second place, we have the fullest prospect of being supplied with the means of a preacher's support. I have said, let it be supposed that of 1300 new members, there should be a permanent increase of only 700, and that these 700 realise one shilling a quarter each - or £35 0. 0 a quarter making a total of £140 a year. The appointment of a single preacher would cost little more than a third of this money; and the surplus might be applied to the liquidation of the debt on two new houses which have lately been built, and in the end would secure a considerable reduction of annual rent, the advantage of which would be greatly felt when the time should come for us to exchange for a married man. The appointment of another preacher would, I think, greatly strengthen our cause in four places at which are above 1000 members, and three of which are visited, on the Lord's Day, only once a quarter.

In the third place I have urged this step as one of policy. . . .

Lastly I have urged the duty of moving anew the spirit of Methodism, taking the utmost possession of the ground which God has so liberally put in our possession.

I have however every reason to believe that the Quarterly Meeting will disregard these considerations, and in the face of the enormous labour which will come upon the preachers and the manifold risks which they will run, conclude to do with two preachers, till they shall have seen the result of twelve months trial, that is, in fact, a year and a half from the present time. Would you, my dear Sir, deem it injudicious in me to determine upon removing from the circuit in that case, or ought I to stay and work it in the unusual way as to ticket-giving to which I have adverted? . . .

10   From Joseph Entwisle[1]   *Bath, June 23, 1831*

. . . The state of the world, of our own country, of the church, and *more especially our section of it – all put together*, would be quite appalling, but for the persuasion of the truth of Psa.97[2] and similar passages . . .

[1] Joseph Entwisle senr., superintendent, Bath circuit, 1829–31. When the Theological Institution was opened in London, he was its first Governor, 1834–38.

[2] 'The Lord reigneth; let the earth rejoice . . .'

I am aware there are great difficulties connected with any plan for the improvement of our young preachers. I trust we shall be divinely directed. Something must be done. Unless the improvement of our young preachers keep pace with the general improvement of Society – our ministry will not be supported. At the same time zeal and activity in doing good publicly and privately must *even increase*, or the Clergy and our brethren the Dissenters will take our glory from us. I should think the time you mention will suit for the meeting of the Committee. . . .

11 To T. Percival Bunting[1]   *Bristol, July 27, 1831*

. . . The Conference met this morning. The votes for the Presidency were as under: For T. Jackson,[2] Lessey,[3] Waddy,[4] 1 each: for Jos. Taylor and Atherton[5] 2 each: for Gaulter,[6] R. Smith[7] and Buckley,[8] 4 each: for Reece,[9] 5: for Burdsall 7: for Tho. Stanley[10] 8: for Jacob Stanley[11] 24: for Treffry 39: for Edmondson 44: and for *G. Marsden* 57. Mr. Newton was almost unanimously chosen Secretary. Mr. Anderson[12] and Mr. Hannah[13] are sub-secretaries. All goes on very pleasantly hitherto. As to stations you have already doubtless heard those about which you are most interested . . .

[1] T. Percival Bunting (1811–86), a Manchester solicitor, 2nd. s. and biographer of Jabez, and a great lay defender of his constitutional policies.

[2] Thomas Jackson (1785–1873), connexional editor, 1824–42. President, 1838 and 1849. Theological tutor, Richmond College, 1842–61. A scholarly man of very conservative political tendencies.

[3] Theophilus Lessey (1787–1841), superintendent, Manchester (Grosvenor St.) circuit, 1829–32. President, 1839.

[4] Richard Waddy (1769–1853), superintendent, Newcastle-upon-Tyne circuit, 1829–31.

[5] William Atherton, preacher, London (Spitalfields) circuit, 1830–31; superintendent, 1831–33. President, 1846. D. 1850, aet. 74.

[6] John Gaulter, superintendent, Manchester (Oldham St.) circuit, 1830–32. D. 1839, aet. 73.

[7] Robert Smith (1769–1847), Governor of Kingswood School, 1820–43.

[8] James Buckley, supernumerary. D. 1839, aet. 67.

[9] Richard Reece, superintendent, Rochester circuit, 1830–32. D. 1850, aet. 84.

[10] Thomas Stanley, superintendent, London (Hinde St.) circuit, 1830–32. D. 1832, aet. 58.

[11] Jacob Stanley senr. (1776–1850), superintendent, Bath circuit, 1831–33. President, 1845. 'An ardent lover of constitutional liberty, he regarded popery as inimical to the rights of man, both civil and religious; and in the pulpit and by the press, he bore a fearless testimony against its arrogant pretension'. *Minutes of the Methodist Conferences* xi. 561.

[12] John Anderson senr., preacher, Leeds (East) circuit, 1830–32; superintendent, 1832–33. D. 1840, aet. 48. See also n. 3 p. 17 *infra*.

[13] John Hannah senr. (1792–1867), superintendent, Huddersfield circuit, 1830–33. Theological tutor, Theological Institution (Richmond branch), 1834–41, (Didsbury Branch), 1842–1866. President, 1842 and 1851.

12   From Samuel Jackson[1]   *Sheffield, March 21, 1832*

[Is willing to accept an appointment at Westminster] . . .

Whatever my talent may be it is unpolished and therefore does best among a poor people. I am cured of the wish to govern a circuit leavened with radicalism. It is distressing to me to hurt even the most mischievous mule in the way I have hurt Geo. Rawlins. That I believe was a public duty. But I will always avoid such duties when I can do it with a good conscience . . . Many luscious compliments were paid me [up to the last Conference] and I was told that my going there [the new Norfolk Street circuit] was a settled thing etc. etc. But having in the opinion of some who are radically inclined, treated some of their old friends with too little mercy – having openly complimented the old trustees for their magnanimity in giving up so large a part of their trust for a public purpose – and having dared to reprove that bitter feeling of hostility towards these old veterans (for such with all their faults they undoubtedly are) with which one or two of the leading men in the new circuit are full to boiling over, and being moreover guilty of many similar indiscretions – beside a whole host of infirmities – I am now politely passed by. This is all right but not palatable . . . [especially as he had apprenticed his son in Sheffield.] . . . You will be glad to hear that after a hard tug, we have gained a vote in the Redhill committee for a weekday evening school in immediate connection with their Sunday School. We shall now have an evening school and I hope ere long a week*day* school for teaching writing and arithmetic, before which Sunday writing will melt away . . .

13   To Edmund Grindrod   *Liverpool, May 1, 1832*

[Stationing gossip] . . . All, with whom I converse, seem to be of one mind, that Mr. Newton[2] ought to be, and will be, our next President. It is *rumoured* in London, but I cannot credit it, that Dr. [Adam] C[larke] says he is not yet a Supernumerary, and avows his *wish* to 'finish his fiftieth year of labours, and his itinerancy, by filling the Presidency for the fourth and last time'!!!

[1] Samuel Jackson, superintendent, Sheffield circuit, 1829–31; Sheffield (Carver St.) circuit, 1831–32. President, 1847. Governor of Theological Institution (Richmond Branch), 1848–55. D. 1861, aet. 75. The letter relates to the later stages of a long campaign by the Sheffield preachers to undermine the independence of the Sheffield undenominational Sunday schools, the greatest of which was at Redhill, and put a stop to Sunday writing lessons. On this see Ward, *Religion and society* pp. 147–9, 173.

[2] Robert Newton was President for the second time, 1832.

We hear delightful accounts of great prosperity from many Circuits. Yet I fear the prodigious amount of emigrations to America, etc., will keep our aggregate numbers low. The Connexion, however, seems to be once more in a *generally* sound and loyal state. The Second London Circuit, I fear, is one exception. The Derby Case[1] proves, like that at Leeds, how much mischief may be done by allowing factious and fanatical men to proceed too long and too far, without timely restraint. It proves also the wisdom and importance of 'Special District Meetings'. They are not enlightened friends of popular rights, who have decried such meetings. I think Mr. Davis should have called one,[2] instead of taking the whole *onus* of anxiety and responsibility on himself. He has been ill used. Macdonald's pamphlets,[3] and that of 'A Minister of Derby', will do good, and help to put matters in their proper light.

I know not how you view the new Irish Education Scheme.[4] The Irish preachers and people are, almost to a man, strongly hostile to it; and so, after much and careful examination, so [*sic*] am I. It seems to me well-intentioned perhaps, but bad in principle, utterly mistaken even as a measure of policy, founded on assumptions instead of facts, and in its *practical* bearings both on strict Catholics, on Protestants, and on the half-enlightened and inquiring class of nominal Papists, who now send their children in large numbers to Bible Schools, inconceivably mischievous. . . .

[1] The expulsion of the 'Derby Faith people' in 1832 led to the loss of nearly half the membership of the Derby circuit, and the creation of a small new connexion of midland circuits. Revivalists and supporters of preaching by women, they are said to have held that 'saving faith is not wrought in the human mind by the divine influence as the gift of God; but is simply an exercise of powers inherent in our nature, and employed at our will'. G. Smith, *History of Wesleyan Methodism* iii (4th ed. London, 1866) p. 171.

[2] John Davis senr. (1780–1852), superintendent, Derby circuit, 1831-32. It was a special District Meeting which had brought on a much larger secession at Leeds in 1828, and Gregory held that the staff of the Derby circuit had avoided much worse trouble by keeping the matter in their own hands. Gregory, *Sidelights* pp. 97–8.

[3] George Browne Macdonald (1805–68), preacher, Derby circuit, 1829-32. His pamphlet against 'the faith people' was entitled *Facts against fiction* (2nd. ed. Derby, 1832). Cf. J. Hackett, *Arminian Methodism miscalled 'Derby faith'* (Derby, n.d. [1832]).

[4] The Irish National Education system, introduced in 1831, attempted to provide a common education for children of various denominational allegiances. The clergy were to provide denominational instruction for children of their own flock on at least one day per week, and before or after ordinary school business (as the managers might determine) on other days. In ordinary lesson time undenominational religious instruction should be given by the teachers, based on a collection of newly translated scripture extracts approved by Catholic and Protestant church authorities. The Irish system (on which see D. H. Akenson, *The Irish education experiment* (London, 1970)) had immediate bearings on the English situation which are discussed in J. Murphy, *The religious problem in English education* (Liverpool, 1959).

14 From Michael Thomas Sadler[1]   *Leeds, September 10, 1832*

My Brother[2] has just informed me that he has seen you this after-noon in passing through Leeds, and that you expressed to him the kindest wishes as to the success of the contest for the representation of this borough, in which, at the instance of a very numerous body of requisitors, I am about to engage. I cannot express how much gratified I feel at this mark of your kindness, as it proves to me that notwith-standing the misapprehensions regarding my opinions and conduct which have prevailed in some quarters, you retain those kindly feelings towards me which I value highly and rejoice to find I have not lost. Prompted by my feelings at this moment I cannot refrain from stating that at no time have I ever written one injurious word against yourself or Mr. Watson,[3] who I find suspected me of having done so, and was therefore perhaps somewhat incensed against me. On the contrary I was

[1] Michael Thomas Sadler (1780–1835), an active Methodist in his youth, subsequently established in his brother's linen firm at Leeds, had reacted emotionally and intellectually against the liberal individualism of the day, and now combined a traditional Toryism with the leadership of the Ten Hours Movement. Deprived of his seat for Aldborough by the Reform Bill of 1832, he was now canvassing for election at Leeds; defeated in December by John Marshall and T. B. Macaulay, he relinquished the leadership of the Factory Movement to Lord Ashley.

[2] Benjamin Sadler, linen merchant.

[3] Richard Watson (1781–1833), the principal Methodist theologian of his day, his *Theological Institutes* being published in six parts, 1823-29. Watson entered the Wesleyan ministry in 1796, desisted from travelling in 1801, and was preacher in the Methodist New Connexion, 1803–07, being received into the Wesleyan ministry again in 1812. On September 16, 1831, when Macaulay and Sadler had begun their canvass in Leeds in anticipation of the Reform Bill passing, Richard Watson had written to John Anderson, preacher in the Leeds (East) circuit, 'on the great question of slave emancipation, I think we cannot for a moment hesitate to give the influence we may have with the people connected with us. Sadler, to say nothing of the ambition which has made him court the high-church and despise us, has never opened his mouth in Parliament against slavery'; to Macaulay's 'venerable father, that great, that sacred cause of negro liberation owes more perhaps than to any other man in the empire', and he himself had committed himself against slavery in Parliament (M.C.A. MSS. Richard Watson to John Anderson [postmarked] September 16, 1831). The following day Watson was called on by Sadler, and learning that his letter had been published in Leeds, he wrote again trying to withdraw the more offensive portions of it (M.C.A. MSS. Richard Watson to John Anderson [postmarked] September 26, 1831). Sadler's present application to Bunting may have borne fruit in the placards posted round Leeds on Sunday, December 9, immediately before the election, by Bunting's especial friend, W. Gilyard Scarth, saying 'that he could not support any man [i.e. Marshall or Macaulay] who was a Socinian, because he denies the deity and atonement of Christ, and that all other questions, secular or sacred . . . sink into insignificance in comparison with this'. The same evening John Anderson, now superintendent of Leeds (East) circuit, 'a man as highly esteemed for his piety as for his zeal in favour of Negro Emancipation, took occasion to reprehend with just severity the conduct of Mr. Scarth in violating the Sabbath by agitating men's minds with electioneering subjects', and repudiated the allegations of unitarianism against the liberal candidates. *Leeds Mercury* December 11, 1832 p. 1.

at the time I was so unfortunate as to fall under his displeasure on that and on some other accounts in which I can aver he equal[ly] mistook my views, attempting, without I trust any reference to electioneering movements, to revive our former intercourse. With Mr. Marsden[1] it had not ceased; – Mr. Watson and myself exchanged our volumes, and I thought had been upon the most cordial terms, when a painful mis-understanding arose, the recollection of which I wish to banish from my mind. I heard of the honor you had done me in attending the House of Commons during a discussion on a subject which I originated and which I continue to have much at heart – and was truly sorry to hear of the accident which had occurred to you in consequence,[2] some time afterwards and when Mr. John Wild said you had recovered. I had often meant to write to you on subjects of, I think, a very important character, and to have engaged, if possible, your influence in at least one cause deeply affecting the happiness, and welfare of the lower classes especially of tender years – but after the unfortunate mis-understanding to which I have alluded I feared had I opened a corre-spondence with you and attempted to obtain your sanction to certain attempts which I contemplated in behalf of the agricultural and manufacturing poor, it might be construed into an electioneering manoeuvre on my part and I therefore resolved to postpone my intention till I could no longer be liable to that imputation, which might perhaps have been naturally enough made against me had I pursued that course: – though nothing was further from my wish than to degrade the sacred function of the ministry to electioneering purposes; otherwise I might have put forth more than one letter of my friend Mr. Marsden, in which his opinion of not only myself but of my two rival candidates is given in no equivocal terms and which would have had great weight in my favour, as he was President of Conference and had travelled here with great acceptance. But on the contrary I never once shewed, much less published them, and I am satisfied that I have pursued the proper course. On the whole you will be pleased to hear that my friends augur most favourably as to my success, though the Unitarians who are here a rich and consequently a powerful body are universally against me, and several of the dissenters.[3] I sincerely apologise for having written so long and rambling a letter. My object in sitting down was to thank you most cordially for your kind wishes, and now that I can do so without its being supposed that I have political views in it (as you have already

---

[1] George Marsden, q.v.   [2] See n. 4 p. 6 *supra*.

[3] The constant theme of the *Leeds Mercury* was that Sadler had deserted his old dissenting connections, and was trying to cover the fact by blackening his opponents as unitarians. *Leeds Mercury* October 20, 1832 p. 5: December 11, 1832 p.1.

expressed yourself as favourable to me) – to beg your acceptance of a few volumes which I have published during three or four years past. To one of these works – that on Population,[1] I earnestly entreat your attention – the principle it enunciates and I hope proves – is I trust that sanctioned by the doctrines and duties of Revelation. The theory I discovered is rapidly gaining ground amidst much opposition and ridicule among those 'who would fain expel GOD and his providence from the world'. Some of the first scientific men of the age have within these few weeks past expressed themselves as entirely in its favour . . .

15 From Robert Wood[2]   *Leeds, September 24, 1832*

. . . *Non-Con-ism*[3] here seems to be almost at its last gasp. A measure exceedingly offensive to Mr. President Matthew Johnson, Messrs. Sigstone, Bell and Yewdall[4] – offensive because criminatory of their proceedings in their June Quarterly Meeting – was proposed in their late Conference – and after a warm debate of two hours, it was put – when the President declared it to be carried – and instantly left the Chair, saying 'Protestant Methodism is at an end!' Much confusion ensued. Attempts were made to restore harmony, but in vain. Another meeting, by which its fate is to be decided, will be held to-night. What the anticipated result is, may be gathered from the fact that application has been this day made, by Captain Sanderson, to Mr. Anderson and myself, to know if the Old Connexion will receive back about 20 Local Preachers and Leaders, and about 200 Members! We have given no positive reply. We think they should *first*, if they believe it to be ⟨thei⟩r duty, withdraw from their present ⟨conn⟩ections – *without* securing '*two* strings ⟨to⟩ their bow' – that none of those who caused, or fomented the disturbances can, on any account, be readmitted – that the others may, if they confess their fault, and pledge their co-operation in support

[1] M. T. Sadler, *Law of population: a treatise in disproof of the superfecundity of human beings, and developing the real principle of their increase* (London, 1830).

[2] Robert Wood, superintendent, Leeds (West) circuit, 1832–35.

[3] Leeds Protestant Methodism, a radical secession occasioned by the introduction of an organ into the Leeds Brunswick chapel in 1827 (see *Early Correspondence* pp. 156–92). The hopes here expressed of the total collapse of the Leeds Protestant connexion proved premature; the connexion threw in its lot with the Warrenite Wesleyan Methodist Association in 1835. In the 1830's Leeds Wesleyanism grew rapidly in numbers, in some measure perhaps at the expense of the Protestants, but after 1840 went into prolonged decline which by 1863 had reduced its numbers to the level of the mid-twenties, despite the doubling of the size of the town and continued chapel-building.

[4] The original leaders of the Leeds Protestant connexion, who had long enjoyed a local notoriety for radicalism, revivalism and opposition to Church rates.

of Methodism as it *is*, and *was* when they left us – that, in such case, Leaders may be received with their flocks, as they will only be bringing back our own. *Members*, of course, agre[e]ably to the invitation of Conference will be accepted – although they have justly forfeited the privilege, by their long delay. But it is a question with some of our best friends, whether any Officer should be received back, except he will come in as a Member. There is certainly reason to fear that if *some* only are received, the rejection of others may occasion uneasiness. We are desirous to 'shew mercy,' as far as we can, without endangering our safety or disturbing our peace. Will you favour me with your opinion as to what had best be done . . .

16   From Joseph Entwisle   *Lambeth, October 11, 1832*

. . . You see how poor Beaumont[1] has committed himself; i.e. if you have seen his sermon as reported by the *Wesleyan Preacher* and the Liverpool *Circular*. Also how Dr. Clarke's friends in the *Advocate* have injured his reputation. Our Ex-President missed his way in giving his *name* to the *Advocate*.[2] . . . I wish much to hear from you the result of the meeting in Manchester . . .

17   From William Leach   *Burslem, October 22, 1832*

. . . Things are improving every Quarter. Within the last few days we have had a very remarkable revival at one of our places about 2 miles from Burslem on the Manchester Road. Two colliers had been playing at cards all the night, and were at their work during the time of preaching in our chapel which is near to the house in which they were. They were cursing and swearing in a dreadful manner; when as they thought lightnings began to dart upon them with a strong smell of brimston[e]. They endeavoured to get to their homes but their horrors followed them. They began to cry for mercy. The neighbourhood was all alarmed.

[1] Joseph Beaumont M.D. (1794–1855), preacher, London (Southwark) circuit, 1831–33. A prominent spokesman in Methodism for liberal political views, he was convicted in his official obituary of infidelity to connexional discipline, and 'indulging an exaggerated sense of personal independence'. *Minutes of Methodist Conferences* xiii. 13.

[2] For the Liverpool *Circular* see n. 2 p. 3 *supra*. The *Christian Advocate*, a savagely anti-Buntingite paper, was edited by John Stephens the younger, the brother of Joseph Rayner Stephens.

No person thought it safe for them to neglect prayer since these men had begun. For several days and nights, nearly the whole population of the place which is considerable, were engaged in incessant prayer. Many of them were two and 3 hours on [their] knees without ever rising. Many of those who were blackened with almost every crime I believe are washed in the Blood of the Lamb. From what I had heard before Sunday last I feared there was a great deal of noise without much that was solid. But on Sunday I had a Love Feast at Tunstall and these persons were many of them present. I think from 20 to 30 of them spoke and gave in general such an account as was to my mind perfectly satisfactory. I do think this is a genuine and remarkable work of God. This will cheer your heart as well as mine . . .

18 From John Beecham

London, 77 Hatton Garden,
December 1, 1832

. . . I am glad to inform you that Mr. Alder has accepted our invitation[1] (subject of course to the usual condition that the Conference see fit to appoint him) and he says his Bristol friends consent to forego their claims on him for another year, but will expect Conference to be favourable to them, and give them in his place, one of three or four whom they will name. Peter M'Owan,[2] Alder thinks, is one of the number. I do hope the Conference will show them special regard in this business. They have certainly acted very handsomely. I learn however that Mr. Dixon[3] is hugely offended that he has not been invited, as several preachers he says had spoken to him on the subject. He surprized some of us at the time when the subject was agitated in the Committee. After Mr. Alder's name had been mentioned and the general feeling appeared to be in his favour, Dixon suddenly bolted out of the room, and it now turns out that he left us in great indignation. Mr. Watson was telling me yesterday, that he has never seen Dixon since, and that he

[1] Robert Alder D.D., preacher, Bristol (King St.) circuit, 1831–33, served in Canada till 1828, and in 1832 negotiated a union between two rival Canadian bodies, the Wesleyan Methodists and the Methodist Episcopal Church (of American provenance). The invitation was to become a secretary to the Missionary Society, a place he held till 1851. Left the ministry 1853, and d. at Gibraltar December 31, 1873.

[2] Peter M'Owan (1795–1870), preacher, Hull circuit, 1830–33. He was in fact stationed in Glasgow by the next Conference.

[3] James Dixon (1781–1871), preacher, London (City Road) circuit, 1831–34 (and actively engaged at this time in demanding anti-slavery pledges from parliamentary candidates [M.C.A. MSS. J. Dixon to Jabez Bunting, November 20, 1832]). President, 1841. Father of R. W. Dixon, author of the *History of the Church of England from the abolition of the Roman jurisdiction* (London, 1878–1900).

understands it is to be a long time before he will have the honour of another interview.

I spent a good part of the forenoon yesterday with George Stephen.[1] He interested me much with his account of the proceedings of the Lords' Committee on the subject of slavery, and of the plots of the West Indians, and the counter-manoeuvres of the friends of the Negro. Lord Suffield[2] acted a very noble part. Stephens [*sic*] showed me *confidentially* a work which he is getting up with a view to bring the evidence produced before that Committee, fully before the public. It is a series of comments and observations on the evidence itself, and will be such an *exposé* of slavery and West India affairs as must make a great impression on the public mind. He is only waiting till the evidence shall be published; and he will then bring his publication out *anonymously*; for of course he does not want it to be known that he is the author. He wrote to Lord Suffield only yesterday, about the publication of the evidence, and he suspects that the West Indians are manoeuvring to suppress it.

I must however give you *a hint* of something still more important. There is something of great moment now in preparation for the benefit of the Negro. We had, last night, a communication from Mr. Buxton[3] giving us to understand that a committee were in negotiation with government – that they were digesting a plan of emancipation – that they agreed in adopting the great principle that Christianity alone could prepare the negroes for the new condition into which they are to be brought – that the greatest encouragement must therefore be given to missionary operations. His object in writing to us is to ascertain how far we will and can concur in giving effect to the plan – what aid we can bring into the field – what we can do in forming a college for the training of a native ministry &c. A boundless prospect of good seems to be opening not merely for the negroes of our colonies, but for the 5,000,000 of the slave population of the world. I cannot however in a few lines, give you an adequate idea of the plan so far as it is at present before us. Its magnitude, its Christian principles, its plausibility, combine in recommending it powerfully to us. Mr. Watson dines with me today, and we shall talk the subject over more fully with a view to an

[1] George Stephen, 4th s. of James Stephen, and legal adviser to the Anti-Slavery Society, which with Quaker support had founded the Agency Committee in 1831, to rouse public opinion by public lectures by paid agents in the country. There is a reference to the disquiet his radical methods caused older abolitionists in no. 23.

[2] Edward Harbord, third Lord Suffield (1781–1835), liberal peer, long almost the sole advocate of abolitionism in the upper house.

[3] Thomas Fowell Buxton (1786–1845), philanthropist, succeeded Wilberforce in the leadership of the anti-slavery party in the Commons in 1824. At the beginning of the parliamentary session following these negotiations, Lord Althorp announced that the government would introduce an emancipation measure.

answer. In the meantime I must bind you, like ourselves, to secrecy. They deprecate the idea of the matter getting wind at present. Mr. Watson will no doubt embrace an early opportunity of communicating with you on the subject, and seeking your counsel. Till then you will kindly keep the thing to yourself . . .

19 From John Beecham   *London, December 22, 1832*

. . . We have not heard anything further respecting the plan of negro emancipation I mentioned in my last, excepting that I learned from the Secretaries of the London and Baptist Societies,[1] the other day, that Mr. Buxton had communicated with them also on the same subject. The more I think of the principle on which the scheme is to be arranged the more I approve of it. It will, and it will not, be *immediate* emancipation. Slavery is to be put an end to at once, but then the negroes are to be indented to toil for a given number of years. As soon as the plan is brought into operation, the negroes will pass from the condition of slavery into a state of apprenticeship; and this middle state is designed to continue no longer than shall be judged requisite for preparing the negroes, by religious instruction especially, for full enjoyment and exercise of all the rights of freemen. After we had given the subject some consideration, Mr. Watson embodied our views at length in a letter to Mr. Buxton in reply to the one with which he had favoured us. In regard of ourselves, he told Mr. Buxton, we could not calculate on greatly extending our West Indian Mission by means of voluntary subscriptions, as our Missionary work, in which we were already engaged would demand the utmost liberalities of our friends – that the best way to help us would perhaps be to build us chapels and provide us residences for our Missionaries, and the chapel rents would in part meet the other expenses – that if the pecuniary part of the question were met, we could perhaps send out twenty additional men per year for a given number of years – and that we could bring over, if means were provided, some of the religious negroes, who might be judged likely to become teachers and train them in this country for the ministry. He cautioned Mr. B. to especially guard against any renewal of a former attempt to place us under the clergy of the establishment, telling him that if we are to be any use in carrying into effect their philanthropic plan, we must as it respects the clergy be left free, and do the good we can in our own way. We have learnt from experience too many lessons to allow our indulging over-sanguine expectations on the subject, but I think it is

[1] I.e. the London Missionary Society and the Baptist Missionary Society.

now pretty certain something must be done, and something very considerable too, and I indulge the more confidently in hope, when I see the parties who are concocting the plan, give religious instruction its just place, and attach to it its full weight of importance in their calculations. Now, as to the indirect good resulting from some such plan being carried into effect, who shall say, that our bringing over negro youths for education for the ministry, shall not give us, almost unawares, what has been so long a *desideratum* with us, a college for training our candidates for the ministry?[1]

We have not heard anything more from Jamaica of importance. We dont therefore know whether the prosecution of the magistrates is going on. I have heard though this week, by the bye, of a matter of moment. Lord Goderich[2] admitted to a gentleman of my acquaintance in an interview he had with him lately, that the Law Officers of the Crown, had been applied to from Jamaica for their opinion as to the Toleration Act being in force, and my friend has since learnt from undoubted authority, though in confidence, that the Attorney and Solicitor General both concur with the Attorney General of Jamaica that the 52 [*sic*] of Geo 3[3] is not in force there, but they differ with him in thinking that neither is the old Toleration Act the law of Jamaica. They however do not decide fully so as to wish their opinion to be made public till they examine the subject more at length. I confess when I read the opinion of the Attorney General of Jamaica at the first, I thought he could not prove the old Toleration Act to be in force there, if he rejected the 53 [*sic*] of Geo 3, and I shall be glad to find our Crown officers giving this as their final opinion, because if the Toleration Act of William and Mary is not in force, for the same reason which I have not room to assign here, neither are the persecuting acts of Charles, and we are thus thrown on the common law, and our missionaries may preach without a license at all, if they only keep the public peace. The planters must mind that they dont push this question of law too far. But I am

---

[1] The reason for this distrust of the clergy was that the colonists had formed themselves into a Church Union to wage war upon the evangelical dissenters who were strengthening their following among the slaves, and in January 1832 destroyed 14 chapels (*Parliamentary Debates* 3s. xiii. 41). On the foundation of the Theological Institution, see below nos. 43 *seq.*

[2] Frederick John Robinson, Viscount Goderich, later Earl of Ripon (1782–1859), Secretary of State for War and Colonies, 1830–33, who tried hard to secure terms of emancipation which would not be too onerous for the planters to accept.

[3] The act 52 Geo. III c. 115, originally drafted by Thomas Allan, the Wesleyan connexional solicitor, and carried with the support of the Liverpool government, to repeal the Clarendon Code. After the defeat of Lord Sidmouth's bill to put down itinerant preaching in 1811, the clergy on many benches of magistrates began to refuse licences under the Toleration Act to Wesleyan preachers, on the ground that they were not ministers of particular congregations. Cf. Ward, *Religion and society* pp. 55–63.

acting on the common principle of putting of[f] the evil day to the last. I am reserving the sorrowful, truly sorrowful, part of my communication to the close. Mr. Watson is in a very alarming state of health. Dr. France was with him the day before yesterday, but I fear his opinion is not favourable. His sufferings are extreme, and are prostrating his strength very rapidly. We have hardly seen him at the Mission House at all for the last three weeks, and he has been so oppressed lately as to prevent his reading or writing, or even thinking. I earnestly pray for his speedy recovery, but I confess I have but slender hope . . .

20   From Agnes Bulmer[1]   *London, January 9, 1833*

Although I suppose you will receive official intelligence of the melancholy event which has taken place, yet I could not feel satisfied without closing my mournful communications by telling you myself that the decease of our highly valued, esteemed, and beloved friend Mr. Watson took place last evening at five minutes past seven o'clock. The final scene (as far as I have been able to learn) was not disturbed by any conflict – it was as tranquil as it had been the 'previous day. The lamp of life quivered in the socket as long as exhausting nature furnished the smallest supply of energy, and then quietly expired. But oh! what a gloom is felt amidst the circle over which its beams have been accustomed to extend! Yet the light of which we have been bereaved is blended with the splendour of heaven – this world is dark to us who remain in it – but the chariot shall ere long descend which I trust will convey us also to the ineffable glories which surround the Redeemer's throne. A standard bearer is fallen in the armies of Israel, but he did not relinquish his colours to the hand of the enemy in the day of battle. The dying testimonies of our departed friend and minister, I trust will remain as seals of the truth in many hearts. But who will be baptized for the dead? . . .

21   From Robert Pilter[2]   *Nottingham, February 6, 1833*

. . . I have no Methodistical or anti-Methodistical news worth sending, but perhaps a sketch of our last Quarter Day's proceedings will interest you. Our numbers had declined nearly 100 chiefly in consequence of the

---

[1] Agnes Bulmer (1775–1836), widow, 3rd. da. of Edward Collinson of London; a leading London Methodist and writer of hymns and spiritual biography.

[2] Robert Pilter (1784–1847), superintendent, Nottingham circuit, 1831–33.

D

'Derby Folks'[1] visiting our circuit and obtaining in five or six places members from us to that amount. We had however, 180 on trial, so that unless the delusion spreads we shall add as many as we have lost. On the Saturday evening previous to the Q[uarter] D[ay] it was whispered that the 'Ballot' was to decide various important questions and that cards were printed that each man might put in his 'Yes' or 'No'. Our usual number, about 90, sat down to dinner. When I proposed Mr. Jerram as one of the Circuit Stewards he rose and said 'that as several persons had mentioned to him the plan of voting by ballot, he had no objection to have it adopted in his case'. A burst of popular-radical applause such as I never before witnessed in a Q[uarterly] M[eeting] followed the proposition. I rose and stated that I had several very strong objections to the cowardly sneaking plan, but as I was to be the object of the Ballot perhaps everything I stated would be construed into a wish on my part to stay a third year, a subject on which I felt perfectly passive: If the meeting would agree to leave the subject open for discussion and not adduce the proceedings of that day as a *precedent* I would agree that, *for that day*, the experiment should be tried. This was agreed to and at it they went tooth and nail, but not till after many strong things had been said against it by others. First they rejected Mr. Burton as Circuit Steward by a majority of *one*. Against Mr. Jerram were 16 '*no's*'. Then the Stewards moved 'that our worthy Super[intendent] should remain a third year', and several very pretty things were said in his favour. The *cards* were distributed. The collectors followed with their boxes. A deep silence prevailed and all waited to hear the important result. I got up and stated the issue '54 say "Yes". 21 say "No" *A minority sufficiently large to send any man from your circuit*'. Then began another uproar. '*What*, was the minority to rule the majority. We never had such an overwhelming majority for any man before. This is the result of the abominable ballot' etc. etc. When I got them calmed a little I told them the *law* and *custom* of the Connexion as to three years stations: at which they looked wondrous wise. I then w[h]ispered to *Clarkson*[2] 'Will you after this stand the ballot. I *cannot* remain with such a large minority'. He hoping of course that everybody would be for his remaining persisted in being ballotted for. The result was 37 for and 27 against (Batty[3] had previously informed the Stewards that he should leave the Circuit on account of his health). I then advised them to cho[o]se a fresh set, but it was moved and carried unanimously that only two preachers should be invited this quarter and the Super and the

[1] Cf. n. 1 p. 16 *supra*.

[2] William H. Clarkson, preacher, Nottingham circuit, 1831–33. D. 1881, aet. 86. Moved to Sunderland after the next Conference.

[3] Edward Batty, preacher, Nottingham circuit, 1831–33. D. 1849.

youngest preacher be left until next Quarter Day. They have obtained a *promise* from P. Haswell.[1] Aylmer was engaged. So stands the matter. I think you never saw children more vexed with their rattle than my dear friends were with the ballot. I think it will not lift its head again in our meeting. 'I guess' the next Quarter Day will reverse the proceedings of the passed [*sic*], but I am very cool on the subject. May God direct my way. Will Halifax or Huddersfield be open?[2] . . .

22   To an unknown correspondent   *n.d or pl.* [*1833*] [*Draft*]

. . . I do not feel it *necessary* or expedient to enter into any electioneering controversy especially with a Gentleman whom I had not the honour to know even by name. To the hundred shameless falsehoods which certain persons have propagated I have not written one line in reply, for the purpose of publication. Some f[rien]ds have printed animadversions on my calumniators but without consulting me; and I am no party to anything which has appeared. 'The honour of Methodism and its Ministers' will be best vindicated if it need any vindication, before the regular authorities of our connexion, who will hear both sides before they even by implication condemn.

I voted conscientiously for Lord Sandon, because I know him to be on the whole almost infinitely more eligible than his opponent, I judge him so not merely or chiefly on political grounds, but on considerations advisedly religious which affect subjects and interests quite as sacred and as momentous, even as the holy cause of negro emancipation. Nay, much as it may surprise you, I was materially influenced in my preference by my regard to the just rights liberties and welfare of the oppressed slaves themselves. The truth is as your letter shews me, that you know very little about Lord Sandon or his opponent, between whom my choice lay; and quite as little about what you assumed to be my political principles; and you violate at once truth and justice, when you state that I 'deemed party feelings and politics too large a sacrifice to be made to the cause of humanity and religion'. Though I decline any further explanation to a perfect stranger *in writing*, I shall be happy to see you, if any opportunity of personal interview should occur. And perhaps I may venture, as you appeal to 'courtesy', to refer you to views

---

[1] John Partis Haswell (1790–1870), superintendent, Edinburgh circuit, 1830–33. 'I am a Wesleyan Churchman, preaching to this day without a licence rather than declare myself a dissenter' (M.C.A. MSS. J. P. Haswell to [T. P. Bunting] September 7, 1868). In 1833 Conference brought about a complete change in the Nottingham circuit staff.

[2] Pilter's next appointment was as superintendent to the Rotherham circuit.

taken by persons nearer to the scene of these farfamed transactions than
yourself, of the conduct I pursued as they have been stated in the
Liverpool Courier of January 11 and January 25, and in letters signed E.
and S. in the *Manchester Times* of January 19 and 26,[1] repeating however
my remark, that I am no party to anyone of those articles, and do not
make myself responsible for them as containing my own exact views and
all the reasons of my vote. I am almost ashamed of myself for having
written so long a letter on such a subject, but trust that you will receive
it in proof that, since you state yourself to be a Methodist and a zealous
friend to the injured African, I am for those reasons,

Sir, Yours respectfully,

23   To John Beecham   *Liverpool, February 19, 1833*

I was on the Cheshire side of our Circuit when your letter arrived.
. . . I may probably be wrong, but to me it appears that there is no
need for hurry [to make representations on the slavery question]; and
that the proposed measure of sending ruled papers by the next parcels to
every circuit, and thus in fact creating suspicion and alarm, if not
clearly *necessary*, would be improper and mischievous. There is no
probability that ministers will announce their purpose to Parliament for
some weeks to come. When it is announced, a considerable time must
undoubtedly be allowed to all parties for consideration and discussion,
and for petition, memorial, deputation, or remonstrance, if requisite. I
think we ought not to *presume* that we shall have cause of complaint; or
at all events, if we privately fear it, we ought to *know* it as a fact, before
we rouse the public to resistance by petition, or make any ostensible
preparations for doing so. This seems to me due in justice to the govern-

---

[1] At the Liverpool election of 1832 the sitting members Wm. Ewart (Whig) and Lord
Sandon (Liberal-tory) were challenged by Thomas Thornely, a unitarian radical, and Sir
Howard Douglas (Tory). The 1831 Conference recommended Wesleyans to give paramount
importance to the slave question in the exercise of the franchise, and Ewart and Thornely,
as protagonists of immediate abolition, called for their support. Having demanded immediate
abolition, Bunting occasioned considerable controversy by causing ministers who intended to
vote for Ewart and Thornely to stay neutral, and himself gave a plumper for Sandon when
his vote was not needed. Bunting's friends as well as his critics wrote in force to the Manchester
and Liverpool press, the letter from 'E' (which in fact appeared in the *Manchester Times*,
January 12, 1833) explaining that the conference statement was not a rule, but advice to be
implemented in the light of local circumstances; that Bunting had obtained an adequate
pledge from Lord Sandon; that in Manchester even the Anti-Slavery Committee supported
the gradual abolitionists; and that unitarians could not be trusted to legislate. Cf. *Manchester
Times* December 29, 1832; January 5, January 19, 1833: *Liverpool Courier* January 16, 1833
p. 24. No letter signed 'S' has been traced.

ment, and will have with them most of the appearance of a christian moderation, so as to strengthen our claims to attention from them hereafter, if we see cause to complain of their project, when announced. I am sure that many of our circuits *would* complain of the expense of ruled paper, if it should turn out not to be wanted. A measure of this sort just now, no necessity being proved or proveable, would injuriously distract the thoughts and conversation of our people, and might so divert them from the best things to subjects much mixed up, in this time of excitement, with the politics of this world, as to injure the work of God. Our duty, and our policy too, require us to be the 'quiet in the land', as far and as long as we innocently can. I decidedly think that the holy cause of Anti-Slavery has already been disgraced and prejudiced in some quarters by the system of 'agitation', after the fashion of Irish Papists and Repealers, which has been employed to promote it. The wrath of man worketh not the righteousness of God. Even the unprincipled *Advocate* confesses, amidst all his threats of violence and blood, that what he calls 'O'Connellizing' in this question has gone far enough at present.

There are some points on which I do not know the views of your Committee; but am not sorry to have an opportunity of expressing my own to you. I think it is a matter of equal importance and delicacy, to consider well and calmly, what are the precise portions of the Slavery Question with which, *as a Missionary Society*, we can properly concern ourselves in any public way. To terminate persecution effectually and at once, – to obtain for the persecuted redress for past wrongs, – and to have the religious liberty of missionaries and of negroes amply secured, so as to facilitate the indispensable work of christian instruction in all our colonies, and protect our Societies in the enjoyment of the Sabbath, and in the free practice of all the duties which the Gospel enjoins on its disciples, – these, and such like things, are clearly not only lawful for us, but obligatory on our consciences. And we may safely and beneficially go further, and declare to the Government and Parliament our full persuasion, founded on long experience, that an early and entire abolition of the state of slavery is indispensable to the full attainment of these righteous objects. Whether we ought, *as a Missionary Society*, to meddle with the *merely civil* or *political* part of the subject, I very much doubt. In our capacity as individuals and as Englishmen, we may do so with propriety. Have your Committee ever gone, or been inclined to go, beyond the boundary now stated? At all events I am strongly impressed, that in all *our* private memorials, or public petitions, whatever may be the proper time, the *religious and missionary* bearings of the subject should be made most prominent, and give the paramount character to our proceedings.

While I much doubt the wisdom, and even the justice, of any un-necessary and premature appeal to our people, *distinctively*, and in their separate congregational character, of course I quite approve of their uniting with other friends of the cause in their respective towns, by signing *general* Petitions. And I am even inclined to think, that if you have not done it already, it would be right forthwith to address a mem-orial to the Government, stating that as it has been officially announced by Lord Althorp that measures respecting the slaves are now actually under consideration in the Cabinet, you feel it due to your missionaries, and to your numerous societies and congregations in the West Indies, earnestly to pray that their religious liberties may receive a full share of deliberation, all intolerant restraints be removed and prevented, a Sabbath secured to them as their undoubted and inalienable right, etc. etc. etc. . . .

. . . Now for the most important request of all, that for consent to be proposed as your colleague and that of Mr. Alder[1]. On this my mind vacillates much; and I cannot yet come to any satisfactory conclusion. I have not heard a word from the Leeds Stewards. Till they in some sense release me, I, of course, whatever I may think, can *say* little or nothing. Many of the preachers, and leading friends of missions in these parts, express themselves strongly in favour of my accepting the proposal, subject to the decision of the Conference. At some times, I am disposed to think that it *is* a call for the sacrifice of private inclination and convenience to public duty. At other times I shrink and waver. Has noone else yet occurred to you of sufficient standing, both in age, and in the public confidence, who would be able and willing to go to your help, if appointed ? . . .

P.S. I was sure, as it has turned out, that the unfortunate division of the Committee on the 17th January, would get into the *Advocate*, and be misrepresented to my injury. I do not feel quite easy, or think it exactly just and right, that the distorted and perverted view given of that affair, in the *Advocate*, and assumed as quite unquestionable by several of its later correspondents, should go uncontradicted or un-explained. Do not the *minority* and especially *you four* whose names are specified, owe this to themselves, to me, and to the missionary cause, itself, if they *really* and *heartily* desire that my name should be officially identified hereafter with the Society. At all events, it should not go uncontradicted that I *immediately* and at once *accepted* the Committee's nomination, as published in the *Advocate* . . .

---

[1] Bunting was appointed a secretary for foreign missions, along with Beecham and Robert Alder, at the Conference of 1833.

24 From John Beecham

London, 77 Hatton Garden,
February 23, 1833 [Draft]

. . . You ask whether I have not yet thought of anyone besides yourself for the vacant Secretaryship, my answer is – no! My decided judgment is, you ought to come, and my personal feelings and wishes are in accordance with my judgment. I well know that the precipitancy of an injudicious brother has placed me under circumstances which are calculated to awaken a doubt in your mind as to whether I sincerely wish to have you as a colleague, should I be spared to be reappointed at Conference. But how could I avoid being involved as I am? At Mr. Watson's death, my mind turned as naturally to yourself, I am persuaded, as did Mr. Lessey's, but at the time of that Committee meeting, I had no opportunity to consult anyone on the subject. What with business pressing on me, and attention to Mr. Watson, and anxiety on account of him, sleep and I, I can truly say, had been almost strangers for some weeks when his death took place. And then the management of his funeral, and business connected with it, as well as the general mission business, pressed as heavily on me till we got him into his grave. Rash indeed then should I have been to have thrown so important a question in such an unprepared state before the meeting; and it would have been especially unkind to yourself, as I had heard (though I had learned no particulars) that a great clamour had been raised against you respecting your vote (for Lord Sandon). My plan was, that as soon as the funeral sermon should be preached, I would have a confidential conversation with you and then arrange with my associates in office not only the *manner* but the *time* of settling the business in Committee; for I could not tell whether your friends, with yourself, would not prefer allowing the clamour to subside a little, before the question should be *formally* determined in Committee, in order to prevent your enemies making the invitation the means of harrassing you the more severely, while as yet the business of your vote was so imperfectly understood. With these impressions on my mind, when Mr. Marriott[1] abruptly asked me near the close of the meeting, whether I did not intend to propose a successor to Mr. Watson before we broke up, not wishing for obvious reasons to give any hint of what I had in view, I answered that I had not sufficient light to warrant my taking such a step, and recommended that we should take a little time for consideration. Am I asked: But why not go along with Mr. Lessey when he introduced the question? I waited a considerable time before I said anything in reply, in order that I might see how the proposal was taken, and it was not till I saw that there

---

[1] Thomas Marriott Esq. (London), member of the Committee of Privileges.

was such a strong feeling of indignation produced against the *irregularity* and *precipitancy* of the measure as to prevent the comfortable settlement of the question at that time, that I complained of Mr. Lessey's procedure, with a hope that he would allow us to arrange to have a special meeting when we might do the right thing in the right way. His peremptory refusal led Mr. Haslope[1] then to declare that he would press his amendment, and take the sense of the meeting. Mr. Haslope told me afterwards, he saw very clearly that several who, he was certain, were your friends, would not vote for Mr. Lessey's motion in order to express their disapprobation of his irregular proceeding; and to prevent so unpleasant a result, he pressed his amendment for a special meeting to afford them an opportunity of expressing their disapprobation of Mr. L's conduct without injuring yourself. And that both the Treasurer and myself formed a right estimate of the motives of the minority is certain; for no men could behave more handsomely; nor did any support the motion for inviting you more heartily than they, when I called the special meeting for reconsidering the subject. You must bear with me in dwelling on those circumstances so minutely. It is necessary for my own vindication. Mr. L. with the best intentions, I doubt not, has inflicted on me a great injury. It was cruel to add to the burden which divine providence had imposed on me, by placing me in an attitude which was capable of misinterpretation, and which might possibly lead to a painful misunderstanding between you and myself. The pain and anxiety which his unfortunate conduct has produced in my mind, have caused my weight of care to press far more heavily and injuriously on me than it otherwise would have done; and nothing but a consciousness of rectitude and integrity has, under the Divine blessing, supported me. That the *Christian Advocate* would make a handle of the business was next to certain and the apprehension of that, ought to have restrained your impetuous friends from acting so as to do you harm. We have not been indifferent to the *Advocate*'s notice of the affair, but how to rectify it has been the difficulty. We could not have published a true account without producing an explosion in the committee. When I called the Special Committee to reconsider the proposal for inviting you, Mr. Lessey cautioned me against casting any reflection on him and his friends, saying he would not answer for consequences if I did. Now although he and I are quite friendly again, I know he has felt so much on the subject, that had we published the most simple and unvarnished statement of the real case, he and his friends Marriott and Smith[2]

---

[1] Lancelot Haslope J.P. (1767–1838) of London; lay Treasurer of the Missionary Society and member of the Committee of Privileges.

[2] Richard Smith Esq. (London), member of the Missionary Committee.

would have felt themselves reflected on by merely telling as much of the truth as would be necessary to make the transaction understood; and we should have had on the first meeting of the Committee after, a more serious collision than before, and which most probably would have greatly increased your difficulties in some way or other. And then our embarrassment has been as great in regard of the *medium* of publication. We have no paper of our own you know to serve our purpose; and what had we to expect from Stephen[s]'s[1] hands when it is his practice to suppress entirely or curtail communications which do not please him, and bestow plentiful abuse on the writers or those whom they advocate? We should get no justice for you from his hands. He would treat us most probably in the same way as others or get up some letter under a feigned name, to counteract ours, and make your case appear worse than before. We know so many of his tricks, that one has no hope of fair play at his hands. And after all, there is one great point admitted in his statement which ought not to be rashly endangered. He distinctly says that the minority *did not object to Mr. Bunting*, but were merely *contending for form and regularity*; and you will perceive that his correspondents take that view of his communication; and attack the *whole* committee for inviting you. Now it would be very painful if, by objecting to his account, we should give Stephens an opportunity of mystifying the subject, and making an impression on the public mind, that some of the minority, at least, were after all decidedly opposed to your appointment to the Secretaryship. Those considerations have kept us silent. We have preferred to remain exposed to reflection and suspicion, rather than make the matter still more trying to yourself. It is evident even to the superficial reader that he only places us in *seeming* opposition to you; and however painful it is to us, we have submitted to that wrong, rather than expose you to some new and more harrassing attack. I hear but one opinion expressed here respecting those who have appeared in the *Advocate* in your behalf, which is – that it would have been far better for yourself if several of these had kept silence, as they have only given Stephens the very opportunity he wished for to lengthen out the controversy and multiply words against you. I have thus stated to you the peculiar circumstances in which the minority have found themselves placed – between two fires, which has rendered it impossible for them to act without the certain risk of doing greater mischief. . . .

[1] John Stephens the younger, son of John Stephens the elder (q.v.), and brother of Joseph Rayner Stephens (q.v.). Editor of the *Christian Advocate*.

25 From John Beecham   *London, 77 Hatton Garden,*
                                             March 23, 1833 [*Draft*]

. . . I feel much honoured by the frank exposition of your views and feelings in reference to the more important business of the secretaryship. Your communication on this subject afforded me unfeigned pleasure; and the Treasurer and several other members of the Committee to whom, as you permitted me, I mentioned the nature of your communication, expressed their great satisfaction at finding that you were so favourably disposed to their application after your interview with your Leeds friends. We are not at all surprized at the reasoning which they adopt; we were prepared to expect that they would dwell on the importance of your Leeds invitation; and we are satisfied with the conclusion to which they have come, that while they will not be parties in releasing you from your engagements, they will not offer any *unreasonable* opposition to your appointment to the Secretaryship. It could hardly be expected that they would concede more than this. We hope that you will not delay much longer to give us your official answer to the invitation, *conditionally* accepting it, and referring the decision of the question to the Conference. You may rest assured that 'the Committee see no cause to withdraw their application' to you, and are fully prepared to urge their request at the Conference . . .

I hope the Slavery question has at length got into a fair train for settlement. Since I last wrote to you those of us who have been able to peep a little further behind the curtain than the public in general, have had great doubts and anxieties on the subject, and we have been apprehensive of a great struggle. It is now however understood that the West India body which had rejected the offer of Ministers, are coming to a better mind; and that they are now hastening to propose accommodation[1] . . .

---

[1] Not only Beecham, but also T. F. Buxton who (as appears from another draft of this passage appended to the letter) was the source of Beecham's inside information, had become extremely anxious at the ministers' delay in announcing their proposals for the abolition of slavery, and on March 19 had refused to withdraw a motion for abolition until Althorp fixed the date on which the ministers would announce theirs. Moreover changes within the government led to the appointment of Lord Goderich, the Colonial Secretary, as Lord Privy Seal, and to the resignation of Lord Howick, his undersecretary. In May the government proposed a scheme for abolition accompanied by a period of indentured labour, rather than the plan of immediate abolition devised by Goderich and Howick, but though (in the words of Beecham's other draft) 'the ministers appear to have been almost staggered by the difficulties which the West Indian body have originated', they had not secured the support of the West Indian interest, which opposed every proposal.

26   From J. Wightwick   *Tenterden, April 3, 1833*

[Enclosing the following unsigned letter]

Being necessitated by business (which came along quite unexpected the preceding evening) to be from home I was unable to attend the Quarterly Meeting this day as I otherwise intended. 3 or 4 of the members whose tickets have been withheld did attend, and, as the consequence of their attending was truly painful, I feel it my duty partly with a view for your information and partly with a view to ease my own mind to drop you a line. The Local Preachers met in the vestry at 2 o'clock and after their business was over the Brethren comprising the Quarterly Meeting met, among whom were three whose tickets had been kept back. Mr. Thomas[1] immediately objected to them on the ground that they were not members, and, as they did not think proper to go out, he adjourned the meeting to the Preacher's House whither all the friends followed him, when such scene took place as I am really ashamed to name. Mr. T. seeing those brethren coming endeavoured to keep them out by the force of his arm and all the assistance his wife could afford, when force was applied to force and Mr. T., without *any* reason, for three or four times cried Murder! Murder!, and actually sent his servant for a constable who came down to Mr. T. to quell the disturbance at a *Methodist Quarterly Meeting*, a thing I presume never before heard of! The Brethren who had entered urged Mr. T. to state by what rule they were thus expelled, *promising* if he would shew them that their expulsion was at all consistent with the laws and usages of Methodism, they would *immediately* and *quietly* retire from the meeting. This he positively and repeatedly refused to do, though they very much wished it. Mr. T. then refused to proceed to business and adjourned the meeting to Wednesday, April 10th, although some of the friends had come 12 or 13 miles to meet him purposely to transact the business of the circuit.

The whole to me, Sir, appears truly awful and I cannot but think it call[s] aloud for the immediate interference of some higher power.

A number of men fearing God, with three ministers of Christ at their head, meet to conduct the temporal affairs of the circuit. 3 of the most respectable (one of 30 years standing and a liberal supporter of Methodism) are thrust out in the most *insulting* manner because they

[1] John Wesley Thomas (1798–1872), superintendent, Tenterden circuit, 1831–33. Thomas's defence was that he was the victim of a malicious conspiracy by schismatically inclined members in touch with the Leeds Protestants; that he was found innocent of all charges by the District Meeting, except those of suspending three members and expelling one without the consent of a Leaders' Meeting; and that subsequently the Leaders declared the guilt of three of these proved. M.C.A. MSS. J. W. Thomas to Jabez Bunting, July 24, 1833.

cannot countenance what [was] wrong. There being no reason given, no cause shewn why [they] should be deprived of one of the most invaluable blessings of life, that of membership, stratagem and force is resorted to, the cry of Murder is heard in the streets, and the head of this ecclesiastical band sends for a civil officer to end the strife and take into custody those men of God; and the affairs are to be entrusted principally to the young and inexperienced, and I may say, some would say unprincipled . . .

[*Wightwick's letter confirms the above account with much circumstantial detail and concludes*]

I believe there are about 80 persons whose tickets are withheld from them in Tenterden and these are those on whom nearly or all that [*sic*] any responsibility rest while in Society in raising contributions for the support of so good a cause as Methodism. However bad it may be used or abused, it is most truly in my idea such a system as has not been since the Apostle's day and is so well calculated to evangelize the whole world. When reviewing the whole I am struck with the amazing providence of God wherein Mr. Wesley was led, in which Divine Providence has brought about such an economy step by step, through [such] a mysterious concurrence of circumstances as strongly stamps it as the *Work of God*. But I have hardly room to say that when an enquiry was made respecting a representative from Hamstreet Mr. T. said 'there were no *Society* there,' so that the whole of that society of 58 members is gone, making the whole, in 3 places only, about 150 members gone whom he considers not members. If it be possible I should be thankful if you could cast the burden and anxiety of this truly painful and distressing case into Mr. Kershaw['s][1] care and attention, for I think care should be taken to preserve your valuable life. For the many losses which the connexion has lately sustained is [*sic*] calculated to humble us, both preachers and people, speaking loudly for us to 'prepare to meet our God'. And you, my dear Sir, are frequently viewing the landscape over and behold your Saviour and the very many dear Brethren in the ministry in the course of your long warfare with Palms in their hands etc. . . .

[1] John Kershaw (1766–1855), sole preacher, Sheerness circuit, 1831–33. Poet and translator of Dante.

27   From James Wood[1]   *Bristol, June 6, 1833*

The Model Deed[2] is I think almost unexceptional [*sic*]. The two points I notice as of most moment and not quite right, are the power of Trustees to enlarge or alter of their own accord, and their power to appropriate surplus funds as they please, provided it be to any of the objects named in the clause. In Bristol we have suffered deeply from the abuse of those powers, and are minus at least £3000 this day in consequence thereof. I am trustee for three of our chapels in Bristol and, of all the meetings that I know of in or out of the Church, the meetings of the Trustees are the worst; I fear it is nearly the same in other places. To men so neglectful I hesitate to grant such powers exclusively. The chapels being strictly the property of the people, though legally that of the Trustees, the people or some body for them ought to have a voice also in reference to alterations of chapels and appropriation of surplus monies. To chapels in large towns this is more particularly applicable.

I beg your kind attention also to the following. Classes are the door of our Society and are perhaps the best social helps in the world to penitents seeking pardon. Band meetings are admirable for persons seeking holiness when under the care of good band leaders: but such are not numerous in any place and numbers of our members are so engaged in public or private business that they cannot find time to meet therein. Public bands are greatly helpful to seekers for purity of heart, but many such are excluded because they do not and cannot meet in a private band. Such persons meet often in classes where neither [the] Leader nor one of his people enjoy that great salvation – their counsel and experience help not such seekers – often their desires for holiness fail, they give up the pursuit and fall back into the common rank which contains many who enjoy not vigorous spiritual health. I know the jealousy of Conference in reference to old rules is very great, but times and circumstances will and are changed. Would not a relaxation of the rule as to public bands (now in many places through the door being so narrow almost nominal meetings only) were relaxed [*sic*] and the Superintendent Preacher authorized to admit to those bands all whom he

---

[1] James Wood (1751–1840), supernumerary preacher in Bristol from 1826. Cf. no. 30 *infra*. Assumed Alexander Mather's administrative functions when he broke down in 1800, and was elected President at the next Conference (1800) and in 1808.

[2] The Conference of 1829 had appointed a committee to prepare a case for examination by the Solicitor General and other eminent counsel upon the security of the Model Deed upon which Methodist Trust premises were held, and which vested the premises in a Trust to permit only preachers appointed by the Conference to preach therein. The proposal was to save expense by making reference to the original deed in subsequent deeds. The Conference of 1832 approved the proceedings of the Committee, and ordered a copy of them, with the Model Deed and a model conveyance referring to it, to be despatched to every circuit. A revised form of conveyance was adopted by the Conference of 1868.

approved who meet in class and are clear as to their acceptance with God, and respecting whom he is satisfied that they cannot meet in private band? Many such would gladly attend the public bands and both be useful to others and get good themselves. We must recollect the far more extensive employment of our people now in Sunday schools, as Missionary Collectors, as Tract Distributors, as members of various committees, than in the earlier days of Methodism, and all this requires more time. But a hint is sufficient – you will see its importance and practicability or otherwise at once and be guided accordingly . . .

28   From James Townley[1]   *Ramsgate, July 1833*

How many have been the painful occurrences which have taken place since I had last the pleasure of seeing you! But how numerous and great have also been our mercies! Our esteemed brethren Clarke, and Watson, and James,[2] and [Thomas] Stanley, and Storry,[3] and a host of others of our endeared associates have been called to their eternal reward, whilst we remain sojourners still on earth! . . .

I cannot, however, remember to whom I am addressing these lines without noticing, with what regret I have seen the attacks made upon one of the most disinterested of men, and greatest benefactors to Methodism, in the newspaper called, unworthily called, the *Christian Advocate*. To the character given of you in the paper of the last Monday in June by a writer signing himself 'A Junior Preacher', I most cordially subscribe; and I constantly regard as one of the most honoured days of my life, when I was favoured, with an opportunity at the London Conference, of moving the thanks of the Conference to you; – believing then, as I still do, that, under God, you have by your various financial regulations and Christian suggestions, been more than the *temporal* rescuer of the Connexion from ruinous embarrassments, and one of the greatest and most active agents in promoting its religious and spiritual character. I trust the prayers of the Church will long be heard on your behalf, and that of the Connexion, and that God will bless you by sparing you with life and health to prosecute your benevolent efforts for the welfare of Methodism. Forgive this honest statement of my views and feelings. . . . I must beg leave to say a few things relative to Methodist

[1] James Townley D.D., educated by Rev. David Simpson, evangelical incumbent of Macclesfield. Became preacher, 1796. Secretary to the Missionary Society, 1827–32. President, 1829. D. 1833, age unknown.

[2] John James, d. 1832, aet. 46. Secretary to the Missionary Society, 1827–32.

[3] John Storry, d. 1832, aet. 50. Former Congregational minister.

affairs, which press upon my thoughts. Much has been said respecting the £2000 proposed to be given for the MSS. and copyrights of our late highly gifted and much esteemed brother Watson. Were these a present purchase as a matter of Trade *merely*, I might be disposed to regard the sum as large; but if a *London bookseller* did not think *£3000*! too much to offer the Rev. T. H. Horne[1] for his 'Introduction to the *Critical* study of the Scriptures'; – and if Mr. Tagg [Tegg] did not think it too much to give a large sum for Dr. Clarke's Commentary[2] – why should we not offer a handsome remuneration to Mr. Watson's family for his valuable and *popular* writings! Besides is it not questionable whether the works of Mr. Watson, which the Book-Room at present possesses, have not already more than realized to the Connexion an amount equal, at least, to what is proposed to be given to his bereaved family? – His *Institutes*,[3] his *Catechisms*,[4] – his *Theological Dictionary*,[5] his *Life of Wesley*,[6] his *Reply to Southey*,[7] etc. etc. have already produced a rich harvest; one may justly expect his *Conversations for the Young*,[8] eulogised even in the *Evangelical Magazine*, as the result of a life of study, his *Sermons*,[9] his *Commentary*,[10] etc. etc. will realize a large amount, to say nothing of the continued and

[1] Thomas Hartwell Horne (1780–1862), biblical scholar, bibliographer and polemic, whose *Introduction to the critical study and knowledge of the Holy Scriptures*, first published in 1818, was frequently reprinted and remained a standard work for over half a century. As a young man, Horne seems to have been an active member of the Methodist Society at Lambeth, and corresponded with Bunting about his plan for a critical edition of the Bible, which eventually grew into the *Introduction*. Joseph Butterworth, the Methodist law publisher, assisted him to find leisure for scholarship first as a private clerk, than as deputy to Adam Clarke as librarian of the Surrey Institution. In 1819, Howley, then bishop of London, ordained him as a literate on the strength of his *Introduction*, and in 1834, hearing that a Wesleyan Theological Institution was to be founded, Horne, still standing 'guard against German neologism and Popery', sent Bunting a present of books for it. M.C.A. MSS. T. H. Horne to Jabez Bunting, December 3, 1806; April 8, 1807; December 6, 1809 (these letters are partly printed in *Life of Bunting* i. 286–288, 293, 355); October 20, 1807; September 9, 1834.

[2] Adam Clarke, *The Holy Bible, with a commentary and critical notes* (8 vols. London, 1810–20). The Methodist Book Room declining to republish a revised version of this work after Clarke's death, James Everett negotiated the sale of the copyright to William Tegg (1776–1845) an immensely successful publisher and bookseller for £2000; he is said to have realised £30,000 on it before he died.

[3] Richard Watson, *Theological Institutes* (6 parts London, 1823–29).

[4] *Catechism of the evidences of Christianity* (1823) reprinted in *Works of Richard Watson* xii.

[5] *A biblical and theological dictionary* (London, 1831).

[6] *Life of Rev. John Wesley* (London, 1831).

[7] *Observations on Mr Southey's 'Life of Wesley', being a defence of the character, labours and opinions, of Mr Wesley against the misrepresentations of that publication* (London, 1820).

[8] *Conversations for the young designed to promote the profitable reading of the Holy Scriptures* (London, 1830).

[9] Watson's sermons were first published as a collection with his *Works* (1834).

[10] *An exposition of . . . St. Mathew and St. Mark, of . . . detached parts of . . . Scripture* ed. T. Jackson (London, 1833).

regular sale of his former works! In addition to all this, who can state
the amount of our obligation to him (and through him to his family)
for his long, laborious, indefatigable, and successful exertions on behalf
of our Missions. He has sacrificed his very life for the interests of
Methodism, and who will withhold a sum from his family to make them
comfortable? It would be a disgrace to the whole Connexion to withhold it. I know that the Book-Committee never thought him remun-
erated for what he had generously, but as many of them thought, with
regard to his family, *imprudently* given. So strong was this feeling, that I
have no doubt Mr. Mason[1] and other members of that Committee, will
recollect, my stating, in his presence, that a sum ought eventually to be
applied to some purpose, gratifying to himself; for instance to the education of young preachers. I name this to prove prospective designs, of
some kind of remuneration; and when cut off in the midst of his days, by
labours too vast and constant even for his gigantic mind, how can we
better testify our conviction of the value of those labours than by a
liberal purchase of those *Works*, which may enrich, as well as edify our
Connexion, when by that purchase we render those comfortable whom
he tenderly loved. But I cannot, I will not believe the amount will be
negatived . . .

29   From James E. Moulton[2]   *Carnarvon, July 13, 1833*

. . . Our friends in this circuit look to you to provide for them next
year. They have not thought it advisable to apply to any one believing
that you would know better than themselves who would be likely to suit
them. This station is an important one, and is likely to become increasingly so. The introduction of English Methodism into the Principality will, I believe, be productive of lasting benefit. This circuit is
rather a trying one on account of the small scale on which things are
carried on; the greater part of the population speaking a different
language, and being completely shut up to his efforts, renders it unpleasant: – there is also much fatiguing travelling: but the friends are
kind, many of them intelligent – and there are great opportunities for
improvement, having very frequently to address the same congregation.
A person of some *mind*, and who has also zeal and energy and a little of
the missionary spirit, is the character for this part of the Connexion. We

[1] John Mason, Book Steward, 1827–64. D. 1864, aet. 82. An intimate friend of Richard
Watson, Mason already enjoyed a considerable reputation for having got the finances of the
Book Room in order, and contributing to the general funds of the denomination from its
profits.

[2] James E. Moulton (1806–66), sole preacher, Bangor (English) circuit, 1831–33.

hope the Conference will not object to appoint a second preacher:[1] our friends feel more and more convinced of its *necessity*, and of the advantage which would result from it. They wish they could do without asking for the £30, but at present they cannot. They confidently hope in the course of time to be able to be independent of assistance from our friends, and the manner in which hitherto notwithstanding the fewness of their numbers they have kept their pledge, affords room to believe that they will not ask for assistance any longer than they find it absolutely needful.

I may here mention that at the last Welsh District Meeting, after Mr. Newton had left (he being obliged to go before the conclusion leaving Mr. Gaulter behind) the proposition was again brought forward that the two English Circuits in North Wales should be connected with the Welsh District; and the old man, who has not often visited Wales, has been talked over into an acquiescence with this proposition, and will I believe support it at Conference. At the last Conference the subject was started, and quashed. Our friends here, and in the other Circuit also, are of the same opinion as before, that to remove them at present from the protection of an English District Meeting, would be most injurious to the rising cause. I need not refer you to the reasons . . . I merely express to you that our friends hope that you will take care of them: being now in a District of which you are chairman they look to you as

[1] Two preachers were appointed to the Bangor (English) circuit for the first time at the Conference of 1833. In letters of September 25 and December 7, 1832, Moulton had already put the affairs of his circuit to Bunting who, as chairman of the Liverpool District, had some oversight of them. The small English causes in Carnarvon, Bangor, Amlwch and Holyhead were growing steadily, and the former found themselves packed beyond capacity in summer, especially on those Sunday evenings when there was no English service at the Church. Even in 1837 the Society membership was only 100 and it was not easy to justify stationing two preachers. The main centres of the circuit were, however, very remote from each other, English residents desired services in the vernacular, but produced few local preachers among their own number, and only two Welsh local preachers were able to 'preach English in some degree'. To put the English work under the Welsh District might not only destroy the claim for additional ministerial assistance on which its survival depended, it might make the appointment intolerable to English preachers. 'Calvinism is rampant in the Principality, . . . especially in the Northern counties: against this Welsh Wesleyanism ought indeed to be the bulwark, and it is to some degree, but not so efficiently as it might be . . . The grand religious defect throughout the whole of Wales is lax notions in reference to the Christian ministry, and here the Welsh Wesleyans have caught the prevalent infection, and the notion of a body of men being set apart entirely for the ministry is what they are very reluctant to admit'. (M.C.A. MSS. J. E. Moulton to Jabez Bunting, May 15, 1837). To these arguments Bunting, who had already secured additional preaching staff for Buxton on the ground of its significance as a watering-place, was sympathetic, and the Bangor circuit retained its second preacher until the Conference of 1842 created a separate English circuit at Holyhead. For other examples of the perennial embarrassments of English Methodism in Wales, see M.C.A. MSS. J. Simon to Jabez Bunting, July 27, 1836; W. Drewett to same, April 9, May 12, 1838; W. Drewett to John Davies, January 23, 1839; Joseph Wood to Jabez Bunting, April 30, 1838.

E

their Protector and trust that you will use your influence in their
defence should it be necessary . . .

30   From P. C. Turner to T. P. Bunting

Bristol,
November 22, 1833

. . . Mr. Scott[1] is a *very* nice man, I like him much and think his views
of Methodist discipline will be serviceable here, we want a larger spice
of Tory principle amongst us, though we have on the whole a very
excellent set of men as managers, among the first of whom is Mr.
Wood.[2] Poor old Mr. Wood is getting very feeble, though not ill – he
retires from his work in fine stile, seems to look at nothing with a
jaundiced eye and rejoices in the conviction that he leaves Methodist
preachers and Methodist societies in a better state than they were in
more primitive days . . . The plan p⟨ropos⟩ed by the special committee
in London for the improvem⟨ent⟩ of young preachers meets with some
opposers here, bo⟨th⟩ amongst preachers and people.[3] My fear is that it
may get into indifferent hands at a future day and b⟨e⟩ ⟨a⟩ manufactory for such 'dashing blades' as come out from the *dissenting colleges.*
From this I sincerely hope we shall be preserved. I think the proposed
scheme will be more expensive than can be conveniently met – but I
must leave it to wiser heads than mine and hope it may be a real
blessing to us. . . .

31   From George Morley[4]

Woodhouse Grove, January 8, 1834

. . . Every Quarter Day in this District has gone off very well, only in
Bradford they passed a Resolution in favour of the Ballott, and in our

[1] John Scott, superintendent, Bristol (King St.) circuit, 1833–36. Cf. n. 1 p. 1 *supra.*

[2] James Wood, supernumerary, q.v.

[3] After formal and informal discussions over several years, the Conference of 1833 appointed
a committee to make proposals for the education of preachers on the list of reserve, i.e. of
candidates already approved for the ministry who were called into service as vacancies arose.
By the end of October the committee had prepared an elaborate report later published as
*Proposals for the formation of a Literary and Theological Institution with a view to the improvement of
the junior preachers in the Methodist connexion*, and, proceeding to recommend the appointment
of Bunting as President, and of others as tutors, encountered the opposition of one of its
members, Dr. Samuel Warren. In the course of the year 1834 growing opposition to the
scheme gathered round Dr. Warren and his friends who finally seceded to form the Wesleyan
Methodist Association. This discontent is extensively illustrated in letters which follow.

[4] George Morley (1772–1843), Governor of Woodhouse Grove School, 1831–43. One of the
early organizers of the Missionary Society, of which he was Treasurer in 1821, and Secretary
in 1824.

own, they would have passed some very violent and insulting resolutions, on the Institution, if the Superintendent would have put them.
But he felt himself obliged to refuse; though he would have allowed
them to express to the Conference, in proper language, their views on
that, or any subject of general legislation, but nothing on the subject of
any distant District, or Circuit, or individual Preacher. They went away
very much dissatisfied and say they shall bring it on again in March.

32   From Samuel Jackson[1]   *Liverpool, January 9, 1834*

. . . I wish you success in your exertions on behalf of the 'Missions'
abroad, and the 'Institution' at home, and shall be ready to promote
both objects as far as my influence extends. I hope you will find time
to bestow a thought upon week day schools at home. You have an
agent for schools in Ireland, why should we not have such an officer in
England, who might be supported for a few years out of the Contingent Fund, study the whole subject thoroughly, organize schools in the
principal towns, on the best principles, which would serve as models,
and be generally imitated in due time? Mr. Comer says the Liverpool
schools this year, will have an income which will meet the expense.
If so who need despair! . . .

33   From Thomas Harris[2]   *Burslem, February 13, 1834*

. . . During the last two months I have had a more than usual load of
care in reference to the affairs of the Burslem Society. It has long been
the wish of our principal friends that the time of our public worship
in the morning should be altered from 9 o'clock to half past 10. The
opposition to this measure has been from the Sunday School, in which
1400 children are instructed, but which has no direct connexion with
the worship of Almighty God. During six months in the year, the elder
children who come to the chapel in the morning in time to hear the
sermon, have a ticket given them which entitles them to learn writing

[1] Samuel Jackson, superintendent, Liverpool (North) circuit, 1833–35. Jackson's lifelong
interest in education led to his election as President in 1847 at the crisis of Lord John Russell's
education plans (*Guardian* 1847 p. 507). Liverpool Methodists had been unusually forward in
opening day schools, and by 1825 they were educating 1420 day scholars as compared with
1000 Sunday scholars. William Comer was a Wesleyan cotton broker of Tory political
sympathies.

[2] Thomas Harris (1791–1863), superintendent, Burslem circuit, 1833–35.

on the Sabbath day. But as a whole the public worship of Almighty God forms no part of the education of the children in the Burslem Sunday School, altho[ugh] the school is the property of the Trustees.[1]

I have just succeeded in obtaining a new Trust Deed for our Chapel and have made 23 new Trustees, but the leaders, at least a majority of them influenced by the school teachers, are pleading their right under the law of Pacification,[2] Viz. That service in Church hours shall only be permitted when a majority of the Leaders on the *one hand*, and a majority of the Trustees *on the other desire it*.

I shall be obliged if Mr. Bunting can inform me if I am right in my interpretation, viz. That the votes of the Trustees and Leaders should be conjoined and the ⟨ma⟩tter determin⟨ed⟩ by the majority. I find that in the trial of preachers for false doctrine etc., preachers, Trustees and Leaders are united in one body and the majority carry the point. Some of our Leaders (who I expect will give up the classes if the alteration is made) contend that a majority of the Leaders separately can control a vote of the Trustees. I am opposing this doctrine with all the prudence and firmness of which I am capable. Am I right?

In desiring the opinion of Mr. Bunting to guide my judgement I wish to act upon my own responsibility without quoting names.

I have found since I commenced this affair that the school has for years been labouring to be independent of the Chapel, and that in a few years they intended building a new school room, upon a separate and independent Trust of the Chapel. Happily this is prevented. In every other part of the circuit we are doing well, and the oppositionists have no sympathy from a single ⟨socie⟩ty in this circuit. . . .

[1] Burslem Sunday School, founded in 1787 on Methodist initiative 'not to promote the religious principles of any particular sect, but setting aside all party distinctions, to instruct youth in useful learning [and] . . . the leading and uncontrovertible principles of Christianity', was one of the largest and most famous of the undenominational Sunday schools, and still paid rent to the Wesleyan Trustees for their premises. For the development of the case, see no. 82 *infra*. On the disorderly state of the Burslem circuit, see *Early Correspondence* no. 84.

[2] The main object of the Plan of Pacification (1795) had been to regulate the terms on which Methodists might receive the sacrament of Holy Communion from their own preachers in their own chapels. The decision as to the administration of baptism, the burial of the dead or the conduct of services in Church hours was made subject to the same procedure, the Leaders and Stewards representing the sense of the people, the Trustees the financial interest in the property. The Plan was intended to settle conditions of practical separation from the Church of England, not the relations between the Methodist Societies and other institutions more or less informally connected with them.

34 From John Beecham   *London, February 21, 1834*

. . . I sit down to communicate to you what we have heard as to our destroyed chapels in Jamaica.¹ The day before yesterday, Mr. Dyer² sent wishing to see some of us. He had ascertained that Mr. Lefebvre³ [*sic*] does not stand in the same confidential relation to Mr. Stanley,⁴ that Lord Goderich's Under-Secretary did to him:⁵ that Mr. Stanley does not advise with him much and that of course Mr. Lefebvre had not much influence. He had seen Mr. Lefebvre, however, and was told that he might be assured nothing would be done at the *Colonial* Office in the business. Mr. Dyer then went to Lord Henley⁶ to get him to lay the case of the chapels before the Lord Chancellor, with a view of getting him to include the amount in the expenses for Education to be met out of the money he has for appropriation. Lord Henley eventually undertook to convey a statement to the Lord Chancellor,⁷ and this he has done, through Mr. Brougham his Lordship's brother.⁸ From Lord Henley Mr. Dyer went to Mr. Buxton, and laid the case before him. Mr. Buxton remembered that Lord Althorp⁹ distinctly promised him, when the one million pounds was granted by Parliament, that the chapel losses should be met out of that sum, and he had it in writing, having put down at the time his Lordship's words that there might be no mistake. Mr. Buxton immediately set off to Lord Althorp who admitted that he had had such conversation with Mr. Buxton, but did not think what he promised amounted to more than that ministers would do what they could to obtain redress for the sufferers. Mr. Buxton then proposed to accompany a deputation from the two Missionary Societies¹⁰ to Lord Althorp and engaged to see Lord Althorp, and arrange with his Lordship to see the

¹ On these see n. 1 p. 24 *supra*.

² Rev. John Dyer, appointed first full-time Secretary of the Baptist Missionary Society, 1818. Found drowned 1841.

³ John George Shaw-Lefevre (1797–1879), said to have been specially selected by Lord Stanley to be his undersecretary at the Colonial Office, 1833–34. Cf. n. 4 p. 52 *infra*.

⁴ Edward Geoffrey Smith-Stanley, commonly called Lord Stanley, later 14th earl of Derby (1799–1869), Secretary of State for War and Colonies, 1833–34.

⁵ On Lord Goderich (1782–1859), Secretary of State for War and Colonies, 1830–33, and his undersecretary Lord Howick (1802–94), see n. 1 p. 34 *supra*.

⁶ Robert Henley Eden, second Baron Henley (1789–1841), master in chancery and specialist in bankruptcy law. Published an important plan for Church reform, 1834. Brother-in-law to Sir Robert Peel.

⁷ Henry Peter Brougham, Lord Brougham and Vaux (1778–1868), Lord Chancellor, 1830–34.

⁸ William Brougham, later 2nd Baron Brougham and Vaux (1795–1886), M.P. for Southwark, 1831–35.

⁹ John Charles Spencer, Lord Althorp, and later Lord Spencer (1782–1845), Chancellor of the Exchequer and Leader of the House of Commons, 1830–34.

¹⁰ I.e. the Wesleyan Methodist Missionary Society and the Baptist Missionary Society.

deputation on Saturday if convenient. In communicating this to us, Mr. Dyer was anxious that we should engage Lord Morpeth,[1] or some other influential statesman to join us in the deputation, thinking it would add weight, and would go to impress the Chancellor of the Exchequer with the idea, that if he refused help, the matter would be seriously taken up in Parliament. That part of the plan which related to our going with them to the Chancellor on Saturday, in company with Mr. Buxton, who had voluntarily offered his services, met our views at once, but the proposal to try to engage Lord Morpeth appeared a very doubtful plan; for it did not appear to me (providing his Lordship should consent to become a member of such a deputation) that we had made up our minds at Hatton-Garden[2] to tell ministers in effect, that if they refused, we should strive to place the strength of Parliament in array against them. However as Mr. Dyer was to hear from Mr. Buxton yesterday, whether his Lordship would receive the deputation, we went down to the Baptist-House, and learned that Mr. Buxton had not been able to see Lord Althorp and fix the deputation for Saturday; but Mr. Dyer told us that in the meantime he had received a message from the Colonial Office, stating that Mr. Stanley wished to see him (Dyer) as this day (Friday) at 12 o'clock. What was the object of Mr. Stanley he could not tell, but he was balanced between hope and fear – fear that Stanley had determined to end the business, by refusing to do anything at all – hope that Lord Althorp had seen and told him, that he found himself pledged with Mr. Buxton and something must be done. (I ought to have told you, that before Stanley's message arrived, Lefebvre had sent for Dyer. He had overheard Lord Althorp and Mr. Buxton in earnest conversation on the chapel business, and he wished to learn from Mr Dyer all the particulars; and he told Mr. Dyer, that if Lord Althorp took it up, all was plain, for he had only to move his finger and it would be done). Mr. Dyer now wished to know from us whether he was authorized to tell Mr. Stanley (in the event of his refusing in the name of the Ministry to do anything) that both the Wesleyan and Baptist Societies were determined to appeal to the justice of Parliament, and would exert themselves to the uttermost to make that appeal effectual. I told him that it appeared to me that there was every reason to hope for the best: that the strong presumption was that Lord Althorp had seen Stanley on the subject; and that he would find things in progress; however, providing that were not the case, I must

---

[1] George William Frederick Howard, known as Viscount Morpeth, later 7th earl of Carlisle (1802–64), Whig M.P. for West Riding 1832–41, 1846–48. Chief commissioner for woods and forests, 1846–50.

[2] Beecham's residence as Secretary to the Missionary Society.

frankly own that I did not conceive ourselves at liberty to authorize him to use the name of the Wesleyan Society so explicitly as he wished; because our Committee had not as yet mooted the question, as to whether we should place ourselves finally in opposition to Ministers and endeavour, by bringing the nation on them, to obtain redress; and moreover that I should question, whether if it came to that, that we must take such steps or lose all, our Committee would not rather suffer the loss of so *comparatively* small a sum rather than proceed to such extremities. He met this by urging that the amount of the sum was not so much the consideration, as the principle which was involved; and that we ought to maintain the principle, he thought, to guard against being injured in future, which we might be, if our enemies saw it might be done with impunity. To this I replied that we were secured against that by the passing of the Riot Act by the Jamaica Assembly, which will give us a claim on the parishes in case of any future loss. In conclusion, I told him, that he might be assured, we should cooperate with them in every possible way short of breaking with ministers on the subject; and that if his interview with Mr. Stanley should prove unfavourable, no unnecessary time should be lost in bringing the subject before our Committee. I feel for them, their loss is so great; it is a life and death question with them. As Dyer said it is more than their whole annual income, and they must have it by some means if it can be got at all. I lay down my pen for a while, awaiting the result of Mr. Dyer's interview with Mr. Stanley . . .

35   From John Beecham   *London, February 25, 1834*

To make sure of hearing the result of Mr. Dyer's interview in time to communicate with you this evening, we went on to Fen Court, and awaited his return from the Colonial Office. He returned between 4 and 5 o'clock, having been an hour and a half with Lord Althorp, Mr. Stanley and Mr. Lefevre. He took with him Knibb and Burchell.[1] At first the ministers appeared high, especially Mr. Stanley, and not disposed to render assistance, stating that it was a very proper question for

[1] Rev. William Knibb (1803–45), Baptist missionary in Jamaica, whose chapel was destroyed in the reaction of 1832; commissioned by his brethren to present their case in England, he did much to convert Baptists to the cause of immediate emancipation. Later turned against the apprenticeship system. Rev. Thomas Burchell (1799–1846), Baptist missionary at Montego Bay, 1824; returned to England 1831 on family business and to answer charges against the Baptist Missionary Society in Jamaica; on his return in 1832 he was arrested and had to leave for New York. Returning to Jamaica in 1834, Knibb and Burchell did much for negro education in organizing Sunday and Lancasterian schools.

the Jamaica legislature to entertain but that the government at home could not be fairly called on to reimburse the Society. Having heard all that Mr. Dyer and his companions had to say, they appeared to enter into the subject more freely; and the result was that they promised Mr. Dyer the matter should be laid before the cabinet, and should be seriously considered. Mr. Dyer seems in good spirits and thinks they have now some good ground for hope. I dont however see that the promise amounts to much more than an expression of the willingness of Lord Althorp and Mr. Stanley to meet the losses if they knew what fund to go to, for that was the difficulty on which they dwelt in the conversation.

On the other hand, Mr. Dyer has ascertained that he has done wrong in letting ministers know, that the Lord Chancellor's plan of appropriating the sum out [of education monies means that] his proposal is made public. The Trustees are much displeased about it; and Mr. Buxton told Dyer it was an outrageous thing to introduce it into the question of chapel losses. I am glad we are out of that scrape; but I certainly did think Mr. Macaulay's[1] mentioning it to ourselves the evening we spent with him, was in confidence and that he did not intend it should go beyond our own private circle. I am glad we have kept to that . . .

36 From James Wood[2]   *Manchester, March 6, 1834*

I take the liberty of requesting your attention to the accompanying resolutions, and of explaining the circumstances under which they are forwarded.

Several individuals, resident here and in Liverpool, members of the Wesleyan Methodist Society, have, for some time, deeply lamented the evident want of some correct and frequent medium of communication throughout the connexion. They decidedly think that the conductors of many of those periodical publications to which large numbers of our people do, undoubtedly, regularly refer for political and general information, are not by any means sufficiently careful as to either the truth or the purity of the impressions which they produce upon the

---

[1] Thomas Babington Macaulay, later Baron Macaulay (1800–59), who shortly afterwards sailed to take an appointment as member of the supreme council of India.

[2] James Wood (1777–1849), partner in the Manchester cotton firm of Wood and Westhead, first president of the Manchester Chamber of Commerce, opponent of free trade and tory politician. A lifelong local preacher, class-leader and friend of Jabez Bunting. For Wood's character and relations with Bunting, see *Early Correspondence* pp. 13, 18–19 *et passim*.

public mind, and that not any of them manifest those distinctively christian principles and feelings which should commend them to the perusal of Christian readers. And they are still more impressively convinced that, if those scriptural opinions, which, as to questions both of doctrine and discipline, we have, as a Society, more peculiarly endeavoured to promote, are to retain any influence upon the conscience and affection of a community, now so vastly numerous and so diversified in character and station – those opinions must be brought under the constant observation of their professors, uniformly and manfully avowed, calmly contrasted with opposing views, and exhibited in their true and inseparable connection with every other subject really affecting the common welfare.

A weekly newspaper seems the most proper method of attempting the objects thus proposed, both because it only could have any chance of substitution for the objectionable matter which finds its way into so many Methodist homes, and because it would afford a proper opportunity of discussing many topics which, otherwise, must totally escape any careful consideration.

These remarks apply exclusively to the Wesleyan Methodist connection. But there is certainly good reason to believe that amongst other sections of the Christian Church, there is ample room for the introduction of a newspaper conducted on the principles laid down in the resolutions, and fit, therefore, for the indiscriminate use of a family.

It is conceived that this desideratum also must be supplied by the publication now contemplated.

Entertaining these views, the individuals alluded to have determined to carry them into practical operation. They indulge the hope that a proprietory unusually large for such an undertaking, while it will diminish the pecuniary risk, will serve also to secure a more than ordinary degree of interest and effort. The capital necessary for commencement has, as it is believed, been accurately ascertained. Ten persons[1] have already resolved to start the enterprise, even should they not obtain any further assistance, and will feel happy to take upon themselves the entire responsibility. But they naturally feel anxious that the feelings

[1] Accompanying this letter, which issued in 1835 in the publication of the *Watchman*, is a printed circular of a meeting of Wesleyan Methodist gentlemen in Manchester, bearing the names of James Wood and Thomas Farmer Esq., London; John Fernley Esq., Manchester; George Heald Esq., Liverpool; James Heald Esq., Parr's Wood [Stockport]; Peter Rothwell Esq., Bolton; Thomas Sands Esq., Liverpool; Joshua P. Westhead Esq., Manchester; Mr. T. Percival Bunting, Manchester. This circular proposed to give Conference confidence in the committee by placing the paper under the management of 5 laymen appointed by the proprietors, and 5 preachers appointed by Conference among whom should be the editor of the *Wesleyan Methodist Magazine*, one of the tutors of the proposed Theological Institution, and one of the general Missionary Secretaries.

and influence of others should be engaged on its behalf, and have therefore agreed that 25 shares of £100 each shall in the first instance be
proposed as the basis of the project. Twelve of these shares are now
taken up, and the remaining 13 they wish to offer to such gentlemen as
they feel persuaded are like-minded with themselves, on the great
principles of Wesleyan Methodism. And through me, they now earnestly
request your concurrence and support.

It is hoped that the resolutions will meet your approbation, but any
suggestions you may make respecting them shall be carefully considered.

With respect to the politics of the proposed paper, the individuals
already embarked in the undertaking are prepared to concede all
personal predilections.

Though some of them entertain strong opinions upon such subjects,
they all concur in thinking that the proprietors of a paper, conducted in
the manner now suggested, may reasonably anticipate success. They
cannot be induced to believe, at least until the trial has been made, that
the fierce spirit of party has yet destroyed the characteristic 'simplicity
and godly sincerity' of their fellow-Methodists. Or if, unhappily, that
spirit has, in some cases, and to a partial extent, pervaded our community, they feel but the more imperatively bound to make one great
effort to recall their brethren to the remembrance of former principles,
and to place public affairs before them in that same light, in which only
even the far less complicated interests of private life can be fairly
estimated, the clear, solemn light of eternity.

As the parties have no pecuniary end to serve, the resolutions are
framed with especial reference to the appropriation of the profits of
the paper to religious purposes. In the selection of the intended
Wesleyan Institution, they have been guided by a deep conviction of the
necessity of such an establishment, and by the persuasion that they
cannot more effectually promote the welfare of Methodism, than by
seeking to perpetuate the usefulness of its living ministry.

It need only be added that the undertaking is commenced with the
determination that, whatever difficulties may arise, it shall have a
fair and long trial. You are cordially requested to engage in it, in the
belief that you will consider it, not as a pecuniary speculation but as a
humble and self-sacrificing effort to do good. The present shareholders
however feel confident of ultimate success. Every possible provision will
be made for limiting the responsibility of each proprietor to the amount
of his share, and, so far as will be consistent with the maintenance of a
select and unanimous proprietory, for facilitating the transfer of shares.

You will oblige the friends of the measure by the free statement of your views respecting it, forwarded to me, High Street, Manchester; and, meanwhile, they request that this communication may be kept strictly private. The fact of the intended commencement of the paper is already known, and need not be concealed. But I am sure you will at once perceive that all details as to its proprietorship and management are matters of confidence between the parties immediately concerned and ought not to be divulged . . .

37   To Edmund Grindrod[1]   *London, March 14, 1834*

. . . Jos[eph] Stephens's[2] Ashton doings fill me with indignation. It is plain he wants us to exclude him. The thing cannot be tolerated. I incline to think that, considering it in connexion with the violent and wholly unmethodistical character of the Resolutions at the formation of the Society of which he is now an officer and agent, a Special District Meeting should *immediately* be called, and give him reproof and admonition, as well as refer the case officially to Conference for final adjudication. Perhaps he would take the warning, and withdraw from the Secretaryship . . .

38   To John Beecham and Robert Alder   *London, April 3, 1834*

. . . Last night, between 8 and 9 o'clock, I received a *second* note from the Colonial Office, stating that Mr. Lefevre wished to see me at 12 tomorrow, on the subject of Negro Education[3] in the West Indies. This of course has deranged all our plans. Mr. Haslope and Mr. Taylor,[4] who were to have gone with me today, have agreed to accompany me

[1] Edmund Grindrod, superintendent, Manchester (Irwell St.) circuit, 1832–35.

[2] Joseph Rayner Stephens (1805–79), preacher, Ashton-under-Lyne circuit, 1833–34. Hitherto somewhat of a martinet in the ministry like his father (cf. n. 3 p. 5 *supra*), Stephens now became subject to disciplinary proceedings for acting as secretary to the Ashton Church Separation Society, and at the following Conference resigned from the ministry under suspension, leading a small local connexion in the Ashton and Stalybridge area. He rapidly achieved national fame as a violent agitator in the Ten Hours, Anti-Poor Law, and Chartist movements, but his radicalism caused speedy secessions among his followers.

[3] On this subject see no. 39 *infra*.

[4] Joseph Taylor, preacher, London (City Road) circuit, 1833–34; superintendent, 1834–36. A year earlier Bunting had suggested that Taylor rather than himself should become missionary secretary, but Beecham wished to keep him for the missionary treasurership and for grooming for the Presidency to which he succeeded in 1834. M.C.A. MSS. Jabez Bunting to John Beecham, February 19, 1833; John Beecham to Jabez Bunting, February 23, 1833 (passages omitted *supra*).

tomorrow; and I have written to Mr. Lefevre accordingly, expressing our request that the explanations we have to give on our Chapel property in Jamaica may be made the subject of conversation in the *same* interview. I have since seen Mr. Dyer and Mr. Ellis.[1] The former is invited to the conversation on Negro Education; the latter is not. The London Society will send in a Memorial on the Marriage Question on Saturday or Monday. Our movement on that point must be made as soon as Mr. Matthews[2] returns. If Mr. Ellis be correct, we need nothing to legalize *past* marriages of slaves; that being done, he thinks, by an Order in Council issued about 1826. It will only be *after* the new Toleration Act comes into operation in August next, that any new declaration or enactment will be needed. This must be thoroughly sifted.[3] . . .

39   To John Lefevre[4]   *London, April 16, 1834 [Draft]*

I have examined with attention the paper entitled 'Heads of a Plan for promoting the Education of Youth in the British West Indies' which you were so good as to communicate to myself and my friends on Friday the 4th Instant; and thankfully avail myself of your obliging permission to lay before you in a written form the remarks which it has suggested to our minds.

1. We have pleasure in expressing our strongest and most decided approbation of the principle adopted in the 2nd Head of Plan viz. that 'Instruction in the doctrines and precepts of Christianity must form the basis and must be made the inseparable attendant of any such system of

[1] William Ellis (1794–1872), chief foreign secretary of the London Missionary Society.

[2] Richard Matthews, a Wesleyan barrister; one of the first secretaries of the Anti-Slavery Society and member of the Committee of Privileges (1833).

[3] Before negro emancipation Wesleyan preachers in the West Indies were under strict instructions to admit or continue as members no persons who lived in concubinage, and performed ceremonies of marriage for slave members which, though not recognized by law, were held to be morally binding and salutary. After emancipation, the former slaves, being no longer chattels but free persons, were able to contract legal marriages, and doubts arose as to the forms of marriage they had accepted as slaves. Moreover, except in Demerara and those Bahama Islands where there were no clergy, only Anglican priests who were few in number might celebrate legal marriages. The Mission House kept the Colonial Office under pressure both to validate past marriages and to secure the legal right to celebrate in future, and on March 15, 1836 Lord Glenelg wrote to the Governors of the West Indian colonies, asking their legislatures 'promptly and diligently [to] apply themselves' in this sense. Cf. no. 112 *infra*.

[4] John George Shaw-Lefevre, undersecretary at the Colonial Office, 1833–34, and younger brother of Charles Shaw-Lefevre, later first Viscount Eversley. Lefevre had a distinguished career in a variety of senior administrative posts, ending as clerk of the parliaments. He was Vice-chancellor of the University of London, 1842–62.

education'. This principle we deem to be of vital importance. Our long experience as a Missionary Society in various parts of the world, and especially among various tribes and classes of *heathen* and other *previously uninstructed* people, has fully convinced us that any education dissociated from religion, or not avowedly and habitually connected with *some* form of Christian profession and discipline, is exceedingly inefficient, and will fail to accomplish, in any large or permanent degree, those objects even of civil amelioration and of social order and security which must be supposed to be contemplated by the state, when it undertakes to afford pecuniary assistance to plans of this description. We respectfully state our earnest hope that no alterations will be made in the plan for educating the negro youth which would so far *generalize* the instruction to be given as in fact to *neutralize* it also as to its moral influence and public benefit.[1]

2. With similar satisfaction we perceive in the 3rd and 4th Heads of the 'Plan' the practical recognition by His Majesty's Government of the obligation implied in the Resolution of the House of Commons of the 12th and 13th June 1833, respecting the *'Liberal and comprehensive principles'* to be adopted in 'providing for the religious and moral education of the negro population to be emancipated'. The best possible way of fulfilling this obligation appears to us to be one which we trust the plan before us is intended to embrace, that of rendering the funds placed at the disposal of the Crown for Colonial Education available for the encouragement and assistance of all denominations of Christians (*without requiring them to abandon or to compromise their respective systems of doctrine and discipline*) upon their proving to the satisfaction of the authorities, that they possess the means of making their several educational agencies to bear upon *such a number* of the whole mass [of the] youthful population which it is desired to benefit, as would justify the Government in granting them a reasonable share of pecuniary aid. We think that the 'liberal' principle requires not merely that the assistance afforded should be extended to Dissenters and Wesleyans as well as to the Established Church, but also that it should be so dispensed as to secure to every class of agents, their own modes of teaching whether by *catechetical instruction* (to which our experience leads us to attach great importance and utility) or otherwise, their own disciplinary regulations, their own forms of devotional exercise in school, and the unfettered exertion of their own pastoral influence and superintendence. A new system of elementary *secular* teaching, and the use of a set of *exclusively scriptural* lessons, *common to all parties*, would doubtless be beneficial as far

---

[1] I.e. that no plan of undenominational instruction on the pattern of the Irish National scheme should be adopted.

as they go; but would not in our judgment be at all equal in eventual efficiency to the still *more* 'liberal and comprehensive' plan of assisting *all* (in proportion to the number of the youth they are able and willing to educate) without imposing any restrictions as to internal religious management, or requiring the least sacrifice of conscientious views or usages.

Such *assistance to all* whose operations are contributory to the general result, on such a scale of extent, both as to the number of pupils and of teachers, as to deserve that assistance, without interference in the interior religious arrangements of any, appears to us to be the plan most just in itself and most likely to promote general peace and harmony.

3. We greatly honour, however, the noble and benevolent object which His Majesty's Government appear to aim at accomplishing in the 5th and 6th Heads of their Plan; viz. the simultaneous establishment of *at least one school* in each of the Districts into which it is proposed that every colony shall be forthwith divided. In this application to the work of Colonial Education of something analagous to the *parochial principle* adopted in the ecclesiastical systems of our own country, our general views and feelings as Wesleyan Methodists would induce us at once to acquiesce, provided that it be accompanied, as in this country, with perfect and unfettered liberty for those who prefer to act on a somewhat different plan, or who, approving of the parochial principle as far as it goes, desire to establish additional means of promoting moral improvement. And our acquiescence and approbation will be still more entire and thankful, if in the plan for colonies provision be made, not merely for *allowing and protecting* but for substantially *assisting*, such additional and supplementary efforts as may be made by any portion of the people themselves, or by the Societies in this country with whom they are connected. We must, however, in frankness express our apprehension, that the District-plan will have to encounter many difficulties; that it supposes an appetite for educational improvement to have been already created more universally than the fact, we fear, will warrant, and that at all events it can be brought into extensive operation only very gradually and at a period too remote to justify its being made the *exclusive* object of the pecuniary support of the Government.

4. If, however, it be determined to try the system of District-schools, we respectfully submit that in the preliminary inquiries proposed by the 6th, 8th and 9th Heads of the 'Plan', it will in our opinion be indispensable to consult the religious views, connexions and preferences, not so much of 'the inhabitants' generally, nor exclusively those even of 'the subscribers', or of 'the persons having charge of the apprenticed

labourers', but also and especially, of the *parents* of the young people, who need and desire education. Where religious principles have already obtained a decided and extensive operation, we are persuaded that a large number of such parents will be found ready and able to enrol themselves in the lists of subscribers; and thus to obtain their due share of consideration and influence. But in the Districts not yet benefited by much Christian cultivation, the case may be for a long time very different. And in all cases we cannot but think that it will be both just and expedient to recognize and exemplify as much as possible the deference due to the parental character and authority, even though the poverty or comparative apathy of some who sustain that relation should prevent for a time their assuming the responsibility of subscribers.

5. But with still greater anxiety we submit to your consideration our earnest request, that whatever may be the religious denomination of the teacher preferred by the majority either of the inhabitants, subscribers, proprietors or parents, for what may be termed the *Primary* School of any District, any other class of Christians who shall desire it, though constituting but a minority, may be *assisted* in building and supporting an *additional* School, in the same District, if that will best serve their convenience, on proving to the satisfaction of the Governor that the applicants represent the wishes of the parents of such a number of children, as may be deemed sufficient to occupy a *second* school, and on their giving the same subscriptions and guarantees as shall be required in the case of the Primary Schools before mentioned.

6. We beg leave very respectfully to state that we deem it most important to have regard in all these arrangements to the *religious liberty and comfort* of those numerous negroes and others, who are already by the exertions of Missionaries brought into more or less intimate connexion with our Christian communities, and to whom the education of their children in the modes they do not approve is an object of conscientious consideration, and with this view we further suggest that, where the parents of the children, for whose benefit any school is proposed to be established, and the resident friends of education who may be disposed to assist them, shall not be found able to raise the *whole* of the sum required for the erection, or willing to give, *alone,* the guarantees demanded for its subsequent support, they shall be at liberty to obtain such further present aid, and such promises of future annual assistance, as may be necessary, from any missionary society in this country which may be inclined to appropriate a portion of its funds; or from any other institution, British or colonial, which may be inclined to promote the object of negro education; and that provision shall be made for extending to such cases the pecuniary

aid of the Government, and for accepting the joint guarantee thus provided.

7. We beg leave to repeat the representation before verbally made to you that, in our opinion, the object of the plan will be greatly facilitated in most cases, if the blank in the 7th Head (in the clause which is to define the period of the guarantee for annual subscriptions) be filled up with the words *three years*, and not with the words *five years*, as at first intimated.

8. Permit me to call your attention to the apparent discrepancy in the 7th, 10th and 12th Heads of the 'Plan'. We respectfully submit, that the requirement, under *both* heads, should be stated as stipulating for the offer of *at least one third* of the first outlay, *and not less than one half* of the annual expenditure, to be raised by the parents and subscribers, or their guarantees; and for the completion of the total sum required by a government grant, to supply the remaining deficiency, after such local and auxiliary contribution shall have been raised to its utmost practicable amount.

9. We think that it should be provided that the 'estimated first cost', mentioned in the 7th Head, must include school-furniture, excepting books and slates. For the article of *benches* etc. for instance, would cost, in many cases, as we are informed, half as much as the building of the school. It cannot be desirable that this peculiarity of West Indian locality should be allowed to operate as a practical hindrance to the introduction of so benevolent a plan. We also suggest that it is at least a matter for consideration whether the words 'books and school requisites' introduced in the 11th Head, might not be better omitted, and the words 'books and slates', substituted; we are advised that everything but books and slates would be easily procured in the colonies, and it will be desirable to make the proposed establishments depend as little as possible on foreign resources of any kind or from any quarter.

10. It appears to be exceedingly desirable that the Government should strongly recommend, if not require, that a separate apartment should be provided in each school-house to be erected by its aid, for the education of females. This would afford facilities for instruction in those arts of useful industry which belong exclusively to females – would diminish the expense of teachers, as female teachers may be obtained for smaller salaries – would at once increase very materially the *supply* of teachers, which will perhaps be found practically a great *desideratum* – and would prevent the incalculable moral injury to be apprehended, especially under the circumstances of this case, from the indiscriminate association of youth of both sexes in the same apartment of the building.

11. To the *principle* of the 13th Head, which respects the dismissal

of teachers in case of malversation or habitual neglect of duty, we cannot have the smallest objection. That part of it which requires 'habitual reserve in reference to the political dissensions of the colonies', and condemns 'needless and improper interference in any political measures by which colonial society or any particular branch of it may be agitated', has our cordial approbation. These are sentiments solemnly inculcated in the Standing Instructions of which a printed copy is regularly delivered to all our *missionaries*; and we shall be glad to extend them to all persons whom we may at any time employ as *Teachers* in schools connected with our Society. But we may perhaps be permitted, after all that has happened, to observe that we lay the greatest stress on the term '*proved* guilty', which is used in the 'Plan', and most earnestly entreat that, however great may be the improvement, of which we rejoice to perceive the indications, in the tone and feeling of some classes of colonists, effectual provision may be made in the details of the 'Plan' for the security of our agents against captious, intolerant, and *unproved* accusations.

12. To one other topic only will I presume to call your attention, but it is a topic to which we attach the highest importance, and to which we are most desirous of attracting the favourable consideration of His Majesty's Government. We earnestly solicit that permission may be given in the case of such schools, as may be, under the arrangements of the proposed 'Plan', connected with our Society and Denomination, for their occasional occupation, in the Districts where we have no chapels, and at hours which will not interfere with any scholastic duties, as places of general religious worship and instruction. For,

(1) The glorious act of last session, when it shall come into operation, will secure to the religious negroes the inestimable boon of a christian Sabbath *in every week*. Hitherto, in practice, many of those on the plantations have not been able to attend public worship oftener than *on one Sabbath in three or four weeks*. The legal establishment in their case of the *common right* of Christians by the laws of God to the enjoyment of a weekly Sabbath will be hailed by thousands of them as one of their best and dearest privileges; and even as to the emancipated negroes generally, it must be held to be of vital importance to the morality, peace, and good order of the colonies, that their exemption from Sunday labour should be turned to the best account, and that, to prevent its perversion to purposes of dissipation and vice, every facility and inducement should be furnished to their attendance on the public worship of Almighty God. In few if any of the colonies are the existing accommodations for such worship adequate in any tolerable degree, especially in remote and rural districts, to the now altered circumstances. To meet *this* exigency is a

F

matter of as much importance as Negro Education itself. May not *both* objects be combined, to some considerable extent, by the permission to occupy school-houses as occasional places for preaching and worship, under the direction of those religious bodies who shall take a share, with the sanction of the authorities, in the work of juvenile education?

(2) It deserves to be considered that in very many cases the disposition of the emancipated slaves, of the free coloured people generally, and of the benevolent public of the colonies, to raise liberal contributions as required by the 'Plan', for the erection and support of *schools* would certainly be stimulated most effectually and extensively, if it were distinctly understood, especially by the country negroes, that they would thus at the same time obtain facilities for the education of the children and opportunities for the attendance of the adults on public worship with an incalculable saving both of the time and of the toil now spent in travelling for that purpose.

I have to apologize for the length of these observations. Perhaps it will be excused if you will have the goodness to reflect that the Society for whom I act has been for more than half-a century successfully engaged in most expensive and anxious labours among the negro population of the West Indies, and is naturally solicitous that the best possible arrangements should be made for the improvement and civilization of a race of men with whose interests the sympathies and feelings of the whole body of Wesleyan Methodists have been long and inseparably identified. From the returns of last year it appears that the number of members in our West Indian Societies then amounted to 31,937 of whom 22,972 were slaves. This number includes *accredited members only*, not their children, nor yet the very large number of persons who attend the public ministry of our missionaries but are not recognized as our regular members. Our missionaries (*all accredited ministers*, not including catechists or any subordinate agents) now amount to not less than 71. Representing therefore the interests and wishes of so large a body of His Majesty's subjects abroad, and expressing the general feelings and anxieties of a still larger number at home, I trust I shall not be deemed to have taken too great a liberty in occupying so much of your valuable time by the statements now most respectfully submitted.[1]

---

[1] Towards the end of 1834 the plan here discussed was accepted by the Missionary Society, and the government promised financial assistance for school-building and the oversight of secular instruction. 24 Methodist day schools were to be erected in approved places, towards the cost of which £5000 was voted in successive parliamentary grants, 1835–36, on condition that a further £2500 should be raised by the Missionary Society. The government made a yearly grant in aid of the schools which began at £1000, but was gradually reduced and terminated in 1846. The wider Methodist hopes of public support were disappointed, the schools were never numerous enough to accomplish the work they hoped for among the

40   From Edmund Grindrod   *Salford, April 17, 1834*

... It is reported that Stephens has introduced the Dissenting Petitions into our congregations and vestries for signatures: this appears to me greatly to aggravate his proceedings. Mr. Newton[1] is about to inform him that this will constitute one of the charges against him. The *Manchester Guardian* of last Saturday informed the public of Mr. S's intended trial;[2] and, I expect, that next Saturday's *Times* at least,[3] will issue its airy fulminations against the District Committee. You know that some of us are too well inured to newspaper calumny, to be deterred by it from discharging our duty to God and his Church ...

41   To James Kendall[4]   *London, April 24, 1834*

... I believe that a great majority of the most thoughtful and influential persons in our connexion, both ministers and laymen, are friendly to the principle of an Establishment, when connected with that of perfect religious liberty and protection to all other denominations. Such is the sentiment ably advocated in a review of Bogue and Bennett, which you will have seen in our *Magazine* for April.[5] I do not think it probable that we can ever *formally* unite with the Church of England, so as to be amalgamated in one Body. The present discipline of that Church must exclude, in a sense, all separatists. But I think we are bound by every principle of consistency, expediency, and duty to maintain the most friendly feelings towards the Church, and to discountenance as far as we

native population, and in 1837 only 36 of the 1266 teachers in Methodist schools received any salary. G. G. Findlay and W. W. Holdsworth, *History of the Wesleyan Methodist Missionary Society* (London, 1921) ii. 319, 322–3.

[1] Robert Newton, preacher, Manchester (Grosvenor St.) circuit, 1832–35. Chairman of the Manchester District, 1834.

[2] The first reference in the *Manchester Guardian* seems to have been a report of Stephens's suspension on May 3, 1834.

[3] The *Manchester Times* April 19, 1834, did not report the Stephens case, but quoted Adam Clarke on the dangers of the establishment principle, and reported a meeting of Birmingham Wesleyans which had demanded the separation of Church and State.

[4] James Kendall (1799–1859), superintendent, Arbroath circuit, 1833–34. Kendall held the view that Methodists, corporately, were betraying the Church establishment, and, in so doing, playing into the hands of radicals in their own ranks.

[5] D. Bogue and J. Bennett, *History of the dissenters from the Revolution to 1808* (2nd ed. London 1833) was reviewed in the *Wesleyan Methodist Magazine* 3s. xiii. 200–211, 277–96, in March and April 1834, in hostile terms. It was claimed that 'the friendly feeling of the Methodists towards the Church has been stronger latterly than in the days of Mr. Wesley; their goodwill for her has increased as she has improved in spirituality and efficiency'. *Ibid.* p. 287.

can without making ourselves *partizans*, that bitter and unchristian hostility towards our two venerable National Establishments which is now too much in fashion . . .

42   From John Bowers[1]   *Manchester, April 29, 1834*

. . . I seize a few moments this morning amidst the proceedings of our District Meeting to acquaint you with the result of our enquiry into the case of Mr. Joseph Stephens. It occupied the whole of our morning sitting and terminated at a late hour last evening. The most important facts of the case he at once admitted, denying only that he had acted in the instances charged *in opposition to any injunction or counsel of his Superintendent*. He was then asked by the Chairman what defence he had to offer for these violations of the laws of Methodism. His answer was 'None, until the facts he had admitted were *shewn* to be violations of law'.[2] This, it was contended, the meeting at that stage of the proceedings was not required to do. At this point he kept 'at bay' for a considerable time, resolutely refusing to say one word until it was proved that his conduct had been 'alien' from Methodism. Dr. Warren[3] who from the first evinced his learning on the subject, here warmly and repeatedly insisted that the meeting was required to produce 'the Statute' which had been violated. After a great loss of time this was attempted, and Mr. S. was again called upon for his defence. He still unaccountably declined to say a word. Upon his retirement which of course immediately followed, we proceeded to deliberate on 'our Judgment'. Mr. Grindrod proposed a series of resolutions which if the time permit before the departure of the mail I will copy. We proceeded to discuss them separately. When the first was moved, Dr. W. again for a considerable time occupied the attention of the meeting, and proposed an

---

[1] John Bowers, preacher, Stockport circuit, 1831–34.

[2] Stephens came to the District Meeting prepared to argue that Conference had never condemned the separation of Church and State, a union of which (at least in its Constantinian form) Wesley himself had disapproved. Once the Meeting had assumed as a premise that to advocate disestablishment was unprofessional conduct in a Wesleyan preacher, he could have no defence. The documents of the case are reprinted in G. Smith, *History of Wesleyan Methodism* iii. 529–31.

[3] Samuel Warren LL.D. (1781–1862), superintendent, Manchester (Oldham St.) circuit, 1833–October 1834. Joint author with John Stephens, father of Joseph Rayner, of one of the standard manuals of Methodist law, and already at loggerheads with Bunting over the proposed Theological Institution. Expelled by the Conference of 1835, he founded the Wesleyan Methodist Association. Seceded to the Church of England 1838; rector of All Souls, Ancoats, 1840–62.

amendment which was seconded by Mr. Everett.[1] Mr. Crowther,[2] here
very seasonably and with very happy effect interposed, and was followed
by others on the great desirableness, at such a crisis, and on a case of
such importance, of perfect unanimity in our decision. Dr. W. and Mr.
E. with very good feeling withdrew the amendment. Each resolution
was then in an harmonious spirit discussed, and adopted *unanimously*.
Mr. S. being called in, the resolutions were read to him, and in con-
formity with the last he was required to give a pledge that he would
forthwith withdraw from the Secretaryship of the Church Separation
Society, and abstain from attending public meetings for any object
similar to that avowed by such an association. He declined 'to give any
pledge with those resolutions'. This was not said in a tone of contumacy
or defiance, but with deep, and (undeniably) unaffected emotion. He
wept profusely. He was expostulated with most tenderly; and *time was
allowed him* (until the close of the meeting) to deliberate on his final
decision. His conduct to those who know him most familiarly has been
perfectly inexplicable. He was disposed at the opening of the case to
quibble and trifle. From this he was quickly beaten off, and did not
again attempt it. He was prepared with a long and elaborate defence:
and I can scarcely conjecture his motive in persisting to withhold every
part of it. The following are the case and resolutions. 1. That Mr. J.R.S.
has attended four different meetings at etc. etc. one of the avowed
objects of which is to obtain the total separation of the Church and
State, and that at these meetings he delivered speeches expressive of his
approbation of that object. 2. That at the Ashton meeting the terms
'Wesleyan Methodist' were on his motion introduced into the preamble
of the Memorial etc. 3. That he announced from the pulpit that a
petition to the same effect lay for signature in one of our chapels. 4.
That he accepted the office of Corresponding Secretary etc.. 5. That he

---

[1] James Everett (1784–1872), at this time supernumerary in Manchester, but appointed by
the next Conference to Newcastle-upon-Tyne (West) circuit. Everett had entered the Methodist ministry in 1806, and, being since 1821 a supernumerary on grounds of ill-health,
was now a book-seller. Despite his pleas of ill-health he accepted innumerable special
preaching engagements, especially Sunday school anniversaries, and began a long series
of publications in the fields of literature and Methodist history. Already a fixed opponent
of Bunting, he was privy to the manoeuvres which took Dr. Warren out of the connexion in
1835, but was stationed by Conference out of the town at the crucial time, and abandoned
Warren at the end. Suspected in the 'forties of being the author of the anti-Buntingite
Flysheets (1845–48) and other works critical of connexional policy, he was expelled in
1849 for refusing to answer questions about his complicity. He then took the lead in the
Wesleyan reform agitations, and became the first President of the United Methodist Free
Churches in 1857.

[2] Jonathan Crowther (1794–1856), preacher, Manchester (Oldham St.) circuit, 1832–35.
Headmaster of Kingswood School, 1823–26.

has thus acted without consulting his Superintendent and contrary to his example and expressed opinion.

Resolutions. 1. That in these proceedings Mr. S. has flagrantly violated the peaceable and anti-sectarian spirit of Wesleyan Methodism so strongly enjoined in the writings of our Founder, enforced by repeated acts of the Conference since his decease, and required as a necessary qualification of every Methodist Preacher, particularly in that fundamental epitome of his pastoral duties contained in the Minutes of 1820, and directed by a standing order of the Conference to be read in every annual District Meeting as solemnly binding upon every minister in our Connexion.[1] 2. That the speeches of Mr. S. are directly at variance with the general sentiments of Mr. Wesley and the Conference and are distinguished by a spirit of hostility against the Church of England highly unbecoming a minister of our Connexion which has always openly professed and honourably maintained great respect and affection for that Church. 3. That as far as his influence extends Mr. S. has committed the character of the Connexion upon a question involving its public credit as well as its internal tranquillity, that he has manifested a great want of deference to the recorded opinions of his Fathers and Brethren in the ministry and a recklessness of consequences as to himself and others by the very active and public part which he has taken in aggressive proceedings against the Church. 4. That he has endangered the peace and acted *prejudicially* to the spirituality of the Connexion by giving occasion to the introduction of unprofitable disputations upon ecclesiastical politics amongst our people, thus trampling upon the directions of the very last Conference in its pastoral address to the Societies, which Mr. S. was bound by his example at least to enforce. 5. That in accepting the office of Secretary etc. he has acted directly contrary to his peculiar calling and solemn engagements as a Methodist Preacher. 6. That the culpability of these proceedings is aggravated by the fact that they were taken without consulting his Superintendent and contrary to his example and expressed opinion. 7. That he be required forthwith to resign his office of Secretary etc. etc. and to pledge himself to take no part etc. etc.. 8. That on giving the above pledge his case be referred to the Conference for a final adjudication . . .

---

[1] The Liverpool Minutes of 1820 gathered up a Conference conversation on the ideals of the ministry begun by Bunting during his first year as President. They contained no political reference, but called on preachers to give themselves 'wholly' to their 'proper work as servants of Christ and his Church'.

43 From Edmund Grindrod   *Liverpool, May 1, 1834*

. . . By this time I presume you will have received a copy of the Resolutions on the case of Mr. J. R. Stephens. They were drawn up by me, but modified and revised by the District Meeting. Stephens made no defence but quibbled most unworthily. Dr. W[arren] moved an amendment which, for its folly and inadmissibility, I could not have expected from the youngest member of the Committee. It was seconded by Mr. Everett, but withdrawn when it was perceived to be against the universal feeling of the meeting. Dr. W. seemed disposed to embarrass us at every point. In the confession of our faith, he could not let the doctrine of our Lord's Eternal Sonship pass without taking exception to its being introduced as an indispensable article in our creed.[1] This procedure produced upon the minds of the Brethren generally an impression greatly to his disadvantage. What Stephens will do I know not. I am of opinion that he will not permanently settle at Ashton, though it is probable that he will cause mischief and division in that circuit before he leaves it.

I must now strive to divest myself of conjectures and speculations as to what will be the consequences of present agitations. I expect the Connexion will have a struggle for it, but I have no doubt of the ultimate triumph of good principle.

44 From John Baker[2]   *Truro, June 16, 1834*

. . . At my coming into this Circuit at Conference last it was intimated to me by the Leaders, both in and out of the Leaders' Meeting, that they wished the large classes to be divided, as the Leaders could not look after the members as they ought to be looked after – they were greatly falling off in their subscriptions and it was thought the introduction of new Leaders into the Meeting would help to infuse fresh life; as this was a ⟨sub⟩ject of conversation in the meeting and *no Leader* raised the least object⟨ion⟩ I took it for granted the thing might be done and certainly would be a blessing.

---

[1] Bunting, Richard Watson and others maintained that Adam Clarke was unsound on this doctrine (cf. n. 2 p. 5) and it had been the occasion of some friction among the preachers. In an *Address to the Wesleyan Conference* (1835) in support of Dr. Warren, the Rochdale Quarterly Meeting made the new 'test' on this subject introduced by Conference in 1827 a prominent ground of complaint against Conference rule. One of the questions now asked of candidates for the ministry at their examination in District Meeting was 'How do you prove the eternal Sonship of the second Person of the Trinity?' E. Grindrod, *Compendium of the laws and regulations of Wesleyan Methodism* (3rd ed. London, 1848) p. 79.

[2] John Baker (1793–1845), superintendent, Truro circuit, 1833–35.

It was decided to divide a large class and a Leader was *unanimously* elected to take the division. It was thought right also that he should meet in the class to be divided for a few weeks and the Leader was requested to prepare the minds of his people for the division; after this it was decided to divide another class and another Leader was *unanimously* chosen.

At a subsequent meeting we received a message from the first class that they had no objection to be divided, but they would have one of two men whom they named as their Leader, and not the man the meeting had chosen; these men were both improper persons and in yielding to their request we should have allowed the people to choose a new Leader instead of the Leaders' Meeting; this therefore I mildly but firmly resisted and the Leaders agreed with me.

We enquired their objection to the Leader we had chosen and they replied nothing whatever, but that he was young (he is about 28, a truly pious and respectable man and has now a very excellent class); in order to remove this objection and meet the case peaceably if possible, we added two old Leaders who had small classes, to the two new ones and gave the choice of 4 classes to the persons thus divided off; we also agreed that only so many should be taken from the classes to be divided, as would reduce their number to 28 in each class and further, that to prevent anything like partiality, the persons should go out by lot; two Leaders were appointed to see this done in each class.

I would just stop here for a moment in my relation to observe that perhaps I gave way here too far, but I found that dividing classes had always been a difficult thing in Cornwall, and in more than one instance had failed, and therefore my object was to establish this great *principle*, that we have a right to divide large classes, and that it was my business in connection with the Leaders' Meeting to elect new Leaders for the divisions and not the people; this principle I endeavoured to keep in view, and I am thankful to add, that it is established in this Society.

But to return, one of these classes was divided, and the members went as desired and are all now among us; in the other class 4 persons who were drawn to leave and one who was not, determined not to yield to the wishes of the Leaders' Meeting; these we afterward found had been stimulated to resist by Sawle and Scott,[1] the two Leaders who have since left us, and who, I shall be able to shew you, had long planned a division in the Society.

I and some of the Leaders have heard that Sawle had been en-

[1] James Sawle and William Scott who invited the Methodist New Connexion to begin work in Truro.

couraging those persons to resist and at our next meeting we conversed on the division of the classes to see if Sawle would object, but all he did was to ask that one of his classes (for he had two) might be opened, but as that class was large and therefore stood on the same ground with the other large classes, we could not consent and that he knew; we found from the Leaders who attended the division that those persons who refused to comply had used language with reference to the Leaders and myself which was really abusive, and that they were determined to set us at defiance and go into [whatever] class they pleased.

This conduct we saw could not be allowed, or we should have to do the same work over again in the classes they would join – the members would move from class to class without any cause when they liked and that dividing classes must be abandoned; we therefore *decided* (Sawle and Scott being present and not objecting a word) *that we could allow them to join no* class but one of the four opened for them.

From that meeting Sawle and Scott went and told these people, they would take any of them; I heard of this and wrote Sawle a note remonstrating with him on the impropriety of his conduct and expressing a hope that he would not persist.

At our next Leaders' Meeting 13 Leaders were present including Sawle ⟨and⟩ Scott; they were asked if they had taken these members; they said they had and intended keeping them; we remonstrated with them and observed that Leaders' Meetings were useless if one or two Leaders might go away and act in direct opposition to the great majority, but they would not hear or be persuaded; I intimated that it would be impossible to recognize them as Leaders if they persisted, at this remark Mr. Budd[1] (who is editor of the *West Briton* Newspaper, the steady opposer of the constitution of Methodism for years and of whom I have no doubt you have heard) took fire and asserted that I had no right to say what should be done with Sawle and Scott if they persisted, that it was the business of the Leaders' Meeting to award the punishment; to this I replied that if this were his doctrine it was not Methodism, and I trusted I knew my duty too well to admit it – that I was there not as a Moderator or as a vote with them, but as a distinct party with distinct duties;[2] in reply he gave us plenty about Popery and that he would call a District Meeting etc. etc., and I saw that by this clamour we were losing sight of the main point and I said in order to come to the

[1] Edward Budd, an Irishman, who had conducted a private boarding-school at Liskeard and then Truro.

[2] The Liverpool Minutes (cf. n. 1 p. 62 *supra*) required preachers to remember 'that we are under solemn obligations to conduct ourselves . . . not as the mere *Chairmen* of public meetings, but as the *Pastors* of Christian societies, put in trust by the ordinance of God, and by their own voluntary association with us'.

point we wished to settle I would in this case waive what was my right (entering my protest in the Minute Book against my compliance being taken as a precedent) and take a vote of the Meeting on this point, 'If Brother Sawle and Scott persist in acting in opposition to their Brethren, shall they be removed from their office or not'. 7 voted for their removal – not a hand was held up for them and the 4 who were neutral had all spoken against their conduct, Budd himself observing, 'If I do not hold up my hand against them, I cannot for them'.

We then tried them again, but they persisted and were accordingly removed from their office and 4 new Leaders, *sound genuine men*, appointed to take their 4 classes.

The next evening Sawle and Scott called a meeting of their members – gave their version of the affair – told them they would meet them apart from us, and did all they could to prevail with them to leave us which a great many of them engaged to do; the best and soundest of them could not be induced to leave us, the rest (among whom there were no doubt a few sincere weak people) did do so to the number of between 70 and 80 and thus the separation was effected.

As to the real cause of the separation, there is now but one opinion among all who know the case, that the division of the class was laid hold of as a handle to effect the division in the Society, which had been planned and determined on long before, and Sawle's object certainly was to make a party large enough to form a separate Society, to whom he was to preach and by whom he was to have been supported; but in this object he has entirely failed, his own supporters thinking that he had not talents sufficient for such an undertaking.

We have proved satisfactorily that Sawle had told some of our Coun⟨try⟩ friends months before I came into the Circuit, that he felt himself w⟨illing?⟩ to leave us and that the impression was following him everywhere, and Scott, more than once during the last year, threw down his book on the table of the Leaders' Meeting when everything did not please him and would threaten to leave [the] Society and take his members with him.

Five months previous to my coming into the Circuit, one of the party (then forming) said to one who still remains with us, 'it was greatly desired that a few like himself would unite and then they might get a chapel for themselves'.

Ten days before the meeting at which these men were removed from their office, Sawle went to Mr. Moyle[1] (a person who has built a chapel on purpose to attempt to break down our mode of Chapel settling and

---

[1] John Moyle appears to have been a candidate for the ministry who, late in 1836, changed his intention to offer himself. M.C.A. MSS. John Davis to Jabez Bunting, January 10, 1837.

who has been keeping open his chapel in opposition to us and our services in the same village and getting Local Preachers from ours and other circuits to supply the pulpit) and assured him that there was to be a division in the Society and that 100 members were about to separate; that if he (Mr. Moyle) wished it he would come and preach in his pulpit and he only regretted that he h⟨ad⟩ not offered his services before; *this we charged Sawle with in the Leaders' Meeting and he did not deny it.*

On the Friday preceding the Leaders' Meeting mentioned above, these persons had a secret meeting and arranged and determined on the separation, from all which it may be seen that the division of the class was a mere handle to accomplish a division in the Society.

I have no doubt the separation may be traced to three distinct causes, each contributing a share.

1. Sawle's wish to be a preacher instead of working at his trade; this has made him a discontented fault-finding man for years; he has some talent as a Local Preacher, and he thought it a great deal more than it really is, hence he has always been endeavouring to lower the preachers in the estimation of the people.

2. The existence and influence of a base democratical spirit which has spurned at order and designated it tyranny, for Sawle and nearly every-man of his party are Radicals and sworn enemies to our discipline.

3. I am sorry to add the neglect of discipline, which has served to foster all these bad feelings and produce such a state of moral decay and corruption as would scarcely be conceived. Take an instance; it was intimated to me that it would be well to make some remarks about family prayer in the Leaders' Meeting. I did so and questioned the Leaders about attending to it, when to my astonishment I found 3 who lived without it, and one of these a man with a large family, attempted to justify the neglect of it.

I wish now to offer a few remarks on the results of this division 1st as it respects those who have left us.

They are erecting a chapel with borrowed money, for they have not obtained enough by subscriptions to pay for the ground on which it is building. The person who has lent the largest sum has a mortgage of the whole and I am told they are in difficulties to obtain money to finish the chapel as none of them are in circumstances to borrow it on their own personal security.

They have obtained a young man from the Kilhamites who preaches to them, together with Sawle and 3 or 4 other local preachers. We hear very little about them and endeavour to go on our way looking to ourselves; I entertain no fears about what the Kilhamites will do. With the present party they can do no harm, and in this sentiment our real friends join.

2nd as it respects ourselves.

Previous to this event our society here could never meet its current expenses and was continually getting into debt; now we have enough and a balance in hand.

A debt of nearly £90 had accumulated on the Circuit in the last 3 years and was increasing, now our income meets our demands.

Our public collections are about an average; the Kingswood [collection] better and the Yearly [Subscription] *more* than was *ever paid in one year by the Circuit.*

We found ourselves 78 members short last Christmas, at Lady-day we were but 35 short and we had upwards of 80 on trial, so that I trust by Conference we shall nearly if not quite have made up our loss.

I have now a Leaders' Meeting willing to support Methodist discipline and though there are 3 or 4 who are disaffected yet remaining among us, their influence is greatly lessened, and with the exception of these we draw together in the greatest harmony.

It is acknowledged on all hands that the work of God in the Circuit has not for many years presented a more promising aspect than at present, the progress of our people in piety is marked and satisfactory, and the members we are adding are I trust coming in the right way.

In our congregation here we have had a falling off and also in the seat rents, but these are gradually increasing again and will I doubt not as winter approaches increase still more.

Sawle published a pamphlet when the separation took place, professing to give an account of the affair, but I do think that a book of such a size from a Christian professor was scarcely ever published so filled with falsehood and misrepresentation; some of our friends wished a reply to be published, but I steadly resisted this, as I knew the object of the party was agitation, and if he could publish 9 falsehoods in the statement, he would not hesitate to publish 19 in a rejoinder, and I persuaded our friends that it was better to leave the matter to God, which I believe all now see to have been the best way.

I have had no unpleasantness in any Society in the Circuit except the one in town, and I was never more affectionately requested to stay in a Circuit another year, than I have been here. I have consulted with my colleagues and we have drawn together in every part of the painful affair.

At our District Meeting held in this town at the close of last month I gave the same statement which I have now given you; there certainly was a disposition manifested by some of the Brethren to find fault with our proceedings if they could, and they resisted any strong resolution being passed in favour of our measures, some of them hinting as a reason that it would bring them in contact with the disaffected in their own Circuits and they wanted to let it pass without notice. However after a long discussion the following resolution was put to the meeting:

'The case of the division in the Truro Society having been heard, the District Meeting is of opinion that the circumstances were such as to render a division inevitable, and they approve of the general measures adopted by Brother Baker and his colleague'.

For this 9 voted in favour 2 against and 7 were neutral. A very distorted account of this meeting has got out into the world, and it is very broadly asserted by the disaffected that I had a narrow escape of being expelled and that my measures had been condemned. This affair has been one of the most painful ever passed through in all my life, my support has been the testimony of a good conscience that I have sought the glory of God and the good of his cause in the whole matter, and that so far as I understand them I have broken no rule or usage of Methodism, but endeavoured as far as I could firmly to support them.

There is one subject more on which I wish to make a few observations. That subject is the case of Mr. Moyle's Chapel.

As this case has been before Conference already, you may perhaps ⟨re⟩collect, that some 3 or 4 years since a person of the name of Moyle w⟨orked?⟩ a division in one of our Societies in this Circuit and built a chapel for the party he had formed; this Mr. Moyle has used all his efforts to prevent new chapels built in this neighbourhood from being settled on the plan of the Connexion and has steadily set himself in opposition to our discipline.

At the recommendation of a Committee appointed by Conference some of our friends built a chapel in the village for the sole purpose of supporting the constitution of Methodism; on this chapel there is a debt of nearly £500 and not one of the Trustees are connected with the place, but all belong to other parts of the Circuit.

When I came to this Circuit, I found that of 70 persons whom he took from us when he separated not 20 remained together, and scarcely any had come back to us, the bickerings of Christian professors had produced more blasphemy and infidelity in the village than we had in the whole circuit. Beside and above all that, from the first the Local Preachers of the neighbouring circuits had supplied this chapel, while we had a chapel of our own in the same place open at the same time.

I spoke to the two preachers who were on our plan on the impropriety of their conduct and they immediately desisted. I wrote to the preachers of the Redruth and Gwennap circuits and requested they would take steps to prevent their Local Preachers from coming, and strange to tell *they refused to take any steps* to prevent them and these men still persist in coming; the District Meeting did not take up the thing as I thought they would have done and the resolution they passed 'directing the Brethren to request these Local Preachers to desist' has had no influence.

Now this is attended with great evils.

This chapel is the ral[l]ying point for disaffection of all sorts – the people who have separated from us go there, our Local Preachers and Mr. Moyle's influence keep up a congregation and this has prevented Mr. Moyle from settling the chapel as it is fully believed he would have done had our Local Preachers desisted.

June 21st.

Since writing the former part of this letter, I have found out that the 4 Leaders mentioned before with Mr. Budd at their head are exerting themselves to get me removed out of the Circuit at the end of the year; they are exasperated because I will not give up the point of awarding punishment, when a Leaders' Meeting has pronounced sentence of guilt: the plea they are using with the Chairman and those whom they wish to influence, is not that I have done wrong, but that as so much unpleasantness has arisen in the Society I ought to be removed, but this [is] all a mere cover, their true reason is, that I have in conjunction with the sound and true men endeavoured to raise up our discipline, and even about the awarding of punishment they do not complain that I have used the right offensively, but that I have no right to use such a power at all, in short that the Superintendent is only to pronounce the sentence which they pass.

There was a day when Mr. Budd (who has been the common agitator of this Circuit for years) and those who are now leagued with him, could impede the progress of right measures in the Leaders' Meeting, but that power has been paralyzed since I have introduced several new Leaders into the Meeting who are sound men. This quite exasperates them; but these men have no party in the Society, for they are less esteemed as Leaders than any others among us.

These disaffected men are expecting an advocate in Brother Thomas Martin my predecessor;[1] he passed through this town a few days since – never called on me to ask a word of explanation – never called on one of our sound leaders, and though he saw my colleague never asked *him* a word of explanation, but he went to Mr. Budd and told him in the presence of my colleague he should be on the Stationing Committee and would take care to speak about my removal from the

---

[1] Thomas Martin (1780–1866), superintendent, Truro circuit, 1830–33; Plymouth circuit, 1833–36.

circuit; I think it will be admitted, that this conduct was to say the least very unkind.

I have said above that efforts are making to accomplish my removal; by the disaffected here and in other parts of the District, and the object (as our friends here observe) is plain; for should I stay and thus with the help of our sound men establish and make good the ground taken (of which I thank God I feel no doubt) it will I hope find its way into the other parts of the district, whereas my removal would be a tacit censure on the steps taken – be a cause of triumph to our opposers and would greatly discourage our best and warmest friends.

Were I to be removed, Mr. Budd would take the ground (right or wrong) that it had been done because I had claimed the right mentioned; few Brethren (likely to come to this circuit) would take up the line just where I may leave it. If they did they would that moment be in the hot water from which I am now happily escaping and without that knowledge of the men which bitter experience has procured for me and if he yielded or *blinked* the question in any way, all that has been accomplished would be lost and the thing thrown back farther than ever; the plain fact is, that this is in principle a Leeds case, only on a much smaller scale.

Now as I have been so affectionately invited to stay and my colleague also – as the Circuit is in a state of peace and the work prospering, and no one wishes this removal but the disaffected and these so very few, I do not think I ought to go . . .

45 To John Beecham   *n. pl. June, 26, 1834*

From the account of Mr. Lessey[1] and Dixon[2] it appears, that the violence of the opposing party at City Road [Quarterly Meeting] last night was beyond all description or precedent. They both say they never saw anything equal to it in any place. They were cheered on to frenzy by Mr. Moore's[3] furious speeches and example. The whole affair was evidently *concerted*, and the meeting partly packed for the purpose. Mr. Lessey attempted to object to the re-discussion at all, on the ground that the *confirmation* of minutes respected only the *accuracy of the entry*, but

[1] Theophilus Lessey, superintendent, London (City Road) circuit, 1832–34.

[2] James Dixon, preacher, London (City Road) circuit, 1831–34.

[3] Henry Mooore (1751–1844), supernumerary, London (City Road) circuit from 1833. An Irishman, and the assistant, travelling companion, amanuensis, literary executor, and biographer of John Wesley, Moore had enjoyed a reputation as a theologian in his earlier years; he had recently fought an acrimonious battle with his fellow-preachers to continue his occupation of Wesley's house at City Road.

did not re-open the subject, especially when no new light could be pretended. But in this he was weakly and very unfortunately over-ruled by Mr. Hunter himself![1] Dixon spoke nobly. Maughan[2] attempted to put him down by clamour, but Dixon's firmness *forced* a hearing. Taylor,[3] in his speech, happened to call their mode of proceeding *insidious*, which Rd. Smith,[4] who was as bitter as gall, resented. At last there were 26 for rescinding the last Quarter's Vote, and 15 against it, including all the preachers, except Mason, who did not vote!! Lessey is vexed at Walton,[5] who did not *speak* at all. Bowes[6] was very determined on the wrong side. Poor Lessey feels it dreadfully. I am truly sorry for him. He talks of leaving; but I think will not in the end see it right to the Circuit to do so. It is a business which would require much deliberation, before [being] adopted; though it would certainly serve them as they merit. It is altogether a bad affair, and the moral effect of it elsewhere will be very mischievous. Hunter led them very much astray, however well-meant his motion, when he induced their consent to have it introduced at all into a Quarterly Meeting.

Now for a stone in the other pocket. We had a full meeting[7] this forenoon, and a delightful one. I first apologized for Walton's omission[8] to Haslope and the other gentlemen. Then, as they had not been consulted before, and we knew not their minds even on the *principle*, we thought it right to allow discussion on that. Entwisle,[9] *Gaulter*,[10] *Cubitt*,[11] *Taylor*, Naylor etc.[12] made very telling speeches. Hoby[13] and

[1] John Hunter, a prosperous retired woollen-draper; d. 1839, aet. 80. A prominent London Methodist, buried at City Road.

[2] Probably Thomas Maughan of City Road, widower of Mary Maughan and father of Thomas Maughan junr., to whom inscriptions were erected at City Road. George J. Stevenson, *City Road Chapel and its associations* (London, 1872) p. 489.

[3] Joseph Taylor, cf. n. 4 p. 51 *supra*.

[4] Richard Smith, a trustee of City Road Chapel; d. 1855, aet. 74. His second wife was Mary Anne, younger and favourite daughter of Adam Clarke.

[5] Daniel Walton, preacher, London (City Road) circuit, 1832–35. In 1848 he was subject to disciplinary proceedings on suspicion of being implicated in the publication of the *Flysheets* (cf. Ward, *Religion and Society in England* p. 263). D. 1862, aet. 72.

[6] George Bowes, class-leader and trust treasurer at City Road. D. 1856, aet. 63.

[7] To discuss the affairs of the proposed Theological Institution.

[8] Daniel Walton was one of the candidates recommended by the Committee for establishing the Institution to serve as a tutor, but was never appointed.

[9] Joseph Entwisle sen., superintendent, London (Lambeth) circuit, 1831–34.

[10] John Gaulter, superintendent, London (Hinde St.) circuit, 1833–36.

[11] George Cubitt (1791–1850), preacher, London (Great Queen St.) circuit, 1833–36. Assistant connexional editor, 1836–42; editor, 1842–50.

[12] William Naylor, superintendent, London (Spitalfields) circuit, 1833–35. D. 1868, aet. 85.

[13] James Hoby, fringe manufacturer; member of the Missionary Committee and of the original Theological Institution committee; trustee and class-leader at City Road.

Elliott[1] were at once quite hearty. Haslope, who at first said, but kindly, that he only came to hear, seemed convinced, and thought we ought to try the experiment, though afraid of the evil of *congregating* young men in one place. Jenkins[2] took much the same ground. At last Elliott moved, and Haslope seconded, a Resolution, expressive of their approbation of the principle of an Institution, and their readiness to become a provisional Committee for carrying it into effect, but proposing to limit it *at present* to about 30 students resident in the Institution House; viz. 16 for Home [work], 10 for Missions, and 4 for Ireland. Farmer,[3] who had gone out for half an hour, came back, and supported this effectively and cordially; offering to afford his pecuniary aid as soon as it would be wanted. It then becam⟨e⟩ necessary to adjourn till Wednesday next. A sub-committee (Farmer, Taylor, Walton, Bunting, Beecham) were appointed to prepare General Rules; and a few more with them to look at Hoxton Academy and report. Mr. Haslope, after having once *adhered*, became a chief speaker, and will soon, I think, be among the foremost . . .

46   From Humphrey Sandwith[4] to T. P. Bunting   *Bridlington, June 28, 1834*

[Is most grateful for the offer of the editorship of the projected newspaper, but must weigh carefully his family responsibilities]

. . . I cordially concur with the Committee in the loud demands of the times for an undertaking of which they have so well chalked out the

[1] John Searman Elliott Esq., London; member of the Missionary Committee and of the original Theological Institution committee.

[2] William Jenkins, supernumerary in London since 1810; practised as an architect specializing in chapel building and repair. Member of the original Theological Institution committee, and addressed one of the early Centenary Fund meetings. D. 1844, aet. 81.

[3] Thomas Farmer Esq., of Gunnersbury; d. 1861, aet. 70. The most prominent Methodist benefactor in the South, and a leading promoter of the Theological Institution.

[4] Humphrey Sandwith (1792–1874), surgeon at Bridlington, and from 1842 lecturer on the theory and practice of medicine at Hull school of medicine. He attracted notice in 1825 as a defender of Methodist church order against Mark Robinson of Beverley (see Ward, *Religion and Society in England* pp. 153–56; *Early Correspondence* pp. 100–114) and published a major unsigned essay on 'Methodism in its relations to the Church and the nation' in the *Wesleyan Methodist Magazine* (1829) (M.C.A. MSS. H. Sandwith to Thomas Jackson, October 1, 1832). Edited the *Watchman* from its beginning in 1835 to 1842. Sandwith was encouraged by a London doctor in the belief that he might succeed as a physician in Town provided his connexion with the newspaper were not general knowledge, and the *Christian Advocate* gave such adverse publicity to the proposed appointment as to make it difficult for him to remain in his practice at Bridlington (M.C.A. MSS. John Beecham to Jabez Bunting, September 1,

G

outline. And though politics are to me a comparatively new field of enquiry, and one which presents many complex questions for discussion, with a deep sense also of my incompetence to do full justice to the wishes of the Committee and the wants of the Connexion, nevertheless I should not object to hazard the painful alternative of a failure. There is enough, I confess, to excite the aspirations of an ambition consecrated to the interests of truth, in becoming the political organ of a Connexion like ours, in which politics are subordinated to loftier principles, and thus what is too commonly the bane of piety, becomes its aliment and support. As to the duties of an Editor not seriously interfering with the practice of my profession or with its studies, but proving possibly a salutary exchange of mental pursuit, I confess myself at a loss now to determine that question, or how far my medical character and reputation might be affected by it. The public are extremely jealous of any interference with a profession to which they judge an exclusive attention essential to its successful exercise. It would seem, in short, as generally understood, that the highest style of the medical character (as for example that of the late Dr. Percival)[1] is formed in the calm retreats of science, undisturbed by the exciting elements of political contention.

I regret, that the claims of my profession will not allow me to leave home for so great distance, and so long a time, as those you mention . . . The only eligible place under the pressure of my engagements, will be for me to give your Father the meeting at York . . .

47 From John Beecham   *Dublin, July 1, 1834*

I am much obliged by your letter although some parts of it were vexatious and trying. I was fully prepared to expect that the result of the discussion at the City Road Quarterly Meeting would be unfavourable. But what were Walton and Mason doing? I wonder Mason did not vote. I find from conversing with the President he has had information from London about the Meeting, and I expect those who are unfriendly to the

1834). He got Thomas Chalmers to canvass non-medical votes in an unsuccessful attempt to obtain a Glasgow medical qualification, by assurances that 'our projected newspaper . . . *would be friendly to the Church*' (M.C.A. MSS. Humphrey Sandwith to Jabez Bunting, October 3, 1834), and then called on Bunting to assist a finally successful application to St. Andrews. M.C.A. MSS. Humphrey Sandwith to Jabez Bunting, October 18, 1834: December 10, 1834: January 3, 1835.

1 Thomas Percival (1740–1804), unitarian doctor in Manchester, to whom Jabez Bunting had been apprenticed before entering the ministry, and after whom the recipient of this letter was christened.

Institution will bruit it abroad as much as possible. The President[1] tells me he has also been informed that some of the preachers in London are unfavourable to the Institution, and among the number is Farrar.[2] The President thinks it is quite an improvement on the original plan to limit the number of students as now proposed.[3] The second part of your letter was very refreshing. It is a *weighty* 'stone in the other pocket', and I do not fear the final result after all the enemies of the Institution can do. I have reminded the President that unless the Conference renounce all pretensions to consistency, an Institution must be had of some kind; that our Conference discussions cannot extend beyond the *details* of the plan – the *form* of the Institution . . . I have talked with Mr. Waugh[4] about our present views on the subject of the Institution. He quite approves of limiting the number of students, and thinks with us it is of great importance to get hold of this place at Hoxton,[5] and commence operations *at once*. I think we can put another 'stone in the right pocket' by some consideration of the subject here . . .

48   To John Beecham   *London, July 3, 1834*

Accept my thanks for your welcome letter just received.

On the morning after I last wrote, Mr. Haslope, Mr. Hoby, Mr. Pocock,[6] Mr. Walton, and myself, went to inspect the Hoxton Academy. It is a charming place for our purpose. There are 27 studies, the very

[1] Richard Treffry, superintendent, Bristol (Langton St.) circuit, 1832–35.

[2] Abraham E. Farrar, preacher, London (Hinde St.) circuit, 1833–36. D. 1849, aet. 60.

[3] The Conference committee drawing up the scheme had originally planned to educate all the preachers on the list of reserve, but finally advocated a pilot scheme for residential seminary training for 30 men, 16 for the home work, 4 for Ireland, and 10 for the mission field. The London preachers were to give an additional examination to the men on the list of reserve, refer the men they thought inadequate back to Conference, keep some in readiness to be called out for immediate service at home or abroad, and appoint the remainder (apart from residents) as non-resident students whose reading was to be directed and examined by the tutors of the Institution.

[4] Thomas Waugh (1785–1873), one of the most distinguished preachers of the Irish Conference, stationed in Dublin, 1831–34. The Irish interest in the subject lay in the fact that the immediate possibility of proceeding with a residential seminary arose from a legacy of £1000 received by the Irish Conference 'to promote the improvement of our junior preachers in Ireland'. This they paid over to the proposed Institution in return for being reserved four places, with a title to more if they paid for the candidates.

[5] See *infra* no. 48.

[6] William Fuller Pocock (1779–1849), architect, a member of the original committee of the Theological Institution. The purchase of Hoxton Academy, an institution which had had a chequered history since its staff developed liberal views towards the end of the previous century, enabled the Institution to offer its first residential accommodation.

things we should like to have, if [we] were about to build, a capital Library Room, shelved round, a large lecture room, two gardens, quite separate from each other, and, in short, every thing ready to our hand. I hope they will give us time to get the decision of Conference, and not let it for a Lunatic Asylum, for which it seems they have an application. There is great *talk* of opposition from certain preachers. But surely the Conference will not now disgrace itself by a retreat. Farrar at first seemed *queer* and *captious*; but at our last meeting was more cordial, or at least *acquiescent*. Stanley[1] was absent!! I wish a vote of the Irish Conference in favour of an *Institution-House* etc. could be obtained. If tolerably unanimous it would tell well . . .

On the 1st day of the Finsbury Election Pownall[2] was 300 ahead. But Wakely and Babbage then *virtually*, though not nominally, retired in Duncombe's favour, who had at the close a majority of 600. Without my consent they published a note I had sent to Pownall. I am not sorry, as it avows a good principle of which I think, religious people need greatly to be reminded. Of course I am lauded in the Conservative papers, and abused, they say, as usual by the *Advocate*. No matter! My sentiments are thus unwittingly circulated at Jack's[3] expense in quarters where they would not otherwise have travelled; and they may d⟨o⟩ well on future occasions . . .

I saw Lefevre on Saturday, and again on Monday; – very kind, but no *official* answer for us from the Treasury, to which our case has once more been referred. I saw, however, at Cambridge a letter from Rice[4] to Mr. Forster,[5] and had certain significant hints from Lefevre, from which I infer fully that we shall only get £1045. I waited till last night, in hope of an official reply. As none came I resolved to go to press. A statement is therefore printed in the July Notices, and in separate circulars, urging a collection on the 1st of August in Great Britain and

[1] Jacob Stanley, preacher, London (Hinde St.) circuit, 1833–36.

[2] A vigorous effort was made by the Tories led by Henry Pownall to capture the liberal stronghold of Finsbury. Bunting wrote a letter of support to Pownall, which was published in the *Standard*, and appeared on the hustings with him. These actions, at a time when J. R. Stephens was subject to discipline for political action on the radical side, occasioned criticism at the following Conference. Bunting then explained that the letter was published without his explicit consent, and that his appearance on the hustings was due to the reluctance of the whig government to begin negotiations upon the assessment of chapels to rates. Pownall, defeated by 680 votes in an election in which the Liberal vote was divided among three candidates, later wrote to Bunting, thanking him warmly for his services, and announcing that, as the opposition of the Dissenters made it impossible for him to succeed, he would not stand again. M.C.A. MSS. Henry Pownall to Jabez Bunting, December 16, 1834.

[3] John Stephens, the younger, editor of the *Christian Advocate*.

[4] Thomas Spring-Rice, later first Baron Monteagle (1790–1866), secretary to the Treasury, 1830–34.

[5] Probably Matthew Forster, prominent West Africa merchant.

Ireland, to be primarily applied to the case of the chapels, and then, if there be a surplus, to the General Purposes of the Special West India Fund[1] ...

I see that Rice told Buxton and the House of Commons on Tuesday night that the Government had made arrangements about the Jamaica chapels *'perfectly* satisfactory' to all parties. What a strange mis-statem[en]t. I am vexed with such a representation ...

49 From Joseph Hargreaves[2]   *Heywood, July 4, 1834*

When I had the pleasure of meeting you at Middleton you kindly encouraged me to write sometime during the year. I have delayed until *now* in hope of being able to communicate some information in reference to the state of this circuit *generally*, and to the conduct of our *principal men particularly*, which if not *important* will at least be *acceptable*, to *one* on whom devolves 'the care of all' our 'churches'. The Methodistical and consistent decision of the Manchester District Meeting in the case of the *great* J. R. Stephens has caused considerable excitement in Rochdale. The 'Radical Memorialists'[3] who affect to despise Conference, and who *really* wish to control its decisions, called a meeting or meetings of their own party, and determined to get up a string of resolutions for the adoption of the Quarterly Meeting; they also agreed to withold their subscriptions from the funds of the Connexion for the present. In consequence of Mr. Cheetham's[4] telling the Stewards, according to agreement in our private Preachers' meeting, that he would leave the circuit if anything was done contrary to the spirit and rules of Methodism, the famous resolutions were never moved in the meeting; but I am sorry to say that our Circuit Stewards and several of the Leaders have refused to pay their subscriptions to the Auxiliary Fund. Some friends who are of a

---

[1] The Missionary Committee claimed that £2090 was needed to restore 6 Methodist chapels destroyed in the riots of 1832. The government proposed to ask Parliament for half this sum if the Missionary Society would raise the rest. On August 1 special collections raised £1600, and when the special fund for West Indian missions and schools was closed in 1835, it exceeded £9100. Findlay and Holdsworth, *History of the Wesleyan Methodist Missionary Society* ii. 319.

[2] Joseph Hargreaves (1806–86), preacher, Rochdale circuit, 1833–34.

[3] In 1829 the Rochdale Quarterly Meeting was rebuked by Conference for sending up a memorial supporting the Stewards and Leaders of Leeds (for whose opposition to the Leeds Brunswick organ, see *Early Correspondence* pp. 156–92) but kept up their opposition till 1832. In October 1835 they began their opposition to the Theological Institution from which developed an open clash with the superintendent minister and one of the most damaging secessions ever to befall a Methodist circuit. See *infra*.

[4] Charles Cheetham (1794–1858), preacher, Rochdale circuit, 1832–35.

better mind have liberally come forward and made up the sum to more than it was last year! The abominable *Christian Reprobate*[1] is read in nearly all our influential families in Rochdale. I am happy in the prospect of leaving at Conference. Mr. Slater[2] who says he was desired by the Heywood people last year, has written to inform the Stewards that he shall not ask for the appointment of Mr. Slack[3] unless they will pay attention to his comfort, and have the house made dry . . . We have been favoured with a measure of prosperity in the Heywood Society, there are six classes and about one hundred members more in this neighbourhood than there were twelve months ago . . .

P.S. I intend to forward by one of the preachers a copy of a pamphlet published at Ashton entitled – *Facts from the press; not fictions from the pulpit.* It has been circulated by some of our *small friends* amongst the enlightened and *liberal* Independents who wish our people to make a stir about Stephens.

50 From John Beecham

Dublin, Saturday noon
[Postmarked July 5, 1834]

I am much obliged by your full and kind letter which I have this instant received. I am sorry that our friend Pownall has not succeeded, though I am not surprized, as I expected his jarring opponents would combine if they saw danger in order to exclude him. I am glad, however, he has made good play and obtained a respectable minority. The publication of your letter will do good I doubt not, and as to the abuse you speak of in a certain quarter, it will do good also, though the author does not intend it.

I am very glad to hear of your proceedings respecting the Institution. I should think the building at Hoxton will be the very thing; and I am more impressed with the reason for our taking it which weighed with us at our meeting before I left home. Let it be once secured and entered on, and the question will then be *practically* set at rest whether we have an Institution or not. Mr. [Robert] Newton is now here; we have talked the subject over. He was greatly chagrined with the *illaterati* [*sic*] of the North Circuit,[4] but heartily approves of what we have agreed on

---

[1] I.e. *Christian Advocate.*

[2] Barnard Slater (1779–1851), superintendent, Bolton circuit, 1832–35, their area representative on the Stationing Committee.

[3] Benjamin Slack (1809–68), appointed preacher, Rochdale circuit, as requested, 1834–35.

[4] I.e. the rowdy proceedings in the City Road Quarterly Meeting, reported by Bunting in no. 45.

respecting the limitation of the number of students, say to 30, and with the proposal to engage the Hoxton building. I have told him my plan to engage some strength for our cause from the Irish Conference and he goes fully into it. I may be deceived in my calculations, but I have good hope we shall find the feeling here generally in favour of the Institution. I suspected there was a reason for Jacob [Stanley]'s absence from the Committee before I left home, and that suspicion is greatly confirmed by his absenting himself a second time, and I incline to think from what you say, that there is something in what the President says about Farrar. But I cannot think it possible the Conference will disgrace itself by retreating on account of such defections and such opposition as we hear of.

You will have heard from the Manchester friends perhaps that Newton has had to go to Ashton. The preachers could not get on, and requested to have a Special District Meeting;[1] but he attended their Quarterly Meeting instead. He says they are in a wretched state. But you will hear all about it. Mr. Newton says he hears Bromley[2] at York is making very unfair representations respecting us, as that it is intended on our side of the 'house' to take high ground and endeavour to throw the Connexion almost, if not altogether, into the arms of the Church, and therefore he urges it as a matter of highest moment to get Jacob elected [President?] in order that his influence may be employed in counteracting our project. When will brethren use common honesty? One knows what to do with open, honourable opponents . . .

51   From Thomas Kaye[3]   *Liverpool, July 9, 1834*

As it is not impossible that you may have heard several versions of the introduction of the Address in favour of the Church into the vestry of Brunswick Chapel for signature, and as I am the party liable to the blame of that measure (if blame there be), I trouble you with this brief statement, in order to put you in possession of the real facts of the case, that the saddle may 'rest upon the right horse.'

It was only about half an hour before service time on the Sunday

---

[1] For quietening the circuit after the trial of J. R. Stephens.

[2] James Bromley, preacher, York circuit, 1833–35. Supported and advised Dr. Warren at the time of his expulsion, 1835. Said to have been the only member of Conference to vote against the expulsion of Samuel Dunn, 1849. Himself expelled after refusing to appear before a special meeting of the Bath District Committee, 1850.

[3] Thomas Kaye, proprieter of the *Liverpool Courier*, of Tory sympathies, Treasurer of Liverpool Brunswick trust.

morning in question that I had put into my hands the Address and sheets for signature, with a request from one of the Secretaries who had the management of the affair, that, if there would be no objection, those of the Congregation worshipping at that or any other of the Wesleyan Chapels who were friendly to the object might be afforded an opportunity of signing the Address. This, of course, was left entirely to my own discretion. I felt no objection – I saw none, nor did I suppose there would be the slightest ground of opposition urged by any individual at Brunswick, the measure being, as I thought then, and still think, in perfect keeping with all the Minutes and addresses of Conference, and, as I believed, in strict harmony with the views and feelings of all the Preachers in our circuit.

If I had thought it necessary upon principle to consult Mr. [Samuel] Jackson, the superintendent that morning (which for the reasons above stated, I did not) there was no time for so doing. As it was, I carried the papers to the Vestry, and there I found Mr. Sands,[1] Circuit Steward, and the two Chapel Stewards. I asked them if there would be any objection to the Address being laid there for signature and the fact announced from the pulpit. After having read it they all concurred in the view I had taken. The sheets were then placed upon the table, and the only hesitation about signing the document was manifested by Mr. Stephenson[2] himself after the morning service, on the ground that it purported to be from the '*Lay Members of the Church of England*'; but upon my pointing out to him the word '*friends*,' which occurred in another part of the Address, and which, I observed, opened the door for him also to express his friendly feeling towards the Establishment, he then subscribed his name.[3] The document bore the signatures of five other Preachers. The sheets were as well signed (I mean as to numbers) as in many of the churches in Liverpool . . .

Mr. Jackson, with his characteristic caution, and wish to avoid the slightest ground of excitement, had, it appeared, fancied it might possibly be made the occasion of getting up a counter-address; but, *entre nous*, – this was an idea probably never thought of by any living soul except himself, and until he had thrown out the hint and had talked about it, and not till then can I conceive there was the most remote probability of anything of the kind . . .

No circumstance, as far as I am capable of judging, has tended so much to raise the cause of Methodism in the estimation of respectable Society

---

[1] Thomas Sands, Liverpool merchant; member of Missionary Committee.

[2] William B. Stephenson, preacher, Liverpool (North) circuit, 1831–34. D. 1866, aet. 64.

[3] This was evidently one of the addresses energetically pushed in the cause of Church defence at this time.

in this town, as this very event, – the signing at Brunswick having been talked about freely, and hailed as a full redemption of that pledge which has for years past been given, that there was no hostility on the part of the Wesleyan body towards the Church of England.

My friend Mr. Stephenson has passed his three years in this circuit with great credit to himself – his congregations have been kept up to the last. He has neutralised if not extinguished the Leeds Street leaven,[1] and has been instrumental in the hands of God, along with his highly respected colleagues, in working a good work, and increasing the members of the Society . . .

52   From Thomas Waugh   *Dublin, July 13, 1834*

. . . The affair was brought under the notice of our Conference, that our proceedings (the Representatives) had their fullest approval – that a deep and *unanimous* anxiety prevails to see the Institution commenced – the money held by us ready to be handed over to the managers as soon as may be necessary, and that we feel deeply grateful for the provision made by your proposed plan for Ireland.[2] The resolution passed on the occasion I shall be prepared to present to your Conference . . .

53   From Joseph Sutcliffe[3]   *Brighton,*
July 17 [1834] [Postmarked]

. . . We have lost three leaders to the Irvin[g]ites[4] and twenty two members including the three leaders, but its effects are not felt either in our *congregation*, or *collection* or *numbers* in society, all of which are in- creased. We should have had, I confess, a greater increase had not those visionary evils happened. I regard their secession as a purifica- tion of the society . . .

Our young men must have scholastic aids, notwithstanding the clamours of local preachers, and the fears of our more pious people. It is

[1] I.e. the radicals who had been creating disturbances since the division of the Liverpool circuit in 1825. See *Early Correspondence* pp. 118–28 and, *supra*, nos. 1, 3, 8.

[2] Cf. n. 4 p. 75 *supra*.

[3] Joseph Sutcliffe, superintendent, Brighton circuit, 1832–35. Wrote a popular *Commentary on the Old and New Testament* (London, 1834–35). D. 1856, aet. 94.

[4] Followers of Edward Irving (1792–1834) who had been compelled to retire from his ministry at Regent Square Presbyterian Church, London, owing to his approval of speaking in tongues. His followers took the title of Holy Catholic Apostolic Church.

the interest of the Trustees to favour the plan, and the edification of the people (now educated at boarding schools) require[s] it. They must either look up to the sanctuary or they will wander elsewhere . . .

54   From P. C. Turner to T. P. Bunting   *London, August 5, 1834*

. . . I am writing in the midst of a spirited debate about Stephens, and therefore I am likely to make all sorts of blunders . . . Stevens's [*sic*] case came on yesterday morning at 9 o'clock the District Minutes were read and *many many* questions asked about the decision they came to, and after the matter had been thus fully explained by various members of the *Dist*[*rict Meeting*] then Stephens was put on his defence, this he attempted to do by objecting to the 2nd and 3rd resolutions,[1] he was repeatedly asked if he stated to the meeting that he would submit to the 7th if the 2nd and 3rd were rescinded, but about this he quibbled – and it came out at last that at the final close of the business he said he would have relinquished his Secretaryship if these said resolutions *had not* been passed. He occupied about two hours perhaps more, and then *retired*. Your father immediately rose and began a glorious speech, which continued perhaps 3/4 of an hour when the time for breaking up came, and he was declared to be *in possession* at 6 o'clock this morning; he began soon after the hour, and continued for about an hour, moving resolutions commendatory of the Dist[rict] – adopting its decisions and offering, on consideration of Stephens pledging himself to behave properly, that he should be restored to his place, and if he *refused*, that his suspension should be continued through the year, with the proviso that if he would give the President the required pledge he shall be authorized to send him to the first vacant place. Bromley moved an amendment, the spirit of which was the removal of the sentence and the restoration of S. to his place. This was seconded but no other preacher seemed to think favourably of it and certainly noone *spoke* in its favour – Mr. N⟨ewton⟩ seconded your father's motion in a good speech[2] . . .

Would you believe that *John* Stephens[3] appeared at the door this morning to demand an entrance into the Conference which of course he did not obtain. I hear he intends to bring a magistrate – *if he can get one* – to forward his purpose. We are in the midst of our work, I hope a decision will be come to today, but at this stage I must leave off . . .

[1] For these resolutions, see no. 42 *supra*.

[2] A list of the speakers follows which adds nothing to the account of the debate in Gregory, *Sidelights* pp. 150–64.

[3] See n. 3 p. 76 *supra*.

55 To James Wood   *London, August 16, 1832*
                                  [*sic – error for 1834*[1]]

It is probable that Mr. Newton, Mr. Crowther and Mr. Bowers will
have communicated to you already the result of the conversation in the
Conference about the Newspaper. Yet I cannot resist the temptation of
stating to you at this my *first hour of leisure* since I saw you in Tadcaster,
the *substance* of what has occurred, leaving you to collect the details from
the friends I have mentioned, and from Mr. Anderson[2] on his return.

My strong impression, I may even say *conviction*, after all the discussions growing out of Mr. Stephens's case, was that it would not be
expedient at present to ask from the Conference a direct and positive
sanction of the paper by a public vote or act. We should probably have
obtained a majority even in that case. But there is a general feeling of
salutary caution, lest we should as a Body be committed to any particular line of party politics,[3] and so injure the character and usefulness
of our ministry, and provoke unprofitable disputations among ourselves
and our people. Now, though there is nothing in our project or purpose
which would really violate this feeling, yet, considering that the paper is
not yet in being, there would have been some even among its friends in
Conference, who would have hesitated about expressing *beforehand* an
approbation of the design. And then I had some doubt also whether,
after all, a distinct promise of encouragement, obtained as it must have
been by something like *pledges* on our part, would not have fettered us
too much in our proceedings, and involved, also, a liability in future
Conferences to the annoyance of much cavil and animadversion from the
few preachers (few, but bold and noisy) who do not agree with us in
opinion on public and methodistical questions. I wished a hundred
times that some of the country proprietors had been present, to decide
for themselves what course we ought to take. I felt my situation to be
delicate and perplexing; but, after consulting with our best friends, did
the best I could. I stated to the Conference the *necessity* and probable
usefulness of such a paper, and the *general principles* on which you intend
to conduct it; disclaimed asking for an immediate vote of encouragement, but announced the project as likely to be executed; asserted the
readiness of the parties to give any reasonable power of interference and
control to the Conference as security for its methodistical character, if,
on seeing it, they should hereafter be disposed to afford to it the benefit of
their patronage and recommendation; and wished to elicit the views and
feelings of the Preachers. The result was most satisfactory. The project

---

[1] The holograph of this letter is at U.M.C. Archives, Lake Junaluska, N.C.

[2] John Anderson, superintendent, Manchester (Grosvenor St.) circuit, 1833–35.

[3] On one of the reasons for this, see n. 2 p. 76 *supra*.

was hailed with almost unanimous *enthusiasm*; and loud calls for its *speedy* accomplishment were made from every quarter of the Chapel. A strong conviction of its necessity and certain success was decidedly expressed, and, though no *act* of the Conference was just now deemed prudent, I was authorized to state to the gentlemen concerned that the Preachers feel the need of such a paper, will look on it with a most favourable eye, will afford every proper facility by our Book Parcels, etc., to the circulation of their prospectuses, and if they find it on inspection to answer to the spirit of its original professions, may *probably* be induced next year to publish a direct recommendation of its general design etc., though still disclaiming any distinct and sweeping responsibility for its specific contents. Now I think this is all we need in the commencement; and shall be happy to know if you and our other friends agree in the propriety of the course which I have ventured to adopt.

As it is not unlikely that Parliament may meet earlier than usual, it would perhaps be well if it could be made possible to begin the paper rather sooner than January 1. This however is open to much discussion. At present and for some months to come, all heads and hands here will be fully occupied with the *Institution*. Mr. Hunter is decidedly of opinion that Mr. Sandwith's engagement in a newspaper would essentially injure his success as a physician. And between ourselves, I incline to think that his services, however valuable, would be bought *too dear* on the liberal terms you have last proposed to him; and that we might possibly get a sufficient editor at a cheaper rate, and without the serious responsibility of moving Mr. S. and his family from his present locality. Some preachers strongly recommend Mr. Gawtress, now connected with a newspaper at Hull and well acquainted with the business. Mr. Grindrod once named him to us; and can tell you all about him. As second man or sub-editor he would at all events be a great acquisition. I congratulate you on our success in regard to the Institution; a success to which the noble list of contributions from Manchester very essentially contributed. Please shew this letter to *Percy*, with my love . . .

56 From Samuel Wilde[1]   *Yeadon near Leeds, September 20, 1834*

You have heard no doubt of the great revival of the work of God in this town and circuit for which I hope we shall never cease to be thankful to God. Such has been the addition to our numbers that our old Chapel

---

[1] Samuel Wilde, superintendent, Yeadon circuit, 1832–35. Retired from ministry, 1853.

will not hold the whole of the members of our Society by some hundreds so that we have been obliged to build a new Chapel . . .

Our Trustees have unanimously desired me to give you a pressing invitation to open our chapel. . . . Do come and see 'the Grace of God' and I am sure you will be glad. I am happy to say that the great majority of our new converts stand fast and we are expecting to have the whole town converted when we get our new chapel opened. As our people are nearly all poor our strength is in our numbers, but, as trade has been very bad in this neighbourhood since we began the erection of our chapel until very lately, many small subscriptions which were then promised will not be obtained for some time to come, so that it is the more necessary that we should have a good opening. Everything considered our people have done wonders so that we hope to have our chapel placed in good circumstances . . .

It is a pleasing fact that our revival has led already to the erection of four new chapels and the enlargement of several more. I am happy to inform you that the appointment of a second preacher to this Circuit by the last Conference is now thankfully accepted by one and all of our people, and they have cheerfully engaged to support him without asking any help from Conference. I am sorry to learn that an individual who happened to be in London at the Conference in opposing the appointment of a second preacher made statements which were by no means founded in fact and I do assure you there is nothing in this Circuit but the most kindly feeling towards the Conference[1] and I hope Mr. Bullivant[2] will be both acceptable and useful amongst us . . .

57 To Edmund Grindrod   *London, September 27, 1834*

I thank you for your two kind sympathizing and welcome letters, the first of which came into my hands late on Monday night, the last, this morning.

[1] In this generation Yeadon enjoyed remarkable revivals every seven years, the most remarkable breaking out in the early weeks of 1834, commencing with the conversion of four members of the preacher's family, and bringing in about 1000 converts in Yeadon and the adjacent villages of Rawdon and Guiseley. According to Gregory, it was proposed in the Stationing Committee to appoint an extra preacher to watch over the flock, and this was carried in Conference despite the remonstrances of the preacher, Trustees and Chairman of the District, Bunting demanding 'less parade about revivals'. Part of the cost of the additional preacher was borne by the adjacent Woodhouse Grove circuit. (Gregory, *Sidelights* pp. 168–9). The appointment of the additional preacher was insufficient to save the day in 1850, when the Yeadon circuit suffered one of the worst of all shipwrecks in the Wesleyan Reform secessions. Ward, *Religion and society* pp. 269–72.

[2] William J. Bullivant, preacher, Yeadon Circuit, 1834–35. D. 1869, age unknown.

At 1 o'clock in the morning of Monday the 15th inst., on my way from Hastings to London, I had the misfortune to stumble against a stone parapet, connected with the steps of the Inn at which the coach stopped. No serious injury was sustained; but one of my shins was broken, and Mr. Hunter rigidly confined me to the sopha almost ever since, allowing me only the last four days to go to the Mission House in a coach for a few hours. My leg is nearly well again; but the want of usual exercise has made me low and nervous, and I am apt to lose my natural sleep, if at all excited. Under these circumstances I have judged it best at present not to read Dr. Warren's pamphlet at all.[1] Perhaps it will be best for me not to be annoyed by it at all, till near the time of Conference when the subject must come of course under public cognizance. This will account to you for my not having sooner written to you.

Great and highly criminal as is Dr. Warren's offence against our discipline in publicly impugning and endeavouring to defeat a measure which the Conference has so deliberately sanctioned, yet I think that suspension, however merited, would be inexpedient.[2] It would give the factious part of the men of his Circuit a pretext, if not a right, of interference, so as to *let them in* as parties in the controversy; for they would expect to have reasons assigned for inflicting on them the deprivation, for so large a portion of the year, of their Superintendent's services. You will see from this that I incline much more to the course suggested in your second letter, than to the one proposed in your first. Official enquiry and cognizance of the offence, an immediate verdict of censure and condemnation as to the pamphlet, admonition to the offender, and solemn warning as to the sin and peril of opposing himself in future by any overt acts to the execution of the Conference's decision – these would all be very proper; and then the whole case might be referred to Conference for *sentence*.

I hope to see Mr. Newton with whom we can talk the matter over more at large . . .

58   From John Beecham   *[pl. illeg., postmark Grimsby]*
September 29, 1834

. . . I have been much gratified with my visit to the North, as it has afforded me an opportunity of making personal observation of the state

---

[1] S. Warren, *Remarks on the Wesleyan Theological Institution for the education of junior preachers: together with the substance of a speech delivered at the London Conference of 1834* (London, 1834).

[2] Warren was in fact suspended conditionally after refusing to take his trial before a Special District Meeting in October 1834. Cf. no. 60 *infra*.

of feeling in some important Methodistical districts on the great public questions by which the connexion has been agitated. I spent the greater part of a day in Hull on my way to Sunderland. A few of the principal friends met me at Mr. Alsop's, and I was glad to find that a very good feeling prevailed among them on Stephen[s]'s case, the newspaper, and the church and state question; and that they are as warmly as ever attached to the cause of Missions. Mr. Henwood[1] was one of the party, and appeared more than ordinarily cordial and alive to the interests of Methodism. I learned more particularly from Mr. Alsop that there is a very good feeling on the subject of the newspaper in Hull; and I should calculate that it will be respectably supported there. At Sunderland I was entertained at the house of Mr. Willam Longridge,[2] who inquired most affectionately respecting your health and welfare. He told me he has sympathized with you so much on account of the persecution you have undergone by the *Christian Advocate* that he has frequently been on the point of writing to you a letter of condolence, but has been restrained by the consideration that your time was too much occupied to attend to such unimportant correspondence as his. He wishes me however to convey to you the expression of his very sincere affection for you and esteem for your public character. He is very much delighted with the decisions of the Conference, and manifests the most lively interest for the Institution. I talked with him and the preachers at large on that subject, and endeavoured to impress them with the importance of making strenuous efforts to raise annual subscriptions for its permanent support. I found that Mr. Longridge had been thinking much on the subject previously, and a suggestion which he offered appears to me deserving of notice . . . that in our principal places the preachers or some of our friends should call on those whom they might think most likely to contribute, and inform them that as we are now making preparations for commencing the Institution we are anxious to ascertain the probable amount of support which will be afforded by the connexion, and would thank them to say what we may put down . . . for them as a yearly subscription, leaving it to be called for say in the month of January. I told Mr. Longridge it had been proposed to publish speedily a kind of circular on the subject with a list of subscriptions already put down, which may serve as a guide to others . . .

On the church and state question, I found the state of feeling in the

---

[1] James Henwood Esq., a Hull class-leader, circuit steward and local preacher; member of the Committee of Privileges from 1835. A banker who began in the Methodist firm of Smith and Thompson and who occupied Wilberforce's old house. D. 1854, aet. 70.

[2] William Longridge (apparently son of Michael Longridge (1757–1815), draper and one of the most important early Methodists in Sunderland) was secretary to the Sunderland Sunday School Union and a prominent Methodist in the town.

North better than I had expected. At Durham they are very well satisfied with their appointment of preachers, and are settling down pretty quietly. Mr. Bramwell[1] is said to be very weary of attending the Independent chapel, and is preparing to return to ours. I learned at Sunderland that a good deal of trickery had been displayed by those who got up the memorial from that place to the Conference.[2] Several who signed it understood that it was a memorial on quite another subject, and have expressed great mortification and chagrin at their having been so duped. I find that the Memorialists of the North are quite surprized at the Conference having taken any notice of their confessedly irregular petitions, and I incline to think it would have been better had the Conference . . . adhered strictly to its principles and rules by refusing to look on these memorials at all. The Memorialists now assume a kind of right to talk and argue on the subject, as the Conference has so far noticed them as to record a resolution respecting them; and I fear this condescension of the Conference will be urged in future as a proof that even *irregular* petitions and memorials obtain *some* consideration and attention from the Conference. On the whole the feeling in Sunderland is very good on the great Methodistical question to which the Memorial referred; and I incline to hope that our ordination service there last week will have a good Methodistical effect in every sense. We had an immense congregation attended on the occasion, and we had certainly one of the most solemn and impressive seasons of the kind I ever witnessed. Great satisfaction was expressed by all I saw and heard of . . .

⟨The⟩ President will no doubt have told you that I wrote to him a few ⟨days a⟩go, more especially on the Gateshead case. The Kilhamites are forming Gateshead into a circuit, and taking Forsyth[3] into their

---

[1] William Bramwell (1794–1882), attorney at Durham 1815; alderman 1835–52; Mayor 1840, 1841, 1845, 1852 and 1853; Recorder, 1860–82.

[2] A *Declaration of certain of the officers of the Wesleyan Society in the Sunderland circuit addressed to the Wesleyan Conference* (January 27, 1835) complained that the preachers had used every means to suppress expressions of view on the Warrenite side of the question, while giving every facility to the other side, and that Special District Meetings composed of preachers only to hear charges against preachers were contrary to the legislation of 1794–95.

[3] Joseph Forsyth, preacher, Gateshead circuit, 1833–34. Expelled with Dr. Warren by a unanimous vote of Conference (M.C.A. MSS. J. Taylor to Jabez Bunting, August 30, 1835), Bunting improving the occasion by an address to the young men on 'the responsibility of Conference as the custodian of the doctrines which had been the making of Methodism' (Gregory, *Sidelights* p. 242); became Methodist New Connexion minister at Gateshead 1835–38, when he retired, undertaking the pastorate of a small Independent church in Newcastle. Parting from them in consequence of fraud perpetrated by one of the Trustees, he had temporary oversight of some separated members of the New Connexion in Gateshead, before joining his brother-in-law's business in Penrith. The Free Church of Scotland proposed to send him as a missionary to Canada in 1847, but went back on the arrangement, and he then hoped for employment in the Methodist Episcopal Church of America in order to pay off his

connexion. Six or seven hundred will most likely go with him. Mr. Keeling[1] thinks, however, that they will not all remain in their connexion; but that if a popular arrangement can be made for Gateshead, many who would be worth keeping may be preserved from going at all, or may be speedily recovered . . .

59   From Jabez Bunting Jnr.[2] to Mrs. Bunting, his mother

100 King St., Manchester, October 18, 1834

Percy[3] is just going to send a parcel to London, and I am reluctant that it should go without inclosing a letter for you. I fear, however, that the fact of its reaching you so soon after Father's arrival at home, will detract from the interest which, under any other circumstances, would belong to a letter from *Manchester*.

What *I*, individually, am fullest of at present, is my recent *Leeds* adventure. I really think, that the two days I spent there on the interesting and exciting occasion of the opening of the new chapel,[4] were, without exception, the *happiest* days of my life. Notwithstanding that Father has doubtless anticipated me in the *leading* particulars of my visit, yet will it afford *me* a retrospective *satisfaction* greater even than, I am persuaded, it can afford you, to communicate a more minute and *circumstantial* detail than *he* would have the time to give you.

On *Thursday* evening, the 9th October, then, I mounted the Miller coach to Halifax, where I had previously arranged to meet Percy and Eliza,[5] the latter going with Mrs. Bealey[6] by way of Todmorden. I reached Lord Street by nine o'clock, and saw Harriett,[7] Eliza, Percy and Miss B. Bentley. William[8] had gone out to preach. I met with a warm

debts (M.C.A. MSS. J. Lowthian to Jabez Bunting, July 31, 1848). Subsequently he became an accredited Wesleyan missionary in Canada West. M.C.A. MSS. Same to same, November 13, 1855.

[1] Isaac Keeling (1789–1869), superintendent, Newcastle-upon-Tyne (West) circuit, 1834–1836; chairman of Newcastle District, 1834. President, 1855.

[2] Jabez Bunting junr., 3rd son of Jabez Bunting by his first wife Sarah Maclardie. D. 1843, aet. 27. This letter gives almost the only insight into the lighter side of Bunting family life and the social side of their church life.

[3] T. Percival Bunting. Cf. n. 1 p. 14 *supra*.

[4] The new Albion Street Chapel in the Leeds East circuit was opened by Bunting and others on October 10, 1834.

[5] Wife of T. Percival Bunting.

[6] Widow of Richard Bealey of Radcliffe; a great Methodist benefactor and friend of the Buntings. Mrs. Bealey was sister to Samuel Warren. Cf. no. 63 *infra*.

[7] Wife of W. Maclardie Bunting.

[8] William Maclardie Bunting (1805–66), eldest son of Jabez Bunting by his first wife Sarah Maclardie. Preacher, Halifax circuit, 1832–35. He travelled 1824–49, when he became

H

reception, and, what was more congenial to my views and feelings just then, some warm tea and muffin. Soon William came in, and his arrival was the signal for discharging our respective stocks of 'news' which during our separation from each other had greatly accumulated. Percy told us about his London visit. I endeavoured to represent the public feeling of Manchester, and gave interesting information as to the state and prospects of different parties, and William discoursed on general topics. Then came supper, jugged hare, cold beef, apple-tart and cheese, then we arranged for our journey the next morning, then had prayer, and last of all went to our respective apartments. *I* slept, or at any rate, had I not been too much excited by the prospect which was to be realized in a few hours, might have done, on a sofa in the front parlour.

Friday morning came, and I arose, unintentionally about *five o'clock* – sat in William's study – played 'my time' as Job calls it, on the organ etc. etc. We had on the preceding night arranged to *leave* Halifax at eight o'clock, and with that view to breakfast at *seven*, and actually, some of our party retired to rest under the delusion that they would do as they intended. About *nine* o'clock or a little after, however, they *did* join myself at the breakfast table, and about *half-past nine*, we set off to Leeds, a distance of 16 miles, part of us in William's carriage and the remainder in a post-chaise. Nothing remarkable occurred on the road, and by dint of hard driving, we reached the chapel just as the Preacher was about to commence his sermon. Mr. Scarth[1] met us at the door and accompanied us to a pew. The chapel was pretty well filled by an attentive and respectable congregation, and presented a very imposing spectacle. I recognized a very great number of preachers, indeed no less than *42* were present at the Friday services, including six or seven dissenting parsons, Winter Hamilton[2] among the number. Father preached, oh most delightfully and *like himself*, from 'God is greatly to be feared in the assemblies of his saints etc.'. After the service we adjourned to the vestry of the adjoining Old Chapel, where a party of 50 dined on a cold collation provided at Mr. Scarth's expense – fowls, ham, beef, etc. etc. Then we went to hear Mr. Galland[3] from 'Who being the

a supernumerary on grounds of ill-health. A prominent Protestant politician, he was active in the Evangelical Alliance from its inception, and succeeded his father as honorary secretary, 1858.

[1] W. Gilyard Scarth (1780–1853), Treasurer to the Leeds Brunswick trustees, prominent Methodist conservative politician in Leeds (cf. n. 3 p. 17 *supra*) and friend of Jabez Bunting.

[2] Richard Winter Hamilton (1794–1848), congregationalist minister at Albion (later Belgrave) Chapel, Leeds from 1815 till his death. In the 'forties he was a prominent Anti-Corn Law politician and educational voluntaryist.

[3] Thomas Galland, superintendent, Halifax circuit, 1833–36. Born at Hull where he possessed landed property, he was educated at Cambridge for the ministry of the established Church, but became a Wesleyan preacher in 1816. Reputed the wealthiest and most Whiggish preacher of his generation. D. 1843, aet. 48.

brightness of his glory etc.' Very many slept. After tea, which was provided as well as the dinner, we once more went to chapel and listened
to Mr. [Robert] Newton, from 'Lord I have loved the habitation of thy
house etc.' – a most Newtonian sermon indeed! After this service a
prayer meeting was opened by Father who prayed most powerfully and
at some length. Then we took a little refreshment in the Old Chapel
vestry and somewhere about half-past ten o'clock Pawr to our great
delight accompanied us to Halifax, where we arrived, tired truly, but
immeasurably gratified at the proceedings of the day – about *one o'clock*.
Again we felt faint and partook of some cold beef and bread, porter,
brandy and water etc. etc. in the kitchen, and at *two o'clock*, I got inside
the mail to Manchester break-fasted at Lime Grove,[1] and took my place,
the first thing, to Halifax for that evening. Mrs. Scarth strongly pressed
myself to go home with her that night and stay over the Sunday, but
my office engagements rendered my compliance with her invitation
impracticable.

Well, on Saturday evening I mounted the Miller again, and reached
Halifax about nine o'clock – found the whole party assembled. It was
rather vile for two or three hours, so vile indeed (I could not tell how)
that I was glad to retire with Eliza into a private room. The fact was
William was poorly, and Harriet anxious about anything and everything. We supped on veal cutlets and ham, had prayer and retired – *I* to
my sofa. The next morning (Sunday) I got up, and in very good time,
set off for Leeds in a small gig, accompanied by Eliza and Percy, myself
in the middle. We missed our way and were obliged to go two or three
miles round. At length we reached the chapel, but to our consternation
found both it and the adjoining Old Chapel quite full. The chapel-
keeper, however recognized us, and found us most eligible accommodation in the vestry, where we could see and hear to our satisfaction.
Father, you know, was the Preacher; his text was 'I am not ashamed of
the gospel of Christ etc.' and *never*, perhaps, did I ever hear him to
greater advantage and profit – he was – it struck everybody – unusually
energetic and impressive – *I* never felt and wept and vowed so much in
my life. The worst was he exerted himself too much. We then as on
Friday dined in the adjoining vestry, though not quite with so large a
party. After dinner, I went with Father to take his place for the next
morning, and afterwards, with him, heard Mr. [James] Dixon from
'Ye are come to Mount Zion etc.', the most evangelical and practical
sermon I ever heard from him. We all took tea at Mr. Geo. Morley's and
then finished up with a sermon from Mr. [Theophilus] Lessey:– the
text 'In this place is one greater than the temple', stopped [at] the

[1] Percy Bunting's suburban house in South Manchester.

prayer meeting for a short time, parted most reluctantly with Pawr, and myself and guardians returned to supper at Mr. Morley's. There we sat talking over the events of the day, and I, having succeeded in getting a place by the mail which leaves Leeds at midnight, arrived at Manchester at six o'clock on Monday morning – very tired, and literally *ill* with excitement. Such was my journey. I have not had a fine time telling it, because I am conscious that a deal of it is old news, and interesting only to myself. I somehow like Leeds Methodism, though it is certainly too noisy and exciting.[1] The people were exceedingly civil to me, at least, those that I know, and I have made many new acquaintances. I have forgotten the chapel. Father will supply my omission – it is large, plain, and when full very imposing in its aspect. The congregations, on the Sunday especially, were overflowing. I sincerely wish you had been there to see and hear for yourself for it is impossible for me to convey an adequate idea of the whole ceremony. *I* shall *never* forget it 'while memory holds her seat', as they say, and if my attendance at it has done nothing *more*, it has at any rate eternally and unchangeably confirmed and increased my Methodistical attachments.

And now poor Pawr – *he* I am sure must have been gratified by the display of good Methodist feeling towards himself, which was evinced both at Leeds and Manchester. I was very unhappy and so were all his friends in these quarters, to see him so depressed. With reference to the immediate cause of his present persecution viz. the publication of Warren's blacking,[2] I dare not trust myself either to speak or write. The feeling of Manchester so far as *I* am competent to judge is very strong, and, of course, with the exception of the vile Oldham Streeters,[3] very unanimous against the cowardly slanderer. I am not at all apprehensive for the result of the crisis, which all parties seem to concur, is inevitable. Everybody in Manchester is in capital spirit and we are all awaiting the impending District Meeting. Crowther's pamphlet[4] accompanies this letter. I have not yet found time to read it – it will do, we may depend upon it, an infinity of good, especially in his own circuit. But what say you to the new honour conferred upon

---

[1] At the previous Conference Jabez Bunting's verdict on the Methodism of Yeadon nearby had been that 'a noisy meeting and a love-feast constitute a great portion of their ordinances'. Gregory, *Sidelights* p. 168.

[2] Cf. n. 1 p. 86 *supra*.

[3] Samuel Warren was superintendent of the Manchester (Oldham St.) circuit from 1833 till his suspension in October 1834, and in September secured the backing of his Quarterly Meeting for his attack on the Theological Institution.

[4] Jonathan Crowther, *Defence of the Wesleyan Theological Institution and the proceedings of the Institution-committee and the Conference* (London, 1834).

Pawr?[1] We dont overmuch like it, though we are glad of the honour, coming as it does at the right time, if any. I suppose others will assume the title for him. I have a great prejudice, somehow, against Methodist doctors . . .

60   From T. Percival Bunting   *Manchester, October 23, 1834*

Bez[2] has communicated to you the proceedings of the District Meeting up to last night. I hastily finish the account.

The Brethren met this morning at nine. At the suggestion of Mr. West,[3] a Deputation, consisting of Messrs. Newton, Hanwell,[4] Crowther, and McKittrick,[5] waited upon the Doctor [Warren] to enquire whether, after the time for deliberation which the interval had afforded, he was still determined not to take his trial. He asked then whether they came with a message from the District [Meeting] for, if so, he must request the presence of a friend. Accordingly in came Bromley. The Doctor requested them to repeat their question which they did. He then told them that the conclusion to which he had come and which was expressed in his letter was unaltered. The Deputation retired and reported the result to the District [Meeting] who after a long but very harmonious discussion, carried unanimously, every preacher voting, three resolutions.

1st. That Dr. Warren be suspended for one month.

2dly. That if he will write to the President within a month, stating his willingness to stand his trial, his suspension shall be removed, and his trial shall proceed unprejudiced by any of his conduct at the present District Meeting.

3dly. That in case of his continued contumacy for a month, he remain suspended until Conference.

After dinner they met again, and prevailed upon Mr. Newton to take the Superintendency of the Oldham St. Circuit. His places in the [Manchester] South Circuit are to be supplied by the preachers in the other circuits and then by a young man to be called out. So this affair ended. The President is to meet the Auxiliary and Circuit Missionary

---

[1] Bunting received the degree of D.D. from Connecticut Wesleyan University, and from the time the distinction became commonly known in the following year was generally addressed by his new title.

[2] Bez, the family pet-name for Jabez Bunting junr., on whom see n. 2 p. 89.

[3] Francis A. West (1800–69), preacher, Stockport circuit, 1834–36. President, 1857.

[4] John Hanwell (1783–1854), preacher, Manchester (Oldham St.) circuit, 1832–35.

[5] William M'Kittrick (1775–1858), superintendent, New Mills circuit, 1834–37.

Committees tomorrow. Should anything particular occur, I will let you know. I believe some of the classes have refused to pay their moneys already . . .

61   From William Vevers[1]   *Woolwich, October 25, 1834*

. . . Some of our respectable friends have enquired of me respecting the matters at issue between Dr. Warren and the Conference, in which you receive your full share of personal insult; but I have invariably satisfied them that *he* occupies a wrong position – and that *you* are the subject of unmerited calumny. I purposely avoid any public allusion to these matters because I know how much easier it is to bring an extraneous subject into a meeting than it is to get it out after it has been introduced.

I avail myself of the present opportunity to assure you that I view with feelings of unmingled indignation the unprincipled attempts which are now made to wound your feelings and lessen your influence. I should have regarded this assurance as a mark of supererogation, if it had not been intimated to me during the last Conference by a friend, that my proceedings were watched – that I stood on the brink of a precipice – that I had abandoned my principles – and that I was about to abandon my party and unite with another! I confess that if I had not for some years ceased to be surprised at any thing which is either *said* or *done* in connexion with Methodism, this intimation would have surprised me. If I know myself, I have never been a party man though I have been one of a party – not because I have been determined to go through thick and thin – but because the reputed head of the party has always been able and willing to assign such reasons for his proceedings as have commanded my conscientious support for his avowed principles and purposes . . .

62   From Charles Prest[2]   *Pendleton, October 30, 1834*

Regarding our important missions as being placed in singular and difficult circumstances, I certainly feel it to be my duty to render them

---

[1] William Vevers, superintendent, Deptford circuit, 1833–35. Vevers had contributed *Observations on the power possessed and exercised by the Wesleyan Methodist ministers* (London, 1828) to the Leeds controversy, and continued to write largely in defence of the Methodist constitution and the Protestant cause. D. 1850, aet. 58.

[2] Charles Prest (1806–75), preacher, Manchester (Irwell St.) circuit, 1833–36. Home Missions Secretary, 1857–75. President, 1862. A staunch Protestant politician.

whatever aid I can, and shall therefore, all being well, be at Stockport on the days you mention . . .

The Methodistic riot at Bridgwater Street[1] was one of the most disgusting scenes I ever witnessed; but it works admirably to the prejudice of the faction. On the whole things begin to assume a better appearance. Many of those friends of Methodism who before that were not inclined to take any part in the strife have put on their armour, and are absolutely rallying round our ancient bulwarks. We shall hold that meeting (i.e. Bridgwater St.) soon and shall take care to prevent, by the police if necessary, a recurrence of the 'most unmannerly and indecent uproar' which then occurred . . .

63 To T. P. Bunting   *London, November 4, 1834*

I have been wishing every day for the last week or two to find time to write to you, but have been defeated in my purpose by the continued pressure of public business. I can now only thank you and Jabez for your frequent and deeply interesting communications,[2] without noticing their sad contents in detail. One topic, however, I feel it imperative to mention to you without delay.

Yesterday I was called out of a committee by Mr. Rance.[3] He seemed, I thought, a good deal embarrassed on addressing me, and with many apologies, hoped I should not be offended by his stating something of importance to one branch of my family, which had lately come to his knowledge, and which he understood was to appear in that night's *Advocate*. I at first rather evaded the communication thus announced, by saying that I never wished to have any conference or explanation with anyone or about anything, which had any reference to or connexion with the managers of that paper, persons with whom I should think it unwise to trust myself alone in a room, and to whose calumnies I was resolved never to reply, at least by any such direct means as would imply a recognition of their honesty or honour. He then stated that the papers which he had attempted to put into my hands came to him, not from

[1] Four days after Warren's suspension, a missionary meeting at the Bridgwater Street chapel in Salford was broken up by his supporters led by a local preacher, Captain Barlow. The meeting was eventually held at a later date with police scattered through the chapel and galleries, but a court for the trial of Captain Barlow fell into such disorder that no verdict could be arrived at in the presence of the accused.

[2] These letters are now lost, and were probably removed from the collection by Percy Bunting after his father's death.

[3] Thomas Francis Rance, surgeon; d. 1843, aet. 55. A prominent London Methodist, and leading advocate of the Centenary Fund, 1838.

the *Advocate* people, but from Samuel Warren,[1] who, he said, had been in his pew the night before at City Road, and had taken the opportunity afterwards of telling him his tale – which tale had evidently made a deep and unfavourable impression – and as he thought that if the affair should appear in the *Advocate* it would be injurious to the character of the [Theological] Institution, he begged me to read the documents. I at length complied, and found that they referred to the calling in of Mrs. Bealey's loan to Sam. Warren.[2] They were copies of your letter to him, dated Oct. 21, and of his letter to Mrs. Bealey, also *said* (but that must be a mistake in copying) to be dated Oct. 21. They were inclosed to Mr. Rance in an envelope, containing the following note:

'My dear Sir,
                    I fulfil my promise of yesterday by handing you the inclosed exact copies of the letters I mentioned, and you have my full consent for shewing them to any one – not excepting Mr. Jabez Bunting – you choose. You will now be able to judge on which side *malice* lies. In much haste, believe me etc., Samuel Warren, 52 Great Coram St., 3d Nov.'

The copy given of your letter is *under-scored* very much, in order to make certain words (such as '*requires* the *immediate* payment', '*forthwith* transmit', '*Theological Institution*', '*that Institution*', '*peremptory direction* to *enforce*', '*Not to admit any delay*' appear more emphatically harsh and severe. At the end of his letter to Mrs. B. is the following note. 'To this letter there was sent an extremely rude reply by my cousin Richard Bealey,[3] distinctly affirming that Mr. T. P. Bunting's letter *was* authorized by Mrs. Bealey: and the £175 was sent by me immediately.'

On hastily reading these papers as we stood on the staircase (for I was wanted immediately in the Committee Room) I told Mr. Rance that I had nothing to do with this transaction, and did not see the object of his making the communication to *me*; that as to Mrs. B., her character

[1] Samuel Warren junr. (1807–77), son of Dr. Warren by his first wife, Anne Williams. He studied medicine at Edinburgh, 1826–27, and became a barrister in London, 1837, but his principal ambitions were literary. It is a curious commentary on the financial embarrassments revealed in this letter that his first successful novel which began as a serial in *Blackwood's Magazine* in October 1839, and was published in three volumes in 1841, was entitled *Ten thousand a year*. Other successful novels and a number of manuals of law and professional ethics followed. Through the influence of Conservative governments he obtained the Recordership of Hull, 1852, and the Oxford D.C.L. degree, 1853. A stout Protestant Churchman, he was M.P. for Midhurst 1856–59, a seat which he vacated for a mastership in lunacy.

[2] This letter, with other details of the case, was printed by Samuel Warren junr. in *More light on the Radcliffe affair* (Manchester, 1834). According to him the loan of £175, now called in, had hitherto been regarded as a gift, made in 1829, to establish him in a legal career.

[3] Son of the Richard Bealey mentioned n. 6 p. 89 *supra*.

was so universally established as to convince everybody that she would not have taken such a step lightly, or without some great provocation or reason; that Mr. Richard Bealey's letter, which might perhaps state the origin and justification of the measure, was *not copied*, a very suspicious circumstance; and that as to you, you were evidently acting *professionally*, and in obedience to official instruction, and would, I doubted not, be able on that ground to defend yourself. I added that it did happen to have *incidentally* come to my knowledge, that a letter deemed very insulting and improper had been sent to Mrs. B. by Dr. Warren, in which he had represented himself and *his family* as unwilling to be under any further obligations to her friendship. (This intimation *you* had give me in your letter). *That* letter, I said, as well as Mr. R. Bealey's, must be before me, before I could fairly form any decided opinion. This seemed to alter considerably Mr. Rance's view of the case; but he still thought that as there was an *appearance* of *great vindictiveness* in suddenly calling in the loan, and by an attorney's letter (which I *think* S.W. had led Mr. R. to consider as having been *by him* rather viewed as a gift than a loan) and as the name of the *Institution* was so emphatically *connected* in your letter with the transaction, it would tell very unfavourably against *you*, and against the *Institution* with the public at large, and operate injuriously on both. He therefore felt it right, out of friendship to me, to tell me that the *publication* was intended; and at length let out the secret, that *I* am charged with having *counselled* and *suggested* the measure which Mrs. B. has adopted, and that is to be alleged as a decisive proof of *my* revengeful and malignant feeling towards *Dr. W.* I told him, that I knew nothing of the step taken, till after its adoption, and then only casually; so that, whether it be right or wrong, I am not accountable. I believe I did in friendly confidence admit to him also (for I must tell you everything I can recollect) that if I had been aware of your intention beforehand, and asked for an opinion, I should, as far as I now see, have advised its non-adoption, under present circumstances, for fear of unfavourable construction; but added that, unless I knew more of Dr. Warren's letter, which I believed to have given great and just offence to Mrs. B., I could not judge of the amount and degree of provocation, nor even, absolutely, of the measure itself adopted in consequence. Mr. Rance went away, apparently relieved, and assuring me that he had only a friendly motive in calling on the business. In about an hour after he sent me the documents, saying 'As I do not wish to retain the letters, have not shewn them to any one but yourself, and have no copies of them, I will thank you to destroy them'. This whole affair greatly distressed me last night. I feared for *you*, as a young professional man; and I deeply felt for Mrs. Bealey. I

for once got the *Advocate* of last night, and was glad to see that the publication is only partially made as yet. Can you do anything to *ward* off
the mischief still threatened? Did Dr. Warren's letter *specifically* and
unequivocally mention Saml. W. as concurring in the abominable insult
thu⟨s⟩ offered to Mrs. Bealey? I think much depends on *that* point. You
say that he represented his *whole family* as concurring. I suspect that
Sam. knew nothing of it, and if implicated at all, he was implicated by
his father without his consent. If so, is not *his* a hard case? You have of
course seen the article about this affair in last night's *Advocate*. *Can* it be
that Rance has told Sam. Warren of his interview with me, and that
Sam. has suspended the leave to publish till he could write to his father,
and obtain particulars about his letter to Mrs. Bealey? I greatly regret
this mixing up of a personal offence with the Institution controversy.
And I do also earnestly wish that *your* name should not, if possible, be
even *professionally* connected with these awful strifes. I fear it may
eventually injure your interests. Let me have your views immediately on
this whole affair, which makes me dreadfully nervous.

   N.B. Can you let me have a copy of Mr. R. Bealey's letter to S.W.? ...

   I received your Saturday's parcel yesterday; but on mature reflexion
have not sent your statements to the newspapers. For, 1., Are you
aware that the charge in the *Times* at least would probably be 10 or 12
guineas? and 2dly, The paper though able and important, and perhaps very fit to be put even into newspapers by the parties themselves
who write in self-defence, contains *direct accusations* against Mr. Bromley
of a very serious character. Now I think that *I* ought to be for many
reasons *no party* to the advertizing of such charges. I wish, if possible, to
take no part either against Warren or Bromley *at present* by any overt
act of direct or indirect hostility, in order that I may not be gagged or
interrupted at the next Conference, on the *pretence* that I have been
already an accuser and a party personally concerned and ought not to
be allowed to sit or speak as one of the judges in the court of ultimate
appeal. You will see the weight of this consideration; and, if you still
wish for the advertisements, get some other agent than myself. Perhaps
Mr. Bowers could do it much more privately, and without risk of subsequent personal annoyance. He is very staunch in the good cause.

   It has given me unfeigned pleasure, my dearest Percy, to find you
so firmly and zealously attached to right principles in this tremendous
crisis, and so helpful to our excellent friends who have to fight in
Manchester the battles of truth and good order. Yet my pleasure, great
as it is, is somewhat taxed, at some moments of gloom, by the fear that
you should be put too prominently in the front lines of the host. You
are yet young; you have the misfortune to bear my unpopular and hated

name, and to be obnoxious on my account to many prejudiced persons; and you have to establish yourself in the world. Is it not therefore expedient that you should, as far as paramount duty will permit, avoid unnecessary prominency in these agitations, and help the preachers *privately* by your talents and sympathy rather than as the *known and public agent* of the party to which you laudably attach yourself? Excuse this suggestion made, I assure you, in the fulness of paternal esteem, and affection. For instance, would it ⟨not have⟩ been better that the circulars of Saturday should have been folded and *directed* elsewhere than at *your* office?

Present my affectionate and respectful remembrances to Mrs. Bealey, and say that I am greatly obliged by her kind and soothing letter, which I shall answer as soon as I can fix on any plan for my journey to Leeds. I fully propose to accept her friendly invitation to the secure and hospitable retreat at Radcliffe. Present circumstances and duties totally prohibit all thoughts of Harrogate for this year. I am very uneasy on account of the vile attacks making on the *Mission Fund* in various quarters. My mind is much harassed, more than I like to confess to everyone; but my bodily health, thank God, is greatly improved since I saw you. We have a frightful press of business just now! Plans for Negro Education, Institution Business, mutinies of Branch and Juvenile Committees etc. etc. etc. But I strive still to trust in God, our sure refuge; though I earnestly covet a private station, were it even 'a cottage in some wilderness' . . .

64   From David M'Nicoll[1]   *Liverpool, November 4, 1834*

As Mr. Ward is preparing a parcel for London, I take the opportunity of sending you a line or two. I question whether you will have time to read more in these days of methodistical warfare, which no doubt has greatly increased your correspondence.

I beg to assure you that your friends in Liverpool, I believe without exception, deeply sympathize with you in this time of persecution, so shamefully and unmercifully inflicted upon you; and I write to say, that nothing of this kind, I am verily convinced, has made the least impression on their minds to your disadvantage; but on the contrary their respect and affection for you are if possible even higher than before. As an individual, I honestly declare, as I often do at present both

[1] David M'Nicoll, superintendent, Liverpool (South) circuit, 1832–34; preacher, Liverpool (North) circuit, 1834–35; superintendent, 1835–36. D. 1836, aet. 54.

among your friends and your foes, that I cannot for the life of me discern the *shadow* of a reason for all this opposition; but rather the strongest reason for gratitude and admiration. Your conscience acquits you, and God himself approves of you, and these are sources of the richest consolation – still you may not be disposed to reject the addition of a little friendly condolence. A reaction must take place, posterity will do you justice, and in the meantime it is yours to '*rejoice* and be *exceeding* glad; for great is your reward in heaven, for so persecuted they the prophets that were before you'.

What is most to be lamented is the shocking devastion inflicted on our beloved Zion. Lord have mercy on those who have been the occasion and the perpetrators of so enormous an evil! That any of them should be Methodist preachers is to us a new and painful reflection.

What is going on in Manchester, you know, I presume, even better than we do in Liverpool.

Secret meetings of conspirators are becoming very frequent here. D. Rowland has had several in his own house, and they have published their laudatory address to Dr. Warren in the *Albion* yesterday. The facts could be proved, even at Leeds Street Leaders' Meeting, but Mr. Marsden[1] will not give his consent to an indictment because he says the meeting would not only have to prove the facts of the case, but also to declare that they were violations of our rules which of course they would not do. I am a very poor Methodist lawyer, but it strikes me that neither the rule, nor usage, nor reason requires this. Mr. [Samuel] Jackson knows not what to do. He thought you had too severe an opinion of those men, but he now finds, to the grief of his heart, that you were right and he was wrong. They have turned round upon him lately, and thrashed him most unmercifully, and gained a perfect victory over him, as perhaps you may have seen in the *Advocate*. The address to Dr. Warren from our men was signed by 34, that of the South by 27. One of their resolutions is to withhold their money, which we find they already act upon. Another is to withhold subscriptions from the Mission Fund . . .

65   From John Beecham   *London, November 15, 1834*

I have found it impossible to get you a copy of our draught ready to send you this evening. Mr. Hannah is now at work writing it out fairly, and 'licking it somewhat more perfectly into shape'.

We have adopted the form of a declaration referring in the preamble

[1] George Marsden, superintendent, Liverpool (South) circuit, 1834–36.

to the circular issued from Manchester announcing the formation of a central association for agitating the connexion[1] and expressing our persuasion of its being the imperative duty of all etc. to avow their sentiments at such a crisis. Then follows 1. an expression of our views and feelings respecting Dr. Warren's venturing to publish his pamphlet against the Conference, thereby assailing a vital principle etc. etc. 2. Disapprobation of his misrepresentations of the proceedings of the Conference; and indignation at his imputation of corrupt motives to the majority. (In a short note at the foot denying the statement that a very large number of the preachers were neutral). 3. Reprobation of systematic proceedings to agitate the connexion – proceedings at variance with the spirit and constitution of Methodism. 4. adopted on the vain and false pretence that the Conference had violated the Plan of Pacification.[2] Included – the Regulation at length, and is shewn 1. That Conference resolution not such a 'rule' as there contemplated to be 'enforced' in the Connexion. No public collection, or in classes appointed; but Institution so far as societies concerned left to liberality of individuals. 2. That even if had been such a 'rule', it not necessary for Conference to wait a year before it acted on; that all which Plan of Pacification says is, that if in 'a given circuit' the *first* Quarterly Meeting object, the rule shall not be enforced during the year, but that even in that circuit it shall be enforced afterward if the majority of circuits are found at the following Conference to concur in it, and 3. that the very rule or law which it is said the Conference has violated expressly condemns the Manchester proceedings, as it expressly enjoins that a dissenting Quarterly Meeting shall not by publications or otherwise disturb the peace of the Connexion on the subject. 5. Condemnation of recommendation to people to withhold contributions etc. that were to be attended to, ruinous consequences to our Trustees, dependent circuits etc. 6. That ever willing to listen to respectable lay friends, and are persuaded that Conference willing to call in their aid and counsel to still greater extent, when proposal made at proper time and by proper persons; but while thus express our determination to maintain the great principles of our constitution etc.

[1] On November 7, 1834 at a meeting of Methodist office-bearers in Manchester, a Grand Central Association was launched to secure open sessions of Conference and 'to obtain from the Conference a disavowal of the powers exercised by the Special District Meeting at Leeds in 1827, and a revision of the rules of 1797, so as to divest them, as much as possible of all ambiguity as to the rights of both preachers and people, which we think is imperatively called for by the transactions of the meeting alluded to; and by the *absolute* decision of the Conference of 1834, to establish a Theological Institution, without consulting the constituted authorities of Methodism'.

[2] See n. 2 p. 44 *supra*.

Conclusion . . . included in a stirring appeal.[1]

I hardly know whether you can make out the above very hastily sketched from memory. Father Gaulter[2] and also Entwisle are in fine tune this morning; and I think all our faces are brighter than they were. A spirit I trust is now roused which will be overruled in its workings to the saving of the Connexion. I had half an hour's conversation last night with Mr. Taylor which was satisfactory to me. He goes with us to the fullest extent. To ascertain that was gratifying. He gave me moreover some little information respecting Mr. Stanley.[3] He was glad to find we were not intending to pass an opinion respecting the propriety of the proceedings of the Manchester District Meeting, as he thought it would endanger our union. Mr. Stanley thinks that the proceedings were too hasty; but I shall hope from what Naylor says that he will concur with us on those general subjects which our declaration includes. And as to Mr. Bromley, Naylor told me, what he says he has never mentioned before, that previous to the last Conference Bromley wrote to him a confidential letter, inviting him to a union for setting wrong matters right. Naylor was so indignant at being thus addressed that he treated the letter with silent contempt. This is one of the facts which go to prove that we have had a system of revolutionizing at work long enough[4] . . .

66   From William Leach   *Wakefield, November 15, 1834*

. . . During the greatest part of the time I have been here we have had great peace. Five better Local Preachers' Meetings, and Quarterly Meetings I never had in any circuit, than those I have had in this circuit. But Warren's business has tended to agitate the minds of some of our people both in Wakefield and in the country. Some of our best friends do not know what to think about the frequent acts of misconduct, and rebellion among the preachers. They say Stephens and Forsyth the

---

[1] This broadsheet was published as a *Declaration of Methodist preachers stationed in London and its vicinity on the subject of a late circular*, London, November 25, 1834.

[2] John Gaulter, superintendent, London (Hinde St.) circuit, 1833–36.

[3] Jacob Stanley, preacher, London, (Hinde St.) circuit, 1833–36.

[4] That there was some kind of conspiracy is made clear in James Everett's private journal. On May 14, 1834 Everett met secretly at Leeds with Warren, James Bromley and Joseph Beaumont, 'to deliberate upon and mature a plan for the purpose of curtailing the power of the dominant party in Methodism, whose arbitrary and crooked policy was becoming more and more apparent, by the manner in which they were forcing upon the people and the Funds an expensive Theological Institution'. John Rylands Library, Manchester. MS. Memoranda Book of James Everett, III May 14, 1834.

last year; and now Warren, Bromley and others. I explain and am able in some degree to pacify some of them . . .

What will the end of Warren's business be? The market men from Rochdale and Stockport are bringing strange tales here about their townsmen going with him. How infatuated they must be. I am sorry to find that the subscribers to Missions in this Circuit are in some cases withholding their contributions. I wish you could so touch the subject while at Leeds as to satisfy these mistaken people . . .

67   From John Beecham   *London, November 18, 1834*

. . . I now enclose a copy of the rough draft which was read at our meeting yesterday, in order that we may have your opinion respecting it before we publish, and may have your sanction for affixing your name to it, if it prove to be what you could wish. Several reasons combined to influence us yesterday, to delay the publication for a few days. In the first place, Mr. Bowers[1] had received a letter from Mr. Scott of Liverpool (to whom he had written on Saturday night) expressing as his opinion that we were yielding to unnecessary alarm, as he had received within the last fortnight letters from 150 circuits, and from their tenour he judged that no *general* or *great* excitement prevails; saying however that when a demonstration of opinion should be necessary he shall concur in it. In the 2d place the President [Joseph Taylor] read a letter from Mr. [Jacob] Stanley in very kind language but expressing his fears that the District Meeting had been called precipitately at Manchester; and Messrs. Gaulter and [Abraham] Farrar were of opinion that Mr. Stanley only needed fuller information to satisfy him, moreover expressing their opinion that Mr. Stanley would go along with his brethren in declaring his determination to adhere to Methodism; and in the 3d place the observations which you kindly forwarded to me respecting our saying anything expressly of Dr. Warren before the expiration of the month, appeared to the preachers to be weighty.[2] Under all the circumstances of the case, it was concluded that we should have the draft amended by Thursday, that we might read it again at the Book Committee[3] (or rather after it) and should meet on

[1] John Bowers, preacher, London (City Road) circuit, 1834–37.

[2] The District Meeting had given Warren a month in which to reconsider his refusal to stand trial.

[3] The London preachers' meeting at the Book Room, the connexional publishing concern, formed a kind of informal cabinet, which constituted most of what central executive government the connexion then had.

Monday next at the Mission House, and *finally* decide upon it. During this interval it was arranged that the President and Mr. Entwisle should wait on Mr. Stanley and have a friendly conversation with him, and we felt that to gain Mr. Stanley was itself a sufficient reason for a few days delay. In the meantime we considered, the *month* would expire, and we should then be rid of the difficulty ⟨your⟩ letter suggests; and what especially weighed with me and others was the delay would afford time to hear from yourself, as to the result of your personal observation in Yorkshire and Lancashire. You would be able to judge more satisfactorily as to whether a declaration from the London preachers is at present necessary, and if so, whether the enclosed *draft* will do. Bowers and others of us think that Mr. Hannah has elaborated it to too great a length – that something more compressed and nervous would be better. Now I have to beg that you will let me hear from you immediately; and please carefully to examine the draft, and suggest all the alterations, as to *matter* and *expression*, which you judge necessary; and *also say whether we may append you name to it*. We must not publish till you have ascertained what the declaration will be, and can thus allow us to print your name.

½ past 5 – I have just been interrupted by Bowers' sending me a letter from Stockport, in which mention is made of the 'Circular' which the 'Central Association' has subsequently published. I feel still more satisfied with our delay of a few days, because our declaration can now be made to refer to it also. You will see that circular before we shall, and it occurs to me that if you can spare time to alter the enclosed draft so as to suit the precise state of things . . . as influenced by *this last circular*, you will do a great service. I am more and more convinced that we must be on our guard as to what we publish . . .

68   From J. B. Holroyd[1]   *Norwich, November 18, 1834*

. . . You are aware that a number of official characters, rank radicals both in politics and religion, have long disturbed the peace of the Society in this city. I am sorry to say that my predecessor[2] gave them too much countenance, till in the spirit of their creed, they would act without him, and such scenes took place as were like anything but Christian conduct. One who had been a leading man among the dissentients, but had sense and piety enough to see that such conduct would soon exterminate all religion, turned round, took Mr. P[owis] under his wing, proposed a

[1] James Briggs Holroyd (1777–1862), superintendent, Norwich circuit, 1834–36.
[2] Henry Powis (1789–1879), superintendent, Norwich circuit, 1831–34.

penny subscription to purchase him a silver teapot, got up a tea-party at the corn-exchange where the pot was presented, to the mortification of the disaffected party, who considered themselves deserted by their leader. From that time a separation was determined upon, as subsequent events have demonstrated, and taking the advice which I understand has been given in the *Advocate*, to make common cause with the Kilhamites, a *secret* correspondence was carried on for two months, in which it was agreed upon, that Mr. G. Beaumont,[1] who was turned out of the Kilhamites' connexion 20 years ago and has kept possession of the chapel ever since, should on his giving up the chapel be received back as a supernumerary with £20 pr. annum. and one Jackson[2] whom the Ranters turned out of their connexion last Conference, is appointed as the stationed Kilhamite preacher at Norwich. All was kept a profound secret until the city was surrounded with placards announcing that the 'New Methodist Connexion Chapel Berr St. would be opened on Sunday October 26th by the Rev. T. Allin[3] from Sheffield and – Jackson from Cambridge'. Great numbers of our people were favoured with copies of Allin's Address to the Methodist Delegates at Manchester,[4] and an Exposition of the principles of Church Government adopted by the Methodist New Connexion. And on the Thursday and Friday after, I received the class books and plans from 7 Leaders, and plans from 5 Local Preachers.

I very opportunely got a list of those who had given in their names to join the Kilhams, through the medium of an old gentleman who has been the principal support of Beaumont, and was greatly mortified that he was not consulted about the arrangements, and finding the names of two Leaders who had not tendered their books and also the names of some others who were not to leave yet. Having respectable evidence to confirm the information I had received, on the Monday evening following, the Leaders' Meeting supported me in demanding the class books from two of them, and to several whose names I had received as having intimated their intention of going after a w⟨hile?⟩ I put the question promptly whether they had any such intention, informing them that if such were their intentions if they did not avow it I could not give

---

[1] George Beaumont, a preacher with the Methodist New Connexion 1815–17, when he desisted travelling.

[2] Thomas Jackson, Methodist New Connexion preacher, Norwich and Yarmouth circuit, 1835–37. Formerly a Primitive Methodist travelling preacher, 1821–34, his last station being at Cambridge. He desisted travelling 1840.

[3] Thomas Allin (1748–1866), one of the leading preachers of the Methodist New Connexion, who tried hard, though with limited success, to secure the Warrenite rebels for the New Connexion.

[4] T. Allin, *To the Wesleyan Methodist Delegates assembled in Manchester* (Sheffield, [1834]).

I

them credit for Christian principles. All denied such intention but one of the Stewards who has since resigned his office. I am happy to inform you that the number of private members that have left, are very few compared with the *officials*, that a blessed work is going on in the city, and our people are all in expectation of a revival . . .

69   To John Beecham   *Manchester, Friday Morning*
                                                     [November 21, 1834]

I am pressed here beyond measure by calls on my time which I cannot resist. I can therefore now only say that substantially I very much approve of your circular; but have hastily scribbled a few remarks and suggestions which I inclose.

Warren's month of grace was a *calendar* month, and does not expire till Monday when the District will re-assemble. There is not the slightest hope of his submission or quiescence. It is, and will be, open, active, bitter warfare, on the part of him and many of his friends. Tonight he is to *lecture* against us in the Music Hall at Liverpool. There is a still worse circular than the one you have noticed, issued by the 'Meeting of Manchester and Liverpool Delegates' or Central Association. I hope to get you a copy. Its preamble is diabolical.

Glorious meetings at Leeds both on Monday and Tuesday. The most enthusiastic and general cheerings and clappings greeted the passing of a unanimous Resolution, applauding the decision of the Mission Committee as to the Institution . . .

70   From John Beecham   *London, November 22, 1834*

. . . We have heard with delight of your good doings at Leeds. Mr. Shaw[1] in conjunction with the other Secretaries, has drawn up an account of the meeting and sent it to me for publication . . . The account will tell most delightfully, I am sure, on the minds of our friends generally . . . Last evening we had the Quarterly Meeting of the London Auxiliary District Committee . . . We had an unusually large meeting, and before we commenced business, one of our staunch friends called me out to inform me that several whom he knew were much dis-

---

[1] William Shaw, preacher, Leeds (West) circuit, 1833–36. This was the one interlude of home service for Shaw during appointments in South Africa 1820–57, after which he returned to serve on the Missionary Committee. D. 1872, aet. 73.

satisfied with the General Committee, and would be at the meeting prepared to object. We however got to work; it of course fell on me to say a good deal; and without detailing our proceedings it shall suffice to say, that the meeting was raised to a tone of enthusiastic feeling, under the influence of which Walter Griffith[1] arose and said he should not think they had done their duty unless they embodied in a resolution an expression of their devoted attachment to the Missionary cause, and their entire confidence in the General Committee. This proposal was warmly received, and the resolution was carried unanimously . . .

We had a very pleasing meeting of the [Missionary] Committee on Wednesday. The education plan for the West Indies on which we had agreed, was warmly approved of, as was also the proposal that Mr. Buxton should be the medium of communicating with Government on the subject. I saw Mr. Coates[2] afterwards. He was delighted with the decision of our Committee, and expressed his strong confidence, that if we (two societies) kept united on the subject, we should overbalance the influence of our friends who wish to have a *liberal*!! mode of education adopted . . .

We had a Book Committee on Thursday at which we talked largely on the present state of Methodistical affairs; and Mr. [Henry] Moore explicitly stated in order as he said to free himself from suspicion that he had no intercourse whatever with Dr. Warren. That Dr. Warren called on him at the Conference, and he told him then what were his views as to Mr. Wesley's intentions respecting an Institution, ⟨bu⟩t that since then, he had had no intercourse whatever with the ⟨Do⟩ctor. He then expressed to the meeting his disapprobation of two or three ⟨m⟩atters, but the old gentleman was answered with such spirit, ⟨th⟩at he gave up, saying, he found he could not obtain a hearing, the tide of feeling being so strong on the other side of the question. And that was the case. The preachers manifested a noble and firm spirit in behalf of Methodism. It was agreed that we meet at City Road on Monday morning at 10 to decide on our prop⟨osed⟩ declaration. I hope to hear from you ⟨w⟩ith adv⟨ic⟩e as to the steps to be taken before the hour of meeting.

We have had very few letters this week. I find that at Truro they have printed Bromley's letter and are circulating it through Cornwall, and by a letter from John Sumner[3] received this morning it appears that they are placarding the walls with it at Darlington and the surrounding villages. He complains very much that our enemies have the

[1] Walter Griffith M.D., a prominent London Methodist.

[2] Dandeson Coates, Lay Secretary to the Church Missionary Society. D. 1846.

[3] John Sumner, preacher, superintendent, Stockton circuit, 1833–35, and Chairman of the District. D. 1837, aet. 46.

field, and wishes Mason would print the letter in the Manchester paper replying to Bromley and send them some thousands of it and other good things to ⟨dis⟩tribute among the people. I will see Mason before I send off this, and advise with him . . .

71   From John Beecham   *London, November 24, 1834*

It is now 6 o'clock, and I have only just got home from the Book Room where I have spent the day. We have gone fully into the subject of the present emergency of the Connexion, and as to what we in London ought *forthwith* to do. The result of our deliberations is almost all I have time to give. We agreed to print and send out with the Book Parcels

  1. 15000 of the *Touchstone*[1]
  2. 3000 of Cubitt's pamphlet[2]
  3. Protest of the July Committee in support of Cubitt against Warren.
  4. Vever[s]'s pamphlet,[3] nearly ready, and said by the Editor to be a capital thing.

All these it is agreed shall be distributed *gratis*, among those who most need them, and who will not perhaps be disposed to buy on our side of the question.

Then as to our Declaration. We have digested it carefully, and the printer is now setting it up. The 'Circular' recently published by 'the Central Association' at Manchester, and which you observed in your letter to me you would send if possible, I regret has not come to hand. We therefore proceeded without it as circumstances admitted of no further delay. Your valuable suggestions have been attended to, and I think you will find that the Declaration has assumed a more perfect form. On the subject of the Declaration having your signature attached to it; all felt the desirableness of having your name; but on the other hand there was but one opinion that we should in some way express our views and feelings in reference to yourself, and the more we looked at it,

---

[1] [F. A. West], *The Touchstone, or free thoughts on the propriety of establishing a Wesleyan Theological Institution* (Manchester and London, 1834). At least three editions of this pamphlet were produced.

[2] George Cubitt, *Observations on Dr. Samuel Warren's pamphlet against the Wesleyan Institution* (London, 1834). At the Conference of 1834 Cubitt had moved 'That the Conference *specially and earnestly* request Mr. Bunting to take the general superintendency of the [Theological] Institution, by whatever name the office might be called'.

[3] W. Vevers, *An appeal to the Wesleyan Societies on the attempt now made to subvert their constitution* (London, 1834).

the more obvious did it appear to us, that we could not have so good an opportunity as this Declaration affords for effecting that object. It was therefore unanimously concluded that your signature should be omitted and that we should embody in our Declaration that vindication which we owed both to *you* and to *ourselves*. We have agreed to print as many copies of the Declaration as will cost at least £140. You will ask, 'But where is the money to come from?' An important question which we did not overlook, but which was immediately set at rest by Mason's proposing (if we approved of it) to find the money to meet the whole expense. He certainly has entitled himself today to our best thanks. He decidedly has taken the lead in proposing *prompt, spirited, liberal* proceedings and offering cheerfully to delay the Book-parcels, in order to the accomplishment of our measures. Of course, his finding the money must be *sub rosa*, or we shall soon have the welkin ringing about the misappropriation of the Book Room funds . . .

72   From J. Taylor
London, November 26, 1834[1]

On the 24th I had Mr. Newton's letter in which, after consultation with the brethren and you, he recommends the intended meeting[2] to consist of all the members of the respective Committees (the Book and Chapel Building Committees excepted) appointed at last Conference, with the Treasurers and Secretaries of the Children's and Contingent Funds . . . You are aware of the reasons which induced Mr. Newton's recommendation, I am not. That plan may be the best. For instance the Committee of Privileges is limited to matters which very indirectly affect our funds. The number of the persons a[bout] 101 gentlemen and 115 preachers, is so large that after deducting sixty for those who may not attend the meeting, 156 is a large number. Are we in no danger from the temper . . . which part of the meeting will bring from the places in which they reside? Is the time not late (Decr. 17)? I want light and shall be thankful for it.

Our Declaration is temperate and signed by all but Mason and Moore, Stanley and Beal.[3] Mr. Vevers sends out a pamphlet, and parcels which will do good. In London we are pretty quiet. From the country I hear only little at present, but there is much uneasiness in several places. The Missionary Committee resolutions are making [an] impression . . .

[1] The holograph of this letter is at Emory University, Atlanta, Ga.

[2] To declare support for the Theological Institution and the Methodist constitution.

[3] William Beal (1785–1872), preacher, London (Great Queen St.) circuit, 1833–36.

73   From John Beecham   *London, November 26, 1834*

I purposed sending you this tonight by the mail, but Bowers and I have been down to Westminster to Cubitt's affording him a little aid, and it is now too late. However as Mr. Hannah has sent you a copy of the Declaration, I am less uneasy at missing the mail than I otherwise should have been.

I spent the whole of last evening about Beal. At the meeting on Monday he proposed an amendment as a substitution for the Declaration, but as noone seconded it he withdrew before the business closed. Mr. Bell[1] was therefore dispatched yesterday when we met to read over again the Declaration and sign it, with a copy to Mr. Beal. I called at Mason's in the evening, and while there, Beal called, bringing back the copy. He said he could not sign it, because such a phrase which he pointed out was too strong. We talked with him on the subject but he went away without signing. I then suggested to Mason that we should see the Editor, and consider whether we should venture to substitute another word which equally expressed our meaning, and try him again. We all agreed on this, and Mann[2] and I set off to Battle Bridge, and told him that in order to afford him every reasonable opportunity, we had agreed to alter the expression as he suggested. This startled him and he then said that there were several other things he objected to, but urged again what he had proposed at the Book-Room, that we would add a note saying 'Mr. Beal was unintentionally absent when the Declaration was finally agreed to'. This we refused of course. We were not to be made parties to such trickery; and afford him an opportunity of standing well with both parties.

Mr. Stanley has pursued a similar course. Instead of sending back the Declaration with his signature, he accompanies it with a note, saying, if he had been present with us and heard the conversations which we have had he should probably have gone with us, and requesting that a note may be added, stating that he was absent through indisposition when the Declaration was agreed to. A very modest request, after a deputation consisting of *the President* [Joseph Taylor] and Mr. Entwisle had visited him, and given him all necessary information on the Manchester proceedings, and the grounds and reasons for the steps we are now taking – and Mr. Gaulter too has visited him, and Mr. Farrar dispatched immediately at the close of our deliberations with a copy of the Declaration! After all this trouble with him, to ask us to become parties to a *practical* lie, in order to enable him like Beal to

[1] Alexander Bell (1788–1851), superintendent, London (Great Queen St.) circuit, 1833–35.
[2] Joseph Mann, superintendent, Newcastle-upon-Tyne (East) circuit, 1834–36. D. 1837, aet. 53.

shape his course afterwards as may prove most convenient and safe is rather going too far. You see however Josiah Hill[1] has given us his name, and we may therefore dispense the better with those who refuse. His name will tell. [William] Jenkins has gone with us like a man, to our surprise. I had expected that he would be on the other side rather. Mr. Moore did not come near us. The President asked him at the Book-Committee, but he said he dared not to come. (He was handled with such firmness at the Book Committee, though respectfully, that he went away weeping).

You will see that the paragraph relating to the influence of the laity has been thrown into a somewhat different form. It was the subject of lengthened conversation. I think all the preachers were in favour of *such an extension* of the influence of our lay-friends as we contemplated when the rough draft of the Declaration was prepared,[2] but after full consideration of the subject, the preachers generally were of opinion, that it would not be judicious at present to talk of our willingness to admit of changes lest we should do harm, by *perplexing our* brethren in the country, who would not be in possession of our *full views* on the subject – and by *encouraging our enemies*, who would lay hold of any such intimation, and speak of it [as] a proof of our fears. And after we read the Circular of the Central Association published in the Liverpool papers, one of which accidentally came to hand, in which they require that the Conference shall give up the provision of the Special District Meeting, it appeared that we ought to be especially careful how we at present talk of a willingness to change, lest it be understood as a kind of admission of our readiness *to listen to such claims as those.* As we cannot yet say what turn things may take or how we might possibly embarrass the *next* Conference by raising undue expectations, it was resolved to repel the charge of our trampling on the liberties of the people and declaring our resolution to maintain *their* rights *equally* with our *own*, conclude with a resolution to stand by the *great principles* of Methodism, leaving to to be determined at a proper time what *modification* in accordance with *those principles* may be necessary. So strong was the opinion of several of the preachers on this point, that I am persuaded

---

[1] Josiah Hill (1773–1844), preacher, Deptford circuit, 1833–36.

[2] At the next Conference it was conceded that all the public funds of the connexion should be expended under the superintendence of committees of preachers and laymen (chosen by the preachers). It was also made impossible for a superintendent to expel members in haste, though he was permitted to refer the disciplinary verdict of a Leaders' Meeting which he thought had acted unfaithfully to the decision of a Minor District Meeting. The law governing the transmission of memorials to Conference (provided they were 'consistent with the essential principles of Wesleyan Methodism, and within the pale of our established constitution') was also clarified.

unanimity could not have been maintained among us in any other way.

I send you a copy of the Notice. I am happy to inform you that the Resolution of the London District Society on the cover is working well in London; and I hope its effect elsewhere will be great. Such a testimony in our favour from men who have their eye constantly upon us, will have its weight, and I hope it will set *an example* to other *sound* committees . . .

74   From Richard Waddy[1]   *Wednesbury, December 2, 1834*

. . . It has pained me much to see that state of agitation into which the Connexion has been thrown by the very *unkind* and I think unprincipled conduct of Dr. Warren. In Dudley the official men are *nearly all* disaffected,[2] this I think would not have been the case (at least to that extent) if Mr. Edwards[3] had been supported by his colleagues,[4] but one of them appears to incline to the disaffected party, and the other to want *nerve*. The District as far as I know is at peace, with the exception of Dudley. There are a few uneasy spirits in most of the circuits, but they are kept down by the *sound principles* of others. There have been strong efforts made to disturb the peace of *this* circuit. Deputations from Dudley have repeatedly visited us. Messrs. Gordon and son[5] etc. were over about eight days ago, waited upon one of the Circuit Stewards, gave him the Manchester resolutions etc., and said they had engaged that they should be put into the hands of every Circuit Steward in the District. They dined at *Mr. Botteley's* at *Hill Top*,[6] one of our Local

[1] Richard Waddy, superintendent, Wednesbury circuit, 1834–37.

[2] One of the most damaging of all the Warrenite secessions was at Dudley (see Ward, *Religion and society* p. 171), and when negotiations between the Wesleyan Methodist Association and the Methodist New Connexion broke down, the Dudley men seceded again and joined the M.N.C. .

[3] Thomas Edwards (1781–1869), superintendent, Dudley circuit, 1833–35.

[4] John H. Rowe (d. 1838, aet. 54) and Benjamin Frankland (1787–1872), preachers, Dudley circuit, 1833–35. At the Conference of 1835 Rowe 'was charged with having announced from the pulpit one of Dr. Warren's agitating meetings, and with having obstructed, instead of helping, his superintendent in enforcing discipline'. Gregory, *Sidelights* p. 202.

[5] John Gordon had resigned from the Wesleyan ministry in October 1834 in sympathy with Joseph Rayner Stephens, and was stationed by the Methodist New Connexion at Dudley early the following year. Most of the rest of his career was spent in and out of the M.N.C. ministry in Ireland. Alexander Gordon appeared as the patriarch of Dudley Methodism at its ceremony of union with the M.N.C.

[6] Hill Top, halfway between Birmingham and Dudley, was missioned for the Methodist New Connexion from the latter, the early services taking place 'in a spacious malt-room, kindly lent by J. Batley Esq.', a Local Preacher. The first chapel was opened on February 21, 1836.

Preachers, a rich man, and a *master* collier who has several of our official men in his employ. He has sent one of his servants through the Circuit with the Manchester resolutions etc. for the Leaders to read in their classes, but I have only heard of one instance in which this request has been complied with, and that was by one of his own servants. I feel at present at a loss how to act. If I take up the subject and proceed to his expulsion, I fear it would be a kind of *rallying point* for the *party*, and produce contention and discord in the Circuit. If I let him alone, he will feel the weakness of his influence and the opposition will die away. I called sometime ago to converse with him, but he was not at home, and I mean to let him feel a little of his own weakness before I pay a second visit.

At and for a short time *after* the Conference I had a plentiful share of abuse from the *Christian Advocate,* but they have of late lost sight of me. Since then, *you* sir have had a plentiful share from them and their friend Dr. Warren. I saw the Birmingham brethren, who with my colleagues deeply sympathize with you, and to assert our *sincere* and *unabating* esteem, if it be at all likely to answer any valuable purpose, we are ready *publicly* to testify our personal esteem, approval of your public conduct as relating to the Body, and our determination to *abide* by the *present Constitution* of Methodism . . .

75   From John M'Owan[1]   *Hull, December 4, 1834*

. . . In Hull we are not yet quite composed. We expect however to escape without a division. Last Friday a meeting of the discontented was held, but in consequence of the strong disapprobation of their measures expressed by many of our friends in the Leaders' Meeting the preceding evening, and the explanation which Mr. Newton gave us during a few minutes as he passed through from Grimsby, they only met to adjourn till the Quarterly Meeting – and we trust that even then there will be no attempt to disturb. The movers are few, and already they have felt their weakness. We wish however that one or two of our respectable men were more cordial, and more cautious in expressing their partial discontent. A *declaration* on the part of the faithful is, I believe, now in preparation which will have a good influence. And we hope to send before the end of the month a tolerably fair list of subscriptions, and a few small donations to the Institution.

We deeply sympathize with yourself, the President, Secretary and

[1] John M'Owan (1791–1876), preacher, Hull circuit, 1833–35.

other brethren who have had the brunt of this battle to bear. They are days of rebuke and trouble, but we believe that God will not only sustain you and bring you triumphantly through, but will also establish our Zion and make her more than ever a praise in the earth . . .

76   From Joseph Agar[1]   *York, December 8, 1834*

. . . The Lord only knows what I have felt in my mind concerning our Methodist Church, and for the souls of our people; we have had out-ward peace for a long time, so men from amongst ourselves must rise up and do all they can to put a stop to the glorious work of the Lord.

The Lord has raised me up a son to be more bold in his cause than I am. I believe I should never have taken that bold stroke that he and the other Stewards did!!! To send that answer to Wm. Wood[2] when he sent them near a stone weight of *Poison* without paying carriage. I should have sent it back and let W.W. pay carriage both ways and sent the answer to himself instead of inserting it in the Manchester paper. It was a bold trial of Bromley[3] and his friends in York. They took fire and such a time we have had in our Society ever since as I never remember. *Oh, this Radicalism* what has thou done in England both in Church and State. Its surprising what hold of the affections he's (Bromley) got here by his fine speeches – my good Ladies etc. etc., but that our Leaders and Local Preachers should be so duped as they have been! Last Wednesday night it was Bromley['s] turn to meet the Leaders. He had been about to muster his partizans, unknown to his colleagues and meant to have carried a vote of censure upon the Stewards for sending the Circular Letter and so to have put in the Manchester paper for to counteract their former letter. You will see in the Manchester paper of Saturday the 6th inst. what I suppose is Bromley's account of the Leaders' Meeting.[4] It was in two of our York Saturday papers.

[1] Joseph Agar (1761–1847), a leading York Methodist who had entertained John Wesley and loved to recall the Methodism of his day. Sheriff of York 1812. Took a case concerning the the liability of chapels to assessment to the poor rate to King's Bench; King v. Agar was a leading case until the law was altered by 3 & 4 Wm. IV c. 30. His son Joseph became a Wesleyan preacher, 1810, and d. 1830.

[2] William Wood, a Manchester manufacturer and secretary of the Grand Central Associ-ation.

[3] James Bromley, preacher, York circuit, 1833–35.

[4] A letter from Bromley to Samuel Warren appeared in the radical *Manchester Times* on December 6, 1834, expressing his dissatisfaction at the way the District Meeting had treated him when he came to support Warren; there was also an unsigned report that the York Leaders' Meeting had attempted to call their Stewards to account for a letter they had written to the *Manchester Chronicle* but were frustrated by the superintendent's refusal to put the motion.

Our *Central Babel* at Manchester[1] has directed all their artillery against our next Quarter Day, *all through the Connexion*. I ask you who has a right to vote upon any subject at Quarter Days. As old Methodist as I am, I do not know. This you will please to inform me and write me all particulars soon as you can.[2] I go about every day to try to keep peace and I fully believe if we had not had Bromley we should [have] both been peaceable and prosperous . . .

77 From Elijah Morgan[3]   *Macclesfield, December 13, 1834*

. . . We are greatly troubled by anti-methodistical pamphlets with which we are inundated from Manchester and need all the help we can have from heaven and earth. The minds of our people are agitated greatly, but I hope we shall not suffer much loss by departure from us. I would rather live under the most arbitrary government on earth than under mob government . . .

78 From W. Gilyard Scarth   *Leeds, December 20, 1834*

I have sent you a Copy of the *Intelligencer*[4] of which I have sent 60 Copies in every direction of the Kingdom, wherever I thought they might be

---

[1] I.e. the Grand Central Association.

[2] The precise constitution of the Quarterly Meeting, the business meeting of the circuit which held the corporate funds and invited and paid the preachers, was, and remained, undefined, a source of considerable inconvenience in a period of conflict. It was generally understood to be composed of office-bearers in the local Societies, but the notion 'that all persons filling these offices should be at liberty to exercise its franchise' was officially discountenanced as 'neither a right nor a safe state of things'. There was in particular much variation of practice in regard to the admission of Local Preachers. In the constitutional rearrangements which were provoked by Warren's revolt, the Quarterly Meeting lost its right to address Conference by memorial on general connexional matters to a Special Circuit Meeting whose composition (of senior office-holders) was precisely defined. Cf. E. Grindrod, *Compendium of the laws and regulations of Wesleyan Methodism* (3rd ed. London, 1848) p. 129; also no. 122 *infra*.

[3] Elijah Morgan (1787–1853), superintendent, Macclesfield circuit, 1832–35.

[4] The *Leeds Intelligencer* December 20, 1834, carried a full report of the violent attempts of the Warrenites to put down Gilyard Scarth and other friends of Conference when they tried to seize the chair at a meeting in Leeds Music Hall and put a resolution that the proceedings of the Wesleyan Methodist Association were 'deceitful and wicked'. 'They, the liberal reformers, wished to try and condemn first, and hear another night! We never recorded a more discreditable proceeding . . . The issue was the defeat of Dr. Warren and his fellow labourers in the work of division and confusion; and we sincerely rejoice at it'. Cf. *Leeds Mercury* December 20, 1834 p. 4.

useful (chiefly to Preachers) which will give you some idea of '*Dr. Warren in Leeds*' and a tolerable correct account of what I believe may be termed as a whole *the most unaccountable of all unaccountables*. We trust we have done service to the good cause (however we so intended, and hope our Master says 'we did well that it was in our hearts') we think we 'stopped the mouths of Lions' but are not so sanguine as to expect they are jaw-lock'd, or that they will never roar again. The advertisement in Baines' Paper on Saturday of the intended visit of Dr. Warren and his coterie a little surprised us, and [we] were very glad that we were before hand with them, in getting our Declaration out the very same paper (I think you will be pleased with such a list of officers, I doubt you will not equal it in any other Circuit).[1] Our Preachers thought in unison with the friends they consulted, they would meet the Societies on the Sunday evening and affectionately advise them not to attend the meeting, and which they did. On Monday however a few of our staunch and warm friends chiefly of the St. Peter's Society, began to think they ought to get up an opposition, and not let the *Agitators* go over the course quite as smoothly as they expected; this feeling was much more excited and strengthened by a placard which was largely posted in every part of the Town on Tuesday-morning (see the report for a Copy). We soon found it was impossible to prevent some of our people from attending the meeting, and expressly with a view to oppose their proceedings, and the matter then before us was, whether we would let these feelings take their course, or we would muster a *respectable* opposition; after due consideration amongst each other the latter course was decided on, and this having partially got abroad on the morning of the meeting many thought it their duty to muster, and at six o'clock, an hour before the commencement of the time fixed, a crowd of Methodists, with many Noncons[2] and others were waiting at the door for admittance, and our friends who got in first soon witnessed the filling of the room, by a very different description of persons than those who were invited in the bill;[3] not Wesleyan Methodists only, but Noncons – Ranters – Dissenters – a

---

[1] *Leeds Mercury* December 13, 1834 p. 4 for advertisement of the Warrenite meeting at the Music Hall. Both the *Mercury* and the *Intelligencer* for that date carried declarations, of the kind now got up in many circuits, from the Leaders' Meeting of the Leeds (West) circuit, and from the Trustees, Stewards, Leaders and Local Preachers of the Leeds (East) circuit, the latter with scores of signatures, affirming their confidence in the preachers and the discipline of the Methodist Society. See also *Leeds Mercury* December 20, 1834 p.4. Ten days later Scarth and his friends in the Leeds (East) Quarterly Meeting displayed their self-confidence by resolving to re-open the Old Chapel, and request the stationing of an additional preacher. M.C.A. MSS. W. G. Scarth to Jabez Bunting, December 30, 1834.

[2] I.e. the Leeds Protestant Methodists who had seceded in 1827.

[3] According to the advertisement admission was to be by Society membership ticket only.

few Churchmen and a rabble of Nothingarians and Nondescripts. The
John Wrigglesworth[1] who proposed the Chairman, had sent in his
resignation as Steward and Class-leader the week before, being offended
by our Declaration, and the speeches which were made in the support of
it; he had we understand a principal share in union with the Non-cons
in inviting Dr. W. to Leeds, and also in the shameful posting Bills about
stopping the supplies when you were with us. A young man of the name of
Parker, a Local Preacher of the West Circuit whom I do not know,
seconded the motion. These I believe were the only two Wesleyan
Methodists who *appeared* in their behalf. Gordon[2] came to me in the
Orchestra when he had finished his speech, and wished to shake hands
with me, which I refused, explaining it was not any thing in the course
of his speech that led me to withhold my hand (nothing personal) but
the *errand* on which he came to Leeds. You will notice, I dare say, what
was more evident at the meeting than can appear in the abstract of their
speeches what a rope of sand they are. I prayed at our Leaders-meeting
on Monday-night that God would '*turn the counsel of Ahitophil into
foolishness,*' and it was responded to by *Amens,* so *many* and so *loud,* you
would have thought they would break the ceiling; and truly they were
manifestly answered. The Liverpool men are thoroughgoing reformers,
wreckless of all consequences, but their *great* gun Rowland was so sore
from his late expulsion that he took up most of his time in showing
(which you have not got in the report) that he had so conducted himself
that our old friend Saml. Jackson whom we had long known and loved,
had *tyrannically* put him out of Society. What a tale to interest such an
audience, and to come seventy miles to relate! Gordon you will see
has been in the moon, and brought down some new discoveries. '*The
Methodist-Conference a Political-union*'! And prove it too! And prove it
from those very premises which every body else thinks prove the
contrary! And then Dr. W. complimenting your humble servant. Ah!
he much mistook his man if he thought he was to be *gagged* with compliments. And O what a scene when he made such a meeting his confession-
box, and asking forgiveness of *them*! Moreover, while he was giving his
quibbling exposition of the law of District Meetings, *Gordon* behind not
far from me answered to what I remarked, that *Warren* was *wrong* in
his interpretation; that what he (Gordon) maintained was that the
Law was wrong, not the usage. I said well I can understand that, but I
cannot understand the Doctor. And now in conclusion let me say, we
did our *best,* according to our *light* and *ability,* and I am satisfied. Perhaps
some good will issue from it, it was a great personal sacrifice on the part

---

[1] John Wrigglesworth, formerly circuit steward in Leeds (East) circuit.
[2] See n. 5 p. 112 *supra.*

of many of us; but if we have been rightly directed, (and I am sure we sought wisdom from above) to God be Glory . . .

79   From M. Ashton[1]   *Liverpool, January 3, 1835*

Of the general or substantial truth of the *Lantern*'s[2] report of D[avid R[owland]'s trial you will be a better judge when you look over these slips.[3] *The Morning Light* will probably shine out on Wednesday next, and the present will be one of the articles. It is from the pen of our highly esteemed but calumniated Superintendent.[4]

The prospects in our North Circuit are beginning to brighten. Our deficiency upon the quarter was only £10, and we know of about £25 Society money withheld to this day by the White Lion Boniface.[5] Only one or two of the malcontents were there and silent as the grave. A strong resolution of approbation and another of sympathy with Mr. J[ackson] was passed in a very feeling manner. At the Local Preachers' Meeting North [Circuit] last night the men (not the Preachers) proposed and passed a resolution that no member of the Association should have his name on the next plan and that every man should answer when questioned about it to the Superintendent's entire satisfaction before his name should be continued.

The late Leaders have used such extraordinary diligence to prejudice their people against the preachers, that they will succeed in drawing off we calculate at the outside 400 members in the North and about 350 in the South.[6] Mr. Marsden[7] is extremely slow, and is trying to save thereby the members, though he will not spare the Leaders; but I think

---

[1] Michael Ashton, a Trustee, Leader and Local Preacher in the Liverpool (North) circuit.

[2] The *Watchman's Lantern* (which ran from December 17, 1834 to November 18, 1835) was a paper published by the Liverpool Methodist radicals in reply to the Buntingite *Watchman*; the local supporters of Conference opposed it with a sheet of their own, the *Illuminator* (which ran from January 7, 1835 to March 23, 1836), for which *The Morning Light* was perhaps a proposed title.

[3] This letter is written on the back of the galley slips of *The case 'without a parallel'; or David Rowland and the Leeds-street Leaders' Meeting, Liverpool*, a pamphlet which ridicules Rowland and the Associationists for making complaints when they had committed aggression against the ministry in the first place. They had tried to get a favourable verdict before the trial by putting up the landlord of the White Lion to move at the outset that the charges were frivolous and vexatious.

[4] Samuel Jackson, superintendent, Liverpool (North) circuit, 1833–35.

[5] See n. 3 *supra*.

[6] Decline in membership (not necessarily the same thing as loss of members) proved to be 670 in the North circuit, and 583 in the South.

[7] George Marsden, superintendent, Liverpool (South) circuit, 1834–36.

he is beginning to see that he must make quicker work to avoid greater mischief.

We had a capital *real* Lovefeast at Brunswick last Sunday afternoon at the same hour that the radicals had theirs in the Music Hall. I have not seen such a lovefeast at that Chapel for numbers and good feeling for many a long day. In fact in the North we are well purged of the pests of our Society, and peace and unity is restoring. In the South only six of the ringleaders are formally expelled as yet and although the Pitt St. Leaders bluster terribly at the expulsion of Mr. Treasurer Cole last Thursday night and vow that they consider themselves expelled and cut off, they take care not to commit themselves formally to the act. But 2 or 3 weeks must settle the whole catalogue of them. They have been scheming to frighten Mr. Marsden but it will not do. If there was one man amongst them worth saving it was Cole, and they have seen his fate and their disappointment almost amounts to madness . . .

Mr. Aitken[1] arrived from the Isle of Man today and on to Burslem where he preaches the anniversary of the chapel sermons tomorrow; Monday Stafford, Tuesday Darl[a]ston, Wednesday Dudley, Thursday Dunstable, and on to Spitalfields on Sunday. He asked me in a very pleasant spirit for a note of introduction to you. I need not say with what pleasure I gave it. His sentiments on the Association are sound enough, but he has more pity for the *misguided* members of it than I think they deserve. But his influence among that ignorant class of otherwise good men is really prodigious and perhaps he might be persuaded to use it for the good of the cause of Methodism. His notions about our finances are of the Bramwellian[2] cast, very well suited for the times of the Millenium, but for these he neither understands nor is very willing to be taught. But his piety and powerful preaching will win him a way amongst our people for good or evil to the cause. May the Good Shepherd direct it in the right one. I most fervently pray that his communication with the London Preachers may be overruled for immediate good . . .

[1] Robert Aitken (1800–73), popular evangelist, whose exclusion from Methodist pulpits was one of the grievances of the Warrenites against the connexional management. Ordained deacon in the Church of England in 1823, he resided in the Isle of Man, and, incurring the displeasure of the Bishop of Chester for irregularities in preaching, withdrew from the Church. Sought to become a Methodist preacher but was never taken into full connexion. Established chapels of his own in Liverpool and elsewhere, but in 1840 returned to the Church and was eventually beneficed in Cornwall.

[2] William Bramwell, Wesleyan preacher with aspirations to be a revivalist. D. 1818.

80   From I. Crewdson[1]   *Ardwick,*
                                            1 mo [January] 5, 1835

May I beg the favour of thy reviewing the accompanying little work
for the *Methodist Magazine.* I ask it with great hesitation being in some
degree aware that thy time and attention which have always many
claims upon them w⟨ill⟩ be unusually occupied at the presen⟨t⟩
moment. If it should be compatible with thy m⟨any⟩ engagements I
should consider it as an *especia⟨l⟩ favour,* but if not, might I then leave it
to thy *discretion,* to put it into the hands of another.

It may not be improper for me to say for the sake of putting thee in
possession of my views, that the object of the work is not to fight the
Hicksites[2] in America, else more might have been said and in stronger
terms in reprobation of their unscriptural notions; but it is, *without
making the application to Friends,* to hold up a *mirror* to them, as well as a
beacon, and especially to promote amongst them the acknowledgeme⟨nt⟩
of the paramount authority of the Holy Scriptures. The Friends in this
country reprobate Hicksism in the abstract, but generally speaking they
know it only by its most revolting features. They are little aware how
nearly allied to it in sentiment (i.e. in its incipient state) many of them
are. If the paramount authority of the Scriptures were once fully
recognised by the body some errors which are now held would it may be
hoped fall as ⟨a m⟩atter of course: this therefore appeared to me like the
first point to be gained, and to contend for it upon the broadest ground
without touching some points which must necessarily follow if this be
recognised seemed more likely to engage the favourable attention of
those who are the immediate objects of the work than if it had gone
more into detail.

Scriptural truth is certainly making its way in the Society [of Friends]
and herein we may rejoice, but on the other hand opposition to it is
assuming a much more decided character than heretofore.

To many who are not intimately acquainted with the views which
prevail in this body, and with the importance which is attached to those
views, some of the remarks in the work must appear like an attempt to
prove that A is the first letter of the alphabet; they can have little idea

[1] Isaac Crewdson (1780–1844), minister among the Society of Friends in Manchester, whose
Beacon to the Society of Friends (1835) enclosed with this letter, called upon Quakers to return
from mysticism to 'a religion of *faith* . . . founded on the *testimony of the Spirit of God* transmitted
to us in Holy Scripture'. This pamphlet aroused such a vehement reaction that the Crewdson
family withdrew from the Society of Friends. See Ward, *Religion and society* pp. 67–9.

[2] American Quaker followers of Elias Hicks (1748–1830), who seceded from the main body
in 1827, and whose views, regarded by Crewdson as equivalent to Deism, were condemned
by the English Yearly Meeting in 1829.

of the hostile feeling with which they will be received by many in the Society.

May I take the liberty of suggesting, th⟨at⟩ if the wor⟨k⟩ defective as it is, should appear to you at all worthy of a favourable notice, the end of the writer (which is to induce the Friends to *think* – to *consider*) would I believe be promoted by the review bearing the evidence of a friendly feeling towards the Society.

I have written to thee *confidentially* and without reserve believing that thy christian solicitude and charity take a wider range than your own body, large as it is . . .

81   From James Allen[1]   *Shrewsbury, January 14, 1835*

. . . I have but very lately been given to understand that some weeks ago Mr. Brocas[2] one of our Circuit Stewards wrote to you and that you have deigned him no answer. I have no doubt that the reason is that what he has written is an outrage upon your views of *right*. I trouble you with this communication in particular to *beg* that you will send him some answer. Because his writing to you shews that you have in some degree his confidence and because a few words such as you could write might have a good influence and you might assign as the cause of your long delay the confounding nature of the sentiments contained in his letter. I know that it is his desire that Methodism should be changed into Kilhamitism and I know that he has been in warm correspondence with the Central Committee in Manchester and has submitted some of his letters to several of our friends in Shrewsbury. But as we have a blessed work of God going on in the town I believe that he was afraid to introduce the subject at our Quarterly Meeting and because he gave up all intention of doing it he kept away from the Meeting and nobody rejoiced in his absence more than myself. There are in Mr. B. some redeeming qualities. His heart is in [the] work of God. He has a chapel adjoining his own house where he has gathered a lovely congregation to which he pays a laudable attention. And out of this congregation he has formed a delightful society which is Methodistically in every respect the

---

[1] James Allen I (1787–1863), superintendent, Shrewsbury circuit, 1834–36.

[2] In October 1835 Thomas Brocas of Copthorne House, Shrewsbury, wrote to the *Christian Advocate* calling for resistance to ministerial tyranny in Methodism. He was excluded by Allen from membership, a sentence confirmed by the President and Chairman of the District; his readmission was called for by a large body of office-holders in the circuit, but in vain. The result was a small secession to the Methodist New Connexion. Brocas unexpectedly arrived to share in the union of the Dudley seceders with the M.N.C. in 1836, and appeared with a Warrenite delegation at the opening of the Hill Top Sunday School in 1837. See n. 2 p. 122 *frina*.

K

best that we have out of Shrewsbury. And he declares he will not rest till they are a hundred strong. He has a very amiable and pious lady for his wife who is a Methodist and his three oldest daughters are members and pious. He is very friendly with me when I meet with him at his house or elsewhere but obnoxious subjects are never hinted at . . .

82   From Thomas Harris   *Burslem, January 22, 1835*

. . . We are happily in tolerable peace and prosperity in this circuit The differences with the school party[1] were settled not entirely to my satisfaction – but perhaps in the best mode, considering all circumstances, and indeed if they had not been settled before the Warrenite foolery and wickedness commenced, I know not what might have been the result.

We have altered the name of the school, to the Burslem Wesleyan Methodist Sunday School. We now commence service at half-past nine instead of nine, and as many of the children as we can accommodate in the Chapel are brought every Sunday morning to public worship. Although they will not allow me to be the regular Chairman of all their committee meetings, yet my right to attend them and take part in all their discussions is conceded. And I am also to nominate two leaders who are to be on their school committee. By the blessing of God the strength of a dominant faction in the school which had long governed the Society is completely broken: I also expect that in a short time the hour of worship will be altered to half-past 10. There is a very gracious revival in the circuit, and we admitted 150 on trial last Quarter. 72 of these were at Hanley. Mr. John Ridgway and Co[2] with all the Kilhamites are stirring up all the strife they can, and are sorely disappointed they did not obtain a number of deserters during our differences. But indeed that party is too well known in this neighbourhood to gain many proselytes from us . . .

[1] See no. 33 and n. 1 p. 44 *supra.*

[2] John Ridgway was one of the Methodist New Connexion representatives who received the Dudley seceders in 1836. The trouble in the Burslem school came the following year when the chapel trustees proposed to remodel the school according to the connexional rules, and end Sabbath writing lessons. The bulk of the school seceded, and opened a new undenominational school, Hill Top, in the presence of an imposing Wesleyan Methodist Association delegation in 1837.

83   To Edmund Grindrod   *London, January 28, 1835*

Your afflictive letter . . . has but just reached me; and it is now nearly post-time. Yet I cannot allow the mail to depart without a few lines of most sincere and sympathizing condolence on an occasion so truly mournful.[1] But what shall I say? Gladly would I suggest any sentiment which might in the slightest degree soothe your spirit under this heavy stroke of the divine hand. You are however happily familiar with all those heavenly consolations from which alone relief can be hoped for. I shall therefore best discharge the duties required from me by our long and cherished friendship by my earnest and unceasing prayers to our common God and Father, that He will effectually apply by his Holy Spirit the comforting promises and revelations of his blessed gospel to the inmost soul of his bereaved and sorrowful servant, and pour into your heart the secret refreshings which are the only balm that can heal a wound like yours. Greatly do I rejoice to learn (for there is 'a joy in grief' and a 'mercy in every lot', however painful) that the 'latter end' of a life so excellent and amiable was peace' and glorious victory through the blood of the atoning Lamb. This is indeed a solace which it would be criminal not to feel and acknowledge with becoming gratitude. He who was the strength and support of your dear departed wife in the hour of her extremity will strengthen and support you also in this and in every future time of need. His own honour, indeed, is graciously pledged to do so; for he has convenanted with us to be our 'God *All-sufficient*'; and now that [He] has dried up the *source* of your highest earthly and creaturely comfort, he will in very faithfulness become to you, more fully and sensibly than ever, the *fountain* of living waters, and grant you a more satisfying fruition of Himself . . .

84   From Robert Pilter[2]   *Rotherham, February 26, 1835*

I hope by the blessing of Him whose you are and whom you serve that you are in good health and spirits and in nothing terrified by the number or malice of your adversaries. Many a fervent prayer to Almighty God is offered on your behalf. At present you appear to me to have gotten out of the forefront [of] the battle and our amiable, excellent, deservedly honoured Newton[3] is become the butt against whom the enemy hurls

---

[1] The death of his wife, Mary, da. of Rev. John Crosby, Wesleyan minister. She d. January 25, 1835, aet. 46.

[2] Robert Pilter, superintendent, Rotherham circuit, 1833–35.

[3] Robert Newton replaced the suspended Warren as superintendent, Manchester (Oldham St.) circuit. He preached under police escort in the Oldham St. chapel, but was hissed and

his fiery darts. May none of these things move him. Did ever you or I or any body else a few years ago think we should live to see the day when Methodism, a glorious system, which we had admired and on account of which we had often blessed God, would be represented by men amongst ourselves as an execrable thing, as bad as Popery. And that Methodist preachers should be represented as a set of unprincipled villains whom it is a merit to abuse or starve! I seem like a man in a dream and can scarcely believe myself awake. I often carry all the parties and persons contending to the Day of Judgment. Great God what disclosures that day will make! Everything is quiet and on the whole prosperous in this circuit . . . I am glad to find by the *Watchman* that the Institution is going on swimmingly. The *Watchman* is over-Toryish for our Rotherham people. I am pleased with the dignified silence it has maintained in reference to the very existence of the *Advocate*. I think he might give us a larger *compendium* of the week's news . . .

85   From Edmund Grindrod   *Salford, March 2, 1835*

[Will Bunting preach for the Irwell St. Trustees who behaved admirably during the late contentions but are in difficult financial circumstances?] . . . Though a few disaffected seat holders have left the Chapel, others have supplied their places, and more sittings are let this quarter than the one preceding . . .

Great anxiety for the suit in Chancery[1] now pending generally prevails. However it may terminate I have faith in God that he will overrule it for the good of our Connexion. I feel a growing conviction that we are called upon to do something to diminish the democracy of our Leaders' Meetings and Quarterly Meetings, and to protect our Connexion from the frequent occurrence of the unhallowed strifes

then abandoned by his congregation; at Oldham Road in the evening, the service was broken up, and, as he left the chapel escorted by a party of friends and police officers, he was pursued down the Oldham Road by a hooting rabble and had to take refuge in the Oldham St. vestry. A month later he was kept out of the Oldham St. pulpit, and Warren preached to a crowded congregation.

[1] Early in February 1835 two bills were filed in the Vice-chancellor's court, one by Dr. Warren, now suspended from his functions as a Wesleyan minister, against the trustees of the Oldham St. chapel, Manchester; the second by four trustees of the Oldham Road chapel and Dr. Warren, against the other trustees. Both applications sought the restoration of Dr. Warren to the pulpits of those chapels as an accredited minister. Failing in both applications, Warren appealed to the Lord Chancellor who, after giving an authoritative exposition of Methodist law and usage, dismissed the appeal.

which now afflict us. But this, I am persuaded, cannot be effected without adopting some regulations at 'Head Quarters' which shall be considered as a boon by the intelligent and well-affected portion of our community. I have thought much upon this subject since I last saw you, and long for an interview with you, on this, as well as on other accounts . . . [Thanks for his sympathy in bereavement.]

86   From John Bicknell[1]   *Hull, March 2, 1835*

I presume that you and other influential preachers will be considering what measures may be proper to be adopted at the ensuing Conference, relative to the present state of affairs in some circuits. Though an humble individual and possessed of very little ability to write upon legislation, I take the liberty of offering a few suggestions that have occurred to me, in consequence of what I have seen *here*. I make these suggestions to *you* rather to any other preacher, on account of Mr. Vevers having stated in his first appeal,[2] that it had been *your* intention to propose to the last Conference 'some alterations of a *liberal* character'. What those alterations might be I know not, and hence can give no opinion about them, but believing that it may assist you and others whom you will consult, to know the general feeling of your Brethren, I am free to avow my conviction, that the Plan of Pacification, as far as [it] relates to the *government of the Societies*, is already *too liberal*, taking the word liberal in the licentious import which the Democracy, both political and religious, of the present day often give to it. That plan perhaps was good for 1795, but it is not so for 1835. I think every intelligent Methodist who has observed the operation of political power in this country during the last few years must be aware that the Reform Bill, a measure most unnecessarily and injuriously extensive, both in what it destroyed and in what it created, has produced, or if not produced, has greatly aggravated and inflamed, such a lust of power in a considerable number of our people, that it is becoming very difficult indeed, in some places, to exercise that pastoral authority, with which I believe the New Testament has invested the minister of Christ, and which is indispensable to order and good government. The Leaders' Meetings, for instance, have in my judgment, greatly too much power, particularly where they have been allowed to remain, as here, altogether. The Leaders' Meeting of this town consists of above 100

[1] John Bicknell, preacher, Hull circuit, 1834–35. D. 1878, aet. 92.

[2] W. Vevers, *An appeal to the Wesleyan Societies, containing a reply to a pamphlet entitled 'An affectionate address of the United Wesleyan Methodist Association'* (London, 1835).

persons, the much greater part of whom come together not to show their classbooks that the preachers may become acquainted with the state of their respective classes, and visit the sick and absentees whose cases may seem to require it, and give them such advice as their office as Leaders often needs, but to *vote* in determining how this and the other shall be done – the government of the Society and its affairs really being much more in the Leaders' Meeting than in the Superintendent. Wherever such a state of things exists, I have no doubt that it is mainly owing to the *injudicious conduct of the Preachers*: it has been my lot to travel a few years with some of the present Fathers of the Connexion, and I have several times been surprised at their bringing matters into the Leaders' Meeting which I thought they should have decided upon their own authority and responsibility. To consult the Leaders on some occasions is indeed very proper – to do it on *all* occasions may give a man a reputation for liberality – and were human nature so constituted that one could be sure it would always stop at *consultation*, it would not be objectionable, but when a number of official persons find they are con-sulted about *every*thing – that this is done not when the Preachers might fall in with them *casually* and *individually*, but in their *collective and official* capacity – and that it is done *repeatedly*, they soon feel their importance, and what at first they were only *consulted* about, they eventually take upon them to *decide* and to *administer*. To withdraw any portion of the power, which has thus been perhaps very undesignedly but very unwarily conceded, is I am aware impossible, but surely greater care ought to be used to avoid the unnecessary introduction of things into meetings that have already engrossed so much ecclesiastical authority. More care ought to be used also in the appointment of Leaders, to ascertain their Methodistical views relative to our constitution as well as to doctrine and general discipline. Could not some regulation be adopted to put Leaders upon a course of *Probation*? While members, and preachers, local and travelling, are subject to a season of trial, persons are placed in the very important office of Leaders, without any trial at all, which I very much lament, more especially as a large portion of them are poor men. In case of any trial, their nomination to the full possession of office should be with the Superintendent, as well as their introduction to it. As another instance of the undue power yielded to the Leaders' Meeting here, and the same I understand is practised in some other Yorkshire Circuits, I may mention that no persons are allowed to have tickets as members of Society, until they have passed that meeting.

My principal object in writing to you is to express my earnest hope that nothing will be done at Conference to diminish the *pastoral* power of the Preachers: taking the connexion throughout I am persuaded that

that power is not at present at all too much. I would say, let it not be given up whatever may be the consequence. I believe that a very large majority of our intelligent and respectable people would be against such a measure: in *this* Circuit, I know they are. There is not one person here who favours 'the Association' who is a subscriber to our funds, with the exception of the Mission Fund. Mr. Cookman,[1] who has occasioned us the most trouble in consequence of his having a better head than any other of the agitators, has not for many years subscribed either to the Schools – to the Chapel Fund – or to the Auxiliary Fund. He is a decided republican, and I have no hesitation in saying that his desire is to destroy the authority of the Superintendent to sentence any convicted person, and to reduce him to a mere *chairman*, who is only to *pronounce* a penalty previously decided upon by a majority of the meeting. I may take the opportunity to remind you that the scriptural and Methodistical right of the Superintendent to *apportion* as well as to deliver a sentence, needs to be more explicitly stated than it is in the Minutes of 1795–7. The want of its being so has occasioned difficulty here as well as in other places. The Minute respecting illegal meetings made in 1795 and explained in 1797, must also be published with the other rules – the omission of its publication having been laid hold of by some charged with that offence, as indicative that the Conference had given it up.

Perhaps all the above may be quite unnecessary on my part, but I wished to express my sentiments on what I believe to be the main but concealed object of the disaffected among us, of those however who have any definite object at heart, for as to lay delegates in the Conference, or what some now call a house of Commons to meet in the same town and at the same time, with the Lords, such a proposition I hope would not be entertained for a moment.

With respect to *yourself* individually, as suffering the largest share of contumely and opprobrium, especially at the commencement of the disturbances of the present Methodistical year, I beg to express my Christian and brotherly sympathy, and the hope that you are not only sustained under it by the testimony of a good conscience, but also that you may be spared among us for yet many years of usefulness . . .

87 From James Dixon[2]   *Liverpool, March 14, 1835*

. . . Hope you will be able to give a good account of Dr. Warren next week – the Lord is I trust on our side, and though not intended, I

[1] George Cookman became a forceful radical member of the newly reformed Hull corporation at the elections of December, 1835.

[2] James Dixon, preacher, Liverpool (South) circuit, 1834–36; superintendent, 1836–37.

should suppose you consider his application to the courts, doing us greater service than we could have done for ourselves. It will I think settle some legal points which were rather uncertain, increase the confidence of our own preachers and people in the stability of our constitution, and prove that we are not a dissenting or rather a *democratic* body.[1] . . .

88   To T. Percival Bunting

London, Wed. Evg.
[Postmarked March 25, 1835]

Before this can reach you, you will have received from Mr. Bower[s]'s[2] *Special* Message the joyful news of the perfect triumph of our good cause. The Chancellor spoke for an hour, most ably, eloquently, argumentatively. ⟨He?⟩ is with you on every *legal* point. The *Watchman* will, I hope, tell you something more; and when we meet I shall be glad to enlarge, although 'memory is almost lost in heedless ecstasy'. To God be the praise! I hope our victory will be enjoyed with humility, moderation, and charity. All our counsel are delighted; and I never saw Mr. Bower[s], calm and philosophic as he is, so visibly and pleasantly excited. There was an immense crowd of listeners; and our mutual greetings were truly joyous . . .

89   From John Waterhouse[3]

n. pl. or d. [Postmarked Birmingham,
April 3, 1835][4]

. . . We are doing very well in this town, we have an increase of 83 members this quarter and 196 on trial. Our Quarterly Meeting was most harmonious. There are however a few *Locals*[5] who are under the influence of Devil's Advocate, and Dr. Warren's party have been trying for weeks to get a Meeting in Birmingham; as yet they have failed. Our

---

[1] On March 5 Bunting had given notice of Warren's appeal to the Lord Chancellor (see n. 1 p. 124 *supra*) to the Liverpool preachers, counselling, 'Let us pray much, and fear nothing' (S.M.U. Dallas, Texas, MSS. Jabez Bunting to J. S. Stamp, March 5, 1835). Dixon's concluding comment blossomed in a tradition of official historiography which held that 'the whole case affords proof of the manifest providential supervision which regulated Methodist counsels, and directed Methodist operations'. Smith, *History of Wesleyan Methodism* iii. 276.

[2] Probably John Bowers, preacher, London (City Road) circuit, 1834–37.

[3] John Waterhouse (1789–1843), superintendent, Birmingham circuit, 1832–35.

[4] This letter is appended to that of Francis Heeley to Jabez Bunting, Birmingham, March 31, 1835.

[5] I.e. Local Preachers.

Rads. dare not shew themselves. They know if I ever get hold of them they go overboard. Dudley is in an awful state, Edwards had to break up their Quarterly Meeting, Stourbridge is in as bad a state, the other Circuits in the District are as far as I can learn quiet . . .

Who is to be President? I have made many enquiries but can get nothing satisfactory. I think it is of great importance to have, at this time especially, a *thoroughly sound man.* Is it possible to succeed with Mr. Grindrod? I have heard that Mr. Reece is spoken of; that I think will not succeed.[1] I see a great difficulty, I wish you could remove it . . .

90 From John Beecham   *London, April 1, 1835*

. . . Dr. Sandwith came yesterday. I have laboured hard to impress him with our views as to what kind of leading articles we are now especially wanting;[2] and I am in expectation that another week's paper will exhibit an improvement in this respect, and that we shall not appear dragging about week[s] behind in our remarks on political events . . .

91 From R. Alder   *Warrington, April 17, 1835*

I have just come over to this place, and snatch a moment to tell you that we have had two glorious meetings at Liverpool. [Missionary] collections I understand were between twenty and thirty pounds more than last year, and the moral influence connected with them is beyond all price. They have quite inspirited our people. The chapels were crowded. A resolution expressive of approval and of confidence in the General Committee was most heartily adopted. There was a forest of hands held up for it. Not one was held up against it. The Agitators[3] held a meeting here last night. If I can only recollect all that I have heard concerning it, I will make you laugh. Their speeches made a few Tories . . .

---

[1] Richard Reece became President for the second time at the 1835 Conference.

[2] In the *Watchman.* Sandwith himself wished to act as Bunting's mouthpiece on, e.g., the Irish National Education question. M.C.A. MSS. H. Sandwith to Jabez Bunting, May 7 [1835].

[3] I.e. the Warrenites.

92   To Samuel Warren   *Manchester, April 21, 1835*[1]

The object of my former communication as to your reputed a[sser]tions
at the Bury Meeting having been fully answered by your positive denial
that you made them I need not enter into any vindication of the
unquestionable veracity of my informants. Your assertion that you do
not believe that any leaves were ever taken out of the Conference
Journal sufficiently establishes that fact:–[2] and [it] should be useless to
moot the question whether or not you have always said so [until other
points of a similar nature which need not be enumerated have first been
settled.]

An acute but perhaps somewhat fanciful friend has suggested that
the last paragraph of your reply conveys a sarcasm, however pale and
indistinct, upon my 'inexperienced youth' [and really I am half inclined
to think that I perceive some sarcasm.] If such was your intention, I
can only assure you in all simplicity that I remember instances in which
I have been so far suspecting and experienced as to detect in individuals
of respectable reputation and of greater pretensions characteristics
which others were much slower in discovering but which all honest
men now cordially unite in most deeply detesting.

93   From James Kendall[3]   *Cockermouth, June 2, 1835*

Your prompt and generous reply[4] to my last year's letter on the subject
of our union with the Church of England encourages me again very
briefly to address you on a point or two of at least comparative
importance.

In the first place, may I with all deference to your matured judgment
suggest the propriety of a revision of those 'Minutes' put into our
hands when received into full connexion, seeing they are incompatible
in their present *form* with our present practical position towards the
Church of England, and *may* if unaltered form the groundwork of
debates not a little dangerous to our stability and comfort as a connexion. Insignificant as I am in the estimation of the Conference I have

---

[1] This text is taken from a very rough draft. The passages here printed in brackets are
crossed out in the MS. There is also much crossing out in the last sentence.

[2] Though the basic legislation of the period following Wesley's death, the Plan of Pacification (1795) and the Regulations of 1797, was published with the Conference Minutes, it
had never been validated by being entered in the Conference Journal. This omission was
rectified at the next Conference (1835).

[3] James Kendall, preacher, Whitehaven circuit, 1834–35.

[4] See no. 41 *supra*.

my opinions and my reasons for their adoption, and though it would be sinful in me to tease *others* with my scruples and fears – I cannot help *at present* regretting that our attachment to the Church of England is so *very theorick.* I know right well that I am suspected of vanity and imprudence in consequence of having exchanged letters with the Bishops of Exeter and Chester respecting Methodism and Churchism, but I never should have thought of this had it not been for my 'Minutes' which I received as 'Rules to walk by'. In writing to you however, I have *done* with my uneasy speculations.

In my present Circuit Dear Doctor we have fierce work which *more than ever* convinces me that thorough-paced Dissenters *holding offices* in our Connexion are no great acquisition to us. I have fought in my poor way many a battle for yourself and the Theological Institution, and have repeatedly *perhaps* imprudently challenged the outrageous defamers of your character and declaimers against the Institution to a public debate. But oh for peace! The Radicals here are in *earnest*, as they not only stop supplies from the funds of Conference but from us poor fellows the preachers. The Vicar of Wakefield preached to the prisoners. If *some* of us have to go much longer without money, there is no saying who may have to imitate him . . .

94   To T. P. Bunting   *London, June 18, 1835*

. . . You must excuse me if I, in the *strongest possible* manner, press on your attention the importance of forwarding in the course of next week, so as to be here before another meeting of the Committee, the donations and first year's subscriptions to the Institution from Mrs. Bealey and family, and *your own.* Mr. Bowers can tell you how the thing was alluded to at our meeting last Friday. With difficulty I obtained an order that the General Notice given in this week's *Watchman* should be the *first* step. Remembering the most unfortunate publications in the *Advocate* about S. Warren's debt, etc. etc., I am, for Mrs. B.'s sake and yours *most anxious* that the thing should never be mentioned in Committee again, except as *settled*[1] . . .

There is a split among the Anti-Slavery friends. Buxton, in the unfortunate absence of Z. Macaulay[2] at Paris, has given himself up too fully to the guidance of Geo. Stephens[3] and the old agitation party,

---

[1] See no. 63 *supra.*

[2] Zachary Macaulay (1768–1838), philanthropist, one of the founder members of the Anti-Slavery Society.

[3] George Stephen, on whom see n. 1 p. 22 *supra.*

who are going to work very indiscreetly. A parliamentary committee for enquiry would have been quite right; but a motion to suspend the grant, *in the first instance*, and *before cause shewn*, is thought outrageous, both by Government, and by some staunch friends of the *original* Anti-Slavery Society[1] . . .

Confidential

95   To T. Percival Bunting   *London, July 9, 1835*

Your letter stating the views of Mr. [James] Wood and Mr. Heald,[2] surprises and pains me. I cannot divine their motives for such a procedure. If such men as they will thus add to our existing mass of perplexity and solicitude, I shall begin to think it time, for me at least, to retire from all further struggle against democratic encroachment. I have for months often doubted whether I ought not to absent myself wholly from the coming Conference, and could easily come to that conclusion.

I have not seen the President's circular to the gentlemen.[3] I should suppose that it sufficiently expresses the object it has in view. Mr.

[1] It is a singular instance of the disarray into which the anti-slavery movement had speedily fallen, that Bunting's report was the reverse of the truth. The old Agency Committee had metamorphosed into the Universal Abolition Society, and was agitating in this cause in both Britain and America. The relatively conservative Anti-Slavery Society held that they had a sufficiently onerous commission to secure effective abolition, and prevent the perversion of the apprenticeship system in the British colonies. Alarming reports of the maltreatment of West Indian apprentices led them to call a convention at Exeter Hall on May 15, as a result of which, on June 19, 1835, Buxton moved in the Commons for the appointment of a select committee to determine whether the planters had met the conditions under which compensation was payable. Readily satisfied with Sir George Grey's assurances on behalf of the government that no serious difficulties had arisen, he withdrew his motion, and privately explained to Macaulay that there was no point in harrying the government until the real counter-attack he expected from the planters took place. To this approach Stephen's Universal Abolition Society was exceedingly hostile.

[2] James Heald (1796–1873), prominent Stockport Methodist, cotton-spinner, philanthropist and banker. For a time retired from business to study for ordination in the Church of England, but returned both to business and to Methodism, becoming Treasurer to the Missionary Society, and a leading supporter of the Theological Institution, especially the Didsbury Branch opened in 1842 near his home at Parr's Wood. Became Tory M.P. for Stockport, 1847–52, but lost the seat on accepting the principles of free trade.

[3] The object of this negotiation was to offset pressure from the Grand Central Association upon the following Conference by securing public testimonies of support from a prior meeting of lay grandees of the connexion, which would show, at the least, that the financial blockade attempted by the Warrenites would be ineffective. It gave incidental confirmation to the Warrenite charge that Methodism was in the hands of a coalition of the connexional management and the rich, but as the letter shows, Bunting's fear was that it might be construed as a concession to democracy.

Farmer (who alone has named it to me) seems quite to understand it, and says that he will attend. I know of no plan or arrangement as to the mode of conducting the proposed meeting; but *suppose* that *a free and friendly conversation* is desired, with men on whose general goodwill and attachment to our essential principles of discipline we judge that we can depend. The objects, I presume (but I do not speak for any but myself), of such conversation would be, to ascertain whether the class of persons invited to attend are prepared conscientiously and cordially to support us, in abiding *substantially* by our present constitution, and in maintaining it against the organized conspiracy which aims at subverting it; to learn from them whether *they* have any feelings of dissatisfaction, on any minor parts of the system, which explanation and argument, or, if they can shew cause for it, some *minor alterations* in administration (not affecting our fundamental position) may remove, so as to secure their hearty and decided alliance in resistance to revolutionary measures; and to ask and obtain their friendly advice and counsel (not *as an official and organized body*, but *as individuals* whom the President and preachers acting with him, are desirous to consult, for the better guidance of their own subsequent conduct) respecting the most discreet and efficient means of securing those great ends which, we *presume*, we are alike anxious to promote.

This is the best general statement I can give in reference to the meeting. If any whom we have counted on as really *with us* are not indeed *decided*, or if they in their hearts prefer a system more *Kilhamitish* and *Allinish*,[1] it is well that we should know it in time, and prepare for the worst.

Mr. Wood has perhaps forgotten that during my two last visits to Manchester *he* twice strongly urged on me the propriety of our taking some means to secure our having *at hand*, at Sheffield, a number of lay-friends; that we might not be abandoned, or seem to be so, to the attacks of the hostile delegates so-called, whose assembly has been so pompously announced. To have 'at hand' such friendly counsel and support as he suggested, seemed to me to be desirable; and probably it was my mention of this to the President that *first* called his attention to the point . . . Is there no *legal* possibility of Warren's dragging us into Chancery again, if the Conference *expel* him? Did not the Vice-Chancellor intimate that an allegation of *'fraudulent' expulsion* would be matter of which the court would take cognizance? If so, should not

---

[1] A reference to Thomas Allin (q.v.) a leading preacher in the Methodist New Connexion founded by Alexander Kilham, in which the Conference was composed half of preachers and half of elected lay representatives. Cf. Thomas Allin, *An exposition of the principles of church-government adopted by the Methodists of the New Connexion* . . . (Sheffield, 1833).

great care be taken to do everything in the most technical and proper way? And would it be well to have a case drawn, and counsel's opinion previously obtained, on that point?[1] . . .

96   From William Jenkins   *6 Red Lion Sqr. [London] July 27, 1835*
[Encloses the accounts of Dr. Coke's legacy for Conference] . . . I feel more than words can describe desirous that the present contentions may end in some explanations and concessions in the *true spirit of the Plan of Pacification* and of the *concessions of 1797* – leaving no power to any person to abridge or cavil at them afterwards, as will satisfy great numbers, if not all, the present discontented – and perhaps if you were to add – 'That all the business of the funds at the Conference be managed by a committee or committees of the people' – this would only ease the preachers, and in no wise affect the great work of God among us . . .

I have no fears that the great cause will sink, it is the Lord's and He will uphold it – but individual souls are precious! I would not part with *one* if possible – and certainly for nothing that is *not vital* to the great trust for *saving souls*, which God hath committed to the Methodist preachers. O that we may never forget or lose sight for a moment of our true calling which is not to mix with worldly schemes or parties, or to rule this way or that way – *but to save souls, to bring them in* if possible, and *never separate any but for sin!*

97   From John Davis[2]   *Penzance, September 23, 1835*
. . . We had a very harmonious [Financial District] meeting yesterday, a great many Stewards present, but our Radicals at St. Austle, Redruth and Helstone are Radicals still – I have recommended firmness and decision to the Brethren in those circuits, but to guard against pre-cipitancy. In several places there is great propect of much good, thank God . . .

[1] Later the same night Bunting wrote by private messenger recommending that the Manchester District Meeting should take counsel's opinion whether their minutes condemning Warren were actionable on the ground of libel. The London preachers 'who are to be in part the judges on the case in Conference should be wholly kept out of the matter'. M.C.A. MSS. Jabez Bunting to T. P. Bunting, Thursday evg. [July 9, 1835].

[2] John Davis snr., superintendent, Penzance circuit, 1834–37.

98   From Robert Wood[1]   *Manchester, October 31, 1835*

. . . At Rochdale, things remain nearly *in statu quo*. At Clitheroe, the crisis is at hand. A Warrenite meeting has been held, at which one or two Local Preachers attended. These, the Superintendent will bring to trial, and an explosion may be then expected. In Bury, a delightful *reaction* has taken place. The Wesleyan Reform Meeting there did us great service. The animus of the Speakers – their misrepresentations and falsehoods – disgusted nearly all their hearers. And the following day (for the meeting was held on the preparation for the Sabbath) the Lord wrought a blessed work in our chapel. Sinners were cut to the heart under the evening sermon, and several cried aloud for mercy. 'O Jesus, ride on!' . . .

99   To Isaac Keeling   *London, November 4, 1835*

. . . I am happy to infer from your statement, that your Answer to Allin is,[2] as the Americans say, *progressing* towards completion. Good general principles of Church-Government are now what is [*sic*] chiefly wanted; and these, I doubt not, you will supply.

The state and prospects of the Connexion, with comparatively few exceptions, appear to have very much brightened since the Conference. In London our few Radicals boast and bluster much, but will I think be able to do but little. I know not one man of real methodistical respectability who is disposed to join their standard . . .

100   To John Beecham   *Manchester, November 16, 1835*

You would hear that we could not get places so soon as we wished, and therefore did not leave London till Wednesday evening. Through mercy we had a safe, though to me a sorrowful journey, marked at every successive stage by heart-rending associations[3] . . .

I . . . return the proofs of the paper on the Pastoral Office.[4] I like it

[1] Robert Wood, superintendent, Manchester (Grosvenor St.) circuit, 1835–38.

[2] Keeling's pamphlet seems never to have been published. An anonymous broadsheet *To the Rev. Thomas Allin* (n. pl. or d.) now printed at Sheffield was probably the work of one of the Sheffield preachers who had their own controversy with Allin.

[3] Sarah Maclardie, the bride whom Bunting had brought to London from Macclesfield in 1804, d. September 29, 1835, aet. 53.

[4] In 1829 Beecham had published the first of the great Wesleyan treatises on the Pastoral Office (cf. n. 1 p. 3 *supra*). He is here recapitulating the doctrine for the *Wesleyan Methodist Magazine*. In an undated letter to Bunting which probably evoked the above reply, Beecham

very much. It is very reasonable, and I think conclusive. I have offered on the margin a few suggestions for your candid consideration, which you will take for just as much as you, on more leisurely reflexion, think they are worth, and no more.

I find it difficult here to get any time for my own work. Every heart knows its own bitterness; and many preachers in the neighbourhood, who are in little local difficulties, and want advice, insist on seeing me.

Things in the methodistical world are much brightening here. All the circuits are doing well; and the preachers please and are pleased. The Rochdale Chapel case is in a train for being satisfactorily settled, and those fine premises rescued from the Warrenites.[1] About half the town Society, it is hoped, will be saved. At Bury there is still some perplexity; at Clitheroe matters will probably find their crisis by an explosion in a week or two. Macclesfield is much improved. Most of the other circuits are peaceful, as far as I can learn.

Aitken[2] has formally resigned his place among us in the Isle of Man, as the condition of his negotiating for the office of a Church Home-Missionary. So bursts this bubble!

Your papers in the [*Methodist*] *Magazine* have maddened the 'Grand' Association people in these parts. They say in their speeches that the Conference has made a great discovery; and that 'the Keys', which no Church but the Romish ever believed to have a real existence, have been found by the Methodists! What a worthless house must *their* Church be, which they thus confess *has no keys*. Is it because it contains nothing worth locking up?

The proprietors here are sadly vexed at the insertion of Mark Robinson's[3] Advertisement of his Books and Puffs in last week's *Watchman*. It is a lamentable blunder. That we should support a paper, in order thus to circulate, at a crisis like this, Robert Hall's[4] condem-

---

had complained 'Alas! my "Pastoral Office"; it swells again beyond bound. What can I do? I think I must finish it in an appendix, in the next year's Magazine'. M.C.A. MSS. John Beecham to Jabez Bunting, n. pl. or d. [erroneously labelled '?1838'].

[1] In September John Sumner, the Rochdale superintendent, declared that unless the officers and members of the Rochdale Society submitted to certain tests 'he would hold no communion with them'. The Union St. trustees went ahead with a reform meeting, and T. P. Bunting, the solicitor son of Jabez, helped Sumner to secure an injunction, forbidding any assembly on connexional premises unless conducted by a minister. For the disaster which subsequently befell the Rochdale circuit, see Ward, *Religion and society* pp. 169–70.

[2] Robert Aitken; see n. 1 p. 119 *supra*.

[3] Mark Robinson of Beverley had attacked ministerial pretensions in a revival of Church Methodism, 1824–25, and had established a short-lived Church Methodist connexion (on which see *Early Correspondence* pp. 98–114). Humphrey Sandwith who had been brought up with him at Beverley first attracted attention by defending the Wesleyan constitution against him.

[4] Robert Hall (1764–1831), Baptist divine.

nation of our system, is really 'too bad'. I hear much, but say little; as I do not wish to blister a part already inflamed and sore. Was Dr. S[andwith] a party to that insertion? I should think not. It shews that there must be a better provision for a constant inspection of all the slip-proofs. I wonder too, that Dr. S. should copy the two letters about Mark's proceedings from the *Record*,[1] without giving at the same time the true state of the case. He ought not to be allowed, and that through our own columns, thus to bamboozle the clergy and the churchmen. Dr. S. had abundant materials for letting out his true character and the utter failure of his schemes, without any libellous intimation, or danger of lengthy and undignified controversy . . .

101   To [James Stephen][2]   *L[ondon], January 9, 1836 [Draft]*

I have the honour on behalf of the Committee of the Wesleyan Mission-ary Society to offer to you, and through you to the Noble Secretary of State for the Colonial Department,[3] their cordial thanks for the prompt and obliging communication of a copy of the paper addressed by Mr. Shrewsbury in January 1835 to Lieut. Col. Smith.[4] That paper was

---

[1] The *Watchman* of November 4 and 11 (pp. 351, 359) reprinted letters from the *Record* alleging that Mark Robinson was collecting money to open chapels the congregations of which should receive preaching from Methodist lay preachers, and the sacraments at the parish church. This enterprise had already failed, though for a time one of the buildings at Beverley had been used by the incumbent as an episcopal chapel.

[2] James Stephen (1789–1859), permanent counsel to Colonial Office and Board of Trade, 1825; under-secretary for colonies, 1836–47.

[3] Lord Glenelg (1778–1866), colonial secretary, 1835–39.

[4] Late in 1835 Beecham reported to Bunting that Thomas Fowell Buxton and the Aborigines Committee had received information from the Cape as to the part played by Methodist missionaries in the Kaffir War of 1834–35, which might lead them 'shortly [to] stop the Kaffir missionaries in their career' (M.C.A. MSS. John Beecham to Jabez Bunting n. pl. or d. [wrongly labelled '?1838']). Bunting then wrote to Stephen (M.C.A. MSS. Jabez Bunting to James Stephen, December 17, 1835) that the Secretaries of the Missionary Society understood the government to have received reports of a letter about the Kaffir war addressed to the Governor of Cape Colony by Shrewsbury, a Methodist missionary lately returned to England, which, if true, were highly censurable; and requested a copy of the letter, so as to set on foot an immediate investigation, the results of which are here reported. William James Shrewsbury (1795–1866), preacher at Boulogne, 1835–36, had served in the West Indies, 1815–24, and in South Africa, 1825–35. Brusquely accused by Bunting on this occasion of Antinomianism, and condemned, as he believed, unjustly in Conference resolutions, Shrewsbury kept away from Conference and official business for years, until brought to seek reconciliation out of sympathy for Bunting's sufferings from the *Flysheets* (M.C.A. MSS. W. J. Shrewsbury to Jabez Bunting, July 7, 1851). Bunting's MS. notes on the case survive, undated, in M.C.A. Sir Harry George Wakelyn Smith (1787–1860) took a leading part in subduing the Kaffirs, 1836, and became governor of the Cape, 1849.

L

submitted at the earliest opportunity to the consideration of the Committee, whose unanimous resolutions on this most painful occasion I take the liberty of transmitting. I inclose, also, a copy of the document which Mr. Shrewsbury delivered to the Committee [meeting], in explanation of his opinions. Though far from satisfactory, it is perhaps only just and fair that you and [Lord] Glenelg, if you deem it expedient, should have the opportunity of becoming acquainted with them.

On one point I feel it my own duty to explain. When the rumour of Mr. Shrewsbury's having written the very censurable paper in question first reached us by the medium of a distinguished friend, it was mentioned that Mr. Shrewsbury had written a 'Letter *to the Governor, Sir Benj. D'Urban,* containing certain advices and counsels on the subject of the Kaffir War'. So the communication of that friend was understood, and *in those terms* substantially the matter was stated by one of my colleagues to Mr. Shrewsbury in a letter of enquiry. To *that* statement it was that Mr. Shrewsbury replied by a denial of his having, to the best of his recollection, written *to the Governor* at all on that subject, not recollecting then, that he *had* sent in writing to *Lieut. Col. Smith* the heads of their previous accidental conversation. When afterwards we obtained and repeated to him a more minute account of the import and contents of the paper, Mr. Shrewsbury instantly recalled the transaction to his memory; at once acknowledged the fact of his having written *to Col. Smith*; and admitted (though he had kept no copy) the substantial accuracy of the statement. He has strangely and grievously erred in this affair; but we who have known him long, cannot for a moment question his veracity, as to the explanation now given of his original disclaimer.

Most gratefully appreciating your friendly attentions to the applications of our Society on this and other occasions, and your personal kindness to myself in forwarding the letter with which by your obliging permission I troubled you, to the Chancellor of the Exchequer. I have the honour to be [etc.]

102 To John Beecham   *Penzance, January 18, 1836*

. . . I am not on the whole very sorry that the grant to our [Missionary] Society is reduced to £3000, as the reduction proportionably diminishes the advance to be made out of our own funds for school *houses,* and leaves more available for *schools themselves* in the country-districts where, after all, they will be most wanted, and where separate buildings need not always be erected.[1]

As to the *distribution* of the £3000 to be effected by a *selection* out of our first list, I must leave it to you, with Mr. Alder, Mr. Hoole, and our excellent Treasurer.[2] I have not now the papers at hand on which alone I could form any opinion as to the most exigent cases. Mr. Taylor's local knowledge will be of great service; and I shall have entire confidence in the rectitude of your united decision. Lord Glenelg's principle is a good one. The benefit should be as much as possible *diffused*. The amended list contained in your letter appears to me, as far as I can hastily judge, admirably accommodated to this principle . . .

103   From Benjamin Clayton[3]   *Kendal, March 9, 1836*

. . . We have hitherto been at peace in this circuit and have some prosperity, though many attempts have been made upon us by the 'Grand Central' men. Thomas Graham!!! who formerly travelled in this circuit came night before last, and spent all *yesterday* in this town, and after a great deal of 'hunting' among the people he contrived to get up a *private* meeting of about ten persons, it was held in the house of a man who was once one of the first Methodists here; but having failed in business, and laid little or nothing to his creditors, he is not allowed to become a member with us at *present*, and is very much grieved because he is not allowed to take the lead in our prayer-meetings in the chapel – the rest who met with them last night are generally men of little influence or character.

I know the *whole affair* about T. Graham being taken to the lock-up house, when stationed at Montrose,[4] and his trial before the Magistrates but will you, dear Doctor, kindly inform me *when* and *why* he at *last left* the connexion? I am not sure whether he intends visiting Kendal again soon to hold a public meeting. We have no fear. I understand T. Graham is on his way for *Glasgow*.

[1] A few days later Bunting commented: 'We have at last got Lord Glenelg's promise of £3000 for negro *school-houses* in different islands, out of £20,000 voted by Parliament for that object; but on the condition that *we* add £1500 to that sum, being one third of the estimated cost of £4500, and undertake the *annual support* of the *schools* which will make a heavy addition to our annual expenditure'. M.C.A. MSS. Jabez Bunting to Robert Wood, Camborne, January 23, 1836.

[2] Joseph Taylor, superintendent, London (City Road) circuit, 1834–36.

[3] Benjamin Clayton, superintendent, Kendal circuit, 1834–37. D. 1851, aet. 54.

[4] Thomas Graham jun., preacher, Arbroath circuit, 1832–33.

104 From J. S. Stamp[1]   *Oxford, March 13, 1836*

. . . I have for some time beheld with anxiety a certain class of young
people, who from education and principle are sincerely attached to the
doctrines and discipline of Methodism, chiefly children either of
members of Society or of regular hearers in our congregations, whose
age or condition in life prevented them from being in the Sunday School,
and whose minds had not received that decidedly religious turn to be
received in close connection with the Wesleyan body, yet were destitute
of that pastoral attention and care necessary to foster the good impressions they had imbibed and to confirm the pious principles they had
received, and for want of which they are frequently at the mercy of
every babbler in Scripture, perpetually shaken with the wind, ever
learning but never able to come to the knowledge of the truth, the
result has been but few, comparatively speaking, of the children of the
Methodists have joined the Society, many are well-wishers, but they
have not fully and decidedly given 'their own selves to the Lord and
unto us by the will of God.' It has long appeared to me that something
might be done to meet the situation of these persons. Some years ago I
read Mr. McDonald's pamphlet[2] and as I can recollect that went too far
on the other side; were his plan to be embraced, and all the children of
the Methodists be considered members of Society, we should commit a
suicidal act, and Methodism strong in proportion as attention is paid to
purity would soon dwindle into 'vox preterea nihil.' Yet were the grand
principle of Mr. McDonald's book adopted, and the youth (I use this
term opposed to the children of the Sunday School whose case the
Conference *has* met)[3] of our congregations brought under immediate
pastoral instruction, without compromising the wholesome discipline of
Wesleyanism, a desirable end would be gained, the importance of this
is obvious. They are too old for the forms of a Sabbath school and are
cordially attached to the constitution and doctrines of Methodism, yet
the general standard of scriptural knowledge among them is defective
and they are of an age more likely to imbibe the pernicious principles of
an ungodly world than at any other period of life, but by an affectionate

---

[1] John S. Stamp, superintendent, Chester circuit, 1835–38. Ceased to be recognized, 1849.
Similar anxieties about the basis of membership and the extraordinary mobility of those who
passed under, and out of, Methodist pastoral oversight, were much more forcibly expressed
in the 'forties. Cf. nos. 242, 246, *infra*.

[2] James McDonald, *An address to the preachers . . . on the necessity and utility of securing to all the
children of Methodists a regular Christian education* (Rochdale, 1821).

[3] In 1827 Conference consolidated recent legislation by which the constitutional authority
of the preachers in Wesleyan Sunday Schools had been steadily developed, and preachers
were invited to make the independent Sunday schools long related to Methodism conform to
this pattern.

and assiduous attention to their spiritual interests, we can little doubt many ere long will be active members of Society, not ashamed to speak with the enemy in the gate; for their benefit these classes are formed. Again though intended primarily for such, not exclusively so, I expect the attendance of the junior teachers at least of the Sunday School, agreeing to the sentiments contained in the Minutes of 1827, respecting the management of these Institutions. I think as pastors of the Society we ought to have some personal acquaintance with the doctrinal views and scripture knowledge of those to whom we intrust the spiritual instruction of 'the children of the Church'; *that* obtained in the quarterly visitation of the classes is confessedly imperfect and limited, supposing all the teachers were members of Society, the greater part of the objects of Sunday school instruction have been solemnly initiated into the Church by baptism, and have a legitimate claim to an interest in the pastoral charge. In accordance with those views I have turned my attention to these institutions in the circuits I have travelled and have had to lament the comparative unfitness of the teachers for their important work; it is true, they are able to initiate them in the regular gradations of reading, spelling etc. and can hear them repeat the catechism, but how few can explain or apply the scripture or the catechism to the understanding of the children. These meetings are open also to junior local preachers and the younger members of Society.

The plan adopted is catechetical instruction, the subject is the New Testament harmonized according to Townsend[1] in chronological and historical arrangement to which is also associated some question from the second or third part of the conference catechism. This gives a Wesleyan character to the exercise and renders more familiar and interesting those excellent formularies. I have hitherto acted independent of printed forms or fixed series of questions and have been guided by circumstances. The leading practical truths of Christianity are exhibited by easy and familiar interrogation and then applied with affection and earnestness to the conscience and to the heart; all gossiping debate is scouted, no question during the meeting is put but by myself, although at the conclusion I have been in the habit of inviting questions from the class, should any part of the subject under consideration be unintelligible, and afterwards have thrown myself open to the consideration of any difficulty met with in their general reading. This in a degree has given me the superintendency of the books read, and a favourable opportunity for admonition and caution against an indiscriminate perusal of works, calculated, if not to poison, to confuse the mind

[1] George Townsend, *The New Testament arranged in chronological and historical order, with copious notes* . . . (London, 1825).

and bewilder the imagination. I confess these classes have added to the labours of the study to maintain variety, but recovering a few hours from sleep is more than compensated by the pleasure taken in these meetings by the young people, my own improvement in biblical knowledge and thus affording greater facilities for pulpit preparation.

The advantages already perceived are various. Several have become in religious character more decided, and by their humble enquiries respecting scriptural doctrine and practice are I doubt not earnest seekers of salvation for whose benefit I am about forming a class of which I shall take the lead. The preacher has been brought into immediate and intimate contact with an important part of his charge, who not only look on him as the pastor of their parents, but in a peculiar sense their own spiritual guide, instructor and friend. And to say nothing of the increased interest with which the public ministrations of the word are attended, our schools are reaping benefit in the instruction becoming more scriptural and practical. Such is a brief account of the objects, plan and advantages of our bible classes. The young women meet on Monday evening, once a fortnight for an hour and a half, the young men on Wednesday evening for the same time, also once a fortnight. The latter are employed on the Gospels – the former with the Acts and Epistles. The reluctance ma⟨nifested by⟩ some to sit as learners has vanished, and all anticipate with pleasure the ⟨former? o⟩bjection raised by some that they will foster pride, and lead to the youth being pushed into office and that we are training them for local preachers is not founded in knowledge. Who are the most eager to fill office in our Societies? I do not hesitate to say – the most ignorant, having generally found those most advanced in Christian experience and scriptural knowledge most backward to fill public stations in the Society. I feel warranted in saying that the common feeling of our young people who attend these bible classes – may be thus expressed – 'I could not have imagined I knew so little before I came to these Meetings.' . . .

105 From Samuel Robinson[1]   *Yeadon, near Leeds, April 16, 1836*

[Will J.B. come and preach for them?] . . . We have 600 members in this village; not the like, perhaps, to be found in the whole connexion of the same amount of population; and our congregations command with very few exceptions the whole adult inhabitants. They are an excellent people, and would be so much pleased with your visit that you could not but be greatly pleased yourself . . .

[1] Samuel Robinson, superintendent, Yeadon circuit, 1835–37. D. 1844, aet. 50.

106 From John Arthy   *42 Upper York Street, Bryanstone Square*
[London], April 25, 1836

. . . Suffer me to intreat you as a father to use the influence God has given you to put an end to the disputes between the Preachers and people, for what could either side gain by victory?

Mr. Wesley in the old Minutes enquires 'how far ought each to submit to the Majority'. Answer: As far as his conscience is convinced, further than this ought to be required of no man. But now our Preachers tell us they are bound to act as they do and cannot help it.

Is this Wesleyan Methodism?

I believe Jesus Christ will put down all rule and authority which encroaches on his own and that speedily. Let me intreat you to discountenance the violence of party spirit and also the practice of speaking evil of such as differ – may yours be the ministry of reconciliation and God and man will bless you for ever. Amen.

107 From William Hinson[1]   *Northampton, June 28, 1836*

. . . In reference to the cause of Methodism in this town and circuit, we have cause for thankfulness that our Societies are still on the increase on the whole, and that all our leading men are attached to Methodism, and most of them, I believe, very firmly. But we have some Local Preachers, most of them poor men, and not of much influence, who are in a measure disaffected to our cause. One or two of these are talking men. Several of these brethren are greatly offended at the terms of admission to our newly constituted Circuit Meeting, as being of too exclusive a character.[2] In appealing (after the final close etc.) the other day, to the stewards etc. it was judged proper to call a meeting to consider the propriety of memorializing the Conference. I believe the only subject will be that of the terms of admission to the aforesaid Meeting.

Our friends thought it better to have a meeting, under present circumstances. The dissatisfied party wanted to have memorialized the Conference from the public Quarterly Meeting. To this I objected, and without much opposition proceeded to the regular business of the meeting. I find that firmness, blended with kindness, are [*sic*] necessary under circumstances of this kind.

I have sometimes been almost at a loss to determine whether or not the newly constituted circuit meeting does away with the liberty

---

[1] William Hinson (1777–1852), superintendent, Northampton circuit, 1834–36.

[2] I.e. the meeting constituted by the legislation of the last Conference for memorializing Conference on matters of general interest. Cf. n. 2 p. 115 *supra*.

formerly granted, to discuss the propriety of any new rule at our September Quarterly Meeting. I have put the question to several of the brethren, but they have hardly known what to say. I do not see that the rule granting the liberty before mentioned at the September Meeting is repealed, but am inclined to think that still in reference to matters of finance, the liberty remains. . . . [What is Bunting's opinion?]

108 From Joseph Sutcliffe[1]   *Rochester, July 11, 1836*

In these difficult times I have my feelings for the Ark, the first care of heaven, and the best care of pastors.

Respecting the glory of the christian ministry, I have spoken out in 20 places of the connexion. It[s] origin is from heaven, and must not be touched with human hands. Christ has delivered to the church the commandment he received of the Father. 'By Jesus Christ are all things, *and we by him.*' Of course, I can not agree that our ministry should be subject to a smoking club, or the radical tongues of the age.

The general complaints are *three* 1. Expulsions; then in cases of appeal, let it be to a full and fair Quarterly Meeting, purified from the jealous and invidious influence of local preachers. Bryant,[2] head of the Bryanites, was expelled by the Camelford Quarterly Meeting for unfaithfulness in a testamentary trust. 2. The long period of ten years before they have a voice at the Quarterly Meetings, or at the other meetings. Would it be safe, surrounded as we are with a majority of hostile Local Preachers, to reduce the years to seven or rather to eight? which would be a fair and equal law for the travelling preachers and the official men; for we are three years preparing at home, and four years in the work abroad; and have no vote in Conference till the fifth year, which makes eight in all.

The *third* out-cry is, that the superintendent has too much power! Beyond that of the love of the people, the superintendent has very, yea very little power. Certainly no man ought to be compelled to give the sacrament to a man who lives in open sin. He must have the power 'to exclude obstinate offenders from our religious fellowship.' *Min[utes of Conference]* p. 155.

---

[1] Joseph Sutcliffe, superintendent, Rochester circuit, 1835–36.

[2] I.e. William O'Bryan (1778–1868), founder of the Bible Christians, a revivalist offshoot from Wesleyan Methodism constituted a denomination, 1819. Before he restored the Irish orthography, his family were known as Bryan or Bryant.

Perhaps an extract from Manchester may give you some light of the feeling in Manchester.

2 Marsden Square July 4

'I have not taken much part in the question of both sides of which much may be said. But if I find any fault it shall be on your side (I wrote about my Bible[1] to him and said some things against Mr. Eckett's[2] proceedings) though I do not intend that knowing the very difficult circumstances in which the Conference has been placed.

Two or three things I will just say. *First*, I think a very little conciliation or appearance of a wish to conciliate, would satisfy eight-tenths of both parties, and dispose many dissentients to return. *Secondly*, your party err here, in supposing that those who remain as members of Society are *thick* and *thin* approvers of current measures, though I could name some that would surprise you, who are very doubtful in the matter. *Thirdly*, the great bone of contention is the subject of the superintendent's power, and the smallness of that of the Leaders and Stewards in circuit meetings, as in the expulsion of members, etc. Beside the opinion prevalent that the last Conference took the opportunity when making concession to legalize certain actions of Distr⟨ict⟩ Meetings of which the people had com⟨plained⟩ as infringements of existing laws. *Fourthly*, I think unless some slight alterations are made, things will continue in their unsettled state from time to time even should the Warrenites remain quiet, which they will not be, unless their case is endeavoured to be met.

Yours etc. etc.

Charles Swallow[3]

I have made this extract which I thought you would like to see in perfect confidence that the communication shall not transpire. Mr. S[wallow] is nephew of the late J. S[wallow] Esquire of Willow-hall, and is confidentially employed in the firm. But no doubt you know him well.

[1] Sutcliffe had evidently written to Swallow about his recently published scripture commentary (see n. 3 p. 81. *supra*).

[2] Robert Eckett (1797–1862), a London Methodist radical, who had joined Warren and became in time the Bunting of the Wesleyan Methodist Association. Cf. n. 3 p. 2 *supra*.

[3] Charles Swallow; probably one of the Manchester cotton dealers of that name.

109   From J. Armitage[1]   *In confidence*
   to Rev. Messrs. R. Reece,   *H[ebden] Bridge [postmarked Halifax]*
   R. Treffry, R. Newton and   *July 16th [18]36*
   Dr. Bunting

Dear Fathers and Brethren

You are already aware of the circumstances of Todmorden Circuit *at least partially so.* You know Brother Wm. Wilson[2] had been one year *on the ground,* Mr. B[umstea]d[3] and self did think that Mr. Wilson was too violent, and we thought it would be better to overcome certain individuals by calmness and perseverance – but to our grief *and vexation* matters grew worse *and worse.* A little while before the March visitation *of the classes,* we 3 preachers met at our house [at] *Hebden Bridge,* and concluded that it would be better to consult the Chairman [of the District], and desire him to select a few of the senior preachers in the neighbourhood in order to consult together on the best mode of proceeding in giving the tickets. The decision of the Meeting was that we should not have any test *in reference to what is called the [Grand Central] Association,* but if the members paid the minimum of Quarterage we should give them tickets etc. etc. It has however so happened that I had another *impression upon my mind,* about the sentiments and conclusion of the aforesaid *social* meeting at Halifax. I thought we was not to interrogate them on the subject of the Association if we did not know whether they was or was not in the Association, but it never entered my mind, *either at the above meeting or since,* that we was to give tickets to those we knew to be in the Association, and more especially so when I read the Minutes of last Conference, see *page 100 etc.*[4] It never entered my head that any Minor or *even* regular District Meeting has any *authority* or right to set aside *either* the letter or spirit of the Minutes of Conference.

---

[1] John Armitage, preacher, Todmorden circuit, 1835–36. Desisted from travelling, 1839. For his views on church discipline, see M.C.A. MSS. J. Armitage to Jabez Bunting, August 5, 1836. In 1828 Armitage begged Bunting to forbid his wife (who created trouble in every Society) access to any manse (M.C.A. MSS, Same to same, October 10, 1828); this created stationing difficulties and he now wished to be reunited with her.

[2] William Wilson (1810–74), preacher, Todmorden circuit, 1834–36.

[3] John Bumstead (1778–1855), superintendent, Todmorden circuit, 1835–38.

[4] The Conference of 1835 unanimously resolved 'that any person who, instead of *peaceably retiring* from our Connexion, if he decidedly disapprove of our system either of doctrine or discipline . . . endeavours to retain and employ his position among us for the purposes of opposition and strife – or who continues, after due admonition to be a member of 'The Grand Central Association' or of any other confederacy formed for the object of systematic agitation – is guilty of a flagrant transgression of that *morality of the New Testament,* the observance of which was a principal condition of his admission into our Society, and must be considered to have justly forfeited his claim to the privileges of our religious fellowship'. *Minutes of the Methodist Conferences* vii. 535.

However it has so happened that it fell to my lot to meet Mr. Wm. Thompson['s][1] class for tickets, one of the most determined foes of Wesleyan Methodism, and one who acknowleded in my own house at H. Bridge that he was in the Association and was not ashamed of it etc. etc. and one *also* who was *self* sent as Delegate to the last Conference *in Sheffield*; with such knowledge *and conviction on my own mind*, could I, *as an honest man to Methodism*, give a ticket without saying a word upon the subject. I frankly confess, both then and *now* and at our regular District Meeting I could not, except the Conference say I must. To the Head I cheerfully and *willingly* submit *and bow*.

As soon as possible I stated to Mr. Bumstead what I had done and also to Mr. Wilson *my other colleague*, who in reply said I had done nobly. We had nothing *now* to do but go on and we should get rid of these radicals etc. etc. etc. I said to my Superintendent, Mr. Thompson, the person from whom I withheld the ticket, being a Local Preacher *also* as well as a class-leader, he should have a notice that his places would be supplied *until a further hearing of his case*. For I repeatedly told him that he was not expelled but simply suspended and that he might have a Leaders' Meeting in which his case might be reconsidered and *determined* accordingly. Mr. Bumstead desired me to drop him a line *on the subject*. I did so, and the following is a copy *verbatim*. Mr. Thompson, Dear Sir, I am directed by the Superintendent of Todmorden Circuit *viz*. The Rev. J. Bumstead to inform you that under existing circumstances, you cannot be allowed to officiate in any Wesleyan pulpit, or [be] in anywise connected with our Society, *whatso[e]ver*, I am one of your best friends, J. Armitage, *Hebden Bridge, February 18, '36*. N.B. If you require another hearing in reference to what took place on Sunday morning *last* in the Wesleyan Chapel *vestry* at Luddenden, Mr. B[umstea]d will call a Leaders' Meeting at this place and hear your complaint and decide accordingly. Your reply by letter to Mr. B. *or self* will be attended to duly. J.A.. *Observe*. The Sunday morning following viz. the 21st of February the following bill was posted up *at our chapels* and circulated:

To the Wesleyan Officers in the Todmorden Circuit. This is to request all the Trustees, Local-preachers, Stewards and Leaders in this Circuit to assemble in the Chapel at Luddenden Foot on Friday next February 26th 1836 at three o'clock in the afternoon in order that I may state to them the manner in which I was left without [a] Society Ticket on Sunday the 14th Inst. by Mr. Armitage the second travelling preacher and also in order that I may lay before them a letter which I

---

[1] Two William Thompsons each subscribed for 100 £1 shares in the W.M.A. chapel built at Hebden Bridge in 1839; the one here mentioned was probably William Thompson of Luddenden Foot, corn dealer, a trustee of the Salem Wesleyan chapel.

received on the 19th Inst. from the same person, by authority *as he writes* of the Superintendent Mr. B[umstea]d, forbidding me to preach in any Wesleyan Chapel under existing circumstances and also in order that I may ascertain whether my Brother officers approve of this *modern summary way* of proceeding and also in order to consult my Brethren in the fear of God as to the subsequent measures which ought to be adopted. I earnestly desire *all officers* to attend. Wm. Thompson Senr., Trustee of 7 chapels, Local Preacher 20 years, Circuit Steward 16 years, Leader upwards of 20 years. Luddenden Foot, Todmorden Circuit, Halifax District, 20th of February 1836. You'll *just* here notice there is only the prohibition of my letter, *under the direction of my Superintendent*, not a word about the antidote, i.e. The offer of a Leaders' Meeting to reconsider the case when and where the whole matter might have been settled amicably if there had been the disposition on the part of Mr. Thompson *to do so*, but it is well known that he has for years been an enemy to Wesleyan Methodism. I could say very much on this subject was it needful but enough at present. Well then no sooner was the above bill posted up and in circulation than Mr. B. and my other colleague Mr. W. set off to Halifax, had an interview with the Chairman. They consult together, *without even saying a word to me upon the subject*, and conclude that it would be best to call upon Mr. Thompson at his own house on their return from Halifax, and inform him that I had exceeded the bounds of my authority, and that he might meet his class and preach as us[u]al, and that a time would be appointed to give him his class tickets. *Accordingly that has been done.* You'll now perceive something of the painful situation in which I was placed, and how the report run through the circuit and *country*, and yet not a single *honest* Methodist said I had done wrong, but perfectly right and that he ought to have been put out of society years ago. Dear Fathers and Brethren you may rest assured that I felt very uncomfortably, *at that time*, and especially in reference to my colleagues when I called to mind how they praised me as soon as I had done the deed, but no sooner was there the appearance of discontent in the disaffected, *only* then I'm left to struggle with the difficulty *single-handed*. I think myself in this affair most shamefully treated – but further when that illegal and *in my judgment at least* anti-methodistical meeting was announced by a *playcard* as stated above – I spoke to Mr. B. and said do not you intend to prohibit that Meeting and state the consequences of holding it. He said no, the Chairman thought it better to say nothing about it, but let it go on. I confess I felt very queer on this subject, and therefore thought I would drop a line to the Chairman. I did so – and the following is a copy. Mr. Chairman, Dear Sir, I am somewhat surprised that you should advise Mr. Bumstead to let the illegal meeting proceed without any prohibition or *injunction*. Supposing I have done wrong *which I do not as yet admit*, is that any rule why another should so *seriously* trespass. I do think, *though in submission to your superior judgment*, that the above case is similar to that at Rochdale though through God on a much smaller scale and should be met as promptly *forthwith*. I simply give these hints that I may stand clear of any blame in this matter, *at least* though the Chapel is not what is called settled *properly*, yet it is settled as well as it could be under existing circumstances, and bears the Wesleyan name on a stone in front, and would in my *humble* opinion, be given to us in any Court of *Justice* in England. I do therefore think that you as Chairman of this District or Mr. B. as the Superintendent of this Circuit, should forbid such an anti-methodistical meeting being held there on the 20th Inst. . . . With reference to withholding a ticket from Mr. Thompson, I could not do otherwise *with my views*, nor am I yet convinced that I have done wrong. If even I had had the same impression as my Brethren seem to have had at the social meeting held in Halifax, *especially* when I am told that our head is a monster and Mr. Wesley was pope and the Conferences are Popes and that we have taken all the power out of the hands both of Leaders' Meetings and every other meeting and that we can and will do as we please and there is no justice can be had off us etc. etc. After such statements of these before *30 or 40* persons and numerous insults in reference to preachers, Districts and Conference etc. etc. I could not the⟨n⟩ nor can I ⟨no⟩w give tickets to such individuals unless some one o⟨r other?⟩ will deli⟨ver m⟩e from all responsibility. If I am wrong I trust the ⟨Lord⟩ will soon open my eyes that I may not repeat these errors. I hope y⟨ou will⟩ not think any worse of me for thus addressing you. I could not be easy ⟨to⟩ let that illegal meeting pas[s] *on and through*, without thus giving my humble opinion on the subject. Hoping to see you soon, when I can more fully open my mind upon passing occurrences. I subscribe myself yours most truly and affectionately. J. Armitage. N.B. I cannot yet think that you and the brethren assembled at Halifax had any design in acting in opposition either to the letter or spirit of the last minutes of Conference, *see pages 160 etc. etc.* Notwithstanding the illegal meeting went on *without let or hindrance*. Since that time Mr. Thompson has had his ticket *given him*, and ordered to go on meeting his class, preaching etc. etc. Even assisting Dr. Warren and a Mr. Mackey of Ireland *but now of Stockport* in opening places of worship etc. etc. *in this circuit*, and now of course Mr. Thompson is expelled which in my opinion, *at least* – had the plan been followed up which I *firmly believe* was begun right, when I simply suspended him by withholding his ticket – had we proceeded *evenly*, *kindly*, and affectionately and, *at the same time* firmly, two-thirds of the present evil would have been prevented *i.e.* my humble opinion, but meeting Mr. Thompson's class and giving him authority to preach etc. *as usual*, strengthened his hands and the cause of Warrenism *abundantly*, that is my decided conviction. I may be very wrong but I think not – and thus for what I did in asking Thompson whether he was satisfied with Methodism as it now is, and whether he was in any way connected with the Association. You'll of course have a notice when the Halifax District minutes are read, you'll just observe I bring no formal charge against any of the Brethren. *Only* I thought it necessary to put into your hands the simple *ungarbled* state of the case. And *now* if my Fathers and Brethren think I have done wrong, I hope they will deal with me according to the merit or *demerit* of my case. I leave myself *with all confidence* in your hands. In the meantime as I have already told the chairman, I consider myself ill used in the whole affair, and as I informed the District Meeting I would not yield to any in attachment to Wesleyan Methodism. I have never sold it yet, *not even for my own flesh*, indeed I never had an equivalent offered for it *in my humble opinion* and therefore it is not likely that I should sell it. And yet I never did hold the rules in one hand and an iron rod in the other, except in extreme cases. 'God is love'. Yes and truth too . . .

110 From Elijah Morgan[1] *Stourbridge, July 18, 1836*

. . . I found this circuit so injured, chiefly by very disaffected Local Preachers who seem to have thought they could do better *without* Travelling Preachers, and who had so prejudiced Trustees, Leaders, Members, seat holders and hearers against us all, that at one time I thought there would be no division but that all with few exceptions would depart from us.[2] This was effected by encouraging the people to read the scandal published in the *Advocate, Lanthorne, Catechisms*[3] etc.; by calling public meetings to make speeches against the Conference and its preachers when all the vile slanders in circulation was retailed with additions; by 'prating against us with malicious words,' in the houses of our people very extensively all over the circuit; and even by *preaching* against us in our own Chapels, taking texts they could make to bear upon us. The following may serve as a specimen and which was preached

---

[1] Elijah Morgan, superintendent, Stourbridge circuit, 1835–36.

[2] The Stourbridge seceders, along with those of Dudley, joined the Methodist New Connexion, and became noteworthy for their evangelism and prosperity.

[3] I.e. the *Christian Advocate, Watchman's Lantern* (cf. n. 2 p. 118 *supra*) and *A catechism for Wesleyan Methodists . . . in three parts* (Liverpool, 1834).

from in more than one of our Chapels, Jer. 10 [v.]21: 'The pastors are become brutish, and have not sought the Lord; therefore they shall not prosper and all their flocks shall be scattered.' This was said to describe the character of our preachers, and to foretell the fate of our people. We are rid of these troublers of Israel and I hope the Circuit will come round in a year or two more. We have always had the undisturbed possession of Brierley Hill and Cradley Chapels. The Stourbridge Chapel we wholly possess and are settling it on new Trustees. Mount Pleasant Chapel is to be settled immediately. There we have only possession when the Travelling Preacher can go and then occasionally very unquiet possession. At Brettell Lane we continued longer than there was any hope of good. At Lye Waste we continued till our friends thought their own lives as well as ours in such danger they could not consent to go any longer. I hope the preachers will leave both these in the hands of the Trustees who would not allow us quietly to possess them any longer, they are deeply in debt. I have done my best in the whole affair. I hope no objection will be made to my leaving this circuit, my health has suffered, my spirits greatly sunk and my character blasted far and near; we are called, thieves, robbers, Conference-Devils and that which is worse than all others in the ears of the people, *tories*. I hope some quiet Circuit will be found for me where I may be respected and do good, for though I leave at the end of one year, yet I have had *five triennial* stations out of the *last seven*. If you will say a word for me it will do me great service, and lay under great obligation . . . [Yours &c]

---

111   From George Taylor[1]   *Helston, July 21, 1836*

. . . The necessity of purging these societies from the horrid leaven of faction has long been seen by all who have known anything upon the subject. The painful task which it has fallen to my lot to perform, I commenced by attempting to bring into our Leaders' Meeting, stewards upon whom I could depend. Six persons were nominated in January last, out of whom the leaders were at liberty to choose two, but they rejected the whole and insisted on the re-election of those [that] had served. They argued, 'the office could not be vacant', and that 'no Leader could be removed etc. but in conjunction with a Leaders' Meeting'. I took my stand on 'the office ceases at the end of the year'. We were thus completely at issue. They would not move, and I *could*

---

[1] George Taylor (1789–1868), superintendent, Helston circuit, 1835–37. For his clash with the Leaders' Meeting, referred to below, see M.C.A. MSS. G. Taylor to Jabez Bunting, January 28, 1836.

not, and do my duty. Every Leaders' Meeting after this till the separation, was a scene of debate. I thought the affair could not be settled without a special district meeting, but both the Chairman and the President thought I must act alone in the business. Painful as it has been I have done so. The March Quarterly Meeting came before I was able to procure new stewards. The Leaders would pay their money to none but the old one, him they sent to the Q.M. charged 'not to pay the money unless he were recognized as steward'. As this could not be done he took the money away again. I took a bill on the Helston Society for the amount of their quarter's payment, and called on the Leaders for the money. Four of them refused to advance it. These I cited to attend a Leaders' Meeting to answer to complaints I had to prefer. When assembled they refused to take their trial, 1st because [they] were of the number of 16 Local Preachers who had just before signed a document agreeing to resign their plans if any one of them should be called to take his trial for any offence before a Leaders' Meeting till they should be first tried at a Local Preachers' meeting. And 2nd. because I would not consent that 'the whole question of fact and damages should go to the jury'. The discipline of the connexion being thus put I thought in abeyance, I at once suspended three of them from membership till they would agree to certain terms proposed to them, binding them in future to refrain from agitation. The others I expelled according to the rules of the last Conference.

At this the faction took offence as I expected. The 16 Locals resigned. Public meetings have been held in many places to 'explain' the conduct of the rads., and to abuse me and the Conference too, and make as wide a separation as possible. In this they have succeeded too well, though not to the full extent of their expectations. Instead of taking away half our members, or breaking up the whole circuit as they seemed to think they should do, only a little more than 200 have gone away; from 60 or [to?] 80 more have been lost in the struggle and now meet nowhere in religious society. The 200 include all, or nearly so, who are disaffected, but by far the greater part are persons led away by the employment of undue influence, or gross misrepresentation. It is said many more will leave if this Conference do not make an alteration in the 'rules'! But this remains to be proved. The things which most annoy us now are the attempts to take away our chapels. The 'reformers' have already got three places of worship altogether, and into four more they force their way for the purpose of holding their religious meetings. The circumstances of these I have stated in a letter to Mr. Davis[1] and should be

[1] John Davis, superintendent, Penzance circuit, 1834–37. Chairman of Cornwall District, 1832–37.

glad of some advice. The local brethren in neighbouring circuits have been exceedingly kind in coming to our help, or our places could not have been supplied. They, some of them, travel 40 miles on a Sabbath to assist us. We can not expect this will last through the winter and on this account we hope to be favoured with a single man as our third preacher. Upon this the Stewards will write. *Your* help in our behalf in this affair would be esteemed a great favour . . .

112   From John Beecham   *London, July 21, 1836*

. . . I am very glad that I sent for Crofts,[1] as I have got so much information from him as to the Governor's scheme of education in the Bahamas, and also respecting the Bill which has passed the Bahama Legislature for confirming all past missionary marriages.[2] This last measure furnishes a triumphant proof of the practicability of what we ask for, and will serve as a precedent to guide the other legislatures, under the direction of the Colonial Secretary in settling the question of past marriages throughout the West India colonies. Regarding the Bahama school system which the Governor has originated, I can only now say, that it is intended to combine the energies and resources of all parties, in order to provide a common form of education for all the poorer classes, whites as well as blacks, in the Colony; and that the Governor is expecting that we shall place the two schools we have engaged to establish under the management and control of the Education Committee. On looking at the whole case, I have judged it proper to communicate again with Sir George Grey[3] upon the subject, and have had an interview with him today. Things have thus got into a fair way for settlement, and I will tell you the particulars, when I shall have the pleasure of seeing you. I am in hopes that I have nearly got through with my evidence before the Apprenticeship Committee. I have taken up the marriage question, the encroachment made upon the religious privileges of the negroes by the distribution of their hours of labour, and the two matters mentioned by Britten[4] to which you referred me in his letter, viz. the state of young children under 6 years of age, and the clause in the Nevis Act which puts it into the power of an unfeeling master to withhold the supply of food from the apprentice and furnish

---

[1] John Crofts (1798–1857), preacher serving in the West Indies, 1820–35, when he returned home, and was stationed by the ensuing Conference at Deptford, 1836–39.
[2] Cf. n. 3 p. 52 *supra*.
[3] Sir George Grey (1799–1882), undersecretary for colonies 1834 and 1835–39.
[4] Henry B. Britten (1804–1887), preacher serving in the West Indies, 1826–36.

M

him with land to cultivate, leaving him and his children meanwhile to
starve. I had a long chat with your friend Lord Sandon, who is anxious
that we should send a missionary, if we have one, from *Jamaica* (to
which colony they are *now* confining themselves) for examination. We
have none save Burrows,[1] and I fear he is not the man; however, I took
a frank from his Lordship for him, and have written him a long letter
for the purpose of sounding him, and when I get to Birmingham I will
consult you as to whether we should trust him or not. I shall be in
attendance again tomorrow at the Committee,[2] but am inclined to
think that I shall not have much more trouble . . .

113   From Thomas Dunn[3]   *n. pl., July 29, 1836*

I shall be obliged for your permission to bring the case of *Royton* Chapel
in the Oldham Circuit before the Chapel Committee. On account of the
infidelity and vile politics of the place we have not been able to have
a congregation there since the agitation caused by J. R. Stephens.

114   From William Horton[4]   *Louth, July 29, 1836*

In support of the application from the Louth Circuit for the appointment of a fourth Preacher,[5] I beg respectfully to submit to your consideration and, if you think it needful, to that of the Conference, the
following statement:–

    1. The Louth circuit, which extends about 22 miles from east to west,
and 12 from north to south, comprises 49 country places in all of which
we have societies, as our schedule now before the Conference will shew.
Of these there are 9 villages, containing 115 members, which are not
visited at all by the itinerant preachers, the tickets being sent by the
local brethren;[6] except in one case, in which the members come to an

---

[1] Thomas Burrows (1807–84), served in various West Indian stations, 1831–36 and 1838–47;
preacher, York circuit, 1836–37.

[2] The Select Committee on the working of the apprenticeship system for which Buxton had
moved on March 22, 1836, and which sat April 19 to August 5, 1836. For its report, P.P.
H.C. 1836 XV.

[3] Thomas Dunn (1793–1873), superintendent, Oldham circuit, 1835–38. Studied under
Dr. Chalmers while stationed at Edinburgh, 1831–33.

[4] William Horton (1800–67), superintendent, Louth circuit, 1834–37. This letter shows
how, in many scattered rural areas, there was little substance in the preachers' claims to
authority based on pastoral oversight.

[5] A fourth appointment was made by the 1836 Conference then sitting at Birmingham.

[6] I.e. Local Preachers.

adjoining village to receive their tickets. Thus it has not been found practicable, either by my predecessors or myself, to extend to these 9 places our personal ministry, or to our Societies therein any thing more than an indirect and defective pastoral influence.

2. At 6 other places, where we have 92 members, we are able to preach only once a quarter, that is, when we give tickets.

3. Five of our principal places, containing 264 members, and a population of 2289, in all of which we have good chapels, are destitute of week-night preaching. We visit them only on the Sabbath Day, and at three of these five places we have only just sufficient time for the performance of our pulpit duties. In all these places scarcely any opportunity is afforded for pastoral attention and oversight.

4. On the other hand, six other places of considerable methodistical importance, containing 269 members, and 2100 inhabitants, have hitherto had no share of our Sabbath labours. In several of these places some of our most respectable and affluent friends reside; and, in all, our cause is likely to be greatly benefited by the occasional services of an itinerant preacher on the Sabbath Day.

5. In the town of Louth we have 700 persons in Church fellowship with us, including 55 on trial. Nearly two years ago my colleagues and myself considered it highly desirable to adopt a regular system of household visitation. We obtained from every Leader a list of the members under his care; we divided the town into 14 districts, each comprising about 20 families, and our rule was to take one of these districts every week. So incessant however are the other occupations of this circuit, and so frequently has the day appointed for these pastoral visits been necessarily taken for other purposes, especially for village missionary meetings, of which we hold 16 in the year, and without aid from other circuits, that, owing to these and other hindrances, our plan of household visitation, though never laid aside, has been but imperfectly prosecuted.

Now, Sir, the appointment of a fourth Preacher to this Circuit will enable us to supply all these defects in our ministerial and pastoral duties. We shall be able at once to abolish the practice of giving tickets by Local Preachers. The places referred to in paragraph No. 1 will receive a sermon from an itinerant preacher, at least once a quarter, and every ticket and note of admittance will be delivered by ourselves personally. Additional preaching will be given to the places alluded to in paragraphs No. 2, 3 and 4, so as to meet their several exigencies; and our plan of pastoral visitation, as to our large and flourishing Society at Louth, will be more regularly and efficiently attended to. To this I may add, as a collateral benefit of no mean importance, that the brethren would have some valuable time for reading and study, of which at present we are almost wholly deprived.

On other particulars bearing upon the subject I need not dwell, you being already in possession of them; such as the great enlargement of the work of God which has taken place during the last two years, our numbers having risen during that period from 1677 to 2161, besides 172 on trial:– the proportionate augmentation of our circuit income, which is more than adequate to meet the expense of a fourth preacher, and fully warrants the pledge which the circuit stewards have given to provide for a fourth family at the expiration of four years:– and the unsound and somewhat precarious state of health, to which I regret to say one of my colleagues Mr. Seth Dixon[1] has for some time been reduced. These are points which will doubtless have their proper influence upon the judgment of the Conference.

In conclusion I feel bound to say that I should not have deemed it requisite to trouble you with this communication, but for the intimation which has reached us that, from an inadequate supply of candidates for our regular work, the Conference will be compelled to refuse some of the numerous applications for additional men. This information has excited much uneasiness among our friends here. They are perfectly unanimous in their views as to the necessity of a fourth preacher; and have never entertained a doubt as to the readiness of Conference to accede to their request. To be disappointed now would not only be painful, but positively injurious. It would be thought hardly right if, while this circuit is contributing liberally to the Contingent Fund[2] (£63 is the sum this year) to extend the benefits of our Wesleyan ministry and ordinances to other parts of the kingdom, its own wants could not be adequately supplied.

Will you allow me to add, as to the selection of a suitable young man, that his pulpit qualifications should be of a superior order, as in Louth he will have to address a congregation, which, in point of number, intelligence and respectability, is certainly not exceeded, and perhaps hardly equalled by any in the County . . .

[1] Seth Dixon (1803–85), preacher, Louth circuit, 1834–37.

[2] The Contingent Fund was originally supported by a subscription made in all the classes throughout the connexion, first appointed by Conference in 1756, and was reinforced by a July collection made in congregations, appointed in 1815, and by profits from the Book Room. The fund claimed to be the biggest of all village preaching associations, but had always had other objects, including the liquidation of chapel debts, the payment of preachers' deficiencies in poor circuits, and securing protection from mob-violence. It thus served as a general financial reserve for connexional purposes.

115 From Benjamin Kirk[1]   *Stalybridge, August 4, 1836*

... I have now resided in Stalybridge about two years. At the time I came Methodism was at a low ebb; the class I joined had only three members, [it has] now twenty four, and with the blessing of God we are still prospering. [At] the last Conference held in Sheffield I strongly urged the necessity of having three preachers. We have had three and with grant of Conference both our finances and numbers have increased ... We are beset by (I will not say enemies) but by Stevenites,[2] New Connection and a host of unitarians. The population of Ashton, Duckinfield and Stalybridge contained in 1821 32,672, in 1831 51,718, being an increase of 19,046. Since then the increase has been in a greater proportion. This circuit contains a population of from 80,000 to 100,000. You will see from this the necessity of having very active zealous good preachers, otherwise we shall sink again and the next fall will be worse than the first. The bulk of the members are poor as respects this world's goods but rich in faith and very zealous for the cause of Christ ...

116 From Barnard Slater[3]   *Macclesfield, September 9, 1836*

Yourself, and Messrs. Entwisle, Treffry, and [Jacob] Stanley, were all acquainted with the foolish, not to say wicked, report in reference to Brother G. H. Rowe,[4] which was sent to our late Conference; and it is but an act of sheer justice to Brother Rowe that you should know the result of our examination of that report; and it is to the honour of Mr. Thorley,[5] our excellent Circuit Steward, that he heartily joins me in this communication, and on reading to him approves of every sentence.

On my return from Birmingham with all convenient speed I convened the parties, heard the accusers of Mr. R. on the subject – which even in itself amounted to but little. But happily for Bro. Rowe, two of our highly respectable leaders walked with him after the sacrament to

[1] Benjamin Kirk, proprietor of Benjamin Kirk & Sons, cotton-spinners, Water Street Mills, Stalybridge. The advice in this letter was repeated in 1838 (M.C.A. MSS. B. Kirk to Jabez Bunting, July 16, 1838) with the additional comment: 'If we had a better house and a more wealthy Society perhaps we should fare better as to preachers, but having 120,000 souls and many perishing for want of instruction, I feel it of more importance than all the riches in the world'.

[2] Followers of Joseph Rayner Stephens.

[3] Barnard Slater, superintendent, Macclesfield circuit, 1835–38.

[4] George Hambly Rowe (1786–1850), preacher, Macclesfield circuit, 1834–36.

[5] Joshua Thorley (d. 1844, aet. 60), converted by Lorenzo Dow, 1804; played a leading part in establishing Wesleyan Sunday schools and the Centenary School in Macclesfield. For 23 years secretary of Macclesfield Dispensary. A class-leader, circuit steward and trustee.

the very door of the gentleman's house where, on his entering, it was said he was drunk; and those Leaders say not only that his walk and his conversation discovered no such thing, but that they named the *topic* of his conversation, which was on a subject of deep interest, and highly appropriate after the solemn ordinance of the Lord's Supper.

The party [was] thus confronted; and on hearing Mr. Rowe solemnly declare that, being unwell during the whole day, he had not tasted fermented liquor the whole day, and that after preaching he took one glass of wine, it was finally concluded that the explanation was satisfactory, and the parties agreed that no more should be said on the subject.

There is a good deal of indignation in the town at the conduct of the teetotal man who originated [the] affair; I believe it will not in the least degree injure Mr. Rowe's usefulness here.

I find however – but this will give *you* no surprise – that the *Kilhamites*, several of whom are *Teetotallers*, are making the best of it for their cause here. Thank God, my dear Doctor, that Wesleyanism does not need to have recourse to such mean and miserable shifts to support its lofty and pure interests. May God make us more and more faithful in the discharge of all its important duties! . . .

117   To James Blackett[1]   *London, September 14, 1836*

I inclose at your request the letter sent to the Conference from Bramley. But I must beg you not to let it go out of your hands or Mr. Newton's,[2] and to return it to me by the first private conveyance that may offer itself. You are of course aware that it is in its very form irregular, because according to the *very Rules of 1797* themselves, if the subscribers wished to protest against the resolutions of 1835[3] being *immediately* binding in their Circuits, the time for that protest was the *September* Quarterly Meeting, not that in *June*. *Not* being suspended in September, they instantly became binding on that Circuit; though there might have been, if regularly desired, a Special Circuit Meeting in July to ask for their modification or repeal by the Conference of 1836. It is therefore in courtesy and kindness, not as a matter of right, that a deputation has been appointed to meet them. I wish that a better spirit and sounder views may prevail among them. As the subscribers are so *many*, is it not

[1] James Blackett (1778–1848), superintendent, Leeds (Bramley) circuit, 1835–37.

[2] Robert Newton, preacher, Leeds (East) circuit, 1835–38. Chairman of Leeds District, 1835–41.

[3] I.e. the new constitutional regulations.

desirable that Mr. Newton and yourself should take some other preachers and friends with you from Leeds, at least as witnesses of what may pass on the occasion?

I rejoice to hear that amidst all this democratic folly you see some tokens of a revival of God's great work in your Circuit.[1] . . .

118   From James Blackett   *Bramley, near Leeds, September 21, 1836*

The Deputation appointed by the Conference viz. the Rev. Messrs. Robt. Newton, Vevers, J. Anderson Senr., Galland and Blackett met the subscribers of the irregular document addressed to you from Bramley at the last Conference.[2] The whole of them were present with the exception of two or three individuals. They were unwilling to say anything until the document were read, and then they found they had been wrong in their assertion, that the connexion was in that dissatisfied state which their memorial intimated. Then the great point was entered upon, which was called by one of the party 'The cardinal point', namely, their deprivation of the high office of *judges* in a *Leaders' Meeting*. We contended they never had it by law, nor by general usage. They might be confident that the latter might have been the case in a few instances in their own circuit; and there might have been some few Superintendents in other places that might have said improperly in a Leaders' Meeting, after that Meeting had pronounced the accused person guilty, 'Well Brethren what shall we do with him', and that was more out of courtesy to the meeting than of considering that they had a right to pronounce the sentence, or fix the measure of punishment. We then shewed that Mr. Wesley had the sole power of expelling members in his hands during his

---

[1] The 'democratic folly' of the Bramley circuit, already revealed in an attempt to establish voting by ballot at the Quarterly Meeting (M.C.A. MSS. W. Vevers to Jabez Bunting, January 2, 1836), inflamed it was alleged by the radical agitations locally of Joseph Barker in the Methodist New Connexion, was violently exemplified in the dreadful breakup of the circuit in the Wesleyan Reform secessions in 1850 (cf. no. 333 *infra*); in 1859 the preacher reported continued 'antagonism . . . from a low radical democratic feeling of great heatedness which shows itself alike about political and religious matters, and is especially strong about the doctrine of a "hired ministry"'. M.C.A. MSS. W. Binning to J. Beecham, November 16, 1850: Henry Beeson to C. Prest, December 5, 1859.

[2] Cf. M.C.A. MSS. W. Vevers to Jabez Bunting, September 27, 1836: 'I presume you have been informed by Mr. Blackett of the result of our interview with the Memorialists at Bramley. I think a little more frankness, and readiness to offer explanations, on the part of Mr. B. would have in some degree prevented the misunderstanding which has arisen. They displayed great ignorance, but little malignity; and though there are still the principles of radicalism among them, yet I think our object was in a very great degree accomplished. Mr. B. attaches great importance to trifles'. Cf. no. 142 *infra*.

life, and so had all the Superintendent Preachers until 1799, and then, a power was given to the Leaders' Meeting, as a check upon the Superintendent in the receiving members into society and expelling them. But the power which the Leaders' Meeting received was limited only, to put a negative upon any person being received into society after having been on trial and the power of acting as a jury to give their verdict, guilty or not guilty. Then the power remaining was in the hands of the Superintendent to fix the measure of punishment, and pronounce the sentence. But if the latter part of the power referred to, viz. that in the Superintendent's hands were given up to the Leaders' Meeting, then that meeting would have all power, and the minister of Christ would have no power to comply with the apostolic injunction, 'Put away that wicked person'; nor could he act as the angel of the Church of Christ.

They said after some considerable retiring small shot, that the Rules were now the Rules of the Connexion (referring to the new regulations of 1835) and therefore, they supposed they must remain, and I think intimated as much as that they would withdraw their opposition. This was not said in so many words; but the intimation given amounted to that. I then as Superintendent of the Circuit rose up and stated to them that I had treated them with all kindness, although they had differed from me in opinion, and I besought them to let us unite together in mutual prayer to God, and go forward with one combined effort to promote the salvation of souls. They then disclaimed a disposition to agitate. And I must say, I have had my mind relieved from a heavy pressure, which a few months ago had nearly taken my life. About 2 months before the last Conference I had inflamation of the lungs etc. and I was for several days on the verge of eternity. My purpose now is to treat the parties as if they had never offended, and do all the good I can both to their bodies and souls, for time and eternity. We prayed, and shook hands heartily with each other and separated. . . .

119   From James C. Hindson[1]

Houghton-le-Spring,
September 15, 1836

I am under the necessity of laying before you the case of two of our chapels in this newly formed circuit. The chapels in question are situated at New Lambton and Philadelphia, two somewhat populous villages, the one about two, the other three miles from this place.

These chapels were built on Lord Durham's property, by his per-

---

[1] James C. Hindson (1800–63), superintendent, Houghton-le-Spring Circuit (which had been carved from the Sunderland circuit at the Conference of 1836), 1836–38.

mission, for the benefit of his Lordship's workmen, by the instrumentality of the Wesleyan Methodists. Towards their erection Lord D. contributed, I believe, timber, stone and tiles; and they cost from £70 to £100 each besides, which was obtained by subscriptions among our people.

Nearly one-half of our Societies in both these places left us during the the recent secession in the Sunderland circuit; and these parties have succeeded (chiefly I believe by means of Mr. Ward of Durham,[1] who is his Lordship's attorney) in obtaining the consent of Mr. Morton, Lord Durham's agent, to their occupying their chapels once at least every Sabbath. At my entrance on this circuit, I paid no attention to the attempts made to obtain Mr. M's consent, any farther than to retain the exclusive occupancy of the chapels, which I have been enabled to do to this day. When I found that they were likely to succeed, I addressed to Mr. Morton the following letter:–

'Houghton-le-Spring, September 9th, 1836

Sir,

I have learned from various quarters that attempts have been made to obtain your consent to the divers⟨ion or⟩ partial diversion of the Methodist chapels at New ⟨Lambton⟩ and Philadelphia, from the uses for which they were origina⟨lly⟩ erected, and to which they have been sacredly devoted to the present time.

I beg most respectfully to say that, as the Representative of the Wesleyan Conference and Connexion in this circuit, it is my *imperative duty* to retain and maintain the exclusive occupancy of all our chapels within the precincts of the circuit.

The two chapels in question, are, as I understand, Wesleyan chapels, held of my Lord Durham, not by any legal instrument, but, by what we all feel to be equally secure, his Lordship's word and honour.

I feel that it would be improper for me at present to enter into a detail of the facts and circumstances connected with the secession of a comparatively small portion of our body in this neighbourhood from the parent community, resting assured that you will receive *ex parte* statements with caution, as we all know that such statements are not infrequently incorrect; and especially when I remember that they are but the charges of a factious or mistaken *few* against a long-established and

---

[1] John Ward, d. c. 1849, prominent Durham Methodist, solicitor and politician. He had been election agent to Michael Angelo Taylor, M.P. for Durham City, 1800–02, and had led local resistance to Lord Sidmouth's bill against itinerant preaching (Ward, *Religion and Society* pp. 52, 58). Wrote a MS. tract on the Sonship of Christ (M.C.A. MSS. B. Slater to Jabez Bunting, February 6, 1828), and, falling out with the Wesleyans, joined the Methodist New Connexion. Cf. *Early Correspondence* pp. 174–5.

well-tried christian community – a community of loyal, peaceable, industrious, and I may be allowed to add, respectable people.

Should you, however, desire any such explanations, they shall be most cheerfully given, either by written communication or personal interview as you may wish.

I am extremely sorry to have to trouble you with this communication, but feel it my duty to make the above statement and beg to subscribe myself,

Your most obedient servant,
James C. Hindson, Wesleyan Minister.'

H. Morton Esq.

⟨The morni⟩ng after I sent the above letter, I learned that Mr. Morton ⟨had⟩ given his consent that the Seceders should worship in our chapels and had ordered our Chapel Steward to arrange with them before next Sunday what part of the day they should have. I delayed till today, expecting a reply to my communication, but received none; and this morning, I thought it my duty to wait on Mr. M., supposing my letter might have miscarried. Mr. Beckwith, Supernumerary,[1] accompanied me. We were received courteously; and Mr. M. intended to reply to my letter today. He says he does not wish to interfere in our matters; and yet he persists in granting them the chapels a part of the Sabbath. To that arrangement, I replied, I could not consent; and that there was only one course left me to pursue, and that was, to lay the whole case before the President of our Conference, and the Committee for guarding the Privileges of our Body,[2] and handed him a copy of the minutes, requesting him to read the names of the gentlemen composing that Committee. He evidently felt himself in difficu⟨lties⟩. We had a good deal of conversation; and I said all that I p⟨ru⟩dently could. But still he was firm to his purpose; and, in the end, I requested that we might be permitted quietly to retain the use of the chapels for ten days, till I could lay the case before the persons to whom it was my duty to apply – to which he readily consented.

These are the leading circumstances of the case. There are many minuter ones which I cannot enumerate; but which have in some degree influenced my conduct. I cannot honourably retain the chapels exclusively beyond the 25th September, and if we in part give them up, I fear it will injure our cause. Our best friends deprecate this course. I

[1] James Beckwith, supernumerary, Houghton-le-Spring. D. 1852, aet. 58.
[2] A Conference standing committee, composed of preachers and leading laymen, created in 1803. Besides guarding Methodist rights to property and religious toleration, it occasionally pronounced on political issues.

have had interviews with Mr. Keeling,[1] and his views are the same as mine. I must also name that there are other *two* chapels in this circuit, held of Lord Durham in the same way and *several* in surrounding circuits; so that, if we yield, noone knows where the matter will end. Lord Durham is in Russia.[2] H. Lambton Esq. M.P. for North Durham, is his Lordship's brother. Whether an appeal to him would secure our object, I cannot tell. Or whether a communication from the Committee of Priv⟨ileges⟩ to Mr. Morton might not be of use. His address is, H. ⟨Morton⟩ Lambton offices, near Durham. We have 24 members at Lambton and 38 at Philadelphia. I am sorry to trouble *you* with this affair; but having so little time, I judged it the best step I could take . . . I fear I shall have to trouble the Committee ere long with the Shiney Row chapel case; but this must lie over for the present. I shall anxiously look for a reply. I ought to have stated that our Leaders at the above places are Lord Durham's workmen; and of course under Mr. Morton.

120   From Abel Dernaley[3]   *Appleby, September 30, 1836*

. . . Perhaps it is necessary for me first to state that a formal division has taken place. About 70 have left us, perhaps near sixty of them have united with the Association, a few have become Ranters, and I believe a few are hesitating as to what they should do. The Association party have got a preacher who I understand is come to itinerate among them. In consequence of the peculiar circumstances of the first chapel mentioned below he preached in it last Sabbath afternoon (which was his first Sabbath) although the preacher appointed was there, and the local brother took the evening. He preached in the same chapel again on Tuesday night, although they knew it was my turn to be there on the following night. The chapel in question is situated in a village called Kirby-thore 5 miles from this. In no⟨ting⟩ the pecular circumstances of the above chapel I would first obse⟨rve⟩ that it was first enlarged in the year 1828. Before its enlargement it was ⟨ ⟩ yards by eight, now it is fifteen by nine. It appears that the old chapel was settled on the Con-ference plan several years before its enlargement, the new part has not been settled. The land on which the new part stands was bought

[1] Isaac Keeling, superintendent, Sunderland circuit, 1836–39. Chairman of Newcastle District, 1834–39.

[2] John George Lambton, first earl of Durham (1792–1840), ambassador extraordinary and plenipotentiary to St. Petersburg, 1835–37.

[3] Abel Dernaley (1797–1866), superintendent, Appleby circuit, 1836–39. (In Hall's *Circuits and Ministers vide sub* Kirkby Stephen which became head of the Appleby circuit in 1877.)

prospectively (several years before the enlargement was actually proceeded with) by the late Mr. John Crosby, father to the Rev. John
Crosby[1] who died on Kendal Circuit a few years ago. Mr. James Crosby
the eldest son, who with another brother (both Leaders) has joined the
Association, states that his father paid for the land himself, and that it
was properly conveyed to him. Now in consequence of this Mr. James
Crosby says that the Chapel is his, he being the heir to his father's property. He further says that if we choose we may preach in it along with
the Association preachers (i.e.) as I understand every alternate Sabbath.
It may be proper also to state that the yard in front (which may be
3 yds wide) is claimed by Mr. Crosby. Formerly there was a parish
pinfold[2] where the yard now is. When the chapel was enlarged old Mr.
Crosby offered a corner of one of his fields to the parish in lieu of the
pinfold and it was accepted. Thus you see on what ground Mr. Crosby
now claims the Chapel Yard. As connected with this chapel we have
now seven members – have lost by the division 21 members. The
Crosbys were the persons who entertained the preachers. The chapel
has a debt upon it of 60£. Mr. James Crosby states that the seat rents
have not covered the interest for some time in consequence of which he
is about 10£ in advance. I have done all in my power to obtain a sight of
the Old Chapel Deed in order that I might give you all the information
possible, but have not succeeded. Where the deed is I have not been able
as yet to learn. Mr. Crosby says it is not in his house, that is all he will
say about it. I believe there is only one surviving Trustee, he however is
one of our *firmest* friends. Should like to know as early as possible what
we shall do with respect to preaching in the Chapel. Shall we mix for a
time with the Association men? or how shall we proceed?

The next chapel is Bolton about 4 miles from Appleby.

It appears that memorial concerning this chapel was sent to our late
Conference, the object of which was to obtain permission from the
Conference to dispose of it according to a certain plan proposed by Mr.
Dent and specified in the Memorial. I would observe that Mr. Dent
(the person immediately concerned) considers the Chapel as being little
more ⟨tha⟩n a family chapel as the village contains only a few houses
⟨and⟩ there are very few inhabitants in the vicinity. As a family they
gave 50£ towards its erection – about 50£ more were raised by donations in the circuit, and there remains on the chapel a debt of between
twenty and thirty pounds. In the Memorial I understand Mr. Dent
proposed to pay back the 50£ collected in the circuit and take the
chapel with its present incumbrance and wished to obtain the per-

---

[1] John Crosby, preacher, Kendal circuit, 1831–32. D. of typhus 1832, aet. 27.

[2] A place for confining stray or distrained cattle etc.

mission of Conference to that effect. I understand also that the Trustees desired the Conference in the same memorial to give them its advice on the subject. The answer of Conference as communicated by the Chairman of this District was as follows, being says the Chairman, an extract from the minutes of the committee who sat on the case. 'That the Trustees of Bolton Chapel in the Appleby Circuit be directed to execute their trusts, and the preachers occupy it as usual'. Since I came to the Circuit Mr. Dent and his class consisting altogether of 10 members principally his own family have left us, according it appears to their previous determination, and such is the influence which Mr. D. has in the place that although I have gone myself to preach I have not had one to hear me. [I] should like to know how to proceed in reference to this Chapel. As the Trustees have been directed to execute their trusts Mr. D. says he expects them to do so. First by giving him security for his money, and 2ndly. by paying interest for the same, and every other expense which may be incurred. Mr. D. has worship now performed in his own house. Before I dismiss this case I would remark that Mr. Dent addressed a letter to our Quarterly Meeting on Wednesday last in which among other particulars it was stated that he Mr. Dent had found out that altho' the Memorial sent by the Trustees had directed the Conference to appeal for further information to the Rev. J. Rigg[1] respecting the chapel he had not been consulted at all on the subject. And it appears from a recent communication received by Mr. Dent from his cousin Mr. Rigg that he (Mr. Rigg) had heard nothing about Bolton Chapel in the Conference. What Mr. Dent has got to say now on the subject will be seen in the following extract from his letter above mentioned. 'I think (says he) that I have good authority for saying there was no legal order from the Conference in reference to our chapel. You know to constitute any act of the Conference legal it must be the act of the majority. I say that the memorial of our Trustees was never read to, nor the judgment of Conference asked upon it, so there could be no legal order from the Conference respecting it. So much for the privilege to memorialize Conference, though they say they are ready to receive communications and attend to them from any number of Trustees or any member of *Society*. True, it is your privilege to memorialize and it is the privilege of Conference either to lay your memorials on the table or throw them under it as it thinks *proper*. In reference to this subject I speak advisedly, I have the authority of a person who I believe attended all the sittings of last Conference and unto whom special reference was made in the memorial of our Trustees and who says (i.e. Mr. Rigg) 'of your chapel I *heard nothing* in the Conference'. I

[1] John Rigg, superintendent, Birmingham (Belmont Row) circuit, 1835–38.

therefore am constrained to say that the direction of the Chairman of this District is either the order of one man or of a select few'. I have thought proper to give the above extract that you may see how Mr. Dent stands affected towards us. It is the opinion of some of our friends that as Bolton never has been nor is ever likely to be of much importance to Methodism only so far as one family is concerned, it would be well for the Conference to accede to Mr. Dent's proposal and appropriate the *refunded* sum to the case of Appleby Chapel by making it a 'Basis or set off' to a subscription among the Trustees and friends which must ere long be opened with a view to liquidate the enormous debt on that chapel which case, indeed, must next be mentioned. The case of Appleby Chapel stands thus. In connection with this chapel there are two dwelling houses one of which is inhabited by the preacher. Indeed, there is another building which was erected for a currier's shop, with a view to accommodate Mr. Broster[1] (now of Lancaster) when he retired from our itinerant work, and which was for a time occupied by him for that purpose. Now it is converted into two small cottages. On these premises there is a ponderous debt of 1150£. Very few sittings comparatively are let, and the number will now be less as several of those who have left us took sittings for themselves and families. There are since the division took place only 13 members connected with this chapel, before the separation there were 22 members. The chairman has informed me that this case must be brought before the Chapel Fund Committee. In order to gain something, a specific sum must be raised. In this I apprehend no small difficulty, as several of the Trustees are dead, and others removed to America, several are very poor, and of the others which are left who are able to do something 4 or 5 are Radicals, who say they will not give a farthing unless the whole be made personal property.

The last case is that of Murton. Three Trustees connected with this Chapel are resolved to be *out* of the Trust, otherwise they will insist on the Chapel being sold according to the provisions of the Model Deed. As this chapel is in pretty good circumstances having only 60£ upon it and paying its way, I think it will be possible to find persons to whom the Trusts may be transferred. Thus I have laid open the above cases as clearly as I could, considering the information I have been able to gain since I came on the circuit. Indeed I am sorry to trouble you with these cases but I stand in need of counsel. Any remarks you may think proper to make will be thankfully received and duly appreciated . . .

[1] Enoch Broster, became preacher 1814, retired owing to ill health, 1824.

121   To Abel Dernaley   *London, October 29, 1836* [*Copy*]

It really has not been in my power, amidst the incessant occupations of the long journey from which I returned only two days ago, to return an earlier reply to your interesting letter. Even now my answer must be brief, and I fear unsatisfactory to you. Unless I was on the spot or familiar with all local circumstances, I can form no very decided opinion on cases where the question sometimes involves points of *legal* nicety, and always the enquiry, not merely what is right and just, but what is *expedient*. It is not every legal right that it is *worth while* to defend by legal processes.

1. As to *Kirby-Thore*. It seems doubtful whether we have any legal right to the *new* part; and if so it would be vain to contest the matter. If people will foolishly build chapels on other people's land or without properly securing them to the Connexion, they must abide the consequences. But I think you should not preach in the chapel *conjointly* with the Warrenites, but seek a place elsewhere. However, the Deed if you could see it and submit it to someone who understands law, which I do not, might lead to some different conclusion.

2. *Bolton*. It is very possible that Mr. Rigg might not attend the Chapel Committee at Birmingham, nor hear the case reported to Conference. He was not always present; having many other things to mind and neither the Conference nor the Committee would wait for him, nor for anyone else. Mr. Dent's complaint on that point is all *trumpery* and founded on 'evil surmisings'. The Memorial was regularly preferred to the usual Committee *by the Conference*; they reported distinctly upon it to Conference and that *Report* was *unanimously approved* and adopted. Possibly the next Conference may think it best, as you suggest, to take Mr. Dent's offer to refund the £50 collected, but I have not authority to alter or modify the actual decision.

3. The case of *Appleby* can only be met in the way you mention, by a liberal subscription, in order to justify your asking help from the Chapel Loan Fund. Were the people *mad* when they built such a costly chapel and premises for so small a society? I should think they were.

4. *Murton*. The right way here is what you propose; i.e. to get new trustees, and get rid of the opposing ones.

For you I feel much. Your situation is perplexing; and you have my sympathy and prayers. But you are at the post of duty; and may expect divine guidance, help and comfort.

122 From Thomas Garbutt[1]   *Driffield, October 21, 1836*

During the agit[at]ions of our connexion by Dr. Warren and his friends, this circuit was exceedingly disaffected. This was altogether confined to the town, and that, to 4 or 5 individuals, but those persons had great influence in the circuit and could carry almost everything their own way. One of them was a circuit, and another, the town, steward. The late Mr. Wm. Harrison[2] was laid aside by severe affliction nearly all the year previous to my coming, and was not able to attend to the concerns of the circuit; during that time the influence of these men had greatly increased. I learned with pain soon after my arrival, that some had withdrawn their contributions from our missions, contributed to support the *Advocate*, and held correspondence with Dr. W. or some of the members of the Association, who encouraged them to agitate. At the first December Quarterly Meeting they commenced their work and proposed certain alterations in our system; those of course I opposed, and would not put any of their resolutions. The Circuit Steward was offended and tendered his resignation. This I most readily accepted and nominated a most excellent man in his place, who was chosen by the meeting. Our friends seeing the object of these men, saw that it was high time to put down the spirit of faction. At the March Quarterly Meeting resolutions were moved (which appeared in the *Watchman*) approving of Methodism as it is, their determination to support it, sympathy with and confidence in you, and Mr. R. Newton etc. The minority was only 4. They testified their confidence in and affection for me, and intreated me not to leave them at the next Conference. I promised to remain, and I am glad that I did. It was painful to be placed in such circumstances but some [one] must have done the work, and the people rejoice that it is done. We have peace in our borders and prosperity in our Zion . . .

Two of the men who have rendered us the most trouble have no office among us, but are Trustees, and they insist *as Trustees* to attend and vote at our Quarterly Meetings. I will than[k] you for your advice on this subject. Trustees were allowed to do so by my predecessor . . . [*Endorsed*] [*To Thomas Garbutt*] Answered Nov. 28. Trustees not members of Quarterly Meetings as such, by our original rule. But usage has in many places practically superseded rule.[3] If in Driffield Circuit the usage for a considerable time has been to admit Trustees, *being members* of Society, I would not advise Mr. G. to attempt an alteration, but meet annoyance with firmness and patience.

---

[1] Thomas Garbutt sen. (1784–1851), superintendent, Driffield circuit, 1835–37.

[2] William Harrison sen., superintendent, Driffield circuit, 1833–35. D. 1835, aet. 63.

[3] Cf. n. 2 p. 115 *supra*.

123 From J. Robinson[1] *Camelford, October 27, 1836*

I am sorry to say that the Wadebridge Chapel case has been pending for several months, and is still held by the Seceders. We have done all we could to obtain peaceable possession, promising 'if they would quietly retire, we would when convenient, free them from their liabilities'. You may not be aware that Rosevear,[2] Davey and Grose,[3] the framers etc. of the resolutions I shewed you when at Bodmin, are Trustees of the above Chapel, and that at their Local Preachers' Meeting, held at Grose's house, the last Monday week, the following resolution was passed, 'Not to yield up possession of the said chapel, and moreover that a subscription be entered into in order to defray any expense that should be incurred in resisting any attempt that might be made to take the chapel from them'. As a copy of the Deed, with every particular, has been sent months ago, to Mr. R. M. Reece[4] and to the late Secretary [of] the Committee of Privileges,[5] I will not any further trouble you than to say, we have preaching in our Circuit Steward's house near Wadebridge, and it is become far too small to contain the congregation, and from circumstances connected with the family we cannot be permitted to preach in the house much longer. We have now 30 members all alive to God. The interest of the chapel is decreasing – the arrears of seat rents are not regularly collected, and some have gone away to the Independent Chapel and taken sittings there, and the Radicals are sneeringly telling the public 'If the Conference could have taken the chapel they would have done so before now,['] and our own people and friends are enquiring 'When shall we have the chapel?'[6] Now my dear and honoured Sir, if anything can be done to set this matter at rest, the sooner the better. At any rate let our sound Trustees be freed from their liabilities and we will do all we can to obtain another, and a larger preaching house. As we have 'a Committee of Privileges['] our own Trustees ought

[1] John Robinson (1786–1865), superintendent, Camelford circuit, 1835–37.

[2] Thomas Pope Rosevear, a wealthy merchant of Boscastle (1781–1853), who led a Warrenite revolt in the Camelford circuit which secured the support of 51 of the 53 local preachers and about 90% of the members. Cf. no. 178 *infra*.

[3] John Davey, yeoman farmer of Trenant, Egloshayle (1792–1863), a trustee and one of the founders of the first Wadebridge Sunday school. Seconded Rosevear's reform resolution at the Camelford circuit Christmas Quarterly Meeting, 1834. William Grose, yeoman farmer of Penpont, St. Kew, local preacher and trustee. Of Quaker origin, he was one of Rosevear's principal supporters.

[4] Richard Marsden Reece Esq., of London, a member of the Committee of Privileges.

[5] William Toase (1782–1863), preacher, London (City Road) circuit, 1834–36.

[6] Rosevear's rebels retained possession of many of the chapels in the Camelford circuit, without legal title, and the tiny Wesleyan rump continued to print their names on the quarterly plan, describing them in a footnote as 'illegally withheld'. T. Shaw, *A history of Cornish Methodism* (Truro, 1967) p. 83.

to have 'fair play'. I know you will pardon my *Lancashire* expressions and rejoice with me when I tell you that I have gone over the ground which Warren and his party went over before, and have realised about 250£ towards building a chapel 40 feet long and 30 broad at Boscastle, where *Rosevear* lives, and we calculate of having only about 50£ debt upon it. To God be all the praise, Amen. If our Wadebridge chapel case be clear, my opinion is that if notices were served the Radicals, with all their ⟨fanaticism⟩, love money too well to resist. The above case has been so long before the public, that if something *decisive* were done, many of the friends in Cornwall would be thankful. By this day's post I have written the Rev. A. E. Farrow[1] and R. M. Reece Esqr ... Hoping that the case may be speedily brought before the Committee[2] and that you may be in London at the time and begging an interest in your prayers . . . .

124   From William Jackson[3]   *Derby, November 1, 1836*

. . . We have not any outbreaking of faction in this Circuit but I am sorry to say some of our Local Preachers have manifested a very bad spirit and have threatened to send for the infamous Dr. Warren. From all I can learn they are a number of the old Faith faction[4] that were improperly brought [in] again and wish to trouble us. We shall endeavour to watch their proceeding and guard against their designs . . .

125   From John Kershaw[5]   *Lynn, November 30, 1836*

. . . In this town, we are not without a strong leaven of Warrenitism. My Colleague and myself have taken little or no notice of [it] in public: we have preserved our discipline entire, and by so doing, and God's blessing, the asperity which existed is very much softened down. Two Local Preachers and eight or ten members of Society have recently withdrawn from us very quietly. In the letter of resignation which the chief of them sent to me he says, 'Methodism is based upon a rotten foun-

---

[1] Abraham E. Farrar, preacher, London (Spitalfields) circuit, 1836–39. Secretary to Committee of Privileges, 1836.

[2] This letter is endorsed in Bunting's hand, 'Referred to the Secretary of the Committee of Privileges'.

[3] William Jackson sen., superintendent, Derby circuit, 1836–39. D. 1863, aet. 73.

[4] Cf. n. 1 p. 16 *supra*.

[5] John Kershaw, superintendent, Lynn circuit, 1835–37.

dation. The storm and tempest of public opinion will soon throw it down and great will be the fall thereof'!! The thing is not worth mentioning in itself, but as I am writing you, your official character demands of me I should make you acquainted with it. Our congregations are very good. Not a pew to be let in the chapel, and but few seats. 'Take courage, and be thankful' – may be our motto still.

126   From Joseph Sutcliffe[1]   *Bayswater, December 13, 1836*

I am happy to learn that my letter to the Earl of Dudley's Steward through the Superintendent has produced the desired effect in the restoration of the Gornal Wood chapel, a building that will contain about 480 hearers.

My letter I confess in a plain narration contained too much *egotism* how the late minister for foreign affairs[2] after the Bible Meeting held me by the sleeve in the ante-chamber while he explained his speech. In about a month I ventured to send my grammar for the good of his Lordship's children, adding that we had 39 members in society at Gornal Wood, and that Sammy's house, a poor collier where they met, would not hold 30. His Lordship at once gave us land. In my letter to the Steward adding, that the day the chapel was opened, Mr. Dalton his lordship's banker, having heard me preach that morning in Dudley chapel, sent me a bank-note £1 for the collection. The Steward felt indignant on reading this plain account, and restored the chapel. Thank God for His grace and justice too. I promised the Dudley congregation that in 2 or 3 years they would see it filled again . . .

I want to see Methodism live when I die . . .

Methodism has now to work its own way with a Socinian and a Calvinistic clergy on the one hand, who steal the rich from us; and with an overflowing swarm of ranters on the other, who gather up the poor. Our Trustees [also offend], by pewing out the chapels and leaving but a *crib* for the poor, and even the crib is in many instances occupied by classes of Sunday scholars in the morning who perfume the house of God with a school effluvia . . .

A dignitary in the church with whom I have now and then changed a letter *asks* whether in case the Methodists wish to come near the church, 'Can you offer a few suggestions on that head, of which I may be permitted to make a quiet use, according to the best of my judgment? If so, I shall be happy to avail myself of them'. He adds, and I was rather

---

[1] Joseph Sutcliffe, supernumerary, London (Great Queen St.) circuit, 1836–37.

[2] John William Ward, first earl of Dudley (1781–1833), foreign secretary, 1827–28.

surprised to find it so, that 'among ye higher clergy, so far as I can judge, there is a good feeling towards the Methodists'. . . .

127 To W. B. Stephenson[1]

London, December 24, 1836
Private and confidential [*Copy*]

. . . I shall drive up to Portland Street, whenever I come; and wish to be *incognito*, till I have seen Mrs. S. and yourself, and made arrangements for accomplishing, with the least notoriety possible, my main objects, viz. to see Mrs. ————[2] and *her children*. Do you know anything of her *plans* for the week after next? Does Father Wood[3] simply mean when he calls her *not intellectual* enough for me, that she is not literary, or much conversant with *books* of general knowledge? Or does he refer to any real deficiency in mental vigour and comprehension? I hope the former is all that he intends to convey. But tell me ⟨c⟩andidly and fearlessly, all you know on that p⟨o⟩int. Does he distinctly say that in addition to her many other eminently good qualifications, she is, though not brilliant in talent or acquirements, *judicious, sensible*, and in domestic life *companionable*. Does Mrs. S. think her, if not lively, yet *cheerful* in her general temper and manner among her intimate friends, and sufficiently *conversational* to recreate the spirits of a man often jaded and worn down by the cares and anxieties of his daily avocations? If you *can* answer by Monday night's post, so that I may get your letter here on Tuesday morning, I shall be greatly obliged; as I much wish now to bring my own mind to an *almost immediate* decision, which is for many reasons desirable. You will easily guess to what side my inclination and wishes strongly lean. Now, my good friends have another hearty laugh at my expense. I hope soon to have the pleasure of laughing with you; though truly it is no laughing matter, but it has strangely been the fashion in all ages, I believe, to treat such affairs with a smile; and you have no doubt had your share of such treatment. Long may you both live and be increasingly happy in each other, in your children and in your God . . .
P.S. As I still wish in the *present* stage of the business and especially till I know something of Mrs. M's mind to keep it perfectly private, tell me *where, when* and *how*, you think it will be most acceptable to herself to grant me the favour of an interview, if I come . . .

---

[1] William B. Stephenson, preacher, Bristol (King St.) circuit, 1834–37.

[2] Mrs. Martin (née Green), widow of an Irish Wesleyan preacher, Robert Martin, who d. 1833, aet. 51. Bunting married her in 1837, and is here seen obeying the fourth of Wesley's *Twelve rules of an helper*: 'Take no step towards marriage without solemn prayer to God, and consulting with your brethren'.

[3] Cf. n. 1 p. 37 *supra*.

128   From James Blackett   *Bramley near Leeds, January 13, 1837*

I am well aware that you were acquainted with the state of this Circuit at the last Conference, when you had received an irregular address signed by 34 persons expressly against the regulations of the previous Conference.[1] There was a deputation appointed to visit this Circuit and the result of that I stated to you in a former letter. I did then hope things would go on better, and that all our officers would fall into their ranks, and do their duty faithfully; but I am sorry to say I am much disappointed. Many of the Leaders never attend a Leaders' Meeting from Quarter to Quarter, and if anything transpires which requires me to act upon the regulations of the Conference, which were confirmed last year, it is almost impossible to act upon them, to that effect, as they ought to be. I have had three cases of moral delinquency, and after much stubbornness in many of the Leaders (for some would not give their opinion at all nor vote) they were found guilty; of course as the offences were of such a character as to merit expulsion, I delayed the judgment, until I could meet the Leaders again, which was three weeks in each case, that intervened; but when I gave judgment, most of the Leaders absented themselves, so that in the last case, which took place last Wednesday evening, there would only two Leaders stop, and one of them was going away; but I prevailed upon him to continue, until I had given judgment, and this was done even without the person who was to receive judgment being present, although I had requested her to be present. You must see from this that it requires much promptitude and firmness, as well as proper recollection to maintain discipline properly in this Circuit. I find also, the Local Preachers are all united, as one man against the Conference. Not one of them takes our Magazine, and they aim at a separate interest from that of the travelling preachers, and the Conference. I have spoken to Mr. Newton the Chairman of our District[2] on the state of parties in this circuit several times, and he has always advised me to go on quietly, hoping the parties would be better by and by. But my opinion is that many of them will never be more Methodistical as long as they live. Our last Quarterly Meeting was held Decr. 26th, and one of the Local Preachers, who takes in the misnamed *Christian Advocate*, and hands it about in the Circuit, rose up, and proposed that Mr. Radcliffe[3] should stay in this circuit a third year, but he said, 'I dont like a friend of mine to be Superintendent'. That needs no comment. However, it was proposed that he should be requested to become Superintendent next year and that Mr. Bromley and Mr.

[1] Cf. nos. 117, 118 *supra*.

[2] Robert Newton, preacher, Leeds (East) circuit, 1835–38.

[3] Charles Radcliffe, preacher, Leeds (Bramley) circuit, 1835–38. D. 1852, aet. 65.

Leroyd[1] should be invited to the Circuit. After this Mr. Radcliffe said, 'I should very much like to stay in this Circuit another year, for I have met with nothing but kindness from the people in this Circuit.' How Mr. R. can separate himself from the Conference and he who has to maintain Methodist discipline as Superintendent of the Circuit I must leave him to determine. He has heard everything against the Conference almost that could be stated, and he himself has remarked to me, that at the June Quarterly Meeting the visages of some individuals as well as their words indicated the greatest rancour and abuse possible; he even said he never witnessed anything like it. Therefore I must say, I am astonished at his speech at the last Quarterly Meeting. I could say more on this subject, but I forbear. I can say this, I have not violated one principle of Methodism, nor will I by the Grace of God although the *unkindness* with which I have met, while supporting Methodism as it is, almost cost me my life last year. If the Conference comply with the request above, I shall only as a sense of duty, express my disapprobation of it, and then leave it, having done my duty faithfully. You must be aware of the situation in which I am placed, therefore, if you will give me any advice how to act, I shall be very much obliged to you. I have steered clear of disputation. I have no quarrel with any one in the Circuit. I have had to be guarded on all points, for the Local Preacher and Leader before referred to, wanted me to decide a case of moral delinquency contrary to the regulations of the Conference. I said, '*No, I can not*'. Perhaps I take up too much of your valuable time, by this long letter; but I thought it right as President of the Conference, you should be informed how things are going on, in a Circuit which was altogether in disorder nearly two years ago, and is not in good order now. My opinion is, that a junior preacher should be appointed to superintend it next year, and he should be one, who well understands Methodism, in all its parts.[2]

129   From Joseph Wood[3]   *Truro, January 23, 1837*

I deeply feel your great kindness in favouring me with an immediate reply to my last communication and I thank you very much for your encouragement. It proved a great relief to my mind that you could approve of my measures in the case alluded to.

[1] Amos Learoyd (1795–1865), preacher, Leeds (West) circuit, 1834–37.

[2] The next superintendent (1837–40) was the veteran John Sedgwick who entered the ministry in 1808 and d. 1852, aet. 73.

[3] Joseph Wood, superintendent, Truro circuit, 1835–38. Became preacher, 1826. D. 1859.

The 'difficulty' of discontinuing the censurable practice of appointing any but ministers to hold love-feasts, will depend mainly I apprehend in the manner in which it is attempted. I should suppose it would be imprudent to endeavour to suppress the evil with *observation*. When I dropped the practice in this Circuit I said nothing to anyone of my intention. It is to be lamented that the matter could not perhaps be made the subject of free conversation even in the Conference, without danger of rendering the evil more difficult to be dealt with. I beg humbly to suggest whether in event of any occurrence rendering it desirable that you should address a circular to the preachers you might not direct our attention to this part of our duty in connexion with the observance of our rule relating to the shewing of society tickets on these occasions, preparatory to some more decisive measure.

In availing myself of your kind permission to state my views relating to our Sunday School regulations, I beg leave to observe that I consider it of great importance that our ministers should, as far as practicable, be connected with *the agency* of every department of the work in their circuits, that committees unconnected with agency, except in particular cases, are generally little other than honorary bodies, or merely committees of review, as the institutions they are appointed to watch over, will proceed, whether their committees meet regularly or not. The preacher who has no power beyond that of chairman of such committees is rather at a point of review than of efficiency, more in a seat of honour than of influence. Thus the parent *Missionary Committee* is great and glorious because it is connected with the agency, and the society could not proceed without it, while its affiliated branches through the connexion, are in the majority of cases feeble and inefficient, the agency lying chiefly with the secretary and the collectors. The same remarks will equally apply to many other committees that might be named. Now by the regulations of 1827 the preacher has no place in the Teachers' Meetings which, having the agency, are the most important. When the committee is called in general but few attend, but the Teachers' Meetings are generally well attended. The preacher in these would get to know, and be brought into immediate connexion with, nearly all of the most promising youth in his society, and from conversation etc. an enduring pastoral relationship might be created, that would operate favourably throughout their future life. But the school conductors, having in these meetings the chief seat, are in some cases desirous of maintaining their sway, and are therefore jealous of the least interference on the part of the preachers. While our youth trained in these nurseries come therefore into our Leaders' Meetings and trustees and Local Preachers' and Quarterly Meetings with minds often imbued with wrong principles, jealous of the pastoral authority, and trained in habits prejudicial to the harmony and prosperity of the church. I also question the propriety of vesting the sole power of appointing teachers in the school superintendent. It will not be known, in general, to the supervising bodies who have the *veto*, that such appointments have been made, and the interposal of authority at that stage of the business would probably lead to uncomfortable feelings among the parties. One chief use of the Committee I conceive to be that they may support right measures if a majority of the teachers should happen to go wrong, and, except in rare cases, they will have more influence by meeting *with* the teachers than by meeting *without* them. I would therefore submit, that every third meeting of the teachers should be called the teachers' Quarterly Meeting, or the Quarterly Meeting of the teachers and committee, that the preacher should have the same place therein as in meetings of the committee and that this meeting shall be open to the members of the Committee. That all persons taken into the school as teachers shall be first received on *trial*, and that the Leaders' Meeting shall have a right, before this Quarterly Meeting, to object to any individual so received, but if no such objection be made, this meeting shall decide as to his fitness to be employed as a Teacher. I would propose that in the Quarterly Meeting the minutes of the intervening Teachers' Meetings be read, and that no regulation be acted upon, *after* the Quarterly Meeting unless approved thereby. I would also recommend that answers be entered to the following enquiries viz.

1. Who that have been taken on trial are now proposed to be received as teachers?
2. What has been the average attendance during the Quarter?
3. What is the number now on the books?
4. How many have left the school and for what cause?
5. How many have been received?
6. What books are wanted?
7. What is the state of the Library? Are any books to be ordered?
8. What is the state of the finances?
9. Have there been any particular indications of good among the children?

This meeting should also determine upon the time of the Teachers' annual tea meeting etc. Such a meeting need not interfere with the duties of the Committee, where there is such a body, and it would in a great degree supply the defect where no Committee exists, and the whole would, I think, be of a simple and practical character that might with ease be introduced into all our schools.

The principles laid down in '27 every right mind must highly approve

of, and the regulations are drawn up with much ability. But these rules
are not likely to be brought into general use except perhaps in our
larger towns. Excellent as they are, they will be considered as requiring
too many officers and will be deemed too complex for general operation.
Nine schools in ten will proceed in their usual manner, and if the
preacher has no place in them of *right*, he cannot exert the influence
which every pastor ought to have over institutions of this kind formed in
connexion with his own church. Forgive my prolixity. The above is the
result of my little experience in these matters. I always find that when I
can lay my hand on the *great agency wheel* I have little trouble with the
other movements of the machine[1] . . .

130   From James Allen[2]   *Windsor, January 31, 1837*

. . . I need not, I am sure, remind you of the peculiar position in which
we stand in this town [Windsor] in reference to our new chapel.[3] I am
prepared to say from great and interesting circumstances which have
occurred in the progress of our undertaking, that the eyes of the Court
are very favourably turned towards us. Nearly every individual, high in
rank, in his Majesty's establishment, is a subscriber to our object; and
as he has so kindly identified himself with us in this matter, it is thought
that upon respectful notice of the opening of the chapel being forwarded
to the castle, some of those gentlemen will avail themselves of the
opportunity of attending the opening services. On the *last* week in May
the Ascot races will take place, and then such will be the *splendid* bustle
of this town and neighbourhood, that it would be folly to attempt to
open the chapel; and shortly after, the new church at Upton in this

---

[1] So explicit a formulation of what might now be described as 'managerial theology' is
exceedingly rare in the Methodism of Bunting's period (though cf. on the side of Methodist
reform, George Steward, *The principles of church government and their application to Wesleyan
Methodism* (London, 1853)) and in the 'forties the preachers are found complaining of being
involved (in Wood's language) with not only too many 'honorary bodies', but also with too
many 'great agency wheels'; the doctrine of the Pastoral Office as orthodoxly expounded
encouraged the multiplication rather than the selection of administrative claims.

[2] James Allen II, superintendent, Windsor circuit 1834–37. D. 1873, aet. 50.

[3] To be opened on May 25. Bunting declined the invitation conveyed by this letter to
preach at the opening services. When the new superintendent arrived in September he
reported gloomily: 'The new chapel presents the prospect, with our present income, of an
annual deficiency of £70. There is a mortgage of £1200 on the premises [£600 of which had
been called in for eleven months]. In addition to which we shall have to borrow or otherwise
provide about £2200 . . . I shall meet the Trustees on Friday, when the Treasurer will present
his balance-sheet, I believe to paralize the whole of them'. M.C.A. MSS. George Jackson to
Jabez Bunting, September 5, 1837.

immediate neighbourhood is to be opened. These facts are thought to prove the time fixed upon as being the most proper . . .

131 From Samuel Wilde[1]   *Carlisle, February 9, 1837*

. . . I scarcely need mention to you the peculiarity of our case. The division which took place two years ago was the worst case in the kingdom. The late trustees laboured with all their might to embarrass the concern before they would give up their trust. Having a considerable sum in hand which was due for interest, they contrived to spend nearly the whole of it in consulting lawyers, and then in order to prevent us from getting a new trust, they spread a report through the circuit, that the circumstances of the trust were exceedingly bad, and would be the ruin of any persons who consented to become trustees. Under these circumstances, with a debt of nearly £3000, and nearly twelve months' interest in arrears, we had to look out for new trustees, and yet by the kind providence of God we succeeded in obtaining a good trust in our own circuit. And I am happy to say that our income this year will exceed our expenditure, and if we have a good Anniversary we shall have an encouraging surplus . . . Our trustees deserve every possible encouragement for the manner in which they came forward to the help of the Lord . . . We have now more than three times the amount we had in Society in Carlisle when we came, and yet we have not received six back from the Warrenites. We have raised more this year for the missions than the circuit ever raised before. During the year we have built a very excellent chapel at Brampton, which is in good circumstances, so that we have cause to 'thank God and take courage'. I am fully persuaded that a visit from you would greatly advance our interest in Carlisle. We have a number of respectable Church people in Carlisle, many of whom would come to hear you preach, and help us with the collection. The most respectable people in Carlisle think better of Methodism now than before the division. The leading men of the party who left us were never much respected in Carlisle. The Warrenites are making nothing out, either in the town or country. In Carlisle they are at sixes and sevens among themselves. They have built a chapel which pleases noone. The principle of it is joint stock, the plan is amphitheatre, the roof is supported by heavy wooden pillars. the light is from the ceiling, and the whole is so low and gloomy that they themselves are sadly mortified that they should build such a chapel. It will hold near 600. They have a debt

---

[1] Samuel Wilde, superintendent, Carlisle circuit, 1835–37.

of near £2000 upon it, and the shares have long been at a large discount. The division in the Appleby Circuit has in a great measure failed. Mr. Dernaley is managing that circuit well.[1] I hope the whole District is improving. At our late Trustee Meeting a vote of thanks to the Legal Committee was unanimously passed for the great kindness manifested in the part it took in the settlement of our new Trust, and yet making no charge . . .

132   From William Constable[2]   *Norwich, February 11, 1837*

. . . It was the avowed intention of my colleague[3] to urge on a correspondence with yourself on the subjects about which he has already written so copiously. Whether he has done this I cannot tell. My views and his on 'certain' questions being so directly antipodes of each other, little is now said by either of us to the other on those subjects. So fully am I convinced of the propriety of the steps taken by the Conference and so cordial am I with the regulations etc. of that body that I can accompany no man one inch in a way of dissent, and I do think it of great importance that the Stationing Committee should know the men with whom they have to deal; otherwise they might place two men together upon the same circuit who on certain questions 'take [the] wrong side,' and then to such circuit painful indeed methodistically would be the result. A fact has recently occurred in this city confirmatory I think of such statement. A short time since some printed papers were sent me to be read in our pulpits calling a public meeting to petition the two houses of parliament for the abolition of church rates. I declined reading such papers, or permitting them to be read. They were not read. A few days after a deputation called at my house requesting my signature to the above petition. I declined giving my signature. Last Saturday papers were sent me to be laid before our three congregations on the following day, Sunday, begging that I would advocate the cause of the abolition of church rates and obtain signatures to the petition. I refused the thing *in toto*. Warmly was I taunted with 'your colleague has signed and

---

[1] See no. 119 *supra*.

[2] William Constable, superintendent, Norwich circuit, 1836–39. Became preacher, 1806, d. 1845. When his health failed in 1844, Constable wrote Bunting a brief outline of his ministry. M.C.A. MSS. W. Constable to Jabez Bunting, June 13, 1844.

[3] Thomas Rowland (1792–1858), preacher, Norwich circuit, 1836–38. He had recently sent huge and querulous letters (M.C.A. MSS. Thomas Rowland to Jabez Bunting, November 25, December 16, 1836) complaining of not being made superintendent at Norwich, denying that he was a tool of the radicals and criticising the Conference claim to appoint superintendents to circuits irrespective of the views of the members. Expelled in 1857, he entered the Wesleyan Reform ministry. Cf. p. 372 *infra*.

warmly enters into the subject.' I am really very sorry for this. The abolition of church rates is I doubt not intended to pave the way for the annihilation of the Establishment, and with such considerations I think no Methodist minister should identify himself . . .

133   From Thomas Smith[1]   *York, February 20, 1837*

Believing that you will kindly listen to anything connected with the prosperity of our connection, I venture to address a few lines to you. You no doubt are aware that Temperance Societies on the Total Abstinence plan are now rapidly progressing in this part of the country. Having joined the one in our city and consequently having become acquainted with the working of this new system, I have noticed continually some circumstances, which I think it proper to apprise you of. One is that whenever these Societies have made any progress, there has been a proportionate accession to the Church of God from the ranks of the tee-totallers. But I have also noticed with regret that in consequence of the zealous and almost general advocacy of tee-totalism by the *Ministers of the 'Wesleyan Association', they* are securing the majority of these new converts, who, along with religious instruction, are learning notions very prejudicial to our own body. I am convinced the 'Association' is thus gaining much strength, and the new converts are sincere, bold, and zealous men who bid fair to make Methodists of the right sort. I feel sorry that we who have so much more influence and such superior accommodation for converts, should lose such men, but it is quite natural for the tee-totallers to flock to those places on the Sabbath, where their advocates preach, and to those Societies who lend their chapels and school rooms. I might mention numerous instances in proof of this, but I fear to trespass on your time. One thing however I may with propriety notice. The Warrenite Minister here is a zealous teetotaller,[2] and they have just had Dr. Warren to a tea party on behalf of their Chapel. This was announced by their minister, *at the Tee-total Meeting*, and the consequence was that many of the tee-totallers were induced to hear the Doctor's advocacy of anti-Wesleyan sentiments, and are beginning to attend their chapel. The tee-totallers are increasing very fast, and I cannot doubt that very shortly considerable numbers of them will embrace some religion or other. I have therefore felt the more anxious, that *we* should 'by any means, save some of them',

[1] Thomas Smith, a bookseller's journeyman, at York.

[2] Thomas Adams Bayley (1816–1901), Wesleyan Methodist Association preacher at York, 1836–39.

and if to the *tee-totallers* we could become as tee-totallers, we should, more easily than any other Society, *gain the tee-totallers* . . .

134   From John M'Owan[1]   *Northampton, February 23, 1837*

I am sorry to inform you that some of our people here, without the knowledge and contrary to the feelings and judgment of both their preachers, have determined on getting up a petition against church rates. My reason for acquainting you is that if you think it of sufficient importance, some honourable member may be instructed to neutralize its influence when presented in Parliament, that it may not be what they wish, an example to other Societies in our Connexion.

The first information I had concerning it was from three of the party (official men, and of some respectability in the town) who called to inform me *that they had determined on the petition,* and as they were aware that some of their brethren differed from their views, they wished my advice how to express that part of it which should define their religious character. This was all on which they wished my counsel. Finding that they were not to be diverted from their purpose, and that they were strongly disposed to use language which would have involved the character of the Society, I was constrained to tell them that if they would not tell the legislature and the public that they were but a part of the Wesleyan Society in Northampton, I should deem it my duty to make this public. That I would not allow either myself or any number of the Society, however small, to be identified with conduct so opposed not only to our private judgment, but to our principles and practice as a religious body. That though they might please themselves with the thought that the petition so worded would only refer to the names affixed to it, they *must be aware* that the public would understand it as the act and deed of the whole Society. That if it were the act of the Society this would be the very expression they would employ. And that therefore they were in duty bound as honest men to use language that would not deceive. They at length gave up this point, and have expressed themselves 'A part of the Wesleyan Methodist Society and congregation in Northampton with *others*' etc.

The truth is they have made it an open and public affair. Anybody and everybody is encouraged to sign it. One notice inviting signatures to it has been exhibited in the window of a shop open for selling goods on the Lord's Day. Of course I need not say that while they have thus

[1] John M'Owan, superintendent, Northampton circuit, 1836–38.

degraded themselves as Wesleyan Methodists, the 'others' form a very considerable portion of the signatures. The Petition gives great pain to a number of our best and most intelligent members – though I fear they are a minority. And perhaps I ought to state that the feeling against the rates has been exasperated by items inserted in the accounts for washing surplices and 5/- for a lad going to a neighbouring plantation for a bough of oak to adorn the statue of King Charles on the 29th May etc. etc. . . .

135   From John Davis[1]   *Penzance, March 3, 1837*

. . . The *Watchman* if I am not very much mistaken is likely by its party politics to cause a great deal of what is unpleasant in this part of the world. Our people in these parts live too near the Bishop of Exeter,[2] and experience too much unfriendliness from his clergy to love, with such a love as the *Watchman* would have them love, the Established Church. He is greatly mistaken as to what is the opinion of our people on the church rate question – and I wish we could banish everything of party politics from among us and that we might be left to stand on our own ground doing our own work in our own way . . .

136   From J. S. Stamp   *Chester, March 16, 1837*

You will perceive by the papers which accompany these few lines what we have been doing in this city in regard to the church rates. On the morning of the day in which the meeting took place, the Chancellor of the Diocese, with whom I have for some time been on intimate terms, wrote me a very respectful note wishing my vote and voice. You are aware what my political sentiments in general are and of course on the subject of the rates in question. Seeing therefore those views nobly advocated in the *Watchman*, especially as it regards the ministerial measure introduced into the House of Commons by the Chancellor of the [E]xcheq[ue]r,[3] I concluded I should not be doing far wrong in accepting our Chancellor's invitation. I send you the *Gazette* which gives an almost *verbatim* report of my speech. I send you also the *Courant*

---

[1] John Davis, superintendent, Penzance circuit, 1834–37.

[2] Henry Philpotts (1778–1869), bishop of Exeter, a pugnacious Protestant high-churchman.

[3] The Chancellor of the Exchequer, Thomas Spring-Rice, proposed on March 3, 1837 that church rates be abolished and the loss of income to the Church made good by the improved management of Church lands.

which only gives an imperfect extract of the address, though noticed more at large in their leader. The meeting was highly respectable, there were nearly *one hundred* of the neighbouring clergy in the room, with the greater part of the gentry contiguous to the city of Chester. You will be pleased to learn also that our people in these parts with but a few exceptions are right minded on this topic. My appearance at the meeting has given general pleasure to our congregation, whilst it has given them to see more fully the relative position of Methodism and the Establishment. The political dissenters of this city with their friends and associates of the Kilhamites are as may be expected very mad at me, but this goes for nothing. I have sent two papers to the *Watchman* office for them to do what they think fit in noticing the meeting or not. Perhaps Mr. W. M. Bunting will see them there . . .

137   From Robert Melson[1]   *Stourbridge, March 18, 1837*

. . . What I witnessed on coming here was almost more than a lover of Methodism and a feeling mind could bear. To say nothing of the chapels taken from us, our chapels which we retained possession of were almost vacated, about 700 of our members were drawn from us, and Methodism was looked upon with contempt by the Christian denominations and public in general. The few good friends who retained their love to Wesleyan principles, modes of worship, and discipline, were indeed in a low and dejected state in general, and many of them I believe were almost in despair in reference to ever seeing the happy returns of former enjoyments. The dissentients built a very good chapel in Stourbridge, I suppose not more than 100 yards from ours. We, however, have great cause of rejoicing and of giving praise to the Lord. Our congregations are greatly on the increase and we are in great expectations of better days. Our friends begin to be much encouraged, and are expecting and believing that in a little our chapels will be again well attended, true religion and Wesleyan Methodism with all Christian principles, practise and enjoyments, will again revive and prosper. . . .

[1] Robert Melson, superintendent, Stourbridge circuit, 1836–38. In 1838 Melson reported that after the loss of 700 members he had brought about some recovery, and accepted an invitation to stay a third year, only to find that steps were being taken locally to remove himself and his colleague. 'Should the Conference remove us [he declared] it will be a complete triumph for three or four of the *worst* friends of Wesleyan Methodism, men who were the *ringleaders* of all the mischief in this circuit' (M.C.A. MSS. R. Melson to Jabez Bunting, July 10, 1838). Conference did not reappoint him to Stourbridge, and he became supernumerary, 1839. He disappeared from the ministry between 1847 and 1853, probably after the episode described in n. 1 p. 396 *infra*.

But Sir, at a meeting of our excellent friends I was requested to write to you to come to our help, as we are going to make a very special effort in behalf of our Stourbridge Chapel in order to get a little of the near £2000 debt removed if possible, and so relieve the minds of our excellent Trustees, who have come forward so nobly in these times of reproach and blasphemy. . . .

138   To George Marsden[1]   *London, March 24, 1837*

. . . I do feel it a great privation that for many years past my public avocations have been so overwhelming as to leave me no leisure for friendly intercourse by letter, even with those I have longest known, and still do most sincerely and cordially love. When I shall be able to disentangle myself from my present situation, I know not. It seems that 'the time is not yet'; but, come when it will, to myself it will be most welcome.

I know of nothing in particular or important in the Connexion more than you learn from the *Magazine* or *Watchman*. The *general* state of things, I think, is peaceful and healthy; but we need a gracious visitation of 'power from on high'.

I am aware that you know of the important step which I have it in contemplation to take[2] (though not for a considerable time to come) and which must permanently affect my personal and domestic happiness. I did not make up my mind, without much prayer and deliberation and enquiry, nor without consulting all my family, and several other friends. I have every reason to believe that I have been led to a right conclusion, and have been very graciously directed. . . .

139   **From William Vevers**[3]   *[postmarked – Leeds, April 20, 1837]*

You will I hope excuse me expressing my surprise on finding that *in London* I am regarded as the writer of the letter in the *Leeds Mercury* relating to the *Watchman*.[4] I should have thought that my past conduct

---

[1] George Marsden, superintendent, Sheffield (Norfolk St.) circuit, 1836–39.

[2] His second marriage, see n. 2 p. 172 *supra*.

[3] William Vevers, superintendent, Leeds (East) circuit, 1835–38.

[4] The *Leeds Mercury*, March 25, 1837 p. 7, carried a letter signed 'Wesleyan Methodist' protesting against the efforts of the *Watchman* to whip up Methodist opposition to the government's plans for the abolition of church rates and for Irish municipal reform. The writer objected also to the tone of the statement that 'the respectable individuals who have lately

would have saved me from such an imputation. As I neither *know* nor *care* who the parties may be by whom I am suspected, I cannot be deemed disrespectful if I say, that even the dread of their frown will not deter me, at the proper time and place, from delivering my opinion on *any* subject connected with the peace and stability of our Body. *I am not the writer* of the article in question – nor had I the *least knowledge* of it till I saw it in the paper. On reading it I recognised the writer – and in a conversation with him, I assumed the fact, which was not denied; but I shall not give evidence against a brother who will I believe at any time avow it.[1] I regret to find that the letter has been printed and circulated very extensively by post. I sincerely assure you that I have not supposed for one moment that you suspected me as the writer of the letter; but I thought it respectful to you distinctly to disavow it.

140   From William Mowatt[2]   *Liskeard, April 25, 1837*

I consider it my duty to lay before you a brief statement of what has taken place relative to a secession of Local Preachers and Members from our Societies in this Circuit. Several persons in the Liskeard Circuit, as far as I can learn, have for some years past been dissatisfied with their preachers, our rules and regulations as a body. Dr. Warren's visit to Liskeard about twelve months ago did not abate this sense of disaffection. Receiving from the last Conference our appointments to this Circuit, we entered upon our work with a determination if possible to promote the peace and prosperity of the people, explaining our rules both publickly and privately, hoping by mild and conciliating steps to bring about a better state of view and feeling with relation to our economy as Wesleyans.

At the first Local Preachers' Meeting which we held, a charge was brought against one of our Local Preachers, Jacob Grigg,[3] for preaching

joined the dissenters in petitioning for the abolition of church rates depart from the public and recognized principles of the Wesleyan body; and that *they are not subject to ecclesiastical censure is a triumphant refutation of reiterated charges of Conference tyranny*'.

[1] Thomas Galland, preacher, Leeds (East) circuit, 1836–38; superintendent, 1838–39. Galland made his position on the Establishment question quite clear to Bunting himself: '. . . I think it is but candid I should mention my regret at the pro-Church meeting in London, which has given occasion for opposite demonstrations which might otherwise have never occurred' (M.C.A. MSS. T. Galland to Jabez Bunting, May 22, 1837). For Bunting's forceful but unsuccessful attempt to browbeat Galland in Conference with this letter, see Gregory, *Sidelights* pp. 237–41.

[2] William Mowatt (1788–1850), superintendent, Liskeard circuit, 1836–37.

[3] Jacob Grigg, local preacher, Liskeard. In 1836 his Local Preachers' Meeting warned him 'as to his preaching among the Warrenites' (P. Bolitho, *Methodism in the Liskeard circuit*

o

amongst the Warrenites. He not being present at the meeting, it was determined that a letter should be sent him from the meeting, expressing disapprobation of his conduct, and if persisted in, [he] must take the consequences. His reply was that he would not be subject to such restrictions, and instead of conducting himself as a Wesleyan Local Preacher, visits the Bodmin Circuit, encouraging and aiding the building, settlement, and opening a chapel in defiance of our Rules, offering no apology for such conduct, but resolving to persist in such practices. In making the Plan I could not employ him any longer as a Local Preacher.

This led the Local Preachers to call a meeting at which they determined, if I did not replace J. G[rigg']s name on the plan, they would resign theirs. Accordingly twelve of the Local Preachers sent in their resignation. For satisfaction to myself and colleague I invited Rev. W. Burgess[1] our Chairman to attend our last Quarterly Meeting, who heard the whole of the case. In a letter to Mr. Currelly[2] he observes 'From what I saw at your Quarterly Meeting and from what I know from good authority relative to many persons in your Circuit, I am of opinion that a secession is inevitable. Indeed when men imbibe and propagate such sentiments as were these avowed, it is plain they are not sound Methodists and the sooner they leave us the better'. They who have seceded are endeavouring to alienate our Societies from us. How far they will succeed is not yet known. We are doing all in our power to counteract the efforts of their proceedings. The chapels which are settled according to our mode of settlement we shall retain with our societies. This we hope. But if we meet with places where our Societies cannot be retained, and [we] have chapels regularly settled in these places, how should we proceed[?] Your counsel under such circumstances will be needed and most cordially received.

We find it difficult in our present situation to supply our chapels. If we could have obtained assistance from you by sending us a young ⟨man⟩ for a month or two until we should get our Society regulated, we should feel thankful. We are afraid it will be impossible to maintain our ground against those who have seceded from us without such aid. The greater part of this circuit is firm and those places free from agitation are prosperous. . . .

1751–1967 (Liskeard, 1967) p. 17), but in 1837 he assisted in the 'illegal' opening of the Warrenite chapel at St. Dennis (*West Briton* January 20, 1837) and was expelled by the writer, his superintendent.

[1] William Pennington Burgess (1790–1868), superintendent, Plymouth circuit, 1836–39. Chairman of Devonport District, 1836–39.

[2] Charles Currelly (1806–68), preacher, Liskeard circuit, 1836–37.

141   From John McLean[1]   *Sheffield, May 8, 1837*

Assured of your concern for the purity of our faith as well as for the preservation of our discipline, I beg to direct your *official* notice to the Tract no 303 entitled 'Baptism not the new Birth',[2] which puts forth views on this subject at variance as they appear to me with Wesleyan and Scriptural Theology. That Baptism *is not* the new birth is true; that Baptism and the new birth do not *invariably* go together is true also; but that an infant *as such* is *incapable* of the new birth as this tract attempts to prove, is a most cruel and God-dishonouring notion – a notion repudiated by Mr. Wesley, by the Church of England, by primitive antiquity, and above all by the scriptures of truth. Upon this subject I have thought and read and prayed very much of late. A number of most sacred associations have been collected around it, which must be my apology if I should seem to attach a degree of importance to it to which considered simply in itself it may hardly be thought entitled. As I would not wish to reflect more upon the author of the tract than is absolutely necessary who probably penned it in haste, and may therefore *in some degree* be excused if he has mistaken sophistry for sound reasoning, I refrain from any further notice of it, only observing that upon his principles it is difficult to imagine how children dying in infancy can be admitted into heaven unless original or birth sin be something widely different from what we are taught to believe it is in the scriptures of truth, the creed of the universal church, and the writings of our Heaven-directed Founder. I trust dear Sir you will bring this matter before the Tract committee, and if the Secretary will communicate the result, I shall be obliged.

It will give you pleasure to hear that all the preachers in both these circuits are well and well-affected. Our people also are prepared to *defend Wesleyan* Methodism against the crudities of the Leeds school. Attempts have been made to sow dissension by means of the *Leeds Mercury* letter, the authorship of which appears to be no secret,[3] but they have happily failed. Nor is it possible that any difference of opinion can arise here unless some preacher should turn agitator. Through mercy

---

[1] John McLean (1806–66), preacher, Sheffield (Norfolk St.) circuit, 1834–37. McLean had been a probationer in Bunting's household and regarded himself as, in a special sense, a protégé of the great man. A violent Protestant politician, and of precarious mental balance, he spent periods in a lunatic asylum.

[2] *Baptism not the New Birth. A dialogue between Peter Martin and his cousin Thomas* (London, n.d.) p. 10 in *Wesleyan Methodist Religious Tracts* vii. 'The change is effected on a conscious recipient: there is an understanding to comprehend, a will to put forth certain necessary acts, and a heart to feel; all of which are wanting in a state of infancy, but all of which are necessary in the new birth.'

[3] See n. 4 p. 184 and n. 1 p. 185 *supra*.

this I believe will not take place. Indeed all the agitation is *sure* to be on the other side. The last letter of Mr. Galland is a piece of most disgraceful impertinency. To put such questions as terminate his letter would in almost any circumstances be pure impertinency. In the present case it is more. It is an attempt to tar and feather our lion-hearted sub-editor and some one or more of the Missionary Secretaries. A puny attempt it is true; but this does not lessen its criminality, and if he does not cry *peccavi* and more than *peccavi* at the next Conference, it will be impossible for you to pass it lightly over. What preacher is safe from the effects of Mr. Galland's suspicions if he be allowed to give mouth to them in this manner? Why there is no telling what sort of questions he may ask when the mood next comes upon him; and we know how much importance a large class of readers attach to charges put even in the form of enquiries.

We understand Mr. Vevers has been proving his attachment to the Church of England by publishing a letter against the new vicar Mr. Hook.[1] Should he not have given the new vicar a little more time and opportunity to state his views? . . . Our prospect as to the work of God in this circuit is encouraging. Congregations are *very* good – a gracious influence rests upon *all* our means, particularly the preaching, and our classes are increasing in number. There is some fear lest the anticipated election should divert the minds of our people from the work of God, but we shall do what we can by the divine blessing to prevent it. We are not without considerable hope that Mr. Thorneley[2] will be returned. . . .

142   From William Jackson   *Derby, May 27, 1837*

. . . At the present we have peace in this circuit but during the year we have had unknown trouble with some of the most captious and designing men I have met with. They have done all in their power to annoy us. Every movement seemed to be the result of some deep laid scheme. Some of them used all their little influence to poison the minds of our people both in the town and country. They had 'stopped supplies', and were inducing others to do it. We reasoned with them and bore with them, at the same time giving them to understand we were determined to maintain the discipline of our connexion. All except one withdrew

---

[1] Walter Farquhar Hook (1798–1875), Vicar of Leeds, 1837–59. Vevers's pamphlet, *A letter to the Rev. W. Hook on his inaugural discourse* (Leeds, 1837), was called in question in Conference, but no charge was pressed. Gregory, *Sidelights* pp. 241–2.

[2] J. Thorneley, defeated conservative candidate for Sheffield, 1837. Cf. Ward, *Religion and society* p. 253.

from us, and he refused to answer charges preferred against him at the Leaders' Meeting and to show his contempt of our authority he attended a meeting at the New Connexion Chapel at the time he ought to have been at our Leaders' Meeting.

I have understood a person of the name of Bennett has written to you against me. He withdrew from our Society, but sometime after he changed his mind and used every means to entangle us in a question about his attending the Church. I kept him to the fact of having left the body in a very deliberate man[ner] after his late Leader had spent half an hour in trying to dissuade him from it. I have had some most abusive letters from him, and in the last, dated May 9th, he slanders many of the Preachers, reprobates our Connexion generally, and concludes with 'farewell Methodism as it is'. This Bennett was one of the ringleaders in the Derby Faith faction[1] . . .

143   From James Blackett   *Bramley, July 14, 1837*

. . . I really think something should be done at the ensuing Conference to rescue this Circuit out of the hands of a party that have for their object the subversion of Methodism in it. I know of no plan so likely as the following viz. to place Wortley and Kirkstall to the Leeds West Circuit, and there have a single man and prepare the way for dividing that circuit. Then place Horsforth to Yeadon and make that a regular two preachers' circuit, whereas now it has only one and a half, as far as labour goes. On the plan proposed Yeadon would receive an increase of member[s] to the amount of 180, and Leeds West would receive an increase of 331 members. The places which would then be taken from Bramley would be better supplied than they can be now, and the advantage to the Bramley Circuit would be to divide the influence of the Local Preachers by various arts and plans taking the affairs of the Circuit into their own hands tho⟨ugh I ?⟩ opposed them, being tired of opposition . . . I am sorry to say that since the December Quarterly meeting Mr. [Charles] Radcliffe is one way or another connected with the opposers of our excellent discipline, and as I stated to you before, he was invited to stay a third year and become the Superintendent. This proposition was made by the person who took the chair at the December Quarterly meeting before I came to this circuit, and passed the resolution to send Mr. Eastwood away at the end of the first year.[2] Mr. Eastwood was

---

[1] Cf. n. 1 p. 16 *supra*.

[2] Thomas Eastwood (1781–1855), superintendent, Leeds (Bramley) circuit for one year only, 1834–35.

then ill and unable to attend the meeting. Mr. Newton knows the person; the next that supported it was the man who takes the misnamed *Christian Advocate* and hands it about in the Circuit; and the third man was the person who proposed the vote by ballot with the intent to pass the inclosed obnoxious resolutions; but I would not suffer it at the first December Quarterly meeting I was at in this Circuit; and the fourth was the person who read those resolutions in the Quarterly Meeting in June 1836, I opposing and contradicting him, and when I found he was in a hurry to put them, being almost out of breath, I was obliged to leap out of the chair and dissolve the meeting. I do not recollect of any other person speaking on the occasion. This was at the December Quarterly Meeting last, and nothing has been said about it since. At that very time, and to those very persons, Mr. R. said 'I should like to stay in this circuit another year, for I have met with nothing but kindness from the people in this Circuit'. The plan would be if the above proposition were carried into effect to have two preachers in the Bramley Circuit with 1330 members of society. I can assure you I have had to stand alone in supporting Methodism in this Circuit. I should have been happy to have had a little more of the kind counsel of our excellent Chairman; but his being called off on the important duties of the connexion precluded that in part; yet I have always found him ready to sympathise and kindly advise, when I could meet with him. . . .

At the last June Quarterly Meeting finding that they had been foiled in various attempts at our discipline, they had recourse to another expedient which was to take £5 pr. ann. from each Preacher's salary. This was carried, and one argument advanced in its favour was, that they might be able to make a present of £5 now and then to a preacher. This was to get him to succumb to them, and that they may be able to reward him, for yielding up correct principles.

144   From John Rigg   *Birmingham, July 15, 1837*

. . . Our Friends in this little circuit have exerted themselves nobly. More money by far has been promised than was ever raised towards the erection of any one chapel in Birmingham. But the trade of the town is almost extinguished. Thousands are thrown out of employment; and merchants of large property are reduced to great difficulty. In consequence of this unlooked for occurrence, much of what has been subscribed cannot be paid at present. The opening services are on all accounts of the greatest importance, and if we cannot obtain suitable help, we must be greatly oppressed. . . .

P.S. Mr. and Mrs. Perks[1] will be glad to see you and any of your family whenever you are in Birmingham or are passing through it.

145   From Samuel Trueman[2]   *Towcester, July 21, 1837*

Had I the talents which many of my Brethren possess or known less of the defective nature of my own, I should long since have addressed you on a subject on which I have felt deeply. I refer to that department of our work which has been characterized our 'home mission'. Except a few bigots of high-church principles, some pseudo-religionists, or covert and unmasked infidels, there are few intelligent and no candid persons in the nation, but what will acknowledge that the moral influence of Wesleyan Methodism in raising the tone of pure religious feeling, in elevating the standard of morals, and exciting to christian zeal, and holy enterprise, has been great; and that not only in our own body but in the establishment and among the various dissenting bodies of the nations.

Our zeal in the foreign missionary department of the work of God is our glory as a Church. That zeal is known in the palace, few cottages in the nation but what has [not] heard of it with admiration, it has been acknowledged in the senate, and no speaker on a missionary platform can do justice to us, or to his subject, without commending it. The government both at home and abroad has approved of it, and all ranks and orders of society have united in praising it; but while we may properly thank God for the grace he has given to us, and the honour which in this part of his work he has conferred upon us, there is in reference to the state of what we term the 'home work' great cause of regret, and before God, and the nation, of deep humiliation. What with our vast system of efficient machinery, notwithstanding the thousands of yearly increase, have we accomplished for the moral and religious improvement of the nation in comparison to what we should have done? Have we not too much retired within our lines, confined ourselves to the securing of our camp, and limited the great power God has given us to mere defensive warfare? While in the foreign work we have been all light, life, fire, and zeal, while others have been illuminated by our light, warmed by the ardour of our love, and stimulated to imitate our zeal, we have allowed others to go before us in the missionary work at

[1] Robert and John Perks are described as 'the Wesleyan potentates of the Wolverhampton of those days'. A. C. Pratt, *Black Country Methodism* (London, 1891) p. 51.

[2] Samuel Trueman (1790–1868), superintendent, Towcester circuit, 1836–37.

home. We commenced the system of village preaching, we have continued it on a large scale, but for several years in work strictly *missionary* we have attempted little and have done less.

We ought to admire the zeal of our dissenting brethren in their Home Mission now in active operation, but we ought to do more than admire. We ought to have this day 100 home missionaries employed in England, and we might soon have them if the subject was brought systematically and fully before our societies and congregations. So far from a home mission on an extensive scale being injurious to the fund of the foreign missionary society, it would greatly augment it. We have been trammelled by a narrow policy, and acted too much on a mistaken idea that our people were doing so much for the *foreign missions* that to call upon them to support liberally *a home mission* would be to damp their zeal and injure the foreign work. The result of an extensive home mission would be the salvation of thousands of souls that in our regular way we cannot get near, the rise and establishment of new societies, the formation of new circuits, and the consequent increase of all our important funds. Could there not be several home missionaries attached to every district? Could there not be a general Committee for the Home mission appointed by Conference[1] and local committees in each district, the local committees to consist of the preachers of the district, stewards of circuits, and influential lay gentlemen to consider the best fields of labour, and for raising supplies for the mission etc. Our influential, and respectable friends would feel deeply and support liberally a mission, the necessity of which they can see from their own thresholds, and the advantages of which would be under their own immediate cognizance; and such would no doubt be the blessing of God upon the home mission if prosecuted aright, that in consequence of the enlargement of the work at home, the resources for our foreign work would be increased an hundred-fold.

My Dear Sir, ought we to be satisfied without having one hundred Wesleyan Ministers in London,[2] and the same number in Leeds, and Manchester. Would not our wealthy friends support liberally a mission for the good of their own city or town? Too many of our people in what is termed respectable circuits are loudly calling for splendid talent, they rather wish the light of the sanctuary to dazzle and astonish like meteors rather than like guiding stars with mild unobtrusive light lead to the Saviour, to *duty*, and to Heaven. It is to be feared that many are sinking into a sickly sentimentality, and hear the word that should save them and others with capricious criticism. A home mission in vigorous

---

[1] The first home missions secretary, Charles Prest, was appointed in 1857.

[2] The Metropolitan Chapel Building Committee began work in 1873.

operation would bring our people out of themselves, lead to that spirit of self denial, sacrifice and zeal, which must be more fully felt by the christian church than it now is, if the world is converted to Christianity, and would lead to that athletic, full grown Christianity, which character-ized our people in the days of Wesley. Instead of the July collection,[1] an annual meeting might be held at which the Missionaries connected with the district might attend and detail their labours and success, and the fund for the home work would be thus made ten times more productive, and by this means, Wesleyan Methodism in a short time might spread through the length, and breadth of the land; and believing as we do that Wesleyan Methodism is pure christianity in vigorous operation, why should not every means be used to accomplish so desirable an object? Every year the Calvinists are narrowing the sphere of our influence, and the experience of twenty years has convinced me that we never do so well where the ground has been preoccupied by Calvinism. Why should we not go before them? Let me entreat you in the name of the perishing thousands of our countrymen to turn your attention more fully to this subject. With the great improvements which you have originated and which, highly as they are thought of, will be more fully so, when you and your labours, are the subjects of history, add a vigorous home mission the to practical working of our system and generations yet unborn shall call you blessed . . .

146   From John Stevens[2]   *Lewes, July 31, 1837*

. . . From the first of my coming to this hour I have met with a suc-cession of discouragements and disappointments. As soon as I have surmounted one difficulty, another has arisen, I was very unwilling to remain here the *third year* and it was not until after several meetings were held that I consented not to oppose the *unanimously* [expressed] wishes of the *officers and leading men in the circuit*. I have laboured harder and done more to advance the interests of Methodism in this circuit than any of my predecessors, and yet it is a melancholy fact that the circuit is in a declining state. The causes of this declension I ought per-haps to have stated in vindication of myself to you, but I could not do it without exposing the flagrant departure from Methodist doctrines and discipline of my predecessors. All this I must leave, and will only state before I enter on other matters that there has been a very good under-standing between me and all the officers of the circuit on all matters till

[1] On this see n. 2 p. 156 *supra*.
[2] John Stevens (1790–1874), superintendent, Lewes circuit, 1834–37.

very lately. I have *always carried every point I desired without opposition*; but now some of the Leaders and many of the people are warmly arrayed against me and the Conference. Much of this I ascribe to the dissenters who are exceedingly bitter against us, and have taken every opportunity to inflame the minds of our own and other people, and to injure us and our cause. Defamatory papers have been distributed and the most infamous reports against the preachers as a body have been put into circulation. I have seen the existence of certain principles in our society and congregation at Lewes for some time past which the two last elections have fully developed. In this town there are 20 of Pain[e']s disciples; these with the unitarians, many of the Independents and Baptists have formed themselves into a political society for the accomplishment of certain objects. To this society I regret to say some of our Leaders and Local Preachers have joined themselves. All our people take the radical side in politics, and as they are exceedingly ill-informed on public questions, they are easily made the dupes of designing men.

A few months ago Mr. Easthope[1] came to canvass this town. Before he came he requested a very respectable brother whose name I shall not mention to write to me for the purpose of obtaining my vote and interest among our people. The brother had mistaken the nature and ⟨tenor⟩ of his opinions. I sent him the Lewes papers containing Mr. E.['s] address and speeches accompanied with a letter in which I stated that I could not support a gentleman who advocated a *Reform in the House of Lords*, the ballot and other to me objectionable measures, and so I told Mr. E. himself. But *his object* was accomplished. He took care to let all *our people know what a high character I had got of him from a Brother preacher.* They voted for him; I could not. This gave great offence to our people and all with whom they acted – *I did not vote at all.*

Soon after the Church-Rate question was agitated. My opinions on the subject were know[n]. But still the dissenters took the opportunity when I was out of the way to bring petitions to my colleague and requested his advocacy in the pulpit on the Lord's Day morning! Richard Martin[2] formerly a preacher among us came to make a speech on the subject. My colleague[3] excused himself by stating I was not at home and there the business rested. Here was another disappointment and offence. About the same [time] a petition for the continuance of Church-Rates was got up at Eastbourne. A foolish youth a member of society wrote a paragraph to conciliate the Church people at that place in a most

---

[1] John Easthope (c. 1810–49) was defeated as a Liberal candidate for Lewes, 1837.

[2] As there was no itinerant preacher of this name, Richard Martin must have been a former local preacher.

[3] William Hill jun., preacher, Lewes circuit, 1836–37. D. 1844, aet. 36.

unguarded and improper manner. This fanned the flame of resentment against [*sic*] still more. I was supposed to be the author of this, and had no means of freeing myself against the charge without doing the young man great injury. Last week came on the election for this Borough. The contest was severe. As I had no means of escaping censures, after serious deliberation I found it my duty to vote for the two Conservative members both of whom promised to vote in favor of the Sabbath question. I *attended none of their meetings*, made *no speeches, wrote nothing, canvassed no one.* I simply voted. *And now I am more spoken against – and hated than sin.* Some will leave the Society, one of the Leaders has resigned – and things look very discouraging. . . . You may form some idea of the state of feeling among us when I tell you that the *Magazine* is dashed to the ground and its politics trampled under foot. Can you give me any advice? . . .

147   To Emma Bunting[1]   *Bristol, August 27, 1837*

My letter of Wednesday would inform you of the important, and to me most happy, event which took place that morning;[2] and Nora who I hope arrived safely on Saturday evening will have given you some further particulars of our proceedings.

It was not till Wednesday afternoon that I learned with an agreeable surprize, that Harriet and Eliza[3] had travelled with their spouses to Bristol, and were at the Gloucester Hotel in Clifton; the very place where *we* had intended to make our first *halt*. This circumstance together with William and Percy's consent to bring their wives to see Cheddar on the Thursday, induced us to give up all our former plans for the week; and we went to Wells where next day we were joined by William, Percy, Mr. Wood,[4] Mr. and Mrs. Bisden, Mr. William Green, Mr. Robert Green, Mr. Parsons, and Chas. Parsons. Mrs. P., Harriet, and Eliza were hindered by some sudden indisposition of Eliza's, which made it more prudent that she should be left at Clutton, where the Manchester party had all called on their way to breakfast according to a previous promise, at Lynch House. We saw the Cathedral, and through Mr. Robert Green's influence, the Palace, as well as Gardens; had a delightful ride to Cheddar, which you *must* see; returned to dinner at Wells; and did not separate till 10 o'clock. Mr. Wood went to Bristol

---

[1] Emma Bunting, third and surviving daughter of Jabez by his first marriage.

[2] Bunting's second marriage.

[3] Bunting's daughters-in-law, Mrs. William Maclardie Bunting and Mrs. T. Percival Bunting.

[4] James Wood, see n. 2 p. 48 *supra*.

that night, to be ready for the Manchester coach on Friday. William and Harriet went to Clifton; Percy and Eliza stayed at Clutton; and *we* at Wells. On Friday all of us but Mr. Wood met to a late dinner at Mr. Robert Green's; and dined yesterday at Mr. James Green's. I think all the strangers on both sides were very much pleased with each other; and all has turned out well in that respect, for which I am truly thankful. But O! what a damper on our comfort did I feel yesterday evening, when, while at dinner at Holcombe, a messenger from Clutton brought me a letter from poor Illingworth,[1] announcing the awful news of his most distressing bereavement, after a union of only eight days with that lovely girl. William, Harriet, Percy, Eliza, and we had carriages at the door to take us to Bath, where we all proposed to have spent the Sunday together. I felt it my duty under the altered circumstances to hasten to Bristol, in order to 'weep with those who weep'. We came therefore to Clutton late last night, and to Bristol early this morning. I have spent the forenoon with Mr. Illingworth, who is broken-hearted. The tale is mysterious and affecting, almost beyond romance itself. They were married on Monday, August 14th, and went to Glastonbury, 5 miles beyond Wells. There they were as happy as earth could make them, and in perfect health, till Thursday morning the 17th, when Mrs. I complained of being a little poorly, and wished to remain a while in bed. On Mr. I's return to her, she in the most calm and heavenly manner possible told him that while she had been alone, their whole future life and history had been made to pass before her mind's eye; that she knew she was about to die; and that he would die soon after her, and re-join her in heaven. To this she quietly but firmly adhered, in spite of all he could say. She said that she had cherished with delight the idea of going to Poplar, visiting the poor and sick, praying with them, and ministering to their wants with him: 'such was not the will of God'. She continued poorly; and two medical men were called in, who *up to Monday night* persisted in the opinion that there was *no danger*; that there was an hysteric tendency; but that in two or three days she would be well. Meanwhile her conversation was almost super-celestial; and her quotations from Scripture (the New Testament being her pillow-companion) and comments upon them, most solemnly delightful. 'Tell everyone', she said, 'that "The blood of Jesus Christ his Son cleanseth *me* from all sin" '. This was her constant testimony. She had no pain, no suffering, no uneasiness, from first to last. It was not like a death; it was a translation. On Tuesday morning at 7, she departed, without a sigh, struggle, or suffering of any kind; and on Thursday her remains were removed to Bristol. There are many most interesting particulars of her

[1] William Illingworth (1806–73), preacher, London (Spitalfields) circuit, 1837–40.

last triumph which must be reserved for personal communication. We are to dine with William and Percy and their wives at Egford tomorrow; but I have promised to come to Bristol to bury her on Tuesday morning early. I expect to return to Egford and Clutton for a day or two and to be in Bristol on Thursday night or Friday morning, to meet the missionaries, and see them embark. And now, dearest Emma, how are you? I have longed for a letter from you, but could not instruct you till today where to address one. Tomorrow night (Monday) without fail put into the post in good time a letter directed to me, at Mr. Stratton's, Cheltenham Road, Bristol. Say fully how your foot goes on, and whether you will be able, as I earnestly hope, to join us in Bristol, by coming with Mr. Beecham[1] on Thursday, or sooner if you can. The sooner the better. Everybody in this country is sincerely wishful to see you; but none more than myself and 'Mamma', who loves you very much. She, with Mr. and Mrs. Parsons and Robert Martin, desire to be affectionately remembered to you. Be sure to lock up the study. Shall I engage a bed for you either at Mr. Roberts's or at Mr. Westcott's for the two or three nights you are with us in Bristol? I rather prefer Mr. Westcott's. Say if you can by what coach you will come. If you cannot decide on Monday, write *again* on Tuesday, and *then* direct to me at John Bisden's, Esqr., Egford House, near Frome, Somerset. Do come as soon as your foot is fit to travel. If you cannot walk, you can ride with me; for I am yet a little lame, but otherwise well and happy.

I am as ever, Your very affectionate father and friend.

148   To Emma Bunting   *Clutton, September 6, 1837*

After a week of deep interest strangely chequered by feelings of solemn sadness, and of great and I hope hallowed enjoyment, I again seize a vacant minute for the purpose of addressing to you a few hasty lines.

Your last affectionate letter greatly relieved me. By this time I hope your foot is quite better. You did quite right, I am sure under all the circumstances, not to risk a journey till you were fully recovered. That pleasure is yet to come; and in a few weeks, I trust, it will be realized.

Tuesday, Wednesday, Thursday, Friday, Saturday and Sunday were spent in or about Bristol by our whole party. We lived all together *very happily* at the Full Moon in Bristol. We all, except Harriet, who was poorly, visited Mr. Irving's on Thursday, where the missionaries for India and their wives met the Missionary Secretaries.[2] One evening

---

[1] See n. 1 p. 3 *supra.*

[2] Jabez Bunting, John Beecham, Robert Alder and Elijah Hoole (d. 1872, aet. 74), missionary secretary, 1837–72.

Messrs. Thorp[1] and three of his dissenting friends, supped with us at our Inn; and *talked* till 2 in the morning. On Friday, Messrs. Beecham, Alder, Hoole and myself had a delightful meeting with the missionaries. Mr. and Mrs. Parsons spent Wednesday and Thursday with us. In addition to all this, Mr. and Mrs. Bisden justly claimed much of our sympathy and attention till Saturday, when the funeral of their sweet girl took place at Hutton Court. On Sunday I went in my scarf etc. to join the Stratton mourners in King St. Chapel [Bristol], and heard Mr. Male[2] preach. On Sunday night William preached a glorious sermon, referring to all the events of the week, on 'The Dead in Christ'. So you see we have been fully occupied. Yesterday we went 35 miles down the Bristol Channel, and took a solemn leave of the missionary party. We had twice singing and prayer; and it was a day long to be remembered. They went off in fine spirits. We returned in Mr. Irving's steamer last night to Bristol; and have just now reached Clutton. This week we are to see Ann Eliza and Mrs. Hale; on Sunday I am to say something about Mrs. Illingworth at King St., Bristol; and then we shall in good earnest think of home, as soon as we can pack up all, pay bills, etc., etc. Possibly on Monday night but more probably on Tuesday as we are inclined to make two days of it, we may see Myddelton Square.[3] Let me have a letter by Friday night's mail, to meet me on ⟨Sat⟩urday, at the Rev. Wm. Lord's,[4] St. James's Square, Bristol.

William is somewhat better, Harriet amazingly so, during the three last days of her sojourn with us. She seemed quite at home with us all. They and Percy and Eliza would reach Manchester last night, and I hope would find their four children all well.

I must conclude, or I shall lose a post. 'Mamma is quite well', and joins me in best love. Tell all enquirers *only* that you expect us at home some time next week. . . .

149   From William Vevers   *Leeds, September 22, 1837*

. . . In the *Leeds Mercury* of last Saturday, there is a very bitter letter, on the painful subject which engaged attention at the Conference.[5] I do not

---

[1] Probably Rev. John Thorp, son of Rev. Wm. Thorp (1771–1833) who exercised a notable pastorate at Castle Green, Bristol, 1806–33.

[2] Matthew T. Male (1811–72), preacher about to sail for Bangalore station.

[3] Bunting's house as missionary secretary.

[4] William Lord (1791–1873), superintendent, Bristol (King St.) circuit, 1836–39. Governor of Woodhouse Grove School, 1843–58.

[5] The *Leeds Mercury*, September 16, 1837 p. 6, carried a long and pungent letter from 'Aliquis' (evidently Thomas Galland) giving his version of his clash with Bunting at Con-

know who is the writer – but it is generally ascribed to Mr. G[alland]. I have seen very little of him since Conference. I am afraid he retains all the bitterness of feeling that he displayed in the discussion in Brunswick chapel. The friends in the West circuit scarcely know how to act with him in reference to the next year. . . .

Two of our local preachers have left us and gone to the Church. Marmaduke Flower, a vain, pedantic schoolmaster having received some attention from the Vicar, and, he says, the promise of a curacy, is one. The other is G. Denham – whose character was under investigation on a moral charge. We have no regret on the subject. . . .

150   From John Beecham   *London, February 28, 1838*

I proceed to write you a few lines sitting in the Committee Room on White's affairs. We have been at work with him now nearly three days. We meet at nine o'clock in the morning, and sit until between two and three. When the end is to come, I am wholly unable to divine. You would smile if you could peep at us. We have got Hannah yoked in for the whole business; the Committee allowing it to be right that we as Secretaries shall be at liberty to act only as witnesses etc.

Well! If you dont mind the Ministers will be driven out of the field before you can get back. They have undergone a series of complete defeats in defence of their Master O'Connell. At the Crown and Anchor Tavern, O'Connell made heavy charges against the Conservative members on Election Committees – Lord Maidstone took it up,[1] and proposed a motion on the subject, when up starts Lord John Russell threatening that if Lord Maidstone persisted in his motion, he would introduce another on the conduct of the Bishop of Exeter (referring to what the Bishop said some 2 or 3 years ago respecting the Roman Catholic members and their oath). This volunteer defence of the Noble Leader of the House of Commons produced no other effect, however,

ference over his *Leeds Mercury* letter of March 25, 1837 (see no. 139 *supra*) and protesting against 'the decided political bias which is cautiously but efficiently given to every recognized instrument of Methodist action upon the societies and the public at large . . . [while fixing] the brand of dishonour upon some obnoxious individual as an incendiary writer and political agitator' who was simply trying to resist political entanglements.

[1] Lord Maidstone (1815–94, succeeded as 11th earl of Winchilsea, 1858), M.P. for Northamptonshire (North) 1837–41, carried a motion that O'Connell be reprimanded by the Speaker, against the government, by 226 votes to 197. The point of the interjection by Lord Howick (M.P. Northumberland (North) 1832–41) was that the present state of the law relating to the trial of elections was indefensible, even if it had been indefensibly described by O'Connell.

than to demonstrate the degradation of the ministers in their sub-jugation to the Great Agitator. Lord Maidstone brought forward the subject, and O'Connell having admitted that he had used his motion, he then submitted a motion to the effect that Mr. O'Connell had been guilty of a breach of privilege, and 2. that he should be reprimanded at the bar of the house. Now mark the subjugation of the Ministry; even Lord Howick allowed himself to be put forward to say that no doubt the language used was censurable etc. but thought it should be passed over, and moved as an amendment the order of the day. Here then came the trial of strength, and the ministerial amendment was lost by a majority of 9. The 1st part of Lord Maidstone's motion was then carried by a large majority; but such a struggle was made to get over the evening before the 2d. part of the motion was put to the vote, that the Con-servative side of the house agreed to an adjournment. Last evening the debate was resumed; and after a variety of desperate manoeuvres on the Ministerial side of the house, the opposition gained *two* more decided majorities, and the 2d. part of Lord Maidstone's motion was carried by a majority of 29, and the culprit was accordingly ordered to appear *this day* at the bar of the house to be reprimanded by the Speaker. It is said, he does not mean to attend in order to provoke the House to arrest him which he (and no doubt from his previous recommendation, Lord J. Russell himself) supposes would excite popular feeling in his favour. We shall see how he will act; and what effect the affair will have on the *stability* of the ministry. Its effect on their *character* cannot be doubted.

Satisfactory intelligence on the whole has been received from Jamaica. Last year we reported the number of members to be 18600, and this year they return 18100, and between 4 and 500 on trial. So it appears Pennock [?] has not run away with the whole Society.

I have learned from Mr. Coates that *Government are assisting* the N.Z. Association to get their Bill into Parliament as a *public* Bill to gain time for them. Dr. Hinds[1] has published a pamphlet in which he refers to Coates and myself. . . .

151   From J. B. Holroyd[2]   *Newcastle-under-Lyme, March 24, 1838*

On my arrival in this circuit I found a new chapel ready for opening, the Deed executed (but not enrolled) by which the Trustees had a dis-

---

[1] Samuel Hinds (1793–1872) later bishop of Norwich. His pamphlet was: *The latest official documents relating to New Zealand*. . . . (London, 1838); Beecham replied with *Remarks upon the latest official documents relating to New Zealand* (London, 1838).

[2] James Briggs Holroyd, superintendent, Newcastle-under-Lyme circuit, 1836–38.

cretionary power to shut out or let into the Chapel any preachers they thought proper. The Chapel was to be opened the second Sunday after I got here, and four separate deputations from the Associationists in the Nantwich Circuit, offered their services in case I refused to occupy the pulpit. After several trying and vexatious meetings, they were at last prevailed with to abandon their Deed and have it settled on one that secures it to the connexion[1] on condition of us paying for the new Deed, which amounted to £10 – part of which we have begged, and the rest my colleague and I have divided between us.

At Audley, which is the second place of importance in the circuit, I found a dilapidated chapel with a debt of upwards of £60 more than the original cost (see an account of the case in the circular published by the Chapel Loan Fund). Here a number of the leading men had imbibed the spirit of the Association, with a strong feeling in favour of the School-party at Burslem,[2] and a forward leader might have taken a majority with him to either party. They had a Sunday School of between 200 and 300 scholars taught in the chapel, and being disappointed in their application to the Chapel Fund for relief, in order to form a new Trust, they were negotiating for ground to build a new School which would have been settled in a way over which we could have had no control. It pleased God that some good was done the first Sabbath I spent there, and I used my influence to get them to defer building the school until another application could be made for a final grant, which if obtained would enable us to form a new Trust, and having plenty of ground for a school on the chapel premises, it would then become one concern. The friends engaged to raise £150, on condition of receiving £100. This was granted last October, and the friends raised £162.12.0 paid off all outstanding bills, and left £460 on the chapel. On making arrangements for building the school, the roof of the chapel was found to be in a very dangerous state. It has been examined by four separate builders, all of whom pronounce it unsafe to worship in. This opinion being known has excited considerable alarm. Every seat is now let and many more are wanted. The society has increased the last six quarters from 156 to 198. After mature deliberation, and having obtained plans specifications and estimates, the Trustees have resolved, that as the roof must come off, and the chapel requires enlarging to accommodate the increasing congregations, that there will be a considerable saving in the expense to enlarge it at the same time with the school, and make the whole one uniform building. They have resolved to accept the tender of a very respectable builder to put a new roof,

[1] On the Model Deed, see n. 2 p. 37 *supra*.
[2] On the Burslem Sunday school case, see nos. 33, 82 *supra*.

P

lengthen the chapel 15 feet, carry out the side galleries uniform with the other, put a singing gallery over two vestries behind the pulpit, build two schoolrooms 30 feet by 16, and complete the whole for £500, the nails to be given by some of our friends who are nailers, and all the sand, lime, and bricks to be drawn to the place gratis. To meet this the Trustees and friends engage to raise £250, and the other £250 to be divided between the chapel and the school, as an outstanding debt, which in a few years they intend finally to pay off. The builder is *bound* to have the chapel ready for opening on Sunday June 24, and I write to request the favour of your coming to open it. . . . When I consider the change in the views and spirit of these people, their zeal and liberality in support of the cause they were recently ready to abandon, the con-nexional influence your visit would produce in a neighbourhood that has been so seriously affected with the Association Spirit, and a visit from you would completely destroy it. Permit me dear Sir most respect-fully and affectionately to entreat you to come and help us. . . . I am happy to inform you that the work of the Lord is prospering through the circuit. Our increase is about 40 since Conference – we have paid off an old Circuit debt, and we have peace. The Lord be praised. . . .

152   To Thomas Binney[1]   *London, April 5, 1838* [*Copy*]

I am obliged by your kind communication dated March 5th. . . .

. . . I deeply feel with you that 'the subject of National Education is one of great importance but of great difficulty', and that 'badly done, it had better not be touched'. My present impression is that if done at all in the present posture of affairs, it *will* be done *badly*. I therefore incline to wish that it may not just now be attempted, especially as I have many fears from the appointment of any such Central Board, as I can hope to see constituted. I do not see any great necessity for the abandonment of the *present* plan, while it is *liberally* administered, that of distributing Parliamentary aid by the executive government to schools of all denominations, where certified as deserving of such aid by either of the two great educational Societies already in operation. I think, however, that the same facilities of recommendation should be extended to *other* recognized bodies besides the National Society and the British and Foreign School Society; and that such an extension is very practicable, and would stimulate, not discourage, the voluntary exertions of all classes of Christians.

[1] Thomas Binney (1798–1874), congregationalist minister at King's Weigh House chapel, London, 1829–69.

I am not, however, obstinately fixed in my opinions. And if, as you seem to think, something to be called *National* 'must be attempted', the plan you have been so good as to send me appears to deserve respectful and careful consideration.[1] . . .

153 From Hugh Beech[2]   *Carlisle, May 22, 1838*

. . . When I first saw the buildings of this city at a distance, my prayer was, Lord give me favour in the sight of the people and double the number of Methodists while I sojourn with them. And I am persuaded my prayer will be answered. I entered upon my work with strong yearnings over sinners. The congregations were very small and in the prayer meetings all was still and lifeless – not an Amen to be heard but what was stifled in bringing it out. I resolved to try to alter this, and began to preach the great truths of the gospel with a heart blessedly imbued with a spirit of meekness and love. We got our friends to pray short, and to go *at* it directly and to give us the privilege of saying Amen by asking for such blessings as we wanted there and then, and while the spirit of prayer was given, and the power of God was felt I gave vent to my feelings in some good Yorkshire *Amens*. The blessed work soon began to move, the congregation very pleasingly to increase, and our prospects to brighten. I found 99 members in Carlisle; and at the last visitation the number was 148. The other parts of the circuit are not doing much, but I have no doubt this city will become a very important station in our connexion. I endeavour so to conduct our Leaders' Meetings and other meeting[s] that 20 years hence they may be what a Methodist preacher could wish them to be. I am laid under deep obligations by the kindness of the Conference in allowing me £10.0.0. towards keeping

[1] In 1838 the Church of England showed signs of developing its education programme, and on the side of the state Russell established the Committee of the Privy Council on Education, and there were suspicions that he was moving towards an English version of the Irish National Education scheme (on which see n. 4 p. 16 *supra*). Others must therefore adopt a policy, and at the Conference of 1838 every circuit was required to appoint an Education Committee with a view to developing its own work. In this letter Bunting gives the impression that his views on the question were much more tentative than in fact they were. Under some pressure from Irish Methodists, Bunting had turned vehemently against the Irish National Education scheme and its supporters in Conference in 1832, and his penchant for full denominational control of schools was strengthened by his successful negotiation with Government about negro education in the West Indies (cf. no. 39 *supra*). In 1839 he launched a great drive to open a pipe-line of government support to Wesleyan schools independent of the British and Foreign School Society which finally succeeded in 1847.

[2] Hugh Beech (1787–1856), superintendent, Carlisle circuit, 1837–39. After serving at Selby, Barnard Castle and Birstal in turn, Beech was disappointed with his Carlisle station.

my pony, without which I could not go into the country parts of the
circuit. But *with* it I go out 4, 5, 6, 7, 8, or 10 miles in the country and
have to return the same evening, for we have no accommodation to
remain all night. Some time ago I went 10 miles and preached and
returned without being asked to take any refreshment, but I was as
happy as I used to be at the hospitable table of Isaac Crowther Esqr.[1]
and thank God that very night several souls were awakened, and
received notes the following month. Our friends wish me to remain
another year with [them] and I have said yes, provided the Conference
continue to help me to do the work as they have done this year. Of
course we find a great difference between this circuit and those in
which we have been for many years. Well, while souls are saved I am
happy anywhere.

I have turned my attention to the state of this District, and at our
District Meeting last week, we thought Whitehaven Circuit should be
divided, and make Workington the head of a Circuit,[2] a married and
single preacher at each place, and by taking Keswick from the Wigton
Circuit where a young man resides, and where he has only one place of
five members besides Keswick to attend to, and placing the young man
in Workington where he will be surrounded by plenty of work, and do
something worth living for – in the event of this taking place Wigton
will have to be a solitary station. But when we look at Wigton, a large
and populous place, I wish something could be done *in* it. I cannot say
what is the reason, but they are extremely low. The above alteration
was agreed to at the District. I am persuaded Whitehaven will be much
more comfortable thereby. We have an increase in the Districts in all
the circuits except in one there was 1 less and in another there was five
less. We have great peace in all our borders. This wilderness will
blossom as the rose. . . .

The object of my writing to you at this time is yet to be stated. At the time
of the soul-destroying separation in this place,[3] of course the singers
went away from us and that part of worship was far from being pleasant
in this large chapel. Many of our new hearers have come from the
church, and our Trustees and friends wish to meet their taste by introducing an organ into our chapel, a subscription has been entered into
and to my astonishment I now clearly see they will be able to place a
good and suitable organ in the Lord's House without leaving any debt
on it. And further I do believe that those who have given to this object

---

[1] Isaac Crowther Esq., of Croft House, Morley. Later a member of the Committee of
Privileges. D. 1850, aet. 81.

[2] Workington was not separated from Whitehaven till 1840.

[3] Cf. no. 131 *supra*.

will not give any less to the cause of God on that account. I was afraid that the measure might prejudice our claims upon the Contingent Fund, and stated the case to our beloved President who approved of the reasons for wishing to have an organ. And as we were prepared to say that no part of the purchase money or that which pays the organist should go out of the funds of the society, he thought they should be encouraged to go on in the matter, and that it ought not to injure our claims on the Contingent Fund. We stated the case at our District [Meeting], the members thereof unanimously agreed to recommend it to the Conference for its sanction. And now presuming on the permission of the Conference our friends intend to have the opening in the latter end of August. I am requested most earnestly to solicit the valuable aid of Dr. Bunting on the occasion to preach two sermons. . . .

154   From George Marsden[1]   *Sheffield, May 29, 1838*

I occasionally look back to former years when our interviews with each other were frequent, and when absent, correspondence in some measure supplied the place of personal interviews; but for some time past we have seldom met excepting at Conference, and then whatever friendship preachers may have, there is little time to express it.

You have again entered into the marriage state, and I hope prove it as in former years to be a source of comfort and happiness; but when we reflect upon the past, and look forward into an eternal world, how soon does everything of a temporal nature pass away. We sometimes love to dwell upon the past, and yet there was something of sorrow connected with the former recollections. . . .

By a letter from our President I hear that either Mr. T. Jackson or Mr. Stanley is mentioned as our next President. I am as fully persuaded as ever, that Conservative principles are not only the principles proper for our body, but that they are founded on the Bible. And I would have all our constituted authorities to keep close to Scripture principles; but if it be true (which I hear) that Mr. Stanley has changed his views, and that he is now what may be called a Conservative as to ecclesiastical affairs, I have no personal objection to his election, for I believe he is a man of piety. The Connexion is in peace, and the Lord is zealously reviving his work in various parts of the country, and I hope there is nothing likely to arise among us to create any uneasiness in our Connexion; on ⟨all⟩ accounts if he is ever to fill the Chair, it ⟨will⟩ be the

[1] George Marsden, superintendent, Sheffield (Norfolk St.) circuit, 1836–39.

proper time. But this is the first time I ever entered on the subject, and I should like to know your views on this business. . . .

155   From John Beecham   *London, June 5th, 1838*

. . . We are suddenly and unexpectedly called into the field again by the New Zealand Association.[1] On Friday I had a hasty note from Mr. Coates saying that on looking over the votes etc. of the House of Commons to his great surprise he found Mr. F. Baring[2] was that very evening (Friday) to move for leave to bring in a Bill for the Provisional Government etc. of New Zealand. I saw him of course almost immediately, and he went off to Mr. Plumptre[3] who could scarcely credit the information until he looked over the Votes, and found that it was 'no mistake'. Sir Robert H. Inglis[4] was also seen, and they engaged to say something on the subject. We did not at all expect that they would oppose the Introduction of the Bill; but they were encouraged when the time came to make a vigorous demonstration of opposition, and 23 voted with them against the introduction of the Bill; 74 voting for it. I understand they are quite encouraged by obtaining such a respectable minority on the spur of the moment against even the introduction of the Bill. The second reading is fixed for the 20th instant.

Mr. Coates and I are bestirring ourselves as well as we can. We are commencing an extensive circulation of our pamphlets; and the point which, with our present light, we are aiming at is to induce our friends to resist the progress of the Bill in the House until there be made

[1] The Aborigines Committee of 1837, reflecting the views of the Evangelical interest at the Colonial Office, was apprehensive of contact between European and uncivilized races when not 'attended by missionary exertions', and wished to keep the latter under the control of executive government. Before the end of 1838 they realized that the Maoris could no longer be preserved from contact with any Europeans except missionaries, and that political authority of some kind must be assumed. In 1839 it was proposed to annex parts of New Zealand to New South Wales, by which time Edward Gibbon Wakefield's New Zealand Land Company had already begun systematic colonization. This forced on the establishment of New Zealand as a Crown Colony. Wakefield was always distrusted by the missionary societies and the Colonial Office, and his first move, here recorded, a bill to establish a colony on the lines advocated by his New Zealand Association (founded 1837), was defeated by government influence.

[2] Francis Thornhill Baring (1796–1866), M.P. for Portsmouth, 1826–65; secretary to Treasury, 1835–39.

[3] John P. Plumptre, M.P. for East Kent, 1832–47. On June 1, Baring secured leave to bring in a bill to establish a British colony in New Zealand. Plumptre voted with the minority against the motion.

[4] Sir Robert Harry Inglis (1786–1855), M.P for University of Oxford, 1829–54. Teller for the minority in the division referred to in n. 3 *supra*.

a full investigation of the whole case. There are two courses, either of which will answer the end i. the appointment of a Committee of Inquiry, ii. asking for the evidence of the Lords' Committee to be laid before the House of Commons. Perhaps the latter would be the preferable mode.

The *Watchman*, this week, will be a New Zealand number.[1] I refer you to it for the division list etc. from which you will learn who are our friends. Lord J. Russell,[2] you will see from the Report, announced the Queen's consent for the introduction of a measure, and Sir G. Grey thought it would be better to allow the Bill to come in, thoug⟨h⟩ he said the government were not pledged to support it. The ministers and their adherents voted for the motion.

I am very much inclined to think it will be well to make personal application when you get back to Sir R. Peel.[3] It would be worth his while to make an effort in such a cause. . . . Poulett Thomson[4] voted for the motion. Will not our Manchester friends help to enlighten him? . . .

156 From John Beecham

London, June 9, 1838

I am literally boiling over with indignation. I have this morning got the New Zealand Bill, and so far as I can judge of it, from the cursory reading which I have given of it, it is one of the most *atrocious* schemes ever masked under the cant of philanthropy and professed regard for religion. I write this at [Humphrey] Sandwith's. I have called on him to say that the thing must be shewn up in the *Watchman* on Wednesday that the country may at once be apprised of what is going on. On Wednesday I judge we must take it up in Committee. The Church Committee[5] have decided to *petition* Parliament as soon as they *see the Bill*.

Our worst fears respecting the scheme are more than realised if I under-

[1] The *Watchman* June 6, 1838, contained a leader attacking the efforts of the New Zealand Association to obtain a royal charter, parliamentary news on the subject, and an extract from a pamphlet by John Beecham, attacking Samuel Hinds's support for the New Zealand Association.

[2] Lord John Russell (1792–1878), Home Secretary and Leader of the Commons, 1835–39; Colonial Secretary, 1839–41, when he resisted the influence of the evangelical Stephen, and made an agreement with the New Zealand Company which led to the grant of a charter.

[3] Sir Robert Peel (1788–1850), leader of the Conservative Party in opposition.

[4] Poulett Thomson, M.P. for Manchester, 1832–39. The bulk of the Wesleyan votes in the Manchester election of 1832 went to the whig pair, Mark Philips and Poulett Thomson. D. A. Gowland, 'Methodist secessions and social conflict in South Lancashire, 1830–57' (unpublished Manchester Ph.D. thesis, 1966) pp. 176, 595–98.

[5] I.e. the committee of the Church Missionary Society.

stand the provisions of the Bill aright. What ministers could think of, in asking Her Majesty's consent to have the Bill introduced, and what Lord J. Russell, and the rest of them could think of, in voting for its introduction, why their sense of right did not lead them to reject the proposal with indignation, it is difficult to conceive. . . .

157 From P. C. Turner[1]   *Devonport, June 13, 1838*

. . . There is some alteration for the better and some prospect of further improvement. The loss of the Rads. has been of incalculable benefit to the circuit; and though they occupy a chapel near to ours at Moricetown, we hear almost nothing of them, and I believe they *do* nothing. They do not want the *will* to do us harm, but through mercy they have not the power. Our District Meeting was a peaceable, I might say a *tame*, one. We had an increase of about 230 members and 440 on trial. Devon is in great want of more preachers. The Liskeard Circuit is fast recovering from the shock it received and Camelford is improving. The other circuits are rising a little. . . .

158 From W. Gilyard Scarth   *Gipton, nr. Leeds, July 23, 1838*

I beg to acknowledge the honour which has been done me by the insertion of my name in the list of Ministers and Gentlemen who are appointed as a Committee to make arrangements for the celebration of the approaching Wesleyan Centenary,[2] and by the special invitation which I have received from the President to attend a meeting of that Committee on Wednesday next. Circumstances which I cannot easily control deprive me of the pleasure which an attendance on such a

---

[1] Philip C. Turner, superintendent, Devonport Circuit, 1837–39.

[2] In 1839 a fund was launched to celebrate the centenary of the formation of the United Methodist Societies, which eventually raised over £220,000. (An earlier proposal to celebrate the centenary of Wesley's ordination in 1825 had been declined as unsuitable). The scheme was promulgated at a meeting of preachers and laymen at St. Philip's chapel, Bristol, on July 25, 1838, an invitation to which is here acknowledged. The committee itself put the emphasis upon a new Theological Institution, a Mission House, and better provision for supernumerary ministers and widows, and, despite Scarth's reservations, the fund made possible the foundation of a northern branch of the Institution at Didsbury. Except during the years 1868–85 when Richmond College was used exclusively for training candidates for the mission field, candidates for home and overseas service were always trained together. Eventually a large sum was also voted for the relief of distressed chapels, and a small one for chapel-building in Ireland.

meeting would have afforded me. This I regret; because I am sensible
of the peculiar advantages which cannot fail to arise from a free interchange of sentiments by personal communication. Yet as I feel a deep
interest in the object for which you will so shortly assemble, I take the
liberty of transmitting my views to you by letter, accompanied with an
assurance that I cherish a hearty disposition to concur in any measure
to which the Committee may deem it most eligible to award its official
sanction.

The Committee will, I doubt not, unanimously agree in the recommendation of those particular exercises of devotion which the occasion
pre-eminently demands. It has pleased God, in His abundant goodness,
to preserve the Methodist United Society for nearly one hundred years,
to favour us at this season after many painful agitations with a remarkable degree of peace and prosperity, and to present to us openings of
usefulness, both at home and abroad, which may be said to surpass all
former parallel. For these things a lively expression of gratitude is most
justly due, in connexion with which may also at the same time be added,
in the several localities of our body, a provision to gladden the hearts of
the poor members of the Society by a day of Christian festivity. But
something beyond this ought likewise in my humble judgment to be
attempted. I have thought of two schemes which appear to me to be of
capital and lasting importance, and one of which I ventured in a
personal interview to mention to you. My purpose is to name them now
with all convenient brevity; and thus to submit them to the candid
consideration of yourself, and the other members of the Committee.
I. One of them is the *formation of a United Establishment for the transaction
of Missionary business, and for the objects of the Wesleyan Theological Institution,
on a scale corresponding to the present claims of the Connexion, and capable of such
enlargement as may also meet its future necessities.* – Permit me, with all
deference to the judgment of others, to advance a few observations on
this subject.

1. It is my decided opinion that the *union* of the two Establishments, so
far from causing a fair ground of objection, would be attended with
*signal advantages. – Great saving of time and trouble would by this means be
secured to the gentlemen who are actively concerned in the superintendency of these
two invaluable parts of our general system.* The President of the Theological
Institution is the Senior Secretary of the Missionary Society; the
Treasurer of the Institution is also Treasurer of the Missions; and the
most efficient men in the London department of our work are members
of both the committees. None but themselves can sufficiently estimate
the convenience which would result from the transaction of the business
of both these Institutions on the same spot. – *No small assistance would at*

the same time be rendered to the Officers of the Theological Institution. They would always have ready access to men for whose principles and character they have the highest veneration, and who would promptly give their counsel in any case of difficulty. I am privy to the sentiments of one of these Officers, and may confidently say that he would hail such an arrangement with the most cordial satisfaction and pleasure.

2. It is also my opinion that the students in the Institution who are intended for the home-work, and those who are intended for missionary service, should continue as heretofore *to be trained and instructed together,* should all be encouraged, as far as possible, to cultivate a genuine missionary character. Is it not desirable that they should be eminently *one*? – that they should, during all their future lives, feel that they are still *brethren*? – and that if any, who at first contemplated the home-work, should be led to offer themselves for the work abroad, they should be furnished with every *facility* and *direction* which wisdom and zeal may dictate?

3. It is farther my opinion, much as I should be gratified on some accounts to see a second Theological Institution in the North of the Country, that there ought to be at present but *one* Establishment of that kind. Two reasons only need to be produced in support of this opinion – *the saving of expense*, and *the saving of official men* who might be needed for the supply of two Theological Institutions, men whom the Connexion could perhaps provide, but whom it could not well spare in a consistency with the due performance of its other momentous services.

II. My second scheme is the provision of what I may call, in mercantile language, a *trading capital* in aid of our missionary operations, a capital of from thirty to fifty thousand pounds. I am fully persuaded that the Missionary Treasurers will at once allow the necessity of such a capital, and will tell you how much anxiety it would prevent, how much interest-money it would save, and how wonderfully it would smooth and facilitate all the proceedings of the Missionary Committee. But on these topics I need not expatiate in a letter to *you*; because you are practically aware of the distressing perplexity which is often created by the want of such a capital.

Difficulties will, however, be started against this project – 'Our people would object to the existence of such a capital.' Why so? Would they then object, in other instances, to a person's having a suitable capital when he has to carry on a series of large and expensive trans-actions, and when, if he cannot fall back upon available resources, he must be subject to continual anxiety and embarrassment? 'But the money could not be raised.' That remains to be proved. A considerable portion of it might, possibly the whole. The mode of effecting this must, of course, be left to the Committee. 'Yet there would be nothing to shew, no permanent monument.' Yes; a monument far more permanent than 'things seen and temporal.' The sum which is now spent, and which on our present system is likely to be spent in interest, would support several additional missionaries, and would assist us to rush into the 'great and effectual doors' which God has marvellously 'opened' to us, and there seize upon monuments of eternal blessing which would be seen when earth and time, and change are no more. O that such a sc⟨heme⟩ could be carried into effect! And why should it not? ⟨Though⟩ silver and gold are the Lord's; and while, by the movements of His Providence and Grace, He teaches us that He 'hath need of them', how easily can he raise up men, where we perhaps should least expect them, and constrain them, by the expansive energy of His own love, to pour their gifts, with full hands and hearts, into His sacred treasury.

Other plans will, no doubt, be suggested to the Committee. I am convinced however that you, my dear Sir, will allow the two which I have introduced here to be distinguished by the strong claims of necessity. The present circumstances of the Missionary Society and the Theological Institution most certainly require them; and they would be a worthy remembrancer of the first centenary of that blessed Work to which our affections and lives are so gladly pledged. To distribute the proceeds of the Centenary among our many existing Societies would answer no great end, and to what other particular Fund can we so properly look? The Chapel-Fund is already proceeding hopefully; the School-Fund may be competently supported, by right exertions, in the usual way; and the Fund for our worn-out Preachers will, I sincerely trust, be taken up by our people, as a matter of ordinary justice, and supplied, in some measure, by regular and enlarged contributions.

You may now ask which of the two schemes above named I should myself prefer? If I yielded to the present emergency of the case, I should most probably reply – the second. But, on mature deliberation, I am inclined to think that the first would lead to the second. Let a united establishment be erected; let it stand forth as a kind of visible security to those who may become, in any way, responsible for the pecuniary interests of Methodism; and let the surplus money be appropriated to the provisions of a trading capital in support of the missions. . . .

159   From Thomas Beaumont[1]   *Bradford, July 31, 1838*

In common with thousands of my brethren, I have looked forward with a peculiar feeling to the important and interesting period of the *Centenary of Methodism* as one which has a *special* claim upon the *sympathies* and *capabilities* of the connexion at large.

To the various projects which have emanated from one and another of our excellent friends, I have not been indifferent or disaffected; and I rejoice in the fact that the schemes for signalizing this event in such a manner as to do honour to the Body, have been variously propounded and zealously advocated. It is not without considerable diffidence that in the midst of deliberations which will be eminent for the precise elements which are the best calculated to lead to the best and the wisest arrangements, I presume to offer my own views and feelings; expecially after having addressed them, at some length, to the respected Editor of the *Magazine* whose judgement has deferred their insertion up to the present time. However I am induced to forego all personal considerations in the matter, principally because I hold it to be the duty, as well as the privilege, of every member of the society to seek by all becoming means to promote the best interests of the body. Whilst therefore I should now rejoice to see the material elements of a 'Theological Institution' disposed so as to form an erection worthy of the genius of Methodism; and also should be equally delighted to behold a complete suite of premises every way worthy of the missionary cause, the fee simple of which should be in the inalienable possession of the Wesleyan Missionary Society; I cannot but think that on the great occasion of the approaching Centenary some more magnificent effort might be made than would be required for either of the objects alluded to, and I hasten therefore to express the views and feelings which have rested upon my own mind. Two distinct branches of our economy have appeared to me to lie in a state of almost hopeless abeyance; and it is in reference to these cases, I now presume to address you.

The first is that of *decayed and supernumerary preachers* who I think have the very highest claim upon the connexion for such a provision as cannot under *existing* circumstances be secured to them; and, the second is that of *distressed chapels* where, from the pressure of a blighting incubus of debt, the cause is in a languishing and almost hopeless condition! I am quite aware of course of the great efforts which have been made for a few years past; and yet in too many cases the very working of that admirable

---

[1] Thomas Beaumont (1795–1859), brother of Dr. Joseph Beaumont, preacher; surgeon at Bradford, 1822–59. Alderman, founder of Bradford Temperance Society, 1830, and author of *An essay on the nature and properties of alcoholic liquors* (1837).

system has only served to lay bare and open some of the very painful cases to which I refer. . . .

What I propose to do with the money, is this . . . To lend out to *distressed chapels* the *amount* of their respective debts at *two and a half per cent*; and out of the sum produced by the accumulated interest, to form a fund for the support of all *supernumerary preachers* who have not private resources sufficient for their maintenance. If the sum of two hundred thousand only could be raised, then, by lending it out to distressed chapels at 2½ per cent, almost every case of that nature would be effectually relieved (and if such an object could be effected what a glorious *reaction* in the fortunes of Methodism would in many cases take place?) and a sum of *five thousand pounds annually* would be thus available for the *support of worn out preachers*! . . .

160 From R. Alder   *77 Hatton Garden, London, January 11, 1839*

. . . My principal reason for troubling you with this scrawl is to send you news from Windsor, from which ancient seat of Royalty Mr. Hoole has just returned, and has brought us not only the pleasing intelligence that the Centenary contributions of our few poor friends there amount to more than £150, but what is better than a large collection, that we are to have a change of Ministry before the meeting of Parliament.[1] That is the reason why Her Majesty left Brighton so soon and so unexpectedly, and has returned to the surprise of everybody, even of ourselves until we were let into the secret, to the New Palace. Lord Stanley[2] is to form the Cabinet, and Sir R. Peel is to take office with him. The Duke of Wellington has promised his support, but will not accept office. This intelligence has been obtained from a good quarter and Mr. Hoole is of opinion that it maybe depended on. Of course we believe it, and have spent an hour in assigning to the probable members of the new cabinet their proper places and when the list is complete we will publish. The report brought from Windsor is certainly corroborated by the facts that the Queen, since her return to town, has been much occupied with affairs of State, and that the council sat upwards of 3 hours yesterday. The debate on the Address in the French Chamber is not yet finished, and opinions are greatly divided as to the result. The more prevalent opinion is, that it will end unfavourably to the existing

[1] Though the government majority in the Commons had almost disappeared, they did not resign until May 1839, when Peel's efforts to form a government were frustrated by his famous dispute with the Queen over the appointment of Ladies of the Bedchamber.

[2] Lord Stanley, a vigorous critic of the colonial policies of the Melbourne government, and Peel's successor as leader of the Conservative Party.

Ministry. The King[1] and his family are greatly afflicted by the intelligence which they have received of the death of his second and favourite daughter the Duchess of Wirtemberg. . . .

161   From James Hearn[2]   *Hatford Rectory, January 14, 1839*

Although I have never had the pleasure of being introduced to you by any of our mutual friends, yet having not unfrequently heard of you through my valued connections the Jerrams of Cheltenham and also through my kind neighbour and friend Rev^d. Charles Jerram[3] of Whitney I have taken the liberty of writing to you. . . .

Oxford is close at hand and I am almost in weekly communication with some of the active members of the University. If Christians (I mean protestants) keep aloof from each other their enemies, the papists, who are a united body will *surely* gain the victory over them. It is quite plain that Popery expects to take the different Protestant bodies in detail as Bonaparte did the nations on the continent. Rome regards our semi-papists at Oxford with exultation and fully expects these men, our Puseys, Kebles and Newmans, to do her work.

The object of the New Memorial at Oxford is not merely to erect a mere testimony of respect to these great men.

It is operating powerfully in rallying a better spirit among the young men at Oxford. No one is aware, unless near enough to observe what is passing, the great influence the pernicious publications have made in the minds of the inexperienced and the uninstructed youths in that university. May I be permitted to *request* your *earliest* attention to this subject, I mean erecting a Church at Oxford to the memory of Cranmer Latymer and Ridley. I have no personal motive to gratify because I took my degree from St. John's College, Cambridge, but to me this is a matter of little moment. Either of those great seminaries of learning is of immense moment in times like these. Pray use your influence at *this time* for the truth's sake! Any communication directed to Rev^d. R. L. Cotton,[4] Worcester College, Oxford.

. . . There is to be meeting to decide whether it is to be a memorial or a Church on the thirty-first instant Jany. – Mr. Cotton is very desirous of

---

[1] Louis Philippe, king of France, 1830–48.

[2] James Hearn (c. 1785–1864), rector of Hatford, Berks., 1836–64.

[3] Charles Jerram (1770–1853), rector of Witney, 1834–53. Jerram had been vicar of St. John's Chapel, Bedford Row, 1824–26, and was a well-known evangelical and church-builder.

[4] Richard Lynch Cotton (d. 1880, aet. 86), fellow of Worcester College, Oxford, 1816–38; provost, 1839–80. One of the leading Oxford evangelicals. Later manager of Gladstone's Oxford election committee.

having a place of worship where the gospel may be preached to the poor – with a *si monument[um] requiras circumspice* at least inscribed in its walls with the names of our ancestors . . . I do hope that whatever be our attachment to our particular communities it will allow of our meeting cordially upon this sacred ground. . . .

162   From John S. Elliott   *London, February 20, 1839*

. . . . Dr. Cooke[1] gave us one of the most clear and forcible exposées of the misprision, duplicity and *inefficiency* (except as an instrument of evil) of the National Board of Education of Ireland that was ever delivered. He animadverted with peculiar but just severity on the sentiment of the Home Secretary,[2] that children between 3 and 7 might with safety be educated in the same general basis, without the knowledge of any distinctive creed. Time permits me only to express my heart-felt desire, not unmixed with a firm belief, that the spirit of counsel and might and knowledge as well as of the fear of the Lord may be copiously poured out upon your Committee and especially on the Governors of our Israel. . . .

163   From John W. Gabriel[3]   *17 Marylebone St., St. James,*
March 14, 1839

. . . . Last evening I had a considerable conversation with Mr. Dunn[4] the Secretary to the Borough Road School during which he deplored the want of union amongst the religious societies. He especially pointed out the great advantages that would result if [they were] united upon the principles of obtaining aid from Government for the establishment and

---

[1] Henry Cooke (1788–1868), presbyterian minister at Belfast, 1829–68, and leader of the evangelical party in the Ulster synod, bringing about the exclusion of ministers of Arian views. This letter was written in reply to a request from Bunting (Duke University MSS., Durham N.C.: Jabez Bunting to A. E. Farrar, February 18 [1839]) to call upon Cooke when he came to address the meeting (here reported) for the Hibernian School Society at the Hanover Square Rooms. Cooke had failed to reply to an invitation to preach for the Wesleyan Methodist Missionary Society at Great Queen St. in April, and in response to the personal application of Elliot and Farrar excused his inability to assist on the ground that he would be out of the country.

[2] Lord John Russell.

[3] John Wild Gabriel, a trustee of City Road chapel, London.

[4] Henry Dunn (1800–78), secretary to the British and Foreign School Society, 1830–57; a consistent advocate of state aid for education. On Bunting's attitude to the British and Foreign Society, see n. 1. p. 203.

support of schools leaving the mode of religious instruction and the regulation and control of the schools entirely in the hands of those religious societies who would appoint responsible committees of their own for this purpose.

He expressed his great desire to work with the Methodist society, and expecially his anxious wish to obtain an interview with you, so that he might converse with you on the subject, and requested me to solicit an appointment from you.

. . . Being devoted to the cause of the religious education of the young I have consented to this if possibly I may in the very smallest degree be instrumental in averting a state national education system and be auxiliary in promoting means by which the extension of a Methodistical education may speedily be effected throughout the land. . . .

164   From Lord Lansdowne[1]   *Berkeley Square, April 16 [1839]*

Although it is impossible to answer all the letters which I daily receive upon the subject of education, I feel the very candid and sensible spirit in which yours is written requires not only an acknowledgement but an explanation. I deeply regret the intolerant spirit by which, in the instances you have mentioned, dissenting children have been deprived of the benefit of a school which has received public aid. I trust they are not common and think a more liberal spirit will prevail with most of the managers of Church of England Schools. It would be very desirable that this should be secured, but the difficulty is, that the National Society have hitherto received assistance without any such stipulation, and that one of their rules is to leave the discretion of the managers of schools under them unfettered in this respect.

If however the strictness of this rule is not relaxed, and it appears in any case that a poor dissenting population is thus debarred from the advantages of education, I am confident that it would be felt by the Committee of the Privy Council to be a reason for extending aid to them in a much larger proportion than is usual to enable to establish a school of their own. . . .

[1] Henry Petty-Fitzmaurice, 3rd marquis of Lansdowne (1780–1863), Lord President of the Council, 1835–41.

165   From Thomas Stead[1]   *Bolton, April 23, 1839*

. . . I am exceedingly anxious to see the total extinction of the disrepu-
table practice of writing on the Sabbath. We have since the last Conference established, or rather, are now establishing, Day Schools on an
extensive scale in connection with our prosperous and strictly Wesleyan
Sabbath Schools at Fletcher Street Chapel, which I am happy to say are
sapping the foundations of the old and notorious school.[2] Could you
possibly pay us a visit, it would greatly strengthen our hands. . . .

166   From Thomas Edwards[3]   *Belper, May 2, 1839*

[Could Bunting preach for their infant school?] . . . We have two
infant schools in this town, one under the immediate patronage of the
Messrs. Strutts, the other supported by the Church, the Methodists and
dissenters generally; and an annual collection [is] made alternately in
the Church, the Independent and Wesleyan Chapels . . .

167   From John Wesley Thomas[4]   *St. Austell, May 7, 1839*

It has been announced by advertisement in the usual way that our
chapel in St. Austell has been licensed for the performance of marriages.[5]
I am desirous that you should know that this has been done by persons
not in connexion with us (and at their expense), in opposition to a
formal decision of a trustee meeting to the contrary. The accompanying
newspaper (*The Cornwall Gazette*) will make known to you other circumstances connected with the transaction. The majority of the trustees

[1] Thomas Stead, superintendent, Bolton circuit, 1838–41.

[2] This derogatory description was of one of the most famous Sunday schools in Methodism,
which in its early days had been an especial favourite of John Wesley, and which had continued
to combine an unusually high rate of recruiting to the Society with the practices, now connexionally frowned upon, of Sabbath writing instruction and substantial autonomy. An
attempt to impose Conference rules in 1833 had led to a large separation of teachers, scholars
and members (cf. Ward, *Religion and Society* pp. 136–7, 172). For Bunting's disapproval of
Sabbath writing lessons, *Ibid.* pp. 135–40.

[3] Thomas Edwards, superintendent, Belper circuit, 1837–40. The Belper situation of mixed
education was precisely the one from which Bunting was trying to escape. He declined the
invitation on May 13.

[4] John Wesley Thomas, preacher, St. Austell circuit, 1837–39.

[5] For about a decade after it became possible to license chapels for the solemnization of
marriages in 1836, Wesleyans generally declined to take advantage of the change in the law.
For the reasons which brought about a change (and which included the impossibility of
preventing undesirable parties securing a licence) see no. 254 *infra*.

Q

have acted very properly in the business; and of the three who voted in favour of the measure, two are not members of the society. Our leading friends, however, are fearful that as the chapel has been licensed, though against their wish, the Civil Registrars may, for their own purposes, intrude into it, with the aid of one or more of their *co-radicals*, the adverse trustees; or through the influence and authority of some future preacher who may be favourable to the new marriage law: and they wish to know how it may be prevented. Taking it for granted (as I do) that the general feeling and opinion of the preachers is against the new law, might not the expression of a decided opinion by yourself or member of the Conference in that assembly, be useful in putting these brethren on their guard who either want information, or whose minds are not fully made up on the subject. For myself, I should be glad to see a minute against getting our chapels licensed; but there may be objections to the publication of such a minute of which I am not aware.

There is another matter in which, although our trustees in St. Austell are disposed to act right, they are just now overborne by the 'pressure from without'. *I allude to Tee-totalism.* More than twelve months ago our Chapel was lent to Mr. Teare,[1] for the holding of a meeting of that kind, but on an application for the use of the chapel a 2nd time, the trustees unanimously refused it, except for a sermon or religious service conducted by some accredited minister; but this was contemptuously declined, and for twelve months we have been maligned and calumniated, in consequence of our alleged *opposition* to Tee-totalism. I am sorry to say that at a trustee meeting last evening, consent was given to the holding a public 'tee-total' meeting in our chapel on the evening of St. Austell feast. That happens to be *our preaching night,* and *it is my appointment.* I thoroughly feel the impropriety of giving up the preaching of God's word, and divine worship for such a meeting. It was the unanimous opinion of preachers and trustees twelve months ago that such a meeting would be *a desecration of the place*; and being still of the same opinion, I am placed in a rather awkward dilemma. I have said that I will be no party to the holding such a meeting in the chapel; therefore, should Mr. Hobson[2] as my superintendent request me to give up the pulpit on that evening I shall do so; otherwise I should not feel justified in doing so.

I do not know whether my view of the subject is right or not; but such

---

[1] James Teare (1804–68), a shoemaker and Methodist local preacher from the Isle of Man. One of the Preston teetotallers, and one of the first two nation-wide teetotal missionaries sent out by the British Association for the Promotion of Temperance in 1836. During his three-month visit to Cornwall in 1838, he made 5000 recruits to the temperance societies.

[2] John Hobson (1790–1863), superintendent, St. Austell circuit, 1837–39.

are the facts, and my sole motive for making you acquainted with them is the hope that in the Conference, or in some other way, your opinion will be made known to the preachers, as to the propriety or impropriety of allowing Tee-total meetings to be held in our Chapels.[1] . . .

168   From Lord Ashley[2]   *n. pl. June 7* [*1839*]

Private & confidential.

I have sent you the *new* plan of Government Education – it is worthy of attention.

You will see that the paragraph marked 1. gives powers for the distribution of public money in support of Popish schools and schools founded on the principles of the Central School-Society.[3]

By paragraph 2 the Committee[4] retain a power of inspecting and, so in fact, controlling the schools which may have received a grant from the national funds. I dont know what the Wesleyan body may think of such conditions; I hope the Church of England will reject them.

Pray be so kind as to shew this paper, as soon as possible to Mr. Newstead.[5] . . .

[1] At the Conference of 1839 (see Gregory, *Sidelights* p. 318) 'Dr. Bunting spoke of "the annoyances arising from teetotalism. There are two points on which we must insist: (1) The use of *bona fide* wine in the Lord's Supper; (2) the not allowing teetotal meetings in our chapels" '. Bunting secured resolutions to this effect, holding that 'we are not enemies to sobriety, but to vituperation'. Another speaker described Cornish Methodism as 'in a state of "fermentation" on the subject', and in 1841 over 850 members left the St. Ives circuit and formed the Teetotal Wesleyan Methodist connexion, with a number of chapels in the St. Ives and Penzance area.

[2] Anthony Ashley Cooper, Lord Ashley, later seventh earl of Shaftesbury (1801–85), evangelical philanthropist. Ashley had already given Bunting personal assurance of his 'high respect . . . for the Wesleyan Body' and subscribed to the Missionary Society (M.C.A. MSS. Lord Ashley to Jabez Bunting, May 1 [1837]), and was to intervene decisively in the Wesleyan negotiations with the government on education in 1847. Cf. no. 278 *infra*.

[3] The Central Society of Education, founded in 1837 by Thomas Wyse to press for the implementation of the principles of the Irish National Education scheme in England.

[4] The Education Committee of the Privy Council.

[5] Robert Newstead (1789–1865), preacher, London (Lambeth) circuit, 1837–40, who bore the principal responsibility in shaping a Wesleyan schools policy over the next few years (cf. M.C.A. MSS. R. Newstead to Jabez Bunting, July 14, 1843). An unsuccessful effort was made by the Education Committee to keep him in London for their own service in 1843. M.C.A. MSS. Same to same, July 23, 1843.

169   From Thomas Allan[1]   F[redericks] P[lace, London],
                                                    June 11, 1839 [Copy]

I have just received a note calling a meeting of the Committee [of Privileges] for tomorrow at ½ past 9 at which time I hope punctually to attend. As I must be in the Admiralty Court between 11 and 12, say a little past 11, I shall be glad if you will be prepared with the Resolutions for the consideration of the meeting. In addition to the objections you will state to the new scheme,[2] I am satisfied we must gravely consider whether we must distinctly take the ground that we renounce all assistance from the government and insist upon our objection to the state being the regulator of the education of the population or disposing of the funds of the country in support of popery or the declared enemies of the authorised version and our conviction of the non-necessity of any general plan. I think I am aware of what can and may be s[ai]d against such a resolution as this and if we adopt it (although you would express it in better words than the above) we must be prepared for all that will be said and perhaps done, but still is a stand to be made? And on what principle? For considering the state of the horizon I have no doubt that all Christians will have to take their station on one side or the other – there will be no medium and therefore, if I am at all right, the sooner we take up our position on a principle from which as Methodists we mean not to shrink the better, and the more we shall influence those who halt between two opinions, or at any rate fight our own approaching battles with greater consistency and under God with more hope of ultimate success. In pursuing such a line of conduct I should hope we shall be well supported both by the preachers generally and the sound and major part of our people; if however I should unhappily be mistaken in this hope, yet we shall have preferred the work of God to Mammon and have recorded a testimony against the loose principles of the day which seem to be leading to awful events. Now before tomorrow think of these things deeply, for considering your influence with the preachers much will depend upon your opinion and recommendation. I dont know whether I am mistaken but I seem to feel as if on such points as these there is not the same decided unanimity of feeling as existed when the battle was fought with Lord Sidmouth.[3] Then we were uncompromising. We ran all risks. We have before us a harder service and should be

---

[1] Thomas Allan, for many years connexional solicitor, and a Protestant politician.

[2] Russell's education proposals of 1839. Among those which survived Parliamentary criticism were the creation of the education committee of the Privy Council, an enlarged education grant, and government inspection of schools.

[3] The defeat of Lord Sidmouth's bill to restrict itinerant preaching, 1811. On Allan's crucial part in this campaign see Ward, *Religion and Society* pp. 57–62.

determined in our principles whatever comes or who can answer for the work of God amongst us?

170   From Edward Baines Jun.[1]   *Leeds Mercury Office*
to Jabez Bunting Jun.   *June 19, 1839*

I am obliged by your courtesy in sending me an authentic report of the speech of your father, the Rev. Dr. Bunting. I was quite aware of his sentiments as to the education of the poor belonging to religious communities, and not to the state. But nevertheless there is a passage in his speech, which we extracted from the *Watchman*, and which I find in the same words in p. 11 of the Report you have sent me, that seems to me fully to justify the remarks we founded on it.[2] The passage begins 'Now, what right has a government to say', etc. and ends 'when we may think it right to do so.' It clearly implies that the Wesleyans, inasmuch as they 'pay' to the support of the School Societies assisted by Government, have as much right as the Church to have their catechism used in those Schools. Now we turned this position against your father – as an *argumentum ad hominem* – by showing that it was just as cogent for the Roman Catholics as for the Wesleyans; and yet he maintained that the former ought to receive no 'public aid' whatever. Here is an inconsistency, as it seems to me; and I do not see how it can be explained away.

My decided opinion is that the Catholics have just as much right to 'public aid' for the education of the children of their poor as the Church or the Wesleyans. I am sorry to find that Dr. Bunting thinks otherwise.

I regret to see that you take in seriousness and as a 'slander' what was meant as an innocent joke, namely, the application of the term 'Bishop' to Dr. Bunting. It was certainly not applied with any intention or feeling that could justify this interpretation. Dr. Bunting's eminence as the acknowledged head (by influence and talent) of the Wesleyan body was the chief provocative to apply this term playfully; added to which was the position in which he now stands as cooperating with the Bishops in their opposition to the Government plan for an Education Board. As to the imputations made by some defunct party among the Wesleyans,

[1] Edward Baines jun. (1800–90), editor of the *Leeds Mercury* of which his father, of the same name, was proprietor. A doctrinaire advocate of voluntaryism in education.

[2] The *Leeds Mercury*, June 15, 1839 p. 4, carried a long leader on National Education, which extensively quoted Bunting's speech in opening the Great Queen St. Day Schools in London, and charged him with flagrant inconsistency in accusing the Government of wrongfully taxing the Wesleyans, since they deprived them of their right to use their catechism in schools, while demanding that Government behave in precisely this way towards Roman Catholics.

they never occurred to me. I hope therefore you will cease to think of this term as having been used offensively. I have a high respect for Dr. Bunting's talents, character, and public usefulness, and am sorry to differ from him in politics. But I am sure you will admit my right to maintain my opinions as stoutly as he maintains his. . . .

171   From John W. Gabriel   *17 Marylebone St., St. James,*
June 25, 1839

. . . It seems to me very important that an organised committee should immediately after the meeting of Conference set about devising the best means of extending education and especially day schools in our connexion and I think a committee upon the model of the Missionary committee would be most effectual for the purpose.[1] By the dissemination of information throughout the connexion a correct idea of the importance of day schools and of the best means of establishing them would be obtained and a corresponding zeal excited. It is important that we should aim at effecting the greatest amount of good at the least possible expense and as we have in almost every large town capacious Sunday school room, suitable for day schools without any increase of rent and mostly idle throughout the week, it is obviously desirable that these should be first brought into requisition.

By the Conferential return there are 3339 Sunday Schools; assuming that one thirtieth part of these are suitable for the accommodation of 200 children each, we then [have] available means for the day instruction of 22,200 scholars. It is very important that we should begin wi⟨th⟩ large schools on account of the receipts from t⟨he⟩ children. Our boys' school at Radnor Street wa⟨s⟩ begun under these circumstances and cost for fitt⟨ing⟩ in forms, desks rails and support of master whilst training £68.12.5; it will seat *at desks* 210, shewi⟨ng⟩ a cost of 6/6 per child.

If it should be thought wise to place the sum fr⟨om⟩ the Centenary fund at the disposal of the propo⟨sed⟩ committee they might afford a powerful stimu⟨lus⟩ to education by making grants after the old Treasury plan,[2] say 3/- per head for every child so accommodated, the petitioning committee guaranteeing to raise the rest and secure the school to the Connexion. This would take upon the above calculation £3330 from the grant, they might then assist the enlargement of schools

---

[1] An education committee was established by Conference in 1837.
[2] Eventually £5051.19.3 was voted from the Centenary Fund to Wesleyan Education.

at 5/- per head and if they should have any left might induce the building of new schools at 10/- per head. Conference would soon find it necessary to have a travelling inspector of the schools from their own body at least in the course of two years and if an annual collection were allowed in the larger chapels we should by these means very shortly outrival the church in schools.

The question of a normal and model school is important as it regards expense and usefulness. At present we have a welcome at the Boro[ugh] Road,[1] but if we set about the matter in right earnest we should very soon inundate them with students. An efficient normal school would cost from £1200 to £1500 annually. Its site would be an interesting question. If resolved upon I think with all deference that Radnor Street cannot be surpassed. It is in a good healthy and well populated neighbourhood, the premises are suitable and capable of great extension at a moderate cost and the school is in a very progressively improving condition. . . .

172   From John McLean[2]   *Sheffield, June 25, 1839*

. . . . We are *delighted* with the truly Wesleyan part you are taking in behalf of our insulted Protestantism, and could you come to Sheffield at this juncture, it would be productive not merely of local but national benefit. May the Lord preserve your health for you have a great work before you. . . . In the meantime be assured my dear Sir that earnest prayer shall go up for you to the God of Protestantism. Galland's letter has opened mouths that would have remained shut; but it cannot harm us.[3] Dan O'Connell[4] has furnished a capital defence for us. We are true

[1] Borough Road was the headquarters of the British and Foreign School Society.

[2] John McLean, supernumerary, Sheffield (Carver St.) circuit, 1837–40.

[3] Receiving one Thursday from the President of Conference a batch of petitions against the government's education proposals to be signed by congregations the following Sunday, Galland took exception both to the object of the petition and to its statement that the 'petitioners had given much and serious attention to the subject', but distributed the petitions without signing himself. When his conduct was impeached in the press, he wrote a long letter to the *Leeds Mercury* (June 8, 1839; reprinted in *Manchester Guardian* June 12, 1839) explaining his position, and complaining that the proceedings looked like the use of connexional machinery for a political manoeuvre. For this outspoken statement his character was impeached in Conference by Robert Newton, one of his circuit colleagues, and the violent scene which followed was terminated by Galland's declining to contest the matter further. Gregory, *Sidelights* pp. 268–78.

[4] Daniel O'Connell (1775–1847), Irish nationalist leader, had published *Letters to the ministers and office-bearers of the Wesleyan Methodist Societies of Manchester* (Manchester, 1839) protesting against their opposition to the National Education scheme in terms similar to those of Edward Baines in no. 170 *supra*. He added, however, that the Wesleyans had never

sons of Wesley on his showing. Well there is no retreating now: at all events, to use a vulgar phrase we must 'go the whole hog'. We have drawn the sword and our only honourable and successful course is to throw away the scabbard. I shall send you by this post a Sheffield paper. It was liberal a few weeks since; but has turned conservative, and is likely to do much good. The chief manager of it is a Methodist and a true man. . . .

173   To Robert Pilter[1]   *London, July 6, 1839*

. . . Now for a word as to the two other points mentioned in your interesting and welcome letter.

1. *New Auxiliary Fund.*[2] I see no material objection to those Circuits, which particularly request it, being left *quite at liberty* to take their own mode of raising their quota; provided they do but undertake that they *will* raise it, in one way or another. This, indeed, was always understood, and is, I think, *implied* in the printed plan; though it would not be well to have it absolutely open, without any *suggestion* at all.

2. *Next President.* From all I have happened to hear, I infer that it will be either Lessey[3] or Dixon.[4] I have a sincere esteem for both; and, considering that the Centenary Year requires a man of peculiar *pulpit* qualifications, think that one of those two should be elected. As at present advised, I give the decided *preference* for *this* year to Mr. Lessey, for the reasons to which you refer. He is the *Senior*; he has rendered many and *long* public services as a visiting preacher; he is, of the two, much more familiar with our general *business*, and has been more in the habit

been friends to religious liberty, that John Wesley had helped to found the Protestant Association which led to the Gordon Riots, and that, if they really objected to paying for false religions, they should oppose church rates. At the 1839 Conference, Bunting accused Galland of O'Connellism, and of keeping 'the same company as Mr. O'Connell'. Gregory, *Sidelights* p. 277.

[1] Robert Pilter, superintendent, Bradford (Kirkgate) circuit, 1838–41.

[2] The 'Merciful Fund', known from 1813 as the Auxiliary Fund, received donations with which to supplement the provision made by the preachers themselves through their Annuitant Society for their widows and superannuated brethren. The committee which launched the Centenary Fund originally conceived as one of its chief objects the raising of a capital sum to permit a more generous provision on a regular scale. To do so, however, would have consumed more than the entire yield of the Centenary Fund, and so the New Auxiliary Fund was raised to be supported by Circuits at a rate of not less than 6d. per annum per member, to be collected (it was suggested) at the first two class meetings in January.

[3] Theophilus Lessey, preacher, Bristol (King St.) circuit, 1838–39. Lessey was President, 1839.

[4] James Dixon, superintendent Sheffield (Carver St.) circuit, 1837–40. President, 1841.

of mixing himself with our affairs in Committees. Mr. Dixon would do well *during* the Conference; but I look to the various and often difficult affairs which the President has to settle in the *intervals* between Conferences. In a little time hence, Mr. Dixon may qualify himself for that class of duties; and I shall be truly glad, if I live, to see him in the chair at a proper period. At present I deem Mr. Lessey the fittest. You have now my frank opinion. But I wish we could, especially *this* year, avoid any appearance of great division of feeling on this matter. . . .

174 From William Dale[1]   *Truro, July 12, 1839*

For several months past I have thought of troubling you with a letter respecting some matters (which to me appear important) connected with Methodism in Cornwall, but have delayed it for several reasons, such as an unwillingness to break in upon your valuable time, and 2nd want of time and ability to do justice to the subjects I wished to bring before you; but recollecting the kind manner in which you have interested yourself for Cornwall on other occasions, I am encouraged to hope you will forgive the trouble I am giving you by this application. Without further preface I shall therefore proceed to lay before you my views on the matters above alluded to.

You have doubtless heard of the glorious revival of religion that has taken place in several of the Cornish circuits, that upwards of five thousand have been added to the Societies in the District since the last Conference. But while with every lover of Zion I rejoice in the work which God has thus wrought I feel exceedingly anxious that the proper measures should *now* be taken to improve the *organization* and to increase the efficiency of 'Methodism in Cornwall'. The time is now favourable for introducing the *proper financial system* and increasing the *pastoral labour*, and both these are essential to the preservation of the souls gathered into the church and the future well-being of the Societies in this District. And here allow me to say that to accomplish these objects it is necessary to have *several superintendents possessing special qualifications for the work sent into the County*, ministers of talents, zeal, and prudence, men who are bent on the improvement of their respective circuits. If this is not done now I am greatly afraid Methodism will be thrown back a quarter of a century. This arrangement may require considerable sacrifices on the part of some of our excellent ministers, yet for such an object I doubt not many will be found ready to make them. The

[1] William Dale, an influential layman of Truro.

importance of suitable superintendents is strikingly seen by looking at two or three of our circuits at this moment. In Camborne Mr. Dunn[1] has succeeded in a great degree in introducing the proper methodistical system of finance and made arrangements for doubling the number of ministers on the circuit. In the adjoining circuit of Hayle which has long been suffering from the want of adequate pastoral care, although there has been a considerable addition to the Societies, no step has been taken to increase the number of preachers. I saw a friend from that circuit last week who stated that in one parish six miles distant from Hayle they had eight hundred members, that they had one chapel with a large Society connected therewith that the ministers were never able to visit. My friend suggested to the superintendent the necessity of getting an additional preacher that these large Societies might be properly watched over. He said it must be left to another year. My friend replied, 'by that time you will not have them to look after'. The same may be said of St. Ives where, notwithstanding the great revival, no steps have been taken to secure additional labourers. The circumstances in which that circuit is placed by the late revival evidently requires a superintendent of no ordinary qualifications. The conversion of the clergyman, the Rev. Mr. Malkin,[2] followed by his great zeal and increasing influence renders it exceedingly desirable that the superintendent may be sufficiently influential to lead Mr. Malkin in the right path. In the late revival many of the most respectable of the town have been converted. How important to train them aright and attach them fully to all the institutions of Methodism. The Rev. H. Williams[3] told me they could not increase the number of ministers without an improved financial system which he had been recommending to them and which some had adopted. If his efforts are followed up by a popular and wise superintendent there is no doubt of success and a blessed improvement in that ancient and important place in Methodism will be the result. I have lately heard they had invited Mr. Saunders[4] of Scilly. If so everybody else knows he is quite unfit for the present circumstances. In Helstone our friends have to contend with a vigorous and influential

---

[1] Samuel Dunn (1798–1882), superintendent, Camborne circuit, 1838–41. Dunn, here seen introducing standard Buntingite administration, turned against the connexional management in the 'forties, and edited an opposition journal, the *Wesley Banner and Revival Record*. Required by the Conference of 1849 to discontinue publication, Dunn refused and was expelled, becoming a leader of the Wesleyan reform movement.

[2] William Malkin (1791–1874), chaplain to the East India Co., 1816–32; vicar of St. Ives, 1833–50.

[3] Henry Wilkinson Williams (1810–98), preacher, St. Ives circuit, 1837–39.

[4] John Saunders (1795–1871), sole preacher, Scilly Islands, 1837–39; superintendent, St. Ives circuit, 1839–41.

party of the [Wesleyan Methodist] Association and will need a good bishop[1] and will by the divine blessing do well with one. The same may be said of that old and important Methodist circuit Redruth. They especially want lively preachers with good sense. St. Agnes is a fine and improving field and has *throughout* perhaps the best methodistical feeling of any circuit in the county. At the end of another year they will (I suppose) have to take a second *married* preacher and it will require great prudence and zeal in the superintendent next year to make the arrangements. An unpopular or injudicious superintendent will throw them into great difficulties. At St. Austle the superintendent will have need of great firmness as well as other qualifications always necessary.

I am astonished at my presumption but pardon me. I do feel that a great effort must be made for Methodism in Cornwall and that it is necessary you should know very particularly the state of our affairs. And I do beseech you to make the *effort now*. I believe there never will be such an opportunity again. I speak advisedly when I say that all the superintendents of the District that change this Conference except the Chairman and Mr. Jewel[2] *must be removed out of the District,* and two or three others when the opportunity arises. I have said nothing respecting Truro though matters are not going on satisfactorily, because I am not prepared to make any practical suggestion, and therefore do not like to trouble you with any complaint.

I ought however to say that some improvements are taking place in the District and let the parties making them have the credit that is due, viz. for the division of the Penzance, Camborne, and Bodmin Circuits, and the proposed division of the District for the missionary work which I hope the Conference will sanction. And we shall be extremely glad to see Mr. Dawson[3] as one of the deputation to our section again before long – and I hope this arrangement will lead to a permanent and complete division of the District, making a *Penzance* and a *Truro* District. I have urged this before but have been met by the remark that the Districts would be so small as to have no weight in the Conference. However that will not now be a matter of very urgent necessity.

And now allow me to refer to another subject that will deeply affect

[1] In the Methodist system 'episkope' or pastoral oversight is vested in the circuit superintendent, who in early 19th century correspondence is occasionally referred to as the bishop, sometimes (as here) seriously, more often with jocular overtones implying that he is an interfering busybody.

[2] John Hobson (1790–1863), Chairman of the Cornwall District, 1838–40. Thomas Jewell (1798–1852), superintendent, St. Agnes circuit, 1836–39.

[3] John Dawson, preacher, Camelford circuit, 1837–39; d. 1875, aet. 63. The implication is that Dawson had been appealing for the Missionary Society in the Truro district.

our Cornwall, the proposed plan for making better provision for the Wornout Preachers.[1] Now I will yield to no man in the Connexion in anxiety to promote the welfare and comfort of our Preachers. Yet I am fully persuaded it is impracticable in Cornwall with our large and poor Societies, and if at all practicable it will quite prevent the increase of preachers on the ground which is so necessary, and is an object so near the heart of many of our friends. And I must beg to observe that this plan of charging according to the number of members falls very hard upon Cornwall. On the Children's Fund[2] the balance paid by Cornwall is more than double that of any other District. These two funds will therefore press very heavy upon Cornwall, unless you can modify it in some way that your wisdom may point out. Cannot you take £40,000 from the Centenary Fund to produce £2,000 a year and one thousand from the Book Room that now liquidates the school debt and get the remainder from the circuits and from the subscriptions to the Auxiliary Fund. In the enfranchisement of towns under the Reform Act, their eligibility was ascertained from two things population and property. Might not something like this be adopted in the present case? Let some scale be devised for taking as the basis of the charge to be – number of members and ministers, and not the number of members alone. At any rate I must beg for the sake of my county, that some arrangement or modification that will make it press less heavily on this District may be adopted.

Having thus freely stated my views on the above subjects, I shall take the liberty of troubling you with a few observations on another subject, now engaging much of public attention, i.e. 'Education'. I felt a degree of gratification on finding that the Centenary Committee had agreed to place five thousand pounds at the disposal of the Education Committee but I wished it had been ten thousand. And from the importance the subject has now assumed, I expect it will be judged that the latter sum will be to small. At one of the centenary meetings held at Bristol last year I ventured to suggest that a model school should be established near the Theological Institution that the students might become acquainted with the best methods of instruction, and so be prepared to assist in introducing an improved system of education in such circuits as may

[1] Cf. n. 2 p. 224 *supra*.

[2] In 1819 Conference established the 'Children's Fund' under which the cost of maintaining preachers' children was divided among Districts in proportion to the number of members. Districts with preachers who had few children contributed to the fund for the balance of their quota; Districts with more than their quota of children to support drew from the fund for the balance. Dale had no just ground for criticism of the oppressiveness of the Children's Fund in Cornwall, since the anomaly arose from the appointment of unusually few preachers in relation to the membership, about which he was complaining strongly.

require it both at *home* and *abroad*, and although the idea did not appear to receive much favour from the gentlemen then present, I do confess that the more I reflect on it the more desirable it appears to me. It seems to me of vast importance that while the students are at the Institutions they should have the opportunity of witnessing the operations of daily and Sunday schools conducted on the most approved principles and methods. I shall therefore rejoice to hear that arrangements are making for the establishment of model daily and Sunday schools in such situations in London and Manchester as will afford the young ministers the opportunities above referred to.[1] . . .

175   From George Cubitt   *London, July 29, 1839*

I have spent three whole days at the [British] Museum, and made some copious extracts. The 'Appeal of the Protestant Association' (praised by Mr. Wesley[2] – in three lines – *Works*, Vol. X. p. 159 – 'To the printer of the Public Advertiser.' –) is a closely printed *Sixty page pamphlet*. I have copied very nearly the whole, only leaving out what was comparatively unimportant, and would bear description. I have read likewise some other very important pamphlets on the subject – one of them *90* pages, small letter and closely lined – strongly on the side of Ministers. I think I have got nearly all that is necessary to elucidate the 'Protestant Association' part of the story. I want, indeed, to find out whether there be in existence any of the resolutions and advertisements of the Association – besides what are quoted by those who give the history of the disturbances. It takes a long while to hunt out these documents; I think, however, it is worth the time and labour devoted to it. My present object is to collect all that I can possibly find to illustrate the history of the Protestant Association for its brief existence, and terribly stormy close; Mr. Wesley's slight connexion with it; and the O'Leary controversy.[3] I shall have a quire or two of extracts, as when

[1] Many of the above points were repeated and amplified by Dale in a letter to John H. James, a young minister on a year's sick leave in London, 1838–39, who transcribed large portions in a letter of his own to Bunting. M.C.A. MSS. J. H. James to Jabez Bunting, July 13, 1839.

[2] For this issue, raised by O'Connell, see n. 4 p. 223 *supra*.

[3] A letter to the press by John Wesley in 1780 denying that a Roman Catholic could give security for his allegiance or peaceable behaviour evoked voluminous replies from Arthur O'Leary, an Irish capuchin (*Miscellaneous tracts . . . in which are introduced the Rev. J. Wesley's letter* . . . (2nd. ed. Dublin, 1781). Both men embodied more of the latitudinarian spirit than commentators in the 19th century cared to admit, and Wesley enjoyed a meeting with O'Leary in 1787. Cubitt published the fruit of his studies in *Strictures on Mr. O'Connell's letter to Wesleyan Methodists &c* . . . (London, 1840).

I have made them at the Museum I must rewrite and arrange them at home. As to what shall be done with them, I shall leave that to be decided by yourself and Mr. Jackson. I think I have nearly gone so completely round the case, as to be able to meet Mr. O'Connell with a denial as brief and as bold as may be judged proper. You will be very much amused with the mass of materials I shall have collected, and whether they should be published in any form, in whole or in part, or only deposited in the Wesleyan archives to guide any future historian of Methodism, must be decided by you when you have seen or heard the papers. I do now think most seriously not only that O'Connell must be boldly confronted, but that the entire case be investigated, and the evidence and conclusion, formed into a sort of Memoir, to go along with other Wesleyan papers. I do not think I shall finish at the Museum for three or four days *yet to come* – and then the rewriting and arranging will take me quite as long.

You shall hear from me in a day or two, after I have *carefully read O'Leary's* Life and tracts (or rather essays) and after I have carefully sought out for the Protestant Association proceedings. . . .

176   From George Cubitt   *London, July 30, [18]39*

Mr. Horne (Hartwell)[1] showed me a volume – Italian – not long ago sent into the Museum Library in which there is a dedication styling the Pope an *earthly* God. On the other side you have the extract from the dedication. I send it as a curiosity and as one of the gathered fruits of my searchings. . . .

Is not this one reason why a Protestant state cannot trust the O'Connell party with the National Education? Seeing that while all *merely divided Protestants* have in common only one God, in heaven and earth, the Romanists are the subjects of a temporal sovereign, not the British monarch, but the Bishop of Rome, their secular and religious head, whom they acknowledge as supreme by styling him, an Earthly *God*? And that, not in some ignorant and distant country, but in Italy itself in the year 1815, Pius VII, the restorer of the priests, is styled, *Deus terrestris*. The book is by the Abbott Mauro Boni, Venezia, Dalla Tipografia di Alvisopoli i Gemnari 1815.

[1] For Thomas Hartwell Horne see n. 1 p. 39 *supra*.

Pio VII Pont. Max.
Terrestri Deo
Reique christianae propugnatori

....

....

Maurus Bonus
devotus majestati sanctitatis ejus
Kal. Januar. an. mdcccxv.

177 From Robert Newstead   *London, August [2], 1839*

Could anything be done at Conference to urge upon the brethren by way of recommendation, the importance of reading at every *Sunday* service, some portion – a chapter at least – of the *Holy Scriptures*? It is a reproach against us among many that we have so little of *God's Word* and so much of man's, in our Sabbath *evening* services. I should think it must be difficult to find a reason *against* it. A conversation on the subject among the miscellanea of Conference would probably help forward, and perhaps issue in a recommendation of, a circumstance so devoutly to be wished. I do think the honour of God is concerned in it, and that such an improvement on our Sabbath evening services would be quickly blessed of HIM. Excuse my suggesting it, as I believe your opinion on the point would have great weight with the Brethren, and I am persuaded these are your sentiments also.

I have been thinking whether on the Committee of Education for the ensuing year it would not be well to have a *working* representation from each circuit in London of *laymen*, as well as ministers. *One* preacher and *two* laymen would do well from each, and be quite enough, with its officers. Several are now on who *never* attend.

In addition to the Ex-President and yourself, I presume, would it not be well to have Messrs. Grindrod[1] and Mason, Keeling[2] and Burgess.[3] Scott[4] and Jackson (S.)[5] will represent the other two circuits, and in addition to Messrs. Farmer, J. S. Elliot, Hoby, Alder etc. etc. Would it not be well to have J. Corderoy, and perhaps the senior Mr. Gabriel, or one of them who represented Radnor St. School, Mr. Luke France, Mr. Birt Senr., Mr. Kruse, Mr. Free, with Dr. Heccatie [?] or

[1] Edmund Grindrod, superintendent, London (City Road) circuit, 1837–40.
[2] Isaac Keeling, superintendent, London (Great Queen St.) circuit, 1839–42.
[3] William P. Burgess M.A., preacher, London (Spitalfields) circuit, 1839–42.
[4] John Scott, preacher, London (Hinde St.) circuit, 1839–40; superintendent, 1840–42.
[5] Samuel Jackson, superintendent, London (Spitalfields) circuit, 1839–42.

Mr. Beckett for Treasurer.[1] That should then become an efficient committee, with any others you might suggest with so much better knowledge of the whole. Twenty men or a few more who would give tolerably fair coverage . . . [would be better than 50 otherwise. More names].

I am not quite sure whether I intimated that the *Archbishop*[2] was himself evidently friendly to the admission of our children to their schools, observing that he believed (*knew*) that it was acted upon in large schools in London, particularly Whitechapel, '*though they had found it extremely difficult to make such rules and arrangements as should meet the question ostensibly*'. If he only were concerned, it would be done instantly I am assured, from his extremely friendly bearing towards us in all the conversation I had with him, a full hour on various topics. He seemed astonished to hear that we *contemplated a £100,000 a year* for our *missions* alone, though he said (evidently alluding to the centenary proceedings) 'you are a very rich people'. . . .

178   From O. Henwood[3]   *Camelford, October 22, 1839*

The peculiar circumstances of this circuit is my apology for thus soliciting your attention as a member of the Chapel Relief Committee. On your return from the west of Cornwall last January I saw you in this town, and mentioned our need of pecuniary aid; you pleasantly replied, 'I suppose Centenary aid.'

In this all but annihilated Circuit we shall raise about 70£, including the collection, for centenary purposes; I for one would gladly have given more, but for our pressing local demands. The number of members was in 1835 reduced from 696 to 59; it has since risen to 200, but chiefly by accessions of poor or young people, who can contribute but little at present. No one at a distance can form an adequate idea of the hindrances thrown in our way by the [Wesleyan Methodist] Association. Nearly all the people of property and influence seceded with Mr. Rosevear; and they still make great efforts to erect their cause on the ruins of Conference Methodism. Railing, proselytism etc., etc., are still in active operation, and have an injurious effect on the minds of some who continue with us. We, however, are gaining ground in public

---

[1] All the names mentioned in this sentence were of prominent London laymen, several of whom were active in the affairs of the Theological Institution and the Centenary Fund, but of whom little is otherwise known.

[2] William Howley (1766–1848), archbishop of Canterbury, 1828–48.

[3] Oliver Henwood (1786–1860), superintendent, Camelford circuit, 1837–40.

estimation and in all our church affairs. To our God and Saviour we ascribe the praise. With a little friendly assistance we hope to do well. I have furnished some particulars of our wants and wishes to the Rev. F. A. West,[1] but presume on your kind attention while I briefly enumerate them in this letter:–

Having to quit the house I now occupy, and no other to be had in the town, we have been under the necessity of building a 'Centenary House' for the use of the Preachers, to accommodate the single man also. The new house is on the Camelford Chapel Trust freehold, and in a good situation. It will cost, including furniture, stable, etc., not less than 350£; but the trustees ought not to have more than 200£ added to their former and present debt of 610£, their income being only 27£ annually. We engage to raise 50£ by subscriptions for this express object, and request the amount of the centenary contributions raised in the Circuit, say 70£. This we consider our *most necessitous case*; and in reliance on connexional sympathy we have erected a better house than we otherwise might have done; it is creditable to our cause but has nothing superfluous, being plain and substantial.

With some difficulty and expense our chapel at Wadebridge was reclaimed from the Association; the debt on it then amounted to 390£, which by subscriptions and collections we have reduced to 340£, besides paying Mr. Reece's bill of £6 – 6 – 0, repairing the chapel, improving the entrance etc. There the Association availed themselves of political excitement and built a large chapel near ours, Sir Wm. Molesworth[2] and the most respectable villagers being either trustees or shareholders. Still our cause prospers in Wadebridge beyond expectation, and if we can have a grant of 40£ to meet the above named subscription etc., it will be a seasonable relief. The income of the chapel is about 12£ a year.

Port Isaac chapel was recovered by my predecessor, Bro. John Robinson; but the garden belonging to it is dishonestly withheld, and [it] will cost money to recover it; we hope to have it shortly. Here also the Association have built a good chapel, they are numerous and bitter, and have secured the political reformers as shareholders. Though the debt on our chapel is only about 130£, we cannot as yet meet the interest etc., and request a grant of 25£.

Boscastle is the residence of our chief opponent, Mr. Rosevear, who

[1] Francis A. West, preacher, Halifax circuit, 1839–42; secretary of Chapel Relief Committee.

[2] Sir William Molesworth, 8th bart. of Pencarrow near Bodmin (1810–55), politician of radical and (it was believed) infidel opinions; M.P. for East Cornwall, 1832–37, and for Leeds, 1837–41. He took 20 £1 shares in the 'Forty Windows' chapel at Wadebridge, so designed that it could be converted into house property if it failed as a chapel.

R

as a merchant and determined adversary has great influence. In this Society we had three local preachers, who have recently removed from the circuit; one of them, Brother Rundle,[1] is at the Theological Institution. Our cause in this place is but feeble; and though 300£ at least was subscribed to build our new chapel there, we greatly need a grant of 25£; a debt would then remain of £100, burden enough.

Pengelly Chapel was taken and retaken, injured, robbed and defiled, during the contest, and has produced no seat rent for some years, until the last quarter or two when a few sittings were let. We have lately entered into a subscription to repair this chapel, and require a grant from your fund of 35£. Here too the Association have built a rival place of worship, within a few feet of ours; but we have a rising school and improving congregation. The present debt is 60£, income, none till lately, now a few shillings.

I have further requested 25£ for Tintagel Chapel, and 20£ for Dinham's bridge or Trelill and pass over two or three other cases, which will require a little aid when the circuit is in circumstances to recover them. I advise our friends to reclaim all the regularly settled chapels in due time. We want more places for our Local Preachers, and more week-night labour for ourselves. We earnestly and conscientiously ask 195£ for present use, exclusive of Tintagel and other chapels yet to be reclaimed. . . .

179 From Andrew Kessen[2]   *Soley Terrace, October 22, 1839*

I wish not to be intrusive, but I think you ought to know in what manner my time is occupied. Since the examination my course of reading has been almost entirely directed by Dr. Hannah's *Letter to a Junior Preacher*.[3] I have had additional engagements of various kinds, but all of them immediately connected with my prospective labours. I trust that the time has not been frittered away.

I allow myself six hours out of the twenty-four for sleep, and the remaining eighteen are employed as follows:

[1] Robert T. Rundle (1811–96); on leaving the Theological Institution in 1840, he was stationed in Canada.

[2] Andrew Kessen (1814–79), missionary in Ceylon, 1840–57; principal of Native Normal School, Colombo, 1853–57.

[3] John Hannah, *Letter to a junior Methodist preacher, concerning the general course and prosecution of his studies in Christian theology* (London, 1836).

	Hours.				
---	Mon.	Tues.	Wed.	Thurs.	Frid.
Priv. Devotion	2	2	2	2	2
Theology	3	3	4	3	4
Hebrew	2	2	1	2	1
Tamil	2	2	2	2	2
Latin	3	3	3	3	3
Greek	3	3	3	3	3
Meals	3	3	3	3	3

Saturday is reserved for pulpit preparation or general reading. Under the head of Theology are comprehended the lectures at Stoke Newington and Hoxton, along with the required time for walking to and from these places. Perhaps the time devoted to Latin and Greek may appear large, but I think it impossible to curtail it, as I wish to read over the subjects of my classical examination before Christmas, that during January and February I may revise Mathematics, Logic and Moral Philosophy. Accordingly I must read every day 500 lines of Latin and nearly as many of Greek that I may perform creditably the following amount.

Five Orations of Cicero; two books of Livy; four books of the Odes; one book of the Satires; one book of the epistles of Horace; the Eclogues, and six books of the Aeneid of Virgil. The Greek Testament; Xenophon's Anabasis; six books of Homer; the Plutus of Aristophanes; The Medea of Euripides.

This is by no means a large amount, but my time will not allow me to undertake any more with sufficient accuracy.

I require the immediate use of some classical books: might I be permitted to bring home a few of the higher authors from the Institution Library? May I request also that I be allowed to proceed with my Hebrew as soon as possible? I am very anxious for improvement, and I hope you will not consider this letter as intrusive. I desire to be fully employed, and to show by some degree of diligence that I am not regardless of my sacred calling, nor unthankful to you for the favours which you have so abundantly conferred upon me . . .

180 From Alexander Strachan[1]   *Macclesfield, November 9, 1839*

[Will J.B. preach for the opening of their large Centenary School?] . . . The school is an elegant building, and will cost £1100. Blessed be God,

---

[1] Alexander Strachan (1793–1865), preacher, Macclesfield circuit, 1837–38; superintendent, 1838–40.

our Societies were never more steady; though they have been severely
sifted by Kilhamites, Atkinites, Owenites, Ranters, Associationists etc.
etc.[1] The number of clergymen in the town have been doubled within
the last 18 months. We greatly desire a copious effusion of God's holy
spirit upon ourselves and our people. . . .

181   From Wm. M. Harvard[2]   *Quebec, L.Cn., November 11, 1839*

[Encloses a sermon (wanting) about the Protracted Meeting with a view
to having it introduced at home so far as J.B. thinks desirable. Two
years ago he sent him an account of such a meeting from the *Christian
Guardian* which was greatly owned of God at Montreal, with the suggestion that it would be profitable to the Connexion if such a Meeting were
refined and treated as an allowable irregularity.]

. . . And though the probability is that the idea has already been found
unsuitable to the position of our home connexion, I would humbly bring
the subject again before you, in connection with the few feeble remarks
which will be found in the accompanying publication.

Our respected brother Lord[3] knows well the peculiar gift this way of
one of our American brethren, the Rev. James Caughey,[4] who attended
a Protracted Meeting at Montreal while Mr. L. was resident there, and
whom Mr. Lord wished to have attached to our body; but his bishop
refused to give his consent. I find Mr. Caughey is contemplating a visit
to Europe next midsummer – in all probability to our next Conference.
He is a devoted and intelligent Irishman, and he wishes to see his native
island once more. By him there is no doubt the Protracted Meeting will
be introduced at home; and I felt not a little solicitous to become an
occasion of the subject previously passing before your mind. . . .

[1] For the troubles of Macclesfield Methodism with radicals, revivalists and the undenominational Large School, see *Early Correspondence* pp. 11–12, 46 n. 3, 76–7.

[2] William M. Harvard D.D. served at Kingston, Upper Canada, 1836–38. D. 1857, age
unknown.

[3] William Lord, preacher, Montreal, 1834–36.

[4] James Caughey (c. 1810–91) whose protracted meetings represented a form of organized
moral pressure for revival of the kind made famous by C. G. Finney, became a storm centre
in English Wesleyanism in the 'forties, Bunting and other advocates of a high view of the
Pastoral Office resenting what seemed to be his efforts to wrest control of the pulpit from its
appointed occupant for weeks at a time, those who opposed Bunting from a radical or
revivalist viewpoint supporting him.

182 From George Cubitt   *London, January 1, 1840*

. . . I have made out my case according to the evidence; and cast some light, I think, on a portion of Mr. Wesley's history not before understood[1]. . .

If, making allowance for deficiencies, my brethren think I have cleared Mr. Wesley's character, and by exposing the nature of papistical attacks done *a little* in support of Wesleyanism and Protestantism, I shall be *very thankful*.

A few days ago, I looked over two pamphlets on the *Scotch Church Question*, by Dr. Chalmers and Mr. Dunlop (Advocate).[2] I expected little more than controversial references, but I found expositions of *general principles* of such deep interest and importance that I resolved to send you my copies the first opportunity. *You ought to read them* (if they have not come your way already) even on public grounds. A view of *the Establishment Case* is given which, I think you will be glad to possess; besides – first – information on the points in dispute – and second – some valuable *inferential* references to questions which concern ourselves. . . .

183 From George Cubitt   *London, January 6, 1840*

[The connexion is in great danger which only Bunting can avert.]

. . . First – As to the danger, I refer to that low Arminianism which, however plausible, is always found to draw away from just and consistent evangelism. Very naturally, the preachers have read the Arminian writers of the Restoration School; and the best of them, when not writing on the questions controverted between us and the Calvinists, *tend* – some of them do *more* than tend – to what may be termed Bishop Bull's school. It must have been the influence of such writings that led Mr. Wesley to consent to the celebrated 'Minutes,'[3] which, though *substantially* right, and even in *expression*, when properly connected and explained, less obscure than they would appear taken absolutely, and in

---

[1] George Cubitt had just received from the binder's the first copies of his pamphlet replying to O'Connell. See n. 3 p. 229 *supra*.

[2] Thomas Chalmers, *Remarks on the present position of the Church of Scotland* (Glasgow, 1839); Alexander Dunlop, *An Answer to the Dean of the Faculty's 'Letter to the Lord Chancellor' on the claims of the Church of Scotland in regard to its jurisdiction and the proposed changes in its polity* (Edinburgh, 1839).

[3] *Minutes of some late conversations between the Rev. Mr. Wesleys and others, in 1744* reprinted in Wesley's *Works* viii. 275–98. The so-called *Large Minutes*, repeatedly revised for publication between 1744 and 1789, are principally concerned with matters of organization and discipline.

their insulated form, are still both unguarded and capable of a very dangerous construction. Then I have latterly noticed the unwillingness to receive the doctrine of hereditary guiltiness, an omission of reference to the original constitution in reference to which the entire human family is guilty and punished (taking depravity itself as the consequence of a judicial withdrawment); I might add a tendency to very low views as to the sacraments. Since Conference at a meeting of the Book Committee the expression has been used – 'We are getting fast on to Oxford Tractism, I think. Even before the Conference a preacher talks about the grace given in Baptism!' And the sentiment – because strongly anti-Church – was *at least* echoed by several. And though Mr. Grindrod, with his usual accuracy, dissented, still, his dissent did not *bear down* the remark. I believe that under God you have been the means of keeping us on the right line through a very dangerous period. . . . I am confident from my own recollection of the manner in which even preachers of note were accustomed to speak some twenty five or thirty years ago, that the doctrine of the Divine Sonship of our Lord was not the only one in which we were in danger of being somewhat warped.[1] Man seems as if he could scarcely avoid error sometimes, but by erring. I think the worst is past. But there wants a *thorough confirmation* – a sort of *final, definite establishment* – of what is on all hands, when cool judgment speaks, and a foolish prejudice is kept down, acknowledged to be right. . . .

One of your sermons might be brought to bear upon it somewhat more fully, and then it might take its place along with the one on Justification. Or a separate edition of Mr. Wesley on Original Sin[2] might be given, with a Preface from you. . . . By God's Providence you are placed in a position in which you could speak thus, and so set the question at rest; and set at rest it ought to be. Ere many years, our doctrinal system will, I do not doubt, have to pass through as close a trial as our discipline has experienced. If, when the trial comes, we are compact at every point, with help from God, we are safe. But if we are unsound even in one point (of course, an important point) there is weakness, and an opening for the admission of the wedge. And where will it stop? . . .

---

[1] See n. 2 p. 5 *supra* on Adam Clarke.

[2] John Wesley, *The doctrine of original sin, according to scripture, reason and experience* (Bristol, 1757) reprinted in *Works* ix. 192–464.

184 From John Hobson[1]   *Redruth, January 27, 1840*

. . . Methodism is rising in the Town; and in one of our country places (Wheal Rose) about 60 persons have during the last fortnight been converted to God. In one house where a number of penitents had met in the day time, to unite in prayer for mercy and salvation, a farmer's wife was crying for mercy; and her husband, who was ploughing with a yoke of oxen, on hearing his good wife praying for mercy, left the oxen to go and pray with his wife and the other penitents; and he remained nearly *six hours* in the meeting; and when his good wife had found peace, the good man returned to the *field* and found the oxen had remained *all that time exactly in the place* in which he had left them!

We have had many interesting incidents of a similar character; and we hope the good Lord will *yet by thousands* convert sinners and join them to Himself and his people. . . .

185 From Robert Maxwell Macbrair[2]   *Newark, March 7, 1840*

Excuse the liberty which I take in asking your opinion upon a short paper which I have drawn up on the subject of National and Religious Education, well knowing the interest you take in this important matter. I find great ignorance prevailing amongst our people upon this subject, whilst some are even beginning to regret that they signed our late petitions to Parliament against the late Ministerial scheme, having been influenced by Dissenters and Liberals (so called) to wish for a plan of National Education which shall *exclude all religious tuition*. Thinking to communicate some just ideas upon this subject, I have just put down a few thoughts upon paper; but cannot of myself form an opinion as to whether they are worth publishing, nor have I any friend here upon whose judgment I could depend.

Education is a subject which has long occupied my mind. My views may appear singular, when I state, that I believe education, properly so called to be yet in its very infancy; since there is no real *training* of the *mind* or *culture* of the *moral nature* in our public and private schools . . .

[1] John Hobson, superintendent, Redruth circuit, 1839–42.

[2] Robert Maxwell Macbrair, preacher, Newark circuit, 1839–40. Macbrair became a preacher in 1833, being appointed to Alexandria, and ceased to travel 1856. A note appended to M.C.A. MSS. R. M. Macbrair to James Everett, Newark, September 20, 1839, describes him as 'some years a Methodist preacher, afterwards a dissenting minister in London. Was abroad as a missionary some time, and published an account of his Travels, &c.'.

Will you be kind enough to give me your frank opinion as to whether publishing the enclosed would be likely to do any good in this way *at this juncture*. And if so, are there any passages liable to objection? . . .

186 From John Baker[1] *Burslem, May 28, 1840*

. . . You are well acquanted with the struggle which took place here about 4 years since to put an end to the overgrown anti-scriptural Sunday School which existed in connection with our chapel;[2] the results of that struggle have been most cheering – Wesleyan Methodism has been relieved from an incubus which paralyzed its energies, and we have now not only a scriptural Sunday School but every part of our discipline is fully established.

In order to meet the objection about Sunday writing, our friends adopted two methods, they teach writing on Monday evening, and we have had a Wesleyan day school established; these have both answered well, and tended to silence the objectors.

There is still a very numerous class, for whom our friends are ⟨a⟩nxious to make provision, I mean children who are only fit ⟨for⟩ an Infant School, and there are some strong reasons why these should be cared for. In consequence of so many mothers continuing to work in the Potteries after they have families and having to leave their little ones to the care of Hirelings, the children are exposed to the worst possible influence. And these children themselves going to work at a very early age, their time at our day school is so short as greatly to lessen the benefit they would otherwise receive, and after once they have entered the manufactory, their attendance at the Sunday school is very uncertain.

Under these circumstances we think a well-conducted Infant School would with the blessing of God be of great importance, and the favour we have to solicit of you is, that you will kindly sanction our efforts, by [preaching two sermons]. . . .

Our friends are exerting themselves to raise Wesleyan Methodism to that rank in this neighbourhood which they think it ought to occupy; the division of the Circuit is working well; we have an increase of 63 members and upwards of 50 on trial. We have increased the seat rents in our chapel £50 during the last year, £1800 have been paid off the debt of the chapel, £450 off the debt of another chapel. We have built an organ which cost about 400 guineas. We are now about to build a

---

[1] John Baker, superintendent, Burslem circuit, 1838–41.
[2] On this issue see nos. 33 and 82 *supra*.

chapel in the suburbs, another is determined on for the opposite side of the town next year, and our friends are looking forward to a third prea⟨cher⟩ for these chapels. . . .

187   From James Wood   *Bristol, July 8, 1840*

Perhaps you may recollect [my] putting into your hands at Sheffield in 1835, various suggestions as to modifications of our rules as a Christian Community. To *one* of these suggestions permit me to draw *your* attention now, that if it meet your approval you may propose it at the ensuing conference just at hand.

I advert to the suggestion about admission to the Public Bands.[1]

These are now discontinued in Bristol, perhaps in other places, and in some places I have heard that meetings of a different character have been substituted for them.

Admission to the public bands is by our present rules restricted to those who meet in private bands but the new engagements from friends as Missionary collectors, Tract Distributors etc. etc. with the altered hours of business and domestic habits deprive very many of the possibility of meeting in private band even if suitable leaders could provide for them.

Those members therefore who are thus circumstanced if they meet in classes where christian holiness is either not insisted upon or not enjoyed by some one at least in the class, are placed in a very disadvantageous position in reference to this inestimable mercy; however alive to God themselves and athirst for holiness they hear little or nothing of it except from the pulpit and it really becomes a question whether this glory of our society is not by this circumstance confined within much narrower limits than otherwise it would be. Solely with a view to give every possible help to all the believers amongst us I respectfully suggest for your consideration the propriety of passing a rule at this Conference *authorizing* (but not requiring unless you think it should be an imperative rule) the preachers at the quarterly visitation of the classes to give band tickets inscribed with the letter B either printed or written to all such as are clear as to their acceptance with God through Christ, and athirst

---

[1] According to the rules 'the design of our [band-]meeting is to obey that command of God, "Confess your faults one to another, and pray for one another, that ye may be healed" ', and admission was restricted to those who could claim peace with God and the witness of the Spirit. Conference regulations of 1806, 1812 and 1821 make it clear that these meetings had flagged, and attempts were made to substitute fellowship meetings of other kinds. Public bands were regulation weekly meetings. Grindrod, *Compendium* pp. 174–7.

for a deeper work of grace, which tickets shall entitle them to the privilege of attending the public bands the ensuing quarter if there be such
in the place and on such a basis of admission as this why should not such
meetings be far more numerous than they now are? And may not a
judicious increase of them be a blessing to the Body? ⟨You wi⟩ll perceive
my Dear Sir this is simply a question of liberty to be given to the preachers for the benefit of the most valuable members of the society to be
exercised from quarter to quarter as they may judge proper . . .

188   From John Beecham   *London, July 21, 1840*

I presume from a note which I have had from Mr. Mathews on returning the answer to the New Zealand Directors which I had transmitted
to him for his perusal, that you learned from him at York that I had been
summoned to attend the New Zealand Committee.[1] On Saturday
morning, I was purposing to write to Lord Howick[2] when on reaching
the Mission House, I found a formal order had been brought there by a
messenger of the House of Commons requiring me to attend the above-
named Committee, on Monday at one o'clock. Having no clue as to
the object of my being summoned, or the course which the examination
would take, I could make but little preparation. However, I attended
at the time, and almost immediately on my entering the cloisters leading
to the Committee Room, I met with Mr. William Gladstone,[3] who told

[1] This letter records an episode in the drive for the systematic colonization of New Zealand
mounted by Gibbon Wakefield and the New Zealand Association from 1837. Strongly
resisted by Lord Glenelg, colonial secretary 1835–39, and his permanent under-secretary,
James Stephen, who were deeply imbued with the Church Missionary Society policy of
excluding settlers in order to leave a free field for the missionaries, the Association got a joint-
stock New Zealand Company formed for colonization in 1839, the country was annexed
early in 1840 and the company's first settlers arrived. On April 15, 1840, a great meeting at
the Guildhall in London called on the government to maintain British sovereignty over New
Zealand, and deprecated convict colonization; on July 7 a Commons select committee was
set up to inquire into the state of New Zealand (among the members of which, mentioned
below, were Lord Eliot, Gladstone, Vernon Smith, Hindley and Lord Howick [*Commons
Journals* xcvi. 503, 523]) which simply published the evidence of the witnesses, the chief of
whom, Gibbon Wakefield, tried to blacken the reputation of the missionaries; this evidence
brought the government to grant a charter to the Company and make it a large land grant.
Beecham's evidence before the committee (P.P. H.C. 1840 VII pp. 549–55) was directed to
the point that the land held by the Missionary Society was exclusively for the benefit of the
natives.

[2] Sir Henry George Grey, Viscount Howick, later 3rd earl Grey (1802–94), M.P. for
northern division of Northumberland, 1832–41; under-secretary for colonies, 1830–33, and as
earl Grey, secretary for colonies, 1846–52. Cf. n. 1 p. 34 *supra*.

[3] William Ewart Gladstone (1809–98), M.P. for Newark, 1832–45; under-secretary for
war and colonies, 1835.

me he thought the examination would be of a general character, and he did not appear to be aware that we were in collision with the New Zealand Company. After he left me, almost immediately Mr. Hindley[1] came out who told me Mr. Coates was under examination, and asked me to go home with him to lunch, as he wished to have some talk with me, and would shew me the evidence which had been printed. He said Gibbon Wakefield,[2] as one of the New Zealand Directors had been examined at great length, that he himself had cross-examined him, and had brought out the fact that they had not given quite a *half-penny per acre* for the land they have bought in New Zealand, and that he had procured an order for the production of their titles. I hastily ran over Wakefield's evidence, and to my surprise found that he had put in our letter appealing to the Directors for redress against Colonel Wakefield[3] in regard to the land at Port Nicholson, and the vile letter of the Directors in answer (which I have now no doubt was drawn up with an especial view to its being laid before the Parliamentary Committee) and that he had subsequently made another vile attack upon us [as?] a Society, representing us as sending men from low stations in life who soon threw off the garb of Missionaries and then preyed upon the natives. One alleviating fact presented itself. Mr. Vernon Smith[4] it appeared interrupted Wakefield as soon as he produced the correspondence between us and the Directors, and put in at once copies of our letter to Lord John Russell[5] and his Lordship's reply, for which very kind act may the God of Missions bless him! But still, what was to be done? There was no answer to the heavy charges contained in the Directors' letter, and in Gibbon's own evidence; and I told Hindley that justice imperatively required that I should be allowed to put in our rejoinder to the Directors, but that not having it with me, I could not produce it, unless the Committee would allow my examination to be postponed. He said he would speak to Lord Eliot,[6] which he did on our return, but as

[1] Charles Hindley, M.P. for Ashton-under-Lyne, 1835 till his death in 1857.

[2] Edward Gibbon Wakefield (1796–1862), adventurer and advocate of colonization, London agent of New Zealand Land Company, 1839–46.

[3] William Hayward Wakefield (1803–48), younger brother of Edward Gibbon Wakefield, colonel in Spanish army, agent in New Zealand for New Zealand Land Company, 1840. Purchased 20 million acres of native land for the Company, a holding cut down by the government in 1840–41 to 283,000 acres. Port Nicholson was the site of the present Wellington.

[4] R. Vernon Smith, M.P. for Northampton Borough 1831 till he became Lord Lyvedon, 1859.

[5] John Beecham to Lord John Russell, June 22, 1840 (P.P. H.C. 1840 VII pp. 609–10), protesting that the good work of the Missionary Society in civilizing the natives was being undermined by the land purchases of the New Zealand Company, who were taking land from the natives with which they had already parted to the Missionary Society.

[6] Edward Granville Eliot, Baron Eliot, later 3rd earl of St. Germans (1798–1877), M.P. for East Cornwall, 1837–45.

it was then only about two o'clock, and they had not any other witness to examine, I was called in, and had a variety of questions proposed to me. No question however was put by anyone that referred explicitly to the Port Nicholson, and I therefore took an opportunity to state that I had reason to believe some correspondence had been laid before the Committee which reflected seriously upon our character, and I begged his Lordship's (the Chairman's) permission to attend the Committee on another day for the purpose of submitting our reply to the Directors' charges. Now Hindley had told me (and indeed I knew it before) that he should subject himself to a reprimand for shewing the evidence, it being contrary to rule; and of course when he told the Committee before I was called in that he had let me see it, he got a gentle rebuke from the Chair as a matter of form. But although the formality of a rebuke took place, Lord Eliot whispered to Hindley to the effect that he was glad that I had got the information; and on my asking for permission to come again with the document, his Lordship very kindly told me he would not put me to the trouble but that I might send any documents I chose to Mr. Gurney,[1] and they should be inserted in my evidence. This was an indulgence I never knew to be granted before to a witness. I cannot tell you now all that passed; indeed I am afraid to see my evidence on paper as it will appear such a jumble of various kinds of matter in one mess. A point or two, however, I must mention. I happened to prepare myself beforehand with the requisite information and when I was asked what land we had in New Zealand, I was enabled to shew that the average price which we had paid for our land at the several stations (excepting Manjunga)[2] was a little more than 5/- per acre – that is a little more than the Government price for land there, and at least $4/11\frac{1}{2}$ more per acre than the New Zealand Company! White's[3] case also I hope I disposed of satisfactorily, through the kindness of Mr. Briscoe[4] and Mr. Hindley; and disproved Gibbon's charge to the effect that White was only one of many, or at least several, Wesleyan Missionaries who had acted in the same way.

In conclusion, for the Mail is closing, I was treated with the greatest kindness by the Committee, which was fully attended. Besides Lord

---

[1] William Brodie Gurney (1777–1855), celebrated Baptist shorthand writer; from 1813 official reporter to Parliament.

[2] Mangunga, the main centre of the Wesleyan mission from 1827, on the west coast of North Island.

[3] William White, till c. 1836 a Methodist missionary in New Zealand, 'represented as being an extensive purchaser of land'; now declared by Beecham to be the only missionary sent out by the Wesleyan Missionary Society to be removed from it and become a land purchaser. P.P. H.C. 1840 VII p. 550.

[4] John I. Briscoe, M.P. for Westbury, 1837–41.

Eliot there were present Lord Howick, Vernon Smith, Mr. Briscoe, etc.

Mr. Briscoe wanted to speak with me, to tell me that his object in questioning me was to furnish me with the opportunity of defence! that he was our friend and wished me to have the chance of reply. He and Hindley too, who was with us at the time, said it was evident that an attempt was made to do us harm, and that he was persuaded an impression would have been made much to our injury, had it not been removed. I thanked him for his kind services in our behalf with a more than ordinary warm[th] of gratitude, for I had found that on a previous day he had obtained some capital evidence in our favour from a naval officer. To both Mr. Briscoe and Hindley, we are greatly indebted on the occasion. Hindley had even visited the Mission House on Saturday for the purpose of preparing me for the examination, but unfortunately I was not there.

Well now, to the point! Hindley said, You may depend upon it, Gibbon will be at you again, your evidence will so pull him; and I begged of him to let me know confidentially should this be the case, that I might return to the charge, and meet him with counter evidence; but then I cannot do this, should I be at Newcastle. What am I to do? . . .

Oh! Ward[1] brought the titles etc. yesterday, and among the valuable goods which they had paid for the land, was a great number of *Jews harps*. . . .

P.S. We have had an interesting interview with Mons. Guizot today.[2]

189   From Corbett Cooke[3]   *n. pl. or d.* [*Conference, 1840*]

The division of the Liskeard Circuit and sending an additional preacher to Kingsbridge with the transfer of a few places from the Ashburton Circuit are matters in which I feel great anxiety, as they appear to me to be so intimately identified with the prosperity of the work of God in that part of the district . . .

Division of the Liskeard Circuit.
Liskeard embraces a tract of country 20 miles in width by 30 in length. It contains 46 chapels and preaching houses and Societies. This Circuit

---

[1] John Ward, secretary of the New Zealand Company.

[2] François Guizot (1787–1874), French statesman, called the October following to the ministry of foreign affairs.

[3] Corbett Cooke (1787–1866), superintendent, Devonport circuit, 1839–41. Too ill to attend Conference in 1840, Cooke addressed this letter to Bunting during the session. The 1840 Conference carved a Saltash circuit from the Liskeard circuit, and made an arrangement by which Kingsbridge, the decayed remnant of the old South Devon Mission, received an additional preacher.

suffered more than any other Circuit in the West except Camelford by the confusions of 1835[1] which was in a great measure the result of the want of pastoral influence in the part of the preachers, they not being able to visit many of the societies more than once a month, and several of them only once a quarter. Within the last three years however a very great change has taken place and the people themselves being convinced of the necessity of a division have agreed to a very equitable one among themselves. They are now building a new chapel at Liskeard where our prospects are encouraging and at Saltash they have purchased property in connection with the chapel for school rooms and are also enlarging the chapel – very considerably. I am afraid if the Conference suffer this opportunity to pass it will be many years before we shall have so favourable an opportunity again. The proposition which has come unanimously and strongly recommended by the District will I hope be granted by the Conference. It appears to me to be a measure that is calculated greatly to extend and consolidate the work. They have at present two families and one single man on the ground. We ask an additional single man so as to have a married and a single man in each Circuit.

Statement of the Case of the Kingsbridge Circuit.
[Showing that in the 16 years 1824–39, of the total expenses of the Kingsbridge Circuit £910. 9. 10, £821. 15. 0 have been deficiencies met by the connexion, and the membership has increased by only 17 (118–135). There is not the most distant probability that the same scale of expenditure for another 16 years would produce any more result. Part of the circuit should be annexed to Ashburton, and the remainder placed on a proper Methodistical basis under a single man.]

190   From Jonathan Williams[2]   *Chelmsford, August 7, 1840*

. . . We want a man that can face some difficulties, and brave some dangers. Foulness Island with 2000 inhabitants composed of thieves, skulkers, smugglers, etc. etc. etc., will demand such a man; and Southend, Leigh, Rochford etc. demand a man of first rate preaching talent.

It is a fact that the Clergyman at Leigh, Mr. Eden,[3] (whose wealth

---

[1] On Rosevear and the Warrenite revolt at Camelford see no. 123 *supra.*

[2] Jonathan Williams (entered ministry 1805; supernumerary in 5th London circuit 1840–47), superintendent, Chelmsford circuit, 1838–40.

[3] Robert Eden (1804–86), rector of Leigh, Essex, 1837–52; bishop of Moray, Ross and Caithness, 1851; Primus of Scottish Episcopal Church, 1862–86.

is immense), is *buying* our poor people by dozens; and the others say 'while he fired *iron* shot at us, we stood fire well; but when he loaded *with silver shot*! – he *thinned* our ranks *frightfully*.'

Essex is however opening up to us; and can we but follow up these openings, ere long it will present a Wesleyan soil very different to that seen hitherto. Mr. Wright offers £10 absolutely, and will double it if needed, or even more! Others £5 each, others £1 – etc. etc. etc. . . .

191 To F. J. Jobson *Clutton, Somerset, September 29, 1840*

The preceding inscription[1] was hastily sketched in a moment of bustle and hurry, shortly before I left Town; but I had not time then even to *forward* it to you as I intended.

Perhaps you will have the goodness to shew it to Mr. Jackson, Mr. Mason, and the other members of the 'Wesley Tomb Sub-Committee'. They will accept it or reject it as they think fit. If they should approve of it or wish any alterations to be made, let me have it by post, to meet me in Manchester on Monday next (or Tuesday) when I expect to see Mr. Farmer, who, as Treasurer of the Trustees must, I believe, assent to whatever we put up.

It might have been much better, had there been more room. But I fear even *this* has a line or two too many for the space. I have unfortunately lost or mislaid the particulars on that point with which you favoured me.

[*Appended*]

This grateful Record
of the place made sacred by the
Mortal Remains
Of the Apostolic and Immortal
Wesley
was first erected A.D. MDCCXCI
But re-edified and enlarged A.D. MDCCCXL
(During the Centenary of Methodism)
At the expense, and under the direction, of
His Sons and Successors in the Christian Ministry,
The Methodist Conference,
In token of
Their filial admiration reverence and love.

[1] Much of the money raised by the Centenary Fund was devoted to the creation of seminaries for ministerial training at Richmond and Didsbury; in this inscription for his

192   To John Beecham   *Manchester, October 7, 1840*

I received your letter this forenoon just as I entered the Centenary Chapel Committee, where I have been employed closely ever since; and I now write in the hurry of its business.

I *fear* the time is not favourable for the formation of an auxiliary at Manchester.[1] Trade is bad and *municipal* as well as political matters are carried very high just now. Yet if *leading* men in the Town of *both* parties could be interested in the matter, it would be done, for there is a good feeling in our favour, and *as yet* the tourists of the *other* Society, Messrs. Birnie and Scoble,[2] have not made any public appearance here. But *out of our own circle* some private *preparation* of people's minds seems to me essential to success. I suppose the Sub-Committee of Secretaries have applied already to known Anti-Slavery Friends in their town and county. That application if not yet satisfactorily answered already, should, I respectfully think, be immediately and *officially* renewed; and much must depend on the response to it. The Bishop of Chester[3] or Lord Francis Egerton[4] would be the best chairman for Manchester, and Lord Sandon[5]

tomb at Wesley's Chapel, also designed as part of the Centenary celebrations, Wesley is associated with the claims to ministerial status of his preachers. C. 1823 Bunting had taken down the original memorial tablet and replaced it with another which omitted a line describing Wesley as 'the patron and friend of the Lay Preachers'. Stevenson, *City Road* p.159.

[1] I.e. an auxiliary of the African Civilisation Society. Having lost his seat in Parliament in 1837, and seen the end of the apprenticeship system in the West Indies in 1838, T. F. Buxton gave his whole energy to ending the slave system in Africa, publishing *The African Slave Trade and its remedy* and founding the African Civilisation Society in 1839. His policy now was to conclude treaties with the African chiefs and promote legitimate trade with government help. At the general meeting of the Society in June 1840, presided over by the Prince Consort, Normanby offered ample government assistance, but negotiations for the purchase of Fernando Po failed and an expedition to the Niger was unsuccessful. (For the failure of this expedition see M.C.A. MSS. J. Beecham to Jabez Bunting, n.d. [1842].) Bunting is here replying to a letter from Beecham written after a committee meeting of the African Civilisation Society, which had urged the formation of auxiliary societies, particularly in Manchester and Liverpool, where Hugh McNeill was reported ready to lead the cause (M.C.A. MSS. J. Beecham to Jabez Bunting, October 6, 1840). The African Civilisation Society was dissolved in January 1843.

[2] 'The *other* Society' was Joseph Sturge's British and Foreign Anti-Slavery Society, which in June 1840 held a World Anti-Slavery Convention in London, which sought by peaceful agitation and collecting information to secure the abolition of slavery throughout the world. In 1840 James G. Birney (1792–1857), an American anti-Garrisonian abolitionist, was taken on a speaking tour through 26 towns by John Scoble, the secretary of Sturge's society, who had been a salaried anti-slavery lecturer for years.

[3] John Bird Sumner, bishop of Chester, 1828–40, a well-known evangelical.

[4] Lord Francis Egerton, later first earl of Ellesmere (1800–57), M.P. for South Lancashire, 1835–46.

[5] Dudley Ryder, titular Lord Sandon, later 2nd earl of Harrowby (1798–1882), M.P. for Liverpool, 1831–47.

for Manchester.[1] Archdeacon Wilberforce[2] or Mr. Cunningham[3] or both would be most important and influential, *with Dr. Lushington,*[4] for both towns.

As to myself, I can do more privately than publicly; and my health is *really* in so failing a state, that I can make no engagements at present for *anything* exciting. I begin seriously to fear that I am almost *done for*. But country-air and quiet, if I can ever manage to get them, may possibly rally me for a while, and restore the tone of my mental energies to something approaching to *par*.

I know not that I can say anything more to the purpose.

O that Sir T. F. Buxton could be induced to give three days to Liverpool, Manchester, and Leeds![5] Those three places would each be the centre of most influential operations in numerous secondary towns. His name would be a tower of strength, and a rallying-point of action in Lancashire and Yorkshire. . . .

193 To John Beecham   *Midsomer Norton, October 25, 1840*

I received your letter yesterday[6] just as I was leaving Clutton for this place, where I preached last evening.

I really find myself unable, without hearing the discussion and argument, to offer any decided opinion on many of the points connected with the new periodical, to which you refer.

As to title, I like *The Friend of Africa* better than *The African*. The latter would have come too near to Bannister's *African Colonist*.

If *in addition* to your present religious motto you could find another fitting one of a general character, that would meet the views of all parties, and more fully express the objects of our Society.

---

[1] *Lapsus styli* for Liverpool.

[2] Robert Isaac Wilberforce (1802–57), 2nd son of William Wilberforce, archdeacon of East Riding, 1841–54, when he entered the Roman Catholic Church.

[3] John William Cunningham (1780–1861), vicar of Harrow, 1811–61, and editor of the *Christian Observer*, 1850–58; an eminent evangelical divine.

[4] Stephen Lushington (1782–1873), civilian; M.P. for Tower Hamlets, 1832–41. Judge of consistory court of London, 1828–58. Member of committee of African Civilisation Society.

[5] Buxton's health was already precarious.

[6] On October 24 Beecham had written to Bunting for advice about the details of the publication which the African Civilisation Society had been discussing. He also reported that the Epping Forest estate for which they had bid £7000 with a view to building a missionary college had been offered for 7000 guineas, the owner to keep that share of the forest which would fall to the estate on enclosure. He added, 'I see clearly that our Treasurer [Thomas Farmer] does not like that side of London'. The Treasurer eventually had his way, and the college was built in 1843 at Richmond, near his property at Gunnersbury.

I prefer 'under the *sanction* of the Society' for the reasons you so well state.

At present a series of occasional papers seems to me to be best, but so printed as that they may form the first volume of a regular periodical in due time.

It does not strike me that for some time to come these papers can be sold extensively, if at all. *Gratuitous distribution*, with a view to excite attention, and assist in procuring subscriptions and forming Branch Societies, seems to me to be the principal object just now. With this view I of course should not think of *stamping* it. A circulation effected in a way similar to that of our *Missionary Notices* would succeed. A small parcel might be sent monthly by the booksellers to every place where we have auxiliaries, and *their* offices would locally distribute them. Murray, Longman, Seeley, Hatchard, and others would, I should think, gratuitously render us that service from philanthropic motives, on proper application. . . .

I think it unfortunate that the Manchester meeting is fixed for a day when Lushington and Wilberforce cannot attend. Mr. Trew's visit, however, sets my mind at rest as to the certainty of arranging a substantially *good* meeting.

With respect to the Woodford Estate, it seems to me, as to you, that it would be folly to quarrel about the difference between pounds and guineas. But I should be very tenacious in refusing to admit the reservation to the present owner of the share of the Forest adjoining to the Estate in case of inclosure. *That* would drive us to Mason's plan, as to the site of ⟨the⟩ new buildings, to which my judgement is irre-⟨con⟩cilably opposed. If that *Reservation* be insisted upon, I should then be inclined, most reluctantly, to abandon the whole. I would give something additional in the first purchase, rather than consent to the reservation. We know not what use Munnies might hereafter make of it. . . .

194   From R. Alder   *London, October 26, 1840*

. . . I know not whether we are to have a European War or not. Thiers and his friends have resigned, and if Louis Phillipe can construct a Conservative cabinet the peace of the world will be perpetuated. But I fear that the late changes in Spain will increase the difficulties of the present crisis. The leaders of the Spanish people do not appear to know what is meant by a state of freedom; and indeed how should they, seeing that they have been trained in the school of Popery or of Infidelity.

We shall be glad to see you, but do not return *too soon*. Enjoy the country while you can, and we will do our best in the meantime. I know not when the Wesleyan Centenary Buildings[1] will be ready, and I have ceased to hope or to fear concerning the time of our removal. The builder is in my opinion too great a man for our architect to manage. . . .

195 From James Kendall[2]   *Market Rasen, November 14, 1840*

Being called to Edinburgh a short time ago (as a witness in a trial of great importance) I was introduced by my friend the Rev. Mr. Guthrie[3] (Minister of Gray Friars) to the Rev. Dr. Chalmers[4] who invited me to breakfast with him. Several literary gentleman breakfasted with us. Our conversation though miscellaneous was interesting – and the subject of the Doctor's letter to you, which accompanies this, formed no inconsiderable a part of it.

The Doctor seemed pleased when I told him that though in our Connexion we gave no encouragement to remonstrances founded on mere whim and caprice, *reasonable* remonstrances received respectful attention from the Conference. Still the sole and exclusive *right* of appointing preachers was with ourselves etc., etc.. The Doctor likes this and while paying all due attention to the 'powers that be' maintains (and as I think very reasonably), the right of the general assembly, or the local Presbyteries to regulate the appointment of ministers to parishes. But as it is not my intention to discuss so important a point as that contained in the Doctor's letter, I must satisfy myself with stating that the letter was given to me by Dr. Chalmers unsealed, that I might read it, and acquaint you with our conversation.

I cannot tell Reverend Sir what are your opinions of the controversy in the Church of Scotland, but for my own part I *at present* incline to think that Dr. Chalmers's opinions cannot easily be subverted. I more-

---

[1] The new building in Bishopgate Street Within, London, to house the offices of the Wesleyan Methodist Missionary Society, built from the proceeds of the Centenary Fund.

[2] James Kendall, preacher, Market Rasen circuit, 1840–41. Kendall's views on the Scots establishment should be compared with those on the English establishment referred to in no. 41 *supra*.

[3] Thomas Guthrie (1803–73), Scots evangelical, minister of Old Greyfriars, Edinburgh, 1837–40.

[4] Thomas Chalmers (1780–1847), theologian, leader of the Disruption in the Scots Church, 1843.

over think that if *as a body* we can help Dr. Chalmers and the venerable Church to which he belongs, we *should* do so. I mean however to be *prudent*. . . .

196   From Abraham E. Farrar[1]   *Bristol, February 15, 1841*

. . . I fear we have not done so well as formerly. Indeed if we except the the addition of above 100 boys and girls to the Society, almost every concern has been declining. After Conference a strong party spirit unfolded itself in favour of noisy and late meetings, which made our young colleague Mr. Griffiths[2] its centre, who became *at once outrageously popular*. Since then, all other congregations, prayer meetings, etc. etc. than those where he has presided, have been comparatively small, and every standing Methodistic institution and interest declining. In fact we have been almost revived into ruin! One fact will shew you the temper prevailing at the beginning of the year. Mr. Lomas[3] entered a pulpit where Mr. G. was expected (Portland St.) and more than twenty moved off at once to seek for *something more excellent*! It is unnecessary to add, that the most judicious of our people have sympathized with us in this state of things; and at the Quarterly Meeting urged us, as far as *they* were concerned, vehemently, to remain a third year. Mr. Lomas has been so long domiciliated in this neighbourhood, as to feel at home; Mr. Stanley[4] philosophically hopes for a more Tory state of feeling; Mr. Hill[5] will, I suppose under the advice of Dr. Prichard, retire from the itinerancy – what I should do, I am utterly at a loss. I have no wish to leave Bristol, but vainly hoping to check the noise and lateness of the meetings, my interference has created me *much ill will*; and unless matters assume a new aspect before Conference [I] may be induced to retire. Mr. Wood has patronized the *revival*, and reflects strongly up on *me* for not joining in such a *work of God*; but is otherwise friendly. . . .

[1] Abraham E. Farrar, preacher, Bristol (King St.) circuit, 1839–42.

[2] Frederick Griffiths, preacher, Bristol (King St.) circuit, 1840–42. D. 1873, aet. 64.

[3] John Lomas (1798–1877), preacher, Bristol (King St.) circuit, 1839–42. President, 1853.

[4] Jacob Stanley sen., superintendent, Bristol (King St.) circuit, 1839–42.

[5] Josiah Hill, preacher, Bristol (King St.) circuit, 1839–42. He became a supernumerary at Haverfordwest, 1842, and d. 1844.

197   From William Lord[1]   *Hull, March 27, 1841*

. . . A pamphlet of Mr. Welch's[2] against the Gown made its appearance
yesterday. It is read with great avidity and will make some impression,
though it is I think a failure. He wishes to excite jealousy among the
Local Preachers, but that portion of the pamphlet is too obscure to be
generally understood without an interpreter.

198   From Abraham E. Farrar   *Bristol, April 5, 1841*

. . . your frequent public reference[s] to the [Mission House] Building *as
the gift of the Centenary Committee*, are well advised; for you probably know
there is a prejudice afloat in the country, as to the extravagance of the
Establishment,[3] which cannot be too soon obviated. I have heard that
it was very gravely *blazoned* in a committee meeting in this city within *a
very few days* – when, however, our Mr. Cruss, who lately made you a
call, gave some serviceable statements in reply; which followed out by
similar statements in other places, will soon leave our *Croakers* without
just ground of cavil. I regret to say we have more than one of this
description here.

We are far from being in a healthy state of religion in this city. Our
young friend Mr. Griffiths who conducts a Revival (so-called) has been
unwittingly the centre of a party, who have not treated the other
preachers very ceremoniously; and who, by canvassing the city, have
just received promises of more than 100£ to support him as a *married
preacher* next year! Meantime, though the numbers in the Society are
nominally increasing, *all* our *funds* (even *our Quarterage*) are diminishing.
I am ashamed to say that in the Missionary department, we are 80£
minus! The Circuit is ruined for want of *more Conservative* feeling. . . .

---

[1] William Lord, superintendent, Hull (George Yard) circuit, 1839–42.

[2] C. Welch, *The silk gown: 'To be or not to be' in our Wesleyan pulpits?* (London, 1841).
Charles Welch, of Nafferton Lodge near Driffield, a prominent Hull schoolmaster (Gregory,
Sidelights p. 67), wrote extensively on Methodist constitutional questions, generally on the
Conference side. A great controversy had arisen in the Hull (Waltham St.) circuit when one
of the Preachers, S. D. Waddy, in defiance of his Superintendent's instructions, adopted the
preaching gown, as 'one of several important organic changes' which must take place in the
churchly character of the connexion. Bunting blocked the development of this controversy the
following Conference (see Ward, *Religion and Society* pp. 254–5). Cf. nos. 200, 202 *infra*.

[3] Methodist radicals continued to find the Mission House irksome, for the basement
premises were let out as wine and spirit vaults.

199   From Thomas Pooley   [*Woodford, April 20, 1841*]

[Protesting furiously against the exercise of Wesleyan discipline; he finds it is laid down that with his present views he cannot have communion with the Wesleyans and must cease from agitating the connexion. He has only just heard of the charge, and has only refused to take intoxicating wine at the sacrament.¹]

... I am happy to say that the word 'universal practice' is wrong, for at Cornwall and many other places I could name, they have banished the destructive cup from the Lord'[s] Table again ... Some of my objections for refusing to take an intoxicating wine at the Lord's Table [are] 1st. I am fully convinced that drunkenness is our national sin, and this has been the cause of producing not less than 99 parts out of 100 of the misery and crime that has afflicted our land. 2nd. I am fully convinced as long as intoxicating drinks are made and sold so long will drunkenness with all its misery and crime prevail and as we have the testimony of the most distinguished medical men that they are not only useless but injurious to all persons in health, taken in ever so small a quantity. Therefore as the drinks are productive of evil in every form and no good whatever I think no one will say it is going too far by saying that the manufacture and vending of such a destructive article which tends only to injure the persons that uses it is both sinful and wicked ... 3rd. I also feel as fully convinced that they are in a direct opposition to Scripture ... is it not inconsistent to expect G⟨od⟩ will pour out his spirit upon us, is it not mockery even to ask him to do so while we are huggin⟨g⟩ our sin instead of putting it from us ... Therefore I now make my appeal from the said Minor District Meeting to a Special District Meeting. ...

200   From Peter Duncan²   *Hull, May 10, 1841*

... You will be glad to know that on this circuit we are in a state of great peace, and that in principle and affection our leading men are more attached to the Conference than any body of 'officials' I ever saw. We shall have an increase of members but it will not be very great.

I suppose you know that we are looking for a stormy District [Meeting]. You have doubtless heard that Mr. Smith³ has preferred charges against

¹ Cf. n. 1 p. 219 *supra*.

² Peter Duncan (1798–1862), preacher, Hull (George Yard) circuit, 1839–41. This letter embodies a characteristic over-estimate of the security of the official position.

³ William Smith (1793–1869), superintendent, Hull (Waltham St.) circuit, 1840–41. Smith's dispute with S. D. Waddy carried curious overtones of a brush he had had with his father, Richard Waddy, at Newcastle in 1831, on which Bunting commented, 'Waddy and

Mr. Waddy[1] principally for putting on the gown without consulting him and persisting in wearing it against his orders. It would however appear that Mr. S. now thinks that such orders have never been given (which is really the case) and therefore last week he sent him his commands to discontinue wearing 'the costume'. Mr. Waddy has of course obeyed, and from Mr. S.'s letter I imagine he intends to withdraw his charges. The matter however has gone much too far to be overlooked, and if I am not mistaken it will be demonstrated that Mr. W. has been worse treated and more falsely represented both in this and other places than most persons can possibly imagine. Meanwhile affairs on the other circuit present a very gloomy aspect. The real friends of our constitution are depressed, and I fear they cannot stand out much longer; and in the affair of the gown they consider that their feelings and those of at least nineteen-twentieths of the society and congregation have been sacrificed to meet the clamours of five or six individuals whose opposition to Methodist preachers has been notorious for the last twenty years. Perhaps you have heard a rumour that from the agitations in the Hull West circuit, it is unlikely the Conference of 1842 can be held here. I have only to say that the principal leaders of the opposition to Mr. Waddy did all they could to oppose the holding of Conference in Hull, but at the meeting which was held on the subject, the representatives of the East Circuit were as numerous as those from the West and the opposition of the party weighed no more than the small dust in the balance. Whatever may be the decision of next Conference respecting the question of gowns, I have no doubt but the case of Hull will be properly attended to and then there will be nothing to fear. . . .

201   From George Birley[2]   *Peterborough, May 15, 1841*

. . . I think you will excuse me if I take the liberty of obtruding upon you the impressions of my mind respecting the working of the new system for supplying the necessities of 'Worn-out Preachers etc.'[3] In this circuit it is true, we have with some difficulty raised our quota, but I learn that this is not the case in several of the neighbouring circuits both

W. Smith, *it is said*, have had a breeze at Newcastle, and ought both to leave; but the former has, as usual, a party of friends who plead for his continuance'. M.C.A. MSS. J. Bunting to E. Grindrod, March 2, 1831.

[1] Samuel D. Waddy (1804–76), preacher, Hull (Waltham St.) circuit, 1840–41. Governor of Wesley College, Sheffield, 1844–61. President, 1859.

[2] George Birley (1788–1867), superintendent, Peterborough circuit, 1839–42.

[3] Cf. n. 2 p. 234 *supra*.

in this District and the Norwich one. So far as I can gather information, the principal difficulty has arisen out of the unsuitableness of the present time of making the application to the classes, at least in agricultural circuits. In the winter season many agricultural labourers have very little employment, and their wages [are] lower, much lower than at other periods of the year. Whereas if the application were made to the classes in the first week in October, as a thank offering for the harvest instead of a New Year's gift (as some have been pleased to call it) our poor members would have had the full employment, and extra wages of the harvest months, besides the fruits of the gleaning by their wives and children. Also it would prevent the Christmas application from injuring the Yearly Collection by placing a vacant quarter between them. And further it would equalise the pecuniary applications of our Connexion. If we take the four months including December, January, February and March, we have at present, in that space of time, two quarterly collections, the application for the Theological Institution, the Chapel Fund Collection, the application for the New Fund, and also putting down the Yearly Collection in the class books; making six appeals in the four months, whereas if we take the preceding four months viz. August, September, October and November, we have only one quarterly collection, and the appeal for Kingswood etc. Schools. I believe if our application had been in [the] autumn instead of having difficulty in raising our quota, we should have had a surplus. I am well aware that in addressing you I am writing to one who by his masterly plans and judicious counsels has done more for Wesleyan Methodism than any man living. . . .

202   From William Smith   *Hull, June 21, 1841*

I dare say you have by this time heard of the decision of our District Meeting in reference to Mr. W[addy] and his clerical costume, and the fate of the charges which I preferred against him for his rash and hasty assumption of that costume, and the pertinacity with which he continued to wear it. Feeling myself injured by the conclusion to which the Brethren have come, and convinced of your freedom from partiality in matters of this sort, I take the liberty to submit the following pages to your consideration. I shall lay the resolutions before you, and, in order the more easily to comment upon them, shall place them in juxtaposition with the charges which I preferred. Before, however, I do this, I must make a few preliminary remarks.

In the *first place*, I, lonely and solitarily, had to contend against five preachers, all committed to the gown question, acting so much in concert as could leave no doubt that the peculiar plan of operation was previously conceived and arranged by them, each knowing beforehand the part he should act. The trial of Waddy was the trial of them all.

In the *second place*, nice and (in Methodism) unheard of distinctions were made between Wm. Lord and the Chairman of the Hull District; and Willm. Smith and the Superintendent of the Hull West Circuit; between opinion and advice; between official communication and friendly request and entreaty. What I said in one place was the saying of W. Smith; if the same had been said in another place it would have been the saying of the Superintendent of the Hull West Circuit. For instance, in his own house, in a friend's house and in the street, I requested and urged Mr. W. to lay aside the robe. This was *unofficial*. If the same had been committed to paper and addressed to him folded as a note; or if it had been uttered in our regular preachers' meeting, it would have been sufficient to give legal authority and importance. Is there a single interval between the last and next Conference in which I am not Mr. Waddy's Superintendent? Ought not the wish of a Superintendent to a helper clearly expressed [to] be equivalent to a command? Does not this anxiety to subtleize look like a preconcerted scheme to blunt the edge of the allegations – to divert the less reasoning and reflecting brethren of the District from the main point of the investigation – and to conquer by evasion? Is it in keeping with Christian simplicity?

In the *third place* social-party conversations were admitted evidence on one side and refused on the other. Opinions and impressions were valid testimony in Mr. W's case, while nothing but facts were deemed legitimate on mine. Is not this an indication sufficiently strong of the *inclination* of the court, and of *him* who conducted the inquiry – and of the destiny of the enquiry itself? Is not selfishness often stronger than piety in pious people? Do not party spirit and personal implication sometimes bias the best-intentioned minds?

In the *fourth place* in order to damage the religious and methodistic character of my witnesses, and thereby weaken their evidence, things irrelevant to the question, utterly unconnected with it, were dragged into the examination, and allowed by the Chairman. Conversations on other subjects at Leaders' Meetings and Quarterly Meetings; sayings uttered in moments of excitement; expressions provoked by insult; irritating irony, and keen and cutting sarcasm were introduced, misconstrued and misapplied for the sole purpose apparently of injuring the reputation and destroying the influence of men who resisted Warren's invasion of your laws and constitution, who support with a liberality worthy imitation your connexional funds and institutions, and who give with a lavish hand at your Missionary Anniversaries; men who respect your rights, venerate your characters, uphold your cause, defend your claims, and submit to your government.

This statement of facts, supported as it will be by documentary evidence, collected and drawn up by some of our principal friends will introduce you to the *animus* of these painful proceedings.

I shall now place in parallel columns the charges and the resolutions of the District upon them, accompanied by a few explanatory notes.

1. *Charge.* With unconstitutionally introducing a gown and bands into the Waltham St. pulpit and preaching in them on Sunday 21st of February 1841.

Resolved, that without giving an opinion as to the existence of any law relative to ecclesiastical vestments as both Mr. Smith and Mr. Waddy up to the time of the latter wearing a gown were *fully convinced* that at the last Conference all laws on the subject were declared to be rescinded, the meeting therefore pronounce him *not guilty.*

I never was '*fully convinced*' of it – but the impression on my mind was that the law prohibiting ecclesiastical vestments was *in the* last Conference declared to be rescinded, not *by* the last Conference. The declaration was not made by the President of the Conference. No vote was taken by him. I think it was yourself or someone else on the platform who audibly asked, Do you declare this law to be rescinded? If you do lift up your hands – and a few obeyed the call. But the official head of the Conference had nothing to do with it. At least so I think. Still however I acted on the presumption that the law was repealed. Accordingly I stated that no Leaders' or Quarterly Meeting could arraign Mr. W. at its bar or pronounce upon the legality or illegality of his conduct, but mainly give an opinion of the mischief which is being produced by the use of the gown.

Granting the law in question to be rescinded, is the constitution of Methodism preserved inviolate by the *manner* of Mr. W.['s] assumption of the robe? Is so serious and sudden an innovation upon the usages of the Connexion no transgression against the principles of its constitution? Is the law of usage on which Lord Lyndhurst laid such stress in his memorable Chancery judgment, and which he considered an integral part of our constitution, *almighty* when applied to the members of our society, and to the Trustees of our chapels, and *powerless* when applied to preachers? Is this 'new thing' the subject of any Conferential injunction, sanction or even law of toleration? I contend, therefore, in opposition to the doctrine embodied in the verdict of the District Meeting that a gown cannot be *constitutionally* used by *any preacher* to preach in till its use has been 'first appointed by the Conference'.

Charge 2d.

With introducing the said gown and bands without consulting me as your Superintendent or otherwise obtaining my consent and approbation.

Resolutions on the 2d. charge

1. That it is distinctly proved that Mr. W. before his wearing a gown had on various occasions in the presence of his Superintendent *intimated his intention* of doing so, and explained in his presence what his reason was for not *more formally consulting him*, and requesting *his consent*; viz. that he (Mr. S) might not be *involved* in any *responsibility*.

2. That he (Mr. W.) had frequently expressed the same sentiments to other brethren in Hull, and that Mr. S. had never signified his disapprobation.

3. Also that at a meeting of preachers of both circuits subsequently, it was further explained to him with which explanation Mr. S. expressed his satisfaction.

The Meeting therefore unanimously pronounce him *not guilty*.

The first resolution contains an implied admission of the charge itself. The words ' not now *formerly consulting* me and *requesting* my *consent*,' when interpreted in the light of truth, mean that there was *no formal consultation* with me, no not the least. Is the *intention* of sometime wearing a gown, *intimated* in a vagrant conversation in a tea party at which I happened to be present but in which I took no part, to be solemnly construed into a formal consulting me and requesting my consent as his Superintendent? And if *intimating* his *intention* cannot mean a formal consulting me and requesting my consent, can that be so interpreted, where the *intention* was not even *intimated*? The *formality* of *intimating* his *intention* to take the gown into Waltham St. pulpit and preach in it on the 21st February 1841 was not so much as practised. Is not this a pitiful attempt to evade the question? Indeed the District Meeting came to the above conclusion in the teeth of Mr W.['s] own confession. He said he never consulted me about it. Further than this, he said he never intended to consult me or obtain my consent; that in what he had done he had acted independently of every person, especially of me – that I might not be involved in any responsibility. Is independently innovating upon the usages of our body connexionally correct? Is it not a serious violation of his ordination engagements? Can a helper do it and be guiltless? Is not Mr. W.['s] plea of not guilty and the District's verdict not only not sustained but contradicted?

Of Mr. W ['s] intention to wear a gown as soon as he methodistically could I have long known. For the last three years he has had a partiality for the robe; and has not, during the time he has been with me, attempted to conceal his intentions. Hence he has since he became my colleague again and again endeavoured to win me over to his view of the question, or to disarm my opposition to it. But that Mr. W. would ever have assumed and worn it without the authority of Conference, or at the least the consent of his Superintendent I never apprehended. Than this nothing could have been more remote from my expectations. Hence whatever was said about it in teaparties or elsewhere, I deemed entirely chimerical – not likely ever to be realized.

That Mr. W. 'had frequently expressed the same sentiments to other brethren in Hull' is very likely, for his talk at table on a long cherished favourite topic is like Benjamin's mess, five times more than the rest of the company – and sometimes a little more than others can endure to hear with patience. I never signified my disapprobation at these social and fraternal outpourings on the subject of the gown, for this plain reason I had something else to do. I could not afford time for so profitless an employment, as that of traversing the streets of Hull after Mr. W. to disapprove of the sentiments which he might express about the gown.

The assertion that I at a preachers' meeting or anywhere else, expressed satisfaction with the gown or with Mr. W. wearing it, with my unchanged strong opinions against it cannot be believed by those who know me. My deep rooted opposition to such a concern as a ministerial garb – as a costume to preach in – my hitherto settled conviction, that its general assumption, authorised by the Conference, would be the forerunner of disastrous consequences to our Connexion, such as destroying our simplicity and thereby subverting our usefulness, will ever interpose a shield between me and such a calumny.

At a preachers' meeting held on Friday the 5th of March I did express satisfaction with the prospect of the gown being set aside during a part of the service of the coming Sunday evening. The truly venerable Mr. Vaughan,[1] on account of the large attendances at our sacramental service, kindly lends us a helping hand in the administration of the elements. Mr. W. was to be the preacher for the night. He having previously declared his determination to put on the gown a second time,

---

[1] Martin Vaughan, supernumerary at Hull from 1824. D. 1846, aet. 84.

notwithstanding my then repeated objection to it – I asked, 'What will you do with Mr. V. in the administration of the sacrament? If you go within the communion rails in your gown, he will not assist you'. 'Oh!', replied Mr. W. 'I did not think of that – What must I do?' After utterance of a few more sentences which savoured of a disposition to dispense with Mr. V.['s] assistance rather than throw off the gown, he said 'If Mr. V. will meet me in the vestry after preaching and say he cannot assist me in the administration of the ordinance if I do it in my gown I will take it off'. 'Very well', I answered 'I am satisfied'. 'Will you tell him so[?]' I said, 'I will.' Who I ask can construe the words 'I am satisfied' in this connection, the only one in which I used them, into a satisfaction with the gown, or with Mr. W.['s] wearing it. I was satisfied with Mr. W.['s] condescension in putting off the gown though it were but during the sacramental service. How much more satisfied should I have been if he had taken it off altogether! Is this fair? Does it not develop a determination to gain a point by pushing truth and justice and strict integrity a little on one side? These christian virtues are not entirely lost sight of, but they respectfully and with some degree of *worldly* politeness request them to move a little to the left that they may have room to pass there. Unchangeably the same they move not, hence those that make the request are driven to take a devious course.

3d. Charge.
With persisting to preach in the said gown and bands after I as your Superintendent had earnestly requested you to discontinue the use of them.

Resolutions on the third charge.
1. That it is clearly proved that the first time Mr. W. saw Mr. S. after his wearing a gown was at the Leaders' Meeting the evening afterwards; that on that occasion Mr. S. distinctly stated he had no authority to require Mr. W. to lay it aside, but *sanctioned* the *right* of the Leaders' Meeting to discuss the 'abstract question' and to give you an opinion upon it.
2. That in the course of the same week the Chairman of the District waited on Mr. S. and informed him that the responsibility lay with him (Mr. S.) and not with the Leaders' Meeting.
3. That at the next Leaders' Meeting Mr. S. sanctioned a formal notice of the introduction of the subject into the Quarterly Meeting. That at the

Quarterly Meeting when the numbers were equally divided for and against the continuance of the gown Mr. S. refused to give a casting vote on either side.

4. That for these reasons Mr. W. did not consider *certain wishes* expressed by Mr. S. for laying aside the gown *official* though he stated his readiness to comply even with them had [he] not put the case into the hands of the said meetings.

5. That after the charges had been sent to Mr. W., Mr. S. did send an official order to discontinue the gown which Mr. W. promptly obeyed. This Meeting therefore pronounce him not guilty of this charge.

1. I am a little at a loss to ascertain what the brethren of the District mean by 'the abstract question'. Do they mean the question of law respecting the use of gowns abstracted from the unseemly manner of its introduction into Waltham Street pulpit on the 21st February, and the bad effects which its assumption originated? Or do they mean the effects of its being so introduced abstracted from the question of law? If they mean the question of law abstracted from the consequences of its assumption, these it was clearly proved to the contrary of the District Meeting's resolution. All the evidence that was brought to bear upon this point amounted to a total and unequivocal disproof of the assertion 'that I sanctioned the right of the Leaders' Meeting to discuss the abstract question and to give an opinion upon it'.

If by the abstract question they mean the question of effects and consequences, the symptoms of evil which its appearance occasioned, then I did sanction the right of the Leaders' Meeting of Waltham Street Society to give an opinion upon it, to state the nature and extent of these effects, and thereupon to pass a resolution, couched in respectful terms, to request Mr. W. to lay it aside till the Conference. I did this because I deemed it a 'subject connected with the proper business of that Society'. See Minutes, 1835.

2nd resolution. This resolution is very warily formed and phrased. It seems to say that the Chairman of the Hull District waited on Mr. S. for the special purpose of informing him that the responsibility lay with him and not with the Leaders' Meeting. It was not so. The object of the Chairman's visit of that week was to talk about Society and Circuit matters in which, as Superintendents, we were mutually concerned, such as the division of Sunday School property etc. The Chairman never made it a subject of conversation in any of his visits to me. Farther, he never of his *own accord* communicated with me on the subject. Judging from his excessive and well-sustained caution, I believe he never intended to converse with me about it. At the time in question we had left my house and were in the street, when I commenced the conversation by making some statements to him of what had passed on Monday night at our Leaders' Meeting. It was not that he perceived me in imminent danger, and wished with affectionate eagerness to stop the downward course of my falling fortunes. This resolution, thus episodically put in, betrays an apprehension that the chairman is not free from blame in this affair, and is shrewdly intended to shew that he is not quite so bad as he appears to be.

The Chairman did inform me that the responsibility lay with me. 'What responsibility?', I asked. He answered the responsibility of preserving the peace of the Society. So I thought. Hence as Mr. W. had said at a meeting of Leaders which was held after the regular Leaders' Meeting of the previous Monday, he would not discontinue the use of the gown, I, in the exercise of my responsibility, thought it right to try what effect a resolution of request from the Leaders would have upon him. He had broken the peace of the Society by the assumption of the robe and its discontinuance alone could heal the breach. In all that I allowed and did I aimed to compass this in the least offensive way.

3. The third resolution under this charge says 'that at the next Leaders' Meeting I sanctioned a formal notice of the introduction of the subject into the Quarterly Meeting'. I did so under the auspices of the Revd. S. D. Waddy. In this I paid more deference to his judgment than my own. He very complacently and with an air of authority pronounced the Leaders' Meeting incapable of entertaining the question; adding it belonged to the business of the Quarterly Meeting in connection with my second year's appointment.

4. That the members of the Quarterly Meeting were not equally divided *for* and *against* the continuance of the gown – that this was not exactly the point will appear from the resolution itself. 'That this meeting, while it repudiates the intention to interfere with the vested rights and privileges of our ministers, feels called upon affectionately to urge upon the Rvd. S. D. Waddy (*out of regard* to the peace and prosperity of the Wesleyan Society in this place) the *propriety* of immediately laying aside the clerical vestments assumed by him in Waltham Street Chapel. It reiterates to Mr. W. the assurance of its christian esteem and confidence, and repeats its already unanimously expressed wish that he will continue his ministrations in this circuit

during the ensuing year'. If the abstract question, gown or no gown, could have been the subject of discussion the resolution would have met with a very different result. The majority against the robe would have been overwhelming. The gown would have been shivered into shreds. But the Meeting feeling from the doctrine which I had laid down at its commencement its incapacity to denounce Mr. W.['s] conduct, and legislatively to set aside the vestment, became confused and perplexed. Availing himself of this, Mr. W. declared their opposition fruitless, for the gown must sooner or later become general in the connexion because it was necessary to the finished dignity of our ministry and to the perfection of our church; that though it cannot be kept out of the next Conference, the Conference will leave the assumption of it to the option of the preachers, and to the guidance of circumstances, and that he did not wish to quit the circuit, yet the passing of the resolution would leave him no alternative. Upon this one of the brethren moved the previous question as an amendment upon the original motion. This manoeuvre divided the meeting in their sympathies with Mr. W. but not in their hostility to the gown. This was strong and inveterate as ever. If the gown is *to be forced* upon us, some of them argued, do what we may, we had better allow it in Mr. W. than run the risk of losing him. Others, and they by far the greater number on that side, voted for the amendment in the hopes that, perceiving the strong feeling of the meeting against the gown, Mr. Waddy would forthwith of his own accord, lay it aside and promptly put an end to a dispute which threatened such sad results. Many of the latter are now under very strong feelings of disgust, because of Mr. W.['s] subsequent conduct.

4. [*sic*] Here my 'earnest requests', which, by the bye, were acknowledged to be so by Mr. W., are pared down to 'certain wishes'. The unofficial times and places in which they were made robbed them of all power over his conscience and justified his resistance of them, so he said. It was in the District Meeting he stated his readiness to have complied with these wishes, had not Mr. S. put the case in the hands of those meetings. I never heard such statement by Mr. W. till it was made in the District Meeting.

4th Charge.

With illegally protesting against my conduct while in the exercise of the functions of my office as the Superintendent of the Hull West Circuit and accompanying it by a line of conduct calculated to injure my reputation and destroy my authority.

On the fourth charge the meeting unanimously resolve *That Bro. Waddy is not guilty.*

In addition to the above resolutions the Meeting deem it their duty to state that while they cannot justify the manner in which the gown was introduced by Mr. Waddy it does not appear that many persons in the Hull West Circuit were at first *violently* opposed to it. But since that time there has been considerable excitement arising principally from the following causes viz. the *imprudent* introduction of the subject into the Leaders' and Quarterly Meetings, the extensive circulation by Mr. Smith and others of an *unfounded* report that the wearing of a gown was only the first of a series of organic changes which would be productive of as great evil [as] had ever taken place in the connex⟨ion⟩; and also the publication of a pamphlet on the same subject by one of the members of the Hull West Circuit.

As far as the conduct of Mr. S. [is concerned] *the Meeting however, have also to state that for sometime he has been suffering under personal and family affliction, which they believe has produced mental uneasiness and depression.* They therefore strongly and *earnestly recommend* to the Conference to pass no censure upon him!!!!!

In a few days, if you will permit, I will send you a note or two on the 4th charge and the resolution connected therewith with the last part of the resolution winding up the affair. I feel it to be very offensive to me. If I deserve censure let the Conference censure me. The argument by which they support their strong and earnest recommendation excites, despite of all my [efforts?] against [it?] the most indignant feeling. . . . [P.S.] I shall appeal to the Conference against the whole affair especially against the resolution which so contemptuously reflects upon me.

T

203   From Lord Ashley[1]   *n. pl., July 11 [1841]*

Confidential

Notwithstanding Mr. Gibson's[2] speeches and principles, he will be returned to Parliament, I fear, by the votes of Wesleyans. I have sent you Mr. Fitzroy Kelly's[3] letter, which describes the state of things. It is a terrible affair. I know full well and appreciate your difficulties.

Pray let me have the letter back again. . . .

204   From George Cubitt   *London, July 21, 1841*

. . . Last night, I received a note from the 'Elders and deacons of the Scotch Church, Regent Square' – inviting me to dine, next Tuesday, with them, and other friends of the church, at the London Tavern, to meet Dr. Gordon.[4]

It seems that a Scotch clergyman from Edinburgh, is to be settled over the congregation in Regent Square. His name is Hamilton.[5] Next Sunday morning, Dr. Gordon is to preach there, and introduce Mr. Hamilton to the congregation.

Now, as we have entered into the Scotch question and as neither *yourself* nor *Mr. Beecham* are in town, I thought perhaps it would be important that some of us should have the opportunity of seeing these good gentlemen, and learning from them the actual position of affairs, and there is no one else for it, but myself. I attach importance to the subject thus, by hearing what these gentlemen themselves say, and reflecting on it in my own leisure, I mean to obtain a more exact acquaintance, with the ins and outs of the question, than mere books could give me. . . .

I hope what we have done will do Methodism good. The *Scottish Guardian* has not only spoken favourably of the Review, of your and Mr. Beecham's attendance of the meeting held at Exeter Hall, and of the

---

[1] Cf. n. 2. p. 219

[2] Thomas Milner Gibson (1806–84), conservative M.P. for Ipswich, 1837–39, now elected for Manchester on a liberal and anti-corn law platform. The point of Ashley's distress is that as recently as 1839 the Manchester Wesleyans had voted almost solidly for the defeated Tory candidate, Sir George Murray. Result: Mark Philips (Lib.) 3695: T. Milner Gibson (Lib.) 3575: Sir George Murray (Con.) 3115: William Entwisle (Con.) 2692.

[3] Fitzroy Kelly (1796–1880), barrister, Conservative M.P. for Ipswich, 1837–41.

[4] Robert Gordon D.D. (1786–1853), minister of the High Church, Edinburgh, 1830; supported Chalmers in founding the Free Church.

[5] James Hamilton (1814–67), assistant minister, St. George's, Edinburgh, 1838–39; minister of Scottish National Church, Regent Square, London, 1841–67.

labours of the *Watchman*[1] in the same cause, but likewise gives this important testimony to Methodism:

'Out of the Establishment, there is no body of Christians comparable to the Wesleyan Methodists in numbers, in piety, and in zealous exertions for the spread of the Redeemer's Kingdom. They have more than eleven hundred Ministers whose faithful labours have surrounded them with multitudes of attached adherents, full of vital energy, in every city, town and village of England. They have long been the salt of the land.' Speaking of the *Magazine*, and earnestly recommending the July Number, he says that it 'circulates throughout their *whole Church*'.

Under all circumstances, had I not better wait over Tuesday, and accept the invitation? . . .

205 From Joseph Wood   *Conference [Manchester], August 11, 1841*

May I beg the favour of your kind attention to the enclosed. I have had no communication with any individual on this subject, but I have much reason to believe that some such journal would be of connexional service.

If you do not disapprove I propose to take steps for promoting some such periodical. . . .

Document appended:– The connexion that exists between the Wesleyan Societies is purely of a religious character. Wesleyanism is inflexible and ardent in its loyalty, but lays no obligation upon its members to adopt any particular plans of political economy, or to attach themselves to any particular party in the state.

In the opinion of many a weekly journal upon connexional principles is a desideratum. To accomplish this object it is proposed to publish a new weekly periodical, to be called *The Wesleyan*[2] to be conducted according to the following regulations, viz.

1. On all disputed political questions it shall be *strictly a reporter*. It will state the leading topics that may engage public attention, and will give extracts from the speeches delivered in Parliament. But in cases in

---

[1] Throughout 1841 the constitutional difficulties of the Scottish Church were very fully reported in the *Watchman* which on July 21 (p. 231) reprinted the views of the *Scottish Guardian* on the growth of the non-intrusion question.

[2] This journal was never launched (cf. however no. 268 *infra*), but the proposal was symptomatic of a recurrent need to find some answer to the radical Methodist publications which could find wider acceptance than the narrowly Tory and official *Watchman*. On March 31, 1841 a correspondent to the *Watchman* (p. 102) had urged the case for a somewhat different journal, an intellectual *Wesleyan Review*, in which politics should be of secondary interest. This aspiration was not fulfilled till the founding of the *London Quarterly Review* in 1853.

which extracts may be given from the speeches or opinions of one party in the state there shall be quotations upon the same subject from the advocates or the opposite side of the question, so as to place such controverted points as may be introduced, in the most impartial manner before its readers, unaccompanied by any editorial remarks.

2. It will 'bid God speed' to the Christian efforts of 'all who love our Lord Jesus Christ', whether connected with the Established Church or with different denominations of dissenters, practically exemplifying the saying of our venerated founder, 'The Friends of all, the enemies of none'.

3. But while it maintains this Wesleyan Catholicity, it will assume in regard of Wesleyanism a decided position, supporting its doctrines, explaining its economy and defending its institutions.

4. *The Wesleyan* will also be a repository of religious and literary information, and will include the usual topics of a religious journal.

5. It is not intended to start *The Wesleyan* in opposition to *The Watchman*, or in rivalry of that periodical. On the contrary it is hoped that both journals may pursue their way with no other but the laudable emulation which seeks to surpass in the advancement of 'whatsoever things are pure, whatsoever things are lovely and whatsoever things are of good report.'

It is proposed that the proprietorship shall be held in shares of £25 each – no individual to hold more than eight shares – that the Proprietory shall appoint a general committee of management, and that this committee shall appoint the Editor and a small acting committee; that none but members of the Wesleyan Society shall be eligible to be chosen upon the committee, or to fill any other office in or under the Proprietory, and should the party cease to be a member of the society after his election to any of these offices, his office shall terminate with his membership.

206 From R. Alder   *St. Ives, November 18, 1841*

. . . They are a pitiful set of radicals agitators and slanderers that have arrayed themselves against the peace and order of our Church in this County [Cornwall], and can do us no harm.

This Town[1] I find is the centre of the movement, and we owe that to injudicious and imbecile Superintendents. This part of our system requires revision. Upon the whole the general interests of Methodism as far as I have yet seen are in a much better state than I expected to find

[1] Cf. n. 1 p. 219 *supra*.

them. Nothing of a religious nature will flourish here but Wesleyan Methodism. It is the will of God that it should be so, and neither human weakness not human wickedness shall long prevail against it in any portion of the County. . . .

207   Address to Queen Victoria,   *London, January, 1842 [Draft]*
signed by Jabez Bunting as
Chairman of the Committee
of Privileges

May it please Your Majesty,

We Your Majesty's loyal and dutiful subjects, being the Committee to whom the Conference of the people called Methodists, in the connexion established by the late Rev. John Wesley M.A., has entrusted the charge of its civil rights and duties, humbly beg permission to offer to Your Majesty, by the direction and on behalf of the said Conference, our hearty congratulations on the recent birth of a Prince, an event which has diffused universal joy through your Majesty's wide dominions.

Deeply sensible of the advantages of an hereditary monarchy, and of a settled and direct succession to the throne, and not less mindful of the blessings which this country has enjoyed under the sway of the House of Brunswick, we hail with delight and thankfulness the birth of His Royal Highness the Prince of Wales as a new pledge of the continuance of the present Royal Family upon the throne of these realms, of the security of our national rights and privileges, and of the prosperity and happiness of *all classes of your Majesty's subjects.* More especially do we rejoice in the additional security now afforded us, that those Protestant institutions which are the truest glory and strongest defence of Your Majesty's throne, and which we regard as the bulwark of our constitutional liberty, both civil and religious, will be perpetuated among ourselves and our descendants to the latest posterity. And we cherish an earnest hope and confidence that under the watchful care of Your Majesty, and of his Royal Highness the Prince Albert, the education of the Prince of Wales will be such as will prepare him to maintain, in every station which he may hereafter be called to occupy, those principles of Scriptural Christianity, by the assertion of which the illustrious ancestors both of Your Majesty and of your Royal Consort have been happily distinguished.

We offer our devout acknowledgements to Almighty God, the author of all good, who has preserved Your Majesty and the infant Prince in the hour of danger; and we humbly pray that he may continue to protect and to guide Your Majesty in all things. May his glorious providence watch over the infancy and youth of the Prince of Wales, and endow His Royal Highness with every needful gift to qualify him for the exalted station to which he is born. And may the great King of Kings vouchsafe to Your Majesty, to your Royal Consort, and to every branch of your illustrious house perpetual favour and benediction!

In the Address which we thus presume to offer, we asssure Your Majesty that we express the most cordial sentiments and wishes of the whole body of the Wesleyan Methodists, at home and abroad.

208   To John Beecham   *Manchester, January 13, 1842*

I have just received your letter, etc. of yesterday; but am really too unwell to be capable of thinking, much less of writing, to any good purpose about anything. . . .

We have had long and to me toilsome meetings this week. I am no longer fit for public life. I *must* retire as soon as possible, or irretrievably lose the frail and little health I have left. Several important affairs, however, are well settled, and some difficulties adjusted. When once the Richmond Branch shall have been opened, I hope I may then with perfect satisfaction leave to others all responsibility about the Theological Institution.

It is plain we can have no more money for the *Bishopsgate Premises,*[1] either for furniture, or as interest, from the Centenary Fund; so that we must be strictly economical in using the resources already at our disposal. Nor shall we *at present* get more than £1000, in addition to the £10,000 already given and paid, towards our Missionary Debt. At the winding-up there will be £1000 more, making £12,000 in all for the debt from the Centenary Fund; a very handsome slice to be sure it is. But as that all goes to make up *past* deficiencies, we must go sternly forward on the *Total Abstinence* principle as to new liabilities, for a considerable time longer. . . .

209   From John Beecham   *London, January 13, 1842*

. . . At the Book Committee on Tuesday the proposal respecting a series of Tracts for the Times was agreed to, and the Tract Committee

[1] Cf. n. 1. p. 251

enlarged to carry the plan into execution. We met yesterday afternoon, and marked out our course of operations. You will be amused to learn that Hannah has consented to write a tract to be entitled *Wesleyan Methodism not Schism.* Jackson takes – The sufficiency and Perfection of the Scriptures; Cubitt, Justification by *faith* an essential doctrine of Christianity.[1] . . . Burgess, Young,[2] Sam Waddy etc. not engaged as writers.

210   From William Hopkins[3]   *Warminster, May 3, 1842*

You will pardon me I am sure for the trespass I make upon your time, when I inform you that I am one of the preachers in the Connexion and seek your advice in a case of emergency. You are doubtless aware that the Society at Warminster sustained great injury during Dr. Warren's agitation [from] which it has not as yet recovered. In addition to which, the Chapel was mortgaged for £300; and nearly all the Trustees are Seceders and until within the last year or two they would not consent to transfer the trust, but are quite willing now. The mortgage is left by Will to three poor families who are desirous of commencing business. They have put the case into the hands of Attornies who are daily threatening us with proceedings. As the money was called in last year, the case should have been recommended to the Chapel Fund Committee but was neglected. However it was presented at the last September District by Mr. Wheeler[4] and I believe brought before the Committee but [I] suppose they had other pressing cases which stood before this. Since then I have written several times to Mr. West and he has at length informed me that the funds are exhausted and there is no probability of obtaining relief till next October. I am told by the Attornies that a gentleman in Warminster has made application to them for a transfer of the mortgage, and I have strong reason to suspect the Rector is at the bottom of it; he is practically a Puseyite, calls us unqualified Teachers and canting Methodists, makes the boast that he shall be able

[1] Ten anonymous *Wesleyan Tracts for the Times* were published in 1842 to controvert High-church claims. No. 2 was entitled *Wesleyan Methodism not a schism*; no. 6, *Justification an essential doctrine of Christianity.* Thomas Jackson is not known to have contributed to this series (which included no title of the kind mentioned), but in this year he did anonymously publish *An answer to the question, 'Why are you a Wesleyan Methodist?'*

[2] Robert Young (1796–1865), preacher, London (Great Queen St.) circuit, 1839–42. President, 1856.

[3] William Hopkins, preacher, Frome circuit, 1841–42. D. 1867, aet. 58. (Hall's *Circuits and Ministers* does not note that the Warminster circuit was united with Frome in 1841.)

[4] Robert Wheeler (1744–1849), superintendent, Frome circuit, 1840–42.

to drive all Dissent out of the Town, and as he is a man of property would glory in wresting the Chapel out of our hands. But I am glad to say the Attornies at present are willing to give us the opportunity of redeeming it. There are two parties that would rejoice in our downfall, the Church and the Seceders. The Dissenters would help us, but if the Chapel is lost, unacquainted as they are with our system, they speak of it as a disgrace that our respectable Body should let a Chapel go in a Town like this when £100 would save it. . . .

Low as the cause is here I believe if things were set straight we should do much better and ultimately rise.

211   From John Hall[1]   *Truro, July 12, 1842*

It is with the utmost deference I ask for a portion of your time and attention at the approaching Conference. My excellent colleague, Mr. Williams,[2] will be removed and we want an efficient successor. I need not remind you of the important central position of Truro in the County of Cornwall, and how many contiguous places are under its influence. Most of the clergy here are rife with the worst parts of Puseyism, and are doing all they can to injure us. I shall not dwell upon other parties but simply state that they are more active and numerous in this town than in any other part of the county. The Trustees here are under very heavy responsibilities, though, I am happy to add, that their circumstances are a little improving. The Methodist Society in Truro is strongly attached to the constitution and economy of our church, and supports it in every way. They responded very cordially by augmented contributions to the late special efforts of the Missionary Committee. All things considered, it has appeared to me that a little sympathy and help would now be well bestowed and as well received.

At the division of the circuit last Conference we were labouring under the pressure of a large circuit debt, which is not yet quite removed, though we have raised by special effort nearly £100 towards it. We are thankful to say, however, that the object of the division has been accomplished in retaining three Preachers on the ground, which otherwise would certainly not have been the case. Though this circuit is now extensive, we are thrown upon Truro chiefly in labour and for the financial support. It had been the judgment of some of our best friends

[1] John Hall (1804–80), superintendent, Truro circuit, 1840–43. Among the names canvassed by Hall in a passage omitted from the letter was James Grose who received the appointment.

[2] Henry W. Williams, preacher, Truro circuit, 1839–42.

that Truro had never been cultivated as much as it should have been. The events of the past year have proved it. While the country has not been neglected the town has been more regarded and cared for. The result is that our successes have far surpassed our anticipations. Methodism now occupies a position in this town it never did before, in numbers, union, and energetic cooperation. We think the present period quite an era in the history of Methodism in this town. Could we have sent us a man of tolerable preaching abilities, fervent christian, and consecrated to the work of saving souls, we think we should see great things. The people are prepared for it. To say nothing of the relief which this would ultimately afford to our Trustees, or the increase of Methodism, it would answer the higher end of spreading vital godliness in an important town, which is threatened with all the evils of popery under a protestant name. . . .

212   From William Dale   *Truro, July 15, 1842*

It is with great hesitation I presume to trouble you with any remarks relative to Methodism in this part of the kingdom. My feeling on the matter has for a long time made me desirous to call your attenton to the subject; but considering the importance of your numerous engagements, I felt unwilling to trespass on your time and attention, and had nearly given up my intention until a friend to whom I had made some remarks on the affairs of our Cornish District replied by saying, 'I think you ought to write Dr. Bunting on the subject.' Acting on this suggestion I must hope that your kindness will pardon me, if I trouble you unnecessarily.

It is painful to witness the defective state of organization and discipline in most of our Cornish circuits arising principally from an insufficient number of ministers, while a very formidable obstacle to improvements in this respect is found to exist in the vicious and unmethodistical system of finance generally adopted. For instead of Weekly Class and Quarterly Ticket Money, either a tax of so much per head is levied throughout a circuit or a specific sum required of each Society, without reference to the increase or decrease of members in the course of the year. Allow me Sir to illustrate the practical working of the latter plan. A circuit with a thousand members has to provide for two ministers. At Xmas the probable expenditure of the ensuing year is calculated and apportioned among the Societies; perhaps in the first quarter there is a revival by which five hundred members are added to the Societies. Still they will continue to pay as before, no larger sum being required. The Leaders neglect to call on the new members who therefore are not trained aright in their first love, at the same time many of the old members consider there is less necessity for their exertions, and the consequence is that the payments of a great number become small and *irregular*; and by the end of the year it is found quite as difficult to raise the required sum from fifteen hundred members as it was previously from one thousand. And thus the matter goes on until there are two thousand members, and then perhaps some Societies feel the necessity of additional pastoral oversight, and propose an additional Preacher. This is immediately met by the difficulty of obtaining the necessary funds; and some persons who have not observed the working of the system are suprised to find that the circuit what [*sic*] formerly maintained two ministers with one thousand members, cannot now do more with double the number.

This is no imaginary sketch but an imperfect description of what often occurs, and it will be readily conceived that where such an increase of numbers is going on, without additional ministers, discipline must be neglected, and our beloved Methodism appears crippled and powerless, and schisms are multiplied, where under a better system it would go on extending its triumphs; but, while I lament the existence of such a state of things in many places, I am very happy to acknowledge that some improvement has taken place in the last four or five years especially in the Camborne Circuit, where the Methodistical system of finance has been introduced, and to a great extent carried out, and consequently they have been able to maintain a greater number of ministers than they could otherwise have done. Yet it is evident to those acquainted with the circumstances that Mr. Dunn's efforts would have been more successful, if the ministers in the neighbouring circuits had made a corresponding movement, and the benefits that appeared in Camborne as the fruit of Mr. Dunn's exertions would have encouraged the right-minded to second the efforts of their ministers in so important a work. As the matter now stands a temptation is presented to the disaffected and negligent in the Camborne Circuit to slide back into the old system. Another lamentable effect of the system I have referred to is that in several important places in the county Methodism appears to have lost in great measure its aggressive character and to have settled down in utter neglect of an increasing 'home population.' Even in Penzance where the inhabitants have increased by many thousands in the last 20 years Methodism has been nearly stationary during that period. Mr. Tarr[1] has been earnestly endeavouring to persuade them to make provision

---

[1] William Tarr, preacher, Penzance circuit, 1841–42. Became preacher 1826; voluntarily retired from the work, 1858.

for hundreds of persons who are desirous of attending the Methodist ministry, but unable to move them, he is so grieved with their apathy that he is about to remove at the end of one year.

And now all the evils arising from the vicious system alluded to are increased by the prevalence of Teetotalism. The alarming state into which this has thrown several of our Societies has been brought about chiefly by the want of uniformity in its treatment by our ministers; for while some felt it their duty rather to prevent its being mixed up with our Chapels, Societies etc., others encouraged it in every possible way, opening the chapels, preaching, lecturing etc., in their own and other circuits, uniting with Warrenites, infidels etc. in advocating this cause, administering the Lord's Supper with Teetotal Wine etc. You Sir can readily judge what the effect of all this would be.

And now Sir allow me to lay before you a few suggestions which have been thrown out by some of our judicious friends who are deeply interested in the welfare of Methodism.

1. It is thought to be highly necessary that the *Chairman* of *this District* should be a *minister of more* than ordinary influence, one who from his talents and character would feel himself able to act independently of local prejudices and jealousies, and to assist by his example and counsel every Superintendent making efforts to introduce Methodistical usages, etc. I should not have made this suggestion were it not understood that our present Chairman[1] is likely to leave the District, and of him I feel bound to say, that in many respects he has done good service to the District. Yet he has not grappled with the peculiar customs to which I have referred. Should it be found impracticable to send such a minister into the county might not Cornwall be placed on the list with Scotland and Wales, and the President or Secretary of the Conference with some other minister be deputed yearly to attend the Cornwall District Meeting. This would make our leading ministers better acquainted with the peculiarities and necessities of Cornish circuits.

2. That it is highly necessary to have an increase of Superintendents of circuits possessing talents, prudence and weight of character that will enable them, cautiously but perseveringly, to carry out Methodist principles and extend Methodism.

3. That whatever regulations the Conference may deem it right to make with respect to Teetotalism, it will be necessary that in Cornwall all our ministers should uniformly act on the same principles.

I think before I conclude I should inform you that there has been a considerable improvement in this circuit and especially in this town

[1] John Hobson was chairman of the Cornwall District, 1841-42.

within the last two years, both with respect to financial regulations and devotedness to the cause of God. As I have extended my letter to this unreasonable length, I will not trouble you with any further remarks on this circuit except to take the liberty of saying that a suitable colleague for our Superintendent, Mr. Hall, will be of vast importance at this time. I think too you will be pleased to hear that Methodism in Truro has not lost its aggressive character, for they are contemplating the erection of a new chapel in a populous destitute and increasing part of the town and that at the Annual Meeting of the Trustees held on Tuesday last, the Trustees voted £100 towards that object.

213   From Charles Janion[1]   *Northwich, July 20, 1842*

You will greatly oblige myself and the friends in this circuit by kindly interesting yourself for a few minutes at the proper time during Conference in the case of the third preacher being continued to the Northwich Circuit. I send you a couple of plans that you may judge (almost at a glance) whether we have not work and opposition enough on the ground to call for the labours of three preachers. The two Association Preachers are at most of the villages in our circuit on the same night that we are; and the Primitives have many chapels and preaching places in the circuit. One of the New Weaver Churches at Northwich was consecrated a few weeks ago, and another, a Subscription Church, 2 miles lower down the river, close by our chapel at Barnton, is to be opened in a few weeks. A new infant school room just opposite to the Preacher's houses in Leftwich, has had lectures in it by the clergy (weekly) for the last several months: indeed many of the clergy about here are indefatigable in looking after their schools, in visiting and lecturing among the people, of their respective parishes. I am surprised when I think of it how we maintain our ground, and might exclaim with the Psalmist, 'If the Lord had not been on our side – Then they had swallowed us up quick'. In March our numbers were 906 and 120 on trial. In June they were 1000 and 159 on trial. And yet owing to the influence of two or three cold calculating spirits in the Quarterly Meeting, they would not venture to give the pledge, nor offer to take the third preacher without some assistance, although they were persuaded it would be very unwise to take away the third man. But they hoped that Conference would still sympathize with them in remembrance of the past. It may be thought by some of the Brethren that if

[1] Charles Janion (1796–1871), superintendent, Northwich circuit, 1839–42.

this circuit can raise in one year (as it did this last) £368.0.0 to the missionary cause, it must possess much pecuniary strength; but this does not follow. It is admitted there are many respectable (though but few wealthy) friends in this circuit; but the true reason why so much is raised for the Mission cause is in the fact that *the good Sisters are very zealous* in the cause! . . . Perhaps no *District* in the Connexion, taken as a whole, has been so torn and tried by Kilhamites, Ranterites and Warrenites (and Latter-Day-Saints I may add) as the Macclesfield District has. . . .

214   From William Barton[1]   *London, August 26, 1842*

. . . There is another matter very well worth the attention of the Committee of Privileges. Just before the breaking up of Parliament a Bill was introduced for the regulation of the health of large towns, and empowering a Committee consisting, I believe, of the Rector and Churchwardens of a parish to open new burial grounds, and to close those now existing in large towns. This will have a most serious effect on the income of some of our Chapel Trusts, and certainly ought to be well attended to. I wish you could get a copy of the Bill, and of the Report of the Committee on which it is founded.[2] . . .

215   From Robert Newstead   *Leeds, October 10, 1842*

. . . One of my principal objects in writing now is to place before you several circumstances in connection with *our* Educational movement. When I *last* met our Committee in London Mr. Farmer brought forward some papers (having then recently visited Leeds) relative to an offered premises suited to a normal school. Copies of the same had been sent to me while at Conference – but I had referred the writer (Mr. Stead the Headmaster of the St. Peter's School here, conducted on the Glasgow System in which Mr. S. has been instructed *at* Glasgow) to the *depending* proceeding of our *to be* appointed Educational Committee; as

[1] William Barton (1803–57), preacher, London (City Road) circuit, 1840–43.

[2] On March 8, 1842, the Commons resolved to appoint a select committee 'to consider the expediency of framing some legislative enactments (due respect being paid to the rights of the clergy) to remedy the evils arising from the interment of bodies within the precincts of large towns', which on 14 June reported that burials (with a few exceptions) should be prohibited within towns of over 50,000 inhabitants, parochial authorities to be entitled to the same fees per burial as at present (*Commons Journals* xcvii. 95, 374–5). In 1843 a bill for this purpose was brought in, but after much opposition from nonconformists and others it was withdrawn.

was also done at our Committee, of course, with Mr. Farmer's full consent.

Recently *two* letters have been addressed to me by Mr. Stone – being most accustomed to write to me as Secretary – urging our *immediately* commencing our operations, and strongly recommending *Leeds* as a very suitable locality for a *Normal School*; and in the second letter (having referred *him* in reply to his first to the *probable* results of the depending Committee), he offers, should the Glasgow Institution be broken up by the Scotch secession, to transfer to us *several of their best masters*. He would rather they should *come to us* than go any where else, though he observes at this *crisis* of educational matters 'they will be gladly caught at by many'. . . .

216   To John Beecham   *Leamington, October 22, 1842*

Many thanks for your kind letter of this morning. I think I am drawing some sensible benefit from my residence in this place. The air is very pure; the part of the town, or rather suburbs, where we lodge, remarkably rural and quiet; and the mineral water gentle in operation yet beneficial. The weather, with the exception of Tuesday and today, has been pleasant on the whole, and favourable for walking abroad. But though better in the early portions of the day, I still suffer frequently from restless and uneasy nights, and have had some return of last winter's bronchial affection, and of rheumatic pain and feebleness in my right knee. Another week here will perhaps shew more clearly whether a protracted stay be likely to be of permanent service to me or not.

We shall fully expect you here on Tuesday. . . . You will much oblige me by bringing with you the *Record* of Thursday, October 21st (*last night's*) as I have had the other numbers, and it is the only paper by which I can now keep up my acquaintance with events of general interest in any connected and continuous outline. Besides, I am wishful to see the *Record*'s promised view of Bishop Blomfield's *doctrinal* views (as developed in his late extraordinary charge) which last night's number contains.[1] . . .

Matters begin to assume the aspect of a very serious crisis, and an immediate one, in reference to the Church of Scotland. Has the *Witness*,

[1] Charles James Blomfield (1786–1857), bishop of London, 1828–57. By an effort of reporting in which it took special pride, the *Record* of October 13, 1842, carried a verbatim report of the Bishop of London's charge; leading articles of October 17 and 20 took issue with the bishop on the question of ceremonies and the doctines of justification by faith and baptismal regeneration. In a letter to the *Record* on October 20, 1842, J. Jordan attacked Blomfield for interpreting the Articles of the Church in the light of the Liturgy and Homilies, instead of the light of scripture. This, he held, was to play into the hands of the Tractarians.

or any other Scottish papers, been sent to us? The proceedings of the
Synod of Aberdeen are ominous of mischief. Has the Conference
Answer to the Assembly's Address ever been forwarded?[1]. . . .

217 From Robert Newstead   *Hackney, November 5, 1842*

I gave myself the pleasure to send you the numbers of the *Scottish
Guardian* which has honourably quoted our educational proceedings and
will, I trust, do us good. Thus some good has arisen in another way from
the subject having been taken up in our *Watchman*. I am glad to perceive
that at least the end proposed has been answered in putting down our
meditated '*agitation*' in London, and I hope many more than ever before
have become interested in our educational movements. I have never had
so many letters within a short period from 1838 as within the last *month*
or so. A great many applications for masters among them. We shall soon
again send out all our men and send in others. Two very fine young men
were examined and passed last week. And we are are going to send one
of our preacher's daughters. Poor *Edwards* too who was dropped at the
Conference has been taken up by us and will, I hope, be fitted by the
Glasgow system for some department of usefulness at home or abroad;
and the man for the school at St. Mary's is just finishing. One was
desired the other day for *Lille*, and I wish we could have met it. However
the only one we had ready declined going. I hope it may still be done.
The *education* business is becoming a formidable matter. The correspondence and financial matters occupy a deal of time, but I am
determined to do all that our funds will permit, while I have yet to do
with it, so as to have a complete plan in full, though limited operation,
and *this* will be no small victory after what it has had to contend with
from 1838. . . . We are also going on well *here*; there is a better spirit in
certain quarters – I find it good to *go on* quietly *without* those who will
not work and this makes some [of] them less independent. I am quite
sure a good *spiritual* work is going on here. All our official men have
agreed to spend an hour – the *same* hour – every week in earnest
prayer for the revival of the work, the outpouring of the *spirit, the finding
of a place* for ⟨a⟩ chapel etc. . . .

[1] No document of this kind was printed with the Conference minutes; but the Conference
address to the Societies rejoiced that 'on several late important occasions, evangelical clergymen of the Church of Scotland have supplied our pulpits. Amid abounding instances of
intolerance and bigotry, it is truly delightful to witness this kindly spirit of mutual recognition
and catholic expansiveness of heart. We hail these instances as precursors of that evangelical
union of the members of Christ's mystic body, which shall one day deprive both Popery and
infidelity of their vaunted arguments'.

218   From John Beecham   *Wesleyan Mission House [London],*
                                            January 14, 1843

I am much obliged by your prompt answer to my letter.[1] I have just seen
Mr. Hamilton again and have copied on a subsequent page the para-
graph in the petition which embodies the request to Dr. Chalmers;[2]
and which I think you will see substantially accords with the brief
description I gave you in my last. I think I told you that the Duke of
Argyll heads the petition, and that Messrs. Plumptre[3] and Hardy[4]
M.P.s had also signed it. Yesterday I find the Hon. and Rev. Mr.
Villiers, Rector of St. George's, Bloomsbury,[5] the Hon. and Rev.
Baptist Noel,[6] Rev. Mr. Beamish of Trinity Chapel,[7] Conduit Street,
the Rev. Mr. Bradley of Clapham,[8] Isaac Taylor of Ongar,[9] and
a few others have added their names. Mr. Hamilton informs me
that he and his friends have been anxious to secure no more than a
very select list of signatures, and I understand that they have now
got nearly the number they wished, about 40 or 50 names. As he is
very anxious to send off the petition today, I have ventured to avail
myself of your kind permission and have affixed your name as well as
my own.

I send you herewith a copy of the *Times* of this morning, containing
the answer of Sir James Graham[10] to the Scotch Memorial etc. Mr.

[1] M.C.A. MSS. J. Beecham to Jabez Bunting, January 12, 1843, a letter the contents of
which (apart from a reference to the Friendly Isles District Minutes) are recapitulated in this
letter.

[2] In 1838 Thomas Chalmers had given a celebrated course of lectures in London, defending
the principles of national establishments. He was now to be asked to define the limits of the
rights of the state over the established church.

[3] John P. Plumptre, cf. n. 3 p. 206.

[4] John Hardy (c. 1773–1855), M.P. for Bedford, 1832–37, 1841–47.

[5] Henry Montagu Villiers (1813–61), rector of St. George's, Bloomsbury, 1841–56; bishop
of Carlisle, 1856; bishop of Durham, 1860.

[6] Baptist Wriothesley Noel (1798–1873), leading evangelical and minister of St. John's
chapel, Bedford Row, 1827–48; became a Baptist, 1848.

[7] Henry Hamilton Beamish, anti-Tractarian controversialist; vicar of Kinsale and incumbent of Trinity Chapel, London, 1832–62.

[8] Charles Bradley (1789–1871), incumbent of St. James's chapel, Clapham, 1829–52.

[9] Isaac Taylor (1787–1865), artist, inventor, and, as author of *The Natural History of
Enthusiasm* (1830), *Fanaticism* (1833) and other works, celebrated as a lay theologian. On staff
of the *Eclectic Review*, 1818; began a controversy with the Tractarians, 1839–40.

[10] Sir James Graham (1792–1861), home secretary, 1841–46. At the end of 1842, following
the decision of the House of Lords in the Auchterarder case, Graham had received a memorial
from between four and five hundred Scots ministers threatening to resign their livings if they
were further subjected to the jurisdiction of the civil courts in matters spiritual. On January 4,
1843 Graham had replied somewhat brusquely that the Kirk was demanding that her proceedings should be beyond the cognizance of the courts of law and was claiming the right to
decide for herself what were spiritual matters and what were not.

Hamilton thinks that there is now only one course left; but is of opinion that the Memorialists will not separate from the Church, before the meeting of the General Assembly, when they will make their act the *Act* of the *Church*, whatever that Act may be.

I very much regret to hear so poor an account of your health. I hope you will take all possible care of yourself and not give way to desponding feelings respecting your inability to do what you could wish. Thank God, I am pretty well, and am endeavouring to clear our way as much as possible, by getting on with our foreign correspondence etc., and preparing for the next General Report. . . .

(Extract from the Petition)
'We deem it desirable that the subject should now be followed up by a further course of lectures on the questions how far the dependence of National Churches upon the state for temporal provision is compatible with their independence in spiritual things: how far these two principles admit of being harmonized – and whether it is in their combined practical operation, that a well-founded expectation may be entertained of most effectively accomplishing under the Divine blessing the great objects of religious establishments in the moral and religious instruction of the community.'

This extract is preceded by a short paragraph briefly referring to the *fact* of Dr. Chalmers having delivered a course of lectures on the Establishment Question; and it is followed by another paragraph, in conclusion, briefly disclaiming all *party*, and *political* motives, expressing also the opinion that the present state of the Scotch Church furnishes an additional reason for such a second course of lectures as is now requested.

219 From Robert Newstead   *n. pl., February 10, 1843*

I am anxious not to take up much of your time yet very much so as to one thing on which I desire your opinion, when you have turned it over in your mind. I *write* a line first to state, that we are miserably cramped by *only* the interest of our educational sum – and cannot take on several admirable men, even now having got a little over the edge of our interest, and must withdraw one man to keep under the mark. Now we are *threatened* with a 'public meeting' early in the spring from our *very small* friends on the ground that we – the Education Committee – are 'doing nothing'. They assert, and it is probably true, that a great deal of money would be given *to school purposes* which would be given nowhere

u

else. We must have funds if we are to go on with a most important work – which already is greatly blest.

Now, would it be well for *us* to have a public meeting – at the Centenary Hall, say – ostensibly to lay before *the friends of Education among us* the work already effected, and the wants of the Connexion, and so *forestall* and *include* these friends who will not be satisfied without some (in their case) *anti-Methodistical* movements. I should be very glad to have your opinion upon the *propriety* of our taking *these matters* into our own hand; and so – perhaps – turning our evil into a good. . . .

220   From William Robert Ellis[1]   *24 Chancery Lane [London]*
March 14, 1843

The London Wesleyan Ministers have recently given a public expression of their feeling in favour of the Scotch Church. Would it be advisable to give those of the general body of the Wesleyans who hold similar opinions an opportunity of making them publicly known to their Scotch Brethren? And if so what mode would be the best for such purpose? A meeting of the Wesleyans friendly to the Scotch Church might be called, and at that meeting the true position of that Church might be explained, and resolutions passed approving of the determination of its ministers; and parties might be named who would receive subscriptions for its support. It is not improbable that such a meeting in London would be followed by similar meetings in the country. Or if it be thought inexpedient to risk such a meeting, might not circulars be addressed to such of the Wesleyans as may be supposed likely to give inviting them to subscribe; or may not some means be adopted enabling the Wesleyans to assist the cause as Wesleyans? If it be thought well to adopt any plan for such purpose is the present the time for its adoption on the principle that *bis dat qui cito dat,*[2] and because the matter is now before the public mind? Or would it be better to wait until the ministers have actually left their livings? Or is the Wesleyan body too little informed or too little interested about the matter to make any attempt to elicit a public expression of its feeling towards the Scotch Church prudent? . . .

---

[1] William Robert Ellis, equity draughtsman and conveyancer; d. 1883, aet. 76.
[2] 'He who gives quickly, gives double.'

221   From William Vevers[1]   *Derby, March 14, 1843*

... I regret to see such an article in the *Magazine* as that in reply to the *Remembrancer* and the *Eclectic*.[2] They deserved and ought to have had a severe castigation – but it ought to have been in a very different style. Such articles do us no credit and produce no good. Though I am put off the Book Committee this year – as a reward I suppose for my conduct last Conference! in reference to the Editorial department[3] – yet that shall not prevent me expressing my unqualified condemnation of such an article both in its style and spirit.

I greatly admire your petition on Scotch affairs, and think with you that a very heavy blow will be struck at the Establishment in this country. The time has arrived when we as a body must distinguish between the Church and the clergy. I am sorry to say that though in towns a few of the clergy are tolerant, yet in the country places they are our bitterest foes. They are certainly the greatest enemies to their own Establishment.

I hope our Committee in London will keep a very vigilant eye upon the Educational scheme,[4] and also upon the Cemetery Bill.[5] Both these subjects ought to be narrowly watched in their way through Parliament: or we shall have cause to regret. ...

222   From Abraham E. Farrar[6]   *Liverpool, March 31, 1843*

To put under your eye a letter of Mr. E. Baines, on the subject of the Bill before the House, I forward you the *Leeds Mercury*, for though I do not sympathize with Mr. B. in either his civil or ecclesiastical *politics*, I may defer to his exposition of a public document – about which I confess I entertain the utmost alarm, shared by thousands in this neighbourhood.[7] And the rather, since the suspicious source from which

[1] William Vevers, superintendent, Derby circuit, 1842–45.

[2] An article 'The *Christian Remembrancer* and the *Eclectic Review*' (*Wesleyan Methodist Magazine* 1843, 3s. xxii. 213–16), replying to those journals' attacks on the Wesleyan ecclesiastical position, took a jocular view of 'the lugubrious, apathy-stricken, and democratic *Eclectic* in the fraternal hug of the fire-and-faggot, blustering and intolerant *Remembrancer*'.

[3] There had been an unpleasant clash between Bunting and the Book Committee on an item of agenda at the Conference of 1842. Gregory, *Sidelights*, p. 336.

[4] Sir James Graham's Factory Education Bill, the education clauses of which roused intense opposition from dissenters and Sunday schools, and were withdrawn, 1843. Cf. no. 223 *infra*.

[5] Cf. no. 214 *supra*.

[6] Abraham E. Farrar, superintendent, Liverpool (North) circuit, 1842–45.

[7] Edward Baines jun. published a long letter to Lord Wharncliffe, Chairman of the Committee of Council on Education, utterly condemning Graham's Factory Education Bill, and claiming that it was concerted between Dr. Hook, vicar of Leeds, and Mr. Saunders, a

it emanates has become matter of some notoriety. It is in fact the production of Mr. Kay-Shuttleworth,[1] from hints and documents furnished
by Factory Inspectors, and put together at the request of the Bishops.
I state it on undoubted authority. Now from such a source what may
be anticipated? The Bishop of London[2] acts only in consistency with
his avowed sentiments, in attempting to gain for the Church *exclusive*
influence, and the whole cannot securely be regarded as less than
designed to upset our institutions in the most populous districts of the
nation, and to strike a blow as fatal (yet more insidious) as the bill of
Lord Sidmouth.[3] The whole party publicly hold and avow that everything good is to be discarded which cannot be brought within the pale
of the Establishment, and that all our efforts put forth during nearly a
century in raising congregations and societies, building expensive places
of worship and collecting thousands of children in Sunday schools,
deserve only to share the fate of the Socialism and Chartism of the day
– and ought to be swept aside to make an open platform for the full
operation of the Oxford Tractarians! Now 'an evil tree cannot bring
forth good fruit'. And though it may seem presumptuous in me to seem
even remotely to suspect that you will not give the subject in your
Committees the most mature consideration, or that you can by any
possibility be warped in your judgments by the insidious mode in
which the measure is put before the Senate, you will grant me credit for
at least being anxious that nothing should be permitted, so far as we can
prevent it, that may impinge upon our Protestant liberties and *Wesleyan
privileges*. I may be too much alarmed; but our politicians have lately
given melancholy proofs that they own no principle in legislation upon
religion beyond expediency, and from some of them I had hoped better
things. . . .

223   From E. Oxley[4]   *Exeter, April 29, 1843*

After a silence of many years, you will be I expect not a little surprised to receive a letter from me. Hibernating with the dormouse, and

Factory Inspector, and was 'a declaration of war against all the dissenters in the kingdom'.
Leeds Mercury March 25, 1843, p. 4.

[1] James Phillips Kay-Shuttleworth (1804–77), doctor and former poor-law commissioner;
first secretary of committee of council on education, 1839–49, and the real creator of state
educational policy. Joint founder of Battersea training college for pupil-teachers, 1839–40.
Created baronet, 1849.

[2] See n. 1 p. 278 *supra*.

[3] In 1811 Lord Sidmouth had promoted a bill, which was defeated on its second reading, to
limit the toleration of itinerant preaching.

[4] E. Oxley, an Exeter doctor.

closely confined for half the year, I know little of what is passing around
me either in the Church or in the world, except what I meet with in the
public journals, or what may reach me through the medium of private
friends whose calls are like angels' visits, 'few and far between.' This,
as you may have already heard, has proved a week of unusual excitement in this city. A meeting has been held in the large Subscription
Rooms (to discuss the Education Bill now pending in Parliament)
which were crowded to suffocation. I take the liberty of forwarding for
your perusal the (Radical) *Western Times.*[1] The Speeches, I am assured,
are faithfully reported, and if so, what are we to expect will be the
conclusions arrived at by the sober, judicious, reflecting, and well-
educated portion of the community, throughout the land? Of the results
here, no local resident can be mistaken in affirming that Methodism and
its interests are, for an indefinite period at least utterly compromised,
withall beyond the grade of lawless, reckless, revolutionary demagogues.

In a city where the Bishop[2] is a proud, haughty, bigoted and intolerant Churchman, of pre-eminent talent of a certain kind, and moreover
one of the first sophists of the age, and where his clergy are too generally
of this kind; I would ask, is the language held by Mr. Chapman,[3] and
more especially the sentiments expressed by Mr. Turner[4] either creditable to the cause of truth amongst us as a Christian Body, or calculated to subserve our best interests, in time or in eternity? A more reckless disregard of prudence and propriety I have rarely known, and a
language more unconstitutional and in worse taste could not have been
employed. The radical portion of the community are, I understand,
overjoyed beyond measure; and some of the leading men amongst the
Dissenters are laughing in their sleeves, to see us at the head of the melee
to take the adversary's fire, whilst they wait to take the spoil.

I am no advocate for crouching to, or courting the countenance of
the Clergy of the Established Church. I believe there has been a great

---

[1] For the great struggle of Thomas Latimer and the *Western Times* against Bishop Phillpotts,
see R. S. Lambert, *The Cobbett of the West* (London, 1939).

[2] Henry Phillpotts (1778–1869), bishop of Exeter, 1830–69.

[3] The *Western Times* April 29, 1843, described the excitement generated by the nonconformist meeting against the Education Bill as equalling in intensity that of the Reform Bill
crisis. It commended Daniel Chapman (1799–1856), preacher, Exeter circuit, 1841–43, for
'following out to its most ultra conclusions, the abstract principle of the right of private
judgment, and unfurling the flag of voluntaryism with a daring intrepidity, which must have
astonished many of the Wesleyans who had been disciplined in the old school'.

[4] Jonathan Turner (1791–1847), superintendent, Exeter circuit, 1842–43, declared that 'if
an endowed establishment cannot exist in this country by allowing an equal liberty and
equal religious privileges with all non-conformist bodies, then, in my opinion, the struggle is
entered upon and never can be abandoned till it lead to the overthrow of the establishment
that provoked it (cheers)'.

deal too much of this in practice, even with some of the wisest and best amongst us. I believe it has done us much harm and has tended to place us in a false position in the opinion of the most judicious in the land. We shall soon, I fancy, be called to pay the penalty of our indiscretion.

In all my controversies with the Clergy (and I have had not a few) I never forgot that I had to do with gentlemen by education, with Ministers of Religion and with men of well-trained minds. And although I could be as uncomprising in defence of what I believed to be right and as pointedly opposed to what I considered wrong, as Mr. Turner or any other man, I was careful to do this in becoming language. Mr. Turner has boasted a good deal in public of his high conservative principles and how efficiently he has served the cause of conservatism in aiding the return of at least one member to Parliament; it may be so. But in his recent speech, he would have done well not to have compromised his consistency. Not a few here, if I mistake not, will have to suffer the consequences of his imprudence. But I must leave the matter in your hands. . . .

224 From John Scott[1]   *London, May 13, 1843*

By this day's post you will receive a copy of our Resolutions, passed unanimously at last Wednesday's Meeting. We had a large attendance of Town members; Messrs. Scarth, Howard, John Burton and Dawson,[2] from Leeds; Alderman Meek[3] from York; and Mr. Walker from Stockton.[4] At the commencement the feeling was very strong, and by some of the speakers expressed in no very measured terms, and our Leeds friends were as warm as any – they seemed little inclined to allow Ministers credit for good intention, and seemed disposed to urge us to declare against any combined system of education, and in favour of grants to educational societies, as the only practicable means of instructing the people. This seemed to be beyond our province, at least at present; and we contented ourselves in renewing our appli-

[1] John Scott, preacher, London (City Road) circuit, 1842–43; superintendent, 1843–45.

[2] Gilyard Scarth, John Burton and J. Howard of Leeds were all members of the local committee of Woodhouse Grove school. Dawson is probably Richard Dawson, brother of Billy Dawson the celebrated Leeds Local Preacher who d. 1841.

[3] Alderman James Meek (1790–1862), originally apprenticed to Joseph Agar of York (q.v.); became Lord Mayor of York in 1836, 1849, and 1851; chairman of both the York and North Midland, and the Newcastle and Berwick, railways.

[4] Walker of Stockton (like John Burton of Leeds) was one of the country members co-opted by the connexional education committee in 1843 to beat up opposition to the education clauses of Graham's Factory Education Bill.

cation to Parliament in the words of our former Petition. The Meeting talked itself into great unanimity, upon the whole, and our friends from the country expressed themselves as perfectly approving of all that the Committees had done, and as highly delighted with the Meeting.

We urged our country friends to see as many Members of Parliament as possible while they were in Town. They had a very long interview with Mr. Stewart Wortley,[1] and he had very very much pleased our friends from Leeds by the deep interest in and great familiarity with the subject which he manifested; and he had so reasoned in favour of a *united system* as almost to persuade them that it was to be preferred. The impression however made upon their minds upon the whole was that probably this measure will be withdrawn. They saw Mr. Beckett,[2] Mr. Alderson and Lord Jocelyn,[3] – I do not know whether any member beside. I trust our Resolutions will meet your approval. In drawing them up we were careful not to commit our cause, by new points or unguarded expression, I trust we have succeeded. Mr. Matthews indicted the legal note at the bottom, and the clause referring to school property. . . .

Afterwards we had a long conversation with Capt. Fitzroy, the New Zealand Governor,[4] and were much gratified with his assurance of aid, in every practicable way, to our missionaries; with the good opinion, even affectionate regard, which he expressed for them and for their labours; and with his enlightened views of the policy fit to be pursued in the general government [of] the country. He seems a Christian man. . . .

225 From John Nowell[5]   *Salford, May 24, 1843*

Permit me to make to you the following confidential communications. I have great reason to fear for the Christian stability of Mr. James

[1] John Stuart-Wortley, later 2nd baron Wharncliffe (1801–55), M.P. for West Riding, 1841–45.

[2] William Beckett (1784–1863), M.P. Leeds, 1841–52. Principal partner in the Leeds banking firm of Beckett and Co.

[3] Lord Jocelyn (1815–54), M.P. for Lynn Regis, 1842–54. Contested Leeds unsuccessfully, 1841.

[4] Robert Fitzroy (1805–65), vice-admiral; commander of the *Beagle*, 1828–36. Governor of New Zealand, 1843–46.

[5] John Nowell, superintendent, Manchester (Irwell St.) circuit, 1842–44. D. 1858, aet. 65. For the liturgy, cf. M.C.A. MSS. Thomas Butler to Jabez Bunting, July 4, 1843: ' . . . A few weeks since . . . I attended morning service at City Road Chapel . . . and arrived in *time* to

Garstang,[1] and am therefore very anxious to effect the proper settlement of the Broughton Chapel as soon as possible; but the parties who have been requested to become Trustees will not sign the Deed till they are certified that the final debt shall not exceed £1000; and as it is understood that it is to be brought to that point at the time of your visit to Broughton, I shall be glad to see you there as *soon* as you may find it practicable.

Permit me further to state, that our Trust concerns in Irwell Street are in a fearful state. Some of the acting Trustees, not members of our society, exercise undue power and influence, so that those who are members, are greatly discouraged and depressed. The Trust is, at the least, £100 a year short of meeting its annual expenditure, the congregations very small, the people very generally, and I *fear, increasingly,* disaffected to the use of the Liturgy, in vain do we strive to keep the *officers* of our church from frequent, and. strong protestations against it, as the great hindrance to the extension of our interests in this locality; and I fear, that the conduct of Ministers in the Establishment is greatly promoting this opposition to *our use* of the Liturgy; and I shall not be surprised if several families go from this Chapel to some other, solely on that account. . . .

226   From John Bowers   *Thorp-Arch, Nr. Tadcaster, June 20, 1843*

I ought not longer to delay a more formal and decisive answer than I was able to address to you in my last hurried letter to the communication with which, as the President of the Theological Institution, you have honoured me; conveying the request of the Committee of its Northern Branch, that I would consent to become (subject to the approbation of the Conference) the successor of Mr. Turner as Governor at Didsbury. . . .

I hope it will not be deemed inconsistent with . . . feelings [of gratitude for the offer, and of concern for my health], that I should nevertheless suspend my acquiescence in the request of the Committee upon such

hear the reading of our incomparable Liturgy (which I was sorry to observe was abridged). I was surprised to find what I may term the Metropolitan Wesleyan Chapel, apparently not above one-fourth filled and I was utterly astonished to witness that during the performance of morning prayer, litany and communion service, individuals were constantly coming in, and by the time these services were concluded, the chapel was tolerably well filled; the interruption to devotion caused by this ill-timed and indecent procedure struck me very forcibly, and led me to conclude that at least three fourths of the congregation would be better satisfied if the reading of the Liturgy were dispensed [with] altogether'.

[1] James Garstang, wealthy business man of Higher Broughton.

conditions as appear to me either essential to the beneficial management of the Institution or to my own freedom of mind, to such an extent at least, as would be necessary to enable me to execute with moderate efficiency the duties of its Guardian. I am sincerely grateful for the kind consideration of my present state of health evinced by the proposal spontaneously made to me by the Committee and mentioned so explicitly in your letter, that I shall be freely exempted from such 'public duties' as would be 'either injurious or irksome to me': but the further conditions in which I await the concurrence of yourself and the Committee, are,

1. That such portions of the building as are appropriated to the residence of the Governor shall be strictly and exclusively in his own occupation; and shall not be considered or made common and public, even for the ordinary purposes of the Institution.
2. That with the view of securing the separation of the Governor's family from the other inmates of the Institution, such arrangements be adopted as to make his residence as distinct and independent as the construction of the building will admit.
3. That the appointment of the Matron be vested in the Governor, subject to the 'veto' of the Committee.
4. That certain alterations be made in the domestic part of the establishment, particularly in the appointments of the kitchen, so as to remove the inconveniences which have been suffered in the past year, and to provide necessary additional facilities for the dispatch of the household work.

Allow me in addition to say that it would be most agreeable to my own feelings, that the support of the Governor's family should be provided for, by an allowance for weekly board, as is usual in the case of Ministers appointed to circuits, rather than from the common stock of provisions supplied for the general use of the Institution; but as objections may exist to a change involving such a departure from the established usage in this and other connexional institutions, I respectfully leave it (though not without repeating strongly my wish upon the point) to further discussion with the Committee. . . .

227 From John Beecham   *Wesleyan Mission House,*
London, June 21, 1843

I snatch a moment to write to you a few lines on Scotch affairs.

The deputation are evidently producing already a considerable effect. On Sunday morning Mr. Guthrie preached, as I am told, a most powerful sermon in Mr. Hamilton's church,[1] which was crowded with that very description of persons whom it is most desirable to interest in the affairs of the Free Church. Several *very distinguished* persons were present.

Last night he preached again at Woolwich. Tonight the first public meeting is to be held at Mr. Burn's Church, London Wall; Patrick Stewart Esq. M.P.[2] to take the chair. I am going thither, and have made a half-promise to say a little on the occasion.

On Friday night, another public meeting will be held in Dr. Leifchild's chapel;[3] and on Monday evening we are to have one at the Centenary Hall. On the subject of this arrangement I need not dwell, as Mr. Farmer writes to you about it by this evening's mail.

The great meeting at Exeter Hall is to be held on Wednesday evening next, as was arranged when you were present at Mr. Nisbett's.[4] The Marquis of Breadalbane[5] has consented to take the chair.

Now my principal object in writing is to convey to you the earnest wish of the Committee that you would endeavour to attend: a wish in which I most earnestly participate. Everything is going on most prosperously; but I feel it most acutely that at so important a juncture I am left so much alone. I am doing my best in a prudent way in meeting with and assisting our friends; but I should like for the honour of our Connexion, and for the advantage of the common cause, that you were with us; and I must beg of you, if you can do it consistently with your health, to get home in time to dine at Mr. Farmer's, with our Scotch friends, on Tuesday, and attend the meeting at Exeter Hall the day after. If you could only move a vote of thanks to the chair, or say half a dozen words at any other period of the meeting, so that we might have your name mixed up with it, I am sure it would be of immense service. Do come if possible.[6]

[1] Regent Square Presbyterian Church. Cf. no. 204 *supra*.

[2] Patrick M. Stewart, Liberal M.P. for Renfrewshire, 1841–46.

[3] John Leifchild (1780–1862), minister of Craven Chapel (Independent), Bayswater, 1831–54.

[4] Probably James Nisbett (1785–1854), bookseller and publisher; one of the founders of the Sunday School Union, and a Sunday school teacher at the Scotch Church, Swallow Street, 1803; for a time a follower of Edward Irving.

[5] John Campbell, 2nd marquis of Breadalbane (1796–1862), a strenuous supporter of the Free Church.

[6] Cf. M.C.A. MSS. Barnard Slater to Jabez Bunting, May 26, 1843: '. . . I hope my dear Dr., that you, or your dear William, or some person of character and name among us, will prepare to present, if possible on the first day of Conference, some suitable resolutions in reference to the deeply injured, but most spiritual and excellent Church of Scotland, by way of sympathy etc . . . The free church of Scotland very much resembles the Wesleyan body now; and Dr. Chalmers and Dr. Hannah hold it appears to me very similar offices.' See also Joseph Lawton to Jabez Bunting, October 7, 1843.

The Marquis of Lorne[1] has sent his adhesion to the Free Church. I am afraid our friends Hamilton, Lorimer,[2] and Burns will have to turn out of their churches shortly. I feel especially for them. . . .

228   From John McLean[3]   *Sheffield, July 22, 1843*

We miss you much and trust you will not make any unavoidable delay in coming down. Our school meeting went off very well upon the whole. They were evidently prepared to give up everything that was required by the Manchester Committee rather than come to a rupture with the Conference, which they begin to see will be more serious in its effects upon their personal importance and the interests of the school than they have the candour to confess. At the same time they contested several vital points, and could they have cajoled or bamboozled us into a quiet surrender of them they would have counted themselves happy; but feeling that they cannot afford to quarrel with us and having discovered after divers skilful and uncommonly *gentle* moves that a few of us remained hard-hearted and stupid, they were fain to concede nearly everything for which we contended, except that the Directors should cease to supply goods to the Institution which, as the Proprietors present did not seem greatly to startle at, we deemed it best not to press. I am sorry that Mr. Farmer exhibited a susceptibility of suspicion as to clerical influence which surprised some of our sound friends and rather strengthened the other party. Yet he acted right in most votes, although some of the Rads contend that on one important question he did not vote at all. I believe they are wrong; but he certainly did not hoist his hand quite half-mast high, and the effect was rather sickening upon some. I wish I could have a more unreserved and cordial confidence in a man who is I believe truly good, and who occupies so distinguished a position among our laymen. Alas I fear we have few James Woods, and I should anticipate ere long a grand assault upon ministerial influence headed by some of our magnates, did I not feel a comfortable hope and persuasion that God will spare you to prevent it. I dont think they would succeed, for although we are doubtless being driven somewhat from our *high* and *holy* position as Wesleyan Methodists (which I much regret),

[1] George Douglas Campbell, Marquis of Lorne, later 8th duke of Argyll (1823–1900).

[2] Peter Lorimer (1812–79), minister of Riverside Terrace Presbyterian Church, 1836 till the Disruption, 1843. Professor of Theology at the new English Presbyterian College, 1844; Principal, 1878.

[3] John McLean, preacher, London (Lambeth) circuit, 1842–44. From 1831–40 McLean had been stationed successively in Sheffield circuits and from 1840–42 had been governor of the Wesleyan Proprietory School, Sheffield.

one of the effects of this very move seems to be an increased tenacity about ministerial power and prerogative. At the same [time] I rejoice that this will be prevented, as I fear I might find it difficult – but I must not go on in this way lest I should give as my deliberate judgment what may be only the effects of morbid apprehension or temptation. I beg pardon for troubling you, but thought you might not perhaps hear about the school meeting from any other quarter. There appears to be a delightful feeling circulating among the brethren. . . .

229   From Edward Corderoy[1]   *9 Walcot Place, Lambeth,*
October 28, 1843

In conversation with Mr. McLean some few evenings since, I intimated a passing wish to lay before you a few thoughts on the subject of our movements in the Wesleyan Connexion in reference to General Education – he reminded me last night of my professed intention, and urged its performance. I have in consequence to solicit your kind consideration of the following observations, more especially as I cannot accept the President's invitation to the meeting on Tuesday next.

1st. I venture to think that notwithstanding the multitude of petitions we presented *against* the Factories Education Bill that our people generally (but specially in the districts where education is most needed) are *not alive to their responsibilities* on *this subject*, nor prepared, either to originate or support, any *enlarged connexional* scheme for Day School Instruction.

2nd. That under recent pressure of commercial difficulty, from which many are only just beginning to feel relief, the resources of a large portion of our community have been contracted and therefore we cannot expect, even if the inclination were present, any very great manifestations of benevolence.

3rd. That from these considerations we are *totally unprepared* for a general subscription list, on any similar scale to that put forth by the National Society; we should, by any attempt to rival this, only shew the want of correspondence between the *number* of our petitions and of our *subscribers*.

4th. That we are equally unprepared for the establishment of an Educational Society, similar [to] the British and Foreign School Society with its normal school etc. Desirable as I admit such a thing to be, if

[1] Edward Corderoy had become a member of the connexional Education Committee the previous Conference; a prominent Methodist benefactor in London, he was also known as a Sabbatarian.

Methodism were ready for its accomplishment, there are *now* the following objections

1st. *The want of funds.*

2nd. The *infancy* of our movements in Day School instruction, for if we have an establishment for *Training Teachers* we ought to have schools to send them to when taught.

3rd. The indisposition of our people, *at present*, to multiply Institutions which shall abstract any more of our ministers from the *Itinerant* work. This is not an objection from merely disaffected Methodists, but one which I think you will find extensively entertained.

5th. That if these things be admitted either altogether, or in part, it follows, that it will be the wisest, safest, and most prudent course to attempt only that which is *immediately* and *without much difficulty practicable*. The evil is one that is present and palpable – it must, if possible be met *promptly*, as well as *effectively*.

The only thing for which, I think, we *are prepared*, is to *promote* and increase the establishment of *Day Schools*, in connection with Local or District Committees. This I think may be accomplished by means within our reach.

1st. I venture to suggest that a fund might be raised, by donations payable before next Conference, to the amount of £10,000 – to this might be added the grant of £5000 from the Centenary Fund, making £15,000, to be disposed of in such a manner, as *that Local effort* may be *best stimulated*.

2nd. In many of our large towns we have the building ready to our hands in our Sunday Schools, these might generally be fitted up for purposes of Day School Instruction at a cost varying according to size and mode from £50 to £90. That from the fund I have proposed, *one fourth*, or *one third*, of the expense might be offered, or a grant of all necessary books and school furniture might be made, on the condition that the Local Committee provided the rest.

3rd. That where no sufficiently commodious building is erected, and we have strength enough to carry on the school by a Methodist Committee, the Local Committee might [be] stimulated to build, by an offer of 5/- or 7/6 for each child proposed to be instructed (the Government give 10/-) the dimensions etc. etc. of the proposed building being accurately tested (the Government papers furnish valuable suggestions on this head). This grant also to be made from the proposed fund.

4th. That where we have not Methodism enough to sustain a school by ourselves, the co-operation of other evangelical denominations should be sought, and that here, if necessary, and under proper limitations, grants should be made.

These suggestions you will perceive, Sir, propose a very different mode of procedure from that which has been hitherto adopted, I do not think the best course has been taken, at all events, that a *better* may now be taken. There are many objections to spending your money in training men at Glasgow.

    1st. The distance prevents any possible effective supervision.

    2nd. The men may be well *reported* of for diligence and attainments, but be totally unfit when brought to the trial, for the *Government* of a school.

    3rd. If the men prove *good* teachers, and a better situation offers you have no hold of them, if *bad* they spoil your work and yet think they have a claim on you – if neither good nor bad, they are *unbearable*, useless to Society and a discredit to their employers. I heard of one the other day who has *already* got notice to quit.

I propose therefore that we leave 'Training' alone for the *present*

    1st. Let us erect School Houses, and transform those already erected for Sunday Schools, to our purpose.

    2nd. Let the Local Committees take either the Glasgow or the British system as they please, or as circumstances determine. The efficiency of the School depends mainly on the character and qualifications of the *Master*, and the real excellencies of *each* system are probably *common to both*.

    3rd. Let us take the agency ready to our hands, *about half the teachers* in connection with the Borough Road School, are Methodist, who would gladly serve their own community in preference to any other.

    4th. Let us cultivate a friendly correspondence, not an identity, with the British and Foreign School Society, that through them we we may obtain a share in the Government grants, that through them we may, if we please, train our Teachers, and *without expense*! and thus without adopting their constitution, may have all that is beneficial in their system. . . .

I move in a different sphere from that in which you live – and mix with a class of lay Wesleyans with whom you do not often meet, and I hope you will pardon me for adding that the proceedings of our Education Committee to the present time have *not* been regarded with *unmixed* approbation, that there is little disposition to favour any *annual* appeal whether by Subscription or collection in our chapels, and that as far as I can learn, there is general wish that we should prove the sincerity of our desire to educate the people by doing that which is practicable *at once*, and leaving to the ordering of providence and the development of time any arrangements for a *complete plan* of *connexional education*. . . .

230 From Edward Morris   *Ruabon, December 1, 1843*

I respectfully beg permission to lay before you some particulars in reference to the subject of education in this parish. I have taken the liberty of addressing you from a persuasion I have that you would be able to afford the information I need and cheerfully to render it. I have no doubt from the position you occupy that you are fully engaged, and it is the importance of the object only that I use as an apology. I have long had a desire to see something done towards the establishment of a Day School upon liberal principles, and did hope that some person of influence would take it up. We are strangers to each other and it may be only right to inform you that I am not a person of influence, but I should from a sense of duty as well as pleasure do all I could for the accomplishment of so desirable an object. At the last census the population was about 11,200, a mining district, principally dependent upon iron and coal works, the body of them are very poor and have suffered very great privations within the last two years from the depression in that trade. We have an endowed Grammar School, I believe about 100£ per annum, with a legacy for the clothing of a number of Blue Coat Scholars, also apprenticing them (the Blue Coat) after being in the School a stated period. Notwithstanding these apparent advantages not more than *12* usually attend. We have a National School, the usual number about 50 or 60, some few of whom are paid for by Legacy, the remaining number paid for by the parents. It is conducted upon the old fashion[ed] system, the Master being Sexton of the parish, Vestry Clerk, Book Keeper to the Coaches etc. etc. etc. The management of the above is in the hands of the Vicar and others connected with the Establishment, and it is expected that all who attend them will also attend the services of the Establishment and learn the Church Catechism. Nine tenths of the population are Dissenters, great advocates for Sabbath Schools, and a people that love their chapels. About September last I wrote to Mr. Dunn on the subject and furnished him with the particulars of the parish. In reply I received a most kind and encouraging letter with instructions how to apply to the Committee of Council. I called a few warm-hearted friends together, we sent a memorial, and in reply I received the following: 'If you are unprovided with a plan for the new School and none of those contained in their Lordships' minutes appears suitable, my Lords will readily afford you the gratuitous services of their architect in the preparation or adaptation of a design, if you will furnish me with a plan of the site and all necessary information as to the accommodation to be provided for the children, Master and Mistress.' From the very encouraging nature of this communication we determined upon making application to Sir Watkin,[1] who is the principal landed proprietor in the neighbourhood, for a site. On Saturday last I received a letter from the Agent in which he states that 'I have been honoured by Sir Watkin's command to inform the School Committee that he will have much pleasure in placing at their disposal a piece of ground for the site of a School House. It now only remains to make choice of the situation and I shall be happy for this purpose to meet the Committee any day most convenient'. I have now laid before you the position of the parish and the favourable consideration we have met with. I think it not out of place to inform you that the Vicar who has recently come amongst us, is decidely opposed to us; he was aware of our intention to solicit Sir W. for land and he saw him the previous week. Sir W. did not hesitate to acquaint us that it was not with the approbation of the Vicar. I believe the impression he made on Sir W.'s mind was that we were too poor to accomplish the object if he gave the land. Sir W. enquired what subscriptions we had. My reply was that the noblest part of our subscription was in the willing heart and ready hand of the people. The whole of the wealthy part of the parishioners attend the Establishment and are much under the influence of the Vicar. He speaks unkind of them who differ from him. He has recently had a new complete set of books for his use in Church with a *cross* on them. He keeps aloof of the Bible Society etc. More I must not say. In my first letter to Mr. Dunn I stated 'that the great body of the people were poor, we have twenty three Dissenting places of worship in the parish, about four thousand children and adults attend the Sunday School. And the assistance upon which I would look for in the neighbourhood would be labour, and every christian Church should be appealed to for the assistance they may be able to afford. I am persuaded that if each church in its separate capacity had the subject brought before them and a list of the labourers, masons, bricklayers, joiners and others who constitute the Church and congregation [were] made out, a very considerable amount would be given and the whole [put] under the management of an experienced builder. I recently intimated something of the kind to a joiner and mason of my acquaintance. The immediate offer I had was from one that he would make two window frames and from the other that he

[1] Sir Watkin Williams Wynn (1820–85), 6th bart. of Wynnstay, Ruabon.

would give a day or two at the building. This is the kind of assistance I mean.' In reply to which Mr. Dunn says, 'In relation to your remarks on the *labour* which would be given, I should say ascertain when you meet *what labour* would actually be given, value it at its fair but full price and count it as a money subscription. It is so to all intents and purposes. Let this mode of proceeding be apparent in your application for Government aid and the Government will I doubt not allow it to be reckoned as money and assist you accordingly. If you find any difficulty in this matter let me know and I will apply personally.' We as far as able [followed] the recommendation of Mr. Dunn and the following is the result. Team Work 100 days at 8/-: Joiners 100 days 3/-: Masons 100 days 3/-: Bricklayers 50 days at 3/-: Labourers 200 days at 1/6: Slaters 10 days 3/-: Glaizer 6 days 3/-: money subscription about 30£: altogether would amount [to] *125£*. The estimated cost for a building for 200 Scholars according to plan and specification of the Committee of Council, 57ft long, 30 wide and 15 high would be about 220£. At present we do not know what amount of assistance we may have from the Committee of Council, and unless we do or from some other quarter [have] very liberal [aid] we shall be unable to have one that will be beneficial to the neighbourhood. We are thus circumstanced. In a population of about 11,200, two churches connected with the Establishment, the usual congregation [is] perhaps 6 or 700, three Sunday Schools that number about 300. The Vicar and his friends are now about to erect a School House in a thickly populated district of the parish, and we shall have more Church and Church Catechism. We have *twenty three* Dissenting places of worship and the usual number attending the services is about *Seven thousand*, and the Sunday Schools about *four thousand* children and adults. *And not one day School*. The parents must either send them to those connected with the Establishment or leave them uneducated. About 60 go to the British School, Wrexham, about 4 miles for them. The circumstances of the neighbourhood is such that the people can do but little and the *active opposition* of the Vicar will influence those who have the ability. Perhaps you are ready to enquire my object in being thus particular. I have within the last few days had an impression upon my mind that it would only be an act of justice to make our case known to you Dr. Read[1] and Dr. Cox,[2] and if there are any *denominational funds* for educational purposes to solicit all the aid that can be afforded. The situation we have made choice of is most central and a healthy spot. I am aware that the Wesleyans and others are making great efforts. If the

---

[1] Probably Dr. Andrew Reed (1787–1862), philanthropist and minister of Wycliffe Chapel (Independent), London, 1831–61.

[2] Francis Augustus Cox (1783–1853), Baptist minister at Hackney, 1811–53.

x

denominational Schools are commenced in this parish I am persuaded we shall have several of them and I have no doubt whatever but they will be of a *piddling* sort. The different denominations in this parish are I think as much united as any in the Kingdom. And it is the desire of my heart that a sectarian character should not be introduced and thus make the breach wider, which good Mr. James of Birmingham[1] and others are so wishful to heal. The promoters of this effort are desirous of seeing one noble well conducted school in a central part of the parish (and we have just the right place for it) for about 200 or 250 boys and those many girls. Thus funds could be raised for remunerating a clever intelligent Master and Mistress and to be conducted on the British System, and a degree of permanence given to the whole.

I am the more desirous of some assistance from the London denominational funds from the very favourable influence it would have upon the ministers and churches in the neighbourhood. London Committees have great influence upon country churches, and it is a very common enquiry, what does *our* Committee do in London? I am sure a contribution from them in aid of our object would set that at rest and we should have the people heart and hand in the work, and thus confer a great and lasting benefit on the neighbourhood. Some of our friends are very scrupulous respecting the Government grant. It appears to me thus that if we do not obtain some aid the whole must yet be abandoned. And I am persuaded that it would be almost impossible to have a more favourable feeling on the part of the people than at present. I shall be obliged for any advice and assistance you may please to favour me with. . . .

[P.S.] I made out a list for Sir W. of twenty-eight resident householders who had *promised to act as Trustees*, and [they are] the most influential persons connected with the Baptists, Wesleyans, Independents, Calvinistic Methodists and the Wesleyan Association.

231   From Thomas Waugh   *Cork, January 8, 1844*

. . . We get on with wonderful quiet as to our good work in the midst of general convulsion, and exposed to a hate growing out of novel high-church assumptions, to which we have not been accustomed. But we 'keep never minding', apply us to our own especial calling, and, thank God!, prosper. Methodism is Protestantism's core in this land, let folks talk as they will. Yet what is to be the issue of our political ferments?

[1] John Angell James (1785–1859), Independent minister at Carr's Lane Chapel, Birmingham, 1805–59; advocate of 'catholic Christianity' and promoter of the Evangelical Alliance, 1842.

The pitch-pot I fear must boil over, thanks to bavolers about liberty in a British House of Commons who make it impossible for any ministry to govern aright. The amount of their patriotism is to shield cut-throats, and leave honest industrious people unsheltered. . . .

232 From William Binning[1]   *Lynn, February 26, 1844*

[Will he preach two sermons for Chapel Anniversary at Lynn on March 24] . . . There are also special reasons in connexion with Methodism in this circuit which I plead as an argument in order to prevail upon you. A spirit of hostility to our economy has long prevailed among a large portion of the members, and still more so of the Leaders and Local Preachers. Discipline has been all but lost throughout the country parts of it. No Leaders' Meetings for years, and that where there has been three, four, and even six Leaders. I have begun however to look these persons in the face, and to grapple with their hostility. The insolent and inveterate opposition I have met with in so doing is beyond what I am able to describe. This has been the case especially as to the New Auxiliary Fund, the pence and quarterage in the classes, and the use of our chapels for Teetotal purposes. In thus attempting to restore discipline and order, I have had to dismiss, to suspend, and to demand written pledges to attention to our laws and regulations for the future. This has occasioned much conflict and uneasiness. I have been misrepresented, insulted, and menaced, in order to intimidate, to disaffect the remnant of the people to me, and to render me odious in the eyes of the public. Through mercy I have been enabled to remain firm and unmoved and something considerable I trust has been gained while nothing as to us has been lost . . . on this ground a visit from you would be of incalculable service . . .

233 From Thomas Waugh   *Cork, June 12, 1844*

On my return from Bandon this morning. . . . I had a note from Mr. Prest,[2] with Mr. M's letter to you. He must be meddling, although I did think after what took place the last Conference that he would have been quiet for a while, and his letters to me during the year partook of the meekest tone. I greatly regret his having written to Sir Robert Peel.

---

[1] William Binning, superintendent, Lynn circuit, 1843–45. D. 1857, aet. 66.
[2] Charles Prest (1806–75), preacher, London (Spitalfields) circuit, 1842–45.

Our plan was to wait till we could see the Bill. I know from former intercourse on the subject that Government had the greatest objection to name any one or two parties. They were *particularly averse from mentioning presbyterians*[1] and in their short Bill so shaped it as to embrace all without naming any. My object then was to have 'The Wesleyans' inserted, that we might at the same time be recognised, and not forced under the protection of 'Dissenters'. The wish to gratify me was expressed, but the above reason for not specifying any denomination given....

234　To James Wood　　　　　　　*London, June 13, 1844*[2]

... I was truly grateful to learn from Mr. Barton, Mr. J. Fernley and Mr. J. D. Burton,[3] that your general health is on the whole improved. God grant that the improvement may be progressive, and long-continued. Of myself I can say nothing very good. I was strangely better than usual for about six weeks from the end of April; but for ten days past have been receding; partly owing to the anxiety and toil connected with this vile 'Dissenters' Chapels Bill'. I fear it *must* pass; but there is some hope of modifying the 2d. and 3d. clauses; yet not much. One modification of considerable value to us as Wesleyans, we have already induced Sir Wm. Follett to insert, on his official authority, in the 2d. clause, as passed through the Committee *pro forma* on Monday last, and since printed. It goes to let in, as evidence of the Founder's intention, not merely, as at first, the 'express terms' of a deed, but also any *reference*, contained in a Deed, to any Book, Document, or Instrument, by which that intention may be inferred. So far, so good for us; as the reference to Wesley's Notes and Sermons may thus be rendered distinctly available. But the measure is *essentially bad*, even as it now stands. I wish it could be

---

[1] Peel's Dissenters' Chapels Bill sought to save unitarians from the loss of most of their Old Presbyterian chapels in England and Ireland as a result of legal actions begun (in the main) by Congregationalists, by providing that where no religious doctrines or mode of worship were prescribed in the trust deed, there should be protection for congregations able to prove twenty-five years of continuous possession. For obvious reasons the government wanted to phrase the bill in general terms.

[2] The holograph of this letter is at U.M.C.A., Lake Junaluska, N.C.

[3] William Barton (1803–57), preacher, London (Great Queen St.) circuit, 1843–46; and two lay pillars of Manchester Methodism. John Fernley was a manufacturer, became Treasurer to the connexional Loan Fund on Bunting's recommendation, and twice resigned in 1837 and 1839 because of private business embarrassments (M.C.A. MSS. J. Fernley to Jabez Bunting, July 4, 1839); J. D. Burton was a calico printer, and member of the family which owned the celebrated printing works at Rhodes.

[4] Sir William Webb Follett (1798–1845), Attorney General, 1844–45.

defeated, if not very materially altered before the 3d. reading. Could not Mr. Entwisle be again written to?[1] . . .

235   From George Blencowe[2]   *Maldon, June 24, 1844*

I take the liberty of asking your advice in the absence of the Chairman of the District in the case which is stated in the following letter which on the 21st inst. I addressed to the Rev. J. Scott.

'I feel myself compelled to apply to you as Chairman of the District for advice under the following painful circumstances.

You must know we have been repeatedly requested by the teetotalers of this place to lend them our chapel for a teetotal meeting or lecture or sermon or even to preach without making it a teetotal sermon. Their great desire has been to obtain it for their advocates on almost any conditions. To these applications the trustees have invariably given a denial not only because the Conference have decided that our chapels may not in anyway be used for Teetotal purposes, but because they consider themselves to hold the chapels for purely religious purposes under the direction of the Conference. They have also seen in other parts of this circuit where teetotalism prevails, confusion and disunion to the same extent to exist in the societies. They have therefore been anxious, while they would not oppose, yet to keep perfectly clear of it *as a society*. And from the plain and decided course they had invariably pursued, they supposed they should have no more applications for the use of their Chapel. They however were greatly surprised about a week since to find a report circulated in the town that the present teetotal lecturer for this part of Essex (who is not a Wesleyan but a Baptist) was to take Mr. Aldis's[3] appointments here on Sunday week. They ascertained the correctness of the report and then desired me to write to Mr. Aldis, stating their decided objection to such a use of the Chapel and in this objection they were joined by *all* the Leaders and Stewards. The ground of their objection was 'That from their knowledge of the people they were sure it would divide and bring confusion into the Society'. The unanimity and ground of this objection I distinctly stated to Mr. Aldis and in their name entreated him not to continue in his determination of

[1] William Entwisle, though supported by Wesleyan connexional influence had finished bottom of the poll for Manchester in 1841, but became Conservative M.P. for Lancashire (South), 1844–47.

[2] George Blencowe, preacher, Chelmsford circuit, 1844–46. Became preacher 1839; d. 1893.

[3] James Aldis (1808–85), superintendent, Chelmsford circuit, 1842–44. The fact that Aldis was Blencowe's superintendent explains why he was appealing for assistance over his superintendent's head.

sending the supply. And requested an answer as early as possible. That letter did not receive an answer. I then wrote another asking an answer by return of post, and this shared the same fate as the former. The friends here from what they have seen of Mr. Aldis at other times conclude from this silence that he intends to send the man. And the trustees are determined to lock the chapel against him. Thus you see I am as the resident minister placed in very unpleasant circumstances. I feel that it is almost impossible to move in the present case and not do harm, and if I were to be quiet I should have a guilty conscience. For I am sure that if we have a teetotal lecturer sent to us instead of Mr. Aldis it will produce such a schism among us as will take years to heal. We are quiet and prospering at present but if we have teetotalism as in some other places in the circuit our peace will depart.

I shall esteem it a great favour if you will kindly inform me what course I had better pursue. I shall most willingly adopt the plans you recommend, be they what they may.

Since I wrote the above to the President I have received a letter from Mr. Aldis in which I am informed that he is unmovable in his determination of sending this teetotal lecturer. . . .

236   From Edward Walker[1]   *Birmingham, July 8, 1844*

It may (and indeed it does to myself) appear somewhat presumptuous for me to write you on this occasion, but at the risk of being thought an officious meddler, I feel disposed to venture very respectfully to address a few thoughts to you which have occurred to me in relation to our approaching Conference.

It has been hinted from some quarter that it is doubtful whether you will allow yourself to be elected to the office of President this year; and if this should prove a well founded rumour, I am quite sure the whole connexion will most earnestly deplore it. I trust and hope however that there is no foundation whatever for entertaining such a doubt, for I would take the liberty to suggest that I think your reelection just now would do honour to a great and good principle; and would act as a breakwater to the rapid flow of what are called liberal principles, but which I think, savour very much of a levelling of those distinctions which to my mind appear manifestly to have their origin with God himself. There are individuals I have no doubt *among ourselves* who would be glad to see the honours of high office with us more extensively distributed; but I believe that in proportion as this spirit grows and obtains practi-

---

[1] Edward Walker (1800–79), superintendent, Birmingham (Cherry St.) circuit, 1842–45.

cally among us we shall in the same proportion lose our dignity, our influence, and our usefulness. We have had the character hitherto of being conservative in our ecclesiastical and, as far as we have at any time meddled, in our civil politics also. But I think we are in some danger of forfeiting this honour. If you submit to become our President which I do devoutly hope and pray may be the case, the object sought in these remarks will be greatly served. The state of your health no doubt will have weight with you in judging of this matter, but as you are able to preach pretty often which I am very glad to perceive from various advertisements it is but right to hope that your strength would be proportioned to your day during the Conference. And supposing your health should slightly suffer, the Ex-President could occasionally take your place and thereby afford you seasons of rest.

Should you decline (which I sincerely trust you will not), there will be sad conflicts of opinion as to who should be President, and no one, be he who he may, will go to the Chair with anything *approaching* to a unanimous vote; nor should I be much surprised if occasion were taken in time to come to object to a fourth election, and so when even Dr. Newton, should his valued life be spared, becomes eligible for re-election,[1] some one else be chosen in his stead. . . .

237   From Barnard Slater[2]   *West Bromwich, July 15, 1844*

. . . I have heard a whisper from a Manchester friend that you are thinking of not attending the Conference. This I sincerely hope is not true. . . . We have been looking to you, I may truly say the vast majority of our Connexion have been expecting you, to once again honour us by filling the chair. Now we are not prepared to fix upon any other fit person. If you dont come then we shall be split into numerous parties. I have heard from several very respectable brethren on the subject, and some urge one brother and some another. I have heard the most about Jacob Stanley,[3] and Wm. Atherton. Of one thing I am certain that if you should not be with us, no other brother will gain any majority of votes to give him to feel that he *represents the Body*.

There, my dear friend, do not give way for one moment to the thought of stopping away. O I pray you dont jeopardise the Connexion! As to

[1] Robert Newton, the only man apart from Bunting to serve a fourth term as President, was brought out of retirement for this distinction in 1848.

[2] Barnard Slater, superintendent, West Bromwich circuit, 1841–44, and old friend of Bunting.

[3] For the case against Jacob Stanley (who succeeded as President in 1845), see no. 154 *supra*.

your *health*, God forbid that we should put it to any risk; but you know the office so well, you are so easy in passing off the business of Conference, you will be so well supported by the prayers of the Brethren who love you much, that you need have no fear – and be assured we will ease you of all the business we can. . . .

238 To Barnard Slater

London, July 23, 1844[1]

I offer you many and sincere thanks for your very kind letter.

I cannot in my present position say much on the subject to which you principally refer. Till within the last 10 or 12 weeks, I had no idea that I should be in such health as would permit me to attend any more Conferences, except perhaps as a brief and irregular visitor. My race of public duty is nearly run. But of late I am certainly very much improved, though still frail and uncertain, and at times incapable of much fatigue or of long and anxious exertion. And the representations of yourself, and many other Brethren, for whose judgment I have great respect, have great weight with me. My own opinion still is that one more physically and mentally competent might and should be selected. To myself such an event would be a great relief, for I sincerely dread the onerous duties and responsibilities of any additional public office. Yet I know not that I should now be quite safe in that peremptory refusal to which at one time my mind was made up. I therefore leave it in the hands of God and of my friends. *Release* would be felt by me to be a great personal comfort. But if *they* deem it proper on public considerations, to require my services, such as they are or can be, I must claim more than ordinary indulgence, and, with that understanding, consent to do all in my power, in return for their persevering and unmerited kindness. . . .

239 From Sir Andrew Agnew[2]

*Lochnain Castle, Stranraer, N.B.,
July 24, 1844*

It needed not the notice of the approaching meeting of your Conference at Birmingham to remind [me?] of the many good services done by the

---

[1] In a postscript Bunting added that this letter was confidential, but might be shown to Edward Walker, the writer of no. 236 *supra*.

[2] Sir Andrew Agnew (1793–1849), M.P. for Wigtownshire 1830–37, the leading promoter of Sabbatarian legislation. Joseph Fowler's Conference journal records of this letter: 'The President [Dr. Bunting] promised to cooperate with him in the good work'. Gregory, *Sidelights* p. 374.

Wesleyans to the cause of the Sabbath.[1] Nevertheless that notice did in legible terms tell of where the same cause would best be served again. Let the subject, I would earnestly request of you, be brought within the *regular annual business* of the Conference, and perhaps there is no point better adapted for bringing out discussion on the *principle* than the great master profanation of the present day, namely the railway trains on the Lord's Day. To this point, as a great national sin, it would be well for the Conference to draw the attention of all their ministers and congregations. Not only for the purpose of warning their own members from sanctioning this national sin by availing themselves of the accommodation wherewith the railway trains *tempt* the unwary on the Lord's Day, but also with a view to induce their more wealthy members to become themselves *shareholders* and proprietors in the *local* railways for the purpose of testifying against this sin against the Law of the Sabbath at all general railway meetings. For there is good hope of inducing many friends throughout the country to do likewise, and this not so much in the expectation of carrying the question by a vote as for the moral influence of such public testimonies, and to save the public mind from becoming reconciled to the sin. May I further take the liberty of requesting you to communicate this suggestion to your President with my respectful compliments, as I have not myself the honour of being acquainted with that reverend gentleman.

It gives me much pleasure to see that for modifying, if not defeating, parliamentary measures the Wesleyan is the most influential section of the Church of Christ. Such a degree of national influence is admirably powerful and fearfully responsible. It is a talent which I am sure you desire to make subservient to the cause of the Lord of the Sabbath, and this can you most effectually do by raising your powerful voice on behalf of the 4th commandment. . . .

It was publicly charged upon the Wesleyan ministers who attended the Conference at Newcastle-upon-Tyne that they had in great numbers made use of the railways in that neighbourhood on the Lord's Day. The Wesleyan minister with whom I conversed, thought that the statement was very much exaggerated. But as he was not able to contradict it altogether he expressed a wish that I should take an opportunity for suggesting at head quarters that it would be well to put the friends of the cause on their guard as the enemy is ever watching for their halting. . . .

---

[1] After the little knot of Anglican evangelicals who took the lead in the cause, the Wesleyan connexional management were the principal Sabbatarian force in England.

240   From Thomas Withington[1]   *Birmingham, August 3, 1844*

I sincerely thank you for the private, the kind and fatherly manner in which you have handed over to me the false and malicious epistle you have received. Your time is too valuable to allow you to listen to the details of this case. I have simply to state that the writer of this is a most depraved person, notorious for his subtlety, falsehood, and indeed for almost every evil work except that of drunkenness. Nothing higher can be said of his morality than that he is a teetotaller and as such has no special regard for the character of a Wesleyan Minister. Towards his late mother, an aged member of our Society, he acted in the most deceitful, dishonest and inhuman manner, so as to make him appear in the estimation of any person who possesses a common share of filial affection, more like a monster than a man. As it respects my conduct towards Line, I shall be not only willing but proud, if requested to submit it to the most rigid scrutiny. . . .

241   From Samuel Dunn[2]   *Halifax, September 14, 1844*

In consequence of the treatment I received in 1842, I have not since attended the Conference.

From the Minutes recently published and which I have carefully read, it appears:–

1. That there are about eleven connexional committees.

2. That there are in Great Britain, one thousand one hundred and twentynine Preachers.

3. That there is a preacher who was admitted into full connexion in 1833, who is now (1) Secretary of the Committee of Privileges. (2) Member of the Acting Sub-Committee of Do. (3) Member of the Missionary Committee. (4) On a Missionary Deputation. (5) Treasurer of the Schools. (6) Member of the Book Committee (7) Member of the Committee of Distribution of the Chapel and Educational Fund (8) Do. of the Institution Committee (9) Do. of the Education Committee.[3]

I may be allowed to add

1. That in 1842, I left in the Dudley Circuit, 1775 members. There are now 1521. Decrease 254.

2. That I left £100 in the hands of the Stewards; they have since been £100 in debt. Decrease £200.

3. That £500 appear on the Missionary report from the Dudley Circuit for 1842. In 1844 £300. Decrease £200.

---

[1] Thomas Withington (1816–95), preacher, St. Austell circuit, 1842–44.

[2] Samuel Dunn, preacher, Halifax circuit, 1842–45.   [3] This pluralist was Charles Prest.

4. That I was unceremoniously – harshly – removed from that Circuit, at the end of one year, but my successors are appointed a third.

Our venerable Founder directed with his dying breath, that all things should be done in Conference 'without partiality, as he had done from the beginning'.

Great is your influence Mr. President in this connexion. Shall it be employed before you are taken to your reward, in endeavouring to maintain the true Wesleyan parity, to the prevention of a dangerous oligarchy? . . .

Endorsed:– Mr. Dunn about Mr. P[rest].

242   From Peter Samuel[1]   *Guernsey, November 12, 1844*

As there is a considerable number of persons in this circuit who for several years have been in the habit of taking the Sacrament of the Lord's Supper with us, without becoming members of our Society or of any other Church, I feel anxious to have your opinion as to the propriety of continuing such a practice. The enclosed tickets will shew that it has been regularly carried on.

It appears to me essential that communicants should be something more than *mere hearers*, that they ought to be recognised members of a church and amenable to discipline. However in so important a matter I tremble lest I should go wrong, and therefore if you will be so kind as favour me with an hint how to proceed so as to preserve the discipline of the Body and promote the salvation of Souls, you will greatly oblige. . . .

243   To John Beecham   *Lynch House, nr. Old Down, Som.,*
                                November 12, 1844 [Copy]

. . . You see I have taken advantage of my preaching-journey to Bath and Bradford, and of my visit to my afflicted sister at Stroud, to execute my long-meditated plan of an *elopement* for a time from London cares and turmoil. I am sorry to be away from head-quarters at this busy and anxious period. But I know not when I could be better spared than now. And my health really and truly requires it. Of late some of my old ailments and infirmities have increased upon me; and even now I am not without indications which threaten, if I am not careful, an

---

[1] Peter Samuel (1802–74), sole preacher, Guernsey (English) circuit, 1844–47.

approaching crisis. I say little about this, because I would not alarm unnecessarily either Mrs. B. or myself; but my friends here have partially
detected the fact. The pure country-air may help me, though the
weather is wet and wintry. At all events I can here overtake the arrears
of my correspondence, chiefly 'presidential'; and so return home dis-
embarrassed. This week I hope to be in almost entire solitude, and to
improve the perfect retirement and insulation which are kindly afforded
to me. . . .

244 From Edward Jones[1]   *Dolgelley, November 15, 1844*

The high-church pusy party *here* being very strong and obstinate, and
just commencing the building of a large *National School* which will take
away all the children of our people if they can succeed; and as we have
none among us able to subscribe anything towards erecting a school of
our own; would it not be advisable for our people to unite with the
other denominations (the Welsh Methodists, the Independents, and
the Baptists) in the *British and Foreign School*, rather than let their
children go to the church school?[2] By uniting with the fore-mentioned
denominations, we could secure the children for our Sunday School,
and our own place of worship; but if they will go to the National
School, we shall have no control over them . . .

245 From Hugh Hughes[3]   *Carmarthen, November 18, 1844*

I know that you will excuse me for troubling you once more with a
letter. I want to know your opinion respecting education or day
schools in Wales. A gentleman of this town of the name of Mr. Cha[r]les,
son of the late Revd. David Charles[4] of this town and a nephew of the
late Revd. Thos. Charles of Bala,[5] called upon me last week and read me

---

[1] Edward Jones, superintendent, Dolgelley circuit, 1843–45. D. 1855, aet. 73.

[2] To a similar enquiry from the superintendent of the Newtown circuit, Bunting had replied
on October 26, 1844: 'If it be *quite clear and certain* that you cannot have a strictly *Wesleyan*
Day School . . . the next best thing seems to be your uniting with such other noncon[formi]sts
as are orthodox and evangelical in their doctrinal sentiments to raise a school on the British
and Foreign system'. Endorsement to M.C.A. MSS. Hugh Carter to Jabez Bunting, October
15, 1844.

[3] Hugh Hughes (1778–1855), superintendent, Carmarthen (Welsh) circuit, 1841–43.

[4] David Charles (1762–1834), a Carmarthen tradesman, and one of the first Calvinistic
Methodist lay-preachers to be ordained, 1811.

[5] Thomas Charles of Bala (1755–1814), brother of David Charles, celebrated Calvinistic
Methodist preacher and founder of schools and Sunday schools.

a letter which he had received from some Committee in London expressing their desire that all denominations should unite as one body to establish and support schools in the principality. Understand me this must be general union through every town and village, and not for us to have one of our own where we can support it, and they have one of their own where they can support it, no, but to unite everywhere or not at all.[1]

To the above question, I could not give him a decisive answer until I should hear from you. My own humble opinion is that we cannot support schools of our own but in very few places, if in any place without some assistance from somewhere. The gentleman named above is one of the most respectable members among the Calvinistic Methodists. I do assure you Sir I was not little surprised in finding that narrow-minded party willing to unite with us at all. We are not quite 20000 members both English and Welsh including Monmouth and Newport etc., while they are upwards of 50000, and perhaps the Independents more numerous than them particularly in South Wales, the Baptists are something like ourselves perhaps. Some of their arguments are that it will be a means of creating more union and love among the different denominations etc. I cannot but wonder at this again, that these people above all, who have been our bitterest opposers, should court our co-operation; but so it is, and it is wondrous in our eyes. It is my firm belief that Wesleyan Methodist[s] have done more good in Wales perhaps than in any other part of the world; the good that it has done here will not be known until that day, when the secrets of all hearts will be manifested. There are thousands [of] members with other denominations that have been convinced under the admirable doctrine of Wesleyan Methodist[s]. We had no places to receive them then, nor had we leaders to guide them. And we were despised by all those that were called Christians. But God was with the lads (as they called us) and through Him we conquered all their prejudices. It is a pleasing thought to know that none of our members and but few of our hearers were with the Chartists, nor with the Rebecaites. Wales was not moralized until you have sent your missionaries here, and the thousands that you have spent here are not lost to Christ. Thousands upon thousands will be praising God to all eternity, for your kindness in sending and supporting those men that have preached them the truth as it is in Jesus. Yesterday

[1] Hughes later explained that in addition to two National Schools in Carmarthen there had long been an undenominational Lancasterian school, the master of which was a member of the English Wesleyan Society, and the committee composed of members of all the denominations, and 'all the minister[s] . . . exophisio'. M.C.A. MSS. H. Hughes to Jabez Bunting, November 19, 1844.

was a week[day]. I was preaching in one of those new places that brother Thos. Hughes (who is a kind of a home missionary) has opened lately; there was a very large congregation there, and some of them testify, that they never have heard the Gospel until now: though perhaps that they have had preaching there 60 or 80 years!!

246   From John Stephenson[1]   *Grimsby, November 27, 1844*

My mind has been for many years impressed with the necessity of our making some better provision for the religious care of the youth of our body. Recent events however have induced me to turn my attention more fully to it, and for some time I have been collecting information on this subject. One question, which I have long felt a wish to have answered, is this, 'What number of Children is there in Wesleyan Families?' . . .

. . . I have [also] added a copy of a note which I have addressed to the Rev. J. Scott, which will put you in possession more fully of my views on this subject, and the data there furnished must I think impress every reflecting mind with its vast importance. . . .

(Copy of a letter to the Rev. J. Scott [n.d.]).

I have taken the liberty of forwarding the inclosed circular to about 40 of the Brethren with whom I am acquainted in all parts of the country. And as Chairman of the Education Committee, I have thought you would excuse me for sending one to you. My object is to obtain data on which may be founded a probable estimate of the number of children there are in Wesleyan families, and who therefore would be properly, or ought to be, a part of our pastoral care. My conviction is that as a body of ministers we have erred in not making more suitable provision for the religious care and culture of the children of our members and for many others who would have been placed under care gladly by their parents or guardians.

According to the proportion of different classes of persons in our Societies in my own circuit I find there are 72 per cent of individuals, coming under the designation of 'Widowers, Widows, Married Men, Married Women'.

Last Conference we had 337598 members. 72 per cent of that number gives 243000. Divide that number by two and it gives the number of persons whom we may reckon as married couples, viz. 121500. Multiply that number by 3, the number of children in each family according to

[1] John Stephenson (1799-1861), superintendent, Grimsby circuit, 1842-45.

the ascertained ratio of the numbers in families (i.e. 5 persons, 2 parents and 3 children), and it gives 364500 children. Divide this by *twelve* years and it gives 30375 youth of Wesleyan parents who are annually entering their 'teens.' *Thirty Thousand* youth yearly rising into life from our own body! And I ask where are those 300000 of this class that have risen up the last ten years. The increase in our Societies in the last 10 years has been in Great Britain 45659, deduct this number from the above and it leaves 254341. Now admit that our increase has consisted entirely of the children of our own members, what has become of the Two Hundred and Fifty Four Thousand! *A Quarter of a Million!* Surely there must be some defect somewhere, or our congregations, if not our societies, and our institutions generally must have felt and evinced the benefit of some proportionate increase and improvement. After reflecting upon the subject long and examining it carefully in various ways I am fully convinced that we ought to have *Catechetical Classes* into which as a matter of course our youth should be introduced, and that these classes should be brought under our care and visited periodically as the classes in our societies are visited. And that by a proper exercise of direct pastoral care over them we ought to try to secure them to ourselves for all time to come.

247   From Thomas Harris[1]   *Macclesfield, December 19, 1844*

I feel rather reluctant to obtrude on your valuable time, but your advice on a subject of importance will greatly oblige me. My predecessor Mr. Jackson[2] printed the large Macclesfield Sunday School[3] on the preachers' plan, appointed several of the Local Preachers to lecture there, and occasionally went himself. Several deputations of gentlemen connected with this school have waited upon me soliciting me to do the same; but I have seriously demurred to such requests. The Secretary has sent me their Trust Deed, Rules and report, which I have carefully read over, and have drawn up a letter stating in as courteous terms as I could my objections to the principle of their school, as not connected with any branch of the Christian Church, and therefore without the influence of any acknowledged pastorate. But I have thought,

[1] Thomas Harris, superintendent, Macclesfield circuit, 1844–47.

[2] Robert Jackson (1799–1881), preacher, Macclesfield circuit, 1841–43; superintendent, 1843–44.

[3] The Macclesfield Sunday School, founded on an undenominational basis in 1796, was repudiated by both Anglicans and official Methodists when it moved into its purpose-built premises (the large or 'Big School') in 1812, over the question of Sabbath writing lessons. Cf. Ward, *Religion and Society* pp. 13, 94–5.

would it be safe for me to visit their school and occasionally preach for them, if they will consent to bring a portion of their children *every Sunday morning* to one of our chapels? If they refuse this my negotiations are at an end. If they yield, it would be a great point gained.

Great efforts have been made of late years to make this Institution entirely a church school and I am informed that the Bishop has given leave to clergymen to lecture there.

But at present there are a considerable number of our members in this school as Teachers who have considerable influence, and they think if I would consent to preach for them occasionally, the Methodist influence would greatly preponderate. The question therefore on which I want advice is this: May I safely go to them occasionally if they will concede to my terms? My own judgment inclines towards this plan, because it would be a considerable coming down on their part, and would open to us a large field of usefulness, at least I think so. Many of the Committee and Teachers are afraid of the Church influence which makes them look to us. And I did not think it right for ever to close the door of access to a thousand children and teachers without seeking counsel. . . .

Endorsed:– [To Thomas Harris]

Ansd. Dec. 26. Would rather decline giving an official opinion, or even private and friendly advice. On all *general principles* should be led to concede nothing which the public could fairly construe into a sanction of the plan of that school. Refer particularly to the absence of all responsible connexion with any branch of the Church, and to Sunday writing and arithmetic. But there *may* be local circumstances which perhaps ought to influence Mr. H.'s decision. With him the decision must rest. Wish he had been unfettered by his predecessor's course.

248   From Thomas Padman[1]   *Thetford, January 7, 1845*

About a year and a half ago a chapel was erected (*and a schoolroom under it*) at Northwold, a village in this circuit about twelve miles from Thetford; it was settled according to the Poll deed,[2] opened by Dr. Newton and the Rev. J. Scott; about six months after, the Rev. I. Whitehouse[3] (my predecessor) was opposed by two of the Trustees in the village in holding a Lovefeast; he required them to show their tickets; the said Trustees declared *they should not* but be admitted without; Mr.

---

[1] Thomas Padman (1785–1855), superintendent, Thetford circuit, 1844–45.

[2] I.e. the Model Deed.

[3] Isaac Whitehouse (1799–1874), superintendent, Thetford circuit, 1843–44.

W. was firm, the Trustees with the congregation left the chapel excepting six with whom Mr. W. prayed and then dismissed them. Since then
the two Trustees, Mr. Walpole, Attorney, and Mr. John Cock, Farmer,
have repeatedly sent our respectable Local Preachers word they were not
to come in their appointments, they had got some other person – sometimes a Baptist Minister or a preacher from some other circuit. About
three weeks ago they invited a Mrs. Stamp[1] a Tee-total lecturer to
lecture and preach in our chapel. I remonstrated with them, but it was
in vain. I wrote Mr. Walpole a kind Christian letter with all the
quotations from our Minutes on the subject of admitting strangers into
our chapels, female preaching, Local Preachers from other circuits and
the resolution of Conference respecting Teetotal lecturers not to be
allowed to lecture in our chapels, etc. etc., supposing Mr. W. and Mr.
Cock had erred through ignorance of our rules; but after all on Sunday
last they sent for Mrs. Stamp to preach to them. The Local Preacher
appointed for the evening went to the chapel at the time; the chapel
was not lighted but the door locked and Mrs. Stamp with a large
congregation assembled in the schoolroom under it to whom she
preached. Mrs. Stamp and her husband were Ranters at Sheerness
where they caused much disturbance and were expelled after ruining
the Ranters' cause in that place. Mr. S. removed to Hull and collected
a few people who are called Stampites; I hear he has since removed to
Liverpool and his wife is going about in Norfolk to sow discord among our
Societies; and I have no doubt to obtain a fixment for herself and
husband amongst our people. I know that she has been in some of our
chapels in the Downham Circuit and made a collection for herself.

I have been more fortunate than some of my Brethren. I have never
met with any thing of this kind before. I know not how to act: I have
not strength of nerve to contend with them. I want your advice. I have
thought if you (as our President) would address a letter to Messrs.
Walpole and Cock, Northwold, Norfolk, it perhaps might prevent
further evil. . . .

Endorsed:– [To Thomas Padman]
Ansd. Jan. 13. 1845.
3 Points involved:

1. Claim *as Trustees* to admisssion into our Society's Lovefeasts. Trustee-
ship *by itself* gives no right to membership; nor to any of the privileges
of membership.

[1] The wife of the Rev. John Stamp, a well-known religious and teetotal revivalist of
Lincolnshire origin. He was stationed at Sheerness in 1838 for three years, and was imprisoned
for open air preaching. In 1841 a chapel was built for him in Hull where he gathered a
society known as the Primitive Methodist New Connexion. In 1843 he became pastor of the
Methodist Revivalists in Manchester, dying of consumption, January 29, 1847, aet. 39.

Y

2. Rejection of duly appointed *Local* Preachers. Said to be settled according to *Poll*-Deed; meaning I suppose the *Model* Deed. In either case, the attempt is unmethodistical, and I believe illegal. The Local Preachers of the circuit ought to go as and *when* planned, and if ejected *legal* redress may, if it be thought worth the while, adopted, should gentler means fail.

3. Invitation of persons not approved by Superintendent to conduct any Public Religious Services on Premises. This cannot be tolerated.

If necessary, call in to the aid of himself and his official friends the Chairman of the District.

249   From William Vevers   *Derby, January 25, 1845*

. . . I spent last Sunday in Manchester, and in the afternoon I went to the opening of the Free Scotch Church, and found Mr. Governor Waddy, in full canonicals, gown and bands! though Mr. Hamilton of London had no gown either morning or evening. What an inextinguishable itching there must be in the Governor's body for the sacerdotal, I beg pardon, according to that eminent *Judge* the Bishop of Exeter,[1] the Literary Robe! I suppose you have heard of the rapid progress of the Sheffield School – alias College – alias branch of the London University!! What next! If this be not making haste hastily, *much too hastily*, I am at a loss to know what the Father meant who said 'Make haste *slowly*'. I think the time has arrived when the heavy drag must be put on all the wheels, or that literary and religious omnibus branch of the no-religious London University will be overturned by the sheer haste of the driver. The next Conference must interfere. I have hitherto gone with the friends of that school, but if my information be correct, I shall now make a dead halt.

I entirely concur with you respecting the necessity of a more vigorous executive during the intervals of Conference, and will most heartily support any plan which commends itself to my judgment. When I saw the advertisement relating to Mr. Caughey at Huddersfield, I felt so keenly the positive contempt thrown upon you, both personally and

---

[1] Henry Phillpotts. The reference, here and in the postscript, is to Phillpotts's efforts to preserve the use of the surplice at the time of the surplice riots. On January 8, 1845, Phillpotts published a letter stating that he had received a copy of a letter from the Archbishop, to the clergy and laity of the Province of Canterbury, and recommending the clergy to adopt the suggestions it contained i.e. to continue the services in their present form, 'provided the doing so does not involve omitting or garbling portions of the offices or the introducing of prayers of private composition'. G. C. B. Davies, *Henry Phillpotts, bishop of Exeter, 1778–1869* (London, 1954) p. 186.

officially, that I could scarcely restrain my feelings, and if I had not known that you are in fact powerless, I should instantly have written to request you to interpose as President, and save the Connexion from this continuous, and I think highly reprehensible, attack upon the fundamental principles of our Connexional Union. But some of the simpletons (forgive me for speaking thus of some of my Brethren) who countenance Caughey cannot or will not see the tendency of their own proceedings. If I had not ceased to be surprised at anything either said or done among us, I certainly should have been surprised at the last Conference, when I heard how the *three grave Doctors of Divinity* (I am sure you are not of the same University!) who sat on your right, were carried away with the declamatory nonsense they heard about Caughey. I was almost ready to wish them all three *un*-doctored, that they might undergo an examination on the first principles of common sense before they could be admitted to the degree of D.D.. I *know* that several of the brethren who are as pliable as willows by the watercourses in the Conference, the very moment they get among the people maintain that any opinion expressed by the President is merely his *private* opinion, and ought not to be regarded as the opinion of the Conference, unless formally confirmed. *I maintain the very opposite*. If spared till the next Conference, I think I shall venture after the election of the President and before we proceed to practical business, to raise the abstract question, and maintain in all its barefacedness that any opinion expressed by the President and not confirmed by a vote of the Conference is a mere piece of wax, to be moulded according to the fancy or whim of each member of the Conference. If I should do this I doubt not but some of the very men who act upon this principle, would be eager to refute me; and would chuckle to find me so thoroughly mistaken. It would really serve some 'tame elephants' right to dig this pit that they might fall into it, and be convinced of their great mistakes in reference to the authority of our President. . . .

P.S. What a mess his Lordship of Exeter has made of his work!

250 To George Osborn[1]   *London, January 25, 1845*

. . . You[2] . . . propose the employment of a Professor of Elocution, and that at an expense of thirty guineas and for *two* lectures in *every* week. I do not decidedly object to this, if you *all* (Dr. Hannah included),

[1] George Osborn (1808–91), preacher, Manchester (Grosvenor St.) circuit, 1842–45. President, 1863 and 1881.

[2] I.e. the committee of Didsbury College, Manchester.

decide on its expediency; but *for myself*, I hesitate to share in the responsibility. *Some* benefit it would probably secure; but are there no dangers connected with *formal plans* of that character, and should not the *General* Committee approve of the experiment before either Local Committee adopts it? The object, to a certain extent, is very important; but could it not, as far as it is really needed, be accomplished by other existing means, less formal and elaborate, and less liable to make *would-be-orators*? Perhaps I am too fearful of abuses; and if I knew more of the plan might think of it with better anticipations. We tried something of the kind at Hoxton for a while seven or eight years ago, but without much advantage; and this may have made me too timid. The same amount of time and pains spent systematically and regularly with the students by those who have charge of them, in kind but very particular and faithful *fault-lopping* (to use Mr. Chappell's[1] phrase) might be made to answer every good purpose. . . .

251   From John McLean[2]   *Edinburgh, January 30, 1845*

. . . I am not without hope we shall get our heads up in this place after all, but we have been all but extinguished during the last six or eight years. The Free Church with the exception of some recent demonstrations on Calvinism, of which we take no notice, is throughly friendly. I have preached in some of their principal pulpits and they are pleased to pronounce me *sound*, which is about the highest compliment current in these regions. The effect of this must in the end be favourable; and if we conduct ourselves discreetly and maintain our interest in the Divine regard I feel confident our position in Scotland will in a few years be improved. I dont think we are called upon (for the present, at least) to extend ourselves beyond our existing stations. The Free Church seems to be God's elected instrument for evangelizing Scotland; but we occupy an important position here notwithstanding; and the Free Church will herself be the better for our presence and efficiency in this country. We keep up to its proper height the standard of experimental Godliness, abate the severity of Calvinism, moderate hostility to the residuary church and from our known friendship for the Church of England (which I trust in God we shall never sacrifice) we are a sort of break-

---

[1] George Chappell (1778–1860), cotton spinner and fustian manufacturer; a prominent Manchester Methodist of liberal political views from the time of his conversion c. 1815. A member of the fashionable Oxford Road chapel from 1826. A member of the Centenary Fund committee; contributed 1000 guineas.

[2] John McLean, superintendent, Edinburgh circuit, 1844–46.

water to the ferocity of their anti-episcopal wrath. Above all we are increasing the amount of living Christianity and thus promoting the Glory of Christ.

Is it indeed true that Jacob Stanley is to be our next President? Has the Bookroom[1] really so decreed it? Alas! Alas! I hope you will not become too good natured in your old days. If that party had generously stood aloof at the last Conference one might have felt inclined to deal kindly with old Jacob. But instead of that they mustered their entire strength and there seemed to me to be more of the animus of the Stephenite struggle[2] in London than I have seen at any Conference since. If you admit his party, stronger at present than they have been for a long time, you will be taking the trojan horse into the city. . . .

252   From William Barton   *King's Cross, February 3, 1845*

In transmitting the usual circular announcing the monthly meeting of the Institution Committee allow me also to remind you of some of the other Committees which I hope you will be able to convene in the next few days. . . .

1. The last Conference directed that letters of Ordination should be prepared for the ministers who were ordained at the last Conference. The Book Committee was charged to prepare them and the following Sub-Committee has been appointed for that purpose:

> The President of the Conference
> The Missionary Secretaries
> The Editor and Assistant Editor
> Mr. Barton

2. A Committee was appointed some two years since and reappointed I think afterwards, [and is] certainly still standing, to consider some expressions in the Rules of Society, in the Band Rules and in the forms of renewing the Covenant. Also to prepare a form of Ordination Service for junior ministers and for missionaries. Also to consider the form of Baptism.

In one of the conversations on the subject of Ordination you made a suggestion as to some religious and public service on the designation of a young preacher on trial to his probationary labours. It has often been upon my mind since and I cannot help believing it would in many instances have a gracious influence on the heart. There is only one other thing that I could desire but I do not see how it could be accomplished.

[1] On the Book Room see n. 3 p. 103 *supra*.
[2] The contest which led to the resignation of Joseph Rayner Stephens.

We have an Annual charge at the Conference; it is reported in the *Watchman* etc. and our people have numerous intimations of what *we* ought to be; they read the exhortations which we receive as to our duties to them but who tells them of their duties to us, except indeed the one enjoined in 2 Thess. 3c. 1vs.[1] I should be glad if suitable exhortations could be addressed to both parties but I do not see how. . . .

253 From John McLean   *Edinburgh, February 6, 1845*

. . . The controversy on some points in debate between different sections of the Calvinistic churches in this part of the kingdom seems to extend. Dr. Candlish's[2] letter which you have doubtless seen has called forth two or three pamphlets; and some here think that we should make our voice heard, but I think otherwise, and being in some power, I hope I shall be able to restrain both their tongues and pens. The extreme voluntaries on the one hand and the Established Church on the other are exceedingly anxious to set us and the Free Kirk by the ears; but I hope we shall *all* become more united. I dont think this controversy will do us any harm if we keep out of it and just preach our own precious soul-saving Gospel.

I wish much you would write me a few lines . . . and as I am in a new and rather responsible situation, I feel in need of such counsels as I know you can give. I have to preach next Lord's Day one of the Jubilee sermons for the London Missionary Society in conjunction with Dr. Candlish and that in the chapel of one of the strongest Calvinists on these parts, so we are not breaking any bones by this controversy. . . . What moving times we live in! Is this increased grant to Maynooth likely to be succeeded by any more specific recognition of Popery by the state, or is it intended whilst it quiets Ireland rather to ward off that? I cant give up my confidence in Sir Robert [Peel] yet; but he would need (as our Scotch proverb says) 'a *lang* spoon that sups wi' the Deil'.

[1] 'Finally, brethren, pray for us, that the word of the Lord may have free course, and be glorified, even as it is with you.'

[2] Robert Smith Candlish (1806–73), Scottish Free Church leader and minister of Free St. George's, Edinburgh, 1843 till his death. At this moment Candlish was actively promoting the Evangelical Alliance.

254   From William Barton   *King's Cross, February 12, 1845*

I send you herewith some resolutions on the subject of Marriage, which, with a few verbal alterations, I drew up last May in the hope that Mr. Prest would bring the subject before the Conference.

Permit me to ask your attention to the following remarks on the subject.

I wish

First, To shew that the Conference should give its sanction to the solemnization of marriages in our chapels.

And this, because,

1. If marriage is a religious contract, and its ceremonies are to be performed by ministers of religion, it seems as a general principle so clear as not to be doubted that they should be performed by the ministers of the parties, and not by ministers by whose labours they receive no spiritual profit, whom they do not regard with affection, and whose teaching they believe to be in many cases unscriptural.

Because

2. Marriages *are* solemnized in our chapels. Whether rightly or otherwise, so it is; and as I think, unless the Conference prohibits its ministers from performing the rite, marriages will be solemnized in our chapels more frequently.[1] I do not think the Conference will so prohibit them. There are so many ministers who have performed the ceremony, and so many others who approve the practice, and but wait for the formal sanction of the Conference, that, if I desired the prohibition, I could not hope for it. It would be better the practice should have the sanction of Conference than that it should be continued under what some interpret as a connivance, and others as a restriction.

Because

3. The Conference *cannot hinder* the solemnization of marriages in our chapels. For any one Trustee, though the others dissent, may procure the chapel to be registered for marriages. He may give his assent to enable parties to be married in it, without their being trespassers; nay further, all parties complying with the necessary preliminaries may insist on being married there, whether strangers not of the denominations connected with the place, or otherwise. It is true the minister of the building cannot be compelled to perform any ceremony on the occasion. But is not this a reason that, at least as to parties connected with our congregations or denomination, the Conference should sanction the performance of the ceremony by its own ministers? Should our chapels be exposed to the constant intrusion of all sorts of dissenting ministers,

---

[1] See n. 5 p. 217 *supra*. From now on Wesleyan chapels were licensed in increasing numbers.

or of all sorts of Local Preachers? And how would this operate in times of commotion such as preceded and attended the Warrenite secession? It is feared that, in such times, what, perhaps, with some trustees, cannot be avoided, would occur to a painful extent.

Because

4. Of the opposition of the clergy to our Connexion. To say nothing of other annoyances they refuse to bury children baptized by Wesleyan ministers, in opposition to the rubrics of their own Church, as explained and enforced by their own Ecclesiastical Courts. It may be thought right to yield to their professions of conscience on this matter; but this will leave marriage as the only rite which they will have the opportunity of performing for our people. We baptize them, counsel and instruct them, and administer to them the Lord's Supper, and the clergy refuse to bury; and if they be yielded to we shall have a large increase of burials. Why then should they be selected to marry if marriage can be as well performed by ourselves?

Secondly I wish to shew that the Act of Parliament authorizing marriages etc. (6 & 7 Wm. IV c.85) is not so seriously deficient as to nullify the reasonings before advanced.

And here I at once admit that the Act *is seriously deficient.* It gives no authority to any minister of religion to marry any of his people, except to the ministers of one favoured section of the Church of Christ. It does not even recognize the existence of any other ministers than those of the Church of England. The presence of a Registrar at the marriage is essential, but the religious ceremony may be employed or dispensed with as the parties may determine; or if such ceremony be used it may be performed by a minister or by the chapel-keeper, or by any chimney sweep who may be passing by.

This state of things is justly offensive:

1. As there is no recognition of any religion existing in the country out of the Church of England, the act does not provide for the celebration of marriages by any *religious* form or ceremony but simply by any form or ceremony. And

2. There is no recognition of any minister of religion but the Established clergy. And all through the ceremony the minister must feel that he is not necessary to give validity to the marriage. That is made valid by the presence of the Registrar, and by the declarations made in his presence; and whatever the parties may feel towards their minister, and however they may regard him as such, *he* is compelled to feel that the law does not recognize him as a minister.

This is justly offensive to the great body of Christian ministers not of the Church of England, and the act should have been more liberal. A very simple enlargement of the terms of the Act would have been sufficient. Instead of saying §20 'according to such form and ceremony as they may see fit to adopt' it might have been 'by such minister of religion and according etc.' to such form or ceremony of religion etc.

This will appear more offensive when it is considered that the attendance of a Registrar to witness the marriage of Jews and Quakers is not necessary.[1] Their own forms are sufficient. This remark is open to exception.

But it ought also to be remarked

1. That the Act does provide for the celebration of marriages in places certified for *religious worship*. So far there is a recognition of religion (*so far only indeed*, for with this exception there is scarcely a hint that there is any religion beyond the Church of England) and as to such places the Act provides for the marriage according to the form and ceremony adopted by the parties; while as to marriages contracted at the offices of Registrars there is no reference to any form or ceremony.

2. No preference is given by the Act to Roman Catholic ministers, although the orders of the Romish Church are admitted by the Church of England to be valid.

3. It must not be forgotten that the Act was intended to provide for men whose consciences or notions are too irregular to be brought within the provisions which would satisfy men of better regulated minds and which they would approve. It is questionable whether, if any provision expressly naming ministers had been inserted in the Act, some dissenters would have accepted it. Some would have said that their ministers should have *no connexion* with the state, and others that there were no such men as ministers, or perhaps that all men are so.

But to return to the consideration of the Act as to the powers which it does give.

Though the Act makes no recognition of any minister not of the Church of England, it is still true that the marriage is actually celebrated by the minister and not by the Registrar; the latter being present only to witness and to register. On this point I confess that a minute investigation of the Act has caused me to change my views. The following are the grounds of my present opinion.

1. A distinction between the solemnization of the marriage and the registry of it by the Registrar is constantly recognized in the Act. Thus §23, every entry of such marriage shall be signed by the person *by* or before *whom* the *marriage shall have been solemnized and* by the *Registrar* and

---

[1] Even under Hardwicke's Marriage Act (1753) which required marriages to be solemnized in the parish church, Jews and Quakers had married according to their own rites under common law authority.

by the parties married. The Licence (Schedule C) grants 'unto you (one of the parties) full licence to *solemnize* such marriage,' and to the Registrar to *register* such marriage according to law. Surely a plain distinction is made between the solemnization and the registry of the marriage, and the part assigned to the Registrar is simply to register.

2. Then again the registry is actually signed by the officiating minister (though it is admitted not as a minister) as married *by me* A.B. (party performing the ceremony). It would be an improvement if an addition were made in the form for a line stating the designation of the party performing the ceremony as 'Wesleyan Minister', or 'Officiating Minister'; and I think the form of the Register (Matthews Pa 132) will authorize this if it does not require it.

From these considerations it is thought it will appear that, though there is no recognition of the *minister*, the marriage is actually performed by him.

It is objected that the presence of a minister is not necessary, but that of the Registrar is, and that therefore, essentially, the marriage is performed by the Registrar and not by the minister.

To this objection it is replied: 1. As above; the Act states the distinction between the two parts of the ceremony in the registered building, viz. the form contemplated, and the declaration prescribed; they are not one act. 2. The declarations necessary to be made in the presence of the Registrar are dictated to the parties by the minister and not by the Registrar, but only in his presence. 3. It might as well be said that the witnesses to the marriage perform the ceremony as that the Registrar does so, for the Act requires the declarations to be made in the presence of such Registrar and of two witnesses. The presence of the witnesses is as essential as the presence of a Registrar, but who would say that therefore they are parties performing the marriage? . . .

[*Paper appended*]

Question: What is the judgment of the Conference on the practice of celebrating Marriages in the Chapels of our Connexion?

Answer. 1. The Conference records its conviction that marriage is a Divine Institution, having the sanction of Holy Scripture as an honourable estate.

2. That, without pronouncing any opinion upon those marriages which, by the laws of our own or other countries, may be celebrated without the observance of religious ceremonies, the Conference expresses its decided conviction that, inasmuch as the marriage of members of the Church of Christ not only binds the contracting parties by their engagements to each other, but by the sanctions of the Word of God and their vows to Him, the forms of marriages should, at least in such cases,

always be accompanied by some religious observances, which may tend to explain and solemnly to impress upon the parties the duties of the marriage state; and that therefore the rite ought to be celebrated by a minister of the Gospel.

3. That the Act of 6 & 7 Wm. IV c.85 entitled 'An Act for Marriages in England' having provided for the celebration of marriages in chapels properly certified according to law as places of religious worship, and several of our own chapels having been registered for the purposes, the Conference expresses its regret that the Act has in some of its provisions a tendency to lessen the sanction of the Word of God to the Institution of Marriage as of Divine Appointment which before existed in this country, and now solemnly charges any of our ministers who may engage in the celebration of marriages in any of the chapels in our connexion to connect with the forms prescribed by the Act such religious solemnities of prayer and exhortation as shall tend to produce a sanctifying influence upon the hearts of the parties, and to remind them that the duties of their new state are solemnly and plainly imposed them by the Holy Scriptures.

255   From William Binning   [*King's*] *Lynn, February 13*, [*18*]*45* (*1*)

... [From Conference] I returned to my Circuit hoping that it would have a conciliatory effect on our disaffected members in reference to the Auxiliary Fund.[1] But to my grief I found them as sullen and obstinate as ever. The mischief lies in a great measure with the Leaders. In some of these cases I have succeeded in getting rid of the Leader, and in others have effected some improvement by dividing their classes; but I have one case that completely baffles me. It is our principal country place. Here we have seven Leaders and 120 members. Of these Leaders five are among the very worst in the circuit, one of the remaining two [is] in all things swayed by them, and the other by no means such as you can have much confidence in, as to regard for our laws etc. This too is the popular feeling of nearly the whole society, and of every one at all fit to make a Leader of. What, Mr. President, would you advise in this case?

On coming to this circuit I found things in general in a most discouraging position. No horse, hence many of the country places visited only when they could command a ride; for that ride they were dependent mainly on the men who were trampling our laws beneath their feet. A wreck of discipline as a natural consequence ensued. After a hard and resolute struggle I succeeded in getting a horse and the whole

[1] Cf. n. 2 p. 224 *supra.*

circuit has for a long time been regularly visited. Most of the chapels had been systematically allowed for Teetotal purposes. To get rid of this nuisance I had a desperate struggle, was traduced, calumniated, insulted, and threatened, for some days in fact seemed to be in danger of being pulled out of my house. After however three weeks ferment of this character, I received from their champion (on whom I had laid hold and from whom I had demanded a pledge of attention to our discipline for the future) the following document which I enclose [wanting], only requesting the favour of its being returned.

About this time I had an application from the same person, stating that my colleague had told him that some element should be provided to meet their scruples as to the wine-question, and to know whether anything of the kind had been done, or was in contemplation. I told him of course we had no authority to introduce any such element into the sacrament of the Lord's Supper nor could I sanction anything of the kind. After some time he and his party went (making a parade of it) and took it at the Ranters' Chapel, being accommodated as to their scruples. I advised with the Chairman on the affair, when it was thought best considering all things to pass the act by, hoping they would either see their folly in the business or take themselves away. They have however revived the question, applied to the Ranter Preachers to administer it to them in a private room of Theed's, and being refused, to the Association Preacher[1] who readily consented and gave it to them on Thursday evening last in the above place. Several of the parties concerned are Local Preachers and some of them Leaders also. The case is aggravated also from the circumstance that at that very time we were holding one of our special services, to which services they not only gave their consent but professed to be highly delighted that such [a] thing was contemplated. Now, Mr. President, what steps am I to take in this affair? And in case of decisive measures shall I be justified in exercising some delay from the circumstances that we have at this time a gracious revival of the work of God in the town, and in some country parts of the circuit. We have had some delightful seasons. Last Sunday was remarkably signal throughout. I preached from Hebs. 10. 38[2] and Ezekiel 9. 3–6.[3] I would just add that with this party Teetotalism is all and in all. Our interest may sink at any time for what they care, except in so far as

---

[1] The Wesleyan Methodist Association preacher at Lynn, 1844–46, was Thomas Vasey.

[2] 'Now the just shall live by faith; but if any man draw back, my soul shall have no pleasure in him.'

[3] The material portion of this passage reads: 'And the Lord said unto him, Go through the midst of the city . . . and set a mark upon the foreheads of the men that sigh and that cry for all the abominations that be done in the midst thereof. And to the others he said . . . Go ye after him through the city, and smite: let not your eye spare, neither have ye pity.'

their favourite object is promoted by their connection with us. They have what they call a Temperance Hall in the town. This place is licensed for religious purposes also, hence it is frequently open or occupied on the Sabbath, at the very time of our services, by some preaching woman or Teetotal lecturer etc. It is moreover greatly embarrassed, the consequence of which is there is almost perpetually for the sake of a penny some hubbub or other going on at it, to our most serious annoyance. . . .

Endorsed:– [To Wm. Binning]

Answered February 14, 1845. Advise firmness, faithful testimony, a little patient delay, warning, private reasoning with the members, gradual introduction of sound Leaders. If these fail, invite the Chairman or obtain a Deputation from the District Meeting to meet the Leaders, and strengthen his hands.

256 From William Binning   *[King's] Lynn, February 13, [18]45 (2)*

May I crave a little further indulgence? I wish to advert to two or three particulars which have an unfavourable influence in reference to the management of this perplexing circuit. One thing is, that hardly any of the men on whom I can depend are working men. Hence when any particular effort is required, I am thrown upon the very parties with whom I am so frequently necessitated to contend. Another thing is the conduct in neighbouring circuits as to Teetotal movements. In some of them, they have the pulpit, chapel etc. at will, and in one our School Room (at a country place) is actually let to them. The consequence is when I make my stand I am confronted with these things, and denounced as arbitrary. The want of a third preacher increases this difficulty. This lack unavoidably throws me upon the services of those men, who are more like an army of locusts in the circuit than anything else. Our Trustees here are able enough to bear the expense, but when they will be willing is another thing. Add to all this the perplexity I have to struggle with arising out of the oddities etc. of one whose name I need not mention. Our friends talk about another year, but really I hardly know how to think of encountering it, and everything like selfishness and party feeling I utterly abhor. I am heartily glad at the appearance of your resolutions on the question of Education. They will help me no little in the management of him on that point. . . .

257 From William Binning   [*King's*] *Lynn, March 4,* [*18*]*45 (1)*

Please accept my sincere thanks for the most valuable advice with which you were pleased to favour me. I availed myself of the first opportunity to apprise the parties of it, to advise with and warn them as to consequences in case of a repetition of anything of the kind.

In a little time I received a request, and then a second, for that part of your letter, after which I called upon Theed and told him I could do no such thing as give up the President's letter, nor was there any call for it, there being but one simple question which they could not but understand. The matter passed on till Thursday last when they had a large muster in Theed's Room, and yesterday I received the result, which you have in the enclosed document sent for your inspection and upon which I affectionately request your decision and advice.

To assist you in your deliberations I beg leave to make a few remarks respecting parties etc. As to Theed, he is a Baptist in principle, a systematic enemy to the Establishment, a demagogue in politics, and has been an agitator in Methodism for years. In the case of Warren, Stevens[1] and Forsyth, he used his utmost endeavours to get the agitators to Lynn, and in other ways to promote strife and division in the societies. The parties to whom he alludes are of the very stamp; the Leaders among them those who have given me endless trouble, and the local preachers (except one or two) such as I hardly know how to find any work for.

A word as to the aspect of things. When I had the former struggle the town was on a ferment; now he cannot get any movement that deserves the name of it. One and another are saying 'we have nothing to say for them now, Mr. Binning,' who bullied and blustered hard enough for them before.

Then as to our real friends, they are exceedingly rejoiced, and thank me most heartily, for what they are pleased to term the firm and judicious manner in which I have watched and struggled with this faction; urge me not to shrink, and beg me to intreat of the President, that his decision be such as to rid them of the mischiefs and that without delay.

As to the number that may leave in case of their expulsion it may perhaps considerably exceed what he states (our friends think not) but then it will only be such as stand in the way of all discipline, who annoy and insult you in the grossest manner, and who do very little for the support of the cause. They are pretty mute save the one cry 'Surely we are not to be expelled without a trial'. A prompt termination is requisite, as I must soon have a new Plan. . . .

[1] I.e. Joseph Rayner Stephens.

258   From William Binning   *[King's] Lynn, March 4, 1845 (2)*

You have of course received my second communication with the document containing the decision to which the offending parties have come. I enclose you another document which will furnish you with further information as to the character of those who will be separated from us in case of decisive measures, which now (from my very heart) I hope will be recommended. I find in fact they are fully calculating upon it themselves, and are telling the people of the forces they expect to number. The utmost that they hitherto speak of is 100. That calculation I should be inclined to think however applies to the town only. Then admitting they muster twice that number in the country (I know our friends expect nothing of the kind), my conviction is that it would be one of the happiest events that could befall us. From the greater part of them you get perhaps threepence per quarter, and scarcely one farthing for anything extra, but your full price of opposition and abuse.

Our friends become increasingly anxious every hour for a separation of the parties from us. . . .

259   From William Binning   *[King's] Lynn, March 8, 1845*

Be so kind as to excuse my further intrusion in this troublesome affair. I have to state that they have actually repeated the outrageous act, that they are talking loudly about being cut off, are canvassing in every direction for forces, but still give it as their opinion that we may be intimidated at the numbers whom *they say* are likely to think and to go with them. Our friends one and all say we have now gone too far for anything that would look like retreat, and that the sooner determinate measures are adopted the better. I think something that would strike off all the official parties concerned would (all things considered) best meet the case. It should not however on any account be a measure that would stop short of this.

Theed's class should have tickets on Tuesday next and by far the greater part of his members are among the offenders. Now, Mr. President, what would you advise me to do in this case? . . .

Endorsed:– [To] Rev. W. Binning, Lynn. Second Series. March 4th, 7th, and 8th 1845. Answer written March 15. *Sent* Mar. 17.

Should not have mentioned my letter to the parties. It was private and confidential, for *his own* guidance *only*. I have no power to decide officially. Before a judicial decision, I must 'hear both sides'. If a 'decision' must be had, the regular methods must first be adopted; viz.

Put the leading delinquents on their trial at the Leaders' Meeting (and if Trustees, the other Trustees must be summoned). Then proceed, according to Minutes of 1835. But, if possible, avoid this crisis for a time, and take the direction of the District Meeting in May, who might appoint a Deputation to Lynn. If delay cannot now be suffered, invite two or three senior Preachers with your Chairman to pay a *friendly* visit soon to Lynn, *or* come to London, and take counsel *here* etc. etc. etc.

260   From James Allen[1]   *Hungerford, March 5, 1845*

Very dear Sir,

The subject of '*Teetotalism*,' so called, is rather vexatiously advocated in this town by a few of our friends, one of whom is rather an influential Leader of our society.

A grand festivity, connected with this cause, is to be held here, on Easter Tuesday; and, in connexion with that occasion, I have been applied to, for the loan of our chapel, in which, the parties applying wish to have a sermon preached in the afternoon to the body of the Teetotallers, *as such*: but, recollecting the fact, that at the Conference of 1841 – at which I myself was not present – resolutions were passed on the subject of Tee-totalism, one of which, I have heard forbids the use of Trust Property for Tee-total meetings, I have declined giving my consent to the parties so applying.

I think it probable, that this refusal may give me some trouble; indeed, already considerable obloquy has been cast upon me, on that account; and, wishing to know the precise grounds on which I stand, so far as the regulations of the Conference are concerned, I wrote to Mr. Barton, as the Journal Secretary, begging the favour of a transcript of the resolutions of 1841, on this subject. He kindly and promptly replied by stating, that he had not the Journal in his possession, and by telling me what the specific points are, to which the resolutions refer. Still feeling uneasy, I wrote to Mr. Mason, begging him, as the possessor of the Journal, to furnish me with a transcript of the resolutions and this morning I received his reply, which is, in substance, as follows:– that he cannot give me the extract from the Journal which I wish, without your consent; that the Conference never intended such resolutions to be made public, otherwise they would have been published in the Minutes, and that, the better way would be for me to state the case to you, and to solicit your advice . . .

In reference to my having a copy of the said resolutions, I am sure you

[1] James Allen [2nd], superintendent, Hungerford circuit, 1844–46.

will kindly excuse my asking, as I do so most respectfully, whether, when resolutions are taken by the Conference, which are not to be published, but only recorded on the Journal, resolutions which, nevertheless, are to control the Preachers in the administration of circuit affairs, it would not be well for those resolutions to be sent to them in the form of a Circular, with the understanding, that they were to be kept secretly, unless circumstances like those in which I think I am placed, should render the opposite course necessary. For I humbly venture to say, that it seems to me to be a hardship, that ministers should be expected to act – frequently in difficult circumstances – conformably to certain resolutions, without those resolutions being fairly and verbatim in their possession. . . .

Enclosed. [To J. Allen. n. pl. March 17, 1845.]

You should not require, nor I give, 'a Copy' of the Resolution specified. You admit that you already know the *purpose and substance* of it; and the Teetotallers have made it notorious by their publications, that the Conference deliberately disapproves of the use of our chapels for assemblies of Tee-totallers *as such.* There were *kind* and prudent reasons for not publishing the Resolution of 1841 in the Minutes. A 'Circular' would soon have become *as* public and as dangerous to peace. The Superintendents have by our *established Rules* the right and responsibility of interfering to prevent the lending of our chapels, even for a good cause, to persons over whose teaching and talking we can have no control, and some of whom have abused the privilege as an occasion for most considerable vituperation and extravagance. Our people are divided as to the *mode* of carrying out the system; and we have no right to give our chapels as the arena or battle-field to one class of the combatants against the other.

The *only* and proper uses for which chapels were built, and the *only* persons who have *legal* authority to use them for those purposes, are sufficiently stated in 'The Model Deed,' page 33. A Superintendent guided by the legal provisions of that Deed, needs no other Document to support him.

This Letter is
Private and Confidential.

261   To George Osborn   *London, May 28, 1845*

I have been very ill of severe bronchitis for the last three weeks; and though, since Monday, improving, am yet nearly a prisoner in my own house, and ordered not to converse on business with more than one

z

person in any one day. I am in fact unfit for all business; and *cannot* at present attend to it. . . .

I now see no objection to an Anti-Maynooth Petition to the Lords from Didsbury [College]. The business is hopeless, unless Providence signally interpose. But it is important, that the *protest* against the abandonment of what is left of our National Protestantism should be as *marked* and *extensive* as possible. This will make the sin in some sense, perhaps, *rather less national.* . . .

262 From Frederick J. Jobson[1]   *Leeds, June 19, 1845*

. . . We are very busy, as you will suppose, in making Conference arrangements. There are about 500 Ministers, who have leave to attend. This is a less number than we anticipated from the central situation of Leeds. You will have received the Conference Plan. Some of us have had considerable difficulty in obtaining an appointment upon the printed plan for Mr. Stanley, it being urged by some of his friends that as he is likely to be chosen as the President,[2] it would not be courteous to appoint him to preach. The objections, however, were at length overcome, as you will perceive by the alteration in the plan. Mr. A.[3] is increasingly spoken of in this neighbourhood; but it would seem to me that his election will be doubtful. There are many I think that will sacrifice principle to feeling; and on the ground that he is the more kind and gentlemanly colleague, etc. vote for Mr. S. Should this be the case, it will be a bad omen, for if the Ministers do not support and honour principle we cannot expect the people to do so. I wish there had been someone entirely free from the objections urged by several of the Elders against Mr. A., to be placed before the coming Conference. That would really have tested the principles of the Ministers, but it seems there is not. As a looker-on (for I am yet in my minority), I should like to see Mr. A. in the chair. He is now a very respectable and worthy man, and would be safe in a crisis, but there are *many* that think 'there are six of one and half a dozen of the other', in this respect, and I fear that partiality will be on the side of Mr. S. There is one circumstance in favour of Mr. A. he is better known in the Northern District than in the Southern, and there will be more Ministers from Manchester, Liverpool, Sheffield, Leeds and York, than from Bristol and its neighbourhood.

[1] Frederick J. Jobson (1812–81), preacher, Leeds (Brunswick) circuit, 1843–36; one of the younger preachers personally closest to Bunting.

[2] Jacob Stanley was elected President at the Conference of 1845.

[3] William Atherton, who succeeded as President in 1846.

You will smile at my writing so many words on this matter; but I am grieved to find so great a defect as to Methodist principle. . . .

The District Meeting was a pleasant one, but we had a decrease of members. This decrease led to a discussion (which I think would be beneficial) on the reaction of American-like efforts to obtain a revival. Mr. Caughey has just commenced his operations at York, where he will probably remain for some months. He was something like 5 months in Huddersfield. Something must be done to prevent the use of one pulpit by one preacher; and he a stranger, for so long a period. . . .

263 From Robert Young[1] *Truro, October 2, 1845*

. . . The discipline [of this circuit] is . . . in a very unsatisfactory state. The average system which has been acted upon in this Circuit and District is full of evil. By the arrangements of the Quarterly Meeting, Societies have had to pay from 1/1 to 2/- per member, *including Quarterly Collections*, and in some cases *grants from Trustees*, and our Rule respecting *weekly* and *quarterly* contributions, [has been] not only neglected but in many cases altogether unknown. And when the Society has increased the average per member has usually been reduced. Nor is this all – but persons have been put out of the Society by the Leaders when they became too poor to assist in making up the required sum. Several such cases have I met with already, and one class Leader had actually crossed the name of his own *pious mother* out of his book, because [she was] too poor to give anything, and the removal of her name would save the Society 1/1 per quarter. Contributions have in many cases been divested of their religious character, and been regarded as mere matters of business; and the Steward who at the arrangement of the averages could drive the hardest bargain was considered by the Society to which he belonged a first-rate steward. . . .

264 From Frederick J. Jobson to [T. P. Bunting]

Leeds, November 1, 1845

. . . We have had Dr. Pusey here all the week, heading the popish services at the newly opened Church.[2] The doings have been offensive to

[1] Robert Young, superintendent, Truro circuit, 1845–48.

[2] St. Savour's, Leeds, built by the private generosity of Pusey, acting nominally for a penitent friend, was consecrated on SS. Simon and Jude's Day (October 28) 1845; during the octave of consecration twenty sermons were preached.

Protestants. I dare say that under one form or another you might count 150 crosses in the church. The altar is in a gloomy chancel screened off with rich oaken tracery from the other parts of the church. It stands on three steps, covered with a blue cloth adorned with crosses, and on it lighted candles. Into the chancel none but the priests go; and they bow before it, as they pass. They have preached (in their surplices) the most mystified stuff imaginable, all on penitence. Within the western door on a large gilt scroll is written 'whoever enters this holy place, pray for the sinner who built it'. And I suppose as the name of the sinner is withheld that scroll will remain, and its inscription, when he shall have gone into purgatory. . . .

265   From Alfred Barrett[1]   *n. pl. or d.* [*October–November 1845*]

Knowing the deep interest which you take in that great scheme for promoting union among Christian brethren which was originated at the Liverpool Conference, I am emboldened to intrude a little upon your time by presenting a few thoughts of my own in reference to this proposed Evangelical Alliance.[2] Being only a junior member of the Committee I do this with great deference, and indeed if communications to the Sub-Committee last formed at Liverpool of which you are a member had not been invited, I should not presume to do it at all. I feel deeply interested in the character and object of this religious movement, and perhaps you will allow that those points in a public question which greatly stir and affect one's mind may claim some attention, though not so much as may be claimed for the suggestions of experience or the decisions of wisdom. And first I will take the liberty to say a little respecting the ultimate constitution or organization of the Alliance. To save your time and my own I will write freely and frankly, and if any expression should escape my pen which is inconsistent with the respect which is due to fathers and brethren or with that divine charity the increase of which we all need, I beg you to attribute it to ignorance, or haste, or anything but a deliberate purpose to commit such a fault.

I will not stand to eulogize the movement; the adhesion of so many of the wisest and holiest men of the present age is eulogy enough. And

---

[1] Alfred Barrett (1808–76), preacher, London (Islington) circuit, 1843–46; one of the principal theorists of the ministry, his *Essay on the pastoral office as a divine institution in the Church of Christ* (1839), *Catholic and evangelical principles* (1842), and *Ministry and polity of the Christian church* (1854) becoming standard texts in Methodist seminaries. He became Governor of Richmond College, 1858–67. Subject to depressive illnesses.

[2] The basis for the Evangelical Alliance was laid at a great meeting at Liverpool in October 1845, clearly just prior to the writing of this letter.

as the object of it must unquestionably be pleasing to God, we must seek to promote it by means which are in harmony with his revealed will.

The thoughts of some amongst us veer towards a sort of Annual Convention which, as far as I can understand, shall involve in connexion with its yearly assembling some matters of minor-convocational inter-course all the year through, but still without any further designation of individuals than what arises out of their voluntary adhesion to the doctrinal basis. This I think objectionable for the following reasons. 1. It does not afford sufficient security for the simplicity, piety and heartiness of the members to be admitted. The basis would not exclude nominal and worldly-minded Christians. Whatever movement in society carries influence and power with it, is watched with great interest by *all* parties and with especial jealousy by *some* of them; and painful experience shews that men will connect themselves with such a movement for the sake of appropriating or diverting its power, who have no sympathy with its pure and simple objects. I should urge this objection *a fortiori* against those who say that no other test of membership is necessary than a mere willingness to attend the religious and prayerful proceedings of the several Committees and appointments of the Alliance. We know many who would tolerate prayer and singing the high praises of God, in order to throw their weight into the scale of their own purposes, who personally care but little for either of these sacred exercises. Association in all its various forms is the order of the day, and men speculate about its probable acts and results as they do about the rise and fall of stocks; and they not only watch it, but in a thousand ways seek to mould and affect it. 2d. Because in such a proposal, the vinculum of the Alliance would chiefly lie in the annual gathering of distinguished Christians and Christian ministers from all parts of the world; and thereby the union would not be intelligent, awake and close enough. We have tried this at our Annual Missionary Meetings for years past with only very partial success. The generous excitement of susceptible minds in a great meeting leads to an expression of mutual charity and love which is not afterwards realized. Men then speak of something which is to be done by man, though it seldom is done, instead of going to the New Testament to learn in what position the whole of what we want is to be effected in us by God. Unless we had sinned against each other and the Head of the Church we had not been in our present position; and we must therefore come to closer quarters with each other, and know how or why this is; and nothing is so likely to cast light upon our whole position, as the mutual confession of our sin before God, in each other's hearing, and the mutual revelation of our heart's desires. The Alliance must be so organized as to afford scope for this, or else we hardly touch our main evil and take but a feeble step towards our desired good. And 3rdly. Because if the efficiency of the Alliance be made chiefly to depend on an Annual Meeting and public speaking, there will not be that *constant* exhibition to the world of Christian unity which we desire, and New Testament charity will not be brought out into that active and practical form in which it labours and stirs to bring others in the same street, village, town or country under its own benign influence. Though an annual meeting or something like it may no doubt be held, yet I would fain hope the Evangelical Alliance would grow so large that no single meeting could properly represent it. We want something which will shew, not only for a week in May, but during every day in the year, what the world has doubted and Popery has denied, that 'we are all one in Christ Jesus'. And we ought in connexion with it to have some simple machinery at hand, by which a fellow Christian, or any number of fellow Christians could be attached, not only nominally and formally, but practically and really into its entire working – could be brought to make confession to God, to hear and join in prayer, and to pant with us for living union. Unless we go as far as this, we do not, as far as the setting up of a great and impressive union is concerned, make any advance beyond *a* Missionary or *the* Bible Society.

Others, Dear Sir, there are among us who think that the growth and expansion of the Alliance might be left to the working of the Divisional Committees; that is, that new members should be nominated by an individual or more, and accepted by a majority – and that in nominating no other respect shall be had than to the generally correct life of the nominee and to his professed correspondence with us of belief. This plan I think is open to the objection already mentioned, of affording no security for the truly religious and sincere design of the adherent, inasmuch as private friendship might commit a fault and the Committee not be able to discover it. And besides this, as persons of various views and feelings could hardly be excluded in such a mode of administration, and therefore not even collisions between worldly and spiritual principles, it would require a cumbrous system of polity, with a strict subordination of offices, privileges and rights to keep up the integrity and united action of the whole; degrees of authority would have to be minutely detailed, and a worldly organization would have to be imitated.

It is far easier to mention objections than to shew how they may be obviated, and I am far from being insensible to the difficulties which in the present state of things attend the formation of an Evangelical Alliance which shall be really an Alliance and really evangelical; but these objections which present themselves lead me to ask, is there no scriptural principle by which we may be guided here? In a case where difficulty presses and that difficulty arises out of our own sins, is it not better and simpler to betake ourselves to a plan owned by our Divine Master, or at least to go as far as possible in that direction, and leave all the consequences with Him? And in that case shall we not find an organization to our hands? In plain words is there any valid reason why the Evangelical Alliance should not adopt denominational communion – the participation of the Lord's Supper according to the mode of the Christian body to which the applicant belongs – as the test *sine quâ non* of membership? We have already acknowledged the 'authority and perpetuity of the ordinance' in the doctrinal basis; and if all this be acknowledged in the abstract, we can hardly shrink from this particular application of the case. We can hardly help seeking for our principle of guidance by appealing to the mind of the great Authorizer on the subject. I may not exactly like the mode in which a Christian brother observes the sacrament or ordinance in question, and may disapprove of certain conventional opinions which it is made in his case to satisfy and seal; but the very fact of his being a communicant in his own body, gives me the highest proof that I can have of his religious sincerity and allegiance to Christ. It is the fact itself which I want, and not his own minute and ultra exposition of it. I adhere I honestly confess to the theory of my friend the Revd. W. M. Bunting which is so happily expressed in his own lines,

> I count each church – its symbols, songs,
> Communion, Elders – mine;
> To all in my charm'd sight, belongs
> Th' identity divine.

But I would not require the Evangelical Alliance at present to acknowledge this theory, especially as one of the fundamental resolutions of the Liverpool Conference has made it inconvenient to do so. I would say, Leave me to my own inference as to whether each *community*, as such, is a member of the body of Christ, but do let me see the individual with whom I am to work, and whom I am to acknowledge as a brother in Christ, subscribe with his hand unto the Lord; that is, acknowledge Christ in Christ's own way. It may be said, that there are many sincere and devout persons of evangelical views who are neither baptized nor do they communicate; but I should say that compared with the great mass of professing Christians holding the truths of the basis who long for union, they are so small, so very small, a proportion, that it would be most unreasonable to suppose that a great, prospective and comprehensive scheme like ours, could legislate for their convenience. On this point history and past divine providence should be consulted; I would not look upon history with the eye of a traditionist or Tractarian, but I would enquire, How many there have been in all ages who, when Christ was faithfully preached and discipline tolerably well administered, believed in Him and yet confessed him not, neither in the initial nor the confirmative ordinance? It is not in our power to ascertain whether an individual be or be not regenerate, nor is the actual attainment of regeneration an absolute requisite for membership with us, any more than it is a necessary requisite for Church membership: but such is the union which Christ pleads for in the 17th of John – so spiritual, so like that of the Father and the Son, and which union we all understand the Alliance seeks – that professing brethren must at least exhibit their *hope* and *purpose* of attaining spiritual life; and unless there were a board of religious examination (a thing by the way it would be impossible to constitute) how could this be exhibited but by denominational communion? There might be a system of registration in connexion with this under the direction of divisional and sub-divisional committees, but I should humbly plead for this New Testament mode of recognition as a main feature in the constitution of individual membership – the communion of the Lord's Supper.

A word in the next place with reference to the basis. It is a matter of devout thankfulness to God that, on such a matter of great delicacy and difficulty, the Liverpool Conference was enabled to come to an unanimous agreement. To undo a work that was done under such a blessed influence and with such a manifest divine sanction, would it appears to me be impious. I take it for granted that on no account could it be proposed to *lessen* the number of articles, by taking any one of them away. That would be to go back again. Unity is nothing in our case, unless it be unity in the truth. It would be ungrateful – a strange undervaluing of the blessing which God has given. And as to the minuter exposition of its articles, in order to take a step in advance, this is too serious a matter to be done lightly; and, considering the present state of men's minds, if to any extent it were proposed at present would I think be premature. If we attempt to find words to harmonize the evangelical Calvinist and the evangelical Arminian, we shall no doubt produce in both a nervousness of apprehension and a fastidiousness of criticism, which will tell unfavourably for our main purpose; as well as awaken an incipient repulsion between the presbyterian and congregationalist, and between episcopalian and both. I quite hope that mutual intercourse and prayer will work amazing changes as to the holding minuter shades of opinion. I am sure it has been so with regard to myself. I am sure that, holding as I do the sentiments of evangelical Arminianism, I have been delighted in intercourse with Calvinist brethren to find in them an approximation to my own views which I did not previously suspect, and in some instances a use of scripture phraseology which was juster and more emphatic that that to which I had been accustomed. But in this way I think the matter must work; we must pray and converse together *without* proposing any minuter exposition of doctrine; we must sit and feast together *without the fear* inspired by having a sword over our heads. We must acquire the *real* approximation, the *real* minuter unity, and then symbolize after.

With regard to the practical objects of the Alliance, I think the formation of the Evangelical Alliance itself is a practical object, and involves in itself every other which a Christian ought to seek. If it were to be formally and specially an Anti-Popish confederation, I fear it would be difficult to keep it free from the distraction and excitement of merely secular politics, and that it would be in great danger of being spoiled as to its religious character by merely secular men, who would have no objection for the sake of minor ends, yea would desire to be, anti-Popish. I fear that it would call up a party on the other side in self-defence, and that a strife which ought to be sacred would have too much the appearance of faction. The Evangelical Alliance might and I think at the same time ought so far to operate upon the nation in its social and political condition as to use its influence to secure the return to Parliament of *Evangelical men* – men who fear God and obey in form at least the gospel of our Lord Jesus Christ, men who will oppose not only the legislative sanction of Popery, but of infidelity, Sabbath-breaking, wickedness, and every form of oppression whether it be civil or ecclesiastical. I would not give up the Anti-, the *aggressive*, character of the movement but I would have it move against more evils than one. Then no worldly faction can be formed in opposition; then God's own witnesses stand arrayed in God's own panoply against error. But I should lay the most stress upon the enlargment and expansion of the Evangelical Alliance itself. Let us get into the position assigned to us by Christ, and we need not be anxious as to what we shall do. When we are right, Christ will work by us in *His* own way and not a way of our devising. Then the world will know that the Father hath sent Him. Let us secure the adhesion of the established-clergy and we protect their fidelity and deprive Tractarianism of its harvests; let us gain the non-conformist ministry and their minds will be no longer embittered by exclusivism; let us gain the Christian laity and we deepen their interest in the ordinances and ministry of the gospel; let us call forth an enthusiastic loyalty to the throne of Christ our Lord, and Popery will be more dismayed than even by an adverse bill in Parliament; let us call forth the meekness and gentleness of Christ, bring all into our own desired position of humiliation before God, and then we bring down upon us that peace and energy which are ever promised to revive 'the spirit of the contrite ones'. More will be done, I think, in this way than would be done by those who were otherwise strong in the battle or swift in the race.

The Liverpool Conference no doubt had a good meaning when it resolved that no compromise of individual opinion should be required of its members. But assuredly this is not so to be understood as that, if an Evangelical Alliance is to be formed, nothing whatever of individual predilection, prejudice or liking is to be given up. Is every view that we hold to be as solemn and as tenaciously held as that we are justified before God by faith in Christ alone? Did St. Paul the Apostle act on this principle in his intercourse with Jews and Gentiles? If there be no compromise I apprehend there must be concession, or there can be no alliance. Clergymen must so far concede as to meet their nonconforming brethren in mutual worship, in neutral places, where they can incur no canonical or episcopal censure; anti-establishment men must lay down their exasperated hostility of manner in stating their convictions; persons separated by a past breach must exhibit their concession in burying the memory of it in oblivion, reviving its disputes no more, and all must concede to each other, as far as may consistently be done in connexion with fidelty to the Lord. In all this, I think the Evangelical Alliance would find its noblest and most efficient course of action.

Dear Sir I have done. . . .

266   From James Kendall[1]   *Chesterfield, January 5, 1846*

. . . A long conversation with Doctor Newton last Friday has convinced me that the Conference must *legislate* in reference to American innovations.[2]

The Chairman of our District, Mr. Farrar,[3] has published plans for special services, doubtless with the very best intentions, but I see *danger* in all this.

A class of men exists among us who if not efficiently superintended

---

[1] James Kendall, preacher, Chesterfield circuit, 1844–46.

[2] Kendall had just written to Bunting to exert his influence with 'the editors of the *Watchman* to insert a letter I have just written concerning Chesterfield circuit and Mr. Caughey'. M.C.A. MSS. James Kendall to Jabez Bunting, December 16, 1845.

[3] Abraham E. Farrar, superintendent, Sheffield (Carver St.) circuit, 1845–48.

will soon bring the *regularly instituted ordinances of God* into utter contempt. These men are always boasting of their doings and making little or nothing of sound and wholesome preaching – and in spite of the fearful declensions taking place in certain circuits which some time since were made red hot with the *ism* – go on in their own ways, no man forbidding them.

I glory in real revivals of experimental and *practical* Christianity, but I abhor self-sufficiency and absurdity.

True it is that at present we have a large increase in Chesterfield, and equally true that my Superintendent and myself have worked hard as well as others to realize this increase. But how things will stand this day three months, or 6 months, we cannot say. I love prosperity, but I do *not* love the practical resignation of pastoral authority.

O how frequently do I long and sigh for the orderly and solemn services of *London* Methodism! ⟨Bu⟩t I must be content to let people do as they like – for this is the present fashion in these parts. . . .

267 From J. C. Leppington[1]   *Liverpool, May 25, 1846*

I am very reluctant to intrude on you, but my concern for the credit of religion and the welfare of Methodism, involved in the proceedings of Mr. Caughey, compels me to do so. Mr. Hetherington[2] from Canada has been breakfasting with me this morning and has suggested what appears to me the most ready way of getting rid of him, if indeed we can get rid of him at all, after the influence he has acquired in this country and the indifference he has shewn to what passed at the last Conference! Mr. H. suggests that some influential or authorized party should write to his Bishop in America, and request his immediate recall on the ground that his longer stay in this country was likely to be injurious rather than beneficial, and not unlikely ultimately to endanger the peace and unity of our body. He thinks his Bishop's name is *Waugh*[3] – a plain, straight-

---

[1] John Crosby Leppington (1807–59), preacher, Liverpool (South) circuit, 1845–47. For similar complaints cf. M.C.A. MSS. James Beckwith to Jabez Bunting, July 6, 1846.

[2] J. P. Hetherington served with the Missionary Committee 1845–46, after being stationed in Canadian circuits, 1828–45. D. 1861, aet. 60.

[3] Beverley Waugh (1789–1858), principal Book Agent of Methodist Episcopal Church, 1832; elected bishop, 1836, and remained with the northern Methodist Church after the secession of the South in 1844. At the Conference of 1846, Bunting moved and carried a resolution that the American bishops be requested to recall Caughey, but the following year it was still necessary to have a Conference Committee on his case, which drew attention to 'a rule of 1797 prohibiting our pulpits to preachers from America who are not duly authorized'. Gregory, *Sidelights* pp. 401, 419.

forward man, and one of the most worthy of the American Bishops – and that he would instantly recall him. Should Mr. Caughey, in that case, decline to return, he would lose his connexion with the American body, and the sanction which that connexion gives him in this country. In his own mind Mr. Hetherington ascribes his own illness *primarily* to the disturbance of mind produced by Mr. C.'s proceedings in Montreal. Mr. Lusher[1] and Mr. H. were travelling in that city. In ten years Methodism had advanced from 60 members and 1 chapel to 800 members and 3 chapels, and perhaps the chief denominational influence in the place. The Society was peaceable, docile and attached to its ministers. Mr. C. paid a visit to a friend, was invited by Mr. Lusher to preach on one occasion, announced that he would preach the following evening, called (publickly) on Mr. L. and Mr. H. to assist him in his prayer meetings which they declined to do, proceeded in his course for about ten days, but not succeeding to his mind, called together the Trustees, Leaders, etc., and told them that nothing could be done if the resident ministers stood aloof. (He had previously denounced them, indirectly but intelligibly, in public). On this they were waited on, and urged, for the sake of the peace of the Society, already endangered, to countenance the proceedings, at least by their presence. This they unwillingly, in the emergency, consented to do. Mr. H. heard him almost constantly for a period of nine weeks; and assigns as one reason for hearing him so much, the necessity of being present to hear what he would 'say about *them*', that if necessary they might refute it. On leaving Montreal, he obtained about £300 to assist him to visit Europe. It would seem that Montreal was the beginning of his wanderings, and perhaps his success here encouraged him to visit Europe. Mr. H. was so unhappy that he declined a third year's station; and Mr. Lusher whom these proceedings found unwell, became a supernumerary at the next Conference.

Amongst other things Mr. Hetherington expresses his surprise that Mr. C. should produce so much *effect* in this country. He did not produce so much in America where these proceedings are more common. Religion, Mr. H. says, is so generally low (that is in true experience) in the States, that these extraordinary proceedings are necessary at intervals to impart even the appearance of life; that there are many such parties there as Mr. C. and many more able and striking than himself even in his own way; that the same people are converted again and again; and that if all the announced conversions could be found, the entire population of the States, would be converted in four years; that they proceed at intervals to this 'converting' work, as deliberately and

[1] Robert L. Lusher, preacher at Montreal, 1837–40, and Quebec, 1840–41. D. 1841, aet. 61.

mechanically, as a builder to raise a house: and nowhere is true and fervent and established piety more scarce, than where these proceedings are most frequent. I must add the following case. In Montreal, Mr. C. had preached from 'This year thou shalt die'. He was subsequently informed by letter supported by the testimony of a female that on the previous Sabbath a young man had been awakened; on Tuesday he was converted; on Thursday he died; and on Saturday was buried. Mr. Lusher and Mr. H. doubting this, went to all the cemeteries but could not ascertain that any such person had been buried. They told Mr. C. and warned him (for he was making public use of the letter) lest the whole should prove a fabrication. Mr. C. was not pleased, but shortly after pointed out to Mr. H. the woman who had given him the information. It turned out that the woman was one of bad character (a prostitute) and had been bribed by some young men to convey this letter; and to give confidence to her statement had been in the religious meetings and even to 'class'! It was in a *class* that she was found, previous to her interrogation! The above particulars I give just as they were given to me in the freedom of table talk and with some intimation that they were confidential, though not entirely so; and I must therefore beg that Mr. H's name may not be connected with them in any way that could make him responsible without his own consent. . . .

268 From Benjamin Sadler   *Myton Circuit, Nr. Warwick,*
July 13, 1846

I am unwilling to intrude upon you knowing that your time must be greatly occupied at this season of the year, I will not in consequence request your immediate reply, which I shall however be glad to receive at your leisure. . . .

The great evil to be apprehended here is the combination of Local Preachers acting together and ruling the Quarterly Meetings; there has been something approaching to faction here from this body and I believe other circuits are injured in the same way.

One of their body (who offered himself to travel a few years ago but was rejected by the District Meeting) is the agent for a lying paper called the 'Wesleyan' which is circulated and read by the Local Preachers. This man has lately been the mouthpiece for every grievance at the Quarterly Meetings, and, as they all attend these Meetings, they have the power to rule on all occasions. My object in writing to you on the present occasion is to ask you who have properly a right to attend these meetings, I have always understood a Quarterly Meeting to be constituted as follows

> The Stewards of the Circuit
> The Stewards of the Circuit Town
> one or two representatives from each Country Society

Am I right in supposing that neither Local Preachers nor Leaders *have a right* to be there[1] . . .

269   From John Partis Haswell[2]   *Bristol, August 10, 1846*

As the President overruled my speaking this evening on the subject of your letter to the Bishop of the Troy Conference[3] I beg as some relief to my much oppressed mind to state my reasons against the proposition:

1st. It does that by a side wind which, if right, ought to have been done by a direct vote of the Conference – it is too superficial not to be seen through by our people.

2d. Mr. Caughey has appeared to me to have been a messenger from God to recall us as a Church to the spirit and self devotedness of our Fathers.

3d. The amazing, unprecedented success of his ministry has already stirred up many both ministers and people to an earnestness not felt before, and in this respect the advantages of his visit will remain when he is gone.

4th. We have a painfully small increase of numbers – but what would it have been had not the *2199 increase* in the four Districts in which he has laboured been taken into the account? For 8 years previous to Mr. Caughey's visit, Sheffield had annually gone down so that the Society was *500* less than 8 years before.

5. Mr. Caughey has stimulated our members to support our ministry in a way they had not done before notwithstanding Stewards and preachers had exerted their utmost influence.

6. The misrepresentations and gross falsehoods which have gone forth respecting Mr. C. have never been exceeded, except in those which have gone forth respecting yourself.

From these considerations I could not but vote against your resolution – and deprecate hasty legislation on a subject so intimately connected with our spiritual interests as a body. Your wisdom could

---

[1] Cf. n. 2 p. 115 *supra.*

[2] John Partis Haswell (1790–1870), superintendent, Exeter circuit, 1845–48.

[3] For the recall of Caughey, see n. 3 p. 339 *supra.*

easily have devised a way by which his piety and talents might have been secured to us in this time of need. My fear is that we shall grieve the Spirit of God by putting away a providential blessing and that our next year's labour, while even humbling ourselves, may have a blight upon it.

Good Father Reece[1] must not flatter us into the idea that we are all revivalists, nor my esteemed friend Scott[2] administer to us the comfort that we are all 'as God made us'. Alas, alas, do one half of us manifest a burning Charity [?]

270   From John Wesley Thomas[3]   *Poole, August 20, 1846*

I venture to address you on a subject connected with the proposed Evangelical Alliance, although I can scarcely doubt that it is one which has already engaged your attention. I beg to premise, however, that in the object and principles of the Alliance I cordially agree, and in its success I take a lively interest; nor am I unaware of those difficulties with which it must have to struggle. My design in writing is to draw your attention (if not already drawn) to a point in which I think the welfare and usefulness of the Alliance concerned, and with a further view to my *being enabled to join it*. Hitherto I have been hindered by what I conceive to be a *defect* or *omission*, which perhaps was unintentional, and which I hope may yet be supplied. I allude to the printed Resolutions of the Conference of the proposed alliance, held in Liverpool on the 1st 2nd and 3d of October last. In the 3d Resolution, the 'matters of Doctrine' – 8 in number – expected to be held by the members of the Alliance are such as will effectually, and very properly, exclude *Romanists, Pelagians, Unitarians* and *Quakers*. But I find nothing in those eight articles that will exclude *Antinomians* from the Alliance! Am I to give the right hand of fellowship to those who teach the flesh-pleasing doctrine, that under the Covenant of Grace, faith is the only duty; that sin can do the believer no harm, nay, that it will promote his real welfare and happiness? Yet in more than one or two instances, my lot has been cast in the neighbourhood of such as have been in the habit of preaching this doctrine to mankind. And if it is less rife at present than in the days of Wesley and Fletcher, if the tendency of the Church is even in the opposite direction, it is hardly necessary for me to remind you, that mankind are apt to go from one extreme to the other, *and then back*

---

[1] Richard Reece, supernumerary, London (Great Queen St.) circuit.
[2] John Scott, superintendent, London (Spitalfield) circuit, 1846–48.
[3] John Wesley Thomas, superintendent, Poole circuit, 1845–47.

again, and that institutions are not for today only, but for *all time*. I can scarcely think that any truly evangelical minister would object to the insertion, in any document that is to form a doctrinal basis, of some clause by which *the obligation of the moral law on the consciences of believers* shall be asserted. To me, the distinct recognition by the Alliance of Christ's *kingly authority* and the universal obligation of his *commands* appears not only a necessary *precaution* against the future inroads of Antinomian error, and an important present *testimony* to the Truth, but also as indispensable to the *character* of the proposed Alliance. . . .

271   From Thomas Waugh[1]   *Bandon, December 28, 1846*

I lose not a moment in replying to your kind, very kind and considerate, communication. As to our general condition, you can hardly conceive the state of this wretched judgement-stricken land. A dense population of paupers, possessed each family of its little hoard of potatoes, [which] was used to lounge the winter away with very little employment, and little caring to be employed as being secure of the means of mere subsistence, has at once had its whole dependence swept away, and starves by thousands. After a world of ignorant bungling, work, such as it is, is supplied to very many, but provisions are gone beyond the reach of their means, and the scenes we are hourly called to witness are heart-rending. Government as such has done nothing or worse than nothing. The sad refusal to interfere with trade as they call it, has thrown us on the tender mercies of a few leading corn dealers, who so employ their wealth and wit, that our markets are just fed so far as that prices cannot fall. Indian corn that ought it is said to be had, bearing a sufficient profit at seven or eight pounds a ton, [is] paying seventeen. Depots ought to have been formed to open on prices becoming ruinously high, which would as in the last year have prevented a world of suffering. God only knows where it will end! The distress is, less or more, felt by all classes, but chiefly by labourers, and very small farmers. An Englishman can hardly understand how the potato was everything to these masses. It fed parents and children, pigs and fowls, on which every little extra comfort depended – its destruction has left them destitute of all. The suffering of last year was partial – now it is universal. Last season committees were formed under the sanction of the Lord Lieutenants of counties and Government. They were generally well chosen and efficient. This year they were called into operation again and set to work, but one of the sudden whims, so frequent and mis-

[1] Thomas Waugh, stationed at Bandon, 1846–49.

chievous among our rulers, led to an order for contracting to a very few each Relief Committee, discharging all ministers save those of the Establishment, Roman Catholic, and Presbyterian, one of each. We had raised a considerable sum by subscription, and employed it [for] the purchase of meal sold at the market price when that was reasonable, and under when prices rose, and thus placed the means of subsistence within reach of the poor. After having covered expenses and losses we had a sum of £600 left, which was handed over to the new committee, they and we believing that an equal sum would be granted by the Government to enable them to continue the plan of relief. However, after the lapse of many weeks during which nothing was done the old committee was called together again and the balance restored. I refused to have anything further to do with it, being thoroughly disgusted with what had taken place – but today I have been so earnestly solicited to take part in the management again that I purpose looking in on the Committee tomorrow. Will you forgive all this rambling which adds little to the information you already have from many quarters, and I will proceed to your queries.

1. I believe there are many cases in which our own poor suffer severely. All trade is injured save that in provisions, the prices of which having become so exorbitant must cause distress. I have had several sad communications from the country parts, but although cases of great affliction do exist, yet among God-fearing people the instances bear no proportion to those among a different class.

2. I know personally very few who take advantage of the public works, but our labouring poor would have a fair share of such employment, if sought after.

3. None of the monies you refer to have reached these parts, so far as I know. I dare say the machinery of the Committees is not fully arranged. Whether it will be sent to the relief Committees, or how disposed of I cannot say. From what I have said, I think none of our ministers and, I fear, few if any of our people are on the Government-appointed Relief Committees. In meeting cases of distress, however, I do hope there will not be much respect of parties or persons.

4. I am sure there is not a circuit in the Kingdom in which there are not special and extraordinary instances where relief is loudly called for, and could be well bestowed.

5. I have no doubt our dear people who are in more comfortable circumstances have already been employed in looking after such as your last query refers to. In this town, although borne on in common with others in meeting the general calamity, a special effort has just been made in favour of our own suffering poor, and I dare say this is widely

2A

done. I am aware applications have been 'unwisely' made [by] certain brethren to benevolent friends in England. On being made acquainted with it I instantly wrote reproving the procedure and remonstrating with the parties – and so pointed out the mischief of such doings that in those quarters I think it will not be repeated. I particularly mentioned the impropriety of goading Mr. Farmer, who is exposed to the worthless as well as the worthy from all quarters. The thing grieved me greatly. If anything be done my most decided opinion is that the whole should be managed by a committee of yourselves, your secretary to communicate with the Superintendents of the respective circuits, calling for detailed accounts of the application of the sums committed to them for distribution. They best know where relief ought to be bestowed, and they should be appointed to convey it. I will answer for your almoners that they will 'quietly and efficiently' meet the wishes of our benevolent [friends] while the kindest feelings of their own hearts will be gratified in being the instruments of comforting those who are ready to perish. In Dublin an effort has been commenced to meet a particular (and I fear exaggerated) case of distress on the Donegal Mission. No doubt there is much privation in that remote district, but that four out of five hundred odd Wesleyans should be in a state 'of utter destitution', as is represented, is impossible. Overstatements are mischievous. Particular parties take up what is connected with especial localities but such will always be the case. Even this would lead me to say that a public fund for general distribution ought not to be committed to a Committee here. The scramble I fear would lead to as much ill as good. 'The peculiar circumstances in need of *special* and *extraordinary* relief' as mentioned by you would, I am apt to believe, be better met in the way I have ventured to suggest, than any other. If you see the wretched applicants that crowd my doorway almost all the day long begging a morsel to eat, it would make your heart sore. We deny ourselves usual gratifications to do something towards meeting their applications. Nineteen twentieths are Roman Catholics. Mrs. W. and Mrs. B. gather all the week's scraps, and make each a boiler of substantial broth which is distributed on each Wednesday and Thursday to those who would starve rather than beg, principally our own people. . . .

272   From William Cooke[1]   *Salford, February 2, 1847*

[Encloses a sermon he preached for their Jubilee.] . . . It breathes a
sincere and ardent love for that great section of the Christian Church,
of which your denomination is the parent, and mine a small filial
branch; and I flatter myself you will not find me wantonly aspersing
others, while attempting to vindicate my own community . . . It is my
admiration of your enlightened judgment and candour, as well as your
christian courtsey and kindness of heart, which induces me to send it. I
have been informed that you, though often calumniated and traduced
as a tyrant, have done more to infuse lay-influence into the proceedings
of the Wesleyan denomination, than any other minister, and I believe
it; and greatly should I rejoice to see the exalted talents and extensive
influence which the Great Head of the Church has given you employed
in promoting such a further modification in Methodism as the principles
of the New Testament sanction, and the matured state of the Wesleyan
denomination, and the general state of society, seem to require. . .

273   From William Vevers[2]   *Hull, March 11, 1847*

I regret to inform you that we held a *Minor District Meeting* at
Epworth on Tuesday last on the case of Mr. E. Usher,[3] when we were
compelled to *suspend him till the Conference*. The chief charge was *intemperance*; but he declared that he never knew what intemperance was! It was
however proved by the production of invoices that from September 2nd,
1846 to February 5th, 1847, a period of five months, he had consumed
in his own house 11 dozen of Porter, 4 bottles [of] sherry, 2 bottles of
Port, $1\frac{1}{2}$ gallons of Whiskey, *9 gallons* of *Brandy*! and $16\frac{1}{2}$ gallons of Gin!!
Yet he has never been seen drunk, though he was always suspected to be
under the influence of liquor: and he declares that he does not know
what intemperance means – as he never was intemperate! The charges
were brought by the Circuit Stewards and that of intemperance was
proved by documents (invoices) produced by them. Messrs. Radcliffe,[4]

---

[1] William Cooke (1814–85), Methodist New Connexion preacher, Manchester circuit,
1846–48; three times President of M.N.C. Conference. Despite the sentiments here expressed,
Cooke identified himself with the policy of allying the M.N.C. with other branches of Free
Methodism, alliances naturally anti-Wesleyan in tone.

[2] William Vevers, superintendent, Hull (George Yard) circuit, 1845–47.

[3] Edward Usher, superintendent, Epworth circuit, 1846–47. Became preacher, 1823;
expelled by Conference, 1847.

[4] Charles Radcliffe, superintendent, Barton circuit, 1846–47.

Goodwin,[1] J. C. Hindson[2] and G. Steward[3] were with me. We were quite unanimous in our opinion on his case. He did not appear to be surprised with our verdict, nor did he appear to regret it. He will not appeal, but will apply to be[come a] Supernumerary. We require a report of his conduct in the interval to be given to the next Conference. . . .

I think I have now arrived at the last verse in the last chapter of the Caughey case. Yesterday the Circuit Stewards called upon me (Messrs. Lofthouse and Field) to speak about next year. They were kind and respectful, and told me that they should be very glad to propose me a third year – but such was the feeling of the Leaders against me on the Caughey case that they knew it would meet with the most determined opposition; but still if I *wished it*! they would propose me. I told them with equal kindness and respect that I was neither grieved nor surprised by such a communication; that I had too much respect for myself and my office to *wish* them to propose me a third year; and that I regarded it as a providential release from an office which of late had been intolerable. About 2 hours afterwards Mr. L. said to me that they *still hoped that* a *reconciliation* might take place as it was only on one point – the Caughey matter – that the friends were dissatisfied. I told him at once it was useless to talk of reconciliation as there had been *no* quarrel; that I had acted from principle; that my proceedings were in harmony with my judgement and that of the Conference; and that I *could* not and *would* not yield the matter in question. He told me that if I would yield on that one point, all would be right; but I told him that was impossible. I believe my colleague Mr. Osborn[4] will share the same fate, and Mr. Steward is so convinced of the radical character of the whole case that he feels strongly inclined to make common cause with us at this crisis. It is not unlikely that we shall all three leave on the Caughey case. . . .

274 From Thomas Cutting[5]   *Bramley, March 13, 1847*

Having employed a part of my leisure in considering the subject of *Day School Education*, whether denominationally conducted or otherwise, and

[1] Josiah Goodwin (1785–1866), superintendent, Howden circuit, 1846–48.

[2] James C. Hindson, superintendent, Gainsborough circuit, 1844–47.

[3] George Steward (became preacher, 1829), preacher, Hull (George Yard) circuit, 1846–48. Steward not only did not leave the circuit out of distaste for Caughey (*vide infra*), but voluntarily retired from the Wesleyan Ministry in 1853, and became the most intelligent apologist for Wesleyan reform. See George Steward, *The principles of church government and their application to Wesleyan Methodism* (1853) and his *Farewell to Wesleyan controversy* (1854).

[4] James Osborn (1809–82), preacher, Hull (George Yard) circuit, 1845–47.

[5] Thomas Cutting, became preacher, 1827; desisted from travelling, 1842.

believing how indispensable for *Methodism* it is that the best *possible* plan should be acted upon and the most cautious steps taken under existing circumstances, I cannot resist the temptation to express to you the gratification I feel (in common with others) at the 'serious considerations', rather than 'hasty adoptions' of our *Education Committee* at the present movement.

I trust that there will be no pandering in this instance to the Anti-Church and State, alias purely Dissenting, objects of the party who are decrying the *government new scheme*! I myself conceive that its *main* principles are *sound*, and such as (if generally understood and adopted) will *prevent in future years* the possible introduction of a *purely secular*, alias semi-infidel, movement. I believe also that the *general* arrangement (if approved and employed by us) will prove itself *permanently* advantageous to *Methodism*, and not antagonistic, as some suppose, and Mr. Baines would have us to believe.

I very respectfully suggest that our great desideratum is, and will long continue to be, an insufficiency of funds, *local* and otherwise, to meet our crying *day school requirements*, and that we NEED such auxiliary aid as the government plan is intended to afford. I could adduce two remarkable instances (yea 3) from this neighbourhood in proof of this, but I flatter myself that your comprehensive and observant mind renders my so doing altogether needless.

I submit whether it would not be 'the more excellent way' for the Educational Committee to look at the proposal of the Government, with a view to *adapt* it (by respectful suggestions, etc.) to the general want of the nation and the general taste of the religious part of it; and that, concurrently with so doing, the following (or some such) outline of *Methodist* cooperation, preparation and defence be considered and adopted.

1st. That we form for ourselves (taking the *Glasgow* system as a basis, and culling from other systems too) '*A Wesleyan Day School System*' wholly adapted to our own connexional views and necessities.

2nd. That we proceed to form a large '*Normal Seminary for Teachers*' and an efficiently organized 'Central Model and Working Establishment'.

3rd. That we avow a connexional *locus standi* as a third or '*Wesleyan Day School Society*' and, as such, claim and partake of our proper annual share of Government aid, as to the *two* existing Societies.

This *triple* adoption it strikes me is most desirable, if not indispensable, as a measure of self-defence; as well as to place the Connexion in the position (for further aggressive influence etc.) which so fittingly becomes it. . . .

275   From William Vevers   *Hull, March 23, 1847*

As I see Lord John [Russell] is determined to press the Educational measure[1] so early as April 19th, I venture to hope that our Committee will be called together without delay. I have written to the President to urge him to call us together on *Tuesday next*. I hope you will concur in this as, if we do anything, no time can be lost.

You will be doubtless surprised to be informed that after all Mr. Bell[2] has consented to invite Mr. Caughey to speak at the Birmingham *Missionary Meeting*! Mr. Brice[3] of Liverpool has actually had Mr. Caughey over to baptize his child! and named it after him! This is too bad. It is time that such men should *not* be allowed to occupy some of our best pulpits and most influential stations. Our Quarterly Meeting will be on Friday next, and from what I have heard since my return home I am confirmed in my determination *not* to allow myself to be nominated for a third year,[4] as I am quite certain that it would afford an opportunity, which some of them would eagerly embrace, to insult me, and abuse the Conference! I think my Colleagues will leave with me – though I believe that every thing will be done to retain them – as Mr. Field and his party think that the retirement of *all* the preachers at once would be such a demonstration of the prevalence of the Caughey influence as would greatly damage them in the estimation of the Conference. Mr. F. will do all he can to secure a Superintendent that he can, as he has done formerly, *manage*.

I regret to see an article in the *Leeds Mercury* on Saturday last, doubtless supplied by our friend who *talked* against the measure in the Committee, but who had not the courage to hold up his hand either for or against our Resolution![5] In that article it is stated that the speakers

---

[1] In successive minutes of the Education Committee of the Privy Council in August and December 1846, Lord John Russell's government moved towards the creation of a body of professional teachers trained partly by apprenticeship in schools and partly in college, and partly salaried and pensioned by the state. The question of which schools would be authorized for the training of apprentices and employment of trained teachers was therefore crucial, but it only came before Parliament in April 1847 upon a vote of the funds to cover the proposals. See *Parliamentary Debates* 3s. xci. 952–1315 *passim*.

[2] Alexander Bell, superintendent, Birmingham (Belmont Row) circuit, 1844–47.

[3] Edward Brice (1810–59), preacher, Liverpool (South) circuit, 1845–48.

[4] 'When one has to do with a set of religious blackguards . . . it is enough to induce any man to wish to labour among a number of *Christian* men'. M.C.A. MSS. W. Vevers to Jabez Bunting, March 29, 1847.

[5] The *Leeds Mercury* March 20, 1847 p. 4, carried a leading article rejoicing that 'the united Committees of education and privileges of the Wesleyan Body, who met to the number of about *eighty* . . . on Tuesday last, came to the conclusion to give their firm and strenuous opposition to the Government measure of education', and gave a very circumstantial account of the opposition to Government led by Bunting, and his preacher son, William Maclardie,

on behalf of *accepting* the measure! were Dr. Dixon, Messrs. Reece, Crowther, Kay and Walker![1] Could anything be more dishonourable in principle, or mischievous in tendency, than to destroy the influence of the *unanimous* decision to which we came by such a statement which proclaims the fact of our want of harmony, and thus destroys our strength! Such a man is utterly unfit to be a member of any Cabinet! and I hope when we meet again we shall have courage to mark with our united censure such a dishonourable act. . . .

276 From Edward Baines   *Leeds, March 23, ⟨184⟩7[2] Private*

You will probably have seen from the London papers that Lord John Russell announced last night his intention to 'persevere' with the Minutes of Council, and to bring forward the Vote for Education *on the 19th of April*!

'A little month', then, and an *Educational Dictatorship* is to be established in England! A measure is to be sanctioned, which will inflict a deeper wound on civil liberty and voluntary religion than any measure of modern times. Education is to be enslaved; the electors and working classes are to be corrupted; and an important and irretrievable step is to be taken towards the State endowment of all religions in this country!

May I take the liberty of entreating, that if you see this measure in the same alarming light as myself, you will *from this moment* devote your whole energies to every lawful and constitutional form of opposition to the Government proceeding; and that you will *not remit your exertions* till either the measure is sanctioned by Parliament, or Ministers are compelled to bow before an overwhelming expression of public opinion.

It is still possible to defeat the measure, but not without efforts altogether extraordinary, and such as can only be inspired by an ardent love of liberty and a strong sense of Christian duty.

It is necessary

To petition both Houses of Parliament, from towns, villages, congregations, Sunday Schools, British Schools, etc.

To send deputations to wait on Ministers and Members of Parliament.

and of the contributions of the conservative preachers named below. Subsequent letters relate the disappointment of the *Leeds Mercury*'s hopes.

[1] James Dixon, preacher, London (Hinde St.) circuit, 1844–47; Jonathan Crowther, superintendent, Stockport (Tiviot Dale) circuit, 1846–47; J. R. Kay of Bury, and William Walker of Bradford; all members of the committees of Education and Privileges. For the suspected source of the leak, see no. 277 *infra*.

[2] This letter is partly printed in the *Life of Bunting* ii. 337–8.

To address urgent letters to your own Representatives, signed by Electors, and especially by their own supporters.

To hold public meetings or deliver public lectures in opposition to the measure.

To form Committees which should meet daily, and organize your entire District for immediate action.

Pardon this intrusion and exhortation from one who is absorbed by a sense of the danger that threatens the country. . . .

277   From William Vevers   *Hull, March 29, 1847*

. . . In the *Leeds Mercury* of Saturday there is a letter addressed to the Editors of the *Watchman*, signed by G. B. Macdonald complaining of the article on our London meeting,[1] as not giving a correct version of the *opposition* of the Committee to the Minutes of Council, but being sadly too tame and calculated to dishearten our country friends. If the article in the *Mercury* last Saturday week, giving the names of the members of the Committee who were *for* or *against* the measure has been really supplied by Mr. McD., as I strongly suspect it was, and in reference to which I shall certainly ask some questions on Wednesday, it is really ridiculous to bluster about the *Watchman*. This is a subject which I think merits the attention of the Committee.

In conversation with our Stewards [at Hull], they professed to be greatly displeased with me, because I spend so much time out of the circuit, by going to London so frequently! I told them that with the exception of the last Sabbath, I had not spent one Sabbath out of the circuit since the Conference! That I had been called to London on connexional business, and that in any other circuit in which I had previously laboured, the friends would have felt it a compliment to find that their Superintendent was regarded as worthy and competent to unite in consultation with his brethren on great connexional and national questions, and that I *could* not, and would not, even for the sake of an invitation to stop a third year in Hull East, give up the right of the Conference to appoint, or my right to accept an appointment, on any Committee, on any matter deemed worthy of attention. . . .

[1] George Browne Macdonald, superintendent, Wakefield circuit, 1844–47. Macdonald had supported Dr. Warren at his trial before the District Meeting, 1835. The *Leeds Mercury* printed letters from Samuel Jackson and Macdonald in its leader for March 27, 1847, stating that reports of the meetings of the united committees of Education and Privileges had much underestimated the determination of their resistance to the government. In fact the negotiation begun in no. 278 *infra* bought off their opposition.

278 From Lord Ashley[1]   *n. pl. April 3, 1847*
                                                      Private and confidential

The accompanying letter [wanting] contains a statement of all the
points discussed between us. I hope that you will be able to make your
communications to the *Privy Council* by Monday morning; the parties
will remain in town so that you may, if possible, receive your answer by
Monday evening.

Would it be possible, as it is most certainly desirable, that your
Resolutions should appear *simultaneously with the reply*, but not before?

Allow me again to impress on you the expediency of putting your
enquiries in the most friendly manner, of assuming, as it were, that
your difficulties will receive a candid attention and satisfactory explanation. I urge this the more earnestly because I am assured that such
will be the case, and it would have been the case with the rejoinder to
the Anti-Maynooth Committee; but they have thought fit, I hear, to
write so imperious a letter that the Government will decline to give any
additional explanations.

You may use this letter, if you desire it, in private conversation with
those gentlemen who accompanied you to my house.

May God prosper the work!

279 From Thomas Cutting   *Bramley, Leeds, May 12, 1847*

I am not wishful to intrude myself upon your valuable time unnecessarily
or unseemingly – but heartily concurring as I do in all the cautionary
and well-principled movements of the Wesleyan United Committees
on the subject of education, and being persuaded that the adoption of
the government scheme *as soon as practicable* will result in a very general
and lasting advantage to the Connexion, I am the more solicitous to
ascertain, if I can be made available in any way to promote the great
Connexional ends the Committees are so industriously and dignifiedly
seeking to promote.

I have long been in correspondence with Lord Morpeth[2] and the
Privy Council Committee on Education and have very recently received
an official notification that I am placed on the *registry* for office under

---

[1] For Lord Ashley see n. 2 p. 219 *supra*. This letter led to the Wesleyan committees' accepting
the government plan in return for assurances that the schools controlled by the Wesleyan
Committee of Education would for the first time be accepted as qualifying for state grants
which had hitherto been channelled through the National Society and the British and Foreign
Society.

[2] See n. 1 p. 46 *supra*.

it, but I so greatly prefer to subserve the school purposes of *Wesleyanism*, that *could* I be employed in *its* service, I could cheerfully forego other considerations.

I feel that I cannot, must not, much longer remain a comparative idler, and yet am as reluctant as ever to engage in merely secular pursuits. . . . [Could he be employed in raising funds for normal schools or as a school Inspector?]

P.S. The events which are occurring around us and the animus of Dissenters, together with their studied influence upon many among us, seem to call for very prompt and vigorous plans being adopted to facilitate a thorough organization of the school movement.

This extensive district moreover requires the very *prompt* and *generous* consideration of the *Educational* Committee. Life or death seems bound up therein.

280   From John Beecham

Conference Chapel, Wednesday morning
[Postmarked, Liverpool, July 21, 1847]

. . . We have had a great deal of plain dealing in the [Stationing] Committee, and certain brethren and their proceedings have been very freely animadverted upon. The two Huddersfield Superintendents,[1] it appeared from the statement of the representative, had most culpably allowed our principles to be set at nought, and the committee decided to recommend to the Conference that the petitions for their reappointment a third year should be refused, and they are put down provisionally elsewhere. This decision was come to in reference to some of their proceedings not immediately connected with Caughey's business. The conduct of Bromley was fully dwelt upon,[2] and it was decided that he could not go to London. Some of us are a good deal encouraged by the firmness evinced by the majority in favour of good principles. It is evidently felt that we have reached something like a crisis, and that principle *must be contended for*, or we shall be *precipitated into a downward course*. . . .

[1] John Hobson, superintendent, Huddersfield (Queen St.) circuit, 1845–48, removed to Taunton; Thomas Dickin (1802–61), superintendent, Huddersfield (Buxton Road) circuit, 1845–48, removed to Doncaster. Both were reappointed superintendents.

[2] James Bromley, preacher, Bath circuit, 1847–50. Ceased to be recognized at the Conference of 1850.

281 **From James Kendall**[1]   *Madely, Ironbridge, August 7, 1847*

I am not a little pleased that you have had spirited discussions on the subject of 'anonymous publications' or '*Flysheets*'. I feared much that the plan so sagely recommended of treating things with '*silent contempt*' would have been adopted in reference to these strange publications. But I now perceive that my Fathers and Brethren are alive to the importance of searching out the authors of such seriously mischievous publications.

On the reception of the 'second enlarged edition' of No. 1 of these 'sheets', I wrote to a popular minister and author of our Connexion *a letter of enquiry*. In his answer he stated that himself and Mr. B. had 'each received copies, but who sent them neither of them could divine', that 'while in Birmingham he had seen Mr. Bell who had been in the Metropolis and who had told him that the impression was that a regularly organized committee existed and that the *Flysheets* were issued by its members' etc. etc.

Since this correspondence I have received another *Flysheet* more elaborate and formidable than the former one; and my impression is that unless the Brethren in Conference are unanimous and decided in entering their protest against these pamphlets we shall soon have more of them.

I may be very properly asked – 'why should *I* trouble my head about these publications and your discussions in Conference respecting them?' My answer is ready. There are Brethren now in Conference who have concluded that *Flysheets* have been sent to me and not to some others, because I am known to be '*tainted*' 'Tainted with *what*?,' I might have angrily asked (but having printed a sermon on peevishness, I am obliged to be good tempered). Yet I still ask, 'with *what* am I tainted?'. Disaffection to the leading authorities in Conference? Is this what is meant? If so let it be *proved*. *Take me up immediately on suspicion*. This is far preferable to taking a man *down* on suspicion in the way of circuits, treating his communications to the *Watchman* and *Magazine* with contempt etc. But if any man suppose that I am *in any way whatever* mixed up with these *Flysheets*, let me be sent for and I will say my Catechism on the subject. There is this infamy belonging to all offensive anonymous publications, that they expose numbers of innocent men to suspicion either as principals or accessories. I am, I suppose too *insignificant* a man to be suspected of writing the *Flysheets*, but yet as there is in them a terrible reflection on the purity of the Stationing Committees, and I

---

[1] James Kendall, preacher, Madely circuit, 1846–49. This letter illustrates the mutual suspicion among the preachers generated by the *Flysheets* (1846–48) which led the 1849 Conference to demand almost unanimously that the authors reveal their identity.

myself have been known to complain lustily of some of my past appointments by those Committees, and have in my possession a letter of a President of Conference to shew that my complaints have been reasonable, some may think me indirectly implicated.

I have however had nothing to do with them, and am profoundly ignorant of the source from which they originate . . .

282   From W. M. Harvard[1]   *Maidstone, January 26, 1848*

Since the adoption by our Conference of the appellation 'Church' as designating our Connexion, and 'Ministers'[2] as applicable to such among us as are wholly separated to holy work, I have considered it desirable that we should gradually and uncontendingly introduce those terms into our Circuit plans as well as our Conference documents.

In Canada I never had any difficulty in so doing; and I am apprehensive that I have over-rated the degree of preparedness of the Methodists of this country to support and uphold their Ministers, *as such*. I hope I am superior to any *personal* feeling on the subject that would render it difficult for me to yield to safe and salutary counsel; and I beg the favour of your indulgent assistance in the most entire confidence, as I am bound of course to act on my own responsibility, and would not think it right to involve your honoured self because of any counsel you might have the goodness to afford me.

On coming to this place in August last, I made my plan as enclosed . . . and heard no objection until at our last Local Preachers' Quarterly Meeting when, with but one exception, and on the part of an honest man from the country, it was by all denounced as introducing novel and unscriptural distinctions among 'brethren equally called of God to the same work'. I found the Conference was an authority but of little weight with them. And one ([J.]Pobjee) was desirous of a public meeting that we might there debate the question, and have it decided by the suffrages of the people; which, I was confidently assured, was entirely against me in this matter.

A few evenings afterwards, they held a meeting in a private house, and of themselves only, when it was proposed to divide the Societies on it. And this was only prevented passing, by a proposal from one 'of

---

[1] William M. Harvard, superintendent, Maidstone circuit, 1847–49.

[2] Cf. the discussion at the Conference of 1848: 'In the character of a candidate, the phrase "*Wesleyan Church*" occurred. To this Mr. G. Osborn decidedly objected. "*I would have us adhere to the Wesleyan phraseology*". Dr. Bunting: 'I think Wesleyan Methodist Church*es* is the more correct. We are members of the *Church* of Christ" '. Gregory, *Sidelights* p. 422.

milder mood', that they would work the plan as usual, but, if the same *distinctiveness* characterised it, that they would print another edition of it *with an altered heading*, and circulate it gratuitously through the Circuit; thus (as they think) escaping the violation of that law which places the making of the plan in the hands of 'the Superintendent or his colleagues'.

I feel in a great strait on this matter, because, while I am not disposed to be subservient to the dictation of men so little justified in their course, either by the laws and usages of Methodism, or by the reason and propriety of the thing itself, yet:–

1. I feel that these are days on which contentions on minor points are to be avoided among us; when probably Rome is so near upon becoming persecutingly rampant in our nation, and will probably soon tread under foot, in one common undistinguishment, every little border of propriety and protection that we and our fathers have with so much fondness endeavoured to rear and to shelter in the length and breadth of the Methodist vineyard.

2. We have a good work of God going on, chiefly among the young people, though not by any means exclusively, nearly a hundred individuals having professed to find peace with God since the Conference. And it is to be feared that this work will be hindered, were we to have any considerable counter-excitement originated.

The Local Preachers have, in addition to a high sense of their own importance, been goaded on by some meddlesome dissenters who have taunted them with this new development of 'priestly domination' and 'tendency to Puseyism' as they are pleased to describe the distinctiveness in question. Without the aid of at least some of these 'local ministers' as they affect to be styled, I shall be unable to supply the country chapels. And they are all bound together by sympathy of view and feeling and by solemn compact and determination to act together.

Having been so long from England, I feel deficient as to the views of those by whom I would fain be influenced in such a case. . . .

Had I conceived that there would have been such an opposition on the part of our local labourers, I should probably have thought it not worth while to have mooted the question here, since we have not a very healthful public opinion hereabouts to appeal to. But having done so (unoffendingly so far as my motive was concerned) I hesitate to retrace my steps, unless advised by those in whose wisdom and prudence I confide . . .

I beg also to say that one of our Local Preachers has avowed his opinion that the ordination of our ministers by the Conference authority is *a mere 'humbug'*. Another (Pobjee) that the proceedings of our Conference are *'inspired from hell'*. Would you advise me to put these men on their trial before the Leaders' Meeting? If so, on what law, and what should be the penalty?

In case they reprint my plan with a new heading, would there be any particular law of the Connexion against them? Or could I go on my way and 'wink' at their perverseness?

283   From W. M. Harvard   *Maidstone, February 1, 1848*

It was truly kind in yourself to favour me with so obliging and immediate a reply. My Local Preachers are determined to act together in this matter, and are resolved that they will work no plan that has the word minister in it unless it includes them as well as ourselves in the same common classification.

Our Circuit Steward, being the most influential man that we have, handed me the following form of a heading with his very earnest recommendation. He [is] the No. 4 on the plan:–

'Wesleyan Plan of the Maidstone Circuit – Places – Appointments – Names'.

This by omitting both '*Preacher*' and '*Minister*' he thinks saves the principle; and if you thought the same, it would of course determine me. Of course *noone* is aware that I have the advantage of communicating with yourself on the subject.[1] . . .

Now I hope that I am not prone to contend for a mere word. But this appeared to me to involve no less a principle than that of ours being a regular and authorised ministry, and which, by my giving up the use of the term in the plan, I am called upon publicly to disown.

Again, our Conference after mature deliberation having agreed to adopt the appellation on the official copy of the stations and in the printed and official copy of the minutes, it appeared to me discreditable and unworthy for a minister – a member of that body, and not a junior – in his individual capacity to yield in his circuit so far to a clamour as to relinquish the appellation, and thus tacitly to reprove and condemn the collective wisdom and piety of the ministry in Conference assembled. . . .

The Local Preachers are, I am sorry to have to say it, to give you a clear view of my case, decidedly reckless on this point, and will divide the Societies on it immediately. The people in the country say they are more indebted to the Local Preachers than to us and that they will not

[1] On February 15, Harvard wrote again asking for a Conference ruling on the phraseology to be employed on circuit plans. M.C.A. MSS. W. M. Harvard to Jabez Bunting, February 15, 1848.

sanction on our part any lording it over their oldest and best and most deserving friends, not to say ministers, for they speak of their apostleship. . . . I should add that the majority of them say that the plan adopted in some of the London Circuits is even more offensive than the one that I have adopted inasmuch as it *proclaims the distinction* at the very head and front of the document. . . .

284 From W. M. Harvard   *Maidstone, March 15, 1848*

I took the liberty to forward to you one of our Circuit plans with the heading so expressed as to omit both the *disputed* term '*Minister*', and the *demanded* one of '*Preacher*'.

With the term 'Minister' three only out of nineteen Local Preachers would work; but by the expedient adopted, the services of eleven were secured. The other eight proceeded to print a plan with their own heading, and which they designated in one of its corners, 'Corrected'. A copy of one of these they sent to me, inscribed to 'Brother Harvard'; one also to each of my colleagues similarly inscribed.

I immediately proceeded to identify the eight transgressors with their transgression, and gave them notice of trial before the Leaders' Meeting for the breach of the rule that says 'the Superintendent shall take care that the Plan for the travelling and Local Preachers shall be made by himself or one of his colleagues'; and suspended them from the plan till the result of their *trial*.

In the trial I found the most essential aid in that most comprehensive and invaluable digest of our rule respecting the trial and expulsion of Members, for which we are so inexpressibly indebted to yourself at the Conference in 1835; and it is to be hoped that you will in like felicitous and all-comprehending style and form do the connexion the service of putting the case of the Local Preachers, the entire case of a nomination by the Superintendent, approval or disapproval by the Local Preachers' Meeting, examination as to our doctrines and usages, the Plan, trial, suspension etc. etc. so as to help our *Ministry proper*, to subordinate this species of our agency to the spirit and genius of our ecclesiastical system, and its own evangelical efficiency. We want something on which to fall back by which we may effectively keep out of the local preachership everyone who really is disaffected to the Conference, and remove if possible any who in process of time may become such.

Some time since one of *our* 'Local Ministers' in making the Kingswood collection in a country-place said: 'You may do as you please, either give or not give as you like. For my part I think our Preachers have money enough and time enough to educate their own children, quite as much as we have'. Such men we ought to be able to *remove*. They are a pest to our country Societies.

The Leaders' Meeting voted them guilty without a dissentient voice. I then signified that according to discipline I should defer the sentence until the following week. Seven of them however insisted on an immediate decision, and, on my non-compliance, then and there tendered me their resignation of membership which I was too happy not to accept.

Previous to their leaving the room, in order to lessen their influence for agitation I said to each: 'Have I not invariably treated you with Christian respect and brotherly kindness?' and an answer in the affirmative was given by each in the hearing of the Leaders.

One of the eight subsequently waited upon me saying that he was assured by one who seemed to be learned in Methodist law that the printing of a plan for their own pleasure would not be an infringement of law, but that since he had found his mistake he truly regretted having taken that step. He made the same *amende* in presence of the Leaders' Meeting, and as he has been of irreproachable character among us for more than 20 years I had pleasure in removing his suspension and restoring him to the plan.

Attempts have been made to bring some of the others back. 'Let them adopt the same course, and my ear and heart shall be open to them'.

The law having been thus far vindicated, and my expedient-plan not giving myself satisfaction any more than some others that had consented to work it, I resolved to make a new one according to my judgment. In doing this I regretted that I could not consult anyone whose view on the general question coincided with my own, most if not all of my ministerial brethren hereabouts so far as I could gather being in favour of my 'giving up', for the sake of peace; and which was often quoted against me by my opponents on the spot.

I candidly disapprove of any public move even in a right direction, by any individual among us without the sanction of a due authority, and I deemed myself safe in that respect in falling back upon the phraseology of our annual Minutes. It did not appear to me so important in Canada; but here where discussion may and will arise it seems desirable specially that our ministers should have some uniform mode; and that, as nearly as may be, with due consideration of weaker brethren, our Plans should be conformed to the phraseology of our Conference Minutes.

Humbly conceiving that in case I should have to defend myself in our Church Courts the following would be the most defensible:

Maidstone Circuit 1848
Plan for the Methodist Ministers and Local Preachers
In the Connexion established by the late Revd. J. Wesley A.M.
Anno domini 1739.

To make a long story short, after secessions from the Plan on account of the above heading, which I personally made known, until I could only make out the document by the aid of Prayer Meetings and special exhorters offered for the occasion, I was suddenly 'brought up', as the phrase is, by our *most* managing and influential man (himself a political conservative) who assured me that if I persisted in introducing the term *'minister'* in opposition to the Local Preachers, on whose list he stands at the head, he and his family would withdraw from us altogether; and that other influential parties had made up their minds to do the same.

He proposed as mediator between the parties that I should head the plan 'Wesleyan Preachers' Plan' or 'Wesleyan Plan of the Maidstone Circuit', and conceded that the designation *'Minister'* might appear at the foot of the plan, as in that of the Tunbridge Wells Circuit, in connexion with the sale of Methodist publications.

I regretted to be obliged to yield, but I saw it would make a serious convulsion in the Society; and having pushed the matter to almost that point, I regarded it right to make the best terms in my power, as in the enclosed plan. In this, I hope only *for the present*, 'Sunday and Week Day Services' occupies the place of *'Ministers and Local Preachers'*. May it please God that soon some worthy successor may find *that simple rechange* accomplishable.

Having to put the ministry at the bottom I thought I would both print it in a larger type and also associate it with *ecclesiastical* rather than *commercial* announcements. Not but that I feel it to be one important part of the legitimate business of a *Wesleyan* Minister to promote in every proper way by his own personal agency, the sale of our connexional publications.

This has been a sore conflict, and coming on so soon after my Canada conflicts has well nigh overset me. On the part of my opposers it has been pursued with so much of cunning and bitterness, and in some instances with the most thorough-paced radical vulgarity.

Most of my flock I am sorry to say are of the class called 'Reformers', and have too little sympathy with either the Conference or with our Connexional interests in general. This fact influenced me in the introduction of the term Connexion into the heading. . . .

I comfort myself with the thought that we have, in this hard-fought battle, gained:–

2B

1. The omission of the term preacher as the general designation of ordained and unordained.
2. The admission of the term Minister.
3. The withdrawment of three or four disaffected men from the Plan without the trouble of excluding them.

285   From Richard Tabraham[1]   *Clitheroe, February 15, 1848*

Venerated Doctor,

Aware of the importance of your engagements, I have hesitated to obtrude a letter, especially as it is *strictly private and confidential*, lest I should burden you, but ease of mind, sincere desire for your *counsel*, and devoted love to our blessed Methodism, have compelled me to conquer my reluctance, and throw myself on your *indulgence*. The subject which has for years engaged my thought and prayers is the position of *Methodism* towards the extraordinary *moral movement*, abstinence from all intoxicating drink. It has always appeared to me that Wesleyanism as taught in Mr. Wesley's writings, the Rules of Society Bands, the Minutes of Conference and occasionally the Magazines and other standard works, contains the germ of this mighty Reformation, the principle of which this is the natural development. So I have viewed it from the beginning. And this has been one great reason why I have held by the cause of *Abstinence* with a tenacious hold, that, as I possibly mistakenly thought, the long continued and unmerited frowns of my still honoured and beloved brethren the ministry, could not shake, though if anything earthly could have done this, their supposed displeasure would have done this. Pardon dear Doctor this personal allusion, it was involuntary as my object is far, very far, beyond my little self or any personal affairs.

The above view established my *early aversion* to all kinds of alcoholic drink. This was increased by the awful instances I have witnessed of ministers, their families, officers, members etc. again and again falling under the power of liquor, the fact that many pleaded the example of ministers and others as an encouragement to drink, and this issued in inebriety, the souls we could not secure for Christ through this fell evil, the hundreds of thousands of pounds which our own ministers and people alienated from Methodism, especially from our *glorious missionary cause* every year to spend upon drink, tobacco and snuff. This I knew well, for while I who *abstained* deemed it an honour to subscribe to every

[1] Richard Tabraham (1792–1878), superintendent, Clitheroe circuit, 1847–49.

fund in Methodism and [£]5. 5. 0 yearly to the missions, and this I did without *property*, and generally in some of the poorest and most toilsome circuits in our blessed connexion, my brethren could scarcely screw out 21/-. Drink, tobacco and snuff swallowed up all in many cases. Pardon this seeming *self*, I wanted the *contrast* of indulgence and self-denial.

Thus influenced, believe me dear Doctor, I have mourned for many years over what has really appeared to me *hostility* as well as apathy to *Abstinence* among many of our leading ministers and some of our official people. I know well that tens of thousands of our best people, many of our ministers and a large portion of the churches of Christ and the thinking portions of mankind cannot account for our apathy, not to say hostility. I could have gleaned *volumes* of remarks, not ignorant censorious, vulgar, and obtrusive – but wise, just, holy, sorrowful observations to sustain what I have stated, but I have avoided such collections lest I should fail under the burthen of sorrow they would induce. He who searches my heart knows that I am deeply anxious for the credit, the progress, the union, the spirituality of Methodism. Were I not I would not pen this communication. This is my spring of action. I beseech you, honoured Doctor, cannot something be done to prevent the world, the Church, our own people from saying at least with seeming truth, that as a connexion, we are, in relation to Abstinence far behind the American Methodists and other churches of Christ, and that we do not in this matter, carry out the principles of our Founder etc. etc., that except we put away this accursed thing we cannot prosper so fully as we might do, that saints and sinners are looking in vain to us for help of the slightest kind, a word, a smile etc.? . . .

I plead not for any folly of Teetotalism, much less for a name. Let both go to their own place. I plead for the wisdom of countenancing Abstinence. Be it *connexional* or otherwise as wisdom shall direct, I am easy. I seek abstinence. I do not *flatter*, I should be ashamed thus to insult the man I love, I think few will charge me with this fault. But, Doctor, you are too far-seeing, too comprehensive in your views, too intimate with the state of affairs, to believe for a moment that the progress of the temperance cause can be stopped either among the public or *our* people. You know it will go on, and whether *we* will or not our people will be influenced by its movements. May I not ask, Doctor, is it not, as far as it is good, of God? If so *you* would not stop it. I know you would rather say, let my tongue cleave to the roof of my mouth rather than utter a word to stop it.

God has given you the influence due to your talents, age, station, to his own gracious bestowments so long continued – your brethren justly love you, and would listen to your far-seeing suggestions. O has not the time come when temperance should be promoted *peacably, connexionally*, by us, in our *schools, congregations*, societies – yea among the preachers? Who knows but you, Doctor, are God's ordained instrument to aid Methodism in the most permanent and effectual manner, in the suggestion of some great connexional scheme, which shall silence gainsayers, rejoice thousands of mourning hearts, save thousands of souls; help all our funds, do immense good, and little harm, and make Methodism an increasing wonder in the world – before He gives you the immortal crown? . . .

286   From Thomas Waugh   *Bandon, February 23, 1848*

. . . My unhappy, guilty, ungrateful, because popishly priest-ridden country! And how is it that in the despite of facts, every public measure is taken to nourish and perpetuate the Godless superstition? Treason stalks abroad in the footsteps of famine and priests and 'patriots' preach hatred to those who have made large sacrifices to save thousands from starvation. Let us cease to be Protestant, and, alas, for Britain! . . .

287   To Jonathan Crowther   *London, February 23, 1848*

. . . I have laid before the Richmond Committee the subject to which the Didsbury Committee kindly requested our attention.[1] We had a long conversation respecting it. We quite agree with you in regretting that we have not so large a number of candidates for our Ministry better prepared by previous habits of thought and by elementary attainments as would be most desirable. But we are generally of opinion that it is very doubtful whether, in the actual state of our Connexion, any such letter as you suggest would be expedient or well received. Mr. Jackson very strongly stated *his* opinion that the former letter, read at your meeting by Mr. Bowers, did considerable harm, by discouraging some young men from offering themselves for our work, who, by patient training, might have become very useful ministers, and was one cause of our subsequent want of a *sufficient* number of persons to supply our Circuits, Missions, and Institutions. We all feel how undesirable it is that such men as our two Classical Tutors should be occupied in giving the *mere elements* of *common* scholastic instruction. But it was thought that this evil would be to a great degree remedied by going to the expense of

[1] I.e. the committees of the two divisions of the Theological Institution.

having at each branch of the Institution an Assistant English Master. On the whole, while obliged by the kind communication of your Committee's views and suggestions, we think that the time is not come for any further movement, tending to restrict or discourage an adequate and abundant supply of ministerial labourers.[1] We cannot, would not, *make* such labourers. We must be content to *take* such as the Providence of the great Lord of the Vineyard is, in his sovereign wisdom, pleased to give us; and then afford them all the help we can for the removal of their defects, and the *improvement* of their talents. At all events, it is not a question on which we should agitate Quarterly Meetings. The *Examination Committee* in July might, however, be urged to discharge very faithfully and carefully the duty of *selection*. . . .

288   From William Naylor[2]   *Manchester, July 4, 1848*

[The South Wales District Meeting] . . . need direction and encouragement, and I am inclined to think the work of God among them would prosper more if the change of ministers between the North and South District was more frequent. In the South certain Brethren will always command the first circuits, and to others Brethren must be sent, however unwilling the Circuits are to receive them. In consequence of this, the work does not prosper. I think of proposing at the conference that after a minister has had three appointments in one District, he should pass to the other. . . .

289   From Joseph Sutcliffe[3]   *Bayswater, August 3, 1848*

. . . In reading Dr. Bangs,[4] a thought has struck me that in England we must have three Conferences; *one* in the north, *one* in the east, and one in the west of England. The absence of some of the brethren in

[1] This proposal was considered by the Didsbury committee on February 25, which agreed 'as to the inexpediency of discouraging what may be called the humbler class of candidates for the work of our ministry, but at the same time . . . [were] strongly of opinion that their initiation into the ordinary branches of knowledge ought, if possible, to be secured on some plan less expensive to, or altogether independent of, the funds of the Theological Institution'. M.C.A. MSS. J. Crowther to Jabez Bunting, March 6, 1848.

[2] William Naylor, superintendent, Manchester (Oldham St.) circuit, 1847–50.

[3] Joseph Sutcliffe, supernumerary. Cf. n. 3 p. 81 *supra*.

[4] Nathan Bangs (1778–1862), celebrated American Methodist preacher and editor of the Methodist Book Concern, New York. Sutcliffe had been much inspired by writing a review of Bangs's *History of the Methodist Episcopal Church* (New York, 1st ed. 1838–41), concluding in a passage omitted above that 'we want reviving with these western lives'.

these times of schism for *six weeks* opens our flanks to the invaders. I find a canon about the year 400 that no bishop should be absent from his charge above *three days*.

In the Norwich district, the loss of more than 500 members was a serious stroke. It was indeed a soft and rainy winter, and the roads almost impassible in certain places; but while the brethren were smoking their pipes at home, the ranters would go and gather up the neglected people. Hence when a chairman is ballotted, he ought to have the *right* of representing his district in the Stationing Committee, and to say to the slothful, 'Brother in consequence of your gross neglect of duty, I cannot recommend you to be the superintendent of a circuit the ensuing year'. The above are not my words, but those of the superintendent of the St. Edmondsbury Circuit whose soul was grieved for the losses. I want Methodism to live when all the old men are gone after Wesley. . . .

290   From Edward Baines   *Leeds, November 24* [*1848*]

A Tory and Whig coalition is forming against Sir Culling.[1] Can you do anything to help us with your friends?

291   From William Barton[2]   *Leeds, November 24, 1848*

You are doubtless aware that Mr. Fitzwilliam has withdrawn from the canvass for the representation of Yorkshire. Sir Culling Eardley has issued his address and will address the electors in Leeds tomorrow morning.

I received a private note from Mr. Baines a few days since asking my opinion as to the probability of the Wesleyans supporting Sir Culling if he were brought out and I replied that I believed many of them and

[1] Sir Culling Eardley Eardley, formerly Sir Culling Eardley Smith (1805–63), a founder of the Evangelical Alliance and advocate of disestablishment, now seeking election to Parliament on a Protestant and Anti-Maynooth platform. Baines's *Leeds Mercury* strongly championed Eardley as a candidate for the West Riding, partly on the grounds of his Protestant and voluntaryist principles, partly to get the Hon. Charles Fitzwilliam out (*Ibid.* November 18, 1848 p. 4). Eardley forced Fitzwilliam's withdrawal, but despite the support of Baines and of many Methodists, including Bunting's son, William Maclardie, he was substantially defeated by the Tory candidate, Edmund Denison, owing, according to the *Mercury*, to whig desertion in country areas where landlord influence was powerful. *Leeds Mercury* November 21, 1848 p. 1: November 25 p. 4: December 2 pp. 4, 7: December 23, 1848 p. 4.

[2] William Barton, preacher, Leeds (Oxford Place) circuit, 1846–49.

I thought most of them would support him heartily; but that I feared there was no prospect of success.

I have just received a note from Mr. Baines informing me

'A Tory and Whig coalition is forming against Sir C. Eardley. May I hope you will write to as many as possible of your ministers and friends to declare decidedly and at once for Sir Culling'.

Sir Culling's address to the electors is of a more democratic character than I can heartily approve, but as he fears God and hates Popery I should be glad to see him in Parliament as the Member for the West Riding.

But why do I trouble you with my wishes about Sir Culling? I wish to ask your counsel. I will regard it as confidential if you wish it so. Would there be any impropriety in the Wesleyan ministers in the West Riding issuing a short address stating their confidence in Sir Culling? It would be an unusual step and might lead to public censure, but the times are unusual and for myself I feel that it would be worse than foolish to petition a House of Commons not to endow Popery and to elect members who will do the thing.

If you are not too busy pray favour me *early* with a few lines in reply. . . .

292   From William Barton   *Leeds, November 28, 1848*

Accept my thanks for your kind letter of this morning.

I enclose Mr. Denison's address which was issued yesterday: on *the* point he is decided and satisfactory and presents a fine contrast to Mr. Fitzwilliam on the main subject.

I saw Mr. William Bunting at the Cloth Hall Yard on Saturday morning; he will probably give you a better account of Sir Culling's address than I can. I may say that it struck me as being gentlemanly, manly and candid. While there was evidently a desire not to offend the mob, I must say I did not think there was an unbecoming truckling to it, and I never heard a speech of that character in which there was so much religious principle so fully, openly and yet unobtrusively brought out.

You will excuse my adding that Messrs. West, Methley, Bacon, Stinson, McAulay[1] and myself met yesterday morning to consider

---

[1] Francis A. West, superintendent, Huddersfield (Buxton Road) circuit, 1848–51. James Methley, superintendent, Leeds (Oxford Place) circuit, 1847–50; d. 1861, aet. 70. William Bacon, superintendent, Leeds (Wesley) circuit, 1846–49; d. 1860, aet. 72. Joseph Stinson, superintendent, Leeds (Brunswick) circuit, 1846–49; d. 1862, age unknown. Alexander McAulay (1818–90), preacher, Leeds (Oxford Place) circuit, 1847–50; President, 1876.

whether we could take any and what steps in aid of Sir Culling. And remembering his *extreme* liberalism at the Cloth Hall on Saturday, his unwillingness to aid the Sabbath cause by legislation, and the new step which we should be taking, the possibility that it might be used as a precedent in a worse cause, the fact that addresses to Wesleyans as such are forbidden, and the possibility that the Conference might think us too presumptuous we determined to do no more than any of us might judge proper in a quiet and individual manner.

I have declined to meet Sir Culling's committee.

If I obtain any papers worth sending I will try and forward them.

Mr. Denison addressed the electors in the Cloth Hall this morning. I was not present. His avowal of opposition to Popery was most decided. . . .

293   From William Barton   *Leeds, December 6, 1848*

. . . I have scarcely any intelligence to communicate respecting the election. You will probably receive it more accurately from Mr. Percy Bunting than from myself. And indeed rumours are so numerous and contradictory that I almost hesitate to say anything. I may express my own serious doubts as to the success of Sir Culling Eardley. For

1. The Tories seem *united* against him, and with them are joined many Whig families belonging to the landed interest. Now let the results of preceding contests for the West Riding guide our judgments. In one the Tories contending against Whigs and Radicals lost by about 500 votes, and in a second and subsequent contest they gained by about the same number. Will they lose when Whigs and Tories combine their influence?

2. The supporters of Sir Culling do not seem to embrace heartily all who call themselves Liberals. I can hardly speak with accuracy as to the reason. At Leeds I should not wonder if the truth were known that the friends of Roebuck[1] in opposition to Sir Culling are so from feelings of wounded pride. Some of them did not support 'Friend Joseph Sturge.'[2] At the next annual meeting of our honourable Town Council

---

[1] John Arthur Roebuck (1801–79), radical politician and M.P. for Bath, 1832–37, 1841–1847, and for Sheffield 1849–68 and 1874–79. Eardley had beaten Roebuck for the liberal nomination for the West Riding.

[2] Joseph Sturge (1793–1859), Quaker philanthropist, anti-slavery agitator, and reformer. Becoming a strong voluntaryist in education, he resigned from the British and Foreign School Society in 1845 when it resolved to continue in receipt of government help, and was adopted as a candidate for Leeds in 1847. Though strongly supported by the non-electors, he finished bottom of the poll.

they were dispossessed of their Aldermanic dignity and now, it is said, they declare they will not submit to the declaration of the Baines's. This however cannot be very extensive in its influence. Another reason separating some of the Liberals from Sir Culling's ardent supporters is, at least so I fear, the prevalent ungodliness amongst us. It is a fearful thought we are not moving on the masses, and the thing called Puseyism is doing nothing for them but giving them the power to read the writings of infidels.[1] For the great mass of the Liberals, Sir Culling is too good a man. They may support him because he is a Liberal but they would rather have had a man like Roebuck. What can we do to save the masses? I am beginning to believe that the only thing which can save the West Riding from the worst effects of infidelity and ungodliness is a glorious revival of religion. Upon the whole I believe Sir Culling's friends are in much better spirits than they were a week since. I have my doubts and fears too as to his success. For in spite of my dislike of his political liberalism I am such an admirer of his goodness and of the principles of the Evangelical Alliance that I can still wish him success.

My object however in writing this letter is to explain how it is that your name appears in the *Leeds Mercury* of Saturday as having written a letter etc.[2] I fancied that I was so cautious that I could not have committed you. I received yours on Tuesday week. I mentioned it to one friend only and he one of the most cautious, least talkative, men in Leeds. But with that gentleman Mr. P. Bunting dined that very day in Leeds; he was afterwards at Sir Culling's committee and in the evening from that committee I had a gentleman (Mr. Scales) requesting that I would give up your letter for publication. I declined to shew it to him and the fact made me so chary about shewing or mentioning your letter that I believe Mr. Methley was the only other person to whom I did mention it. On the Thursday Mr. Scales again waited on me for the letter and brought one from Mr. P. Bunting to Mr. Baines urging him to obtain it. Of course I was not to be moved, but I feared that the *Mercury* would have something in respecting you. I was glad to see it in a form so mild and inoffensive. I have now told you the history of that paragraph and shall deeply regret if I find it occasions you any annoyance. . . .

[1] A reference to efforts of the vicar of Leeds, W. F. Hook, to secure a national education scheme.

[2] In the leader on the West Riding election (*Leeds Mercury* December 2, 1848 p. 4) Bunting is quoted along with Edward Bickersteth, Pye Smith, Edward Miall and Dr. Price, as having written privately in support of Sir Culling Eardley.

294   From William Bond   *Bury, February 23, 1849*

. . . Unsworth is situated about a mile and a half from Radcliffe Close and is I believe next to Bury the oldest Methodistical station in this circuit, being visited by several of those venerable ministers of ours, now gathered to their rest, who in their early days laboured in and around Manchester as Local Preachers. For some time there was a prosperous cause there, but owing to various causes, principally the prevalence of infidel political radicalism, the cause of God declined, and for many years barely maintained its existence, so that about 4 or 5 years ago, there were only about that number in Society.

From that time however . . . it began gradually to improve; and about 3 years ago it pleased God to pour out his Holy Spirit on the place, a great number were brought under the converting power of God's grace, and the result was in due time the Society rose to above a hundred members.

Soon after this the necessity of providing a more commodious place of worship in a better situation was felt and the erection of a new chapel was determined on. . . .

295   From John Farrar[1]   *Richmond, March 10, 1849*

I enclose a Bill which has been freely circulated in Richmond. The subject is producing great excitement here, especially among the Dissenters; and some belonging to the Establishment do not like it. If the Bill should pass, the demand upon the [Theological] Institution will be serious, as we are rated at £1000 or £1200. We cannot appear in alliance with the Dissenters in opposition to it in this place; but can nothing be done in our defence? Richmond is now well supplied with clergymen; the present Bill proposes no addition to the number, but simply an increase of emolument. . . .

296   From John Beecham   *London, Friday evening.* [*27 April 1849*]

Just a line to save this post. They have had an awful Quarterly Meeting at Hinde Street.[2] Samuel Dunn[3] was proposed in opposition to Hard-castle,[4] and carried amidst a storm of 'stamping', 'shouting', 'yelling',

[1] John Farrar (1802–84), classical tutor, Richmond College, 1843–57. President, 1854.
[2] Otherwise the London (sixth) circuit.
[3] Samuel Dunn was expelled at the following Conference.
[4] Philip Hardcastle (1804–64), preacher, London (Spitalfields) circuit, 1846–49.

such as is rarely witnessed. Only three had either the disposition or heart to vote against. Abraham E. Farrar[1] is excited and distressed. He and the Stewards appear to have been taken wholly by surprise. But it is evident that there must have been a secret plotting. I have had a long private talk with Thomas Jackson, who grows more confident than ever that decisive measures must be adopted, and he is rather pleased with this Hinde St. affair thinking it will hasten a crisis. . . .

297 From John Kirk[2] to T. P. Bunting   *Stockport, n.d.*
[Postmarked:– May 17, 1849]

We have just concluded Mr. Walton's case.[3] It has occupied us about an hour this morning. There has been a very free and independent expression of opinion on the part of several brethren. On the motion of Dr. Hannah the Minutes of the Minor District Meeting were again read, except the 'Letter of reproof and admonition', which at Mr. W's request was not read. This over, Dr. Hannah, moved two resolutions of which the following is an exact copy, except the two '*determinations*' which are given in substance.

1. That this meeting expresses its high estimate of the care, patience, and impartiality with which the members of the Minor District Meeting have investigated this painful subject, and its grateful satisfaction in the Christian spirit and ability with which the minutes and other documents have been prepared.

2. That this meeting accepts the report of the Minor District Meeting; approves of the two determinations suggested at the last sitting, to wit, (i) That Mr. W. be admonished by the President of the next Conference for his departure from the rule of Christian truth and simplicity. (ii) That he is declared to be disqualified for the present for the office of Superintending a circuit:– and recommends the said determinations to the adoption of the Conference.

Before these resolutions were put Mr. Walton claimed a right to be

[1] Abraham E. Farrar, superintendent, London (Hinde St.) circuit, 1848–49.

[2] John Kirk (1818–75), preacher, Manchester (Oxford Road) circuit, 1846–49.

[3] Daniel Walton, superintendent, Bolton circuit, 1847–49. Walton and the recipient of this letter, Percy Bunting, were the parties to a *cause célèbre* which contributed greatly to the unsettlement of the Methodist ministry. A young minister in the York circuit, William Radcliffe, claimed to have seen a MS. on the study desk of Walton, his superintendent, which contained a passage he had seen in the *Flysheets*. Months later he disclosed this to Percy Bunting, and Walton was brought before Minor District and District Meetings and subjected to the penalties here reported; after a full day's discussion at the following Conference the proceedings were confirmed. Walton was never again a superintendent.

heard, not in defence, but on the motion before the meeting. This was thought improper, the right was refused, but he was allowed, by a formal resolution, the courtesy of a few observations on the point. He charged to be careful what we did as we should have to defend it before the Church and the world, declared his innocence, and made a few other observations of an unimportant character. The resolutions were then passed *nem. con.*, one or two of the Brethren not voting.

Mr. Osborn has given notice of a general resolution on [the] *Fly Sheets*, which was very cordially hailed. . . .

298   From Frederick J. Jobson[1]   *Stockport, May 17, 1849*

. . . The principal subject of interest in this [District] Meeting, of course, has been – Mr. Walton and the *Fly Sheets*. He has been perseveringly obstinate throughout the meeting, and most impudent in his defiance of us. His tact[ic?] was to pass by this meeting altogether, saying, he should make his appeal to the Conference, and seek a new trial, where he should obtain an impartial jury. But the members of the Minor District Meeting, very properly, called for an expression of the judgment of the meeting on their conduct – for it was evident that the design was to render them odious to the public, which would be much more easy to do, than to obtain the condemnation of the public of 60 or 70 ministers. After some difficulties, occasioned by Mr. Bowers's superfine sense of honour – who was, at first, for the passing of the report of the Minor District Meeting on to the Conference, without expressing any judgment on it, the meeting unanimously passed the two following resolutions.[2] . . .

These were moved by Dr. Hannah, seconded by Mr. Bowers (who gave up his objections, and seemed desirous of recovering the confidence and approval of his friends) and supported by Mr. Vevers. All voted for them except Mr. Rowland, who did not vote either for or against the resolutions. Mr. Walton very imprudently said he did not object much to the resolutions as he should be glad to receive good advice from Mr. Fowler[3] or any other good man who might be in the chair. This was intended for a nomination of Mr. F. for the President – but it will

[1] Frederick J. Jobson, preacher, Manchester (Oxford Road) circuit, 1846–49.

[2] As in no. 297 *supra*.

[3] Joseph Fowler (1791–1851) superintendent, London (City Road) circuit, 1848–51; Chairman of London District; Secretary of Conference, 1848. Fowler was expected to be a serious contender for the Presidency in 1849, but was too ill to attend Conference at all. Gregory, *Sidelights* pp. 444–45. (This work was based on Fowler's Conference diary.)

injure Mr. F. for it had the contrary effect to that intended. I am glad to see that the subject is prudently, and yet boldly put forth in this week's *Watchman*. I believe that Messrs. J. and H will be elected,[1] if their friends are awake. Mr. Naylor has shewn some pettishness, and was disposed to complain of our desertion of him; but I think he is nearly pacified, and hope he will unite with us for Mr. Jackson. I hear they have passed a resolution at the Macclesfield District Meeting in favour of the 'Declaration'.[2] The *Wesleyan Times* rages greatly this week. It is evidently prepared for the District Meetings. There is a complaint against Bro. A. Bell[3] for imprudencies at Glasgow. 1. Kissing a lady in his bed-chamber – when bidding her 'good-night'. 2. Exposing his person to the maid-servant. The 1st of these, it is said, he admits as an imprudence, the 2nd he denies. I hope there will be no trial. . . .

299 From John Beecham *Mission House, London, May 26, 1849*

I am much obliged by your kind note of the 23rd instant, communicating the suggestion of another sympathizing friend as to whether it would not be desirable to publish something from the Mission House, with the view of correcting the injurious misstatements in the re-published 'Fly-Sheets', relating to our House-Expenditure, and our alleged extravagant personal expenses as Secretaries.[4] I think it would be desirable on some grounds to do so; but you justly remark 'It is a delicate matter for you to touch'. This is the real fact of the case. It would not be a difficult question to handle if it related merely to salary. Each Mission-ary Secretary, in common with the Book-Steward, Editors, and Theo-logical Tutors, is paid, in lieu of Weekly Board, and quarterage for himself, wife, and one servant, thirty-seven (37) pounds, ten shillings per quarter. And as I have only one child for whom I receive an additional allowance, you will at once see that any junior brother-Minister in one of the regular London Circuits, with a family of four or five young children, has a larger annual salary than myself. This part of the subject might thus be explained in a few words. But in order more fully to meet the objections urged on some other points it would be necessary to enter into so many minute, and in some respects delicate

[1] Thomas Jackson and John Hannah were elected President and Secretary respectively at the Conference of 1849.

[2] At the Conference of 1848 George Osborn had moved that the preachers be called on to declare that they had nothing to do with the *Flysheets*.

[3] Alexander Bell, superintendent, York circuit, 1847–50.

[4] The *Flysheets* had made a particular set upon the administrative expenses of the Mission House and the 'luxury' enjoyed by the Mission Secretaries.

details as to make it impossible for me to submit a full explanation to the public eye, without feeling that both myself and the religious body to which I belong were humiliated by the exposure.

Take for instance the subject of Rent, Taxes, House Bills, Rates, Coals and Candles. It is easy to correct a great mistake into which our opponents fall, when urging their complaint on this point. They entirely overlook, for the occasion, the fact that the houses of the Secretaries are not intended merely as private dwellings for themselves, but also as official residences for the reception of Missionaries; it having been deemed from the commencement of the Society, very desirable that the young missionaries, especially, about to embark for Foreign Stations, should, while in London, be immediately under the eye of the secretaries. This being the case, our houses are much larger (mine is in fact two houses in one) and the Rent, Taxes, [&c.] much higher than would be requisite, were our residences intended merely for ourselves and our own families. In like manner, it would be rendered obvious to reflecting persons that the expenditure on coals and candles must be proportionately increased for missionary use, but to make this fully understood by all, it might be needful to describe the circumstances in which sick missionaries arrive from the mission-field, and frequently require light and fire in their rooms by night, as well as by day, before one could impress any persons with a correct idea of the excess of expenditure in these articles, occasioned by the temporary accommodation of missionaries. If the whole case could be minutely explained, it would not appear to anyone acquainted with London rents and taxes, and the price of coals, that thirty or thirty-five pounds per quarter, was an extravagant expenditure for a double-house and taxes, a corresponding extra expense for fire and light in the apartments of missionaries, and a proportionately larger House-Bill, Insurance etc. A little further consideration would be sufficient to convince any candid person how exceedingly injust it would be, to represent all this amount as laid out upon myself and family, when a large proportion of it has been incurred for the accommodation of missionaries.

Take again the 'Repairs of Secretaries' Houses, and additional Furniture' as the heading in the Society's Report has been generally expressed, for the sake of brevity. The expense of furniture, it is evident, must be much more considerable in such a *public* house as mine, than in a mere *private* dwelling. But I would not enter into details respecting the wear and tear of furniture, and especially the injury done to carpets, floor-cloths, and bed-rooms by the luggage of missionaries and their families, going out and coming from abroad. Respecting repairs, I may add, that if we did not meet some part of the expense ourselves, we should have to pay a corresponding additional rent. I know that my landlord would require an increase of rent not far short of the entire sum which has been expended for my house in repairs and furniture, in the last year.

The amount appearing as paid to me in my account, for the last year (1848) is – for salary including the allowance for two children and postage and washing, say 175£; for Rent, Taxes, Furniture, Repairs, Coals, Candles, etc. say 165£; and for Doctors' Bills 20£, altogether about 360£. But I and my family have not cost the Society all this sum. It includes also the expense of additional rooms and furniture, with increased rates and taxes, for the use of missionaries, and the cost of coals and candles required in their apartments. The sum which I have mentioned (I have of course omitted merely official incidental expenses) is all that can with any plausibility be represented, in any way, as my income; from which, however, must be made, as I have shewn, a very large deduction for the expense incurred for missionary accommodation. Then again, another set off must be taken into the account. I only receive the usual circuit allowance for one servant, but it requires an additional woman servant, and occasional extra-help, to keep the large house which I occupy in decent order; and it costs me forty pounds per annum, out of my own pocket, for the wage and living of my additional servant, and the occasional charwoman which it is necessary to employ. It may be said, however, that the profit arising from the board of missionaries is sufficient to meet this. But what there is in such a remark might easily be made to appear, if a feeling of delicacy did not prevent me from entering into details. It might be shewn that for the board of a healthy man, accustomed to active, country-life, considering the London prices of provisions, or for a sick missionary returning from a foreign climate, who needs special attention and care – one guinea per week would not yield much profit. But our housekeeping book shews it to be the fact, that, after deducting the extra expense for my domestic establishment, which I have had to pay out of my pocket, I did not receive quite ten shillings per week for each missionary who was accommodated at my house during the last year. So much for my profit! If missionaries are provided for in the style of comfort which I ever wish them to enjoy under my roof, there will not be found much opportunity for making profits even under the most favourable circumstances.

How does my income compare with that of others in somewhat similar circumstances? now becomes a relevant question.

1. How does it accord with that of secretaries of kindred institutions? They generally receive in cash a salary of at least 300£ per annum; and some of them have time allowed to attend to a pastoral charge also, and

receive an additional income for their respective churches. I should be content to receive 300£ a year, and provide everything for myself and family, without having any additional income as a regular Minister.

2. How does it compare with the income of other public officers of our own body? I regard it, as not even equal to some. I should prefer to be placed on the same footing with the Governor of the Theological Institution; to have a family-table provided for me, as well as a house, and receive a fixed yearly amount, out of which I should have nothing to find except clothes and books.

3. How does it agree with the income of my brethren, the ministers in our regular Circuit-work? If my brethren candidly take into account the greater expense in apparel which, in our public situation, we must necessarily incur, with the more frequent claims upon our hospitality; were they to look over my list of private subscriptions and donations, shewing the numerous appeals to our charity, made upon us as public men, a considerable number of which a regard for the credit of our Society is alone sufficient to compel us to meet, they would find reason to conclude that many of ministers, in our best Circuits, have, to say the least, as much available income as the Missionary Secretaries.

Looking at my connexion with the Missionary Secretaryship, as a question of profit and loss, the fact forces itself upon my attention that, whatever have been its advantages, I have sustained this twofold loss. I am not *justly* chargeable with extravagance in either my personal or family expenditure; but I have spent, since I came to the Mission House in addition to my official income, 600£ of my own little private property, which I think my circumstances ought to have been such as would have enabled me to reserve for my children. And I have suffered irreparable loss in my better half. By her unremitting attendance by night as well as by day to the sick-bed of a retired missionary's wife, my own dear wife contracted an illness which brought her, at the time, to the verge of the grave, and has left her in such circumstances of delicacy and constant liability to suffering, as to cut her off, to a great extent, from the ordinary enjoyments of social life. . . .

P.S. My best thanks for your persevering endeavours to put down that system of secret slander, which, if not destroyed, will destroy Methodism.

300   From William H. Clarkson[1]   *Derby, July 14, 1849*

As I know you take a very deep interest in whatever relates to Wesleyan Methodism and have long and strenuously endeavoured to promote its

---

[1] William H. Clarkson, superintendent, Derby circuit, 1847–50.

best prosperity, I deem it right to lay before you in confidence what relates to the case of Mr. Dunn,[1] that you may have an opportunity of judging of the truth of the propositions which in the shape of charges I preferred against him at the District Meeting, with the judgment passed upon his case. The propositions were my own composition and therefore whatever defects they contain they are all my own.

I think they were all clearly made out, if the Conference would deem the resolution passed concerning the declaration protesting against the *Fly Sheets* to have been a *bona fide* resolution of Conference which some have taken upon themselves to deny because the declaration was not signed by the President and Secretary.[2] I enclose therefore the propositions and reference to the proofs which with the help of a *Banner*[3] you will clearly understand. Mr. D. I am sorry to say manifested a very obstinate and untractable spirit, despite of all the remonstrances of the District, besides appealing against its judgment and going on still with the *Banner*. Such reckless conduct reminds one of Samuel's words, 'rebellion is as the sin of witchcraft'.[4] I hope however the time is come when the Conference will take decisive measures to prevent the house being divided against itself and to make the minority quietly and peaceably submit to the majority. . . .

Charges preferred against Brother Dunn

That the *Wesley Banner*, edited by Brother Dunn, contrary to the laws and usages of the Wesleyan Connexion, does,

I. Appeal to the Wesleyan Societies at large and to the world, against the decisions of the Wesleyan Conference, in a manner calculated to excite disaffection in the minds of many against the constituted authorities of the Connexion; and to endanger the peace of the Connexion.

The principle here contended for is that the minority should peaceably submit to the decisions of the majority – this principle [is] violated in the *Wesleyan* [*sic*] *Banner* see *Banner* preface page 1 Jany. – Jany. Page 11 – April Page 52 etc.

II. That it is designed to review the proceedings of Conference and remonstrate against any measures it may pass, which are not in accordance with the views of the authors of the *Wesley Banner*. *Banner* January,

---

[1] Samuel Dunn, superintendent, Nottingham (North) circuit, 1847–49. Dunn was expelled by Conference, 1849.

[2] For this declaration, see n. 2 p. 373 *supra*.

[3] Dunn disclaimed connexion with the earlier *Flysheets*, and began a paper of his own, *The Wesley Banner and Revival Record*, taking the view that reform and revival were both frustrated by Bunting's institutionalism.

[4] 1 Samuel xv. 23.

Introduction or preface Page1 'The conductors of the *Wesley Banner* etc. etc. *Banner* March page 37, letter on the late Conference'. Review of the Manchester Minor District Meeting before its proceedings were finished on the case of Mr. Walton 'See *Banner* February Page 21'.

Advertisement of the *Wesleyan Times* Newspaper see in the *Wesley Banner* advocating sentiments not to be admired and not contradicted or disowned by Mr. Dunn in any after number of the work.

See '*Banner* for February, advertisement at the end!'

III. That it attempts to change the laws and usages of the Conference by appealing to the Wesleyan Societies at large and to the world instead of making propositions of change to the Conference only.

Election to certain offices by ballot – See '*Banner* March Page 38 being the latter part of the letter signed "One of the Conference"'.

IV. That it asperses a large majority of the Conference who have signed the declaration protesting against the *Fly-Sheets*, and deems them by this cause to have degraded their ministerial character.

See '*Banner* page 53' letter signed 'Saml. Dunn from my study March 13th 1849'. Marked insinuations against those who have signed the declaration. See '*Banner* May page 69. Weighty sentiments'.

Copy. Decision of the Nottingham and Derby District upon the preceding charges.

Ques. Are there any objections to any of the ministers in this District? A. The following charges were preferred against Brother Samuel Dunn by Brother Clarkson viz. (the charges here omitted see before)

This meeting having heard the charges preferred by Brother Clarkson against Brother Dunn and having at great length and at various sittings of the District Committee heard Brother Dunn in reply to these charges – it is in evidence

1. That Mr. Dunn did on the 11th inst. communicate to the Editors of the *Wesleyan Times* Newspaper that he had received notice as one of the editors of the *Wesley Banner* of four charges to be preferred against him at this District Meeting – that Mr. Dunn has during these proceedings intimated that the acts of the District Committee would 'go before the world' that the meeting must 'take care what it does' and that no power upon earth shall 'prevent him from judging and acting for himself in matters of this sort'.

2. It is further in evidence that Mr. Dunn is the avowed and ostensible Editor of a monthly periodical called *Wesley Banner* which periodical is now extensively circulated in our connexion, that the tendency of this publication is to promote strifes and divisions, that it greatly 'endangers the peace' of our Societies, and is dividing our people both in sentiment

and feeling, of which we have some painful instances in our own district. 3. That after long and patiently considering all the circumstances of this case several of the senior ministers in this Committee and others expressed a strong wish were it possible to have the whole matter by mutual concessions and agreement amicably settled – the state and circumstances of our Connexion did in their judgment justify this feeling – *whereupon* Mr. Clarkson expressed his willingness to withdraw all charges against Mr. Dunn on condition that the *Wesley Banner* (to which cause of complaint referred) be at once given up. This proposal was most strongly and affectionately urged upon Mr. Dunn both from the Chair and by almost every minister in the meeting. This recommendation Mr. Dunn positively declined.

Under all these circumstances and after long and prayerful deliberation on this subject we are of opinion

I. That the publication called *Wesley Banner* and edited by Brother Dunn ought to be discontinued.

II. That in accordance with this opinion Brother Dunn be required immediately to suspend its publication.

III. That in case this publication continues to be edited and published by Mr. Dunn, that the whole matter be referred to the Conference.

Copy of amendment.

Moved by Brother Griffith,[1] seconded by Brother George[2]

'That these resolutions cannot be received by this meeting inasmuch as they do not contain a verdict upon the charges brought against Mr. Dunn but on the contrary, introduce fresh matter of charge of which he has received no notice and in reference to which, as far as these new charges depend upon Mr. Dunn's statement, he denies ever having uttered the sentiments attributed to him; and has affirmed again and again that if he did he recalled them as he never intended to utter them, and never so much as had the sentiment in his mind; and moreover because no evidence has been adduced to shew that the effect of the *Banner* has been to disturb the peace of any society'.

Remark.

Only the mover and seconder and a young man of the name of Robson[3] held up their hands for this resolution. . . .

[1] Probably William Griffith jun. (1806–83), expelled the following Conference; superintendent, Ripley circuit, 1847–49.

[2] John C. George (1803–59), superintendent, Grantham circuit, 1847–49.

[3] William Holmes Robson (1810–89), preacher, Melton Mowbray circuit, 1848–50. It is an illustration of the burden of seniority in the Wesleyan ministry at this time that after 14 years' service Robson was still described as 'a young man'.

301 From R. Alder *Derby, August 29, 1849*

You will receive by this post a copy of the *Derby Mercury* of this day containing a letter from Mr. Clarkson on the case of Dunn etc., and an excellent leading article on the same subject. It is really to the point, and coming as it does from a disinterested observer, I send it not only for your information, but because I think it would be well to reprint it in the *Watchman*. The excitement here amongst a certain class of our people, acted upon by Local Preachers, is considerable, but by no means alarming; albeit Griffith and Dunn have been so long in this neighbourhood. The respectable and really influential, and useful members of our Body in this place are all right and steadfast in their attachment to the Conference. Unless I am greatly mistaken the storm in this locality will, ere long, blow over. . . .

302 From William H. Clarkson *Derby, September 13, 1849*

. . . I will endeavour briefly to lay before you the present state of the Derby Circuit and would feel greatly obliged for any suggestion you could make to me under present circumstances, and you may rely upon my confidence in *not* making any such communication known.

When I first entered upon this Circuit, between 30 and 40 Local Preachers had given up their Plans, because my predecessor, Mr. Stevenson,[1] had altered the heading of the plan, but he being advised by some of the fathers of the connexion to resume the former heading, the Local Preachers also resumed their labours. Yet this made them feel that they were of great importance, and led them to conclude that they wielded a great power. I found them not in very good temper, but they did not offer me any insult. It pleased the Lord greatly to prosper his work among us, and all things for the last two years have gone on very peaceably. The Local Preachers have kept to law and rule, and given me no trouble. Indeed the great increase of members of society, the excellence of the congregations and the flourishing state of the finances left them no room to complain.

But no sooner did they learn that Messrs. Everett, Dunn and Griffith were expelled from connection with the Conference, than they called a public meeting at which resolutions simply expressive of sympathy for them were moved, but the movers and seconders of these resolutions made remarks condemnatory of the proceedings of Conference, and

[1] John Stephenson, superintendent, Derby circuit, 1845–47. Derby was one of the chief centres of the Wesleyan Reform movement, which took 40 of the 60 Local Preachers and about 700 members.

sufficient, we think, to make out a good case of charge against 3 at least of the parties, two of whom are the most mischievous men in the Circuit, Messrs. Hawgood[1] and Topham. My colleagues and other friends with myself have conversed on the subject, and the conclusion to which we are come, is, that should we take this step and could we even obtain a verdict of the Leaders' Meeting to convict the parties, yet that the result would be the loss of 30 Local Preachers, as we have the fullest reason to believe that they would make common cause with the expelled; beside some class leaders who would join them, which would occasion the loss of a great many members and the expelled would be held up as martyrs to philanthropy, to the Wesleyan connexion and the whole world. We could well spare about 20 Local Preachers if they would only go away quietly and alone and the Circuit would be all the better for it; but in this state of irritated feeling, which is experienced by many well-meaning but ignorant minds, a great loss would be sustained and Mr. Griffith, who, I am informed, is about to take a house in Derby, would, I presume, take them under his care. We have therefore paused and hesitated to take such a step. I had much conversation with Dr. Alder on this subject, and he thought we were acting rightly in pausing for the present.

A declaration has just been issued in the *Wesleyan Times* signed by 36 officers of the Derby Circuit 22 of whom are Local Preachers determining to do their utmost to obtain the abrogation of the law by which Mr. Everett was expelled. These I may say are the tail of the Circuit. All our influential friends are most steadfast. Mr. German, one of our Circuit Stewards, went to the meeting called to sympathize with the expelled, and made a noble speech against their proceedings, and is exerting himself in every way to support the Conference. A man of the name of Mant [?Marsh] who signs himself in the declaration 'Society-Steward' is only the Steward of a small village society.

I have thought whether it would be well at the approaching Local Preachers' Meeting to ask those men who moved the resolutions at the public meeting, whether they would give any satisfaction as to their future course and engage not to attend any meetings on methodistical affairs, not regularly sanctioned by the Superintendent and presided over by himself or one of his Colleagues. I expect they would refuse to answer the question. Then charges might either be brought against them at a Leaders' Meeting, or I might decline giving them any appointments on the plan because of my want of confidence in them. As to

---

[1] Hawgood, who took the chair at a meeting of 'the expelled', August 21, 1849, was a rag-and-bone dealer, of St. Peter's Bridge, Derby. The meeting was fully reported in the *Derby Mercury* August 22, 1849, which also carried a long letter from Clarkson.

those who signed the declaration I need only give them a very few appointments to places of small importance. Any measure which would lead them to leave of their own accord without expulsion would perhaps be attended with less inconvenience than actual expulsion. Would you be so kind as to say whether you think I should be fully justified in taking these steps, and I will take care to act on my own responsibility.

Many feel great indignation against me and several radical families have absented themselves from my ministry since Conference, because I brought charges against Mr. Dunn at the last District Meeting, and he and Mr. Griffith have been expelled; nevertheless, in despite of all odium, I am determined, the Lord being my helper, to do calmly and firmly whatever I believe to be right and fitting in the present exigency. To have established the law of enquiry and to have cast off three great troublers of our Israel, we must perhaps be willing to endure present circumstances and for the sake of the feeble-minded to bear a little more than in ordinary times, until present effervescent feeling has evaporated.

I am sorry to say Mr. Griffith is coming to preach for the Baptists at Mr. Pyke's Chapel on Sunday next in this town. How disgraceful is the conduct of the dissenters toward us at this time. But they and the radical party among us will struggle hard in the contest, for they clearly see that the law which has expelled Mr. Everett will be the death blow of all agitative and divisive measures among the preachers, and will confine each man to his special calling and work, the preaching of the everlasting gospel, and the saving of souls from death. . . .

303   From William Horton[1]   *Edinburgh, September 13, 1849*

. . . The entire press of Scotland, so far as it has yet spoken, is against us. At least I know of no exception. In the United Presbyterian Magazine there is a very bitter article. The Free Church Magazine too which came out on Saturday last has a short notice of the 'Wesleyan Schism', though comparatively moderate in its tone. I have solicited Dr. Begg[2] to write a leading article for the *Witness*, on the right side. He has the proposal now under consideration. He told me that Dr. Candlish is studying the question. . . .

[1] William Horton, superintendent, Edinburgh circuit, 1847–50.
[2] James Begg (1808–83), left the Church of Scotland at the Disruption; minister of Newington Free Church, 1843–83.

304 From Frederick J. Jobson[1]   *London, September 25, 1849*

I write a hasty line or two to say how we are going on Methodistically in London. Friday last was a very good day. The attendance at all the services was large, and the religious exercises very profitable. City Road chapel was crowded at the 10½ o'clock service, and nearly all the chapels in London filled at the evening prayer-meetings. On Saturday, the Committee preparing for the meeting of Local Preachers in London[2] were very diligent in making applications for places of meeting. They wanted to arrange in time to advertise in the *Wesleyan Times* of Monday; but this they could not accomplish, though they have taken a liberty, and advertised in that paper for services in places not yet promised to them. They want Queen Street Chapel for a sermon to be preached to them by Dr. Melson,[3] Jervin Street School Room for their business-meetings, and City Road chapel for the Sacrament of the Lord's Supper, which they propose should be administered to them by the Revd Messrs. Reece, Sutcliffe and a Minister of City Road Circuit. This all seems very good; but I confess I am more afraid of the result of this movement than I am of the one by Messrs. Everett, Dunn, and Griffith. If they gain the *appearance* of Connexional sanction they will add to their number *many*, who would have stood aloof without it. They will then be more formidable in opposition, when we shall deny them what I under-stand them to propose and request, an annual application to the Methodists for pecuniary assistance of their fund. And, when organised, and agreed in their plans, even the well-disposed will unite with the others in complaints, and opposition. They will also keep up the *Wesleyan Times* after the Everett agitation shall have ceased. *I* would not have given them any chapel, so as to allow the *appearance* of Connexional sanction – for by yielding to expediency, at the present, I doubt not, future difficulties will be increased; but I am almost alone in this opinion and must submit. I believe Mr. Lomas has promised Queen Street Chapel. The Trustees of City Road and Jervin Street must decide respecting the use of their chapels.

The President's pamphlet is now fairly afloat.[4] 4 or 5000 had been

[1] Frederick J. Jobson, preacher, London (City Road) circuit, 1849–52.

[2] Local Preachers, whose attempts to organize charitable assistance for those of their number in distress had for years been resisted by the itinerants (cf. *Early Correspondence* pp. 7, 138, 200), were now successful in launching the Local Preachers' Mutual Aid Association; but ministerial opposition was sharpened by the fact that the L.P.M.A. refused to deny its charity to expelled Local Preachers.

[3] Dr. Melson was a popular Local Preacher of radical religious views from the Birmingham (West) circuit. His sermon on this occasion was printed in *Report of the proceedings of the first aggregate meeting of local preachers for the formation of a Mutual Aid Association* (London, 1849).

[4] T. Jackson, *The Wesleyan Conference, its duties and responsibilities: with a vindication of its recent acts of discipline* (London, 1849). [Mr. Herbert] *A dialogue between a member and his leader in*

ordered on Saturday from the circuits – I have advertised it in some 30 Newspapers and in nearly 20 periodicals, and have sent the pamphlet to many editors. I sent you a copy of the *Britannia* in which you would see the article favourable to our cause. I hope we shall have several others, as the result of sending to editors. A Mr. Herbert, Solicitor of Chelsea, has published a good little Dialogue Tract – I have ordered 1000 for distribution – as I have also done of Mr. Horton's – also 500 of Macdonald's. Mr. Lomas has written another letter, which his brother is to print; and Macbrair has sent the copy of a two leaved Dialogue. The *Exposure of Misrepresentation and Falsehood* is out – also *Opinions of the Press.* I put into the latter the article from the *Britannia*. The orders for all, at present, perhaps, amount to 14 or 15000; and *many* thousands will be sent without orders. I will order a parcel of the publications to be sent off to you today. I am most at a loss for the names and residences of respectable parties, not within Methodism, to whom the President's pamphlet should be sent. Can you suggest any names to me? . . .

305   From William H. Clarkson   *Derby, September 27, 1849*

. . . Our Local Preachers' and Quarterly Meetings went off much better than we expected.

At the Local Preachers' Meeting, I introduced the investigation of character with remarking that the three points of inquiry were in reference to doctrine, moral character, and attention to appointments, that the laws of the connexion had been broken by those who had taken an active part against the Conference in the late public meetings and in signing the declaration, but that these being breaches of the general laws of discipline they did not seem to come under any of our present inquiries, and that therefore I should not refer to them in the calling over of the names but that every one of them was amenable to be called to an account at any Leaders' Meeting by anyone who chose to bring a charge. Afterward one of the Brethren inquired what I should do then in a case of immorality. I replied a Local Preacher may be tried for

the Chelsea circuit (Chelsea, 1849). William Horton, *Methodism and liberty, or friendly hints addressed to the members of the Wesleyan Methodist church who demand certain alterations in its polity and laws* (London, 1849). John Lomas, *Further thoughts on certain recent decisions of the Wesleyan Methodist Conference* (London, 1849) (a sequel to *Thoughts* . . . [1849]). [R. Macbrair] *A short dialogue about Conference and the expelled* (n. pl. or d. [London, 1849]). G. B. Macdonald, *A candid reply to certain inquiries relative to the proceedings of the Methodist Conference held in Manchester 1849* (London, 1849). *Exposure of misrepresentations and falsehoods* (London, 1849). *Opinions of the press respecting the recent expulsions* (n. pl. or d. [London, 1849]).

immorality either at a Leaders' or Local Preachers' Meeting. This I think was conceded.

When we had gone through the regular business of the meeting I laid down the laws as to holding meetings reading from the Laws of Pacification and the Law of [18]35. On these subjects I spoke at considerable length, advised them strongly and affectionately against any farther violation of law, at the same time commending them for their conduct during the past two years. In the course of speaking I also assured them that if the law were violated they must take the consequences of it, that I was responsible to the Conference for the execution of those laws, and that certainly the present state of things could not be continued. Only one or two made some remarks and the meeting concluded in peace as it was begun and continued. At the Quarterly Meeting by request I entered into the same subject of law, and addressed the meeting with words of peace, still informing them that I was responsible for the execution of the laws. There is no reason to doubt that they had come prepared with a resolution of their views on the late expulsions, and wished to know if they could there express their opinion on the subject. I informed them that the Conference reserved exclusively to itself the right of dealing with its own members, and that they did not receive addresses on that subject. This appears to be the point that pinches them the most. Mr. German made a good speech on the question. Since the Quarter Day they have been telling the people that they may think on the subject but cannot speak. One private member we have lost and may lose more. There are a few Local Preachers among us who would not I am sure be satisfied with any concessions the Conference might make except that of allowing them to trample it under their feet. I have read the President's pamphlet and an admirable one it is – comprehensive, conclusive, sufficient. We have got 100 to circulate, and I am glad he has left out the names of the expelled.

There is advertised a meeting of the Local Preachers at City Road for the purpose of forming a Friendly Society or Club and Dr. Melson is to preach on the occasion. I look as many others with great suspicion on this movement.

The Local Preachers here ask for a vestry to hold their periodical meetings in and have applied to me for leave. I have told them that I will consult with a Trustee Meeting on the subject. I should like information as to the manner in which we should act in this case. . . . It does seem to me that the vestry should only be conceded on two conditions, 1st That one of the ministers preside at every meeting. 2nd. That they keep only to their own proper business of accounts connected specially with their society. . . .

306   From William H. Clarkson   *Derby, October 1, 1849*

The enclosed I think will furnish an answer to the question I put to you in my last. Mr. Turner has cut it me out of a newspaper and we think you should see it. It is part of Mr. Dunn's speech delivered at a breakfast meeting at Chesterfield.

We are all surprised that the conveniences of City Road should be conceded to the Local Preachers to work out their pecuniary scheme in which we have always feared that they have intended mischief – that mischief is now developed by Mr. Dunn and is I have no doubt the prime object of this movement.

After this speech from Mr. Dunn no accommodation will be afforded the Local Preachers in our vestries to hold their meetings, yet I am inclined to think that the loan of the premises at City Road will tend to mislead many of our Preachers. The onward and reckless course of the expelled ministers daily demonstrates to us, I think, that the Conference has only done its duty in reference to them, and many I believe before next Conference will have their eyes opened to see the fact. . . .

P.S. I wish it could be so ordered that the Editor of the *Derby Mercury* could have a *Watchman* newspaper regularly forwarded, as he has already done us great service and is ever ready to aid us.

Enclosed newspaper cutting:– The Rev. Samuel Dunn felt great hesitation in recommending his friends to pursue any definite course. A meeting of delegates was expected in London, and until they had met and calmly weighed the whole matter it would be better to wait that they might act in concert with other parts of the country. They might however safely urge that Conference should sit with open doors. (Cheers.) Dr. Dixon[1] said four months ago, without reference to them, but comparing England with America, 'the time must come when Conference must be open to the public'. At least one advantage would be gained by admitting the public – it would make gentlemen of the preachers. The scenes of the last Conference would not be repeated. There was nothing in the deed of settlement to prevent them opening their doors, and this would be a very important point gained. Another object should be the appointment of laymen for treasurers; this was desirable from what had taken place during the last year. He could mention a preacher that had between one and two hundred thousand pounds, which passed through his hands annually. He did not hint that he embezzled any part of it, but it was unseemly that a minister of the gospel should be up to the

---

[1] James Dixon had been a Conference delegate to the Methodist Episcopal Church of America in the 'forties and admired what it preserved of Wesley's original intentions. J. Dixon, *Methodism in America* (3rd ed. London, 1849).

neck in pounds, shillings and pence from one end of the year to the other. (Cheers.) Next week delegates from the Local Preachers would meet in London from different parts of the country to establish a fund for their relief, and for other objects. Afterwards the delegates would meet to consider what changes should be asked for in the Connexion. A committee would sit for the next twelve months at Exeter Hall, to see friends from the country and to answer letters, composed of Local Preachers and other officers in the London circuits. He thought they need not be afraid of expressing themselves on this question. The Chesterfield friends had done honour to themselves; and if they were cautious and kept upon the line, the superintendents would be cautious in laying hands upon them. Not one of the committee at Exeter Hall had been touched. The avowed editor of the *Wesleyan* is a Local Preacher, and lives within a few doors of the Doctor, and although the *Wesleyan Times* is called a vile production, the editor passed the quarterly meeting without one word being said. Mr. Dunn gave several instances in which he had been invited to preach in Wesleyan pulpits since his expulsion, and said in one case an officer was called upon for contributions to the Worn-out Preachers' Fund, but said he had nothing for that object, but that he had given £2. 2s. for the fund for the expelled ministers. He was called upon to pray afterwards, and he prayed ardently for the ministers who were so unrighteously expelled. (Cheers.) He mentioned these things to show the feeling which prevailed, and that if cautious they had nothing to fear. Mr. Everett was in York, Mr. Griffith in the neighbourhood of Derby, and he should remain in London; he thought it best therefore that they should mutually agree to consult the London committee as much as possible as to future proceedings. (Cheers.)

307   From R. Alder   *London, October 2, 1849*

I trust that you are deriving much advantage from your visit to Buxton, and that you will return greatly improved in health and strength. We have been much occupied yesterday and today with the intended alterations in Post Office business on the Lord's Day, having been waited upon by a deputation from some of the officials of that establishment at the Book Room, which deputation had waited upon the Bishop of London[1] and Dr. Pye Smith,[2] who have promised their support and cooperation. A great meeting of City bankers and merchants etc. is to be

[1] Charles James Blomfield.
[2] John Pye Smith (1774–1851), eminent nonconformist divine; theological tutor at Homerton College, 1806–51.

held at the Hall of Commerce tomorrow for the purpose of petitioning the Government against the threatened evil. I forward by this post a copy of the *Morning Herald* from which you will perceive the view taken of the measure in that quarter. We are anxious to obtain your authority for appending your justly influential name to our petition, and I enclose a copy of it for your information. As the task of preparing it was devolved chiefly upon myself, I may state that although [it was] drawn up with great haste, I have been careful to verify the matters of fact which are embodied in it. Can you send the desired authority by return of post [?].

Everything is going on much as usual. The Sheetites[1] *alias* Cheetites are still at their occupation, but it will not last unless we help to keep their shop open. There is a capital notice of the President[']s defence in the *Record*. The Local Preachers are to hold their Great Meeting this week. This is a suspicious movement; but the Lord reigneth and blessed be our Rock. . . .

308   From William Horton   *Edinburgh, October 27, 1849*

. . . I send you by the same mail which will convey this, a copy of the Free Church Magazine for this month – published last week. The article on the Wesleyan Conference is from the pen of the Rev. W. G. Blaikie,[2] the editor. He applied to me about a month ago for information on the subject, having previously read my pamphlet. I found he was solicitous to ascertain the true character of the *Fly Sheets*. I lent him the first number, and very gladly communicated to him all the information he sought. He candidly admitted that the short notice which appeared in the Free Church Magazine for September and which was decidedly opposed to the Conference, was premature. He has this month, you will perceive, got nearly right.

Dr. Candlish has given forth no 'deliverance' yet upon the question. Nor have I yet had an opportunity of seeing him. But I am told, I think on good authority, that, in conversing with a friend, Dr. Cunningham[3] said most explicitly that the Conference was right; that in its power of inquiry it possessed an advantage over the Free Church; that the Presbyterian system in Scotland sprang up during a period of great political excitement, and largely partook of the political element; that

[1] I.e. the supporters of the *Flysheets*.

[2] William Gordon Blaikie (1820–99), Scots divine; Free Church minister of Pilnig, 1844–1868. Editor of several journals; professor of apologetics and pastoral theology, New College, Edinburgh, 1868–97.

[3] William Cunningham (1805–61), Free Church controversialist; professor of church history, New College, Edinburgh, 1845; principal, 1847.

this has always hampered them; but that Methodism arose as a purely spiritual system, free from all political entanglements, and based solely upon New Testament principles.

If these are Dr. Cunningham's sentiments, I should rejoice to have publicity given to them. But he may not think it expedient to make an open declaration of them. It appears to me that the leading men of the Free Church entertain more favourable views of Methodism than they think it right to express. They know that such views would be found to clash with the stupid prejudices which generally prevail in Scotland in regard to us. A change however in the right direction is unquestionably in progress. We are becoming better known, and more respected. And the day will yet arrive when we shall receive from the Free Church and the other churches of this country, expressions of friendliness more satisfactory than any thing that has yet appeared. . . .

309   From John Geden[1]   *Hammersmith, November 7, 1849*

Some remarks which you made on *Monday* at the Book Committee, led me to think what more could be done to conciliate the *sincere* but misled among our people, who think that they are not *sufficiently represented* in the Conference, and there is one thing [that] has *occurred* to me, of some importance which I now take the liberty of suggesting to you, and it is, to *allow* the *Circuit Stewards* who may be *present* at the *District Meeting*, to *vote* with the *Ministers* for the *Representative*.[2] Serious objections to this may very possibly exist, but they do not present themselves to my mind. As the individual chosen has to *represent* the *Circuits* as well as the *Ministers*, and as the Circuit Stewards are *generally* men in whom we can *confide*, I have been induced to make this communication – especially as I think I have observed in *past times* that when *unreasonable* and *impracticable* things have been *clamoured* for, this has not *deterred* you from proposing any *reasonable* concession. . . .

[1] John Geden (1793–1872), superintendent, Hammersmith circuit, 1847–50.

[2] The Conference Stationing Committee which appointed preachers to their circuits was constituted by a representative from each District, elected by ballot of all the members of the District Meeting in full connexion; together with the President and Secretary of the preceding Conference, one of the Missionary Secretaries, and one of the officers of the Theological Institution.

310   From John Rigg[1]   *Bath, November 16, 1849*

. . . The expelled[2] were here on Wednesday last, and held a public
meeting in the Assembly Rooms. Mr. Dunn was the guest of Mr.
Bromley,[3] and he and his family were on the platform, by the side of the
Trio, and in the midst of those who have signed the Memorial.[4] Is Mr.
Bromley's conduct consistent with the voluntary pledge which he gave
at the last Conference? He will say I doubt not that he entertained Mr.
Dunn as a private friend. But must such conduct be endured? Such
conduct excites in me unutterable loathing and abhorrence. All the
Trustees of King Street Chapel, save one, are loyal, and no Leader of
any importance connected with it has signed the stupid thing sent to the
President. The Trustees and Leaders connected with Wale St[?] with the
exception of Mr. Phipps, Mr. Batchelor, and one or two more are
resolved to have lay delegation.[5] Had the minister residing amongst them
been loyal nothing of this would have happened.

Many years ago I heard you say in Conference, You have fought and
won your great battle with Kilham.[6] Your next great battle will be
with the Local Preachers. So it has come to pass. Everywhere they are
the leaders in the movement. Can anything be done to improve this
part of our system, by far the weakest and the worst. We have a fair
opportunity, for they are openly aspiring after supreme authority. The
great majority of our Trustees will be found trustworthy. They know
well that if they are to have Local Preachers often in their pulpits they
will soon be crushed to death with debt. I hope the President,[7] his long-
headed brother, Mr. Scott,[8] and especially yourself will think on this
subject.

On Monday last I received an anonymous letter with a card enclosed,
in which the writer tells me that, understanding that I was the principal
means of the expulsion of the Rev. S. Dunn a man on whom I am not
worthy to look, he had out of pure good will, sent me the enclosed, that
I might therewith hang myself at once: for Mr. Dunn was coming to

[1] John Rigg, superintendent, Bath circuit, 1847–50.

[2] 'The three expelled' (by the Conference of 1849) were James Everett, Samuel Dunn and
William Griffith.

[3] Cf. n. 2 p. 354 *supra*. Soon afterwards Bromley refused to appear before the Bath District
Meeting, and was himself expelled.

[4] Numerous memorials to the Conference or to the President were drawn up in the circuits
stating grievances or demanding organic reform.

[5] I.e. lay representation in Conference.

[6] Alexander Kilham (1762–98), founder of the Methodist New Connexion, 1797, in which
the Conference was composed half of preachers, half of lay representatives.

[7] Thomas Jackson.

[8] John Scott, superintendent, London (Islington) circuit, 1848–51.

Bath on Wednesday, and then perhaps I should do it in a rage. The poor creature signed himself

A member of the Methodist Society. . . .

311 From Odden Hambrook   *n. pl. December 4, 1849*

. . . I need not in adverting to the distressing circumstances that disturb the Body, attempt to assign the moving cause; but for my own part consider that it arises from the prevailing and popular notions of governing that obtain in our days. The Wesleyan system is and ever was Conservative; and in our day religious men seem so carried away with what I consider in a great measure are speculative views, that they desire to apply the same principles, or rather experiments, to the Church of Christ, not considering that order and oppression are wide as the poles asunder. But one thing I have seen, both in a confined and also extensive scale, that Liberal opinions (so called) are coupled with absolute despotism. . . .

312 From George Greenwood[1]   *Bingley, January 4, 1850*

. . . As it regards changing the constitution of Methodism, perhaps I may be allowed to say that it pleases me *as it is*. Should any attempt be made to introduce lay delegates into the Conference, my vote would be given most decidedly against it. I never was an agitator, but about 15 years since (when I knew very little of Methodism) being dissatisfied with it, though recommended to the ministry by the Quarterly Meeting where I resided, I resigned and retired. My first sermon as a Minister, was preached in one of the pulpits of the New Connexion, in Liverpool, where the late Mr. Watson[2] exercised his splendid talents. There, and in Huddersfield, the following year, had I the opportunity of seeing reformed Methodism in full operation; and I will say that the best *cure* for a man who is not satisfied with *Old* Methodism is to try some branch of the *New*. He will find, under the new system, rivalries, not very peaceful, respecting who shall be delegated to the Quarterly Meetings and the Conference, respectable and leading individuals in Circuits forming constituencies in order to secure their election to one or both, and each individual shielding his friends and supporters from the lash of discipline should they be charged with any breach of morality.

[1] George Greenwood (1809–65), preacher, Bingley circuit, 1849–52. Preacher in the Methodist New Connexion 1835–38, when he entered the Wesleyan ministry.

[2] Richard Watson, Methodist New Connexion preacher in Liverpool, 1806–7.

Admit laymen into the Conference and we destroy the foundation of Methodism – the whole ecclesiastical superstructure will fall into ruins, and our present economy cease for ever. A new fabric will be built, but let us bear in mind who will be the workmen and what the material. How different, when finished, from the old one!! We shall have Super-intendents *in* our Circuits but they will not be Superintendents *of* our Circuits – they will be such but in name. They must preside in the local meetings only in their turn, must submit to allow Quarterly Meetings to make them their preachers' Plans, and must go to Conference *only* when they are elected. Ministers of all grades must become amenable to a society or a Quarterly Meeting, and at the latter, once a year, undergo such an examination as the following. 'Has he lived as well as preached the Gospel?' 'Has he attended to our discipline?' 'Is he in debt?' These questions are moved by laymen, whether enlightened or ignorant, whether prejudiced against him or unprejudiced. They are moved one by one, either in the negative or the affirmative, put to the meeting by a layman, who then takes the chair, and carried either for or against the minister. If for him, he receives a certificate of good conduct which is forwarded to Conference; if against him, I can only say 'Poor fellow!' I know from *observation* and *some* experience that all this places the minister in a sort of fear during the year, injures his faithfulness and usefulness in the pulpit, and cripples him in the exercise of discipline. More might be said, but it is unnecessary at present. If, however, such a question should be mooted at the next annual District Meeting, it would then perhaps be my duty to say all I know, and to try to point out *why* the work of God does not prosper under these *new* systems. *There is a cause.* Pardon this liberty, dear Sir, taken by one who thinks he has a right to conserve and defend the privileges pledged to him when he was ordained a minister of Methodism *as it is.* . . .

P.S. I hold several letters from ministers wishing to escape from these *New* Methodisms, asking my advice etc. . . .

313　From William Lord　　　　　*Woodhouse Grove, February 1, 1850*

. . . Several of our circuits in these parts are very wrong. Bramley is in a sad state, but I hear some of the agitators are coming to their right mind. Politics has *prepared* the minds of some for their bad work, and *Barkerism*[1] has prejudiced the mass against ministers. Leeds, Bradford,

[1] Joseph Barker (1806–75), a political and ecclesiastical radical, had been expelled from the Methodist New Connexion ministry in 1841, taking with him about one third of the membership. In the mid-'forties he leaned towards unitarianism, and in 1848 was imprisoned as a political agitator. As a boy he had been brought up a Wesleyan at Bramley.

Keighley, Bingley, Pontefract, and several other circuits are upon the whole peaceable. All our leading friends, or nearly so, are sound. I fear politics, railway speculations, self-importance, etc. have predisposed many of our respectable people, not remarkable for spiritual religion, to enter into the movement, at Huddersfield, Wakefield and Halifax; and I do not see how they can retreat unless God vouchsafes to our Societies in those places a remarkable visitation of the Spirit. May this be the case! I hope and pray that you may be supported in this day of rebuke and blasphemy. . . .

314 From James Heald   *House of Commons, February 27, 1850*

I arrived here safely about 4 1/4 o'clock. You will have seen the results of Fox'[s] motion last night.[1] I saw Lord Ashley as soon almost as I had entered the precincts of the House. He advised earnestly that the Government should be left to reply to the motion in the first instance – but after a considerable pause they still shirked it, until Sir R. Inglis[2] compelled Lord John [Russell] to speak. After his statement we all thought it best to refrain and wait the printing of the Bill. Lord Ashley spoke to me today very kindly and freely. He says he believes there never was an instance before of the kind, the Government actually applauding Fox, and with great favour supporting a Unitarian in bringing in a bill whose special operation, if not object, will be to degrade religion and exalt above it what is secular. He says we must now prepare for a serious, solemn and conscientious deliverance of our sentiments upon the grave matter involved in the measure. My candid opinion as well as serious apprehension, said his Lordship, is that this is the beginning of the end which has so long threatened us. I have engaged him to attend a meeting at the National Club to confer upon the best mode of preparing for the struggle. My own opinion is (in confidence) that after what is felt to be the virtual defeat of the Government on Disraeli's motion and the determined action of the Protectionists on Monday night, the Government will bid high for the support of the extreme movement party in the hope of retaining their seats. I shall be

[1] William Johnson Fox (1786–1864), unitarian preacher of South Place chapel, Finsbury, and M.P. for Oldham, 1847–63. On February 26, 1850, he obtained leave to bring in a bill to promote the secular education of the people in England and Wales. *Parliamentary Debates* 3s. cix. 27–59.

[2] Sir Robert Harry Inglis (1786–1855), evangelical; tory M.P. for Oxford University, 1829–54. Inglis compelled Russell to make a statement; the latter asked the house to receive Fox's bill, but was non-committal about its substance, saying that the religious societies had made progress with national education, though not as much progress as had been hoped for.

2D

glad to see you again in London and will send you a copy of the Bill as soon as it is printed. My opinion is that our first plan would have been the best and to have made Fox'[s] motion and speech the occasion of boldly and promptly setting forth right principles.

Mr. Scott was present at the debate. . . .

315   From Peter M'Owan[1]   *Liverpool, March 5, 1850*

. . . Pitt Street Chapel [Liverpool], you are aware, has been for some time back the weak point of our circuit. The population around it has become to a great extent Irish, and of course Popish; and the neighbourhood has become proverbially poor, squalid, noisy, and every way uninviting. These changes have led to the diminution of our congregation, and to the removal of our more respectable friends; so that without special aid from other quarters the Trust must be ruined. Our effort to reduce the debt does not proceed so auspiciously as we anticipated; and indeed there is some danger of its miscarrying altogether. . . .

316   From Robert Newstead[2]   *Woolwich, March 9, 1850*

Having intimated to you that *Dr. Carlisle* had in an inflammatory letter to a local print *called* for a meeting at which he might declare his sentiments of abhorrence at the treatment of the expelled men etc., I hastily write a line to describe *its results*. The agitators have at such call paid us a visit! A meeting has been *secretly* got up. No *intimation* of such purpose being given till *yesterday morning early*, the town was placarded for a meeting at the Town Hall in the *evening* – 'to hear the statements *and to elect delegates for this Circuit'*!!!

The meeting has accordingly been held. Only Mr. Dunn attending and holding forth, as usual, for *two hours*. Griffith did not come, and I am glad to inform you, such is the state of our Society here, that *only the same two men* (Local Preachers) who took part at the Greenwich Meeting, could be found for Chairman and the *only* speaker besides Mr. D. *These 2 men also* were then *elected for delegates*! – one being a common *labourer* in the Dock Yard – the other a very humble Linen-Draper, men of no sort of influence or power in the Society, *the whole of which* – so far as I know – *are firmly attached to our cause, and look upon these proceedings with mingled indignation and contempt*. Dr. Carlisle was it is believed present but, from

---

[1] Peter M'Owan, superintendent, Liverpool (South) circuit, 1847–50.

[2] Robert Newstead, superintendent, Woolwich circuit, 1849–50.

some cause, after all did not speak! We believe that the demonstration has left little or no impression of the kind contemplated. Two less important and powerless men could not have been chosen (*they tried hard for better!*) to represent a meeting (*not our Society*) made up of all sorts of people, many of whom were common soldiers. There is no doubt the meeting was thus secretly and *suddenly* arranged, and close on the eve of the Sabbath to prevent any counteracting measures. I trust it will do very little harm and will make our friends more decided still. . . .

317 From William H. Clarkson   *Derby, March 27, 1850*

I am sure you will be glad to learn that yesterday we had a Quarterly Meeting of the most gratifying and satisfactory kind in which we carried all our measures most triumphantly; and what was still better the Lord was with us and a very gracious divine influence and almost oneness of spirit pervaded the meeting. Messrs. Turner and German were re-elected to be Stewards, with only four dissentients, resolutions passed approving of Methodism as it is, condemnatory of the proceedings of the late so-called delegation meeting, approving of the manner which the Circuit finances had been managed; and strange to say a resolution was carried approving of the manner in which I had carried out the discipline of the connexion with only one dissenting voice, and he is one of the self-styled delegates, who is on Monday evening next to be deprived of his office as Leader. We had about 60 present of our friends from all parts of the Circuit who went away much encouraged and refreshed in spirit, amazed at the things they had seen and heard. Against no proposition were there more than four hands held up. These resolutions were ordered by the meeting to be published in the *Watchman* and *Derby Mercury* newspapers. I therefore refer you to the *Watchman* for a sight of them as well as some remarks made by Mr. Shaw[1] which will be inserted in another part of the paper. At our Local Preachers' Meeting we removed from the office of Local Preacher Mr. Woolhouse, one of the delegates, and I suppose he will leave us entirely. He is a rabid radical and annoyed us much in the Local Preachers' Meeting, but he had no place among us in the Quarterly Meeting. With regard to our finances about 40 friends have engaged to subscribe certain extra sums quarterly which will be continued as long as needed. The result was that the income of the current quarter was about £3 more than the

---

[1] The pledges of loyalty of the Derby Quarterly Meeting opposed by never more than 4 in a gathering of 60 were published in the *Watchman* March 27, 1850 p. 97. Shaw's remarks did not appear.

expenditure. I am quite of the opinion that if the Preachers throughout the connexion would only exclude the worst radicals who have committed themselves, we should have before Conference a healthy state of things throughout the connexion, and the men that would be applying for reforms would have no place among us. What a state we should now have been in on this Circuit if discipline had not been exercised! We have refused tickets to all who have refused to contribute having been before accustomed to do so. By 6 expulsions, some incidents, and prudential arrangements, I gained not less than 16 this Quarter in favour of Conference measures. . . .

318   From Robert Melson   *Handsworth, April 13, 1850*

I have oft thought it to be my duty to address you with a letter, as I find it to be impossible to obtain access through the medium of Secretary or President to the Wesleyan Conference.

In '47 I wrote what I then thought, and still think a very appropriate and important letter to the Conference,[1] addressed it to Mr. S. Jackson, who was then in the chair, but it was not permitted to be heard. Had it been read and acted upon, I believe that we should never have been brought into the woefully deplorable state into which we are now plunged as a *noble branch* of the Church of Christ, and out of which the *Lord alone* can deliver us!

You Sir, have known me many years, and now know me to be an old man and an aged Methodist preacher. Of course you will excuse me in addressing a few words to you in expression of my views and *feeling heart*. That you have *very great power* or influence over your brethren you must know of a certainty. And, indeed, this is a *fact* which has for a long time been believed by the connexion generally, and is now proved to demonstration! I envy you not. But Sir, I shall beg and beseech you to *use* your influence *without delay*, in putting a stop to the dreadful work of *devastation* that is now going on through the length and breadth of the Connexion. It is in you, Sir, just now, *Aaron-like*, to stand between the dead and the living and stay the plague!!!

    [1] This immense and passionate letter (M.C.A. MSS. R. Melson to the Wesleyan Conference, August 2, 1847) called for reform, a complete change of Mission House staff (including Bunting), an end to institutionalization and a return to primitive simplicity in Methodism. On April 26, 1850, Melson wrote to Bunting again, protesting that he had received no acknowledgment of his original letter, and ascribing the chaos in Methodism to Bunting's constitutional legislation: ' . . . consider the awful state of things into which we are brought! by *whom*! and by *what means*! Look at the laws of '35, like a man of understanding, and as becometh the *Premier* for such a wise, holy, just, kind merciful, loving and powerful body of people as the Wesleyans . . .'.

I beseech you Sir, for the Lord's sake, and for the sake of precious and immortal souls, and for the sake of righteousness and peace in the earth, to do this! It is in your power! It is your *duty*! It will redound to your honour and happiness! It will be a blessing to you in life! In death! Before the bar of God! And through all eternity!!! . . .

319   From William Vevers
Wesleyan College, Taunton,
May 6, 1850

. . . Surely such exhibitions of christian feeling as those exhibited in Exeter Hall must enlighten and disgust every man not quite a maniac! I marvel at the Dissenting brethren, who, while they profess to be horrified with our tyranny in our expulsions, have on the *same principles* performed a much more atrocious act of tyranny by the exclusion of a Minister and *entire Church* from the Congregational Union in Manchester in the case of Dr. Nolan.[1] I do not blame them for what they have done, but they have not acted on the *merits* of the case. Their act of discipline has been grounded on the *refusal* of Dr. N. and the Church to *submit* to the terms of the Union, the very principle on which we as a Conference acted. They denounce us – and doubtless applaud themselves! I feel strongly inclined to fire some grape shot into the camp of our fickle and false friends. . . .

320   From Joseph Sutcliffe
Bayswater, June 17, 1850

. . . Some years ago, I remember hearing you say, that the next struggle would be with the Local Preachers. That day is now come, rough and bitter enough. The brethren in the United States, have got that conflict over. Dr. Bangs in his history[2] names 30 or 40, and over 50 locations in one year.[3] It was easy to augur that the number of located men, and half of them in holy orders, would come to mischief in the issues.

[1] E. H. Nolan, formerly secretary of the Irish Evangelical Society, gathered a new congregationalist meeting in Manchester in 1838, and the handsome Ducie chapel was built for him in York St. in 1840. Dr. Nolan 'attracted large congregations for many years, but a cloud rests upon the close of his ministry. He resigned in 1853, and for twelve months the chapel was closed'. B. Nightingale, *Lancashire nonconformity* v. 196–7.

[2] Cf. n. 4 p. 365 *supra*.

[3] For many years terms of ministerial service in the Methodist Episcopal Church of America were very hard, and neither manses nor allowances for wife and family to which the preachers were legally entitled were generally forthcoming. The result was that most of the preachers were single men, periods of service were short, and it was normal for a preacher when he

The located men having married, got short of land with their wives; and others, having taken stores (shops), wants followed, debts in trades. And then *to see* young men then trusting the Lord for bread, and themselves in the background, they spontaneously raised a revolt in all the large towns, complaining in bitter words that they had not been recalled into [the] work and new churches. Truly the Bishop could not recall them. They had located without leave, leaving the superintendents in Districts to fill up circuits, and obliging him to send exhorters rather than preachers, who in turn became able ministers, and neither the Bishop nor the stewards seemed in haste to recall the runaways from them, so they were obliged to remain with [their] own choice. Hence I augur it will be the same with our Local Preachers, who cannot as they would take their turn in all the chapels.

Hence I would say, with deference, that you must go on with your work, and keep the staff in your own hand but make all concessions that can be done with safety to the chief pastors in the church. . . .

321   From Robert Maxwell Macbrair[1]

Nottingham,
July 5, 1850

I beg to submit to your judgment the outline of a scheme which I have long thought of, and which I have often heard mentioned by others as very desirable. The time seems to be *come* for having a *Wesleyan* weekly journal – not to supersede the *Watchman*, but to prevent other newspapers which do incalculable harm to our Connexion. The *Watchman* is upheld for the purpose of Conservatism and is not read by the majority of Methodists. I have heard many of our people who now read *Kaye's Times*[2] say, that they would gladly take in a journal which was not connected with any kind of *Politics*. Other people object to those usual appurtenances of a modern newspaper, 'dreadful accidents, murders, etc. etc.', and would like a paper which might be unreservedly placed in the hands of their children, for their information and profit.

The present generation *will* read newspapers, so they ought to be furnished with one to which no moral or political objections could be made, which would be interesting and instructive to all readers, and to the educated young in particular. Such a journal would soon *swamp*

wished to marry to 'locate', i.e. to drop out of the itinerant ministry, settle in one place, and acquire a home and settled work. Despite Sutcliffe's pessimism 'located' ministers, continuing to serve as local preachers, did an immensely valuable work for their church.

[1] Robert Maxwell Macbrair, preacher, Nottingham (Halifax Place) circuit, 1848–51.

[2] Presumably the *Liverpool Courier* published by the conservative Wesleyan, Thomas Kaye.

Kaye's Times, and prevent the establishment of another of like principles; and would eventually find its way into religious families of all denominations. . . .

322 From John Rigg

. . . I look forward to the Conference now so near with deep and often with painful anxiety. What is to be done with Dr. B?[1] Shall a minister who is the friend of revolution, and revolutionists be allowed to escape without censure and be continued in the important office which he sustains? If so, then will our discipline receive a wound which no art will be able to heal, and every superintendent must hereafter be allowed to do what is right in his own eyes. On the other hand to depose the Doctor from office only would be productive of results which one does not like to think of. Could a middle course be pursued? Could the Doctor be censured, but allowed to retain his present position with the forlorn hope that he may 'tak' a thought and min' '[?] And then there is another doctor[2] on whose consistency and Methodistical soundness, I have ceased to place any reliance. If Methodism be destroyed, it will be by the hands of its ministers.

In this Circuit we are a little better. The backbone of the faction is broken. But we shall probably see a few convulsive struggles before it gives up the ghost and its discordant voice shall cease to grate upon the ear.

Not one of the three delegates from this city has been put upon his trial. My reasons for not placing them at the bar were the following. Two of them must have been brought before a tribunal, three-fourths of whom are their friends, and accomplices; and a trial would to them have been a triumph. The other might have been convicted for he is amenable to the King Street Leaders' Meeting. But to have punished him whilst the others were not called to an account would have been wrong and injurious. Mr. Bill was not present to receive his ticket, and as he has ceased to worship in our chapels, I did not leave it for him. The other two I have seen, and they assure me that they will not disturb the peace of the Society, but either quietly submit or peaceably retire. A second special meeting of the District Committee would have been most injurious. I detained the Circuit Stewards, but no memorial was proposed. Mr. Bromley's[3] salary has not been paid. The Circuit Steward

[1] Dr. Joseph Beaumont, preacher, London (Hinde St.) circuit, 1848–49; superintendent, 1849–51. Cf. n. 1 p. 20 *supra*.

[2] Perhaps Dr. Robert Alder who withdrew from the ministry in 1853.

[3] For Bromley's misdeeds see n. 2 p. 6, n.2 p. 354 *supra*.

expressed a strong desire to pay it; but added that as Mr. B's friends had thought proper, with hardly an exception, either to withhold their contributions or greatly to reduce them, he could not pay the salary out of his own pocket. . . .

323   From Joseph Richardson   *Leeds, July 12, 1850*

I think it important that you should know that the Government are contemplating a measure that will seriously affect our *Trust Property* as a Connexion. Doctor Sutherland[1] paid a recent visit to Leeds and most other large towns by the direction of Government to explain their views and collect information on the subject of intramural interments, with a view of removing them from all large towns etc.[2] When in Leeds he sought an interview with the Mayor, the Town Clerk and the Chairman of the Burial Grounds Committee of the Town Council.

As the Chairman of that Committee I met him with the other parties. After he had explained the Government plan and received from us all the information he could, he made the following statement, and it is to that I wish to direct your attention. '*The Government intend to give compensation to the clergy for the loss of their burial grounds*,' etc. etc. I then said, I am a Wesleyan, and then went into detail at great length showing the injustice of giving compensation to the clergy for the loss of their grounds if we were not also compensated for ours. I also followed him down to his inn and pressed this subject on his attention by various arguments, after which he said he now saw the subject as I saw it and thought we had as fair a right to compensation as the Church had, and he would make the representation to the Earl of Carlisle,[3] who had charge of the Bill, as strongly as I had made it to him. He took notes of my statements. I told him it would be a great hardship to take away our Burial Grounds which we had bought and paid for as Wesleyan property without compensation, to which sentiment he gave his full assent. . . .

[1] John Sutherland M.D. (1808–91), sanitary reformer and inspector under the Board of Health.

[2] Under two acts to amend the law concerning the burial of the dead in the Metropolis (15 & 16 Vict. c. 85 [1852] and 16 & 17 Vict. c. 134 [1853]) the Queen in Council was empowered on the representation of a Secretary of State to close any cemetery or to forbid the opening of any new cemetery in any part of the metropolis.

[3] See n. 1 p. 46 *supra*.

324 From John Moore   *Leeds, July 13, 1850*

. . . I am anxious to disabuse your mind in reference to your late visit to Leeds, fearing that you have left it under a wrong impression, which is exceedingly probable from the unparalleled adulatory treatment you met with when here. Now I will take upon myself to say (and I speak advisedly) that if instead of your just preaching an odd sermon in Oxford Place Chapel, you had taken the Music Hall for one evening and invited fair open and candid discussion from the Methodists of Leeds upon the points of *very serious* difference which at present unhappily distract the Methodist Society, that you would have done more good than by any other means whatsoever! If you have done nothing wrong why are you and your Brethren so reluctant in coming forward to vindicate your characters against the heavy allegations brought against you? It need not be a long business to set the whole machinery of Methodism right again if truth and honesty are the mainsprings, but if they are wanting it will take a long time, *if ever* the machine can be got to work again!!

If you had adopted the course herein suggested, and had been able to prove to the Society your innocence of what is laid to your charge, you would unquestionably have produced a feeling of the highest satisfaction in this important town and one which would have thrilled through the Connexion like lightning. And allow me to tell you, Sir, that until you come forward in some such manner, and put to flight the odium resting upon you, you need not look for peace in the Society, nor have you a right to expect it. You forget that this is the 19th century, or at least your proceedings would lead to the supposition that you do, and men are not to be treated as mere animals or brutes of burden.

Do not I pray lay the flattering unction to your soul that all the Methodists in Leeds are fools, they do not I can assure you believe either the Pope of Rome or yourself to be infallible at least the majority of them do not! –

In conclusion I would earnestly recommend you to light your pipe (if you smoke) or the fire with the piece of paper containing the '*Address*' you got given at the Leeds breakfast as it is certainly of no higher value[1] . . .

---

[1] Great efforts were made at this time to produce demonstrations of lay support for the connexional leadership.

325 From Charles Cornell   *96 Eastgate, Rochester,*
                                                    July 15, 1850

. . . I have been a member for nearly 40 years. Many times Circuit
Steward of this Circuit. I am a superintendent of a large Sabbath
School and a Leader of 2 Classes, which have contained 60 members,
and *without in any way* mixing with the agitating party which is rending
our Society, I have been able quietly to get at the mind of those who are
less informed and also of the sentiments of those who are *neutral*. Again,
as I have had opportunity as I have come in contact with many of our
ministers, I have elicited their views on the present and recent course of
our Methodistic administration, and I feel bound to communicate the
result of these inquiries to you, it being allowed on all hands that you
stand possessed of a power *in Methodism* not known since the days of our
venerable founder, and therefore a *right* or *wrong* turn of the helm in our
present critical affairs may either be for *much good* or much *ill*.

I find that though a large portion of our people in this circuit have
kept aloof from signing papers or going [to] the meetings of the adverse
party, yet it is quite clear they would hail with gladness, a *gentler* and
more *liberal* procedure on the part of those whose place it is to take the
lead in our Conference.

The ministers, of whom I have met with many, take the same view.
This is so general and unequivocal that I sometimes fear that yourself
with those in your own immediate confidence and of consequence
looking at our affairs through *one* medium *only*, may not be aware of the
real state of our people's minds. I am quite sure and I speak advisedly,
that should our beloved ministers carry their purposes in accordance
with the past, *with a high hand*, it will produce such a shock, from which
as a *People at present constituted*, we shall never recover.

It would ill become me to say *what should be done*. But I believe from
my heart that out of the many thousands of our Israel, *you* are by God's
Providence the *only man* that could at this awful juncture *turn* the
adverse stream *into* its right direction and produce peace in our distracted Church. Perhaps you would have to sacrifice much as it
respects party friends, but it would be a glorious result, one that would
close your long and useful life with a glory that would *never go out*.
Naaman once listened to a little maid and was cured – despise not the
reasoning and advice of an individual who loves our Zion, and fears
for her safety and who truly loves and reveres yourself. . . .

326 From Henry J. Davis   *Lawley Street, Birmingham,*
July 22, 1850

Before you descend to the grave, which if you had done so the day you
entered the ministry, would have been a blessing to thousands, I wish to
appeal to you (if there is any grace left in you) to retire from the priest-
hood. Many daily pray to God to take you hence, many curse your
name and memory as a character who has made more infidels than all
the deistical writers put together. Your system through life has been the
aggrandisement of yourself and family. Nearly all with whom I converse
look upon you as a thorough heartless villain, hoping you will repent
and cry for mercy, that mercy you never yet bestowed on any one. . . .

327 From Allen B. Sprigg   *Bedworth in Coventry (Hinckley Circuit),*
September 28, 1850

At a meeting held in St. Mary's Hall Coventry last night, the Revd. S.
Dunn made the following statements, nearly verbatim. After stating the
circumstances attendant upon his expulsion, and the course he has for
many previous years pursued in the Conference relative to the laws of
1835, etc. 'Now (said he) the last Conference have passed a law which
is one of the greatest pieces of Jesuitry that ever existed. Tired of the
publicity which proceedings in our ecclesiastical courts have obtained,
they have passed this law to get rid of trials, and to give them power to
expel you if you refuse to answer "Yes or No" to any question your superintendent asks you, so that if he were to ask you next Tuesday evening,
"did you attend the meeting at St. Mary's Hall on Friday night?", if you
say No, you defile your conscience; if you say Yes, he can suspend or
expel you; if you refuse to answer he can do the same. And so far does
this power of questioning extend, that if he thinks the wife of one of you
Leaders or Local Preachers dresses too fine, he has the power to ask you
what her dress has cost you for the last twelve months and to demand an
answer; and if you refuse to answer he can suspend or expel you'. Not
being satisfied with this version of Methodist law, I told one of the
friends at the close of the meeting that I believed Mr. Dunn was wrong
and was asked by him to go to the house at which Mr. Dunn was entertained and tell him what I thought. I did so, and he persisted in those
statements and averred that not only has a Superintendent a right to
put *a question* on a particular point but *any question* he thinks proper. As I
could not believe this construction of the law even then, he said 'Well
you write to the President and ask him if this is not the case'. I prefer,

however, writing to you. I have been a Leader and Local Preacher nearly 17 years and have no object to serve by this enquiry but that of truth and righteousness. I do not like to hazard a public contradiction on my own views, and shall therefore feel obliged if you will be so kind as to state whether there is an ulterior principle contemplated by the Declaratory Rule 'vide. Minutes 1850 pp. 185 at bottom',[1] conferring such powers as those named by Mr. Dunn. . . .

328   From Abraham Watmough[2]   *Longton, October 11, 1850*

At the close of all the other matters at our late Quarterly Meeting, one of the Reforming Party (of which I am sorry to say a great majority of the meeting was and is likely to be composed) referred me to page 185 of the Minutes of the late Conference, and observed that the article '4. *Trial of members*' was a new rule; and that therefore it was to be subjected to the judgment and decision of that meeting according to a former rule of Conference of 1797, as to whether it should have any force in this Circuit, during this year.

They kept us in debate about this matter, and others of a kindred kind, until past ten o'clock, at which time the meeting was adjourned till the beginning of next week, when the matter should be brought to a close.

Can you, my dear Sir, give me any light or advice which will be serviceable in this case?

They will have a great majority as to numbers in our next meeting; and if they really have a right, according to the rule of 1797, vol. I page 376, which they plead,[3] and upon which they intend to act in reference to the rule of last Conference referred to above (and so far as I am able

---

[1] This seems to refer to the Declaration of Wesleyan ministers of 1849, reaffirmed by the Conference of 1850 and reprinted as an appendix to the Minutes. This affirmed that 'to the Conference alone belongs the determination of the conditions on which ministerial recognition and fraternity are accorded; and that for the proper exercise and discharge of this important function, it must possess the right which it has exercised from the very beginning, of personal examination, whenever it shall judge it to be called for'.

[2] Abraham Watmough (1787–1863), superintendent, Longton circuit, 1850–51.

[3] In 1797 it was 'determined that if at any time the Conference see it necessary to make any new rule for the Societies at large, and such rule should be objected to, at the first Quarterly Meeting in any given circuit; and if the major part of that meeting, in conjunction with the preachers, be of opinion that the enforcing of such a rule in that circuit will be injurious to the prosperity of that circuit, it shall not be enforced in opposition to the judgment of such Quarterly Meeting, before the second Conference. But, if the rule be confirmed by the second Conference, it shall be binding on the whole Connexion'. Conference Address to the Societies, Smith, *History of Wesleyan Methodism* ii. 707.

at present to see into the case they have full power to do so) it will suspend the exercise of discipline *in all cases whatsoever* in this circuit during the year, or, at least, put it entirely into the power of any accused party absolutely to do this, and that in the most summary manner they could desire or conceive. For they will have nothing to do but as follows, which also is evidently the plan they intend to pursue, namely,

1. To put the veto upon the new rule, as they call it.
2. Then take whatever course they think fit, and to do so with absolute impunity during the year. Because,
3. If they should be brought to trial for anything they may do or say, either in reference to reform agitation or any other thing, they will only have to refuse to admit or deny the allegations, in which case the 'authorities' (i.e. not only the minister, but all others) will not be at liberty to assume the guilt of the parties in question, and neither is any evidence to be brought forward; and so *nothing* can be done to stop them, at least for one year!

This, Sir, is evidently the view they take of the matter, and what they are intending to do; neither can I see how this can be prevented if the rule of 1797 be a rule still in force, which I suppose is the case. So that by the passing of the rule of last Conference raising the law of the *Trial of members*, and forming a *new rule* upon it, and by the veto intended to be passed upon the *new rule*, by these two things put together, I am thrown into the utmost difficulty, and greatly distressed about the matter and know not what to do. Because if the party can by virtue of the rule of '97 suspend the rule of the last Conference referred to above, and so put an entire end to discipline for the space of twelve months, what am I not to expect, and what course shall I be able to take, in a circuit like this? . . .

329   From Peter Duncan[1]   *Bath, November 7, 1850*

. . . We are not yet in a position to give you any correct account of the state of the circuit. I think our loss of members in town and country as compared with the March returns will be about 300, though not more than half reside in the town. We shall lose about 16 Leaders and 14 out of twenty-five Local Preachers. We shall have to drop one or two country places which however had never been of any service, and a public room which was rented in a distant part of the city we are likely to lose, through very dishonourable conduct on the part of some who

[1] Peter Duncan, superintendent, Bath circuit, 1850–53.

have left us. We are now busy with the Sunday school department which we are resolved not only to reform but to renew.

I am however thankful in being able to say that there is no probability of our peace being materially disturbed. We experience great kindness on the part of our people and were it not for the crushing debts on the chapels we should have nothing to fear. . . .

330   From James Hoby[1] *10 Mecklenburgh Street, London, December 5, 1850*

I have just been reading an article in the *Watchman* of yesterday on the respective merits of Independency and Connexionalism, it is the second number on the subject. I feel deeply impressed with the belief that if these two numbers could be a little condensed and printed and sold as a tract, at a cheap rate, they would be very useful just now. The Independents are very fond of praising our system, as a specimen of Mr. Wesley's skill and foresight, and then asserting that it is not a Scriptural system, and trying to weaken the attachment to, and confidence in, it to their own advantage. I learnt from a friend that a son of our respected minister Mr. Rigg wrote these essays and that his health does not allow him to do much at present.[2] I think he could produce a tract of moderate size containing the very essence of these articles with the passages of Scripture at length. I do not know that what may be called controversial tracts on the subject of church government have yet been issued by the Tract Room, but I believe they must be hereafter, and if our preachers generally would recommend such a tract as this, it would enable many of those who have neither time nor mind to study the subject at length, to give scriptural reasons for the system they have adopted. It is very evident to me that one reason why the agitators succeed so far as they do, is the great ignorance of so many of our people of the really scriptural principles on which our economy is based and of their inability to perceive that, whilst reformation and greater improvement alone are talked of, the object is really to make Methodism a democratic system, a thing without scriptural warrant and I believe likely to be of very short duration. . . .

[1] James Hoby, a class-leader at City Road, London, and a member of the connexional committees of Education and Privileges. D. 1863, aet. 75.

[2] James Harrison Rigg (1821–1909), son of John Rigg (q.v.), was a supernumerary for a year, 1850–51; he wrote further papers on these themes in the *Wesleyan Methodist Magazine* 1885–86, which were the basis of his book *A comparative view of church organisations, primitive and protestant* (3rd ed. London, 1897).

331   From Thomas Waugh   *Bandon, March 18, 1851*

. . . We have much to depress, and a little to encourage us in this unhappy land. God blesses the labours of his servants on several circuits,
but on others the vile *Times* is foisted, and wherever read poisons. Whilst
Popery is truckled to, and protestantism insulted by the powers that be!
Oh, were political popery as promptly and strictly dealt with as political
protestantism, matters would present a different aspect. Nothing could
be more easy than for a firm and impartial government to keep this
land in order. A suitably qualified minister, supported by a British
House of Commons, could do anything; but a sickening liberality has
all but murdered genuine liberty. I wish the folks on your side the water
would be taught that there is a protestant, as well as a popish Ireland,
and not insist on mixing us up with all that we detest. . . .

332   From Robert Insley[1]   *London, May 8, 1851*

. . . I need not tell you what the general grievances are, the Laws of '35
first in not allowing the Quarterly Meetings direct to memorialise the
Conference, it is considered an infringement of their liberties, and the
Leaders' Meeting not to be their own judge of cases brought before them.
These local meetings must have a more extensive knowledge of the
characters brought before them than a stranger, which must of necessity
make inquiry of some person resident on the spot. You may ask, is all
this to be done for one Circuit? I answer *No*, the agitation is very
extensive and what is wanted for one will equally apply for all, and
[be] hurtful to none. I have examined the rules or laws for [17]95, 6 and
7, and am satisfied they were settled upon a good foundation, leaving
the people sufficient liberty to manage their own affairs, and not
to infringe upon the fundamental principles of sound Wesleyanism
determined by Mr. Wesley and his Assistants. The Conference have a
sufficient guarantee against lay delegation, and their District Meetings,
and the funds, the people dont want new laws but to abide by the good
old ones. Since I saw you I have thought much about the case and
come to the conclusion, that the most satisfactory way to settle the
business would be to repeal nearly the whol[e] Laws of '35 with the
exception of those parts embodied from the before-mentioned years and
the second clause of the Resolution of *'35* Page 115[2] which clause
should never be lost sight of. Had that been acted upon there would not

---

[1] Robert Insley, the oldest Leader of the Hinde Street Society.

[2] This clause rehearsed the rule of 1794 that the Preachers must consult Leaders and
Stewards before expelling a member.

have been so many *expulsions* of late in the Connexion. The noble-minded men that composed the Conferences of those years 95, 6 and 7 have left in the *Minutes* a lasting monument of a *dignified character* worthy of imitation to all succeeding generations. *Yes,* they trembled at the thought of a division and its consequences, the wheat was so *precious* to *them,* they *paused* before they cast out the tares. There was no striving for the Mastery, but for union of action with the Body, and a willingness to make every sacrifice on their own part for the sake of peace to the Connexion. The Committee by Ballot[1] of '95 had the desired effect, so that both sides were satisfied, and the Delegates returned the Conference a letter of thanks, and if the Conference of '51 can be prevailed upon to act in the spirit of their own Resolution of '35, Page 115, it would produce the Methodism of former times, priest and lay would be one and no longer twain, and last not least the character of the Conference [would rise] in public estimation. . . .

333   From William Binning[2]   *Bramley, July 10, [18]51*

The talk is very loud and sanguine in this quarter about wonderful concessions to be made by the coming Conference. But I have seen enough during the past year to impel me to say, if the Conference move at all, *surely* it will be in the other direction. Can the Laws of 1797 be swept away, or so modified as to amount to something like that? These with the insertion of them in class books have given me endless perplexity, and brought torrents of abuse upon me in almost every direction. There is really no keeping Methodism strictly and properly with them as they are. If possible let something be done to remedy this evil, but for God's sake, let there be no movement in the other direction.

There wants some distinct and stringent measure to enable us to get rid of those Leaders who allow the expelled still to meet. The thing is rampant here, while they glory in it, and set you at defiance. And where you have a Leaders' Meeting or majority of it like-minded, how are you to get rid of them with things as they are? Do my dear Sir, think of and press something of the kind.

I have had a terrible year with the radicalism of this distracted place. Abused, calumniated, involved in the midst of violent mobs, and denounced as being too bad even for hanging, reduced in allowances to

---

[1] The reference here is obscure; the composition of the committee of delegates of trustees whose negotiations with Conference led to the adoption of the Plan of Pacification, may have been determined by ballot.

[2] William Binning, superintendent, Bramley circuit, 1850–51.

the lowest pitch, and now deprived even of that, and seem to have no likelihood of getting it, unless you can help us from the special funds. I do hope the Conference will give me a Circuit with tolerable allowances, or with my family I shall be involved in difficulties beyond recovery.

The parties that have been doing their utmost to damage me by memorial to the President, and otherwise, I am sorry to say are directly or indirectly mixed up with the faction that has given me so much trouble. In this hot conflict in fact I have had no direct support but from Brother Willcox,[1] and in some high quarters worse than no help at all. . . .

334   From George Heap[2]   *No. 1, Kingston Place, Leeds,*
July 26, 1851

It perhaps is necessary that a stranger to you should apologise for addressing you on a subject on which your conduct in future will have a mighty influence for *good* or *evil*. The only apology I have to offer is I am about *your own age* and an *Hebrew* of the Hebrews. . . . [and] no stranger to you or your old friends . . . Now then to the point, after all I have seen for half a century I must say this is the most important time that Methodism ever saw. I am well acquainted with all the circumstances which led to the division of 1797 when the *Conference denied* the people preaching in Church hours and having the Lord's Supper at their Preachers' hands, believing Mr. Wesley's words [that] if they left the Church he was afraid God would leave them. There were only 2 sermons preached on [the] Lord's Day at that time and only one chapel. I always attended with my parents. Suppose you had taken Mr. Wesley's advice, would you have had 6 large Chapels in Leeds at this time? I say No. It is rather singular that the founder of Methodism should be born in Hepworth [*sic*], and the reformer of Methodism [Kilham] should be born in the same place, and that the Law of 1797 which was made in Leeds that year, should be so pleaded for at this time. I am sorry to see it so often set aside which is one great cause of the *present agitation*. I now write to request you to use your influence to get all the Preachers to act upon that law and not on [that of] 1835 (if the parties have seen each other in private and fulfilled the Law of Christ first, see Matthew 18 etc.). I hope you have read Mr. Daniel Walton['s] Counsel of Peace. I hope you will take his advice and meet the people. Both must give way

---

[1] Robert M. Willcox (1815–93), preacher, Bramley circuit, 1849–51.

[2] George Heap, a Leeds layman, third-generation Methodist, and intimately involved in Leeds Methodist affairs for half a century.

2E

or the consequences will be awful. I believe instead of us being 56,000 deficient in members, next year at this time we shall be 156,000. I beg you will not depend on rich men, I know them all here. Mr. Wesley warns you of your danger when they *become necessary*. I also warn you not to lean on this arm of flesh, they cannot make Local Preachers, or Leaders. What can you do without them? They are the bees and without them Methodism would soon die out. Not many rich, not many mighty are called. God hath chosen the foolish things of this world to confound the wise, and God hath chosen the weak things of this world to confound the things that are mighty. There are no set of men [who] would be better attended to than Methodist Preachers if they would do as Messrs. Pawson,[1] Hanby,[2] Brown,[3] Entwisle[4] and others did, in visiting from house to house, which I am sorry to say is now so much neglected. The visits are in general to the rich. It has given me *great pleasure* to read the speech you made in Manchester last week where you say you have been a reformer 40 years. I have been one 50 years out of 70, and [am] more than ever convinced that you must infuse more Lay Delegation into the system if you wish for permanent peace and prosperity. There were some good suggestions given you by men of known worth at Manchester. *This is a favourable time* to make improvements. I am glad Mr. Heald has spoken as he has; if you and Dr. Newton *join him*, you will make a *great impression on the Conference*. People *read* and *think* more than they once did; I have been at the Sabbath Schools above 50 years and I am at it yet in Woodhouse, and hear and see how things are going on. I hope you will follow Sir Robert Peel's example and attend to the Voice of the People, recollect they want no other *doctrine, no other Hymn Book*, or any other means of Grace than those God has so long blessed and will bless as long as they are properly used and attended. I am glad so many expressed their wish to free the Preachers from attending the serving tables.[5] This may be done, and would relieve many who want that relief and who would be more in *their place and element* in attending to *spiritual matters*. I hope Divine providence will spare you to see peace restored and a greater union between the Preachers and the people, without this they labour in vain. . . .

[1] John Pawson, leading Methodist preacher. D. 1806, aet. 68.

[2] Thomas Hanby, who at the time of his death in 1797 was reputed to be the oldest Methodist preacher.

[3] Perhaps Isaac Brown who d. 1815, age unknown.

[4] Joseph Entwisle, see n. 2 p. 8 *supra*.

[5] I.e. performing diaconal duties of business management in the church.

335   From James Loutit[1]   *Louth, December 17, 1851*

There are certain notorious and inveterate agitators in this circuit whom I cannot rid Methodism of but by a trial. I am shut up to this course – verdict or no verdict – or stand still and see the church alienated, and finally carried off by an organized opposition, conducted by persons who are at present officers and members with us. In a trial every point will be disputed. I have certainly had some experience in these matters in and out of Methodism; but the wording of some of the rules – no doubt definite enough for the law of love – is loose, and I have so much confidence in your judgment as to induce me to solicit your opinion and advice which I feel assured, for the sake of the good cause, you will favour me with.

In 1794 it was agreed that no Trustee (however accused or defective in conforming to the established rules of Society) shall be removed from the Society unless his crime or breach of the rules of the Society be proved in the presence of the Trustees and Leaders. Min. Vol. 1 p. 300. And this in the preamble to the rules of 1835 is declared to be 'a distinct and special provision'. Min. Vol. VII. 578. In 1797 *no person* was to be expelled for immorality, till such immorality be proved at or 'to the satisfaction of' of a Leaders' Meeting. 1797–1835 Min. Vol. i. p. 375. VII. 578. And in 1797 the IVth Article of an official 'Letter to the Methodist Societies' is entitled – 'In respect to the *appointment* and removal of Leaders, Stewards and Local Preachers'. In the body of the regulation it is provided that 'no person shall be appointed a *Leader* or *Steward,* or removed from his office, but in conjunction with the Leaders' Meeting; but in Article 2, while it is said that 'no person shall *receive* a plan as a Local-Preacher without the approbation of a Local-Preachers' Meeting' (Min. 1. 8º p. 375) there is no express arrangement for his *removal.*

At last in 1835 the uniform usage of the Body was declared to be that 'continued absence from the class-meeting or other means of grace without any sufficient reason, or some manifest breach of the laws of God, or of the particular rules of our own connexion, is usually in such cases reported by the Class-Leader to the preacher, at the time of Quarterly visitation. If there be no denial of the fact or satisfactory defence of the charge on the part of the member, or of his friends who may be present, and if the preacher in the case of alleged crime or misconduct be [not?] of opinion that the offence is one of such grave and serious character as to require some public testimony of disapprobation, the immediate exclusion of the negligent and offending member has usually resulted quietly, and as a matter of course, by the

[1] James Loutit (1801–85), superintendent, Louth circuit, 1851–52.

Preacher withholding his Society-Ticket, and erasing his name from the class-book. But if the member so charged deny the allegation of a wilful neglect of our peculiar discipline as to class-meetings, etc. or of a breach of some law of scripture, or rule of Methodism, and *demand* a trial – then the trial must be forthwith conceded'. Vol. VII p. 579.

From this – and from the preamble reciting the provision for Trustees, and not making it an exception – it would appear that *all members and officers* are alike subject to the regulation of 1835; that the preacher may withhold 'Society tickets' from *any or all* as an interim measure; and that in *any case* a trial must be *demanded'*.

Will you favour me with your opinion –

1. Whether the declared usage and rule of 1835 applies, to all 'Society Officers' – in particular to '*Leaders, Stewards, and Local Preachers*' as well as to members? In other words am I justified, for a sufficient cause, in *withholding a ticket, and erasing from the Class Book* from any one of them, and leave it [to] *them* to 'demand a trial'.

2. Must the Society officer, Leader, Steward and Local Preacher in order to his removal *from office* as well as membership, be *twice tried* for the *same* offence? In such cases this seems absurd and inexpedient. It is more: one Court might with the same evidence pronounce opposite judgments! Would it not be better, at least in cases involving ecclesiastical existence, first to deal with the accused either as a member, or simply on a given charge, leaving the *issue* of the trial itself to determine its application; or by retention of his ticket (if that course be lawful) or trial? And *report that* decision to the *officers'* court as the ground of their action?

3. Should the officers, Leaders, Stewards or Local Preachers refuse to part with the suspended or severed 'Member', is not the remedy to call in the 'Chairman [of the District]' who is authorised to visit officially any Circuit in his District (Min. Vol. X p. 90) and if that fail, then summon a special District [Meeting]?

I imagine that the Minor District does not apply to officers refusing to separate a brother *from office*.

4. Does the case of Trustees for whom 'a special and distinct provision' was made in 1797 . . . form an exception to the law of 1835? i.e. must Trustees in all cases have trial in the *first instance*?

5. In the case of a Trustee being put upon or demanding a trial who is so for X or XII chapels, as in Louth Circuit, yet *not* being a Trustee of the Chapel where he is a *Leader* or a *Member*, are the Trustees of all these chapels, or only a portion of them, and if so what portion, to be associated with the Leaders' Meeting? It will be remembered that the court appointed to try the accused Trustee is composed of '*The Trustees*

and Leaders'. Does this mean *the Trustees of the chapel where* the accused is a member or all his Co-Trustees in the Circuit? Or all his Co-Trustees in England?

I need not say that in these enquiries I seek not to create but to anticipate and be prepared for objection. Knowing how our proceedings will be tested, and that many of our brethren *themselves* hold and act upon opinions the very opposite of each other, I am desirous of obtaining the best advice, wishing to do what is right and being easy as to the issue. As I purpose putting Henry Boothby Junr. on his trial in a few days I shall be happy to receive an *early answer*.

A separation in Louth is not only unavoidable but desirable. . . .

336   To S. R. Hall[1]   *Manchester, December 18, 1851*

I am honoured by the invitation of your Education Committee, so kindly conveyed to me by yourself. But though the spirit is willing, the flesh is weak. My state of health, though improved, to some extent, and several disabling infirmities, which are increased rather than diminished, put it out of my power to undertake any such service. I cordially wish you success in this most important undertaking, and kind regards to Mrs. H. . . .

337   From George Birley[2] to T. P. Bunting   *Market Rasen, August 24, 1853*

You may probably have heard that this circuit is one of those which has nearly been reduced to a wreck by that wicked system of Ecclesiastical Chartism which has been disturbing our beloved connexion more than three years.

When the agitation commenced here, there were 1250 members in the circuit; but these are now reduced to 594!!!

Amongst the other painful results of this diabolical agitation, I found our chapel affairs in a sad state. In some instances the Trustees have never had a meeting since the chapels were erected. And most of the others had not had a meeting for five or six years. In this state of affairs, I and a few of the excellent right-minded Trustees who remain, deem it expedient to consult you professionally respecting the best course to be

[1] Samuel Romilly Hall (1812–76), preacher, Leeds (St. Peter's) circuit, 1851–54.
[2] George Birley, superintendent, Market Rasen circuit, 1852–54.

pursued. A considerable number of our Trustees have become 'Reformers', and some of them are very active and zealous ones.

The chapel at Tealby is one about which I am very anxious. In point of importance it is the second place in the Circuit. It was a considerable time after I came here 12 months ago that I could find the Deeds. They are however now in my possession. It is a rather voluminous affair, the Solicitor's bill which accompanies the documents is £26. 8. 4.

The Trust Deed bears date March 31st 1819. There were 15 Trustees; 7 of these are deceased. One is a man superannuated and unable to take care of himself, who has had nothing to do with Methodism for many years. One (if I [am] rightly informed) has never acted as a trustee. Another resides in a distant part of the kingdom, and four others wish to resign their Trust. Two of these are leading 'Reformers' and none of them members of our Society. There is only one man in whom I can confide. But the worst of all is, the Deed *is not* enrolled in Chancery!!! The debt for such a chapel is small; not much more than £100. The note is only signed by two of the Trustees, and one is a leading 'Reformer' and is very anxious to get out of the concern. He knows nothing of the worthlessness of the Deed. Can you inform me by what method this Chapel can be secured to the Connexion?

The second case is in the large and respectable village of Birrbrook (9 miles from Louth). This is the worst place in the Circuit for the 'Reform' mania; there were more than 200 members and a crowded chapel here; the number in our Society now are 35, and Sunday congregations range from 40 to 70 persons. The majority of Trustees are 'Reformers'. The Trust Deed *is not* enrolled in Chancery. They know this, but are not aware of the power this fact gives them. They consider that the only advantage they gain by this unhappy omission, is preventing the Superintendent from attending their meetings or having any voice in the transaction of Trust business. They hold Trustee Meetings regularly, but the Superintendent is never informed of them. They also prevent the Superintendent from having a sight of the Deed. Can you suggest anything in this case?

We have eleven other chapels *regularly settled*, connected with which we have 'Reformers' who are Trustees. We are anxious to free ourselves from them, and we believe it is practicable. In that case, is there any legal method by which we can appoint substitutes for them without the expense of New Deeds?

Some of our friends have suggested a plan for the whole of the properly connexional chapels in the Circuit to be placed under one consolidated Trust. I believe the whole of the debts on these chapels does not amount to £2000. I fear there are serious legal difficulties in the way of such a measure. I will thank you to favour me with your opinion on this matter. . . .

338   From John McLean[1]   *Lincoln, November 17, 1853*

It is said by those who wish to rescind or to violate clause 30 of the Deed of Settlement of the Sheffield Proprietary School

1. That the connexion with the universities alienates the pupils from Methodism. This I am certain is not the fact. That Wesleyan children will from time to time become Churchmen, either with a view to the ministry, or the pursuit of the higher prizes of scholarship must be expected. But this happens in Dissenting Schools of the same order. It is an effect produced on the minds of Wesleyan parents and children by the perusal of Mr. Wesley's works before they are placed under the care of the Sheffield masters and is to my knowledge, the reason why they are sent there, in preference to schools of a different description. In so far as the distance is lawfully diminished between us and the church, and a conciliatory spirit produced in our children by the connexion with the universities or in some portions of the Church people towards us by the same cause, we cannot but as true Wesleyans and Catholics rejoice. But the allegation that it alienates our children is false. The contrary I believe to be the fact. It conciliates a certain portion of the Wesleyan children who are of a weak or aspiring temper of mind to their own people. When they find a distinguished graduate willing to work with and for Methodism, it has the effect of making them the more ashamed to leave it; and it has a still better effect upon a higher class of pupils.

2. It is alleged that a connexion with the University of London, or perhaps, through a headmaster, with Dublin, is enough. Now I would not wish to say anything needlessly against the London University of which my own son is an undergraduate; but surely Wesleyans cannot yet be willing to forget that it is eminently under Roman Catholic and and Unitarian influence. Who knows yet what it really is, beyond the examining body, which of its own sort is no doubt very good. It is yet to be proved that the parties who made the Proprietary School one of its colleges took a wise step.

As for Dublin University, if any man having sufficient qualifications, is wishful to come from that University, there is provision made for a very easy passage through Oxford or Cambridge, and the same is true concerning the University of London. . . .

The only hope of preserving the noble position of the school is in

[1] John McLean, supernumerary, Lincoln circuit, 1852–55.

such men as Mr. F[armer]. The movement to rescind or violate the 30th clause is I believe greatly promoted directly, but chiefly indirectly, by such men as Samuel Griffith[1] at Bristol and Sibly[2] at the Taunton School. These find a ready sympathy in liberal or sectarian Methodist preachers and Kingswood scholars who naturally crave (the latter) after the situation either for themselves or some of their old school fellows. But surely we are not to be led away from our connexion with the national seats of Protestantism and Learning by such selfish considerations. Let these Methodist lads who have got much more out of Methodism already than they are likely soon to return, learn to glorify God and serve their country by cultivating the disinterestedness of John Wesley and of his true successors the Wesleyan Conference. . . .

339   From William H. Rule[3]

14 City Road [London],
July 10, 1855

No doubt the Committee of Privileges will enter into correspondence with the Lords who are in charge of both the Registration and the Religious Worship Bills,[4] and I earnestly hope they may do this without delay. I send you a note from Lord Shaftesbury, as it recognises a distinction between *public* and *private* places which the law should make.

If you make any use of this note in the Parliamentary Sub-committee on Thursday, pray observe that the mention of *Quarter Sessions* is obviously a mistake in haste of writing a note not meant to be official. His Lordship has been paying earnest attention to the Act Victoria 15 & 16 cap. 36[5] and knows all about the administration of these affairs by the Registrar General. The truth is that people in general know nothing of this last act, and 'Quarter Sessions' rings in the ear still.

I trust we shall get rid of the *penalty*, which is a last vestige of the Conventicle Act, with the policy of that legislation. . . .

[1] Perhaps error for William Griffith (1777–1860), supernumerary at Bristol, and father of William Griffith junior, the reformer (1806–83).

[2] Nicholas Sibly (1780–1862), supernumerary, Tavistock circuit, from 1845.

[3] William H. Rule D.D. (1802–90), connexional editor, 1851–57.

[4] On July 10, 1855, Lord Brougham moved and carried the second reading of a bill to correct a drafting error in the Registration Act of 1852, which, by rendering the registration certificates of Bishops' registries and Quarter Sessions null and void, and transferring them to the Registrar-General, had unwittingly exposed thousands of dissenting chapels to the penalties incurred by contravening the Toleration Act, and rendered the marriages solemnized in them null and void at law. *Parliamentary Debates* 3s. cxxxix. 657–9.

[5] An act to amend the law relating to the certifying and registering places of religious worship of Protestant Dissenters (1852).

340   From John McLean[1]   *Edinburgh, August 18, 1855*

You will not I am sure suppose from my letter of yesterday that I have turned democrat since I came to Scotland, which it must be admitted is a region perhaps somewhat unduly charged with that spirit. I quite believe in the sentiment which your enemies charged you with when I had the honour of living under your roof, and of which I think you have no reason to be ashamed, that Methodism is as opposed to democracy as it is to sin. By which I understood you to mean, that Methodism was unmistakably and irreconcilably opposed to democracy as a system of government. But I also believe that you recognize the existence of a Christian people or flock as distinct from the Pastors; and that next to the glory of God all church arrangements should be made with a view to their benefit. Neither do I doubt that any powers which might with safety be put into the hands of the flock would by you be most freely and gladly consented to. In England, however, you are accustomed to regard the flock or people or congregation as embodied or condensed (certainly *you* never thought that they were *represented*) in the Leaders' and Quarterly Meetings etc. For the south of the Tweed this perhaps is the best, because in truth I fear you have given such powers to those meetings that I greatly doubt whether without the hazard of some fearful tumult you could apportion any of them to the congregation. In Scotland it is different, because our entire ecclesiastical system may be considered to be yet in a state of solution; and also because in this country the existence and rights or, as it would be more Wesleyan and scriptural to call them, the duties of the congregation are universally acknowledged. In the Free Church as well as in the Established Church this is undoubtedly the case. So also in the United, and other Presbyterian sections. You have no parallel to this state of things in England. Now I recommended the Veto Act in yesterday's letter with a view to this peculiar condition of religious opinion and society on this side of the Tweed. I do not deny that I should without scruple place it myself upon much higher ground than that of *mere* expediency, though of course I am too established a Wesleyan to suppose that the scriptures make this or any similar detail of church arrangement imperative, except where the prosperity of the work of God demands it. The reality of a *visible* Church, should I think be carefully kept up, along with the reality (not of an *invisible* Church, as our Calvinistic friends are too apt at once to run the thing to) but of a *spiritual* and *converted* church such as I believe we have; visibly embodied in our own beloved and precious Methodist societies.

Now such a regulated power of vetoing a minister as I described in my last might I think be safely and very advantageously committed to

[1] John McLean, supernumerary, Edinburgh circuit, 1855–66.

our congregations in Scotland. They are all supposed to be baptized.
We admit their children to baptism. They are thus with their families,
members of the visible community of Christ's people, even if they do not
feel themselves worthy to be communicants. I am not sure whether the
Free Church extends the veto law so far; but I am satisfied that it might
be done with our system of Government with perfect safety and advantage. As for having lay Elders in this country, that I believe is absurd
and unscriptural, and I am yet to convince that Mr. Wesley ever gave
the slightest sanction to it. That our Presbyterian friends emerging from
Roman Catholic errors three hundred years since should have fallen
into this Protestant error, is no reason why any section of the followers of
John Wesley should adopt it. But a proper recognition of the Congregation, would have the effect I believe of making one class of our lay
officers more decidedly spiritual, while it would render another class
more exclusively secular and financial, agreeably as I cannot but
believe with the state of things in the *primitive Church* and *certainly* in our
primitive Methodism. Have you not noticed how the godly men of
business of Mr. Wesley's days got superseded by the spiritual men, and
how the secular spirit, accumulated upon our poor but pious leaders
thereby, has been exploding in our Leaders' and Quarterly Meetings
whenever the external atmosphere has become favourable from that day
to this? . . .

341   From P. Duncan[1]   *Manchester, July 14, 1856*

The late examination of students at Didsbury has been the means of
awakening some anxious and painful feelings in my mind. Their knowledge of the Holy Scriptures we found so lamentably defective, as that
we were forced to notice it in the Report. It was the subject of much
conversation at the Committee which met only a few days afterwards.
In the intervening space I had not time to arrange any plan which
might to some extent meet the case. In a conversational way, I did
indeed suggest a few things some of which met with the hearty approval
of Dr. Hannah, who also complained of the defect, but who most
clearly shewed that it was beyond his power to provide anything like an

---

[1] Peter Duncan, superintendent, Manchester (Oldham St.) circuit, 1853–56. Continuing
concern on the matters raised in this letter is indicated by the action of another member of the
Didsbury College committee in forwarding to Bunting 'an important report of the sub-
committee of the Free Church [in Scotland] on the training of students in theology, in which
there is a lengthened paragraph on the importance of instructing them in the English Bible'.
M.C.A. MSS. J. Gilchrist Wilson to Jabez Bunting, November 24, 1856.

adequate remedy. . . . I propose that it should be recommended to the Conference

1st. To institute a *weekly* course of lectures and examination on the books of the Holy Scriptures; and that the Governor be appointed to the duties of this important department.

2dly. To institute a course of lectures on Ecclesiastical History to be delivered *fortnightly*, that a minister from an adjoining circuit be appointed to undertake it; and that this, as well as the preceding arrangement, appear in the Minutes of the Conference and the printed Reports of the Institution.

3rdly. That the time for the annual examinations in Theology be extended to four days or longer if necessary; and that the examiners in their report distinctly state their opinion of the acquirements and proficiency of the students in the following branches respectively according to the time they may have resided in the Institution viz.

(1st)   The Evidences of Christianity; embracing the Divine Authority and Inspiration of the Holy Scriptures.

(2dly) The Doctrines, Duties and Institutions of Christianity; especially such as hold a prominent place in the first four volumes of Sermons and other standard writings of the Revd. John Wesley.

(3rdly) Biblical Criticism; including a knowledge of the writers, the authenticity, history, and other leading contents of the books of the Old and New Testament.

(4thly) Ecclesiastical History.

4th. That the local committee be directed to appoint two ministers and two other gentlemen from their number to be present at all annual examinations. . . .

342   From William M. Harvard   *Liverpool, August 5, 1857*

[Full account of an ordination service at Conference, and the speeches of the American Deputation and their announcement of European Missions] . . . The Bishop [Simpson][1] added that he regretted to find that a minister from their body had recently arrived in this country from whose proceedings we might possibly suffer some degree of inconvenience (Mr. Caughey); that in such a case their church had no jurisdiction since Mr. C. was merely a Local Preacher and could only be

[1] Matthew Simpson (1811–84), Methodist preacher; President, DePauw University, 1839–1848. Bishop, 1852. Outspoken opponent of slavery; reputed the most influential American Methodist of his day.

called to order by his own particular Quarterly Meeting; that Mr. C. had called on him on a matter of courtesy, and he had enjoined upon him not to engage in any services in this country but such as he might be invited to conduct by the official members of this Conference, though he feared with no good effect.

It is said that one of the principal Reformers of Sheffield met Mr. Caughey on Sunday the day of his arrival here and that he accompanied him home. . . .

343   From John Dury Geden[1]   *Didsbury, November 9, 1857*

Some few days since a deputation of Students waited upon me requesting that I would undertake to instruct a few of their number in *German*. I have since conversed with Dr. Hannah and Mr. Bowers on the subject of their application; and as we do not feel at liberty to act in a matter of this sort without your knowledge and approval, I write to ask if you will oblige us, as early as may be convenient to you, with your judgment on the question. Dr. Hannah and Mr. Bowers are agreed with myself on the following points:–

1. That, if German be taught at all in the Institution, it must not be taught privately, but must form part of the curriculum.

2. That the study of the language should be restricted to the older and riper students, and not be allowed to interfere in any way with the existing theological and literary courses.

3. That German is of great value for purposes of ministerial scholarship, and that, unless the state of public feeling be deemed a sufficient reason to the contrary, it is desirable to give it a place among the studies of the Institution. . . .

344   To John Dury Geden   *London, November 14, 1857 [Copy][2]*

Your letter has claimed and received my very serious consideration; . . .

My *conclusion* is that I cannot at present consent to be a party to the adoption of the proposal made by some of the Didsbury Students, even

---

[1] John Dury Geden (1822–86), preacher, Manchester (Oxford Road) circuit, 1853–56; Assistant classical tutor, Richmond, 1847–51; classical tutor, Didsbury College, 1856–83.

[2] This, Bunting's last letter still extant in the connexional archives, was written in a very infirm hand indeed. Geden replied that he, Bowers and Hannah heartily concurred in Bunting's judgment. M.C.A. MSS. J. D. Geden to Jabez Bunting, November 23, 1857.

as modified in your statement of it; and I regret that it should have been mooted.

My *reasons* for this conclusion are such as the following, viz:

1. Considering that the introduction of a German Class into the programme of Studies officially sanctioned at Didsbury must in all consistency be followed, if solicited, by a similar extension of the programme at Richmond, I think that we have no *right* to take such a step without consultation of the General Committee of the Institution. The *curriculum* authorized by the Conference and accepted by the Connexion, and virtually approved by all the annual contributors, is that announced and described in Dr. Hannah's defensive pamphlet.[1] The summary of recognized studies *may* possibly by common consent, after due deliberation and approval by the Conference, be enlarged by the addition of new and different courses; but *not*, I think, without such consent.

2. The studies already sanctioned, some of which are even now but inadequately provided for, are in all reason quite sufficient to occupy the *whole* time and utmost diligence of our pupils during the too short duration of their present term of residence, limited to three years and practically often (much too often) reduced by various exigencies or influences to two years. Surely no student who knows himself or duly ponders the solemn work for which he is preparing, will say that he has *time to spare* for what is at best a merely secondary and supplementary acquisition, which may well be postponed to a period of greater leisure, when *essential* attainments shall have been mastered and matured in future life.

3. I am convinced that the addition of German to our recognized studies would, after recent occurrences in the ecclesiastical world and in some collegiate Institutions, be viewed by our people at large with *extreme jealousy*, and might lead to financial difficulties not to be risked for any such object. This jealousy would not be *wholly* without foundation. Think of what has happened at Oxford, but especially at St. John's Wood and at the Lancashire College;[2] and beware! You cannot, I fear, give a possible advantage to *the very few*, without exposing *the many* to dangers which at present they may be ill-prepared to encounter.

Other reasons for my conclusion have occurred to me in the course of

---

[1] J. Hannah, *A letter to a junior Methodist preacher, concerning the general course and prosecution of his studies in Christian theology* (3rd. ed. London, 1853).

[2] Samuel Davidson, professor of Biblical literature and ecclesiastical history at Lancashire Independent College, 1843–57, was a close friend of a number of German theologians of relatively conservative views, but his contribution to volume two of the 10th edition of Horne's *Introduction to the Sacred Scriptures* (1856) occasioned great alarm to members of his college committee, and he was brought to resign his chair.

my thinkings on the subject; but my impaired memory fails to recall them at this moment. The above are I think, sufficient. . . .

345 [Draft by Isaac Keeling[1] for Dr. Bunting's memorial in City Road Chapel]

Because
it is for the common good
that eminent worth and great benefits
should be acknowledged and remembered,
this tablet is erected by the Wesleyan Ministers,
in memory of the reverend
Jabez Bunting D.D.
Gifted
with large powers of mind, and with intrepid and persistent energy, and
with masterly and persuasive eloquence; religiously trained
by pious parents, and early brought under the abiding influence of personal
godliness; he was, as a christian minister and pastor, mighty in dealing
with the conscience, and proclaiming the saving tenets of the gospel, and tenderly
faithful in feeding and guarding the flock of Christ.
To the councils of the churches
and to the organization and direction of christian and philanthropic enter-
prises, he brought the practical sagacity of a statesman, the comprehensive
and far-seeing wisdom of a legislator, and the moral fervour of a pure and
commanding character.
The Wesleyan Missionary Society,
and other important institutions of Methodism, owed chiefly to him, as a
wise master-builder, their sage and broad foundations, and their
well adapted and enduring structure.
His catholic spirit
found congenial elements and fellow labourers, among the founders of
the Anti-Slavery Society and of the Evangelical Alliance.
Loving
all who love our Lord Jesus Christ in sincerity, he dwelt among his own
people; who claimed his services, as the President of their Conference for
the fourth time in the year 1844, and as the President of the Wesleyan
Theological Institution, from its commencement in 1834 to the close of his
long and useful course.
He died in perfect peace,
on the sixteenth day of June, 1858
in the eightieth year of his age
and the fifty-ninth of his ministry.

[1] Isaac Keeling, superintendent, London (Islington) circuit, 1855–58.

INDEX

Watson, Richard, letters by, 17n.3; mentioned, xiii, 17 and n.3, 18, 21–3, 25, 31, 38–9, 40n.1, 63n.1, 391 and n.2; his writings, xiii n.3, 17n.3, 39 and nn.3–10, 40

Waugh, Beverley, 339 and n.3

Waugh, Thomas, letters by, 81, 298–9, 299–300, 344–6, 364, 407; mentioned, 5, 75 and n.4, 344n.1

Wednesbury, 112 and n.1

Welch, Charles. 253 and n.2

Wellington, Duke of, 213

Wells, 195

Welsh Assembly, xxi, 275

Wesley, John, xi, xiv, xvi, 6 and n.3, 36, 59n.5, 60n.2, 62, 71n.3, 107, 114n.1, 130n.2, 143, 149, 159, 172n.2, 187, 193, 208n.2, 217n.2, 223n.4, 224, 229 and n.3, 237 and n.3, 238, 247 and n.1, 269, 300, 307, 343, 361–2, 366, 386n.1, 406–7, 409–410, 415–17, 419

Wesley Banner and Revival Record, 377 and n.3, 378–9

Wesleyan Methodist Association (Warrenites), xv, xx, 4n.1, 10n.1, 19n.3, 42n.3, 60n.3, 88n.2, 105n.3, 112n.2, 115n.4, 116n.1, 119n.1, 121n.2, 122n.2, 129 and n.3, 132n.3, 135–6, 145n.2, 150, 162–4, 167, 169 and nn.2, 6; 170, 178, 180 and n.2, 185 and n.3, 186, 201, 204, 227, 232–4, 236, 275–7, 298, 324 and n.1

Wesleyan Methodist Magazine, 49n.1, 59 and n.5, 73n.4, 120, 135n.4, 136, 173, 184, 195, 212, 267, 283 and n.2, 355, 362

Wesleyan Missionary Society, xi, xviii, xxi, xxii, xxiii, 9n.2, 11n.3, 21n.1, 29, 30n.1, 31–4, 38nn.1, 2; 42n.4, 43, 45 and n.10, 46 and n.2, 47, 49n.1, 53, 58n.1, 72n.13, 73n.1, 77n.1, 80n.1, 99–100, 106 and n.1, 107, 109, 129, 132n.2, 137–9, 175, 188, 208–11, 215n.1, 222, 232, 242n.1, 243n.5, 244n.3, 251n.1, 272, 277, 280, 339n.2, 373–6, 389n.2, 422; Mission House, xvi, xxi, 25, 52n.3, 86, 104, 208–12, 242, 245, 251 and n.1, 253 and n.3, 270, 289, 373 and n.4, 396n.1

Wesleyan Reform secessions (1849), xv, xvi, xx, 6n.2, 61n.1 85n.1 159n.1, 380n.1, 382–3, 390, 394, 397, 413–15, 420

Wesleyan Times, 373, 378, 381, 383, 387

Wesleyan Tracts for the Times, 270, 271 and n.1

West, Francis A., 93 and n.3, 233 and n.1, 271, 367 and n.1; his writings, 108 and n.1

West Briton, 65, 185n.3

West Bromwich, 303 and n.2

Western Times, 285 and nn.1, 3

Westbury, 244n.4

Westcott, Mr., Bristol, 197

Westhead, Joshua P., 48n.2, 49n.1

West Indies, xxiii, 11n.3, 22–4, 30, 51–8, 52n.3, 77 and n.1, 107, 132n.1, 137n.4, 153 and nn.1, 4; 203n.1, 248n.1

Westminster, 15, 110

Westminster Normal Institution, 1n.1

Wharncliffe, Lord, 283n.7

Wheal Rose, nr. Redruth, 239

Wheeler, Robert, 271 and n.4

White, William, 199, 244 and n.3

Whitehaven, 130n.3, 204 and n.2

Whitehouse, Isaac, 312 and n.3, 313

Wightwick, J., letter by, 35–6

Wigton, 204

Wigtownshire, 304n.2

Wilberforce, Robert Isaac, 249 and n.1, 250

Wilberforce, William, 22n.3, 87n.1, 249n.1

Wild, John, 18

Wilde, Samuel, letters by, 84–5, 178–9; mentioned, 84n.1, 178n.1

Willcox, Robert M., 409 and n.1

Williams, Anne, 96n.1

Williams, Henry Wilkinson, 226 and n.3, 272 and n.2

Williams, Jonathan, letter by, 246–7; mentioned, 246n.1

Wilson, J. Gilchrist, letter by, 418n.1

Wilson, William, 146 and n.2, 147–9

Windsor, xxi, 177 and nn.2–3, 213

Wirtemberg, Duchess of, 214

Withington, Thomas, letter by, 306; mentioned, 306n.1

Witness, The, 278, 282

Witney, 214 and n.3

Wood James Manchester cotton merchant, letter by, 48–51; letters to, xviii n.4, xxii n.1, 83–4, 300–1; mentioned, 48n.2, 49n.1, 132, 133, 195 and n.4, 196, 291

Wood, James, preacher, letters by, 37–8, 241–2; mentioned, 37n.1, 42 and n.2, 172 and n.3, 252

Wood, Joseph, letters by, 41n.1, 174–7, 267–8; mentioned, 174n.3, 177n.1

Wood, Robert, letters by, 6–7, 19–20, 135; letters to, 139n.1; mentioned, 6n.5, 19n.2, 135n.1

Wood, William, 114 and n.2

Woodford, 249n.6, 250, 254

Woodhouse Grove, 42 and n.4, 85n.1, 198n.4, 286n.2, 392

Woolhouse, Mr., Derby local preacher, 395

Woolwich, 94, 290, 394 and n.2

Workington, 204 and n.2

Wortley, Yorks., 189

Wortley, John Stuart, 287 and n.1

Wrigglesworth, John, 117 and n.1